Athletic Sports In America, England And Australia ... - Primary Source Edition

Harry Clay Palmer, J. Austin Fynes, Francis C. Richter, William Ingraham Harris, Henry Chadwick

Nabu Public Domain Reprints:

You are holding a reproduction of an original work published before 1923 that is in the public domain in the United States of America, and possibly other countries. You may freely copy and distribute this work as no entity (individual or corporate) has a copyright on the body of the work. This book may contain prior copyright references, and library stamps (as most of these works were scanned from library copies). These have been scanned and retained as part of the historical artifact.

This book may have occasional imperfections such as missing or blurred pages, poor pictures, errant marks, etc. that were either part of the original artifact, or were introduced by the scanning process. We believe this work is culturally important, and despite the imperfections, have elected to bring it back into print as part of our continuing commitment to the preservation of printed works worldwide. We appreciate your understanding of the imperfections in the preservation process, and hope you enjoy this valuable book.

Game of the Chicago and All-America Teams, at Crystal Palace Grounds, London.

ATHLETIC SPORTS

HISTORY...

LACROSSE, ... , ROWING AND ...

THEIR ...

BY

REPRESENT...

MANAGE...

ASSISTED BY ...

THE WHOLE ... ELE...LY IL...TRATED.

UNION PUBLISHING HOUSE
NEW YORK

ATHLETIC SPORTS

IN

AMERICA, ENGLAND AND AUSTRALIA.

COMPRISING

HISTORY, CHARACTERISTICS, SKETCHES OF FAMOUS LEADERS, ORGANIZATION
AND GREAT CONTESTS OF BASEBALL, CRICKET, FOOTBALL,
LA CROSSE, TENNIS, ROWING AND CYCLING.

ALSO INCLUDING THE

FAMOUS "AROUND THE WORLD" TOUR OF AMERICAN BASEBALL TEAMS,

THEIR ENTHUSIASTIC WELCOMES, ROYAL RECEPTIONS, BANQUETS, GREAT GAMES PLAYED
BEFORE NOTABLES OF FOREIGN NATIONS, HUMOROUS INCIDENTS,
INTERESTING ADVENTURES, ETC., ETC.

BY

HARRY CLAY PALMER.

REPRESENTING THE "NEW YORK HERALD," "BOSTON HERALD," "CHICAGO TIMES" AND "SPORTING LIFE"
IN THE "AROUND THE WORLD" TOUR.

J. A. FYNES,   FRANK RICHTER,
MANAGING EDITOR, "NEW YORK CLIPPER."   EDITOR OF "SPORTING LIFE."

W. I. HARRIS,
THE EMINENT EXPONENT OF BASEBALL.

ASSISTED BY QUIGLEY AND HANLON, ON AQUATICS; PRIALL, ON CYCLING; BANSHEE
AND KELLOGG, ON TENNIS; AND OTHER LEADING AUTHORITIES
ON ATHLETIC SPORTS.

INTRODUCTION BY HENRY CHADWICK.

THE WHOLE MOST ELEGANTLY ILLUSTRATED.

UNION PUBLISHING HOUSE,

NEW YORK.

Entered according to Act of Congress, in the year 1889, by
HUBBARD BROTHERS,
In the Office of the Librarian of Congress, at Washington, D. C.

INTRODUCTION.

BY HENRY CHADWICK.

THE inauguration of the last decade of the Nineteenth century finds athletic field sports in the very zenith of their popularity, alike in republican America as in the colonial provinces of the British empire. A quarter of a century ago, England monopolized the honors in the great arena of athletic games throughout the civilized world; but now, not only does the new England of the American continent devide those honors with the mother country, but the greatest of the English colonial possessions, Australia has entered the lists in successful competition.

The spirit of the existing age undoubtedly favors the plan of a judicious combination of physical recreative exercise with mental culture in order to attain the best results in our system of education. In fact, the experience of the last quarter of a century of American progress in refined civilization has conclusively shown, that the cultivation of the physical faculties, must keep pace with mental culture in order to reach the highest point of excellence in the education of our youths.

In the race for the laurels of the arena of athletic sports, there is, of course, a liability to go to extremes, as in every other struggle for supremacy; but the happy medium in this pursuit, unquestionably recognizes the fact that out-door recreative exercise must go hand in hand with the cultured growth of the mind. The moral aspect of the case too, is one which gives hearty encouragement to national sports and pastimes as essential to the healthy and proper growth of our young people. The inhabitants of our large American cities, have, up to a recent period, lacked a healthy physique as a rule. This has been largely due to the fact that their mental powers have been allowed to draw too largely on the nerve forces of their bodies; and the result has been that the middle period of life has seen thousands carried to premature graves who, with proper attention to physical exercise and recreation in youth and early manhood, would have reached a healthy old age, ere, "the sere and yellow leaf of time" had made itself apparent. In fact, costly experience has taught us as a people, that our old time American system of "all work and no play;" of over taxing the mind at the expense of a neglected physique, is a very short-sighted policy; and very characteristically we have profited by experience and gained wisdom in this respect; and hence the increased and growing popularity of out-door sports for men as well as boys, and also of physical exercise for the fair sex as well, throughout the cities and towns of the North American continent.

It is a peculiarity of the growth of athletic games in the civilized portions of the globe, that most of the field sports in vogue on the American continent are practically known only to the English speaking people of the world. The game of *Cricket*, familiar on every field where the English language is spoken, is a novelty to the nations of the European continent; as is also *Base Ball, Lacrosse, Foot Ball*, and all of the most popular of our manly games of ball. But this condition of things is not likely to mark the future history of modern civilized countries. As each nation advances in its progress towards refinement, increased attention to healthy and manly sports must follow. France, so deficient in regard to national sports and pastimes, finds it essential to take measures looking to the adoption of English and American field games as part and parcel of an improved system of public education. The same policy will naturally be pursued by others of the European nationalities. In Germany, while our field games have hitherto been unknown in that country, athletic sports have found public favor to a considerable extent. But in no decade of the present century has such progress been made in popularizing Anglo-saxon field sports on the continent of Europe, as within the past few years; and especially during 1888 and 1889. In fact the great event in the modern history of athletic sports, was the grand tour of the civilized world, made by the party of base ball missionaries under the leadership of Mr. A. G. Spalding, which did more in six short months to advance the popularity of our American national game throughout the world, than had previously been accomplished in a whole decade.

The distinctive feature of this work is its chapters on the rise and progress of our national game of base ball, from the time of the organization of the first National Base Ball Association in 1857, to the culminating point of the world-wide reputation it attained as the leading American field sport, which was secured by the grand tour of the civilized world by its greatest professional exemplars in 1888-9. There is one consideration which the recent history of the professional branch of the fraternity has made very prominent, and that is the well merited reputation the game has achieved, through the effective legislative work of the National League of professional clubs, of being the most honestly conducted public sport now in vogue. In this great essential, of having the game played in its integrity by its professional experts, it stands side by side with the national field game of England, the glorious old sport of Cricket. It has been the misfortune of nearly every other sport in which professionals have taken part within the past decade, to be lowered in public estimation through the evil influence of the pool gambling which has been such a curse to every sport with which it is connected. The National League at the very outset of its organization plainly perceived that in order to establish professional ball play in public favor, with the very best class of patrons, it must give the death blow to pool gambling in order to secure a permanent existence; and the League has always been and always will be a deadly foe to this evil.

In the preparation of a volume of this comprehensive character, it became a necessity for the publishers to obtain the editorial services of the best known writer in each branch of athletic sport. That this has been well done, from the general editorship of Mr. Fynes through the entire list of his assistants, will be conceded by every one familiar with the leading writers in these several connections.

It affords the writer of these introductory words, who has reached the standing of a *veteran* in these lines, great pleasure in bidding these pages *bon voyage.*

PREFACE.

BY THE EDITOR.

It seems to me that if this book stands for anything, it is a significant tribute to the American public's amazing growth as an intelligent, generous and enthusiastic promoter of athletic sports. Within these hundreds of pages you may read of the origin and development of a variety of pastimes; yet they have been treated of only in outline, and not a third part of all the forms of exercise and diversion popular with us has it been possible to deal with in the limitations of space necessarily set by the publishers.

Still, this volume will go far toward placing in a permanent form some impartial impressions and accurate records of our chief sports. It is due to the publishers to say that they have entered into the spirit of the work with a fine sense of its importance, and with generous coöperation in all its details; and for this, too, lovers of athletic sports everywhere have to be especially grateful, since their literature hitherto has been peculiarly ephemeral and economic.

The selection of writers has been made with care, with a view to an authoritative treatment of the subjects assigned to them; and it is believed that the reader's verdict will endorse the editor's judgment. Certainly there has been no lack of research, or of zeal, on the part of the several contributors, all of whom are writers for the daily newspaper press, thoroughly in touch with their respective subjects, and, therefore, peculiarly valuable as commentators.

Though each writer has been somewhat circumscribed in the space allotted, there has been no loss of harmony or of sympathy in the general handling of the work. It is believed that Mr. Harris's sketch of the wonderful progress of the game of baseball will be read with conspicuous interest, because it is the most careful and most complete paper upon that subject ever put into type. Mr. Harris acknowledges his indebtedness to Messrs. Albert H. Wright and W. M. Rankin, both of the *New York Clipper*, who placed at his disposal valuable statistics and facts relating to the earlier days of the baseball game.

J. AUSTIN FYNES.

January, 1890.

CONTENTS.

PREFATORY.

	PAGE
Introduction by Henry Chadwick	5
Preface by the Editor, J. Austin Fynes	8
Table of Contents	9
List of Illustrations	11

I.
BASEBALL.
BY W. I. HARRIS.

PART I.—Origin of the Game	23
PART II.—History from 1845-1868	28
PART III.—Professional Baseball Established	37
PART IV.—The National League	59
PART V.—The American Association	130
PART VI.—The National Brotherhood	144

II.
THE "AROUND THE WORLD" TOUR.
BY HARRY C. PALMER.

Organization of the Tour	151
Across the Continent	162
In California	189
San Francisco to Honolulu	200
At Honolulu, Sandwich Islands	206
Honolulu to New Zealand	228
The Samoan Islands	233
At Auckland, New Zealand	235
Auckland to Sydney, N. S. W.	239

CONTENTS.

	PAGE
Sydney	241
On to Melbourne, Victoria	253
Melbourne to Adelaide	265
Ballarat	268
Back to Melbourne	271
On the Indian Ocean	282
Port Adelaide	287
Ceylon, with its Strange Sights	293
From Ceylon to Egypt	304
The Gulf of Aden	310
The Red Sea and Suez	311
Cairo	316
The Pyramids and the Sphynx	323
In the Suez Canal	340
On European Soil	344
Naples, Pompeii and Vesuvius	347
Rome and the Coliseum	363
Florence	376
Pisa, Genoa, Nice	381
Monaco and Monte Carlo	383
Guests at Monte Carlo	389
On to Paris	391
In the French Metropolis	392
The English Channel	402
In Old England	404
London	405
Bristol	416
Back to London	420
Birmingham	422
Sheffield and Bradford	423
Glasgow	424
Manchester	425
Liverpool	426
On the Irish Channel	428
Belfast	429
Dublin	430
Callan, Kildare, Kilkenney	432
Cork and Blarney Castle	437
Queenstown	439
Homeward Bound	441
Home Again	442
Banquets, Receptions, etc.	444
The Tour Ended	460

III.
LAWN TENNIS IN ENGLAND.
BY "BANSHEE."

	PAGE
PART I.—Gentlemen Players	461
PART II.—Lady Players	474

IV.
LAWN TENNIS IN AMERICA.
BY T. A. KELLOGG.

PART I.—Early Players and Games	484
PART II.—Tennis Tournaments	489
PART III.—Excellence of the Game	504
PART IV.—Ladies and Gentlemen as Players	512
PART V.—Delightful Associations of the Game	516

V.
LACROSSE.
BY J. ALLEN LOWE.

The Game in Canada and Elsewhere 519

VI.
POLO.
BY E. L. SNELL.

History and Description of the Game 544

VII.
FOOTBALL.
BY FREDERICK R. BURTON.

The Old Game and the New 549

VIII.
COLLEGE BASEBALL.
BY J. B. MORSE.

Origin and Spirit of the Game 559

IX.
THE PRESS AND SPORT.
BY FRANCIS C. RICHTER.

Influence of the Press on Sport 569

X.
SKETCHES OF BASEBALL WRITERS.
BY W. I. HARRIS.

Portraits and Biographical Sketches 575

XI.
AQUATICS.
BY W. S. QUIGLEY.

PART I. —Amateur Oarsmen 611
PART II. —American College Contests 625
PART III.—English College Contests 631
PART IV. —Improvements at the Oar 634
PART V. —Famous Oarsmen 645

XII.
NED HANLAN ON ROWING.
BY HARRY C. PALMER.

A Personal Interview 649

XIII.
CRICKET.
BY J. A. FYNES.

View of the Game in England and America 681

XIV.
'CYCLING.
BY F. P. PRIAL.

PART I. —Development of the 'Cycle 685
PART II. —The 'Cycle Trade of To-day 689
PART III.—Choice of a Wheel 692
PART IV.—Growth of 'Cycling Influence 695

XV.
APPENDIX.

Statistics of Baseball 699
Scores of Games in the "Around the World" Tour 708

Illustrations.

Baseball at Crystal Palace Grounds, London (Illuminated Plate)	*Frontispiece.*
	PAGE
Athletic Baseball Club (Full Page)	22
Baltimore Baseball Club (Full Page)	31
Brooklyn Baseball Club (Full Page)	41
Chicago Baseball Club (Full Page)	51
Cleveland Baseball Club (Full Page)	62
Columbus Baseball Club (Full Page)	71
Indianapolis Baseball Club (Full Page)	81
Kansas City Baseball Club (Full Page)	91
Louisville Baseball Club (Full Page)	102
Philadelphia Baseball Club (Full Page)	111
The Late Charles J. Ferguson	116
Pittsburgh Baseball Club (Full Page)	121
Saint Louis Baseball Club (Full Page)	131
Washington Baseball Club (Full Page)	141
Game on the Philadelphia Grounds (Full Page)	147
Around the World Tour Poster (Full Page)	150
Albert G. Spalding	152
Leigh S. Lynch	154
Professor Bartholomew's Specialty	161
Practical Joking in the Sleeping Car	166
The Mascot's March to Victory	169
Ed Hanlon's Great Catch	175
In a Hurry to Catch the Conveyances	177
Home Runs of a Startling Sort	180
Currecanti Needle	184
The Mascot in Repose	186
Healy's Day-dreams Rudely Broken	187
The "Alameda" at her Dock in Honolulu	208

ILLUSTRATIONS.

	PAGE
Royal Hawaiian Band	210
King Kalakaua and his Suite (Full Page)	211
Hawaiian Family Eating Poi	213
Coast Scenery near Honolulu	216
Throne Room of Palace, Honolulu (Full Page)	217
Statue of Kamehameha, the Conqueror	219
Hawaiian Lady in Riding Costume	220
Royal Night Feast at Honolulu (Illuminated Plate)	225
Cutting "Pigeon Wings" before King Kalakaua	227
Cricket on Shipboard	229
Captain Morse, of the "Alameda"	231
Bird's-eye View of Auckland and its Harbor	235
Headlands of Sydney Harbor	239
Panoramic View of Sydney and its Harbor	241
A Colonial Thoroughfare	242
Mr. Daniel O'Connor, M. P., Sydney, N. S. W.	243
His Worship, Mayor Harris, of Sydney, N. S. W.	244
Base Sliding as Australians Saw It	246
Farm Cove	248
Bathing Beach at Cougee Bay	249
Town Hall of Melbourne, Australia	254
Major Wardell, Secretary Victorian Cricket Association	255
Grand Hotel, Melbourne, Australia (Full Page)	257
Grand Stand, Melbourne Cricket Grounds	260
Baseball Tourists at Melbourne	261
Exposition Building at Melbourne	264
Professor Bartholomew	265
Botanical Garden, Ballarat	270
A Jolly Party at Fern Glen	273
Native Australian Woman and Babe	274
Native Australian Man and Boy	275
Flight on a False Alarm	277
The "Salier" at her Dock, Port Melbourne	281
Captain Thalenhorst	283
The Mascot's Humiliation at the Punka Rope	286
Amusements on Shipboard	287
Carrying Out the Sentence	291
Fishing Boats of the Cingalese	294
The Jolly Jinrickshaw	297
Business Booths in a Columbo Street	298
Religious Procession at Columbo, Ceylon (Full Page)	299
Snake Charmer and his Pet	302
The "Essex" (Full Page)	305

ILLUSTRATIONS.

	PAGE
City of Suez	312
The Great Suez Canal	313
Irrigating Machine of the Nile	314
Egyptian Woman with Face Ornaments	315
Creating a Panic at an Egyptian Station	316
Dancing Girl at the Eldorado, Cairo (Full Page)	319
MacMillan and Palmer Mounted for a Ride	321
A Camel Train	324
The Tourists Mounted for the Pyramids (Full Page)	325
Bridge of the Nile	328
The Contest of the Camels	329
The Sphynx in Lively Company (Full Page)	331
At the Foot of the Pyramids	334
The Khedive of Egypt	335
Passenger Boat of the Nile	336
Common River Boats of the Nile	337
An Egyptian School	338
A Barber Shop in Cairo	339
Khedive's Palace (Full Page)	341
Healy Settling the Egyptian Peddler	343
Sorrento, the Palisade City of the Mediterranean	347
Via Roma, Naples	349
Remains of the Amphitheatre, Pompeii	350
The House Ruffa, Pompeii	351
Street of Plenty, Pompeii	352
Railway up Mount Vesuvius	353
A Peep into Vesuvius	355
San Carlos Theatre, Naples (Full Page)	359
Court of San Martino, Naples	361
Novel Conveyance	362
The Corso of Rome	363
Front of St. Peter's	365
Ruins of the Forum	366
Tourists in the Coliseum (Full Page)	367
Interior View of the Coliseum	369
The Arch of Titus	370
The Arch of Septimus	371
Rome from the Shore of the Tiber	372
Ready for Play in the Villa Borghese (Illuminated Plate)	373
The Appian Way	375
Column of the Conception	376
Front of the Duomo, Florence	377
Statue of Michael Angelo	378

ILLUSTRATIONS.

	PAGE
Bird's-eye View of Florence (Full Page)	379
Panoramic View of Monaco	383
Casino of Monte Carlo	384
Ante-room of the Casino	385
Main Hall of the Casino (Full Page)	387
Panel Decoration of the Casino	390
Panel Decoration of the Casino	391
Notre Dame, Paris (Full Page)	393
Eiffel Tower	395
The Column of July	396
Arc de Triomphe	399
Mr. C. W. Alcock	405
The Tourists at the Club House, London (Full Page)	409
Fac-simile Card of the Prince of Wales	411
The Club House	414
Dr. W. G. Grace, the Famous Cricketer	416
His Royal Highness the Prince of Wales (Full Page)	417
Special Train of the Tourists	422
The Irish Jaunting Car	429
An Ivy-covered Castle	431
Phœnix Park, Dublin	433
Sackville Street, Dublin	434
Grafton Street, Dublin	435
Blarney Castle	437
"A Fine Ould Irish Gintleman"	438
The "All-Americas" after Reaching Home	443
Dr. James Dwight	485
Joseph S. Clark	487
R. Livingston Beeckman	490
Richard D. Sears	492
Henry W. Slocum, Jr.	494
Champion Tennis Tournament, Newport, 1889 (Full Page)	495
Thomas Pettitt	498
Fred. S. Mansfield	501
Howard A. Taylor	503
E. G. Meers	506
Q. A. Sh w	508
Dr. George Beers	521
In Full Run at Lacrosse	523
Wm. G. Hodgson	524
William A. Davis	526
Ross Mackenzie	533
Montreal Lacrosse Team, Champions, 1889 (Full Page)	535

ILLUSTRATIONS.

	PAGE
William L. Maltby	538
Wm. D. Aird	539
Brilliant Dash in Polo (Full Page)	545

PORTRAITS OF BASEBALL WRITERS:

Henry Chadwick	575
Alfred H. Wright	577
Ren Mulford, Jr.	580
Albert Mott	581
Simon Goodfriend	582
Frank H. Brunell	583
Henry F. Boynton	584
Harry M. Weldon	585
Byron B. Johnson	585
Thomas S. Fullwood	586
John P. Campbell	587
Harry C. Palmer	588
John D. Pringle	589
William M. Rankin	589
Philip F. Nash	590
Alfred R. Cratly	591
Walter O. Eschwege	592
Peter J. Donohue	593
O. P. Caylor	594
Jacob C. Morse	595
Charles J. Merrill	596
Alexander M. Gillam	596
John H. Mandigo	597
Robert M. Larner	598
Charles F. Mathison	599
George H. Dickinson	600
Edward S. Sheridan	601
Francis C. Richter	602
William D. Sullivan	603
Joseph C. Pritchard	604
George E. Stackhouse	605
William M. Crounse	606
Horace S. Fogel	608
William I. Harris	610

Harvard Crew at their Training Ground	629
Ned Hanlan, ex-Champion	650

ILLUSTRATIONS.

	PAGE
Hanlan's Victory at the Centennial	659
Hanlan's Reception at Toronto	662
Hanlan Playing Dead	669
Rowing Course at Melbourne	675
Main Street, Ballarat	676
Cricket Game at Lord's, London (Illuminated Plate)	680

THE ATHLETIC TEAM, APRIL, 1889.

I.

BASEBALL.*

PART I.

THE great national sport of the American people is distinctively and almost exclusively the game of baseball. This is not the opinion of a crank. It is a fact admitted by everybody save, perhaps, a limited number of the followers of the turf—its only rival. But there is really no comparison between the two species of amusement in their extent and popularity, and the causes which give them prominence. The one great mainstay of horse-racing is the gambling element that is inseparably connected with it. Take away the betting, and horse-racing, except among a comparatively small minority of its votaries, would fade away like the leaves before the chilling blasts of winter. Not so with baseball. It needs no such adjunct to endear it to the populace. It is engrafted into the hearts of the people. To slightly change a saying of the great master of dramatic literature—

> "Age cannot wither it, nor custom stale
> Its infinite variety."

Time has made no marks upon it to its deterioration. Like the work of the great Bard of Avon, the more one sees of it the more one wants to see. A love of the game has invaded every domestic circle in the land. It furnishes its own attractions, its own excitements; it depends upon no outside influences, other than local pride, for its hold upon the affections of Americans; it is the noblest of manly exercises, and while

---

* By W. I. Harris.

at times it has been defiled, the blotches have been removed from it; it is played on its merits, and it stands to-day the purest sport that the sun shines upon that contains professional experts among its exponents.

The progress of baseball in America has been truly phenomenal, and the hold it has obtained upon the affections of all classes increases rather than diminishes. Its popularity with the masses is extraordinary, as the great crowds which attend scientific exhibitions by first-class teams easily show. A recent illustration of the remarkable interest displayed in the game was the excitement and interest attending upon the playing of six games between the New York and Boston teams, near the close of the season of 1889. At three of these games, played in Boston, the attendance was 31,767, and at the three contests in New York City these figures were exceeded by 115. The total for the three games was 31,882. The final game in New York was witnessed by at least 16,000 people. Of these, 14,364 went through the turnstiles, and the balance viewed the conflict from the bluffs overlooking the new Polo Grounds. And this vast crowd paid from fifty cents to one dollar each for the privilege they enjoyed. These figures have been beaten two or three times, so far as single games go. Over 25,000 people were present on the old Polo Grounds, Decoration Day, 1886, to see the New York and Detroit teams play; over 15,000 witnessed a game in 1888, between New York and Chicago; fully 22,000 people saw the game Decoration Day, 1889, at Brooklyn, between the St. Louis and Brooklyn teams, of the American Association; but, for six successive contests between the same two clubs, the figures in the New York-Boston series of 1888—63,649 paying spectators—have never before been equaled.

The history of ball-playing dates back to the ancients. The lads of Greece and of Rome played a species of handball, but it is doubtful if they, or even the French boys who played handball in modern times, ever dreamed of the baseball of the present day. The origin of baseball is in dispute, and the question will probably never be positively settled. Several writers contend that it came from the old English game of "Rounders," and there is some evidence to that effect. Others are equally positive that the game is entirely an American product, and the evidence adduced is quite as strong, indeed stronger, that this theory is the correct one. To the average devotee of the sport the question does not assume much importance. Only a minority know anything about it, and the vast majority care less. They know they have it, they like it, they wouldn't be without it, and are quite content to believe that the game is a home product. Without wasting valuable space upon the long arguments pro and con, it is enough to say that the concensus of research and opinion justify such a belief as having fact for its foundation.

Baseball was not born. Like Topsy, it "growed." The first games played were no more like the present scientific game of ball than the New Amsterdam of the Dutch settlers was like the New York of 1889. The primitive game was first played in this country, so far as it can be ascertained, as far back as the beginning of the nineteenth century. It undoubtedly originated among the schoolboys of that period. John M. Ward, who is one of the most ardent advocates of the American origin of the game, claims that "Cat" ball was the foundation upon which improvements have been made, and the game brought by evolution to its present almost perfect condition. Certainly, there is ample evidence that this game of "Old Cat," and variations of it under various names, was the forerunner of the present national game. As the pastime was improved and extended, it attracted the attention of older heads, who saw the opportunity it afforded for healthful, enjoyable and manly exercise, and realized somewhat the advantages to be derived from a code of regulations to govern its play.

The first regularly organized club of which we have any record was the Knickerbocker Club, of New York. That organization was purely an amateur one, and took form in the year 1845. The rules prepared by the Knickerbockers were very primitive, but were considered quite complete and thorough in those days. The framers of them looked not to the future, and, indeed, it is well that they did not, for to have loaded down the game at that time with any of its present technical and complicated rules would have been to crush it at once. It had to grow in popular favor, and the mission of the Knickerbockers was to start the ball rolling and establish a basis. To do so it was necessary to simplify the game, and they performed their part of the programme. Fate had designed them grandly, and they builded even better than they knew.

Hence the regulations were simplicity itself. The pitcher, who is to-day the king, was then of very little importance. He had not demonstrated what a factor he was in the game, and the pioneer rule-makers gave him almost unlimited license. The only restriction was that he must pitch the ball, and not throw it. The other details were quite as simple. They were few and explicitly stated, and the game prospered under them for six years, during which time the Knickerbockers had a practical monopoly of the field, so far as systematic organization was concerned; but the interest in the sport was growing steadily, and soon other clubs sprang into existence. Among them were the Gotham, Eagle, Empire and Mutual clubs, playing at Hoboken, on the Elysian Fields there; the Baltics of Harlem, Unions of Morrisania, and the Atlantic, Excelsior, Putnam and Eckfords, of Brooklyn. The interest in the game did not languish, and soon efforts were made to bring the methods of playing it to a national standard.

From 1851 to 1857 it was played differently in different sections. In New York they had the game inaugurated by the Knickerbockers; in Philadelphia a species of "Old Cat," called townball, predominated; and in Boston another version was played. In 1857 a move was made toward making the sport a national one by a convention of the representatives of ball-clubs, and the adoption of a set of rules which were intended to govern the game in all sections of the country. This convention was held in New York City, and sixteen clubs took part, nearly all of which were located in the cities of New York and Brooklyn.

The organization, then perfected, was known as "The National Association of Baseball Players." Twenty-five clubs from various parts of the country sent delegates. A code of rules was adopted, and baseball formally took its place as the recognized national sport of America. The new association met once a year, and a committee of its delegates revised the rules. The game was making rapid strides when the Civil War broke out, and for a time, although the association was kept intact, the game languished. But at the close of the war it took a new start, and from 1865 to 1870 amateur baseball flourished and spread itself in every direction. As an evidence of the rapidity with which the game has become popular, it may be stated that the association had increased from 25 clubs in 1858 to 202 clubs in 1866, with delegates from organizations in Pennsylvania and the West, representing fully two hundred clubs more. And these clubs were located in eighteen States and Territories. Amateur baseball was at the pinnacle of its greatness. It soon became evident, however, that teams of adults, to be successful, must make a business of ball-playing. But players could not afford to do that without some remuneration, and, as a result, most of the so-called amateur teams soon had among their members men who received compensation in one way or another for their services. This practice became so frequent that various attempts were made to curb it from time to time, but none of them proved successful. Finally, in 1868 the National Association was forced to recognize the professionals as a class. So fast did they multiply after this, and so expertly did they play the game, that the amateurs could make no headway, and soon professional clubs were in operation, and openly known as such, everywhere. The most famous of these was the Red Stockings, of Cincinnati, whose wonderful record of 1869, during which they played without a defeat, has never since been equaled. It took just about three years for professional games to crowd out amateur contests as the premier attraction. The last useful convention of the Amateur Club Association was held in 1870. The following year saw the organization of a professional association, and witnessed the first recognized championship contest in America. Since that period amateur baseball has flourished, and amateur clubs have multiplied until their name is legion; but amateur teams, except in the contests of those representing the great colleges of our country, have ceased to attract national attention, although they still excite local enthusiasm and stir up home pride. There is no question that amateur games create intense feeling and rivalry in their respective localities, and will continue to do so as long as baseball shall maintain its popularity; but public attention is now monopolized by professional experts, who have made the game a scientific exhibition of skill such as the originators of the sport would scarcely have believed to be possible.

The first professional association lasted five years. Then came the National League of Professional Baseball Clubs, which ruled the sport with a strong hand and purified it from the taint of dishonesty. That organization for seven years claimed and exercised exclusive jurisdiction over the sport. Then came the organization of the American Association, which has, since 1883, divided with the League the responsibility of conducting the game upon its present honest and remunerative basis.

PART II.

The missionaries of baseball were the amateurs who introduced the game and carried it along from 1845 to 1868. Before considering the progress of professional baseball playing in this country, the work of these pioneers and the events of their times should receive proper attention. No attempt will be made at detailed description. The early history of the game up to the time it began to assume importance enough to receive the recognition of the press has been briefly told in my introductory chapter. This one will be devoted to outlining the principal events of the period from 1857 to 1868, when amateurs ruled the game, and amateur baseball was truly in its glory. This period of twelve years was what might appropriately be described as the infancy of the sport. That infancy was limited really to seven years, for baseball was comparatively stagnant during the five years of the Rebellion. But in the three years succeeding the war much was done to popularize the game, and its spread during that time was remarkable.

The first match game of ball of which we have any accurate record, took place at Hoboken, N. J., June 19th, 1846. The contesting clubs were the Knickerbocker and the New York. This was the first game played under regular rules. From that time to the formation of the National Association there were no recognized contests to settle the question of either State or National superiority.

The first regular baseball convention ever held took place in New York City, May, 1857. The following clubs were represented by two delegates each: Knickerbocker, Gotham, Eagle, Empire, Putnam, Baltic, Excelsior, Atlantic, Harmony, Harlem, Eckford, Bedford, Nassau, Continental, Union and Olmypic. The second convention was held on March 10th, 1858, at which, in addition to the above clubs, delegates from the Metropolitan, Columbian, Osceola, Oriental, Stuyvesant, Hamilton, Pastime, Liberty (of New Brunswick), Monument, Amity, St. Nicholas and Mutual were present. These clubs formed "The National Association of Baseball Players for 1859." It was not until the first year that this organization assumed jurisdiction over baseball that there was anything like a championship contest played.

At that time baseball was mainly confined to New York State, although Massachusetts, by the establishment of the Olympic Club of Boston, in 1854, had begun to show an interest in the sport, and in 1857 Boston had a number of clubs, among them the Elm Tree, Green Mountain, Olympic and Trimountain, the latter being the first Boston club to join the National Association. These clubs, however, played under the rules of the New England game, which differed from those of the New York game.

In New York State the feeling of rivalry between the clubs of New York and Brooklyn was as intense then as it is to-day. The crack teams of that day were the Atlantic, Excelsior, Putnam and Eckford, of Brooklyn, and the Knickerbocker, Eagle, Gotham and Empire clubs, of New York. It was decided that the best test of superiority would be shown by a series of games between picked players from each. Both cities selected their best men, and in 1858 occurred the first series of games ever played for a championship. These games were played on what was known as the "Fashion Course," Long Island. The first one, played July 20th, 1858, was won by New York, by a score of 22 to 18. The teams for the first game were made up as follows:—

New York: Pinkney, 2b.; Benson, c.f.; Bixby, 3b.; De Bost, c.; Gelston, s.s.; Wadsworth, 1b.; Hoyt, l.f.; Van Cott, p.; Wright, r.f.

Brooklyn: Leggett, c.; Holder, 2b.; Pidgeon, s.s.; Grum, c.f.; P. O'Brien, l.f.; Price, 1b.; M. O'Brien, p.; Masten, 3b., Burr, r.f.

The second game was played August 17th, and was won by Brooklyn. Score, 29 to 8. In this contest both teams had new men, and there was a general change of positions. The same may be said of the third match, which was won by New York, 29 to 18. This gave the palm to the Gotham amateurs.

Some of these early champions have passed over the river. Those of them who are now living are still baseball "cranks." Two of them are still identified with the game. One is Richard Pearce, better known as "Dickey," who played as short stop for Brooklyn in the last two games, and who was afterward one of the greatest of professional players of his day. He is still interested in the game, and is occasionally seen upon the field in the capacity of Umpire. The other is Harry Wright, of the New York, the same man who is now manager of the Philadelphia team, and whose name is a household word among the patrons of the sport. It may be noted that Mr. Wright's record in the first game was five outs and no runs, which probably accounts for the fact that he did not participate in the other two games. In fact, Harry was at that period more of a cricketer than a baseball player.

Among individual teams the Atlantics of Brooklyn were considered the crack team of all, a reputation they sustained in many a hard fought battle for many years with their New York rivals, the Gothams. In 1860 the Excelsior of Brooklyn made a stand against the Atlantic and practically wrested the supremacy from them. They arranged for a series of games, the first of which the Excelsior won, 23–4. The second contest fell to the Atlantic, 15–14. The third game was unfinished. It was played on the Putnam grounds, but at the end of the fifth inning the Excelsior refused to play the game out, claiming that the crowd was so prejudiced in favor of the Atlantic that it was impossible for the Excelsior to win. The score was then 8–6 in favor of the Excelsior. The two clubs never played together after this. After this series the game had quite a boom, which was materially increased by a successful trip made by the Excelsior through New York State and to Philadelphia and Baltimore.

In 1861 another match game was played between the combined talent of the Brooklyn clubs on one side and New York on the other. This game was arranged by Henry Chadwick and it took place on the Elysian Fields at Hoboken, October 21st. The best men of the Atlantic, Excelsior and Eckford represented Brooklyn, and their opponents were selected from the Mutual, Knickerbocker, Empire, Gotham and Eagle clubs. Harry Wright played third base for New York, and Pearce was catcher for Brooklyn. It was a memorable game, and was witnessed by over 10,000 people. The game is known as the "Silver

THE BALTIMORE TEAM, JUNE, 1889.

Ball Match," as a silver ball was given to the victors by the New York *Clipper*. The Brooklyn won, 18 to 6, clinching a decisive victory by scoring eight runs in the eighth inning.

In the West and in the South the game was beginning to obtain a foothold when the war broke out and all progress was stopped. In the East the Atlantic held the supremacy until 1862, when the Eckford won the nominal title of champions. They held it during the year 1863, and went through the season without a defeat. In 1864 the Atlantic again won the championship, and during the seasons of '64 and '65 did not lose a single regular game, a feat unprecedented in the history of the game. But it should be remembered that these clubs did not play over a dozen games each during each season. The Atlantic won again in 1866. In 1867 the Union, of Morrisania, won a series from the Atlantic and became the champions of the United States.

The year 1867 was a notable one in the annals of the game. In it the baseball supremacy so long held by Brooklyn clubs was wrested from the City of Churches, and the first great baseball tours were made that did so much for the material progress of the game. It has been said that the tour of the National Club, of Washington, was more efficient in booming the game than all that had been done in the five years previous to its inception, and there is a great deal of truth in the statement. Another great match between Brooklyn and New York, known as the Masonic Match, was arranged in the season of 1867. It was played August 8th, at Morrisania, on the Union Grounds. The New York men won, 13 to 7, which was a remarkable score in those days of a lively ball and straight-arm pitching. Among the men on the New York team afterward prominent as professionals were Pike, Birdsall, Hatfield, and Pabor. Among the Brooklynites who became famous were Joe Start and Bob Ferguson.

The four great teams of the day were the Atlantic, of Brooklyn, Mutual, of New York, Union, of Morrisania, and Athletic, of Philadelphia. The struggles of these clubs were fierce and generally close. The make-up of the four teams in 1867 is here given:—

Atlantic—Pearce, s. s.; Smith, 2 b.; Crane, c. f.; Start, 1 b.; Ferguson, 3 b.; Mills, c.; Galvin, Kenney, r. f.; McDonald, l. f.; Zettlein, p.

Mutual—Hatfield, 2 b.; Waterman, 3 b.; Devyr, s. s.; Watts and Martin, pitchers; Pike, l. f.; Hunt, c. f.; Bearman, 1 b.; Jewett, c.; McMahon, r. f.; Zeller, fielder.

Union—Goldie, 1 b.; Martin, 2 b.; Pabor, p.; Austin, c. f.; Akin, s. s.; Birdsall, c.; Ketchum, 3 b.; Beals, r. f.; Smith, l. f.

Athletic—Kleinfelder, 1 b.; McBride, p.; Reach, 2 b.; Wilkins, s. s.; Fisler, 3 b.; Sensenderfer, l. f.; Berry, c. f.; Radcliff, c.; Cuthbert, r. f.

The Atlantic won their series from all of these clubs except the Union. For ten years the Atlantic and Eckford had held the championship for Brooklyn. July 31st, 1867, the Union defeated the Atlantic, 32 to 19, and finally won the championship by beating them a second time, on October 19th, by a score of 14 to 13. During this season the Union won one game from the Athletic, by a score of 101 to 13. Such a score nowadays would be an impossibility. Imagine a professional team of the present day making 101 runs in six innings! The fact shows what enthusiasts the players were in those days. One of the peculiarities of baseball then was the method of settling the championship. One team, in this case the Atlantic, were the acknowledged champions. Any team that could win two out of three from the Atlantic became champions, no matter how many games they might previously have lost to other clubs. In 1867, previous to defeating the Atlantic, the Union had lost a series to the Irvington, Athletic, Union of Lansingburg, and Mutual, and yet were styled champions. In 1866, the year previous, the Athletic played through the season with only two defeats, once by the Atlantic and once by the Union.

There will always be a question as to the real supremacy of the Atlantic in that year. They went to Philadelphia to play a game but there were so many people on the grounds that after one inning had been played the game was given up. Over 40,000 people are said to have been present, the majority on the outside from which they could overlook the field. As the admission fee was merely nominal, the size of the crowd has seldom been questioned. When the game was played off the Athletic won, 31 to 12. About 2000 people paid $1 a head to see the game within the gates, while thousands witnessed it from the outside. A quarrel over the gate receipts prevented another meeting between the two clubs that year.

The great event of 1867 was the now celebrated tour of the National, of Washington. This was notable for being the first extended trip through the West of an Eastern club. The National were mostly men employed under Government at the Capital. When compared with the baseball trips of this decade the tour of the National Club seems trivial, but at that time and in those circumstances a trip of that nature by an amateur club was an achievement of unusual importance, and the influence it had upon the progress of the game was hardly appreciated even by those who conceived and carried it out. The National left Washington July 11th, 1867, and proceeded direct to Columbus, Ohio, where they won their first game from the Capital Club, by a score of 90 to 10. From Columbus they went to Cincinnati and took a game from the Cincinnati Reds, for which the famous Harry Wright was pitcher. The other games were played at Louisville, Indianapolis, St. Louis and Chicago.

The players who made this pioneer trip were W. F. Williams, p., law student; F. P. Norton, catcher, treasury clerk; G. A. E. Fletcher, first base, clerk in 3d auditor's office; N. C. McLean, clerk, 3d auditor's office; E. A. Parker, l. f., clerk, internal revenue department; E. G. Smith, s. s., clerk, 4th auditor's office; S. L. Studley, r. f., clerk in treasury department; N. W. Berthrong, c. f., clerk of comptroller of currency; G. Wright, second base, clerk, 238 Pennsylvania Avenue; A. V. Robinson, clerk; George H. Fox, third base, graduate (1867) Georgetown College. The trip cost the club nearly $3000, as they did not take gate receipts.

The team played ten games altogether, winning nine of them. The record of runs made shows the vast difference between baseball then and now, when almost the acme of perfection in rules and in scientific play has been reached. The one game lost by the National was at Dexter Park, Chicago, where they were beaten by the Forest City, by a score of 29 to 23. In that game the pitcher of the winning club was a man who is to-day the head and front of professional baseball in this country, Albert G. Spalding of Chicago. Another man who participated in the game against the National was Ross Barnes, afterward acknowledged to be the king of second basemen in his career with the Boston Club. The largest score made by the National was at St.

Louis, where they defeated the Union of that city, 113 to 26. And this with the mercury registering 104° in the shade. Their most decisive victory was at Chicago, when they defeated the Excelsior, champions of the West, 49 to 4. The National, in the ten games, scored 735 runs to 175 by their opponents. That the ball was lively, the fact that 32 home runs were made by the National fully attests. George Wright made 15 of these and George Fox 10. As a testimonial of the speed of Mr. William F. Williams, of the National, it is noted that only two home runs were made off his delivery by opposing clubs. Williams was a terror. The historian saw him pitch at Washington, and, in common with other small boys, firmly believed in the statements made by a verse-writer of those days, whose effusion began something after this style:—

> "Billy Williams, he
> Could split a two-inch plank."

But the swiftest delivery of Williams did not equal the pace of the balls thrown overhand now-a-days.

This memorable tour was planned by Colonel Frank Jones, of Washington, a noted Treasury official of that time. The Nationals were really the nearest approach to a truly amateur team that then existed in the East. George Wright was then, to a certain extent, a professional, and afterward openly became one whose celebrity and superiority were never questioned as long as he remained in active service. He is to-day the head of a flourishing sporting goods house in Boston. Of the others, none of whom ever became professionals, Mr. Williams is now a prominent and successful official in the United States Treasury at Washington, and Mr. Berthrong is a successful artist in Boston. The team was accompanied on its trip by Henry Chadwick, as the representative of *The American Chronicle, Sunday Mercury*, etc.

For some years previous to the celebrated trip made by the National, the practice of paying certain players for their services was in vogue in two-thirds of the so-called amateur teams in the country, and many were the efforts made by the National Association to preserve the amateur character of the game, but all efforts in this direction were useless. A way was found to get around the rules, and all the clubs had professionals employed. This was especially true of the Athletic Club, which won the championship in 1868, receiving the gold ball offered as a trophy by *The New York Clipper*. The Athletic team was substantially the same as it was in 1867, although some of the men changed their positions. *The Clipper* medals for individual excellence in their positions were won as follows: McBride, pitcher, Radcliff, catcher, Fisler, first base, Reach, second base, Sensenderfer, centre field, of the Athletics; Waterman, third base, Hatfield, left field, Johnson, right field, of the Cincinnatis; and George Wright, short stop, of the Unions of Morrisania.

At its meeting in 1868 the National Association decided to divide the players into classes, and for the first time recognized professionals. This was the beginning of the end of the National Association as an amateur body or as a guardian of the baseball interests of the country. Its mission had been fulfilled, and, although its jurisdiction was acknowledged during the next two years, the professionals monopolized the attention of the country, and amateur clubs soon ceased to be of any national importance.

PART III.

Professional baseball was officially established in America in the fall of 1868, when the National Association recognized it by dividing players into two classes. The first regular professional team was the Red Stockings, of Cincinnati, organized and captained by Harry Wright. This famous team has the unequaled record of completing an entire season without a defeat. It is true that the Eckfords, of Brooklyn, did not lose a game in 1863, but it is also true that they only played nine match games. It is a fact, also, that the Atlantics, of Brooklyn, won 19 games in 1864, without losing one. But neither of these records equal the performance of the Cincinnatis, who won 56 games and tied one without a defeat. It has been asserted by some writers that the Atlantics also played through the season of 1865 without a defeat, but this is not strictly true, because the records of the

Atlantic Club show that the club was defeated by the Gothams 39 to 19, January 16th, at Hoboken. This game was played on skates. A number of such games were played in the East, but after a thorough trial the sport in that direction was abandoned, and baseball on ice has never been revived.

Some idea of the difference between the lively ball of 1869 and the dead ball of 1888 is shown by the run columns of the champion clubs of the two years. In 57 games the Red Stockings made 2,389 runs. In 1888, the New Yorkers, in 137 games, scored only 659 runs. From this it may be figured that the proportion of runs, games being equal, would be about nine to one in favor of the lively ball. The great superiority of the Red Stockings over their opponents was shown by the fact that the aggregate score of the losing teams was only 574.

The members of Harry Wright's great team, with the salaries they received for their services, were:

Harry Wright, c.f.,	$1,800	Fred. Waterman,	$800
George Wright, s s.,	1,800	Douglass Allison,	700
Asa Brainard, p.,	800	A. J. Leonard,	700
Charles Gould, 1b.,	800	C. A. McVey,	700
C. J. Sweasy, 1b.,	700	Hurley,	600

This made a total of $9,400 for the entire team.

The salary list of the Boston team of 14 men, in 1889, was $40,000, and that of the New York team of 16 men reached $45,000. The pitcher was not so important in 1869. Then Brainard received $14 a game. In 1889 Tim Keefe received a salary of $4,500, and, as he pitched about 45 times, his work netted him $100 a game.

The Red Stockings had a regular picnic in the West, and then defeated all their Eastern rivals, although some gave them a hard squeeze. Their closest game was with the Mutuals of New York, whom they defeated 4 to 2, a phenomenally low score at that time. They also defeated the Forest Citys of Cleveland, Haymakers of Troy, Atlantics and Eckfords of Brooklyn, Athletics of Philadelphia, Nationals of Washington, and Forest City of Rockford, Ill. These were the great teams of that day. The Rockfords came the nearest to beating the Reds, having them 14 to 12 in the ninth inning, but the Reds got the necessary three runs and pulled the game out of the fire. On the Rockfords were "Ross" Barnes, Addy, Hastings, and Al Spalding, all of whom became famous players a little later.

The wonderful success of the Red Stockings led to the establishment of similar clubs in all sections of the country, and in 1870 there was at least a score of purely professional teams. A dozen of these achieved national reputation. Among them were the Athletics, Atlantics, Chicagos, Forest Citys of Rockford, Forest Citys of Cleveland, Unions of Morrisania, Olympics and Nationals of Washington, Marylands of Baltimore, Mutuals of New York, and Haymakers of Troy. The Red Stockings, of course, continued in the field. It should be said that the element of greed had not at that time entered very largely into baseball. No one thought of making a fortune out of it. All that the backers of the clubs were anxious about was to pay expenses. Indeed, in some places the members of the clubs, being for the most part well to do, didn't mind putting up a few dollars for their fun. They rather liked the assessments for deficiencies, and were really agreeably disappointed if there were none to pay. It will be understood that at that time baseball had not become a business as it is to-day. Individuals were not running the clubs. That is to say, the officers were not owners, most of them being responsible to large memberships. During 1870 the Cincinnatis, who were probably as successful as any team in the way of gate receipts, took in $29,726.26, and expended $29,724.87. In other words, the club's surplus on the season was only one dollar and thirty-nine cents. Of course, admission charges were small in those days, a quarter being the maximum, and the accommodations were not what they are in these days of magnificent pavilions. Some of these teams worked on the co-operative plan, but the leading clubs paid the men regular salaries.

The Atlantics won two games out of three from the Red Stockings, in 1870, one at Brooklyn, 8-7, and one at Philadelphia, 11-7. They were beaten at Cincinnati, 14-3. This gave the Atlantics the championship. The Atlantic team, the last one worthy of the name, was made up of Ferguson, c.; Zettlein, p.; Start, 1b.; Pike, 2b.; Smith, 3b.; Pearce, s.s.; Chapman, l.f.; Hall, c.f.; McDonald, r.f.

It was in this year that the term "Chicago," for shutting out a team, originated. On July 23rd the Mutuals went out to Chicago and defeated the Chicagos 9 to 0, and the expression "they Chicagoed the Chicagos" was used then. It spread everywhere, and since then a shutout has been called a "Chicago."

The Red Stockings were disbanded in 1870, most of the players going to Washington. Those who went to the Capital were Allison, Brainard, Sweasy, and Waterman. Allison was the only one of them who played any ball worth mentioning after they left the great team. The Wrights, Leonard, Gould, and McVey went to Boston, and did exactly the opposite from their recent partners, founding the great Hub team, which held the championship so many years. Brainard of the old Reds is dead. The Wright brothers are yet prominent figures in the game and trade. Andy Leonard is a clerk in the Water Board of Newark; Gould is a deputy sheriff at Cincinnati; McVey runs a saloon at San Francisco; Hurley is a lawyer in Cincinnati; Waterman and Sweasy are hustling against fate. When last heard from one was in Cincinnati and the other at Providence.

Among the best-known players of 1870 were Higham, Holdsworth, Gedney, Birdsall, and Pabor, of the Unions; Force and Berthrong, of the Olympics; Hicks, Glenn, and Hollingshead, of the Nationals; Ferguson, Zettlein, Pike, Hall, Chapman, Pearce, and Start, of the Atlantics; Wood, Myerle, Treacey, and Cuthbert, of the Chicagos; Jim and Will White, Pratt, Sutton, and Allison, of the Clevelands; Reach, McBride, and Malone, of the Athletics; McGeary, Fisher, York, and McMullen, of the Haymakers; Charles Mills, E. Mills, John Hatfield, Nelson, and Eggler, of the Mutuals; Mathews and Carey, of the Marylands. Of the stars of 1870, Jim and Will White, Nelson, and Force are still playing ball. Sutton and Harry Wright are managers, Ferguson, Pearce, and Mathews are umpires, George Wright and Al Reach are sporting goods manufacturers, Mr. Reach is president of the Philadelphia League Club, and Mr. Pike, a Brooklyn merchant.

Professionalism grew apace, and certain far-seeing men connected with the clubs of the day became satisfied that, as baseball was bound to be a business of itself, the professionals should have a league of their own. This suggestion was put into shape by N. E. Young, then secretary of the Olympic Club, of Washington. The suggestion was

THE BROOKLYN TEAM, APRIL, 1889.

boomed by Mr. Wright in the Philadelphia *Mercury* and Mr. Chadwick in the *Clipper*, and the result was the organization of the first professional association at 840 Broadway, New York, March 17th, 1871. The new body was called the National Association of Professional Ball Players. The delegates were James W. Kerns, Athletic Club, Philadelphia; J. W. Scofield, Union Club, Troy; Nicholas E. Young, Olympic Club, Washington; Alex. V. Davidson, Mutual Club, New York; William H. Ray, Eckford Club, Brooklyn; Harry Wright, Boston Club, Boston, and Forest City Club, Rockford, Ill.; J. F. Evans, Forest City Club, Cleveland; J M. Thatcher, White Stocking Club, Chicago; and Oscar R. Hough, National Club, Washington. Mr. Kerns was elected president, Mr. Evans vice-president, Mr. Young secretary, and Mr. Scofield treasurer.

The Association authorized a championship title, and provided for a pennant, or, as they called it officially then, "a championship streamer." This streamer was to go to the club winning the greatest number of games from other clubs entered. The rule read: "The series for the championship to be best three in five games, each club to play best three in five games with every other contesting club, at such time and place as they may agree upon." At this first convention no regular schedule was adopted. Clubs announced such and such dates, and they were agreed to or changed, as the majority decided. All clubs entered were to pay an entrance fee of $10.

It is interesting to note that this convention adopted the first rules for the government of players. They provided that no player under contract with one club should play with another until his first contract was honorably canceled; that in case of a dispute between clubs over a player, each club was to select the president of another club and these two a third, and the board so selected was to settle the question; that in a dispute between player and club both parties were to be heard and settled by the committee on championship. This primitive board of arbitration had the power to dissolve a contract. These rules are quite simple alongside the complicated baseball laws which eighteen years of experience have shown to be necessary.

The contestants for the first actual pennant known—the game under the new championship rules—were the Forest City Clubs, of Rockford and Cleveland; Kekiongas, of Fort Wayne, Ind.; Haymakers, of Troy; Olympics, Mutuals, Chicagos, Athletics, and the Bostons. The Athletics won the championship. They won 22 games and lost seven. Boston was second, with 22-10. The champions were Malone, c.; McBride, p.; Fisler, 1b.; Reach, 2b.; Meyerle, 3b.; Radcliff, s.s.; Cuthbert, l.f.; Sensenderfer, c.f.; Heubell, r.f. Bechtel and Tom Pratt were substitutes.

The Boston team of 1872 was practically the same as that of 1871. It consisted of C. A. McVey, c.; A. G. Spalding, p.; Chas. Gould, 1b.; Ross Barnes, 2b.; Harry Schafer, 3b.; George Wright, s.s.; Andrew Leonard, l.f.; Harry Wright, c.f.; Fraley Rogers, r.f.; David Birdsall and John J. Ryan, substitutes. This team, which Al Wright, of *The Clipper*, pronounces to have been the greatest ever organized, easily won the championship in 1872. This strong club was organized January 20th, 1871. The team varied some during the next four seasons, but the principal players were the same, and it was continuously successful. It is of importance to note here that the year 1872 was the first season when pitchers were openly permitted to use an underhand throw in delivering the ball to the batsman.

The great umpire of the day was "Nick" Young, now President of the League. He officiated in the most remarkable game played by the Bostons in 1871. It was with Chicago at Boston, September 5th, and was won by Boston. Chicago made one run in each of the first three innings, and when the fifth opened Boston had failed to score. In that inning, however, they got in a couple of runs, and had three men on bases when Charley Gould came to the plate and knocked the ball over the left field fence, bringing in four runs and winning the game, for neither side scored after that.

It should be noted that baseball had by this time become very popular among the Canadians, and in 1872 there were good teams established at London, Guelph, Toronto, Dundas, Ottawa, and Montreal, that at Guelph, the Maple Leafs, becoming quite famous. The Bostons made a trip through these cities in 1872, and fairly slaughtered them, defeating the Dauntless Club by a score of 68 to 0. The Maple Leafs were the only club to make any headway, and they were beaten 29 to 7.

The season of 1872 saw five new clubs in the Association. They were Baltimore, Atlantics, Troys, and two from Washington, the Olympics and the Nationals. The two latter, however, were rank failures. The Nationals didn't win a game, and the Olympics won only two, and both of those were from the Nationals. There were really only five clubs in it. They were the Bostons, Baltimores, Mutuals, Athletics, and Troys, and they finished in that order, Boston winning, with 39 games won and eight lost. Their nearest competitors were the Baltimores and Mutuals, with thirty-four victories each. The Baltimores lost 19 games against 20 for the Mutuals, and therefore took second place.

The Bostons, in 1873, won 43 games and lost 16, winning the pennant from the Philadelphia Club with 36 victories and 17 defeats. In that season the series was raised from five to nine games, and unless four were played with each club they could not be counted. The new men on the Boston team that year were Jim White, John Manning, James O'Rourke, and C. J. Sweasy. Bob Addy took Manning's place in the latter part of the season.

The other clubs in the Association that year, besides Boston and Philadelphia, were the Baltimores, Mutuals, Athletics, Atlantics, Washingtons, Resolutes, and Marylands. In this year John Burdock, Dickey Pearce, Remsen, and Pabor were members of the Atlantic Club. Devlin, afterwards disgraced for crookedness, was a substitute on the Philadelphias of 1873. It was thought that the Philadelphias would win the pennant in that year, but they failed because of dissipation in the ranks. The members were Malone, c.; Zettlein, p.; Mack, 1b.; Wood, 2b.; Meyerle, 3b.; Fulmer, s.s.; Cuthbert, l.f.; Treacey, c.f.; Bechtel, r.f.; Devlin, substitute.

The three leading clubs in 1874 were the Bostons, Mutuals, and Athletics. The Chicago Club, which had been knocked out by the great fire in 1871, now came to the front once more, and Hartford also entered a club, making the Association consist of eight clubs. Boston again won the championship, winning 52 games and losing 18. The Mutuals were second, 42-23; Athletics third, 33-23. The Philadelphias, Chicagos, Atlantics, Hartfords, and Baltimores finished in the order named. The series of games was increased to ten in this year. The only change in the Boston team was that McVey was put into the outfield, and two new men, George Hall and Thomas Beals, were utilized as substitutes.

Among the players of 1874 were many who are star players to-day. The Association clubs for that year were as follows:

Mutuals.—D. Allison, c.; Matthews, p.; Start, 1b.; Nelson, 2b.; Burdock, 3b.; Carey, s.s.; Hatfield, l.f.; Remsen, c.f.; Higham, r.f.; Bellan, substitute.

Athletics.—Clapp, c.; McBride, p.; Fisler, 1b.; Battin, 2b.; Sutton, 3b.; McGeary, s.s.; Gedney, l.f.; McMullen, c.f.; Anson, r.f.; Sensenderfer, substitute.

Philadelphias.—Hicks, c.; Cummings, p.; Mack, 1b.; Craver, 2b.; Fulmer, s.s.; Holdsworth, 3b.; York, l f.; Eggler, c.f.; Bechtel, r.f.; Pabor, substitute,

Chicago.—Malone, c.; Zettlein, p.; Devlin, 1b.; Meyerle, 2b.; Force, 3b.; Peters, s.s.; Cuthbert, l.f.; Hines and Treacey, c f.; Glenn, r.f.; and Pinkham, substitute.

Atlantic.—Kessler and Fleet, c.; Bond, p.; Dehlman, 1b.; Farrow, 2b.; Ferguson, 3b.; Pearce, s.s.; Booth, l.f.; Hodes, c.f.; Chapman, r.f.; Clack, substitute.

Hartford.—Barnie and Hastings, c.; Stearns and Fisher, p.; Mills, 1b.; Addy, 2b.; Boyd, 3b.; Barlow, s.s.; Tipper, l.f.; Pike, c.f.; Hastings and Fisher, r.f.

Baltimore.—Snyder, c.; Brainard, p.; Gould, 1b.; Manning, 2b.; White, 3b.; Gerhardt, s s.; Ryan, l.f.; Dean, c.f.; Bielaski, r.f.

Boston.—McVey and White, c.; Spalding, p.; O'Rourke, 1b.; Barnes, 2b.; Schafer, 3b.; Wright, s.s.; Leonard, l.f.; Hall and H. Wright, c.f.; White and McVey, r.f.; Beals, substitute.

The public interest in professional baseball had largely increased during these years, as shown in the attendance at the games, and the space given the sport in the newspapers of the day, but neither the attendance nor the newspaper notices were anything like what they are at the present time. The clubs, too, in 1874 were making a little money, and would have made more if the public had not, about this period, began to evince more or less suspicion as to the absolute squareness of the games, and the National Association began to grapple with the gigantic evil which required three years to eliminate it from professional ball playing, and which was largely instrumental in leading to the dissolution of the Association itself. This dark shadow, however, was then hardly perceptible, but it was there just the same, and was soon to make itself noticed by everybody. The profits of the clubs were not large enough, in spite of the enthusiasm, to add a great deal of the salary paid to players in 1869. This is shown by the salary list of the Boston Club in 1873-4. Pitchers had advanced in skill, and were more costly. Brainard, the Cincinnati champion, in 1869, had $800. Spalding, in 1874, received $1,800, and Jim White got the same amount. It will be seen that in five years the battery had assumed such an importance that pitchers and catchers went up one hundred and twenty-five per cent. in salary. The other members of this great team were paid as follows: O'Rourke, $800; Schafer, $1,200; Leonard, $1,400; Harry Wright, $1,800; George Wright, $1,800; Birdsall, $1,000; McVey, $1,500; Barnes, $1,800; Beals and Hall, about $500 each. The total for the team was a few dollars short of $16,000. It may be stated, as illustrating the wonderful advance the sport has made in Boston in fifteen years, that while the surplus of the Boston Club over all expenses in 1874, was $833.13, in 1889 it was surely not less than $100,000. The actual gate receipts in 1874 were $19,005. In 1889, 295,000 people paid fifty cents admission each to the Boston grounds, and thirty per cent. of these, about 89,000, paid an extra twenty-five cents to the grand stand.

The most notable event of 1874 was the visit of the Boston and Athletic Clubs to England. This trip was outlined very early in the season, and A. G. Spalding was sent to England in February to make all the arrangements and report as to the feasibility of the trip. Mr. Spalding was warmly received in London. He was accompanied by Mr. Briggs, a member of the Beacons, of Boston. They got up two teams of cricket and football players, and played the first game of baseball ever played in England at the Cricket Oval at Lords, February 27th, 1874. Spalding was pitcher for one side, and Briggs was catcher for the other. Mr. C. W. Alcock, now editor of *Cricket*, a leading cricket organ in London, did the pitching for Briggs' side, and they won the game, 17 to 5, in six innings.

On Mr. Spalding's nine was E. Pooley, a cricketer and a member of the then celebrated All-England Eleven. Mr. Alcock was engaged as business manager, and it was decided to make the trip, Mr. Spalding returning to America in time for the work of the championship season.

The two teams and their friends sailed July 16th, from Philadelphia, on the steamship Ohio. There were so many in the party that they required the entire cabin for their accommodation. The Athletic contingent numbered thirty-eight persons, including the following players: McBride, Clapp, Anson, McGeary, Sutton, Battin, Gedney, McMullin, Murnane, Fisler, and Sensenderfer. Al Reach remained at home, on account of business engagements. The Boston contingent included the following players: Harry Wright, George Wright, Spalding, Barnes, Schafer, McVey, Leonard, O'Rourke, Hall, Beals, Kent, and Sam Wright. Jim White declined taking the trip, and Kent of the Harvard College team took his place. Sam Wright, a younger brother of George and Harry, was drafted into service, in order to take part in the cricket games.

The only correspondents who took part in this trip were Alfred H. Wright, then representing the Philadelphia *Sunday Mercury* (now baseball editor of the New York *Clipper*), and H. S. Kempton, for the Boston *Herald*. The Bostons were in charge of Colonel Charles H. Porter, then President of the National Association, and now Mayor of Quincy, Mass. The Athletics were in charge of David F. Houston, a director of the club, who died in February, 1889.

Among the gentlemen who made the entire trip were Joseph B. Rockhill, William Milligan, and Charles J. Cragin, now leading merchants of Philadelphia; Dr. E. A. Pope, of Boston; George W. B. Taylor, of Philadelphia, the largest tin importer in the United States; J. O. Egerton, of Boston, and Fred Alden, of New York. The tourists arrived in Liverpool July 27th, and they played the first game three days afterwards. It was won by the Athletics in a close game of ten innings.

The record of the games played in the trip follows, as also the positions filled by the respective players.

BASEBALL.

No.	Date.	Where Played.	Result of Games.
1	July 30	Liverpool, England, ...	Athletic 14 v. Boston 11
2	" 31	" "	Boston 23 v. Athletic 18
3	Aug. 1	Manchester, England, ...	Athletic 13 v. Boston 12
4	" 3	Lord's Ground in London, England, . .	Boston 24 v. Athletic 7
5	" 6	Prince's Ground in London, England, . .	Boston 14 v. Athletic 11
6	" 8	Richmond, London, England, ...	Athletic 11 v. Boston 3
7	" 10	Crystal Palace Ground, London, England,	Boston 17 v. Athletic 8
8	" 11	" " "	Athletic 19 v. Boston 8
9	" 13	Kennington Oval, London, England, . .	Boston 16 v. Athletic 6
10	" 15	Sheffield, England, ...	Boston 19 v. Athletic 8
11	" 16	" "	Boston 18 v. Athletic 17
12	" 20	Manchester, England, ...	Athletic 7 v. Boston 2
13	" 24	Dublin, Ireland, ...	Boston 12 v. Athletic 7
14	" 25	" "	Athletic 15 v. Boston 4

Totals—Athletics, 161 runs; Boston, 183 runs.
Victories—Bostons, 8; Athletics, 6.

The correct positions of the players in a majority of the games were:

BOSTON.	POSITIONS.	ATHLETIC.
James H. O'Rourke,	Catcher,	James E. Clapp.
A. G. Spalding,	Pitcher,	James D. McBride.
Calvin C. McVey,	First Base,	West D. Fisler.
Ross C. Barnes,	Second Base,	Joseph Battin.
Henry Schafer,	Third Base,	Ezra B. Sutton.
George Wright,	Short Stop,	M. H. McGeary.
A. J. Leonard,	Left Field,	Albert W. Gedney.
Harry Wright,	Centre Field,	James F. McMullen.
George W. Hall,	Right Field,	A. C. Anson.
J. F. Kent,	Substitute,	J. P. Sensenderfer.
Thomas L. Beals,	Substitute,	Timothy J. Murnane.

In addition to the fourteen games of ball, the Americans played seven cricket games, in which they were successful, defeating with ease the Marylebone, Prince's and Surrey Clubs in London, the Sheffield Club in Sheffield, the Manchester Club in Manchester, and the All-Ireland Eleven in Dublin, while the game with the Richmond Club was drawn on account of rain, although much in favor of the visitors. The Americans, however, had a great advantage over their English brothers, who very generously allowed the visitors eighteen men against twelve British cricketers. The scores made are here given.

AMERICANS V.	AMERICANS			OPPONENTS		
	1st	2d.	Tot.	1st	2d.	Tot.
Aug. 3, 4–12 Marylebone Club on Grounds at Lord's,	107		107	105		105
Aug. 6, 7–11 Prince's C. C., at Prince's,	110		110	21	39	60
Aug. 8–13 Richmond C., at Richmond,*	45		45	108		108
Aug. 13, 14–11 Surrey C. C., at Oval,†	100	111	211	27	2	29
Aug. 15, 17–12 Sheffield, at Sheffield,	130		130	43	45	88
Aug. 20, 24–11 Manchester, at Manchester,	121	100	221	42	53	95
Aug. 24, 25–11 All-Ireland, at Dublin,	71	94	165	47	32	79
Total,	684	305	989	303	171	564

* Unfinished innings, only six wickets down.

† Second innings unfinished, only four wickets down.

Financially, the trip was a failure, so far as England was concerned, but the clubs managed to pay expenses from the receipts of exhibition games in this country. The receipts were:

July 13—Farewell game in Boston,	$1,253.24
July 15—Farewell game in Philadelphia,	2,648.82
Sept. 10—Reception game in Philadelphia,	1,321.50
Sept. 12—Reception game in Boston,	1,612.00
Four games in United States,	6,835.56
Games in Europe,	1,679.70
	$8,515.26

A careful estimate of the value of the 1874 tourists as ball players, is found in sketches of the men written at the time, by Henry Chadwick. These interesting details are taken from De Witt's "Guide:"

"Harry Wright—Captain Harry is the oldest baseball player of the party, and though he was first known on the turfy field as a cricketer —he succeeding his worthy father as the professional of the St. George Club—he began to play as a baseballist in the Knickerbocker Club before any of his companions knew how to play ball, Harry having played the game for twenty years past. He first became noted as captain of the famous Red Stocking nine, of Cincinnati—a nine which went through the season of 1869, playing games from Maine to California without sustaining a single defeat. Harry wisely studied up the standard books on the subject, adopted the suggestions he read,

THE CHICAGO BASE BALL TEAM, SEPT., 1885.

and practically carried out the theories taught in them; to which he added his own skillful ideas. As a trainer and captain of a baseball nine he stands alone; his high character, honesty of purpose, and aptitude in governing his men with kindness, making him very successful. As a player Harry, though beyond the baseball boundary in age, is still able to hold his own with the best in his position; while his success in training his nine has led to his being able to fly the champion pennant for his club for three years. He is highly and deservedly esteemed in Boston and throughout all the baseball cities of America. He is the 'coacher' of the Harvard College baseball nine, the champion of the American colleges for years.

"Spalding is justly regarded as one of the most successful of the strategic class of pitchers. In judgment, command of the ball, pluck, endurance and nerve, in his position he has no superior; while his education and gentlemanly qualities place him above the generality of baseball pitchers. As a batsman he now equals the best of what are called 'scientific' batsmen—men who use their heads more than their muscle in handling the ash. His forte in delivery is the success with which he disguises a change of pace from swift to medium, a great essential in successful pitching. Spalding is a thorough representative of the spirited young men of the Western States, he being from Illinois.

"O'Rourke is a fine general player, and especially excels at first base, a position in which a man has to catch the swiftest of thrown balls, either almost out of reach above his head or on a sharp rebound from his feet, while standing with one foot on his base. On an average the first baseman generally handles the ball which puts out half the men in a full game. O'Rourke has put out over 20 players out of 27 in a match. He is a quiet, gentlemanly Connecticut youth, with Irish blood in his veins, and, therefore, full of pluck and courage.

"Barnes is regarded as a model second baseman, being very active in his movements, keen of sight, sure in picking up 'grounders' and holding difficult 'fly' balls, and well up in all the points of 'second base' and 'right short' fielding; besides being an effective batsman. He is the pet of 'Young Boston,' and deservedly popular at the 'Hub.'

"Schafer, the third baseman of the Boston Club, is a fine general player, but not so strong in his position as some in other nines. He, however, makes some wonderful plays at times, and his average in putting men out by sharp pick-ups and good throws equals the highest. He is a smiling, good-humored Pennsylvanian, and quite a favorite with the 'Reds.'

"George Wright is generally regarded as a model baseball player, especially in his responsible position of short stop, and until he injured his leg he had no equal in the position. He is a jolly, good-natured youth, full of life and spirit, up to all the dodges of the game, and especially is he noted for his sure catching of high balls in the infield and for his swift and accurate throwing. At the bat, too, he excels, while as a bowler, fielder, and batsman in cricket he ranks with the best of American cricketers. He comes of real old English stock, his father being a veteran English cricketer and formerly the professional of the St. George Cricket Club of New York.

"Leonard is of Irish birth and parentage, though brought up from boyhood in New Jersey. He is one of the finest outfielders, being a sure catch, an excellent judge of high balls, a swift and accurate long-distance thrower, and very quick and active. As an infielder, too, he excels, as also at the bat and base running.

"McVey, the heavy weight of the Boston team, is from Iowa, and he is another specimen of how they build young men in the 'far West.' He is the change catcher of the nine, and very efficient in the position, while in the outfield he is also a valuable man.

"Hall is a young engraver of New York, and one of the finest of outfielders; very active and quick, a sure catch, a sharp base runner and a fine general player.

"Beals is one of the class of natural ball players, a splendid outfielder and very quick in his movements in the field. Tommy is quite a pet with the Boston ladies, and always elicits smiles of favor from the fair spectators who gather on the grand stand at the Boston Club matches.

"Sammy Wright is the junior of the Red Stocking team—a pretty little ball player and a good little cricketer, too; a promising successor to his older brothers when they retire from the field.

THE ATHLETIC BLUE STOCKINGS.

"Clapp, the regular catcher of the Athletic nine, is cool, reticent, plucky, enduring, and a very able player in his position. He hails from Connecticut, the 'Nutmeg' State, and is a very quiet representative of the talkative Yankees of that section of the Republic. He surprised the cricketers of England with some of his 'red hot' catches sharp from the bat, balls which come like a flash to the hands—and sometimes to the nose and eyes of the catcher.

"McBride—'Dick'—his name is not Richard, but Dickson—McBride is the veteran baseball pitcher of America, and the most experienced man in his position, he having been the regular pitcher of the Athletic Club since 1860. Possessing speed, pluck, and wonderful endurance, together with a thorough command of the ball, and being well up in the points of the game, he stands to-day without a superior in the position in real strategic play in pitching. He always plays to win; and, when only fairly supported, generally brings his nine out victorious. His special aim for the past three years has been to get the pennant from the rival Red Stocking nine. Dick is a good cricketer, too; in fact, that was his little game before he played baseball. McBride is from the Quaker City, though having nothing of that peculiar sect in his ways, except that he is a good 'friend.'

"Fisler is a model ball player in his remarkable coolness and nerve. Quiet, unobtrusive, and reticent, one would never suppose him the player he is. No one is more highly esteemed in the baseball fraternity than 'West.' He excels in almost any position, whether behind the bat, on a base, or in the outfield.

"Battin is the 'colt' of the Athletic team, and quite a promising young player. There is, however, room for him to improve, and no doubt his second season as a professional will see him 'well up in his class.'

"Sutton ranks as one of the best third base players in the country, and it is the most difficult position to fill in the infield, the hottest balls being sent there and the most difficult balls to catch and pick up, while the longest and quickest throwing in the infield is made from third base. His throwing is at times wonderful in its speed and accuracy.

"McGeary is not only a very active and efficient 'short stop,' but a capital change catcher, his style of play in the latter position being quite peculiar. No pluckier player stands behind the bat, he also being noted for his sharp catches of 'fly tips.' He is a Pennsylvanian by birth.

"Gedney is the post-office clerk of the New York State Senate and one of the finest of left fielders, being an excellent judge of high balls and a sure catch, especially in taking balls on the run.

"McMullin occupies the position of centre fielder, where he is very active and efficient. He is also a change pitcher with a left-hand delivery, when one is needed. Last season he led at the bat, being very successful in 'fair foul' hitting, or what cricketers would call 'snicks to short leg.'

"Anson is the heavy weight of the Athletic nine, and plays on the bases as well as at right field. He is the least active fielder of the nine, but excels in heavy batting. He is quite a fine billiard player, and can make a good score in either the French or American game, as can half the entire party for that matter, any style of ball playing coming handy to them.

"Sensenderfer, surnamed 'the Count,' is the handsomest centre fielder of the nine of 1872, and a very fine player in his position, besides being the ladies' man of the club.

"Murnane is a good first base player, as well as outfielder, and is active and efficient in other positions."

The year 1875 was a critical one for baseball, and proved that the National Association had grown too unwieldly to be longer a factor in the sport. It was the last season of that organization, and the Bostons again won the pennant. Thirteen clubs took part in the contest. Of these, six were new teams. They were St. Louis, Red Stockings of St. Louis, Washingtons, Centennials of Philadelphia, New Havens, and Westerns of Keokuk, Ia. Not one of these new teams played out its full quota of six games required by the association, and the Atlantics were in the same boat. The slang term, "in the soup," was not current then. If it had been, it would surely have been applied to the team which dragged so low the title which Brooklyn had regarded for so many years with so much pride.

The Boston team, which walked away so easily with the last pennant given by the National Association, included White, c.; Spalding, p.; McVey, Barnes, Shafer, basemen; George Wright, s.s.; Leonard, O'Rourke, Manning, fielders; Beals, Harry Wright, Heifert, substitutes.

The Athletics of 1875 were McBride, p.; Clapp, c.; Fisler, 1b.; Craver, 2b.; Sutton, 3b.; Force, s.s.; Eggler, c.f.; Hall, l.f.; Anson, r.f.; Bechtel, substitute.

The new teams of 1875 were made up as follows:

St. Louis.—Bradley, p.; Miller, c.; Dehlmar, 1b.; Battin, 2b.; Hague, 3b.; Pearce, s.s.; Cuthbert, l.f.; Pike, c.f.; Chapman, r.f.

New Haven.—Luff, p.; Banker, McGinley, and Keenan, c.; Gould, 1b.; Somerville, 2b.; Latham, 3b.; Geer, s.s.; Ryan, l.f.; Tripper, c.f.; McKelvey, r.f.; Barlow, substitute.

Red Stockings.—Blong, p.; Flint, c.; Houtz, 1b.; Sweasey, 2b.; Ellick, 3b.; Redmund, s.s.; Craft, l.f.; Morgan, c.f.; Orrin, r.f.

Washingtons.—Stearns, p.; McCloskey, c.; A. Allison, 1b.; Brady, 2b.; Doescher, 3b.; Dailey, s.s.; Parks, l.f.; Hollingshead, c.f.; Kessler, r.f.

Centennial.—Bechtel, p.; Fields, c.; Abadie, 1b.; Somerville, 2b.; Craver, 3b.; Radcliff, s.s.; Treacy, l.f.; Warner, c.f; Mason, r.f.

Atlantics —Clinton, p.; Knowdell, c; Cassidy, 1b.; Fleet, 2b.; Nichols, 3b.; Moore, s.s.; Pabor, l.f.; Magee, c.f.; Boyd, r.f.

The Centennials played only a few games. They really had but two players of much account. Those were Craver and Bechtel. The Athletic Club wanted these men, and paid $1,500 to get them. This transfer, the first sale of players on record, broke up the Centennials entirely, and they disbanded May 26th. The details of this deal are somewhat shady, because it was not exactly in accordance with the custom of the times. Two wealthy members of the Athletic Club put up the $1,500, and it was paid over to an official of the Centennial Club, who pocketed the funds and managed to have the contracts of Bechtel and Craver cancelled. It is a peculiar fact that neither of these men did the Athletic Club any good. Craver was crooked. Bechtel took Anson's place so often on the Athletic team that Anson got very sore, and it didn't require much coaxing on the part of Chicago to get him away from the Athletic Club.

The first three decades of baseball in America are closed with the records of the clubs in the five campaigns of the National Association:

1871.	Won.	Lost.
Athletic,	22	7
Boston,	22	10
Chicago,	20	9
Mutual,	17	18
Olympic,	16	15
Haymakers,	15	15
Cleveland,	10	19
Kekionga,	7	21
Rockford,	6	21

1872.	Won.	Lost.
Boston,	39	8
Baltimore,	34	19
Mutual,	34	20
Athletic,	30	14
Troy,	15	10
Atlantic,	8	27
Cleveland,	6	15
Mansfield,	5	19
Eckford,	3	26
Olympic,	2	7
National,	0	11

1873.	Won.	Lost.
Boston,	43	16
Philadelphia,	36	17
Baltimore,	33	22
Mutual,	29	24
Athletic,	28	23
Atlantic,	17	37
Washington,	8	31
Resolute,	2	21
Maryland,	0	5

1874.	Won.	Lost.
Boston,	52	18
Mutual,	42	23
Athletic,	33	23
Philadelphia,	29	29
Chicago,	27	31
Atlantic,	23	33
Hartford,	17	37
Baltimore,	9	38

1875.	Won.	Lost.
Boston,	71	8
Athletic,	53	20
Hartford,	54	28
St. Louis,	39	29
Philadelphia,	37	31
Chicago,	30	37
Mutual,	29	38

1875.	Won.	Lost.
New Haven,	7	39
Red Stockings,	4	14
Washington,	4	22
Centennial,	2	13
Atlantic,	2	42
Western,	1	12

PART IV.

The second section of the constitution of the National League of Professional Baseball Clubs has been aptly termed the cornerstone of honest baseball in America. The beginning of this famous document explains in brief and concise form the cause which led to the formation of the league. Here it is: "The object of this organization is to encourage, foster, and elevate the game of baseball.

"To enact and enforce proper rules for the exhibition and conduct of the game, and to make baseball playing respectable and honorable.

"To protect and promote the mutual interests of professional baseball clubs and professional baseball players.

"To establish and regulate the baseball championship of the United States."

The National Association meant well enough, but it was not based on the right principle. It had served its purpose and outlived its usefulness. It had grown to such unwieldly proportions that a reform in its methods was practically impossible. Another thing was the preponderance of Eastern influences, and this was an evil that sat heavily on the Western members. This fact was largely instrumental in the movement initiated by the late William A. Hulbert, of Chicago, which resulted in the organization which for fourteen years has held jurisdiction over the sport, and made it what it is to-day.

The main cause, however, for reorganization was the rapid decadence of popular belief in the purity of the game. Pool rooms flourished in every city, and the professional gamblers were generally thought to be, and to a large extent were, manipulating the games. There were too many clubs; the system of admitting new clubs was defective, and the absence of any set schedule of games made the championship too much dependent upon the caprice of managers and the lack of discipline; while a contempt for the association's weak methods made the players more susceptible to dishonest influences.

In the fall of 1875, William A. Hulbert conceived the idea of the

National League and, with some assistance from A. G. Spalding, whom Mr. Hulbert had just engaged for the Chicago team, formulated the document which afterwards became the constitution of the new league, and which contained the section quoted as the introduction of this chapter.

It is fitting here to pay a tribute to the memory of the lamented Hulbert. He was a man of great energy and peculiar temperament, and was possessed of just the leaven of positiveness, aggressiveness, and rugged honesty necessary to carry out the vast design he contemplated. He was a reformer in just the ratio that the situation called for. Liberal and progressive in his ideas and methods, he was the right man in the right place, and while he lived he was practically the dictator of the baseball interests of the country, and that without being a tyrant. Writing of him in a recent article in *The Cosmopolitan*, Mr. A. G. Spalding penned these lines:

"He had the true interests of the game at heart, and anything that savored in any way of corruption or dishonesty found in him a vigorous enemy."

Mr. Hulbert died of heart disease in 1882, and the league passed this resolution:

"*Resolved*, That to him alone is due the credit of having founded the national league, and to his able leadership, sound judgment, and impartial management is the success of the league chiefly due."

That resolution, added to Mr. Spalding's tribute, forms a grand and just epitaph for the Father of the League.

In December, 1875, Charles A. Fowle, of St. Louis; John A. Joyce, of Cincinnati; William Haldeman, Thomas Sherley, and Charles E. Chase, of Louisville, met Mr. Hulbert and A. G. Spalding in Louisville, and decided to break away with their clubs from the national association. The eastern clubs were communicated with, and on February 2nd, 1876, the National League of Professional Baseball Clubs was regularly organized at the Grand Central Hotel.

The Chicago, Louisville, Cincinnati, and St. Louis clubs were represented by Messrs. Hulbert and Fowle, both of whom are now dead. N. A. Appollonio represented Boston; William H. Cammeyer the Mutuals of New York; George W. Thompson the Athletics of Phila-

THE CLEVELAND TEAM, JUNE, 1889.

delphia, and Hon. Morgan G. Bulkeley, now Governor of Connecticut, looked after the interests of the Hartford Club. Mr. Bulkeley was chairman, and Harry Wright, secretary. The constitution prepared by Mr. Hulbert, was adopted with slight changes. Mr. Bulkeley was elected president, and N. E. Young, secretary. The salary attached to the latter office, which has been held by Mr. Young ever since, was $400. At the present time Mr. Young's salary is $4,000.

The new constitution revolutionized the loose system which had heretofore prevailed. The entrance fee, which had been $10, was raised to $100. The new association, from being an association of players, became a league of clubs. It was provided that no city could be a member unless its population reached 75,000. It was also agreed that no club could be admitted from any city that was less than five miles from any city then a member. This vested proprietary territorial rights in each of the league clubs. Other reforms were the adoption of a player's contract which did much toward abolishing the system, then a crying evil, of clubs robbing each other of their best players. This was the first step toward the reserve rule. Players were to be expelled for breaking contracts and dishonesty, and when expelled were to be forever after debarred from employment by league clubs. Gambling and liquor selling on club grounds was abolished, and players were made subject to expulsion for being interested in a bet, or for purchasing pool tickets. Thus was started the great major organization. The leading magnates of 1876—the presidents of the clubs—were: Athletics, Thomas J. Smith; Boston, N. A. Appollonio; Chicago, W. A. Hulbert; Cincinnati, J. L. Keck; Hartford, M. G. Bulkeley; Louisville, W. N. Haldeman; Mutual, W. H. Cammeyer; St. Louis, J. R. C. Lucas.

The players of the teams of 1876 are given below. It will be observed that there were a number of changes, the prime one being the transfer of Boston's big four—Spalding, White, Barnes, and McVey—to the Chicago Club.

Chicago.—A. G. Spalding, p., captain and manager; James White, c.; Anson, 3b.; Ross Barnes, 2b.; C. A. McVey, 1b.; J. P. Peters, s.s.; J. W. Glenn, P. A. Hines, and R. Addy, fielders; J. F. Cene, Oscar Bielaski, and F. H. Andrus, substitutes.

Hartford.—Robert Ferguson, captain and manager; D. Allison, W.

A. Cummings, Thomas H. Bond, E. Mills, John J. Burdock, Thomas Carey, Thomas York, J. J. Remsen, J. Cassidy, Richard Higham, and W. H. Harbidge.

St. Louis.—S. W. Graffen, manager; George W. Bradley, Lipman Pike, E. E. Cuthbert, J. V. Battin, R. J. Pearce, J. W. Blong, D. J. Mack, Thomas P. Miller, H. T. Dehlman, M. H. McGeary, and John E. Clapp.

Boston.—Harry Wright, manager; J. E. Borden ("Josephs"), T. H. Murnane, T. L. Beals, H. C. Schafer, A. J. Leonard, J. H. O'Rourke, J. F. Manning, F. T. Whitney, George Wright, John F. Morrill, Lewis Brown, and T. McGinley. W. R. Parks also played a few games.

Louisville.—J. C. Chapman, manager; James A. Devlin, W. Scott Hastings, Chas. N. Snyder, W. L. Hague, J. Gerhardt, Chas. Fulmer, Arthur A. Allison, J. C. Carbine, George Bechtel, J. J. Ryan, W. H. Holbert, W. Somerville, and H. Collins. J. S. Clinton also played a few games.

Mutuals.—W. H. Cammeyer, manager; Robt. Mathews, N. W. Hicks, Joe Start, James Hallinan, A. H. Nichols, E. Booth, W. H. Craver, James Holdsworth, Fred Treacey.

Athletics.—Alfred H. Wright, manager; Alonzo Knight, W. R. Coons, W. D. Fisler, W. Fouser, D. W. Force, George Zettlein, E. B. Sutton, G. W. Hall, Levi Meyerle, David Eggler, Fergus G. Malone.

Cincinnati.—C. H. Gould, manager; S. J. Fields, W. C. Fisher, C. J. Sweasy, H. Kessler, E. Snyder, C. W. Jones, R. Clack, D. P. Pierson, A. S. Booth, Henry Dean, William Foley.

Harry Wright, A. G. Spalding, C. H. Gould, Robert Ferguson, and S. C. Chapman were playing managers. A. H. Wright, W. H. Cammeyer, and S. M. Graffen did not do active field duty.

Of these men of 1876 thirty-one are still directly connected with the game. Paul Hines, Anson, O'Rourke, Charley Snyder, J. F. Morrill, and Jim White are in active league service. Reach and Spalding are club presidents. George Wright is selling baseball goods. Al Wright and Tim Murnane are active newspaper writers. Harry Wright, Chapman, Sutton, and Burdock are club managers, and the two latter are still playing ball. Force, Battin, Remsen, Holbert, Kessler, Jones, Gerhardt, and

Bradley are playing in minor organizations. Knight, Manning, Furguson, Cuthbert, Bond, Clinton, Pearce, and Mathews are umpires.

Each club was required to play ten games with every other club. The result of the season's play gave the championship to the Chicago Club. The record follows:

THE CHAMPIONSHIP RECORD FOR 1876.

	Chicago.	Hartford.	St. Louis.	Boston.	Louisville.	Mutual.	Athletic.	Cincinnati.	Games Lost.	Games Won.
Chicago, ...		6	4	9	9	7	7	10	14	52
Hartford, ...	4		4	8	9	4	9	9	21	47
St. Louis, ...	6	6		6	6	6	8	7	19	45
Boston, ...	1	2	4		5	8	9	10	31	39
Louisville, ...	1	1	4	5		5	6	8	36	30
Mutual, ...	1	4	1	2	3		3	7	35	21
Athletic, ...	1	1	0	1	2	4		5	45	14
Cincinnati, ...	0	1	2	0	2	1	3		56	9
Games Lost, ...	14	21	19	31	36	35	45	56	257	257

Ross Barnes led the league batting averages with .403. The next five men were: Anson .342; Clinton .338; James White .335; Hines .330; O'Rourke .312. The leading fielders were: First baseman—Fisler .978; second basemen—Gerhardt .950; third basemen—Battin .867; Short stops—Peters .932; Left fielders—Leonard .913; Centre fielders—Hines .917; Right fielders—Cassidy .998. George Washington Bradley led the pitchers, with an average of one-twelfth of an earned run to a game. Allison stood at the head of the catchers, with .844.

At the annual meeting at Cleveland, December 7th, the Athletic and Mutual Clubs were expelled from the league because they failed to play out their scheduled games in the final series to be contested in the West. The Athletic and Mutual Clubs, realizing the weakness of the league circuit, and knowing that none of the clubs had made any money in 1876, did not believe extreme measures would be taken, but they failed to understand the determination of the men who had organized the league. Hulburt, who managed things about as he liked, insisted on expelling the delinquents, and it was done, the league deciding to continue with six clubs only. At this meeting Arthur H. Soden was one of the representatives of the Boston Club, and A. G. Mills of the Chicagos. It was agreed to pay the umpires $50 per game, and Secretary Young's salary was increased to $500. It was also agreed to respect all contracts with players made by league or non-league clubs. William H. Hulburt was elected President, to succeed Mr. Bulkeley.

Baseball was not confined to the league in 1876. There were a large number of non-league clubs of professional players who made very good records in that year. Among them may be noted the Actives, of Reading, Pa.; Buckeyes, of Columbus; Fall River, Rhode Islands, Providence; Crickets, of Binghamton; Stars, of Syracuse; Indianapolis, St. Louis Reds, Quicksteps, of Wilmington, and the Alleghenys.

The season of 1877 was one of the eventful and interesting years of the league, and one of the darkest periods in the history of the game. Its progress was retarded, and at one time it seemed as though there might be a retrograde movement; but firmness and promptness saved the day, and, although financially the season was a failure everywhere, still, many valuable lessons were learned, and the foundations were properly laid for the great success which was afterwards attained, and which has ever since been held.

The Cincinnati Club was unable to weather the financial storm, and although the team of 1876, with the addition of Hicks, Mathews, Foley, Hallinan, and Pike, and without Gould, Fields, Fisher, Sweasy, Snyder, Jones, Clark, and Pierson, played a good many games, the club did not count in the championship, as its games won were thrown out because of a failure to pay the annual dues, which, under the rules, forfeited membership in the league. The championship was won by the Bostons, who were strengthened by gaining Jim White back from Chicago, and adding to the team Morrill, Brown, Will White, Bond, and Sutton; Manning, Borden, Whitney, Beals, and Parks retiring. The record follows:

THE CHAMPIONSHIP RECORD FOR 1877.

	Boston.	Louisville.	Hartford.	St. Louis.	Chicago.	Games Lost.	Games Won.
Boston,		8	7	6	10	17	31
Louisville,	4		6	10	8	20	28
Hartford,	5	6		5	8	24	24
St. Louis,	6	2	4		4	29	19
Chicago,	2	4	7	8		30	18
Games Lost,	17	20	24	29	30	120	120

The Boston team was made up as follows: Thomas H. Bond, p.; Lewis Brown, c.; Timothy H. Murnane, 1b. and c.f.; George Wright, 2b.; John F. Morrill, 3b. and l.f.; Ezra B. Sutton, 3b. and s.s.; A. J. Leonard, s.s. and l.f.; James H. O'Rourke, c.f. and l.f.; James White, r.f. and c. Will White was a substitute, and Harry Schafer also played a few games. Harry Wright was manager of the team.

The Louisville team was composed of Devlin, Craver, Hall, Crowley, Schaffer, Latham, Chapman, Snyder, Hague, Gerhardt, Nichols, and Ryan.

The new men in the Chicago team were C. C. Wait, G. W. Bradley, and H. W. Smith. White, Cone, Addy, and Bielaski were the 1876 players who signed elsewhere, or were not wanted.

The Hartford lost Cummings, Bond, E. Mills, Remsen, and Higham, and gained Cassidy, Larkin, Joe Start, and Holdsworth.

St. Louis gained F. C. Nichols, Force, M. C. Dorgan, Remsen, and Craft. They lost Bradley, Miller, Pike, Pearce, Mack, and Cuthbert.

In the averages for 1877, Jim White stood first in the batting, with .385. Larkin had the least average of base hits to a game, and Charley Snyder, of the Louisvilles, had the best catching record, .913. Craft led the first basemen, with .965; Burdock, the second basemen, with .905; McGeary, the third basemen, with .907; Force, the short-stops, with .903; Glenn, the left fielders, with .941; Remsen, the centre fielders, with .902, and J. White, the right fielders, with 954.

Two new minor organizations were started in 1877. One was known as the League Alliance. It consisted of thirteen clubs, and its arrangement of pennant games was very irregular; indeed, there was no specified number of games prescribed. The clubs played as often as they could, and a series of games consisted of whatever number any two clubs found it convenient or desirable to play. The Red Caps, of St. Paul, won the pennant of this irregular association, with a team in which Salisbury and Gross were the battery, Gault, 1b.; Miller, 2b.; Ellick, 3b.; McClellan, s.s.; Ely, A. Allison, and Birmingham in the field. This organization slipped out of sight after 1877, but was revived in 1882, when the Metropolitans and the Philadelphias played a series for what they called the League Alliance championship. It was won by the Metropolitans, with this team: Lynch and O'Neill, pitchers; Reipschlager and Clapp, catchers; Reilly, 1b.; Larkin, 2b.; Hankinson, 3b.; Nelson, s s.; Kennedy, l.f.; Mansel, c.f.; Brady, r.f.

The first International Association was organized at Pittsburg, February 20th, 1877, and was made up of clubs from Canada and the United States. The home products were the Alleghenys, of Pittsburg; Live Oaks, of Lynn; Buckeyes, of Columbus; Rochesters, New York; and Manchesters, New Hampshire. The Canadian clubs were the Tecumseh, of London, and the Maple Leaf, of Guelph, Ont. This organization lasted through two seasons. The Tecumseh Club won the championship in 1877, with a team of players, some of whom afterwards became famous. Fred. Goldsmith was the pitcher; Phil. Powers, c.; George H. Bradley, 1b.; Dinnen, 2b.; Doescher, 3b.; Somerville, s.s.; Joe Hernung, l.f.; Wagner, c.f.; Knowdell, r.f.; Reid and Harvey Spence, substitutes.

The second year of the International, and its last under that name, witnessed quite a change in its circuit. The clubs were the Tecumseh, Allegheny, Manchester, Buffalo, Syracuse, Rochester, Utica, Hornellsville, Springfield (Mass.), Lowell (Mass.), and Hartford. The New York *Clipper* offered a silk pennant to the champions and a gold badge to the player having the best fielding average in each position. The Buffalo Club got the pennant, with Galvin, p.; Dolan, c.; Libby, 1b.; Fulmer, 2b.; Allen, 3b.; Force, s.s.; Crowley, l.f.; Eggler, c.f.,

McGunnigle, r.f.; Mack and McSorley, substitutes. The gold medals were awarded to Henry McCormick, pitcher for the Syracuse Stars; Mike Dorgan, catcher for the Stars; Steve Libby, first baseman for Buffalo; Barnes, second base for the Tecumsehs; Doescher, third base for the same club; Force, short stop for Buffalo; Hornung, left fielder for Tecumseh; Danny Richardson, centre fielder for Utica, and W. H. McGunnigle, right fielder for Buffalo. Of these prize winners, McCormick is dead; Barnes, Libby, and Dorgan have retired; Hornung, Richardson, and Force are still in harness; Doescher is an umpire, and McGunnigle is a manager.

The event of the year 1877 was the action of the Louisville Club in expelling four of its players for selling games. The men expelled were A. H. Nichols, William H. Craver, George Hall, and James A. Devlin. The best account attainable of this affair was written by Charles E. Chase, a director of the Louisville club. His story of this memorable affair is given word for word:

"All who are familiar with matters pertaining to the national game will remember that the Louisville league club of 1877 was by many degrees the strongest aggregation of players ever, up to that time at least, brought together in one team, and very early in the season it was considered a foregone conclusion that the Louisvilles would win the pennant 'hands down.' As the Louisville club was not formed until late in the fall of 1875, the first season's team was not a strong one; in fact it was made up mostly of material cast off by other clubs, but by retaining the best of that year's nine, and strengthening it by such additions as Hall, Craver, Latham, Crowley, and Schaffer, the team of 1877 became almost invincible. Devlin and Snyder constituted a battery beyond comparison, while Latham, Gerhardt, Craver, Hague, Hall, Crowley, and Schaffer not only ranked among the highest in fielding ability, but as wielders of the bat they could not be excelled, and they worked together like a piece of finely modeled machinery in which each part contributes its share in forming a perfect whole. By the middle of the season it was conceded by all that the Louisville club had taken such a lead it could not be headed, and its phenomenal success is what brought about its ultimate ruin. In those days pools upon the games were sold in every pool room throughout the country, the same as pools upon racing events are sold now; but the Louisville club had become such a strong favorite that betters could hardly be induced to risk their money against it, even at very long odds. The gamblers recognized in this situation of affairs a chance to reap a rich harvest upon a small investment, and they at once set about 'subsidizing' some members of the nine.

"About the middle of the season our third baseman, Hague, had a boil make its appearance under his left arm, and this almost totally incapacitated him from playing. As none of our substitutes were strong infielders, and as we could not afford, at that 'stage of the game,' to weaken our team, we cast around for some one to guard the third bag until such time as Hague should be able to resume his position. George Hall, then the captain of the nine, advised most strongly that we secure Albert Nichols, formerly of the Mutual club, but who at that time was playing in Pittsburgh; and, as Hall recommended him as being a very fine fielder and strong batter, our manager, Mr. Chapman, was authorized to secure him at once. From the time of Nichols' employment dated the series of unlooked for events which robbed Louisville of the championship and caused the disbanding of that noted club.

"By the withdrawal, early in the season of 1877, of Si Keck's Cincinnati team from the league, the west was left with an uneven number of clubs. This very naturally placed the original schedule of games in a terrible snarl, and, in order to carry out the schedule, the new club formed in Cincinnati was permitted to play out the games of the old organization; but such games were not to count in the championship race. The new Cincinnati team was by no means as strong as the league clubs, and yet the Louisvilles, which had no difficulty in defeating the Chicagos, St. Louis, and Bostons, seemingly could not win a game from the Porkopolis boys. Indianapolis also had a club formed of 'scrub' talent, yet the 'Louisville Giants' lost more games to them than they won, as was also the case with the Alleghanys.

"When the 'coming champions' started upon their last eastern trip they had some twelve games to play, out of which they had less than half to win in order to insure them the pennant, for it was almost an assured fact that they could win a majority of the games they had yet to play in the west. The Hartfords, then playing upon the old Mutual

THE COLUMBUS BASEBALL TEAM, SEPTEMBER, 1889.

club grounds in Brooklyn, had before capitulated to the 'Giants' without much of a struggle, and it was considered certain that at least four out of the six games with that club could be counted as victories, while at least one-half should be won from the Bostons.

"The first of the series were played in Brooklyn, and the morning the first game was to be played I received an anonymous dispatch from Hoboken (the pool rooms having been driven out of New York, the pool sellers took refuge across the river), stating that something was wrong with the Louisville players, as the gamblers were betting on the Hartfords, and advising me to 'watch your men.' Presuming that this despatch was from some 'crank,' I paid no attention to it, but when I learned that afternoon that our club had been badly defeated, I came to the conclusion that possibly the game might stand investigation. When the full reports were received that night, I was surprised to find Hague left off and Nichols put in his place at third base, and I also found that it was through errors of Craver, Hall, and Nichols that the game had been lost. I at once telegraphed Manager Chapman, asking why Nichols had been substituted for Hague, and he replied that Hall had requested it, giving as a reason that as Nichols was a Brooklyn boy, he naturally wanted to play on his home grounds. This answer seemed sufficient, and my suspicions were for the time being allayed. Upon the morning the next game was to be played my anonymous correspondent again wired me from Hoboken that the Louisville-Hartford game was to be crooked, and the Louisvilles lose. And lose they did, through errors of Devlin, Hall, and Nichols. It is hardly necessary to say that Manager Chapman was immediately notified not to permit Nichols to participate in any more games. This was the commencement of the last eastern series of games, and when the Louisville club returned home it had only two victories placed to its record.

"The directors of the club were now fully convinced of the existence of some crooked players in the nine, but how to ferret them out was the great difficulty. To John A. Haldeman, the present manager of the Louisville *Times*, and who was at that time the official scorer of the Louisville club, must be given the credit of first putting the management upon the trail of the players who had participated in the 'boodle;' for, as he was a fine player himself, had watched the games closely, and was thoroughly posted in regard to what each player was competent of doing, he detected Devlin and Hall in one of their successful attempts to throw a game in Indianapolis, and, even at the risk of getting a severe thrashing, he accused them of it boldly.

"Upon the club's return from Indianapolis, Devlin called at my office. I at once charged him with having thrown the games in Brooklyn, and, while he stoutly denied ever having thrown a league game, he acknowledged to having pitched carelessly when playing against outside clubs. I told him that I wanted a full confession, and gave him until 8 P. M. to think over the matter. When I reached my hotel at 6 P. M., I was surprised to find George Hall waiting for me, and he at once opened negotiations by saying: 'I know I have been doing very wrong, but, as God is my judge, I have never thrown a league game. If I tell you all I know about this business, will you promise to let me down easy?' Although I had at that time no positive evidence connecting Hall with the selling of games, I thought it the best policy to make him believe otherwise, and with that end in view I replied that, as I was already fully acquainted with the part he had played in the nefarious business, I could make him no promises. This mode of procedure worked even better than my most sanguine expectations, for, taking it for granted that Devlin had divulged all, and desiring to place himself upon an equal footing with that celebrated pitcher, he commenced to enumerate the games in which he had played crooked, and also told of the part Nichols had taken in acting as a go-between. Fortified with Hall's confession, I was fully prepared to meet Devlin later in the evening, and by a series of cross-questions I forced him to divulge the entire plot.

"Hall claimed that Nichols first proposed the selling of games, but I have reason to believe that Hall commenced playing crooked even before he became a member of the Louisville club. Devlin acknowledged that Nichols first approached him in Pittsburgh, and told him that Hall had broached the subject to him; that Hall came to him the same day and said they could make $100 apiece by throwing the game, and, as it did not count in the championship series, it could not be looked upon as dishonest. In the light thrown upon matters by future events,

I had every reason to believe that, at the time Hall urged me to engage Nichols, he did so knowing that his influence over the young player would make him a good tool in his projected nefarious designs upon the championship; and I also have reasons to believe that Nichols was not innocent of selling games while a member of the old Mutual club, a fact which Hall was probably acquainted with.

"The night following that upon which both Hall and Devlin made their confessions, the entire team were summoned to meet the directors of the club at the president's office, and they were then requested to sign an order upon the Western Union Telegraph Company, giving the directors permission to inspect any and all dispatches received or sent by them. They were told that if they were honest men they could not object to having their dispatches inspected, and that the failure of any member to sign the order would be construed into an acknowledgment of guilt, for which the player would be at once expelled. With one exception they all signed the order. That exception was Captain Craver, and he was immediately expelled. John A. Haldeman devoted several days to searching for the telegrams sent and received by the members of the club, but they implicated none but those already known to be dishonest (below I append a copy of some of the telegrams), and a week later a thorough investigation took place, conducted by the Hon. Asher Caruth, our present Congressman, which resulted in the expulsion of Devlin, Hall, and Nichols, Craver having been expelled, as before stated.

"Of all the money this rascally gang received, and it must have been a large amount, it was proven that Devlin received but $100, for once in the power of Hall and Nichols they forced him to throw games under threats of exposure."

The telegrams which caused the downfall of the conspirators follow:

PHILADELPHIA, PA., Sept. 13.—*Jas. Devlin, of Lou. B. B. Co., St. Cloud Hotel, Louisville:* Lost heavy to-day on your letter. Make it a point to give me something on Friday and Saturday to get square. Answer as soon as you can on Friday.
BOSNEY.

LOUISVILLE, Sept. 16.—*James McCloud, No. 141 Broome st., New York City:* We have not heard from you as to your promise. D. AND H.

LOUISVILLE, Sept. 16.—*James McCloud, 141 Broome st., N. Y.:* At Cincinnati to-morrow. Sash. D. & H.

["Sash" was the word denoting that the Louisvilles would lose.]

PHILADELPHIA, Sept. 22.—*James A. Devlin, St. Cloud Hotel, Louisville:* Cannot you fulfill the promise? FRED.

BROOKLYN, N. Y., Sept. 19.—*A. H. Nichols, Lou. B. B. Club, Burnet House, Louisville:* Is Cincinnati sure? How much do you want? All right if sure.
P. A. WILLIAMS.

PHILADELPHIA, PA., Sept. 26.—*James Devlin, St. Cloud Hotel, Louisville:* Every one here had the Chicagos to win to-day. Who sent the tip? The pool box had the order to buy three hundred. Chicago favorites two to one. B. J. DOYLE.

NEW YORK, Sept. 17.—*James Devlin, St. Cloud Hotel, Louisville:* I sent you a registered letter from Pittsburg. Will wait answer home. JAMES MCCLOUD.

NEW YORK, Sept. 29.—*A. H. Nichols, 225 Broadway, Louisville:* Letter received. Everything understood. Telegraph early. I go to Philadelphia. Answer 133 Duffield street. P. A. WILLIAMS.

BROOKLYN, N. Y., Oct. 1.—*A. H. Nichols, 225 Broadway, Louisville:* Nothing from you as yet. Send answer to Bloom's court. P. A. WILLIAMS.

LOUISVILLE, Sept. 29.—*William A. Powers, Busch Hotel, Hoboken, N. J.:* Buy Louisville to-day to win. A. N.

HOBOKEN, N. J., Oct 1.—*A. H. Nichols, Louisville B. B. C.:* Nothing from you yet. Is contract complete? Answer Busch's Hotel. P. A. WILLIAMS.

BROOKLYN, N. Y., Oct. 1.—*A. H. Nichols, Louisville B. B. Club, How Hotel, St. Louis:* Nothing from you yet. Answer same as Saturday. P. A. WILLIAMS.

"To the credit of the Louisville club, be it said that it was the first and only one in the league which had the courage to expel a player for crooked playing, for there were several members of other clubs who were known to be equally guilty, but their club managers were afraid to take action against them. That the expulsion of the Louisville players had the effect for a time of retarding the popularity of the national game, and causing the public to be suspicious of all players, there can be no doubt, for while it had been suspicioned that some players in the league were crooked, it had never been proven, and was, therefore, only a suspicion. Nevertheless, the action of the Louisville club resulted in placing the league upon a more solid foundation, and, no doubt, placed a quietus upon dishonest playing."

At the annual league meeting of 1877 the action of the Louisville club in expelling these players was approved. The Cincinnati club was reinstated; St. Louis resigned; Indianapolis, Milwaukee, and Providence were admitted; and Hartford was dropped from the league. The clubs at this meeting were represented as follows: Providence, H. B. Winship; Indianapolis, W. B. Pettit; Milwaukee, W. P. Rogers; Cincinnati, J. M. W. Neff; Louisville, Charles E. Chase and C. W. Johnstone; Boston, A. H. Soden and Harry Wright; Chicago, Messrs. Hulburt, Mills, and Spalding.

There were six competing clubs for the League championship in 1878. Boston again proved the victors, with Cincinnati second. The record of games was:

THE CHAMPIONSHIP RECORD FOR 1878.

	Boston.	Cincinnati.	Providence.	Chicago.	Indianapolis.	Milwaukee.	Games Lost.	Games Won.
Boston,		6	6	8	10	11	19	41
Cincinnati,	6		9	10	4	8	23	37
Providence,	6	3		6	10	8	27	33
Chicago,	4	2	6		8	10	30	30
Indianapolis,	2	8	2	4		8	36	24
Milwaukee,	1	4	4	2	4		45	15
Games Lost,	19	23	27	30	36	45	180	180

There were a few changes in the winning team from that of 1877. The new men engaged were John Burdock and Charley Snyder. Lew Brown and the White brothers went to other clubs. The teams of 1878 were:

Boston.—Harry Wright, manager; George Wright, s.s.; O'Rourke, c.f.; Morrill, 1b.; Manning, r.f.; Burdock, 2b.; Leonard, l.f.; Schafer, substitute; Sutton, 3b.; Bond, p.; Snyder, c.

Cincinnati.—James White, r.f.; M. J. Kelly, c.; Pike, c.f.; Geer, s.s.; J. F. Sullivan, 1b.; Mitchell, c.f.; Will White, p.; Charley Jones, c.f.; Gerhardt, 2b.; McVey, 3b.; Dickerson, l.f.; Pearce, s.s.

Providence.—D. Allison, c.; Fred Carey, s.s.; Richard Higham, r.f.; Tim Murnane, 1b.; Tom York, l.f.; Paul Hines, c.f.; Fred Nichols, p.; Lew Brown, c. and l.f.; Sweasy, 2b.; Hague, 3b.; John Ward, p.; Pike also played a number of games at second base.

Chicago.—Robert Ferguson, s.s. and captain; Anson, l.f.; Start, 1b.; Cassidy, r.f.; Hankinson, 3b.; Remsen, c.f.; J. P. Reis, substitute; McClellan, 2b.; Frank Larkin, p.; Harbidge, c.; Hallinan, substitute.

Indianapolis.—John Clapp, l.f. and c.; John Nelson, sub.; Craft, 1b.; Joseph L. Quest, 2b.; James McCormick, p.; Frank S. Flint, c. and l.f.; Edward S. Nolan (the original "Only" of baseball nomenclature), pitcher; F. J. Warner, s.s.; E. N. Williamson, 2b.; George Schaffer, r.f.; R. E. McKelvey, c.f. Hallinan also played a few games.

Milwaukee.—Charles W. Bennett, c.; Peters, 2b. and s.s.; S. H. Weaver, p.; J. Hoodman, 1b.; W. B. Foley, 3b.; W. H. Holbert, r.f.; W. T. Redmond, s.s.; G. Creamer, 2b.; Abner Dalrymple, l.f.; Golden, c.f.; Ellick, Jennings and Knowdell and Bliss played a few games each.

During the season Nolan, pitcher of the Indianapolis team, deserted his club. He was expelled for so doing, and the expulsion was afterwards ratified by the league. It was during this year that the league clubs were prevented from playing exhibition games with non-league clubs on league grounds during the championship season, and also from playing such club prior to the championship season with the exception of local teams. This latter rule has been since modified.

The champion players, so far as records can ascertain them, were in 1878 as follows: Dalrymple of the Milwaukees, the tail-end club, led the batting averages with .356. John Ward, of the Providence team, was the leading pitcher, the best percentage of base hits made against him being .233. Charley Snyder, of Boston, led the catchers with .841. The best men in the other positions with their averages were: First base—Sullivan (Cincinnati) .974; second base—Burdock (Boston) .917; third base—Hague (Providence) .918; short stop—George Wright (Boston) .947; left field—Jones (Cincinnati) .893; centre field—Remsen (Chicago) .934; right field—George Schaffer (Indianapolis) .844.

The season of 1878 was nearly as disastrous financially as that of 1877, but such a healthy tone of public feeling toward the sport, and increasing belief in its integrity was shown, that the club owners were much encouraged, and made preparations for another eight club league. At the annual meeting, held in Cleveland, December 4th, 1878, the Indianapolis Club resigned, and the circuit was filled by the admission of clubs from Cleveland, Buffalo, and Syracuse. The Milwaukee Club afterward failing to come to time, the Troy Club, of which Gardner Earl was the founder, was taken in to fill the vacancy.

The Umpire question was as troublesome in 1878 as it is to-day, and an attempt was made to straighten things up by having the first regular staff. There were twenty umpires appointed from which clubs were to select.

The year 1879 was notable for the fact that George Wright—the greatest player of that day, who had been the mainstay of the Boston team for so many years—left Boston, taking O'Rourke with him, and, joining the Providence Club, led its team to victory after a hard fight with Boston, Chicago, and Buffalo.

The record follows:

THE CHAMPIONSHIP RECORD FOR 1879.

	Providence.	Boston.	Chicago.	Buffalo.	Cincinnati.	Cleveland.	Troy City.	Syracuse.	Games Lost.	Games Won.
Providence,		8	7	6	10	8	10	6	23	55
Boston,	4		4	9	7	10	11	4	29	49
Chicago,	5	8		6	3	8	8	6	32	44
Buffalo,	6	3	6		7	8	11	3	32	44
Cincinnati,	2	5	8	3		8	9	3	36	38
Cleveland,	4	2	4	4	4		5	1	53	24
Troy City,	2	1	3	1	2	6		4	56	19
Syracuse,	0	2	0	3	3	5	2		27	15
Games Lost,	23	29	32	32	36	53	56	27	288	288

The champion team consisted of J. M. Ward and Robert Mathews, pitchers; Lewis J. Brown, c.; Joe Start, 1b.; M. H. McGeary, 2b; W. L. Hague, 3b.; George Wright, s.s., captain and manager; T. York, l.f.; Paul Hines, c.f.; James H. O'Rourke, r.f. Toward the end of the season Emil Gross, c., and John Farrell, 2b., replaced Hague and Lew Brown.

The Boston team contained some new material. "Sadie" Houck, a Washington boy, was put in as short-stop. Jones, of the Cincinnati team, John O'Rourke, Hawes, and Coggswell were also engaged. Curry Foley was signed to help Bond out in pitching.

The Chicago team was also changed. Ferguson, Harbidge, Remsen, Cassidy, Start, McClellan, and Reis went elsewhere. The Chicago absorbed most of the Indianapolis team of 1878. The team was: Larkin, p.; Flint, c.; Anson, 1b.; Quest, 2b.; Hankinson, p. and 3b.; Peters, s.s.; Dalrymple, Remsen, George F. Gore, George Schaffer in the field, with Williamson alternating with Hankinson at third base.

The new men on the Cincinnati team were Barnes, Peter Hotaling, Lew Dickerson, M. E. Burke, and W. B. Foley. The four new teams were made up as follows:

Buffalo.—Jas. F. Galvin and W. H. McGinnigle, pitchers; John C. Rowe and Clapp, catchers; Oscar Walker, 1b.; Hardy Richardson, 3b. and 2b.; Charles Fulmer, 2b. and 3b.; David Force, s.s.; Joseph Hornung, D. Eggler, and W. Crowley, fielders.

Cleveland.—James McCormick, p.; Andrew Gilligan, c.; Thomas J. Carey, s.s.; C. M. Eden, r.f.; W. C. Riley, l.f.; R. M. Mitchell, p.; M. J. Kennedy, c.; W. B. Phillips, 1b.; George A. Strief, c.f.; F. J. Warner, 3b.; J. W. Glasscock, s.s.

Syracuse Stars.—Henry McCormick, p.; M. J. Dorgan and W. H. Holbert, catchers; W. W. Carpenter, 1b.; Jack Farrell, 2b.; C. A. Allen, 3b.; J. Richmond, s.s.; M. R. Mansel, l.f.; W. Purcell, r.f.; J. McCullar, c.f.; Woodhead, 3b. Creamer also played a few games with the Stars.

Troy.—A. Hall, c.f.; G. W. Bradley, p.; C. Riley, c.; H. Clapp, l.f.; C. P. Hawkes, 2b.; Hermann Doescher, 3b.; Ed. Caskens, s.s.; Thomas Mansel, l.f.; J. Evans, r.f.; P. McManus, sub.; J. Shupe, sub.; D. Brouthers, 1b.

During the season McKinnon was expelled from the league for an alleged failure to keep his contract with the Syracuse Club. This club was dropped from the circuit in the Fall of 1879, and the Worcester Club was admitted to fill the vacancy.

THE INDIANAPOLIS TEAM, SEPTEMBER, 1889.

Anson led the batsmen in 1879 with .407, the largest record made up to that time, and the same player led the first basemen with .974. John Ward again stood first among the pitchers, the percentage of base hits off his delivery being .241. Flint had the best catching average with .830. The other leading fielders were Quest, 2b., .946; McGeary, 3b., .916.; George Wright, s.s., .926; Jones, l.f., .933; Eggler, c.f., .918; Evans, r.f., .885.

The most important legislation of 1879 was the adoption of the first reserve rule, which has been the pillar of professional baseball. It was in the shape of a signed agreement by the terms of which each league club was permitted to reserve the services of five men for 1880.

In 1879 the International Association was succeeded by what was called the National Association, organized Feb. 17th. This minor league lasted two years. All the clubs were from Eastern cities. The clubs in 1879 were Albany, Holyoke, Washington, Worcester, New Bedford, Springfield, Manchester, Rochester, and Utica. The Worcesters drew out and joined the league in 1880. The Albanys won the championship with Keenan, c.; Critchley, p.; Tobin, Dunlap, Burns, basemen; Say, s.s.; Hanlon, Thomas, Rocap, fielders. D. Sullivan, Tom Mansel, and A. Clapp played part of the season with the Albanys. In 1880 the Nationals, of Washington, won the National Association pennant with Lynch, p.; Snyder, c.; Powell, 1b.; Gerhardt, 2b.; Morrissey, 3b.; McClellan, s.s.; T. Mansel, Baker, and Derby as fielders.

The first exclusively Western league was organized Jan. 2d, 1879, at Rockford, Ill., with four cities. They were Rockford, Davenport, Ia., Dubuque, Ia., and Omaha, Neb. The Dubuques finished in first place with a team which consisted of Reis, p.; Thomas Sullivan, c.; Lapham, 1b.; Tom Loftus, 2b.; J. Gleason, 3b.; Billy Gleason, s.s.; Alvaretta, Comiskey, and Radbourn, fielders, and Taylor, substitute. Of these men, Loftus, Bill Gleason, Comiskey, and Radbourn have since become famous.

Early in the season of 1880, the league determined to eradicate, as nearly as it was possible to do so, the drunkenness and other dissipations into which certain players fell towards the end of each season whose clubs had no longer a chance to win the championship, or who felt that they were sure not to be engaged for the next season. To do this, and to correct other abuses which had grown up, the Constitution was amended in such a way as to give clubs the power to suspend players during the season without pay, and to suspend them for the following season if it was thought advisable. The changes made gave the clubs these extraordinary powers that they might exact from the player satisfactory service during the time of his contract, so far as the player was personally able to give it. These changes were fully explained in an admirable address to the players, prepared by the league at a special meeting held at Rochester, Feb. 26th, 1880. On the same date another evil, the practice of negotiating with players before the close of the season, was abolished by an agreement between the clubs not to negotiate with any players for 1881 prior to Oct. 23rd, 1880.

The league championship in 1880 was won by the Chicago club, as shown by the record:

THE CHAMPIONSHIP RECORD FOR 1880.

	Chicago.	Providence.	Cleveland.	Troy City.	Worcester.	Boston.	Buffalo.	Cincinnati.	Games Lost.	Games Won.
Chicago, ...		9	8	10	10	9	11	10	17	67
Providence, ...	3		9	7	6	7	10	10	32	52
Cleveland, ...	4	3		9	6	7	9	9	37	47
Troy City, ...	2	5	3		5	5	11	10	42	41
Worcester, ...	2	6	6	7		8	3	8	43	40
Boston, ...	3	5	5	7	4		9	7	44	40
Buffalo, ...	1	2	3	1	9	3		5	58	24
Cincinnati, ...	2	2	3	1	3	5	5		59	21
Games Lost, ...	17	32	37	42	43	44	58	59	332	332

The champion team consisted of Corcoran and Goldsmith, pitchers; Flint, c.; Anson, 1b.; Quest, 2b.; Williamson, 3b.; Burns, s.s.; Dalrymple, Gore, and Kelly, fielders; T. L. Beals, substitute.

The new club, the Worcesters, had for its team: J. L. Richmond, p.; A. J. Bushong, c.; G. Creamer, 2b.; Arthur W. Whitney, 3b.; A. A.

Irwin, s.s.; George A. Wood, l.f.; Lon Knight, r.f.; Harry D. Stovey, c.f.; F. C. Nichols, p.; Charles W. Bennett, c.; Sullivan, 1b.

Brown and Jim O'Rourke returned to the Boston club. Another new man on the Hub team was Phil Powers, who was engaged as a catcher. Hawes and Snyder retired from the team. Foley, Bond, Morrill, Burdock, Sutton, Houck, Jones, and John O'Rourke continued with the team.

The Providence team included Bradley, Ward, Gross, Start, Farrell, McGeary, York, Peters, Hines, and Dorgan.

The Clevelands had J. McCormick, Kennedy, Phillips, Fred Dunlap, Hankinson, Glasscock, Edward Hanlon, Hotaling, Schaffer, A. Hall, and Barney Gilligan.

Cincinnati was represented by Clapp, J. Manning, W. White, C. M. Smith, S. Wright, Leonard, Carpenter, Purcell, Mike Hansel, J. Riley, and C. Riley.

The Troy contingent included Holbert, Welch, Larkin, Coggswell, Ferguson, Dickerson, Caskins, Gillespie, Connor, Cassidy, Evans, and Harbidge.

The Buffalo team was made up of J. C. Rowe, Charles Radbourn, Crowley, Hornung, Force, Hardie Richardson, Thomas Poorman, Walker, Sam Crane, McGunnigle, and Esterbrook.

Gore, of Chicago, led the batting averages of the league in 1880, with a percentage of base hits of .365. In the fielding averages, Sullivan, of Worcester, led the first basemen with a percentage of .982; Burdock, of Boston, the second basemen with .922; Williamson, of Chicago, the third basemen with .893; Force, of Buffalo, the short-stops with .924; York, of Providence, the left fielders with .932; Hines, of the same club, the centre fielders with .925; Evans, of Troy, the right fielders with .906; and Bushong, of Worcester, the catchers with .845. In pitching, Corcoran, of the Chicago team, had the best average in percentage of base hits off his pitching.

The Chicago club made a little money this year, but it was the only club that did. In consequence of an agreement made in regard to the sale of liquors in club grounds, the Cincinnati club forfeited its membership, and at the annual meeting of the league in New York, December 8th, 1880, the Detroit club was elected to take the place of Cincinnati. At this meeting also the league passed a resolution that they would never remove the black list from Devlin, Hall, Craver, and Nichols, and that they would not even entertain any further appeals in behalf of these delinquents. It might be said here that Devlin, who died a few years ago, made a solemn appeal just before he died to have the stain taken off his character, but the appeal was refused.

In 1881 the Chicagos again won the championship with the same team as in 1880, with the addition of a substitute named Piercy.

THE CHAMPIONSHIP RECORD FOR 1881.

	Chicago.	Providence.	Buffalo.	Detroit.	Troy City.	Boston.	Cleveland.	Worcester.	Games Lost.	Games Won.
Chicago,		9	7	7	8	10	6	9	28	56
Providence,	3		5	8	6	7	9	9	37	47
Buffalo,	5	7		9	3	8	7	6	38	45
Detroit,	5	4	3		7	8	7	7	43	41
Troy City,	4	6	9	5		5	6	4	45	39
Boston,	2	5	4	4	7		8	8	45	38
Cleveland,	6	3	5	5	6	4		7	48	36
Worcester,	3	3	5	5	8	3	5		50	32
Games Lost,	28	37	38	43	45	45	48	50	334	334

The other teams were made up as follows:

Boston.—James E. Whitney, Snyder, Morrill, Burdock, Sutton, George Wright, Hornung, Richmond, Crowley, Thomas Deasley, and Thomas Bond.

Buffalo.—Galvin, Lynch, Foley, Peters, J. O'Rourke, T. J. Sullivan, Rowe, Jim White, H. Richardson, J. H. Morrissey, D. Brouthers, Force, and Purcell, with James O'Rourke as captain and manager.

Cleveland.—McCormick, Kennedy, Phillips, Moynahan, Dunlap, McGeary, Glasscock, Purcell, J. J. Smith, Schaffer, Remsen, John Clapp, Bradley, Taylor, and Nolan.

Worcester.—Richmond, Bushong, McCormick, Creamer, Carpenter, Irwin, Stovey, Carey, Dickerson, Hotaling, Nelson, Dorgan.

Providence.—Ward, Gross, Radbourn, Gilligan, Start, Farrell, J. Denny, McClellan, Hines, Mathews, York, and Brown.

Detroit.—George H. Derby, C. W. Bennett, J. J. Gerhardt, C. Reilly, Bradley, Wood, Hanlon, Knight, L. J. Brown, Powell, Houck, Weidman, Knight, F. Whitney. Manager, Frank Bancroft.

Troy.—Welch, William Ewing, Connor, Ferguson, Hankinson, Caskins, Gillespie, Cassidy, Evans, Halbert, and Keefe.

In the batting averages, Anson was first with .399. Anson also led the first basemen with .975; Quest, the second basemen with .929, and Williamson, the third basemen with .909. The three leading fielders were Hornung, .947; Hanlon, .896; and Dorgan, .907. Force headed the short-stops with .945. The best pitcher was Radbourn, the percentage of base hits off his pitching being .227. Charley Bennett, with .896, was the king of catchers.

In April, 1881, the New York, Metropolitan, and Quickstep clubs of New York City; the Athletics, of Philadelphia; Atlantics, of Brooklyn, and Nationals, of Washington, organized what was known as the Eastern Championship Association. Only three of the clubs completed their schedule. They were the Metropolitans, Athletics, and Atlantics. The Nationals went under early in the season. A club representing Albany was taken in, but it fared no better than the Nationals. The Metropolitans made the best record, winning 32, and losing 13 games. The winning team was: Daly and Poorman, pitchers; Hays and Dorgan, catchers; Esterbrook, Bradley, and Muldoon, on bases; Say, short-stop; Kennedy, Clinton, and Roseman, in the out field. Other men who played on the team were Nagle, p.; Boyle, p.; D. Sullivan, c.; Powers, c.; Nelson, s.s.; Mansel, c.f.

In 1882 there was no change in the league circuit. April 10th, President Hulbert, the founder of the league, died at Chicago. In June, at a special meeting of the league, Richard Higham, an umpire, was expelled, on charges made by the Detroit club, of collusion with pool gamblers.

The Chicago club won the championship for the third time.

THE CHAMPIONSHIP RECORD FOR 1882.

	Chicago.	Providence.	Buffalo.	Boston.	Cleveland.	Detroit.	Troy City.	Worcester.	Games Lost.	Games Won.
Chicago, ...		8	6	6	9	8	9	9	29	55
Providence, ...	4		6	6	8	9	9	10	32	52
Buffalo, ...	6	6		5	6	5	6	11	39	45
Boston, ...	6	6	7		7	8	4	7	39	45
Cleveland, ...	3	4	6	5		4	9	11	40	42
Detroit, ...	4	3	7	4	7		8	9	41	42
Troy City, ...	3	3	6	8	2	4		9	48	35
Worcester, ...	3	2	1	5	1	3	3		66	18
Games Lost, ...	29	32	39	39	40	41	48	66	334	334

The only new man on the Chicago team was Hugh Nicol. The other teams were as follows:

Providence.—Radbourn, Gilligan, Start, John Farrell, Denny Ward, York, Hines and Tim Manning, Nava, C. Carroll, and A. Whitney.

Buffalo.—Galvin, J. Rowe, Brouthers, H. Richardson, Force, Purcell, Dolan, O'Rourke, Foley, the one-armed curve pitcher Hugh Daily, and Burke.

Boston.—Whitney, Buffinton, Deasley, Mathews, Burdock, Merrill, Rowen, Sutton, S. W. Wise, Hornung, Hotaling, H. M. McClure, and Whiting.

Cleveland.—McCormick, Kennedy, Phillips, Dunlap, M. Muldoon, Glasscock, Thos. J. Esterbrook, Doescher, J. Richmond, Shaffer, John Kelly, Briody, Bradley, Tilley, D. Rowe, Dwyer, McGunnigle, and Willigrod.

Detroit.—Geo. E. Weidman, S. W. Pratt, McKenzie, M. J. Powell, Johnny Troy, J. F. Farrell, Foster, Wood, A. Whitney, Hanlon, Robinson, Knight, McGeary, Derby, and Bennett.

Troy.—Welch, Keefe, Ewing, Halbert, Harbidge, Connor, Ferguson, J. J. Smith, Fred Pfeffer, Gillespie, James Roseman, and Cassidy and Egan.

Worcester.—L. Richmond, Bushong, Coggswell, Creamer, Fred

Mann, Irwin, Stovey, Evans, Bond, John J. Hayes, Corey, Mountain, O'Leary, Smith, McLaughlin, O'Brien, Clinton, Clarkson, Halpin, Merrill, and John Irwin.

Brouthers, of the Buffalo club, led the batting averages for 1882 with .367. Brouthers also led the first basemen with .974; Burdock, of Boston, leading the second basemen with .929; Ewing, of Troy, the third basemen with .889; McGeary, of Detroit, the short-stops with .935; Hornung, of Boston, the left fielders with .930; Esterbrook, of Cleveland, the centre fielders with .893; and Evans, of Worcester, the right fielders with .910; Bennett, of Detroit, led the catchers with a percentage of .874; while Corcoran, of Chicago, led the pitchers with a percentage of base hits off his pitching of .208.

The second Northwestern League was organized at Chicago, October 27th, 1882. The clubs entered for the pennant in 1883 were: Peoria, Springfield, and Quincy, in Illinois; Bay City, Grand Rapids, and East Saginaw, Michigan; Fort Wayne, Indiana; and Toledo, Ohio. Toledo won with the following nine: O'Day, Moffit, and Cushman, pitchers; Lockwood and Walker, catchers; Lane, Barkley, and Martin, basemen; Miller, short-stop; Tilley, Welch, and Poorman, fielders.

A minor league, named the Inter-State Association, was organized November 9th, 1882, at Reading, Pa. The following clubs constituted the membership in 1883: Active, of Reading; Anthracite, of Pottsville; Harrisburg, of Harrisburg, Pa.; Merritt, of Camden; Trenton, of Trenton, N J.; Brooklyn, of Brooklyn; and Quickstep, of Wilmington, Del. The first season was marked by the disbandment of the Merritt club, July 20th, 1883, and ended with the Brooklyn club in possession of the pennant, after a close struggle with the Harrisburg team. The champion team: Kimber and Terry, pitchers; Farrow and Corcoran, catchers; Householder, Greenwood, and Fennelly, on the bases; Geer, short-stop; and Smith, Walker, and Doyle, in the outfield. Egan, Manning, Schenck, Smith, Morgan, Luff, and Williams also took part in games during the season.

In 1882 the Metropolitans won the League Alliance Championship, as has already been noted.

The year 1883 saw a big boom in the attendance at ball games. The public was excited to such a degree by the closeness of the league contest that about all the clubs made money, and the game got a footing that has steadily increased ever since. At the annual meeting of the league, held at Providence, Dec. 6th, 1882, Troy and Worcester resigned their membership, and New York and Philadelphia were added to the circuit. A. G. Mills was elected to succeed Mr. Hulbert as president, and N. E. Young was for the seventh time re-elected as secretary. John B. Day and C. T. Dillingham represented the New York club, and A. J. Reach the Philadelphia club. A great many applications were received from players who had been suspended from time to time, asking reinstatement. The following were received back into the fold, and forgiven: John E. Clapp, E. J. Caskins, S. P. Houck, Lipman Pike, Lew P. Dickerson, M. J. Morgan, J. J. Fox, E. Nolan, W. Crowley, Lew Brown, E. Gross, Alex. McKinnon, Phil. Baker, C. W. Jones, and J. J. Gerhardt. None of these players had ever been charged with crooked work. All of them had been punished for minor offenses. Herman Doescher was expelled for peculiar financial methods. It should be said, in justice to Mr. Doescher, that he was afterwards reinstated and served the league as an umpire during two seasons.

On March 17th, 1883, the Arbitration Committee of the two major leagues met in New York City, and the system of piracy of players, which prevailed and was then a crying evil, was abated for all time by the adoption of a document then called the tripartite agreement, now known as the National Agreement. The men who formulated this document, which has been the safeguard of the game, were A. G. Mills, A. H. Soden, and John B. Day, representing the league; O. P. Caylor, William Barnie, and Lewis Simmons, representing the American Association; and Elias Mather, of the Grand Rapids, Mich., club, acting for the Northwestern league. A. G. Mills was chairman, and O. P. Caylor, secretary. No history could possibly be complete without the text of the agreement, which is the Blackstone of baseball law. The document, which includes amendments made up to 1889, follows:

THE NATIONAL AGREEMENT OF PROFESSIONAL BASEBALL CLUBS.

THIS AGREEMENT, made between the Association known and designated as the National League of Professional Baseball Clubs of the one part, and the Association

THE KANSAS CITY TEAM, SEPTEMBER, 1889.

known and designated as the American Association of Baseball Clubs, of the other part, witnesseth, that:

I. This document shall be entitled The National Agreement, and shall supersede and be a substitute for all other Agreements, similarly or otherwise designated, heretofore existing between the parties hereto.

II. *a.* No contract shall be made for the services of any player by any Club member of either party hereto for a longer period than seven months, beginning April 1st, and terminating October 31st, and no such contract for services to be rendered after the expiration of the current year shall be made prior to the 20th day of October of such year, nor shall any player, without the consent of the Club to which he is under contract, enter into any negotiation or contract with any Club, Club agent, or individual for services to be rendered in an ensuing year prior to the said 20th of October. Upon written proofs of a violation of this section the Board of Arbitration shall disqualify such player for and during said ensuing year, and shall inflict a fine of five hundred dollars, payable forthwith into the treasury of the Board, upon the Club in whose interests such negotiations or contract was entered into.

b. Every regular contract shall be registered and approved by the Secretary of the Association of which the contracting Club is a member, who shall forthwith notify the Secretary of the other Association party hereto, and the other Club members of his Association.

III. When a player under contract with or reservation by any Club member of either Association party hereto is expelled, black listed, suspended, or rendered ineligible in accordance with its rules, notice of such disqualification shall be served upon the Secretary of the Board of Arbitration by the Secretary of the Association from whose Club such player shall have been thus disqualified, and the Secretary of the Board shall forthwith serve notice of such disqualification upon the Secretary of the other Association party hereto. When a player becomes ineligible under the provisions of this Agreement, the Secretary of the Board of Arbitration shall notify the Secretaries of the Association parties hereto of such disqualification, and from the receipt of such notice, all Club members of the parties hereto shall be debarred from employing or playing with, or against, such disqualified player, until the period of disqualification shall have terminated, or the disqualification be revoked by the Association from which such player was disqualified, or by the Board of Arbitration, and due notice of such revocation served upon the Secretary of the other Association, and by him upon his respective Clubs.

IV. On the tenth day of October in each year the Secretary of each Association shall transmit to the Secretary of the other Association a reserve list of players, not exceeding fourteen in number, then under contract with each of its several Club members, and of such players reserved in any prior annual reserve list, who have refused to contract with said Club members, and of all other ineligible players, and such players, together with all others thereafter to be regularly contracted with by such Club members, are and shall be ineligible to contract with any other Club member of either Association party hereto, except as hereinafter prescribed.

V. Upon the release of a player from contract or reservation with any Club member of either Association party hereto, the services of such player shall at once be subject to the acceptance of the other Clubs of such Association, expressed in writing or by telegraph, to the Secretary thereof, for a period of ten days after notice of said release, and thereafter if said services be not so accepted, said player may negotiate and contract with any other Club. The Secretary of such Association shall send notice to the Secretary of the other Association of said player's release on the date thereof, and of said acceptance of his services at or before the expiration of the ten days aforesaid. Provided that the disbandment of a Club or its expulsion from membership in either Association party hereto shall operate as a release of all its players from contract and reservation, but the services of such players shall at once be subject to the acceptance of the other Clubs of such Association as hereinbefore provided.

VI. Each Club member of either Association party hereto shall have exclusive control of its own territory, and no Club shall be entitled to membership in either Association party hereto from any city or town in which a Club member of either Association party hereto is located. *Provided* that nothing herein contained shall prohibit any Club member of either Association party hereto from resigning its membership in such Association during the month of November in any year, and being admitted to membership in the other Association, with all rights and privileges conferred by this agreement.

VII. No game shall be played between any Club member of either Association party hereto, or any of its players under contract or reservation with any other Club or "team" while presenting in its nine any ineligible player. A violation of this section shall subject each offender to fine or expulsion in the discretion of the Board of Arbitration.

VIII. Each Association party hereto shall have the right to make and enforce all rules and regulations pertaining to the control, discipline, and compensation of all players under contract with and reservation by its Club members, provided such rules and regulations shall in no way conflict with the provisions of this Agreement.

IX. A Board of Arbitration, consisting of three duly accredited representatives from each of the Associations parties hereto, shall convene annually at a place mutually to be arranged, and shall organize by the election of a chairman, secretary, and such other officers and committees as to them shall seem meet and proper. They may make, and from time to time revoke, alter, and repeal all necessary rules and regulations not inconsistent with this Agreement, for their meetings, procedure and the general transaction of their business. Their membership on said Board shall be determinable at the pleasure of their respective appointing Associations upon duly certified notice thereof. A quorum shall consist of at least two representatives from each Association, and all questions shall be voted upon separately by the respective delegations, and no such changes or additions shall be made unless concurred in by a majority of the delegates of each Association.

X. In addition to all matters that may be specially referred to them by both of the Associations parties hereto, the said Board shall have sole, exclusive, and final jurisdiction of all disputes and complaints arising under, and all interpretations of this Agreement. They shall also, in the interests of harmony and peace, arbitrate upon and decide all differences and disputes arising between the Associations parties hereto and between a Club member of one and a Club member of the other Association party hereto. Provided that nothing in this Agreement shall be construed as giving authority to said Board to alter, amend, or modify any section or part of section of the Constitution of either Association party hereto.

The change in the name of this document was made so as to admit all associations to its benefits. Any minor league may become parties to it by subscribing to what are known as Articles of Qualified Admission to the National Agreement, which provide for the settlement of all matters between the major and minor leagues, and define the rights and privileges of each. Upon payment of an annual sum per league, the clubs in each minor league are allowed to reserve fourteen players. The sum which gives minor leagues absolute protection is $1,000, if said association be composed of four clubs; $1,500, if composed of six clubs, or $2,000 if composed of not more than eight clubs.

The original National agreement provided for the reserve of eleven men. The number was increased to twelve at the annual meeting in 1883, and was a year later increased to fourteen.

The championship season of 1883 was notable for the closeness of the fight between the four leading clubs. The number of games necessary to constitute a series was increased this season from twelve to fourteen.

THE CHAMPIONSHIP RECORD FOR 1883.

	Boston.	Chicago.	Providence.	Cleveland.	Buffalo.	New York.	Detroit.	Philadelphia.	Games Lost.	Games Won.
Boston,		7	8	10	7	7	10	14	35	63
Chicago,	7		7	6	9	9	9	12	39	59
Providence,	6	7		6	7	9	12	11	40	58
Cleveland,	4	8	8		7	7	9	12	42	55
Buffalo,	7	5	7	7		8	9	9	45	52
New York,	7	5	5	6	5		6	12	50	46
Detroit,	4	5	2	5	5	8		11	58	40
Philadelphia,	0	2	3	2	5	2	3		81	17
Games Lost,	35	39	40	42	45	50	58	81	390	390

The winning team comprised M. Hines and Hackett, catchers; Buffinton and Whitney, pitchers; Morrill, 1b.; Burdock, 2b.; Sutton, 3b.; Wise, s.s.; Hornung, l.f.; Smith, c.f.; Radford, r.f.; with Brown, substitute.

The Chicago team consisted of Corcoran, Flint, Anson, Pfeffer, Williamson, Burns, Dalrymple, Gore, Kelly, and Goldsmith.

Providence was represented by Radbourn, Gilligan, Start, J. Farrell, Denny, A. Irwin, Cliff, Carroll, P. Hines, Richmond, Cassidy, Sweeney, and Nava; Harry Wright was manager.

The manager of the Detroit was J. C. Chapman. The players were Weidman, Bennett, Powell, Jos. Farrell, Houck, Wood, Hanlon, T. Mansell, R. S. Burns, S. Trott, and Jones.

Frank Bancroft piloted the Clevelands with this team: J. McCormick, Chas. Briody, Phillips, Crowley, Dunlap, Muldoon, Sawyer, Glasscock, York, Evans, Daily, Bushong, and Bradley.

Jim O'Rourke was the playing manager of the Buffalo team. His men were Galvin, J. White, Kennedy, Brouthers, Richardson, Lilley, Derby, J. Rowe, Cushman, Foley, Eggler, Schaffer, and Force.

The first New York team consisted of Welch, Clapp, Ward, Ewing, Troy, Hankinson, Caskins, Gillespie, Connor, Dorgan, Humphreys, Pearce, and James E. O'Neil.

The first Philadelphia team, which finished last, was managed by Robert Ferguson. The players were John F. Coleman, F. C. Ringo, John Manning, Sid. Farrar, Warner, W. H. McClellan, Purcell, John Nagle, Doyle, E. W. Gross, Harbridge, Hagan, and Fred. Lewis. It is only fair to Ferguson to say that a harder team to handle has never before or since been gathered. Only four of these men are now, at the end of six years, playing ball, and only three of them, Purcell, McClellan, and Farrar are doing so with success.

In 1883 Brouthers, of the Buffalo club, again led the batting averages, his percentages of base hits being .371. In the fielding averages Morrill, of the Boston club, led the first basemen with .974; Farrell, of Providence, led the second basemen with .925; Denny, of Providence, the third basemen with .875; Glasscock, of Cleveland, the short-stops with .918; Hornung, of Boston, the left fielders with .936; Hines, of Providence, the centre fielders with .913; Evans, of Cleveland, the right fielders with .902; Bennett, of Detroit, the catchers with .859, and McCormick, of Cleveland, the pitchers with an average of earned runs off his pitching of 1-35 to a game, this criterion of pitching being first introduced in the league records this year. He also led in having the smallest per cent. of base hits off his pitching, viz.: .209.

The year 1884 was a lively one for the clubs and the players. Public interest was excited to that pitch in 1883 that everybody had visions of a rainfall of gold, and great preparations were made to reap the harvest. Altogether there were twelve associations in operation, comprising almost a hundred clubs. It was in this year that Henry V. Lucas took hold of the ill-fated Union Association, and ran it in competition with the league and the American Association. It was a gigantic scheme, and started off with much promise; but it failed completely, and its projector lost his fortune in the scheme, and finally had to retire from baseball, broken in purse and spirit.

The Union Association was organized at Pittsburgh, September 12th, 1883. At first there were only six clubs, but afterwards the number was increased to eight. H. B. Bennett, of Washington, was president, and Warren White secretary, but at the first annual meeting the association was reorganized and St. Louis was taken in, the Richmond, Va., club, which had helped organize at Pittsburg, dropping out. Mr. Lucas was elected president, J. Pratt vice-president, and Mr. White secretary. Mr. Lucas became the prime mover. His scheme contemplated the abolition of the reserve rule, which Mr. Lucas considered as an outrageous and unjustifiable chain on the freedom of the players. He expended a great deal of energy and time, and soon had his new league in trim for a start.

The cities agreed upon for the circuit were Washington, St. Louis, Altoona, Pa., Boston, Baltimore, Cincinnati, Philadelphia, and Chicago. It was given out that over fifty league players would break their contracts, but when the time came for a show of hands there was quite a hitch. The men who had promised declined for the most part to keep their word. The first recruit Mr. Lucas got was Tony Mullane, of the St. Louis Association Club. He was given $1,000 advance money. He weakened, however, before the season opened. Mr. Lucas, however, succeeded in persuading Fred Dunlap, of the Clevelands, Sam Crane, of New York, George W. Bradley, "Orator" Shaffer, Fred

Shaw, and one-armed Hugh Dailey to join fortunes with the association. In July Mr. Lucas negotiated with Sweeney, the Providence pitcher, who went on a "grand good time," and made himself so obnoxious by his actions, and his refusal to play when wanted, that he was blacklisted. Sweeney joined the St. Louis Unions. The final capture of league players occurred August 8th, when the Cincinnati Union club persuaded McCormick, Briody, and Glasscock to desert the Cleveland club. All these players were expelled by their clubs.

The association season was a disastrous one. They couldn't fight the League and American Association with the young players they had, and the public seemed to lack confidence in the organization. None of the clubs made any money, and only one, the National, paid its expenses. Only five of them played out their schedule. They were the St. Louis, Cincinnati, Boston, Baltimore, and National, of Washington, and they finished in the order named, Boston and Baltimore being tied for third place. The St. Louis team was made up of Sweeney, Boyle, Hodnett, and Werden, pitchers; Dolan, Brennan, and Baker, catchers; Quinn, 1b.; Dunlap, 2b.; Gleason, 3b.; Whitehead, s.s.; Dave Rowe, Schaffer, and a battery player in the field.

The season of the Union clubs opened April 17th. Within six weeks the Altoona team gave up, and was succeeded by Kansas City. The Keystones, as the Philadelphia club was called, lasted until August. When it disbanded Mr. Lucas persuaded the Wilmingtons to desert the Eastern League and join the Union. They did, but gave it up in September, and were succeeded by a club located at Milwaukee. Chicago weakened in August and transferred its team to Pittsburgh, but that city wouldn't support the team, and it was disbanded September 19th. St. Paul supplied the vacancy in the circuit. The association was disbanded January 15th, 1885, as only two of the clubs were willing to continue for a second season.

The men who were prominent in the Union Association are given as a matter of record: St. Louis—Henry Lucas and Theo. Benoist; Chicago—A. H. Henderson and E. S. Hengle; Cincinnati—Justus Thorner; Philadelphia—Thos. J. Pratt; Baltimore—I. W. Lowe and B. F. Matthews; Washington—H. B. Bennett and M. B. Scanlan; Boston—Frank E. Winslow, George Wright, and T. H. Murnane; Altoona—W. Rilz.

The National League expelled the deserting players and went along the even tenor of its way, playing out a very exciting and profitable season. The result was in doubt until August, and even then it was a question of the endurance of one man. That man was Charles Radbourn, of the Providence team, and he won the pennant for his club. He pitched 74 games and won 62 of them, his opponents averaging only a fraction over one earned run to a game. This is all the more remarkable from the fact that Radbourn pitched in 37 consecutive games during August and September, and won 32 of them. He lost only one game in August to New York, the score being 2 to 1.

THE CHAMPIONSHIP RECORD FOR 1884.

	Providence.	Boston.	Buffalo.	Chicago.	New York.	Philadelphia.	Cleveland.	Detroit.	Games Won.	Per ct. Won.
Providence,		9	10	11	13	13	13	15	84	.750
Boston,	7		9	10	8	13	14	12	73	.650
Buffalo,	6	6		10	5	11	14	12	64	.570
Chicago,	5	6	6		12	14	8	11	62	.550
New York,	3	8	11	4		11	11	14	62	.550
Philadelphia,	3	3	5	2	5		10	11	39	.340
Cleveland,	3	2	2	8	5	6		9	35	.310
Detroit,	1	4	4	5	2	5	7		28	.250
Games Lost,	28	38	47	50	50	73	77	84	447	

The Providence team consisted of Radbourn, p.; Gilligan and Nava, c.; Start, 1b.; John Farrell, 2b.; Denny, 3b.; Irwin, s.s.; C. Carroll, l.f.; Hines, c.f.; Radford, r.f.; Bassett, substitute. Sweeney pitched in 24 games, winning 16 of them. He retired from the team in July and deserted to the Union Association.

The other league teams were made up as follows:

Boston.—Buffinton and Whitney, pitchers; Hackett and Hines, catchers; Morrill, 1b.; Burdock, 2b.; Sutton, 3b.; Wise, s.s.; Hornung, James H. Manning, Crowley, and W. P. Annis, fielders. E. Moriarty and M. Barrett also played a few games.

Buffalo.—Galvin and Serad, pitchers; J. Rowe and George Meyers, catchers; Brouthers, 1b.; H. Richardson and Collins, 2b.; J. White, 3b.; Force, s.s.; Lillie, Eggler, and O'Rourke, fielders.

Chicago.—Corcoran, Goldsmith, Clarkson, pitchers; Flint and Kelly, catchers; Anson, 1b.; Pfeffer, 2b.; Williamson, 3b.; Burns, s.s.; Dalrymple, Gore, Kelly, and Sunday, fielders. W. H. Kinzie played 18 games as short-stop. M. Depongher, H. W. Graham, Thos. F. Lee, G. W. Crosby, G. Whitely, also signed, but participated in few games, some of them not in any.

New York.—Welch, Begley, and Dorgan, pitchers; Ewing and Humphries, catchers; McKinnen, 1b.; Connor and Ward, 2b.; Hankinson, 3b.; Caskins and D. Richardson, s.s.; D. Richardson, Gillespie, Morgan, Connor, and Ward, fielders. D. Creedon, C. F. Jones, D. N. Tarbox, and M. Kennedy were signed, but seldom played.

Philadelphia.—Ferguson, William Vinton, McElroy, and Coleman, pitchers; Crowley and Ringo, catchers; Farrar, 1b.; Andrews, 2b.; Mulvey, 3b.; McClellan, s.s.; Fogarty, Purcell, John Manning, and Coleman, fielders. J. F. Cahill, J. J. Remsen, L. Daniels, James Donahue, G. Ingraham, G. Patrick, E. S. Ford, Hallen, W. N. Chatfield, J. W. Knight, J. F. Waring, and F. Riley, were signed, but not played.

Cleveland.—Harkins, McCormack, and Moffat, pitchers; Bushong and Briody, catchers; Phillips, 1b., H. W. Smith, J. H. Ardner, Pinkney, 2b.; Muldoon, 3b.; Glasscock and Smith, s.s.; Evans, Busch, Hotaling, Harkins, Moffatt, and William Murphy, fielders; James McGuire, J. R. Hoyle, L. D. Drake, H. Arundel, C. H. Evenson, and D. W. Mulholland were signed, but not used. Glasscock, Briody, and McCormick deserted to the Union Association about the middle of the season, and were expelled from the league. Fred Dunlap had been reserved for 1885, but joined the St. Louis club in violation of his reserve.

Detroit.—F. W. Mienke, Shaw, Weidman, Getzein, and Brill, pitchers; Bennett and Gastfield, catchers; M. P. Scott, 1b.; W. Geirs, Jones, and Kearns, 2b.; Joseph Farrell, 3b.; Meinke, Cox, and Baker, s.s.; G. Wood, Hanlon, and Weidman, fielders. A. L. Richardson, W. F. Prince, W. S. Walker, and C. S. Maxwell each played a few games. Shaw deserted to St. Louis and was expelled.

THE LOUISVILLE TEAM, SEPTEMBER, 1889.

The reason so many extra players were signed by the league clubs was to prepare against possible desertions to the Union Association.

In 1884 O'Rourke led the batting averages with .350. In the fielding averages Start, of Providence, led the first basemen with a percentage of chances accepted of .974; Burdock, of Boston, led the second basemen with .925; Sutton, of Boston, the third basemen with .906; Smith, of Cleveland, the short-stops with .904; Hornung, of Boston, the left fielders with .913; Fogarty, of Philadelphia, the centre fielders with .915; and Evans, of Cleveland, the right fielders with .911; Hackett, of Boston, led the catchers with .879; and Radbourn, of Providence, the pitchers with an average of runs earned off his pitching of but 1.15 to a game.

The Northwestern League started the season of 1884 with twelve clubs, but gradually dwindled down by disbandment and otherwise until only three of the original members remained. This association was reorganized in 1886, when it included the representative clubs of Duluth, St. Paul, and Minneapolis, in Minnesota, and Eau Claire, Milwaukee, and Oshkosh, in Wisconsin. The championship was won by the Duluth club with the following team: Baldwin, Watson, and Fitzsimmons, pitchers; Legg and Traffly, catchers; Van Zandt, Reid, and O'Rourke on the bases; Manning, short-stop; and Jones, McMillan, and Cody in the outfield.

The Eastern League was organized in 1884, when the Trenton club won the championship with the following team: Murphy, Weidel, and Doyle, pitchers; Knowdell and Grady, catchers; Miller, Myers, and Shetzline on the bases; Smith, short-stop; and Reccius, Grady, and Brouthers in the outfield. The other championship teams were: 1885, National, of Washington, Barr and O'Day, pitchers; Fulmer and Cook, catchers; Baker, Knowles, and Gladmon on the bases; White, short-stop; and Burch, Hoover, and Powell in the outfield. 1886, Newark, J. Smith, Pyle, and Knowlton, pitchers; Daly and Trott, catchers; Tucker, Greenwood, and Burns on the bases; L. Smith, short-stop; and Annis, Casey, and Coogan in the outfield.

The season of 1885 saw another change in the National league circuit. Cleveland was obliged to withdraw. When it became evident that the league would admit Mr. Lucas and his St. Louis club to membership and possibly pardon the deserters, President A. G. Mills, who was bitterly opposed to such a scheme, resigned as President. The three offices of President, Secretary, and Treasurer were combined in Nicholas E. Young, and he has ever since remained a qualified Pooh Bah of the league. After a series of five special meetings, running into the month of April, Mr. Lucas was taken in, and the deserters were forgiven. The St. Louis club was admitted March 5th. April 18th Briody, Glasscock, McCormick, Shaffer, Dunlap, and Sweeney were reinstated. The first three men were fined $1,000 each, and Dunlap, Shaffer, and Sweeney were fined $500 each.

The Chicago team won the championship in 1885, as the record shows:

THE CHAMPIONSHIP RECORD FOR 1885.

	Chicago.	New York.	Philadelphia.	Providence.	Boston.	Detroit.	Buffalo.	St. Louis.	Games Won.	Per Ct. Won.
Chicago,		6	11	11	14	15	16	14	87	.777
New York,	10		11	12	13	12	15	12	85	.759
Philadelphia,	5	5		8	9	9	11	9	56	.509
Providence,	5	4	7		7	9	13	8	53	.482
Boston,	2	3	7	9		7	10	8	46	.411
Detroit,	1	4	7	6	9		5	9	41	.380
Buffalo,	0	1	5	3	6	11		12	38	.339
St. Louis,	2	4	6	8	8	4	4		36	.333
Games Lost,	25	27	54	57	66	67	74	72	442	

The pennant race was a walk-over for Chicago and New York, and up to the very close of the season the result was in doubt. The New Yorks finished the season with four games at Chicago. They needed three of these to make them champions. They had previously beaten Chicago nine out of twelve games, and looked on victory as a sure thing. Chicago, however, defeated New York three straight games. The league teams for 1885 were:

Chicago.—Clarkson and McCormick, p.; Flint and Kelly, c.; Anson, Pfeffer, and Williamson on bases; Burns, s.s.; Dalrymple, Gore, Kelly, and Sunday, fielders. O. P. Beard, C. Marr, E. E. Sutcliffe, and Joe Brown were also given a trial.

Boston.—Whitney, Buffinton, Morrill, Burdock, Sutton, Wise, Hornung, Manning, J. A. Davis, Hines, Deasley, M. M. Hackett, W. H. Hackett, W. M. Nash, Thos. Poorman, Thos. McCarthy, Richard F. Johnston, and Thomas F. Gunning, Purcell, and Whitely.

Buffalo.—Rowe, J. A. McCauley, Brouthers, Richardson, White, Myers, Force, Wm. Crowley, J. J. Lillie, E. J. Hengle, R. Blakeston, and J. Connor, and Stearns, Conway, and Wood. Galvin and Serad were the pitchers.

Detroit.—Weidmann, Bennett, Chas. Getzein, Scott, Mienke, Farrell, Wood, Hanlon, J. F. Morgan, C. H. Morton, and Marr Phillips. Baldwin, McGuire, M. McQuery, Crane, Quest, Donnelly, Halpin, and J. Manning (also with Boston).

New York.—Welch, Hope, Ewing, Connor, Gerhardt, D. Richardson, Gillespie, James O'Rourke, McKinnon, Keefe, F. Deasley (also with Boston), Esterbrook, Ward, and Dorgan.

Philadelphia.—Ferguson, Vinton, E. M. Daily, A. Cusick, Andrews, Mulvey, C. J. Bastian, Purcell, E. E. Foster, A. Myers, C. W. Ganzell, Thos. J. Lynch, J. Clements, E. Nolan, J. Manning, James Fogarty, and Sidney Farrar.

Providence.—Radbourn, Gilligan, Start, Farrell, Denny, Irwin, Carroll, E. N. Crane, C. F. Daily, Radford, C. E. Bassett, Michael Murray, F. L. Shaw, Knight, and Hines.

St. Louis.—H. T. Boyle, G. F. Baker, F. W. Bandle, W. O. Donnell, F. P. Sullivan, J. F. Staples, F. Lewis, J. Quinn, W. H. Colgan, Sweeney, Briody, Sutcliffe (also with Chicago), Emmet, Seery, Shaffer, and D. Rowe.

Connor, of New York, led the batting in 1885 with .371. Baldwin, of Detroit, led the pitchers with 1.35 earned runs per game, and Bennett, of the same club, stood first among the catchers with .885. The leading fielders were: 1b., McKinnon, .978; 2b., Dunlap, .933; 3b., D. Richardson, .950; s.s., Glasscock, .917; outfielders, Knight (24 g.), .957; Lewis (45 g.), .957; D. Richardson (18 g.), .950; Gillespie (102 g.), .941; Fogarty (89 g.), .940; O'Rourke (112 g.), .939.

The Southern League was organized in 1885, when the Atlanta club won the championship with the following team: Dundon, Bauer, and Sullivan, pitchers; McVey, Mappes, and Clark, catchers; O'Brien, Bittman, and Cleveland, on the bases; Cahill, short-stop; and Goldsby, Jevere, and Silch, in the outfield. The Atlantas again won the pennant in 1886, with this team: Gunson and Mappes, catchers; Wells and Conway, pitchers; Lynch, Stricker, and Lyons on the bases; Cline, short-stop; and Purcell, Shaffer, and Williams doing the work of the outfield.

The New England League and the Eastern New England League were organized in 1885. The latter was the stronger, its championship being won by the Lawrence club, of which Walter Burnham was manager. Quite a number of other small State leagues were formed in 1885.

On the Pacific Coast the game flourished splendidly, and the Haverly club, of San Francisco, held the field against all others. Hamilton won the championship of the Canadian League. It is notable, too, that in 1885 the game began to be played in Cuba, in Australia, and the Sandwich Islands. The sport grew in popularity, and the season of 1886 was most successful from every point of view. The only two associations which did not manage to play through the season without a break were the Southern and Eastern leagues. The various clubs, during the season, played an aggregate of over 3,000 championship games.

The National League circuit was once more broken up by the retirement of Buffalo and Providence. The vacant places were filled by Kansas City and Washington. The Detroit club was greatly strengthened this year by the great deal engineered by Fred. Stearns, by which the quartette of players from the Buffalo club, known as "the big four," White, Rowe, Richardson, and Brouthers, were captured for the Detroit club. With these great players the Detroits made a pretty fight for the pennant, and would have won it from Chicago had they been able to make any headway against the Philadelphia team in the last two months of the season. But they couldn't seem to do anything with the Phillies in the windup, and so, after a hard struggle, lost the pennant by a narrow margin.

BASEBALL.

THE CHAMPIONSHIP RECORD FOR 1886.

	Chicago.	Detroit.	New York.	Philadelphia.	Boston.	St. Louis.	Kansas City.	Washington.	Games Won.	Per Ct. Won.
Chicago,		11	10	10	12	13	17	17	90	.726
Detroit,	7		11	10	11	15	16	17	87	.707
New York,	8	7		8	11	15	15	11	75	.630
Philadelphia,	7	7	8		10	12	14	13	71	.623
Boston,	6	6	6	3		11	11	13	56	.479
St. Louis,	4	2	3	6	6		12	10	43	.352
Kansas City,	1	2	3	2	6	5		11	30	.242
Washington,	1	1	3	4	5	8	6		28	.235
Games Lost,	34	36	44	43	61	79	91	92	480	

M. J. Kelly, of the Chicago team, led the batting averages with .338; Baldwin, of the Detroits, led the pitchers with an average of 1.57 earned runs to a game; Bennett led the catchers with .912. The other leading players were: Farrar, 1b., .979; Bastian, 2b., .944; Denny and Esterbrook tied for 3b. with .895; Force, s.s., .908. The crack fielders were: Baker (21 games), 1.000; Fogarty (56 games), .953; Dalrymple (82 games), .952; D. Richardson (58 games), .951; Hornung (94 games), .947; Manning (26 games), .945; Thompson (122 games), 945.

The champion team included Clarkson, McCormick, and John Flynn, pitchers; Kelly, Flint, and Moolie, catchers; Anson, 1b.; Pfeffer, 2b.; Burns, 3b.; Williamson, s.s.; Dalrymple, l.f.; Ryan and Gore, c.f.; Sunday, r.f.

The Detroit team included Baldwin, Getzein, Twitchell, and J. Smith, pitchers; Bennett and Ganzel, catchers; Brouthers, 1b.; Dunlap, H. Richardson, and S. M. Crane, 2b.; White, 3b.; Rowe, s.s.; James Manning, H. Richardson, and Conway, l.f.; E. Hanlon, c.f.; Sam Thompson, r.f. Others who played a few games were: Gillen, c.; Shindle, 3b.

The New York team included Keefe and Welch, pitchers; Ewing, O'Rourke, and Deasley, catchers; Connor, 1b.; Gerhardt, 2b.; Esterbrook, 3b.; Ward, s.s.; D. Richardson and Gillespie, l.f.; D. Richardson, Ewing, and O'Rourke, c.f.; Dorgan, r.f. Among the players tried were Devine, Devlin, Bagley, and S. J. Corcoran.

The Philadelphia team included Ferguson, Casey, and Dailey, pitchers; Clements, McGuire, and Cusick, catchers; Farrar, 1b.; Bastian, 2b.; Mulvey, 3b.; A. Irwin, s.s.; Wood and Dailey, l.f.; Andrews and Dailey, c.f.; Fogarty, Ferguson, and Dailey, r.f. L. Titcomb, Strike, and McCarthy were also tried.

The Boston team included Radbourn, Stemmyer, and Buffinton, pitchers; Daily, Tate, and Gunning, catchers; Morrill and Wise, 1b.; Burdock, Morrill, Sutton, and Wise, 2b.; Nash and Sutton, 3b.; Wise, Nash, Sutton, and Morrill, s.s.; Hornung and Sutton, l.f.; Johnson, c.f.; Poorman and Sutton, r.f. C. J. Parson, a pitcher, was also given a trial.

The St. Louis team included Boyle, Healy, and Kirby, pitchers; Myers, Graves, and Dolan, catchers; McKinnen, 1b.; Crane and Quinn, 2b.; Denny, 3b.; Glasscock, s.s.; Seery, l.f.; Quinn and McGeachy, c.f.; Cahill, r.f. Mapplis, Bauer, Reardon, Murphy, and Pelouze also played a few games.

The Kansas City team included Whitney, Conway, and Weidman, pitchers; Briody, Hackett, and Ringo, catchers; McQuery, 1b.; A. Myers, 2b.; Donnelly, 3b.; Bassett and Radford, s.s.; Lillie, l.f.; D. Rowe and Conway, c.f.; Radford and Whitney, r.f. Baker, c.; McKeon, p.; and King, p., were also tried.

The Washington team included Robert Barr, F. L. Shaw, Madigan, and Gilmore, pitchers; Gilligan, Hayes, Decker, and Oldfield, catchers; Baker, Kreig, and Hines, 1b.; John Farrell and Knowles, 2b.; Knowles, Gladman, and Hines, 3b.; Force, Corcoran, Houck, Baker, Hines, Shoch, Ed Crane, and Cliff Carroll, fielders. Of the players who were given trials by Washington during the season were: McGlone, 3b.; Daly, p.; Fuller, p.; Keefe, p.; Goldsby, f.; Kinslow, c.; Winkleman, p.; Fox, p.; Henry, p.; Wise, p.; O'Day, p.; Whiting, c.; and Gallagher, s.s.

Clubs of Denver and Leadville, Col., Leavenworth and Topeka, Kan., St. Joseph, Mo., and Lincoln, Neb., organized the Western League in March, 1886. The Denver club won the championship with the following team: Tebeau, McMillan, and Mountjoy, pitchers; Lanser, O'Neil, and Hunter, catchers; Straub, McAndries, and Phillips on the bases; Meinke, short-stop; and O'Brien, Ryan, and one of the change pitchers or catchers making up the working force in the outfield.

The International league, organized in 1886, was composed of six clubs in New York State and two in Canada. Originally the New York State League, on the admission of clubs from Hamilton and Toronto, Ont., its name was changed to that of the International League. The result of the championship was in doubt up to the close of the season, when the Utica club won the pennant, with a team including Serad, Pendergrast, and Mattimore, pitchers; McKeough, Hofford, and Toy, catchers; Latham, Hengle, and Shindle on the bases; Halpin, short-stop; and M. Griffin, T. Griffin, and Carroll doing duty in the outfield.

The Portland team, under the management of Harry Spence, won the New England League championship; Duluth won the Northwestern League pennant; Denver the Western League championship; Atlanta the Southern League pennant; and Newark took the honors in the Eastern League.

It was during 1886 that Hermann Doescher was reinstated and acted as a league umpire.

It was in this year also that the league became aware of the existence of a secret organization among the players known as the Brotherhood of Ball Players. This organization, which has made so much trouble for the league, and which has since endeavored to carry its members into an organization inimical to the league, was really organized in the fall of 1885. Its career is treated of in a separate chapter beyond.

There was another shake up in the league circuit in 1887. Kansas City and St. Louis had played the limit, and gave up the fight. Pittsburg and Indianapolis were admitted to fill the vacancies. The season was a good one for the clubs, financially. The Detroit won the league pennant, although closely pushed by Philadelphia, after which came Chicago.

THE CHAMPIONSHIP RECORD FOR 1887.

	Detroit.	Philadelphia.	Chicago.	New York.	Boston.	Pittsburg.	Washington.	Indianapolis.	Games Won.	Per Ct. Won.
Detroit,		10	8	10	11	13	13	15	79	.637
Philadelphia,	8		6	10	9	12	13	17	75	.610
Chicago,	10	12		11	9	5	11	13	71	.587
New York,	8	7	6		10	12	10	15	68	
Boston,	7	9	6	7		11	10	11	61	
Pittsburg,	4	6	12	6	7		9	11	55	
Washington,	4	3	7	8	7	9		8	46	
Indianapolis,	3	1	5	3	7	7	10		37	
Games Lost,	45	48	50	55	60	69	76	89		
Games Played,	124	123	121	123	121	124	122	126		

The Detroit champions were Getzein, C. Baldwin, Weidman, P. Conway, and Twitchell, pitchers; Bennett, Ganzel, and Briody, catchers; Brouthers, 1b.; Dunlap and H. Richardson, 2b.; White, 3b.; J. Rowe, s.s.; H. Richardson and Twitchell, l.f.; Hanlon, c.f.; Thompson, r.f. Shindle played 19 games at third base. Beatin, Gruber, and Burke each pitched a few games. Sutcliffe was tried as catcher.

The other teams of 1887 were made up as follows:

Philadelphia.—Buffinton, Casey, and Ferguson, pitchers; Clements, Gunning, and McGuire, catchers; Farrar, 1b.; McLaughlin, Bastian, and Ferguson, 2b.; Mulvey, 3b.; Irwin and Bastian, s.s.; Wood, Andrews, Fogarty, Dailey, and Buffinton, fielders.

Chicago.—Mark Baldwin, Clarkson, and Van Haltren, pitchers; T. Daly, Flint, Darling, and Hardie, catchers; Anson, Pfeffer, Burns, and Tebeau, basemen; Williamson, s.s.; M. Sullivan, Ryan, Pettit, Van Haltren, and Darling, fielders. Pyle, p.; Geiss, c.; Sprague, p.; and Corcoran, p., played a few games each.

New York.—Keefe, Welsh, George, and Weidman (also Detroit), pitchers; Murphy, Brown, Deasley, and O'Rourke, catchers; Connor, 1b.; D. Richardson, 2b.; Ewing, O'Rourke, and Rainey, 3b.; Ward, s.s.; Gillespie, Gore, Tiernan, Dorgan, and O'Rourke, fielders. The following played in a few games each: Gerhardt (1), Roche (1), Sworbach

THE PHILADELPHIA TEAM, MAY, 1890.

(2), Casey (1), Becannan (1), Mattimore, p. (8), Nelson (1), Hatfield (2), Titcomb, p. (9).

Boston.—Radbourn, Madden, Stemmyer, and R. F. Conway, pitchers; Daily, Tate, Kelly, and T. J. O'Rourke, catchers; Morrill, 1b.; Burdock and Kelly, 2b.; Nash, 3b.; Wise, Sutton, and Wheelock, s.s.; Hornung, l.f.; Johnston, c.f.; Kelly, Wheelock, Sutton, and Conway, r.f. Morgan, Murphy, Poorman, and Higgins were under contract, but released early in the season.

Pittsburg.—Galvin, Morris, and McCormick, pitchers; Miller and Carroll, catchers; McKinnon, Barkley, and Carroll, 1b.; Barkley and C. M. Smith, 2b.; Whitney, 3b.; Smith and Kuehne, s.s.; Dalrymple and Beecher, l.f.; Beecher, Carroll, T. Brown, Miller, and Fields, c.f.; Coleman and Brown, r.f. Bishop pitched three games. A. J. Maul, pitcher, fielder, and 1b., played in 16 games.

Washington.—Whitney, O'Day, Shaw, and Gilmore, pitchers; Mack, Gilligan, and Dealey, catchers; O'Brien and Kreig, 1b.; J. Farrell and A. Myers, 2b.; Donelly 3b.; Farrell, Dealey, and Myers, s.s.; C. Carroll, Hines, Shoch, and Dailey (also Phila.), fielders. Crane (7), Wright (1), and J. Irwin (8), played a few games.

Indianapolis.—Boyle, Healey, Moffitt, and Shreve, pitchers; G. Myers, Hackett, and Arundel, catchers; Shomberg, 1b.; Bassett, 2b.; Denny, 3b.; Glasscock, s.s.; Seery, McGeachy, Johnson, Tom Brown, Frank "Gid" Gardner, Polhemus, fielders. The following men played a few games: Morrison (6), Leitner (8), Fast (3), Kirby (8). All four were pitchers.

The batting averages in 1887 included bases on balls as base hits. Maul, of Pittsburg, stood first (16 games) with .450; Anson (122 games) second, with .421; Brouthers (122 games) third, with .419. Thompson, of Detroit, led the league in actual base hits with .375; Ferguson, of the Philadelphia team, was second, with .341; Maul ranked third, with .281; and Anson stood fourth, with .334. Pete Conway, of Detroit (25 games), led the pitchers with 2.35 earned runs to a game; Boyle (38 games) had 2.42; and Clarkson (58 games) had 2.81. Bennett led the catchers, with .905; Morrell, 1b., with .985; Dunlap, 2b., with 953; Whitney, 3b., with 924; Smith, s.s., with 922. The four leading fielders were Gillespie, .946; H. Richardson, .936; Fields, .935, and Hornung, .934.

The men who represented the new clubs were W. A. Nimick, A. K. Scandrett, and J. Palmer O'Neill, Pittsburg, and John T. Brush, Louis Newberger, and John H. Martin, Indianapolis.

There were two things in the season of 1887 which created much excitement and comment. The first was the sale of M. J. Kelly's release to Boston, the Chicago club receiving $10,000 in cash for the transfer, and Kelly's salary was nearly doubled by the transaction. The second event was the recognition of the brotherhood by the league, and the adoption by the league of a contract prepared by the players.

Other big deals were made for players. Pittsburg paid Detroit $5,000 for the transfer of Dunlap, and Boston put out $3,800 for the release of Sowders, a minor league player.

The various important minor league championships in 1887 were won as follows: International Association, Toronto; Southern League, New Orleans; Western League, Topeka; North-Western League, Oshkosh; New England League, Lowell; Ohio State League, Kalamazoo; Central Pennsylvania League, Shamokin; California State League, Pioneer.

In 1888 the league circuit remained intact, and all the clubs made money except Detroit, Washington, and Indianapolis; but the losses of these even were not very serious. The attendance at the games were the largest ever known; the contest for supremacy was a hot one between four of the clubs, and the result could not be foretold until the last month of the season was well started.

Early in the spring, the Boston club succeeded in purchasing the release of John Clarkson from the Chicago club, paying therefor the sum of $10,000. It was thought that with the assistance of this great pitcher the Boston team would win the championship; but, although they made a brilliant start, winning something like a dozen straight games, they failed to secure the pennant. They played steadily during May and June, then internal dissensions broke up the team, and in July they won only 5 games out of 23. The New Yorks, who were far behind, made a grand rush, commencing July 4th, and, by winning 54 out of 78 games in the last four months, captured the pennant.

THE CHAMPIONSHIP RECORD FOR 1888.

	New York.	Chicago.	Philadelphia.	Boston.	Detroit.	Pittsburg.	Indianapolis.	Washington.	Games Won.	Per Ct. Won.
New York,		8	14	12	11	10	14	15	84	.641
Chicago,	11		8	12	10	9	14	13	77	.510
Philadelphia,	5	10		9	7	15	13	10	69	.531
Boston,	8	7	9		10	10	11	15	70	.522
Detroit,	7	10	11	8		10	11	11	68	.519
Pittsburg,	7	11	6	8	10		14	10	66	.493
Indianapolis,	5	6	4	9	8	6		12	50	.370
Washington,	4	6	9	5	7	9	8		48	.358
Games Lost,	47	58	61	63	63	69	85	86		

The New York champions were Keefe, Welch, Crane, Titcomb, and George, pitchers; Ewing, Brown, and Murphy, catchers; Connor, D. Richardson, Whitney, Ward, and Hatfield, infielders; J. O'Rourke, Gore, Tiernan, Slattery, and E. E. Foster, outfielders.

Chicago.—M. Baldwin, Tener, Krock, and Van Haltren, pitchers; T. Daley, Flint, C. A. Farrell, and Dell Darling, catchers; Anson, Pfeffer, Burns, and Williamson on the bases; Sullivan, Ryan, Pettit, and Hugh Duffy in the field. Among the men signed who were given a trial were: C. E. Hoover, C. W. Sprague, C. R. Brynan, Wm. H. Clarke, Mains, and Gumbert.

The new men on the Philadelphia team were: A. B. Sanders and Wm. Gleason, pitchers; Schriver and Decker, catchers; and Delehanty and Hallman, infielders. James A. Tyng and C. S. Childs were given a trial. It was during this year that the Philadelphia club experienced the greatest loss in its history in the matter of players. This was the death of its star pitcher, Charles J. Ferguson, who was a wonderful pitcher, a splendid infielder or outfielder, and a batsman of great ability. He was a magnificent general player, and had marvelous control of the ball when pitching. It was this man's remarkable work that knocked the great Detroit team, the strongest batting aggregation ever gotten together, out of the pennant in 1886.

Boston had new men in Clarkson, Klusman, Joe Quinn, William Sowders, Irving Ray, Glenn, and Tom Brown.

The Detroit team was changed very little. The new men were all used as substitutes at second base and in the field. They were Nicholson, Campan, and Scheffler.

Pittsburg signed a number of new men, including Hardie Henderson, Jacob Beckley, William Farmer, Staley, McShannic, and Cleveland (who played early in the season with New York). Of these only

THE LATE CHARLES J. FERGUSON,
Star Pitcher of the Philadelphia Club.

Staley, pitcher, and Beckley, first baseman, amounted to anything. The latter was the find of the year, finishing second among the batsmen.

Indianapolis added T. J. Esterbrook, R. D. Buckley, Louis Schoeneck, Con. Daily, S. Burdick, and Paul Hines to its team.

The new men on the Washington team were W. E. Hoy, Walter Wilmot, Frank Gardner, M. J. Murray, Tug Arundel, William Widner, and William Fuller.

Anson, of the Chicago club, led the batting averages with .343, and Beckley, of the Pittsburg, was second with .342. Keefe, of the New York club, led the pitchers with a percentage of 1.5 earned runs per game. Buffinton was second with 1.63, and Walsh was third with 1.7. Bennett, as usual, led the catchers with a percentage of .941. The leading men in the other positions were: Anson, 1b., .985; Bastian, 2b., .946; Nash, 3b., .913; Denny, s.s. (23 games), .916; Keuhne, s.s. (63 games), .915; fielders—O'Rourke (87 games), .959; Tiernan (113 games), .959; Glenn (19 games), .956; Sanders (25 games), .955; Hornung (107 games), .947.

The New Yorks won the World's Championship from St. Louis in 1888, quite as easily as Detroit had done so in 1887.

The trip of the Chicago and All America teams around the world took place in 1888–9. Soon after the tourists started the New York club made an agreement with the Washington club, by which it was agreed to release John M. Ward to Washington for the sum of $12,000. This was the largest sum ever accepted for the release of a player. The offer was a *bona fide* one, and the money would have been paid had not Mr. Ward, on his return home, positively refused to go to Washington.

The league season of 1889 was made remarkably interesting by a general evening up of the playing strength of the teams. This was accomplished by the disbandment of the Detroit team and the admission of Cleveland to the league. Four of the Detroit stars went to Boston, one to Philadelphia, three to Pittsburg, and the balance to Cleveland.

This deal so strengthened the Boston team that it was considered almost a sure winner by a large majority of the people, particularly as the disturbing elements of the team of 1888 had been either eliminated or smoothed out. Public expectation became very near being gratified. So close and bitter was the battle that the result depended upon the games played on the very last day of the season. Another remarkable thing about the contest was that the games of the last day were necessary to settle the order of the first six clubs, something hitherto unprecedented in the annals of the sport. The New York team won the pennant, and also won the World's Championship from the Brooklyns, champions of the American Association.

THE CHAMPIONSHIP RECORD FOR 1889.

	New York.	Boston.	Chicago.	Philadelphia.	Pittsburg.	Cleveland.	Indianapolis.	Washington.	Games Won.	Per Ct. Won.
New York,		6	13	12	12	14	13	13	83	.659
Boston,	8		10	13	16	12	10	14	83	.648
Chicago,	5	7		9	10	11	13	12	67	.508
Philadelphia,	7	6	10		9	9	13	9	63	.469
Pittsburg,	7	3	9	9		13	10	10	61	.462
Cleveland,	4	8	9	10	7		9	14	61	.459
Indianapolis,	7	10	7	4	10	10		11	59	.440
Washington,	5	5	7	7	7	3	7		41	.331
Games Lost,	43	45	65	44	71	72	75	83	518	

The teams and managers for 1889 were made up as follows:

New York (Champions of the League and of the World).—James Mutrie, manager; Welch, Crane, O'Day, and Keefe, pitchers; William Ewing, captain; W. Brown and Murphy, catchers; Connor, Dan Richardson, Whitney, Ward, and Hatfield, infielders; O'Rourke, Gore, Tiernan, and Slattery, outfielders. Titcomb, Foster, and George played in a few games, but were released early in the season. Harry Lyons played in a few games, although never regularly signed. Wagenhurst, the Princeton College player, was regularly signed, but did not participate in any championship contests, and was released at the same time with Foster and Titcomb.

Boston.—James A. Hart, manager; Clarkson, Radbourn, Madden, Sowden, and Daley, pitchers; Bennett, Ganzel, and M. J. Kelly (captain), catchers; Brouthers, Quinn, Nash, Ray, and C. M. Smith, infielders; H. Richardson, Johnston, Kelly, and Tom Brown, outfielders. Sowders played part of the season and was released to Pittsburg.

Chicago.—A. C. Anson, manager and captain; Tener, Dwyer, Hutchinson, and Gumbert, pitchers; Farrell, Darling, Sommers, and Flint, catchers; Anson, Pfeffer, Burns, Bastian, and Williamson, infielders; Van Haltren, Ryan, and Duffy, outfielders.

Philadelphia.—Harry Wright, manager; Buffinton, Casey, Sanders, and Gleason, pitchers; Clements, Schriver, and Decker, catchers; Farrar, 1b. (captain); Delehanty, Hallman, and Myers, 2b.; A. Irwin and Hallman, s.s.; Wood, Delehanty, Fogarty, and Thompson, fielders. Pete Wood and other young players were signed but were given very little opportunity to show their worth. Day and Anderson, two young pitchers, were taken from the Cape May club near the close of the season and did very good work.

Pittsburg had a very long list of talent. It started out with this team: Galvin, Pete Conway, Norris, and Staley, pitchers; Miller, Carroll, and Fields, catchers; Beckley, 1b.; Dunlap, 2b.; Kuehne, 3b.; Smith, s.s.; Fields, l.f.; Hanlon, c.f. (captain); Sunday, r.f. Accidents soon broke the team up and many changes were made. Carroll and Fields played nearly every day and so did Miller. Maul was also used a great deal as a fielder. Toward the end of the season Sowders was secured, Smith went to Boston, and Rowe and White, who had been released to Pittsburg by Detroit, consented to go to the Smoky City. Pete Conway was of no use to the team, as he was unable to pitch more than one or two games. Quite a number of young pitchers were tried. Among them were Krumm and Dunning.

Cleveland.—Thomas Loftus, manager; O'Brien, Gruber, Beatin, and Blakely, pitchers; Snyder, Zimmer, and Sutcliffe, catchers; Faatz, captain and 1b.; Stricker, 2b.; Oliver Tebeau, 3b.; McKean, s.s.; Twitchell, l.f.; McAleer, c.f.; Radford, r.f.; Gilks, substitute.

Indianapolis.—Boyle, Getzein, Burdick, and Rusie, pitchers; Con. Daily, George Myers, Buckley, and Sommers, catchers; Schoeneck and Hines, 1b.; Bassett, 2b.; Denny, 3b.; Glasscock, s.s.; Seery, Hines, McGeachy, Andrews, and Sullivan, fielders. Frank Bancroft was manager and Glasscock, captain. Glasscock held both positions during September and October.

Washington.—John Morrill and Arthur Irwin, managers and captains; George Keefe, Haddock, Fersen, Healy, and Krock, pitchers; Mack, Clark, Tom Daly, and Ebright, catchers; Morrill, Wise, A. Myers, Sweeney, John Irwin, Carney, Arthur Irwin, and Mack, infielders; Wilmot, Hoy, Beecher, Mack, Sweeney, and Schoch, outfielders.

Daniel J. Brouthers, of the Boston team, led the batting averages in 1889 with .373; Keefe led the pitchers in smallest average of earned runs to games played, and Charley Bennett led the catchers with .916. The best players in other positions were: Anson, 1b., .982; Dunlap, 2b., .949; Denny, 3b., 913; Bastian, s.s., .919. Fielders—Gilks (29 games), 1,000; Fogarty (128 games), .960; Delehanty (29 games), .956; McAleer (109 games), .955; Maul (61 games), .946; Sunday (80 games), .945; Ganzel (21 games), .943; Radford (136 games), .942; Hardie Richardson (46 games), .941.

The various championships of the principal minor leagues in 1889 were won as follows: Western Association, Omaha; International Association, Detroit; Atlantic Association, Worcester; Tri-State League, Canton; Inter-State League, Springfield; New York State League, Auburn; Middle State League, Harrisburg; Michigan State League, Saginaw.

The event of the year was the desertion of the league by its players in a body. The influences that led up to this action by which the players sought to break down in a day what it had required so many years of patient endeavor to build up, are said by the deserters to reach back through many years, and to be due to abuses which, it is alleged, were caused and fostered by the reserve rule, and reached a culmination in the classification rule adopted at the annual meeting in 1888.

The ball players' brotherhood was formed for the purpose of protecting the players against the abuses complained of, and did its first work in that direction when, in the fall of 1887, as has already been detailed, the officers of the organization persuaded the league to draw up a new contract in which the rights of the players were better understood than under the form of contract previously in vogue. The word "persuaded" used here is the way the league men look at it. The players claim that the league was compelled to grant the concessions asked by them. To a certain extent the league was obliged to give in to save trouble at that time, but it should be said in justice to its officials that they offered no objections to making the reforms that were granted. They even went so far as to say that they would consider a substitute for the reserve rule if the players' committee could suggest one. That committee, composed of Messrs. Ward, Hanlon, and Brouthers, were

THE PITTSBURGH TEAM, AUGUST, 1889.

obliged to admit that they could not suggest anything that would take the place of the rule that had proved the firmest anchor that honest baseball ever had attached to it. When the new contract was finally adopted the full amount of each player's compensation could not be written into it, because the National agreement contained a $2,000 salary limit clause. One of the objects of the players was to perpetuate their large salaries, and in order to accomplish this they had inserted in the contract a clause providing that no player could be reserved at a less salary than that named in the contract. The only thing that stood in the way was the salary limit, and the league verbally agreed to do what it could to have this limit abolished.

With this the players were satisfied. At the next meeting of the Board of Arbitration the league officials endeavored to carry out their promise to have the salary limit stricken out of the National Agreement. The American Association representatives, however, refused to agree to it, and the limit remained. The players were very much exasperated over this, as they were obliged to sign contracts at $2,000 and to make outside contracts for all compensation received by them over that sum. They accused the league of bad faith, and charged that by diplomacy the objects of the new contract had been defeated. There were a good many threats as to what the Brotherhood would do, but nothing was done. At the annual meeting in 1888, the Indianapolis, Pittsburg, and Washington clubs made a demand on the league for a scheme that would limit the salaries of the players, which were growing to such a degree as to make it impossible to run their teams, as they claimed, at a profit. The pressure was so great that the league yielded, and adopted a classification rule. This divided the players into five classes. Class A was to receive $2,500, Class B $2,250, Class C $2,000, Class D $1,750, and Class E $1,500. It was agreed between the clubs, however, that this classification should not apply to players with whom they then had agreements, or to players with whom they should make agreements, or to whom they felt under moral obligations to do so, previous to December 15th, 1888, and it was provided that certain players, then absent from the United States on the baseball tour around the world, should have two weeks after their return in which to arrange matters before they should be subject to classification.

Under the operation of the new law, few of the star players, and only a small number of those who were not stars, were classified. Indeed, if we are to believe the league officials, it was not intended to affect any but the young players who should come into the league from time to time, and to curb the tendency to unduly increase the salaries of those men who were already in. This new law, if persevered in, however, would in a few years have brought salaries down in a very large degree. The players made a pretty stiff remonstrance, through newspaper interviews, to the classification scheme, but the Brotherhood did not officially oppose it, because their leader, John M. Ward, was in Australia. Had Ward been in this country, it is more than probable that the men would have refused to sign their contracts, but the rest of the Brotherhood officers did not have the courage to make a fight. The scheme was a bad one, as the league men now freely admit. It was practically a dead letter from the first, except with the weak clubs. When Mr. Ward returned from his trip the players had signed contracts, and nothing could be done. The Brotherhood was braced up in every direction, and Ward advised a strike, or, at any rate, the leaders were inclined to order one. It was finally agreed to take a vote of the men as to the wisdom of having a general strike on the Fourth of July, unless the classification rule was rescinded and certain other alleged grievances were adjusted. This vote was taken, and resulted in the negative. This was done, of course, *sub rosa*. Action was then taken openly. The leaders were appointed a committee to present the grievances to the league. President Young, when applied to, appointed a league committee to hear the players, but when Mr. Ward asked for an immediate hearing, Mr. Spalding, the Chairman of that Committee, declined to meet the Brotherhood until fall. This reply is said to have been the last straw that broke the patience of the players. At any rate, they immediately, with great secrecy, began to arrange for a complete secession from the National League. The newspapers exposed the plan about a month before the playing season closed, but it was generally discredited, because the players and their backers persisted in denials that any such scheme had been agreed upon. As soon as the season was over the players threw off the mask, and admitted their purpose.

On Monday, November 4th, 1889, the Brotherhood met at the Fifth Avenue Hotel in New York, and announced themselves in the following address to the public:

To the Public: At last the Brotherhood of Baseball Players feels at liberty to make known its intentions and defend itself against the aspersions and misrepresentations which for weeks it has been forced to suffer in silence. It is no longer a secret that the players of the league have determined to play next season under different management, but for reasons which will, we think, be understood, it was deemed advisable to make no announcement of this intention until the close of the present season; but now that the struggles for the various pennants are over, and the terms of our contracts expired, there is no longer reason for withholding it.

In taking this step we feel that we owe it to the public and to ourselves to explain briefly some of the reasons by which we have been moved. There was a time when the league stood for integrity and fair dealing; to-day it stands for dollars and cents. Once it looked to the elevation of the game and an honest exhibition of the sport; to-day its eyes are upon the turnstile. Men have come into the business for no other motive than to exploit it for every dollar in sight. Measures originally intended for the good of the game have been perverted into instruments for wrong. The reserve rule and the provisions of the national agreement gave the managers unlimited power, and they have not hesitated to use this in the most arbitrary and mercenary way.

Players have been bought, sold, and exchanged as though they were sheep instead of American citizens. "Reservation" became with them another name for property right in the player. By a combination among themselves, stronger than the strongest trust, they were able to enforce the most arbitrary measures, and the player had either to submit or get out of the profession in which he had spent years in attaining proficiency. Even the disbandment and retirement of a club did not free the players from the octopus clutch, for they were then peddled around to the highest bidder.

That the player sometimes profited by the sale has nothing to do with the case, but only proves the injustice of his previous restraint. Two years ago we met the league and attempted to remedy some of these evils, but through what has been politely called "league diplomacy" we completely failed. Unwilling longer to submit to such treatment, we made a strong effort last spring to reach an understanding with the league. To our application for a hearing they replied "that the matter was not of sufficient importance to warrant a meeting," and suggested that it be put off until fall. Our committee replied that the players felt that the league had broken faith with them; that while the results might be of little importance to the managers, they were of great importance to the players; that if the league would not concede what was fair we would adopt other means to protect ourselves; that if postponed until fall we would be separated and at the mercy of the league, and that, as the only course left us required time and labor to develop, we must therefore insist upon an immediate conference.

Then, upon their final refusal to meet us, we began organizing for ourselves, and are in shape to go ahead next year under new management and new auspices. We believe that it is possible to conduct our national game upon lines which will not infringe upon individual and natural rights. We ask to be judged solely by our work, and, believing that the game can be played more fairly and its business conducted more intelligently under a plan which excludes everything arbitrary and un-American, we look forward with confidence to the support of the public and the future of the national game.

THE NATIONAL BROTHERHOOD OF BALL PLAYERS.

On Wednesday, November 6th, delegates representing the eight chapters of the Brotherhood met with representatives of the capitalists in the cities selected for the circuit, and informally organized the Players' National League. The delegates were:

STOCKHOLDER.	CLUB.	PLAYER.
E. A. McAlpin,	New York,	J. M. Ward.
Charles B. Cory,	Boston,	D. Brouthers.
Henry M. Love,	Philadelphia,	C. G. Buffinton.
Unknown,	Brooklyn,	E. Andrews.
Unknown,	Pittsburg,	E. Hanlon.
A. L. Johnson,	Cleveland,	John Stricker.
M. Shire,	Buffalo,	John Rowe.
John Addison,	Chicago,	Fred Pfeffer.

After a two days' session the conference was adjourned until January 7th, 1890, without having formed an organization. This course was taken, so say the Brotherhood men, on the advice of their lawyers. Meanwhile the several clubs will perfect their organization, and in January the new league may be put into permanent operation.

The new scheme contemplates an eight club league. There will be a prize fund of $20,000, to be distributed among the first seven clubs at the end of the playing season, and there will be a co-operative sharing by the players, in certain contingencies. These benefits are provided by means of a pooling scheme. The pooling is done on a basis by which a club that is making money is sure of a fair interest on its investment before its players shall share in its profits. Each club stands on its own basis. After all expenses and a contribution of $2,500 has been made to the prize fund, the first $10,000 of profit goes to the stockholders. The next $10,000, or any part thereof, is to be put into the pool to be divided pro rata among the players of the club making the profit. A second pool will be made of all profits or any portion thereof exceeding $20,000. This second pool will be divided—half to the club and half to the players. It will thus be seen that no club will contribute to the support of another club. As a return for a possible share of the profits the players take a chance of sharing the losses, as all expenses and salaries are to be paid from gate receipts, the stockholders being expressly relieved from liability by the contract signed by player and club.

The government of the league rests in a central board, composed of the president of the league and two directors, one a player and one a capitalist from each club. If any player is dissatisfied with his location he may apply to the board to be transferred, and if the request is granted the player will be transferred without the payment of any consideration to the club losing his services. All contracts are to be made for three years, and a player cannot be released until after the first year has expired, and not then if he has kept all covenants and is able and willing to play good ball.

Severe penalties are provided for players who are guilty of drunkenness or crookedness. The profits to be derived from all ground perquisites, such as refreshments, cigars, liquor, and score-card privileges, belong to each individual club, and all clubs may make individual contracts with their players, who are to have the same salaries they received in 1889, except such as were cut down by classification, and all players suffering from such injustice are to have the salaries received by them in 1888, but there is nothing to prevent the clubs from paying larger salaries if they desire to do so. Such are the main points of the contract which was agreed upon at the meeting of November 6th, and which the players have since been signing. It is understood that the men who played in 1889 for Indianapolis are to play in the new Brooklyn club, and the Washington players, including White and Rowe, are to represent Buffalo.

What steps the league will take to make good the defection of its players cannot now be more than guessed at. When the annual meeting of the organization is held, November 13th, it will be too late to record its action in this volume. Some indications have been given of the policy likely to be pursued. The fight will begin with law suits. Under section 18 of the contract prepared by the Brotherhood and signed by the players, the league clubs are given the right to reserve the players for the season of 1890. The league has been advised by eminent lawyers in all sections of the country that it can hold its players under this section, and enjoin them from playing with the Players' League. The Brotherhood lawyers are said to have given opinions just the reverse. The question will be settled in the courts.

At its annual meeting, November 13th, 14th, and 15th, the National League acted promptly. They undid the unwise legislation that had caused most of the trouble, although it was like locking the stable door after the horse had been stolen. The classification rule was abolished and the sales system so modified that hereafter the player will purchase his own release and share in the purchase-money. The only case of injustice reported under the Brotherhood contract was that of Sutcliffe, of the Cleveland team, who claimed that he had been obliged to play for $250 less than in 1888. Although it was shown that Sutcliffe did not sign a Brotherhood contract the league directed that the money should be paid him on the ground that he was entitled to it under the spirit of the agreement with the players.

The league, at this meeting, admitted Brooklyn and Cincinnati to membership and will play the season of 1890 with a ten-club circuit. A law committee was appointed and a committee on negotiations. The first will endeavor to enforce section 18 of the Brotherhood contract against the players, and the second committee will arrange for the signing of young players.

A number of players have declined to sign Brotherhood contracts, and these, with the men who refused to join the new movement from the first, will form the nucleus for the National League teams of 1890. The men who up to November 25th had signed to stick by the league were Anson, Hutchinson, and Burns, of the Chicago team; Clarkson and Ganzel, of the Boston team; Decker, Clements, Schriver, and Gleason, of the Philadelphia team; Sowders and Sunday, of the Pittsburgh team; McKean, Beatin, Zimmer, McAleer, Glasscock, Boyle, Sommer, Russie, Buckley, and Denny, of the Indianapolis team. Tom

Daly, a member of the Brotherhood, refused to go to the city his organization assigned him, and on November 9th signed a contract with the Brooklyn club, then of the American Association.

The Players' League were more successful. They claimed to have signed seventy-four players November 25th. Thirteen of these are American Association men. The list as given follows, with the association players in italics:

New York.—Ewing, Murphy, Welch, Keefe, Crane, O'Day, Connor, D. Richardson, Whitney, O'Rourke, Slattery, and Gore.

Brooklyn.—Ward, Andrews, Seery, Bassett, *Bierbauer*, McGeachy, and *Tucker*.

Chicago.—Pfeffer, *Baldwin*, *King*, *Boyle*, Dwyer, Tener, Bastian, Bartson, Darling, Farrell, Williamson, *Latham*, Ryan and Duffy.

Cleveland.—Snyder, Stricker, Sutcliffe, and Radford.

Buffalo.—Wise, J. Irwin, A. Irwin, Mack, Carney, G. Keefe, Beecher, Rowe, and White.

Pittsburgh.—Hanlon, Staley, Beckley, Kuehne, Galvin, Miller, Morris, Fields, Dunlap, and Maul.

Philadelphia.—Wood, Thompson, *Milligan*, *Cross*, Hallman, *Foreman*, Buffinton, Farrar, Myers, Mulvey, *Shindle*, *Griffin*, Delehanty, and Fogarty.

Boston.—Kelly, *Kilroy*, Brouthers, and *Stovey*.

In closing this history it is proper to state that the officials of the National League say that they were ready to hear the Brotherhood, and would undoubtedly have abolished the classification scheme and tried to redress the alleged grievances of the players. It is also proper to state that the players say that they were satisfied that they would have been fooled again, as they claim to have been in the past.

Will the players be able to smash the fabric which has been raised by years of care, patience, and skill? Time alone can determine.

PART V.

The American Association was organized at Cincinnati, O., November 2d, 1881. The honor of suggesting it and of carrying the suggestion into reality belongs to Justus Thorner and O. P. Caylor, neither of whom is now connected with the organization. The season of the Cincinnati league club in 1880 was very disastrous, and the club went into bankruptcy. Four hundred dollars was needed to satisfy a judgment for lumber. This money was put up by Messrs. Thorner, Caylor, Louis Kramer, John Price, George Herancourt, and O. B. Long. Aaron Stern, the present owner of the Cincinnati club, afterwards purchased Price's stock. A team was organized and played Sunday games principally. Caylor and Thorner talked over the idea of a new baseball association, and finally called a meeting at Pittsburg. When they arrived at Pittsburg, accompanied by Frank B. Wright, they found that no one else was on hand. They were bound to have an association, so they interested H. D. McKnight in the scheme, and, after wiring other clubs for proxies, held a meeting in Mr. McKnight's office. There the scheme was outlined, and a call was issued for a meeting at Cincinnati, November 2d. This meeting was held and permanent organization effected with H. D. McKnight, president; J. H. Pank, vice-president; and James A. Williams, of Columbus, secretary. The clubs represented at this meeting were as follows: Cincinnati, Messrs. Thorner, Caylor, and Long; Athletics, Lew Simmons and Charles Mason; Eclipse club, of Louisville, J. H. Pank and J. W. Reccius; Alleghany club, of Pittsburg, H. D. McKnight; St. Louis, Chris. Von der Ahe and D. S. Reid; Brooklyn, William Barnie; Philadelphia, Charles Fulmer. The Philadelphia club was ruled out and the Athletics were admitted. In the spring Mr. Barnie could not get backing in Brooklyn, and Baltimore, represented by Henry C. Meyers, was admitted.

Most of the teams of the first season were made up of entirely new men. The only old timers were Cuthbert, Seward, Bill Gleason, of St. Louis; Carpenter, Fulmer, White, and Snyder, of Cincinnati; Critchley,

THE ST. LOUIS TEAM, SEPTEMBER, 1889.

Keenan, and Taylor, of the Alleghanys, and Sam Weaver and George Latham, of the Athletics. The association made itself quite solid with the public by adopting a twenty-five cent tariff.

The first season of the new association was successful beyond the expectations of its projectors, and gave promise that their desire to rival the National League as a major organization would eventually be realized. The first champions of the association were the Cincinnatis. The team consisted of W. White and H. McCormick, pitchers; Snyder and Powers, catchers; Stearns, 1b.; McPhee, 2b.; Carpenter, 3b.; Fulmer, s.s.; Sommer, Macallai, and Wheeler, fielders; Luff and Kemmler, substitutes. Carpenter and McPhee are still playing on the Cincinnati team.

THE PENNANT RECORD FOR 1882.

	Cincinnati.	Athletic.	Eclipse.	Allegheny.	St. Louis.	Baltimore.	Games Won.	Games Lost.	Games Played.	Per Ct. Won.
Cincinnati,		10	11	10	10	14	55	25	80	.680
Athletic,	6		11	6	11	7	41	34	75	.540
Eclipse,	5	5		10	9	13	42	38	80	.520
Allegheny,	6	10	6		10	7	39	39	79	.500
St. Louis,	6	5	7	6		13	37	43	80	.460
Baltimore,	2	4	3	7	3		19	54	74	.260
Games Lost,	25	34	38	39	43	54	233	233	468	

The association's success made it easy to get new members, and in 1883 clubs were admitted from New York and Columbus. The New York club was called the Metropolitan, and was represented by Walter Appleton. John B. Day was also interested. The Baltimore club did not please the association, so it was frozen out, and a new club, located in Baltimore, represented by William Barnie and A. T. Houck, received the franchise. The association this year got into a quarrel with the National League about the players. The controversy resulted in the tripartite agreement, which gave the parties to it protection for their players. Nearly all the association clubs were profitable in 1883, except possibly the Metropolitans. The pennant was won by the Athletics, after a close fight with Cincinnati and St. Louis. The Athletics had this team: Matthews, Carey, Bradley, and Jones, pitchers; O'Brien and Rowen, catchers; Stovey, 1b.; Stricker, 2b.; Bradley, 3b.; Carey, s.s.; Birchall, Blakiston, Knight, and Crowley, fielders.

THE PENNANT RECORD FOR 1883.

	Athletic.	St. Louis.	Cincinnati.	Metropolitan.	Louisville.	Columbus.	Allegheny.	Baltimore.	Games Played.	Games Lost.	Games Won.	Per Ct. Won.
Athletic,		9	5	9	7	13	12	11	98	32	66	.670
St. Louis,	5		6	11	8	11	12	12	98	33	65	.660
Cincinnati,	9	8		4	10	11	9	11	98	36	62	.640
Metropolitan,	5	3	10		6	11	9	10	96	42	54	.560
Louisville,	7	6	4	7		9	11	8	97	45	52	.530
Columbus,	1	3	3	3	5		10	7	97	65	32	.330
Allegheny,	2	2	5	5	3	4		9	98	68	30	.300
Baltimore,	3	2	3	3	6	6	5		98	68	28	.290
Games Lost,	32	32	36	42	45	65	68	68	389	389	389	

In 1884 the association undertook the gigantic task of conducting a twelve club league, and failed, although some of the clubs made a profit. Wheeler C. Wikoff succeded Mr. Williams as secretary. The four new clubs and their representatives were: Washington, L. Moxley; Brooklyn, Charles H. Byrne; Toledo, W. J. Colburn; Indianapolis, Joseph Schwalbacher. The Washingtons didn't last beyond August. They were represented by the Virginias, of Richmond, Va. The first seven clubs made a good race; the others were hardly in it. The Metropolitans, James Mutrie manager, won the pennant with this team: Halbert and Reipslager, c.; Keefe and Lynch, p.; Orr, S. Crane, Esterbrook, Nelson, and Troy, infielders; Kennedy, Roseman, and Brady, out-fielders.

THE PENNANT RECORD FOR 1884.

	Metropolitan.	Columbus.	Louisville.	St. Louis.	Cincinnati.	Baltimore.	Athletic.	Toledo.	Brooklyn.	Virginia.	Pittsburg.	Indianapolis.	Washington.	Games Won.	Games Lost.	Games Played	Per Ct. Won.
Metropolitan,		5	7	5	6	5	8	5	9	2	9	8	6	75	32	107	.700
Columbus,	4		5	5	7	4	5	8	7	2	9	8	5	69	39	108	.638
Louisville,	3	5		5	5	4	6	9	6	4	8	9	4	68	40	108	.629
St. Louis,	4	5	5		6	5	7	5	7	3	9	6	5	67	40	107	.626
Cincinnati,	4	3	5	4		6	4	7	8	4	8	9	6	68	41	109	.623
Baltimore,	5	6	6	5	4		3	5	5	5	9	9	2	63	43	106	.594
Athletic,	2	5	3	3	6	7		6	6	2	8	6	7	61	47	108	.564
Toledo,	4	1	1	5	3	5	3		4	4	5	6	5	46	58	104	.442
Brooklyn,	1	3	3	2	2	5	3	4		3	4	7	3	40	64	104	.384
Virginia,	0	2	1	1	0	0	0	0	2			4	2	12	30	42	.285
Pittsburg,	1	1	2	1	1	0	2	5	6	1		6	4	30	78	108	.277
Indianapolis,	2	2	1	3	1	1	4	3	3	1	4		4	29	78	107	.271
Washington,	2	1	1	1	0	1	1	1	1	0	1	2		12	51	63	.190
Games Lost,	32	39	40	40	41	43	47	58	64	30	78	78	51				

Toledo resigned in the fall, and so did Columbus. The latter club sold its players in a lump to the Allegheny club. Indianapolis and Richmond were dropped, and the association was reduced to eight clubs. The pennant was easily won by St. Louis in 1885, Cincinnati being a poor second, and Pittsburg a bad third. The champions were: Foutz, Caruthers, and McGinnis, pitchers; Bushong, D. Sullivan, and Broughton, catchers; Comiskey, 1b.; Robinson, 2b.; Latham, 3b.; Gleason, s.s.; O'Neill, l.f.; Welch, c.f.; Nicol, r.f. This team, with some changes, won the association pennant in 1886, 1887, and 1888. The new men in 1886 were Kemmler, c., and Hudson, p., Broughton and Sullivan retiring. In 1887 King was added to the pitchers and McGinnis and Kemmler dropped. The new men were King, p., Boyle, c., and Sylvester, fielder. In 1888 the Brooklyn club paid St. Louis $8,250 for the release of Caruthers, $5,500 for Foutz, and $5,000 for Bushong. The Athletic club gave $3,000 for the release of Welch, and $1,000 for Gleason. It was thought that this would knock out the St. Louis team, but it didn't. Captain Comiskey hustled, and won the pennant for the fourth time, with this team: King, Hudson, Chamberlain, and Devlin, pitchers; Boyle and Dolan, catchers; Comiskey, Robinson, Latham, Kerr, White, and McGarr, infielders; O'Neill, Lyons, and McCarthy, outfielders.

THE PENNANT RECORD FOR 1885.

	St. Louis.	Cincinnati.	Pittsburg.	Athletic.	Brooklyn.	Louisville.	Metropolitan.	Baltimore.	Games Won.	Games Lost.	Games Played.	Per Ct. Won.
St. Louis,		10	10	12	12	9	12	14	79	33	112	.705
Cincinnati,	6		9	9	11	8	10	10	63	49	112	.562
Pittsburg,	6	7		6	10	10	7	10	56	55	111	.504
Athletic,	4	7	10		5	8	11	10	55	57	113	.401
Brooklyn,	4	5	6	11		10	8	9	53	59	112	.473
Louisville,	7	8	6	8	6		9	9	53	59	112	.473
Metropolitan,	4	6	8	5	8	7		6	44	64	108	.407
Baltimore,	2	6	6	6	7	7	7		41	68	109	.376
Games Lost,	33	49	55	57	59	59	64	68				

In the spring of 1885 the association expelled James Mutrie, manager of the Metropolitans, and fined him $500, for aiding in the signing of Keefe and Esterbrook with the league. This action resulted in a row with the Metropolitans, and the association voted to drop them from membership and admit the Nationals. The courts, however, granted an injunction against this. The injunction was made permanent, and the association was shown that Erastus Wiman was the owner of the club. After these things were settled up Mr. Mutrie was relieved of his disabilities, but the fine was not remitted. The decision in this case, made by Judges Thayer and Arnold, December 19th, 1885, laid down the principle that no club can be expelled from a baseball organization without notice and trial. At the annual meeting S. W. Barkley, a player of the St. Louis, was suspended for a year and fined $500 for duplicity in signing contracts with both Baltimore and Pittsburg after he had been released by St. Louis, and accepting advance money from both clubs, and then repudiating his contract.

In 1886, as a result of the Barkley case, President McKnight was deposed from office, and Wheeler C. Wikoff was made president. Barkley brought a suit against the association, and a compromise was effected by which his fine was reduced to $100 and he was reinstated.

THE PENNANT RECORD FOR 1886.

CLUBS.	St. Louis.	Allegheny.	Brooklyn.	Louisville.	Cincinnati.	Athletic.	Mets.	Baltimore.	Games Won.	Per Cent. Won.
St. Louis,		12	13	9	15	15	16	13	93	.669
Allegheny,	8		12	12	13	11	12	12	80	.584
Brooklyn,	7	8		13	13	11	10	14	76	.555
Louisville,	10	7	7		10	9	11	12	66	.485
Cincinnati,	5	7	7	10		10	13	13	65	.471
Athletic,	5	8	7	11	10		12	10	63	.467
Metropolitan,	4	8	9	8	7	8		9	53	.393
Baltimore,	7	7	6	7	5	8	8		48	.366
Games Lost,	46	57	61	70	72	73	82	83	544	

In 1886 there were a few events that should be noted. The *Cincinnati Enquirer* brought charges of crooked playing against Tony Mullane, of the Cincinnati club. The association investigated the charges and found them wholly false, and exonerated Mr. Mullane. Bushong and Latham, of the St. Louis club, had a fistic argument in the Baltimore grounds. Charges were brought, the men pleaded guilty, apologized to all concerned, and were fined $100 each. It was in 1886 that a number of clubs endeavored to evade the National Agreement stipulation, prohibiting the signing of players before October 20th. This was done mostly by clubs in the league, the New York club being the greatest transgressor. The object was secured by making personal contracts with the men by individual directors of the clubs. Such an outcry was raised against this system by press and public that when it came to the point none of the clubs tried to hold the men so signed.

In the fall of 1886 the Pittsburg club withdrew from the association, and Cleveland was admitted to fill the vacancy.

The season of 1887 was financially one of the best on record. The pennant race was simply a walkover for the St. Louis club. Three other clubs, however, had an interesting fight for place.

THE PENNANT RECORD FOR 1887.

	St. Louis.	Cincinnati.	Baltimore.	Louisville.	Athletic.	Brooklyn.	Metropolitan.	Cleveland.	Games Won.	Per Cent. Won.
St. Louis,		6	16	13	12	16	14	18	95	.704
Cincinnati,	12		9	8	11	13	17	11	81	.600
Baltimore,	3	11		7	14	10	15	17	77	.570
Louisville,	7	12	11		11	12	12	11	76	.559
Athletic,	8	9	6	8		8	11	14	64	.481
Brooklyn,	4	7	9	8	10		9	13	60	.448
Metropolitan,	5	3	4	8	7	9		8	44	.331
Cleveland,	1	6	3	8	4	6	11		39	.298
Games Lost,	40	54	58	60	69	74	89	92	536	

After the close of the season the Brooklyn club, besides buying the releases of Caruthers, Foutz, and Bushong, of the St. Louis club, purchased the players and franchise of the Metropolitan club, paying therefor the sum of $25,000. The Association made a big effort to place itself on a par with the league. The price of admission was raised to fifty cents for 1888, and the four of the greatest umpires then in the business, John Gaffney, John McQuaid, Robert Ferguson, and Herman Doescher, were hired at very large salaries. Two of these, Gaffney and Doescher, were taken from the league. The league retaliated by hiring John Kelly, the association player, manager, and umpire. This man was then and is now undoubtedly the greatest umpire that ever stepped on the field.

The season of 1888 was not very profitable to most of the clubs, owing to the increase of tariff. The Baltimore and Athletic clubs were so severely boycotted by the public that the association was forced to return to the twenty-five cent tariff. It should be said, however, that the cities of Brooklyn, Cincinnati, and Cleveland took kindly enough to the larger rate. Kansas City took up the vacant franchise of the Metropolitan club in 1888. The pennant-race was a warm one, but the St. Louis team for the fourth consecutive time carried off the prize.

THE PENNANT RECORD FOR 1888.

	Athletic	Brooklyn	Baltimore	Cincinnati	Cleveland	Kansas City	Louisville	St. Louis	Games Won	Per Cent. Won
Athletic,		8	14	10	13	14	15	7	81	.609
Brooklyn,	12		12	14	16	11	13	10	88	.629
Baltimore,	5	8		6	10	11	11	6	57	.423
Cincinnati,	10	6	14		10	15	16	8	79	.594
Cleveland,	7	4	9	7		10	8	4	49	.374
Kansas City,	3	9	8	4	9		6	4	43	.326
Louisville,	5	7	9	3	8	12		4	48	.360
St. Louis,	10	10	14	10	16	16	16		92	.681
Games Lost,	52	52	80	54	82	89	87	43	537	

In the fall of 1888 the Cleveland club withdrew from the association and joined the league. Columbus took the vacant place.

The season of 1889 was an exciting one, and so much bad blood was engendered that the association became very near being wrecked. The fight for the pennant was between Brooklyn and St. Louis. It looked for a month or so as if St. Louis would have as easy a victory as usual, but the Brooklyn team captured the prize in the most terrific contest known in the annals of the association. There were endless charges of unfair treatment made by Brooklyn against St. Louis, and *vice versa*. The troubles culminated in a game at Brooklyn, where Captain Comiskey took his team off the field. This game was given to Brooklyn by the umpire, but, at a special meeting of the association at Cincinnati, a "combine" was made by certain clubs against Brooklyn. This "combine" practically refused to consider any but ex-parte evidence, and deprived the Brooklyn club of the game to which it was plainly entitled. Finally Brooklyn won the pennant with this team:

R. L. Caruthers, W. H. Terry, M. F. Hughes, and Lovett, pitchers; R. H. Clark, Visner, and A. J. Bushong, catchers; D. L. Fontz, 1b.; Collins, 2b.; G. B. Pinkney, 3b.; Geo. J. Smith, s.s.; Wm. D. O'Brien, l.f. (captain); John S. Corkhill, c.f.; Thomas P. Burns, r.f. Manager, William H. McGunnigle.

THE PENNANT RECORD FOR 1889.

	Brooklyn.	St. Louis.	Athletic.	Cincinnati.	Baltimore.	Columbus.	Kansas City.	Louisville.	Games Won.	Per Cent. Won.
Brooklyn,		8	12	15	12	11	16	19	93	.679
St. Louis,	11		9	12	12	14	14	18	90	.667
Athletic,	7	8		11	11	12	12	14	75	.560
Cincinnati,	5	8	9		11	11	14	18	76	.547
Baltimore,	8	7	8	8		12	11	16	70	.519
Columbus,	8	6	8	9	8		9	13	61	.439
Kansas City,	4	6	8	6	7	11		13	55	.399
Louisville,	1	2	5	2	4	7	6		27	.196
Games Lost,	44	45	59	63	65	78	83	111	547	

Some of the clubs which had proved too much for the Brooklyn club at Cincinnati now got to work to form another "combine" to leave Brooklyn out in the cold for 1890. They couldn't get quite votes enough to do it. When the annual meeting was called together November 13th, 1889, at the Fifth Avenue Hotel, New York, St. Louis, Athletics, Louisville, and Columbus formed a combination and sought to elect Z. Phelps, of Louisville, president. Brooklyn, Cincinnati, Baltimore, and Kansas City wanted S. C. Krauthoff, of Kansas City. The election of Mr. Phelps meant that Brooklyn and Cincinnati would receive the worst of every point that could be raised. There was a deadlock, four votes to four, which lasted through two days, during which time something like forty ballots were taken. The deadlock was finally broken by the resignation of Brooklyn and Cincinnati, both of which immediately joined the National League. The next day Kansas City resigned and joined the Western Association. Baltimore made application to the National League, but that body was averse to allowing the Washington club to sell its franchise. Later on the Baltimore club resigned and entered the Atlantic association, making a deal for the transfer of some of its best players to the Washington club.

The secession of these strong clubs, especially of Cincinnati and Brooklyn, financially the best in the circuit, reduces the association to

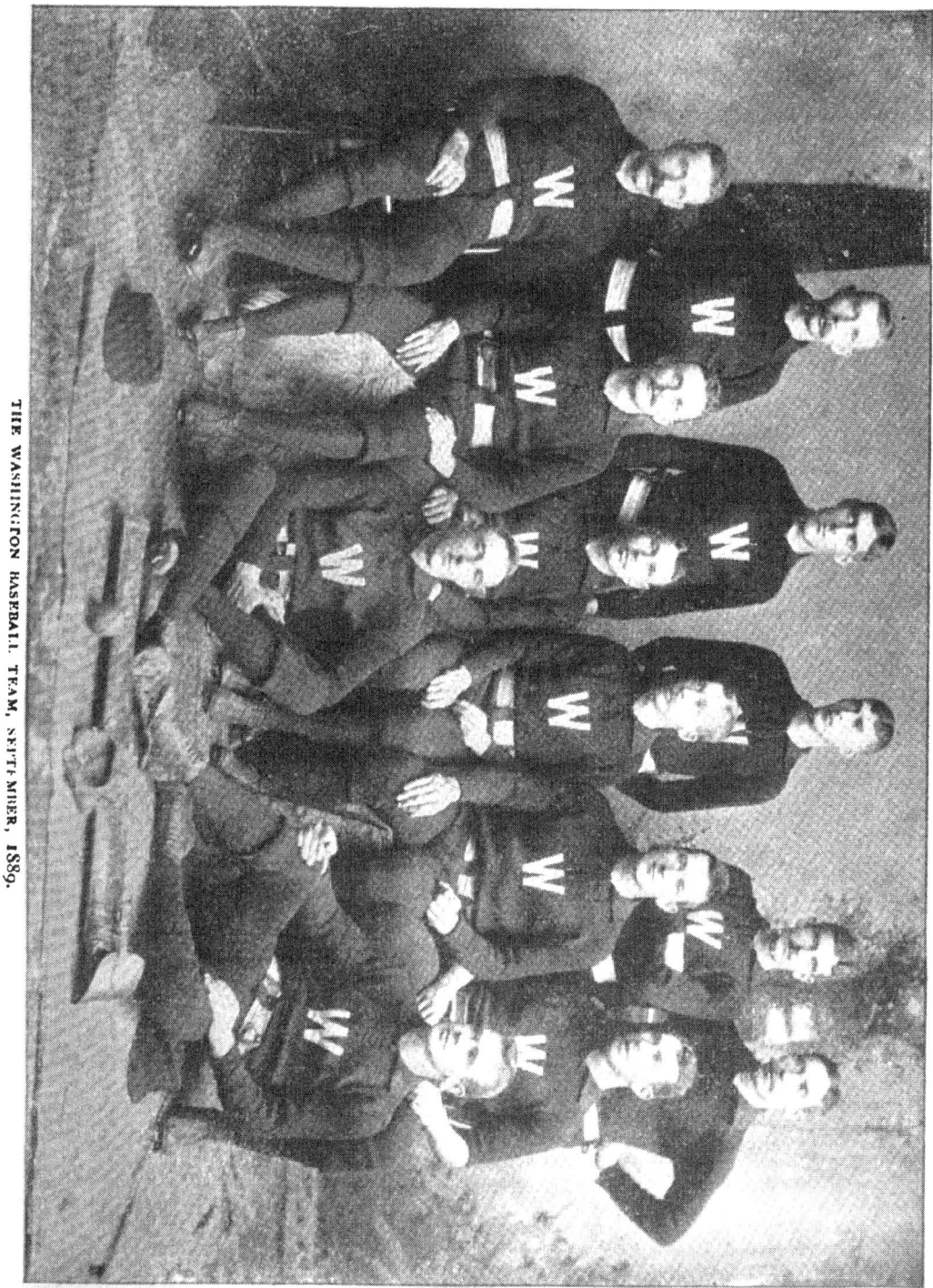

THE WASHINGTON BASEBALL TEAM, SEPTEMBER, 1889.

a position of insecurity it has never known before. It will force all the remaining clubs to reduce their salary list and sell off the releases of some of the star players, and thus aid the National League in its fight against the Players' League. Thus, after eight years of success, we leave the American Association struggling, as some leading baseball men affect to think, for its very existence.

Here are the leading players of the association, in the different positions since its organization:

BATSMEN.
1882. Browning, Louisville,
1883. T. Mansell, St. Louis,
1884. Esterbrook, Metropolitan,
1885. Browning, Louisville,
1886. Orr, Metropolitan,
1887. O'Neill, St. Louis,
1888. O'Neill, St. Louis,
1889. Tucker, Baltimore.

PITCHERS.
1882. Dorr, St. Louis,
1883. Mullane, St. Louis,
1884. Hecker, Louisville,
1885. Ramsey, Louisville,
1886. Ramsey, Louisville,
1887. Smith, Cincinnati,
1888. Terry, Brooklyn,
1889. Stivetts, St. Louis.

CATCHERS.
1882. O'Brien, Athletic,
1883. Wolf, Louisville,
1884. Milligan, Athletic,
1885. D. Sullivan, St. Louis,
1886. Traffley, Baltimore,
1887. Milligan, Athletic,
1888. Donohue, Kansas City,
1889. O'Connor, Columbus,
" Keenan, Cincinnati.

FIRST BASEMEN.
1882. Lane, Allegheny,
1883. Stovey, Athletic,
1884. Orr, Metropolitan.
1885. Scott, Allegheny,
1886. Orr, Metropolitan,
1887. Reilly, Cincinnati,
1888. Andrews, Louisville,
1889. Reilly, Cincinnati.

SECOND BASEMEN.
1882. McPhee, Cincinnati,
1883. McPhee, Cincinnati,
1884. Creamer, Allegheny,
1885. Barkley, St. Louis,
1886. McPhee, Cincinnati,
1887. Bierbauer, Athletic,
1888. Barkley, Kansas City,
1889 McPhee, Cincinnati.

THIRD BASEMEN.
1882. Battin, Allegheny,
1883. Battin, Allegheny,
1884. Battin, Allegheny,
1885. Hankinson, Metropolitan,
1886. Whitney, Allegheny,
1887. Lyons, Athletic,
1888. Shindle, Baltimore,
1889. Pinkney, Brooklyn.

SHORT-STOPS.
1882. Mack, Louisville,
1883. Nelson, Metropolitan,
1884. Houck, Athletic,
1885. Whitney, Allegheny,
1886. Smith, Allegheny,
1887 Gleason, St. Louis,
1888. Farrell, Baltimore,
1889. Fuller, St. Louis.

CENTRE FIELDERS.
1882. Macullar, Cincinnati,
1883. Maskrey, Louisville,
1884. Browning, Louisville,
1885. Welch, St. Louis,
1886. Welch, St. Louis,
1887. Corkhill, Cincinnati,
1888. Welch, Athletic,
1889. Corkhill, Brooklyn.

RIGHT FIELDERS.
1882. Blakiston, Athletic,
1883. Corkhill, Cincinnati,
1884. Swartwood, Allegheny,
1885. Corkhill, Cincinnati,
1886. Corkhill, Cincinnati,
1887. Wolf, Louisville,
1888. Hogan, Cleveland,
1889. Wolf, Louisville.

LEFT FIELDERS.
1882. Sommer, Cincinnati,
1883. Kennedy, Metropolitan,
1884. Kennedy, Metropolitan,
1885. Sommer, Baltimore,
1886. O'Neill, St. Louis,
1887. O'Brien, Metropolitan,
1888. Stovey, Athletic,
1889. Hornung, Baltimore.

This list is official, except for 1889, which is made up from unofficial averages.

PART VI.

The National Brotherhood of Baseball Players was organized by John M. Ward, in October, 1885. That is to say, he then began to put into operation the association which has since become so powerful. It was started secretly by Ward among the members of the New York team. It is a remarkable fact that, beyond a few rumors, no definite information reached the public as regards the Brotherhood, although its projectors worked indefatigably for ten months, perfecting the organization. Finally, through the *Sporting Life*, the details were given to the public August 4th, 1886, in the form of an interview with Ward, written by J. F. C. Blackhurst, then New York correspondent of *Sporting Life*, and the attorney of the Brotherhood.

The Brotherhood was organized with chapters in each league city. Its objects—I quote from the constitution, which has been kept a secret until very recently, when the enterprise of the *Sporting Times* and the treachery of a member brought it to light—are given as threefold:

"To protect and benefit its members collectively and individually; to promote a high standard of professional conduct; to advance the interests of the 'National Game.'"

It is provided that only league players may be members. Each chapter has a president and a secretary. Each chapter elects a representative, and these representatives form a council which holds executive and judicial functions. It has power to decide disputes between members, and between members and the league. The officers are three: president, vice-president, and secretary-treasurer. They are elected by the various chapters, although the nominations are made by the council.

The beneficial part of the scheme is set forth in article xii, which reads:

"A Relief Committee, to consist of three members, representatives of chapters, shall be appointed annually by the president of the

Brotherhood. It shall receive an application for relief from any member, and, upon receipt of such, at once inform itself of the applicant's circumstances. If it be found that he is sick or injured, and without means of his own, the committee shall grant him assistance in a sum not to exceed ten dollars per week, dating from the time of application, and continuing for so long a time as such assistance is necessary."

Every member of the order is required to take the following oath, prescribed by the constitution:

ARTICLE VI. SECTION 1. The candidate, having been regularly elected, shall appear before the president of the electing chapter, at a meeting of that chapter, and take the following oath:

" I (candidate giving full name), do solemnly swear:

" To strive to promote the objects and aims of this Brotherhood, in accordance with its Constitution and By-laws;

" Never to take an undue advantage of a brother in good standing;

" Never to permit an unjust injury to be done to, or continued against, a brother in good standing, while it is in my power to prevent the same;

" To assist a brother in distress;

" To render faithful obedience to the will of the Brotherhood, as expressed by the decrees of the council, or by a vote of my chapter.

" To all this I make my solemn oath to Almighty God, and in the presence of these witnesses."

Such briefly are the objects and general plan of the Brotherhood. In his interview of August 4th, Mr. Ward was asked: " Do you think the reserve rule will be attacked?" To which he answered: "I can only express my individual opinion. Speaking, however, from my own standpoint, and from my impressions as gathered from an association with the players, I should say that it will not be. I believe that a majority of ball-players regard the reserve rule as a necessary institution, though they may consider that some abuses have arisen under it." This was precisely what Mr. Ward said, because the interview was submitted to and approved by him before it appeared in print. Circumstances seem to argue that Mr. Ward was not over sincere in 1886; at any rate, he experienced a wonderful change of heart, for in 1889, three years later, we find him doing his utmost to smash " the necessary institution."

It took the whole of the year 1886 to get the Brotherhood in running order, and the playing season of 1887 was well under way before the players got ready to make demands for the redress of their alleged wrongs. In the fall of 1887 they were recognized by the league at its annual meeting after Mr. Ward had assured the league that the Brotherhood men were free agents, and that the reserve rule was not menaced. The result of the meeting was the adoption of a new contract prepared and presented by the Brotherhood and accepted by the league. Section 18 of this contract gave the party of the first part (the league) the right to reserve the party of the second part for the year next ensuing. This is the clause under which the league now proposes, if sustained by law, to hold its players for the season of 1890.

Just previous to the adoption of the new contract, in an interview Mr. Ward said: "In order to get men to invest capital in baseball, it is necessary to have a reserve rule. Some say that this could be modified, but I am not of that opinion. How could it be modified? Say, for instance, we began this season by reserving men for only two, three, four, or even five years. At the expiration of that period players would be free to go where they pleased, and capitalists who invested, say $75,000 or $100,000, would have nothing but its ground and grand-stand. Then, again, players have agreed that this could be overcome by making the length of reservation vary. It could not, and would cause no end of dissatisfaction. It would be unfair to reserve one man for two years and another for five. The reserve rule, on the whole, is a bad one; but it cannot be rectified save by injuring the interests of men who invest their money, and that is not the object of the Brotherhood."

It will be seen in the light of recent events that Mr. Ward has changed his mind on this subject very materially.

The adoption of the classification rule in 1888 roused the Brotherhood to action. During last summer there was almost a strike. Indeed, a vote was taken whether or not the players would strike on July 4th, but it was voted down. Then a committee of the Executive Council asked the league to appoint a committee to hear their grievances. This committee, consisting of A. G. Spalding, J. I. Rogers, and J. B. Day, got from Mr. Ward a partial statement of what the grievances

OPENING GAME ON THE PHILADELPHIA CLUB GROUNDS, SEASON OF 1889.

were, and then decided that no harm would be done if they were to wait until the annual meeting. The players were informed of the decision. They were very angry, and said they couldn't wait; they must be heard at once. The league committee said they should be heard at the annual meeting. This refusal was just the kind of an excuse needed by the more aggressive players, and they secretly proceeded to arrange to desert the league and form a new organization. The desertion was formally completed when, on November 4th, 1889, the Brotherhood announced its purpose in a letter to the public. This was followed on November 6th and 7th, by an attempt to organize the players' league. Formal organization was not effected, because the Brotherhood's lawyers advised against, claiming that it would not be legal until the different clubs were properly incorporated. All other matters were agreed upon, and a meeting will be held December 10th, 1889, to adopt a constitution and formally organize.

The players' league consists of eight clubs in New York, Brooklyn, Pittsburgh, Chicago, Philadelphia, Boston, Cleveland, and Buffalo. The players will receive the same salaries they had in 1889, except those men who were affected by classification. They will get the salaries paid them in 1888. The profits of the club will be divided by a plan which gives the first $10,000 to the club, and the second $10,000 to the players. All over that sum is divided between capitalists and players, and half of the capital stock may be owned by players. No arrangement is made for the division of losses other than that the capitalists must stand them to the extent of their liability, which in most cases is $20,000, but they are not liable for salaries, which are to be paid from gate receipts.

The Brotherhood is well backed, and expects to start in business next spring, unless the league lawsuits prevent. There are, as yet, no known capitalists behind the Brooklyn and Pittsburgh clubs. The other capitalists financially interested in the players' league are Cornelius Van Cott, E. A McAlpin, C. B. Talcott, and Alexander Meakin, of New York; C. B. Cory, Julian B. Hart, John C. Haynes, George Wright, John F. Morrill, Dr. Bartlett, C. B. Prince, Fred E. Long, and Arthur Dixwell, of Boston; J. C. Rowe, James White, M. Shirer, and C. R. Fitzgerald, of Buffalo; Thomas Johnson and A. L. Johnson, of Cleveland; C. A. Wiedenfeller, J. M. Murdough, and John Addison, of Chicago; E. H. Wells, J. Elliot, John Vanderslice, Henry M. Love, H. L. Taggart, Ben. E. Hilt, J. W. Allen, W. H. Whitall, H. W. Disston, and J. E. Wagner, of Philadelphia. The men back of the Brooklyn and Pittsburgh clubs are the Brotherhood men of means and repute, whose names will be made public at the proper time.

The Brotherhood men all signed agreements with the capitalists in September, 1889, by which the scheme was to be co-operative among the clubs, and the players were to be hired from year to year. But when they came together November 4th, after the players had announced their secession, the capitalists insisted on changing the Brotherhood scheme, which made the strong clubs help support the weak clubs, and on having a three years' contract. The Brotherhood yielded, and the contract was drawn accordingly. Upon going to press about seventy-five men had signed these contracts, and Mr. Ward and the other leaders expect to sign at the very least one hundred players who were with the National League in 1889.

For Baseball Statistics, see Appendix.

THE "AROUND THE WORLD" POSTER, DONE IN COLORS.

II.

THE "AROUND THE WORLD" TOUR.*

THERE have been some noteworthy tours in the history of modern athletics—tours that have commanded the interest and attention of the English-speaking, athletic-loving nations of the world. England's cricket teams have visited those of Australia, and Australia has likewise invaded England—a fact that not a few of old England's representative batsmen and bowlers remember with feelings of mingled regret and pleasure; Ireland has sent her cricketers to America and America has flashed her most promising colors upon the great ovals of the British Isles; Ned Hanlon has crossed the Atlantic and Pacific to do battle with English and Australian oarsmen in their own waters; and an American wheelman has encircled the globe with the track of his bicycle. All these tours excited international interest, and their heroes were in each instance the recipients of many courtesies and kind attentions during their stay abroad and upon their return home.

During all of this time, however, the national game of the Americans —save in a single instance—had never been carried beyond its own shores. It is a matter of history that in 1875 the old Boston and Athletic teams, embracing A. G. Spalding, Adrien Anson, Harry and George Wright, and others of America's crack professionals of those days, journeyed to England for the purpose of showing Englishmen the beauties of the American game. At that time, however, baseball had only just entered upon the remarkable era of public favor and prosperity that has since marked its development in America, and it is safe

---

* By Harry Palmer, the "Around the World" Tour correspondent of the *New York Herald.*

to say there was not one Englishman out of every ten thousand who had even the faintest conception of the theory of the game, for no information bearing upon it had ever been sent to England previous to the advent of the American teams on British soil. In 1875 sentiment was not ripe for the successful introduction of our great field sport into any foreign country, and this fact made itself apparent to these touring players before they had been long in England. They were most hospitably received, however, and did it fall within the province of this chapter to speak more fully of that trip, much 'might be said of the courteous treatment accorded the Americans by the London cricketers and their friends. That tour is memorable, even if only because of its pioneer character.

ALBERT G. SPALDING.

The great tour of the winter of 1888–89, however, causes our first invasion of England to be almost forgotten, for it stands to-day, as it must for many years to come, far and away the greatest, most successful, and most noteworthy tour ever attempted in the history of athletics. The leader of the English tour of 1875 was also the leader of the world's tour of 1888. The English tour, however, was in reality but a mutually agreed upon and experimental trip, undertaken with very vague ideas as to what the result would be, artistically or financially. At that time Albert Spalding was the young, popular and hard-working pitcher of the Boston Red-Stockings, with little more than his energy, ambition, and love of the game to draw upon for the success of the trip. But how differently he organized, planned and conducted the tour of 1888-89. As the possessor of ample means, absolute control of two well-selected professional teams, under contract to him for the faithful observance of his wishes, took the place of the mutual-arrangement aggregation of 1875, while the same great lubricator of all worldly enterprises—gold—rendered possible the employment of experienced assistants, the provision of comfortable, and for the most part luxurious accommodations, and in fact rendered practicable the tour of the world by representative American teams.

The financial outlay of such an immense undertaking was necessarily very great. Mr. Spalding thought of this at the time he conceived the plan. He also realized that the receipts from such a trip could not be figured upon as a factor in its success. Unfavorable weather might prevent no small proportion of the appointed games; thousands of unprofitable miles would have to be traveled; and, worse than all, a lack of interest or a failure of the people in Australia and in Great Britain to understand and enjoy the game, might result in financial disappointment in the only countries included in the tour wherein there were grounds for hope of receipts. The financial failure of the trip seemed not improbable. Indeed, it was predicted by many.

The projector of the tour did not, however, look upon it as a money-making venture, and it was probably because of this that unfavorable predictions did not discourage him or affect his plans. On the contrary, as the arrangements progressed the more liberal and broader-gauged they became. It was early determined that there must be no lack of means and no hesitancy in disbursing them, and there was none. Mr. Spalding for obvious reasons practically shouldered all financial responsibility, and at no time was money withheld or wanting when the welfare of the tour demanded its expenditure. The journey across America from Chicago to San Francisco, was made in special and luxuriously-appointed dining and sleeping coaches; the best hotel and steamer accommodations that money could secure were enjoyed throughout the journey, and the tour of England and Scotland was made in a style that attracted as much attention as did the players themselves. In a word, a deposit of $30,000 in a Chicago bank as a "tour fund." with almost unlimited means behind this deposit, gave the party every reasonable assurance that a lack in this respect would not detract from their enjoyment.

Associated with Mr. Spalding was Leigh S. Lynch, the well-known dramatic manager and formerly the associate of Mr. A. M. Palmer in the management of the Union Square Theatre. Lynch during his dramatic career had made the journey to Australia several times; was possessed of a wide acquaintance in the colonies, as well as valuable experience in the management of such parties; and was altogether the man to assume the business management of the enterprise. At this time nothing had been said of a tour of the world, Mr. Spalding's only thought at that time being to cover Ausltralia and New Zealand thoroughly. As will be seen in the following pages, however, the journey had not progressed far before he had pretty well decided to return to America via the Red Sea, Egypt, Europe, and the Atlantic ocean.

LEIGH S. LYNCH.

Once decided upon, preparations for the big trip were actively begun, though for fear of possible rivalry in the field, publicity was for the time avoided. Manager Lynch started for Australia in February of 1888, to secure exclusive control, for baseball purposes, of the Australian and New Zealand cricket grounds. Drawings for attractive lithographs and announcement posters were at once begun, and this taxed the best skill of designers and lithographers. The outcome was indeed a work of art, picturing all the players in various attitudes of the play, and giving other attractive views calculated to arouse interest wherever seen. These posters preceded the party everywhere, and did much to arouse public interest.

The all-important work of selecting the teams was also taken under consideration. This was no easy task. On the contrary, it was an exceedingly delicate undertaking. Not only must the men selected be the best exponents of the national game, but they must combine with their ball-playing ability, intelligence, good address, good habits, and good morals, qualifications not easy to find combined in any class of men. Confident that the trip would develop into one of international importance and interest, and that it would attract the attention of all English-speaking nations at least, Mr. Spalding was determined to take no chance of bringing discredit upon the party through the careless selection of his players. This point he kept in view not only during the time of selecting, but from the time the party left Chicago until it reached it again after having completed the circuit of the globe. The result was that the splendidly proportioned, well-mannered score of ball players was warmly welcomed and greatly admired in every country they visited as a representative and typical body of Americans, while, at the same time, they gave exhibition after exhibition of ball playing that will rank with the best ever seen upon American soil, even during the championship seasons.

One would naturally suppose that an opportunity to see Australia would be eagerly seized upon by every clear-headed, intelligent American who could possibly avail himself of it, and yet to Mr. Spalding's surprise he experienced serious trouble before the work of signing his men had been completed. The Chicago team, or rather ten of its ablest members, signed at once, and were eager for the trip. It was not so, however, with the All-American team, which it was intended should be composed of one or more players selected from the representative teams of the country. No difficulty was experienced in signing them, but after they had signed, visions of sea-sickness, of death upon foreign shores, and of disasters upon the ocean, began to arise before the eyes of some of the men, and two or three of them suddenly discovered insurmountable obstacles to their joining the party. Michael Kelly, of Boston, for instance, had entered into business in New York, and was consequently unwilling to leave, even though he had signed a contract to do so. Tiernan, of New York, sent a telegram, in which he declared his inability to go, as he was "ill." Others were afflicted with sick mothers, and still others suddenly determined upon hasty marriages, until, at one time, it looked as though no team could be organized to oppose Chicago on the tour. Those who were willing to be persuaded, however, finally tossed their fears over their shoulders, and those who would not be persuaded were left behind, their places being filled by equally capable men.

In April, Lynch returned from Australia, and the plan of the tour having long since been made public, it became a never tiresome subject for comment and discussion in baseball circles throughout the United States, while the Australian press began to show an interest in the enterprise that augured well for its success in the Antipodes. The games of the world's championship series between the New York and St. Louis teams prevented Captain Ward and pitcher Ed Crane, of the New Yorks, joining the party at Chicago, but they overtook the company before it reached Denver; Herman Long, of Kansas City, Ed Hengle, and Frank Flint, of Chicago, accompanying the party until the arrival of the New Yorkers. Thereafter there was no break. After a farewell game upon the League grounds in Chicago, on the afternoon of October 20th, the party traveled by easy stages across the continent toward San Francisco, playing en route at St. Paul, Minneapolis, Omaha, Des Moines, Hastings, Denver, Colorado Springs, Salt Lake City, Los Angeles and San Francisco, finally sailing from "Frisco" Sunday, November 18th, for the Sandwich Islands, New Zealand and Australia. The Chicago, Burlington and Quincy Railroad had provided for the party two magnificently appointed special cars—a dining and a sleeping car—and upon these the journey was made in truly luxuriant style as far as Denver. Special cars upon the Denver and Rio Grande, and Central Pacific roads carried the party the balance of the journey. After two weeks of never-to-be-forgotten attentions and courtesies, including banquets, theatre parties and ball playing upon the Pacific coast, we boarded the steamship Alameda for the first sea voyage of the tour. Leigh Lynch had preceded the party in order to prepare for its arrival at Honolulu, Auckland and Sydney, and the management promised to fall, for a time at least, entirely upon President Spalding's shoulders. Fortunately for all concerned, however, "Jim" Hart, at that time the popular and energetic manager of the Milwaukee team, who had consented to accompany the party as far as St. Paul, was prevailed upon to continue his journey in a managerial capacity to the Pacific coast. Hart subsequently proved one of Mr. Spalding's most valuable lieutenants, his ability, experience as a manager, and wide acquaintance proving of great service.

To a description of the charming tour across the prairies and through the mountains of America; of the royal reception tendered the party by His Majesty King Kalakaua in the Hawaiian Islands; of the generous hospitality of the Australians; of the adventures and experiences of the Americans in the spice-scented island of Ceylon, in Egypt, in Arabia, through a delightful section of continental Europe, and in the British Isles, the following pages are devoted.

THE PARTY.

On the evening of October 20th, a few days after the close of the season of 1888, two magnificently equipped railway coaches stood in the Union depot at Chicago, their sides ornamented by long banners of white linen upon which had been inscribed the words, "Spalding's Australian Baseball Tour." No other cars had ever stood in the great station similarly decorated, and yet no inquiries were made by the hundreds who crowded the platforms, for every well-informed traveler knew that the Chicago and All-American ball teams had played their farewell game upon the Chicago grounds that afternoon and were about to take their departure for Australia. Hundreds of baseball enthusiasts, including scores of the personal friends and admirers of the departing players, crowded the station, and it was not until a few minutes before leaving time that the members of the party bade a final farewell to the crowd, and, together with their more intimate friends and relatives, passed through the gateways and sought the neighborhood of their train, where they said their last farewells to mothers, wives, and sisters. Perhaps no time could be more favorable for the introduction of the reader to the individual members of the party than when, having stored valises, uniform bags, and sundry packages away in their respective sections, the boys awaited the signal for departure.

Inside the car stood Captain Anson and his wife; she, tall and fair-haired like her husband, with big blue eyes and a complexion typical of this particular charm in American women. Near them were seated Mr. and Mrs. Ned Williamson, the kindly face and big muscular body of the famous short stop bending over the fair head and pretty face of the Southern girl he had made his wife six years before. Further on stood Tom Burns, the quiet-mannered man-of-many-friends among ball players, in conversation with George Van Haltren, the well-proportioned and active Californian who has made an enviable reputation with the Chicago Club. "Van," by the way, accompanied the party only as far as San Francisco, his home. At the far end of the sleeper stood Tom Daly and Mark Baldwin, inseparables, and as we afterward learned, the leading spirits of the party in mischief and practical joking. Out upon the forward platform, blonde "Jimmy" Ryan leaned against the break-wheel conversing with two pretty girls, whose faces shone under the prismatic rays of the center-fielder's magnificent scarf-pin; while just beyond, Fred Pfeffer, faultlessly attired, stood looking alternately at the toes of his patent leathers and admiring the faces of half a dozen Chicago beauties upon the other side of the railing. Out-fielders "Mart" Sullivan and "Bob" Pettitt, both "Yankees" from the hills of New England, and both fair-haired, muscular, and splendidly proportioned, pressed against the railing for a last farewell. Catcher Fred Carroll, broad-shouldered, muscular as a blacksmith, and handsomely dressed in a light traveling suit, together with Tom Brown of the Bostons, chatted and laughed with George Wood and Captain Fogarty as the quartette stood beneath one of the big electric lights of the station. Wood, a blonde, and Fogarty, dark-complexioned, dark-haired, and dark-eyed, are, like Baldwin and Daly, chums. Both are members of the Philadelphia team and both are typical ball players of the higher class, in manner and appearance. Fogarty is an Irishman possessed of an inexhaustible fund of wit, a cheery presence and a handsome face. Save upon two occasions, once on the Pacific and once in crossing the English Channel, he was one of the well-springs of life to our party. Wood was more quiet, but as fond of life as his chum. Frank Silvester Flint, or "Old Silver," as he was known among the party; John Tener, of the Chicagos, tall, dark, and slender; Captain Ned Hanlon, of the Detroits; Manager Jim Hart; Hermann Long, of Kansas City, and tall, blonde-headed John Healy, of Indianapolis, are comparing their watches with the big clock on the station wall, while among them all, passing from group to group of the party, with a kindly word here and there and an all-seeing eye to the details of arrangement, is Mr. Spalding, President of the Chicago Club and projector of the tour itself. He came through the gates half an hour ago supporting upon his arm a stately, handsome, venerable lady, nearly as tall, robust and fine-looking as himself. This was Mrs. H. I. Spalding, Mr. Spalding's mother, and through the many miles of travel, as well as among the many attentions and courtesies showered upon us during the tour, the stately presence, snow-white head, and kindly face of this honored lady ever swayed a genial and restraining influence over the more impulsive members of our combination, and lent that air of distinction which the presence of a stately woman alone can impart.

Such was our party as it stood in the depot awaiting the first turn of the wheels upon that memorable tour, and it subsequently proved a most congenial and delightful party for all. It could not well have been otherwise, in view of the principles which guided Mr. Spalding in his selections, and during the entire journey around the world not an unpleasant incident, nor a serious difference of opinion occurred to mar the pleasure of the tour. Later on, at Denver, the party was augmented by John Ward, the well-known captain of the New York team; Ed Crane, the genial "tenor-pitcher" of the "Giants," whose excellent voice helped us to while away many a pleasant hour on deck; "Billy" Earle, the enthusiastic little catcher of the Cincinnati team, whom we picked up at St. Paul, and James Manning, the popular captain of the Kansas City. In addition to these were Newton Macmillan, correspondent of the *New York Sun*, Mr. Goodfriend, of the *Chicago Inter-Ocean*, and the writer. Harry Simpson, of the Newark team, accompanied the party as Mr. Spalding's assistant, and afterward, remaining in Australia, did much toward helping the growth and development of the game there.

At Denver we were joined by Leslie Robison, Jr., of Peoria, Ill., who accompanied the party for the pleasure to be had out of the journey. Mr. Robison was a somewhat delicate looking young man, with a plethoric purse and a generous nature. That he was made welcome, goes without saying. At San Francisco the party was still further increased by Irving W. Snyder, of New York, and George Wright, of Boston. Snyder and Wright formed the third brace of inseparables in our party—"Two Dromios" in fact, who suffered and enjoyed every hour of the journey in close companionship.

Perhaps, however, the two most interesting members of our combination—interesting not only to us but to the people of every country we visited—were the "Professor" and the "Mascot."

For the edification of readers not versed in baseball lore it should be stated that the mascot has become quite an important institution among the professional teams of America. He may be a boy possessed of some special attainment or physical peculiarity, or he may be a bull-pup with a prominent patch over his left eye. It matters not whether a mascot be brute or human, so long as his presence upon the players' bench insures a victory—in the minds of the players—to the team with which he has cast his fortunes and in whose favor he exercises the influence he is supposed to have with Dame Fortune. We picked up our mascot, Clarence Duval, at Omaha, a little, slenderly built, impish-faced negro, with a remarkable talent for plantation dancing, "hoe-downs" and "walk-arounds," and the gift of baton twirling to a degree well calculated to make the average drum-major wild with envy. A French actress making a tour of the Western States, and with whom he had traveled for some weeks as an attendant, had discarded him in the wilds of Nebraska and we picked him up en route. Subsequently he was rigged out in a red coat, gold lace, tight-fitting white trowsers and high-topped patent leather boots, and other paraphernalia of a drum-major's make-up, and led the teams upon the field for their games, walking in front of the line and swinging his silver-tipped baton in a style that never failed to excite enthusiastic applause. On shipboard he danced for the party, his music being the rhythmic clapping of hands by expert members of our party. The little beggar danced for King Kalakaua, amused the Prince of Wales and King Humbert of Italy, and afforded his fellow-tourists no end of diversion. Subsequently, however, he proved a deserter.

And now a word about "Professor" Bartholomew. "Proff," as the boys soon learned to call him, was certainly as original, adventurous and queer-lingoed a resident of Michigan as ever went beyond the shores of his own country. The "Professor" was a balloonist who had broken nearly every bone in his body and gouged out one of his eyes by falling into a tree-top during his professional career. Nothing deterred, however, by his disastrous exploits of the past, he was still following the life of an aeronaut when he met our party in San Francisco. His proposal to make the tour with us to Australia was accepted by Mr. Spalding, and the "Proff" accordingly became one of the party. His specialty, that of parachute leaping, was comparatively new in the Antipodes, and his trip was a success, artistically and financially. It was indeed a thrilling sight to see him ascend, swinging to the trapeze bar of his balloon, until he became but a speck against the blue sky, and then suddenly leap from his perch out into space, clutching the bar of his parachute which trailed after his rapidly descending figure until the air caught its folds and spread it out like a big umbrella above him. The daring fellow, as soon as the parachute had opened, would then go through a series of nerve-thrilling gymnastic performances that rarely failed to make more than one of his spectators turn their faces away in fear. A typical Yankee, with all the characteristic curiosity of New Englanders, he was a source of much amusement to our party, and an object of real interest to the people on the other side of the world. We were all thoroughly sorry when in Ballarat the "Professor's" descending parachute hurled him against the zinc cornice of a roof and cut a big gash in both legs below the knees. He recovered during the voyage across the Indian ocean, however, and was soon as quizzical, curious and originally funny as before the accident.

THE "PROFESSOR'S" SPECIALTY.

Frank Lincoln, the American humorist, was one of us as far as Australia, but did not continue further. Leigh Lynch and Mrs. Lynch, *nee* Anna Berger, the celebrated cornetist, joined us in Australia, completing the party, which was but little changed during the remainder of the tour.

But while I have been introducing my readers to the members of our party, the big station bell in the depot has sounded the time of our departure, and the train moves slowly past the platform, while hundreds of handkerchiefs flutter a farewell, and the first mile, in our journey of thirty-two thousand miles, has begun.

ACROSS THE CONTINENT.

Many American readers have taken the trip across the continent to California and the Pacific slope, and will therefore be familiar with not a few of the scenes through which our party passed. Let me say here, however, that no American can form any adequate idea of the grandeur and extent of his own country until he has made this journey. The days of the bison, the Indian scout, and the red raiders of the immigrant settlement are over, it is true, yet on every hand one sees evidences of a life so entirely different, so crude, when compared with methods and surroundings of an existence in the large cities of the East, that the people, their striking characteristics, their broad Western accent, their evident thrift and enterprise, and the apparent, though as yet imperfectly developed, resources of the country, are as interesting a study as any to be met with in a journey around the globe.

Our party, too, were making the trip under exceptionally delightful conditions. With our magnificently equipped special cars we wholly ignored the hotels en route. Our coming having been well heralded at each point, as well as our intention announced of crossing the Pacific to Australia, local enthusiasm had been aroused all along our route, and we were the recipients of marked attentions which assumed a public character before we had progressed very far upon our journey. At each city our arrival was awaited with impatience; the press, not only of the West, but of the entire country, watched our progress from day to day, the correspondents of our own party alone representing nearly thirty of the leading papers of the Union. It was pleasant to be thus anticipated; to feel that timbrels were being sounded in honor of our arrival, and that thousands of honest regrets followed us upon our departure; it was pleasant to be made much of; it was delightful to travel in such regal style, and altogether no lighter-hearted, more thoroughly satisfied party than ours, ever crossed the continent.

We left Chicago Saturday evening, October 20th, at 7 o'clock, and arrived at St. Paul the next morning. The trip from Chicago was filled with pleasant incidents up to the midnight hour. At each station we found enthusiastic crowds assembled, anxious for a glimpse at the party, and each assemblage gave us a hearty cheer as our train pulled out of the local station. Had we left Chicago in the morning our journey to the "Twin Cities" must have been one continuous ovation. We took dinner upon our dining-car, the "Cosmopolitan," shortly after leaving Chicago, and with that meal our party became a unit of congeniality and pleasant anticipation. After the tables were cleared, it quickly became apparent that every man of the party was provided with an entire poker outfit. To those of my readers who do not approve of card playing this may appear as a reflection upon the moral tone of our ball players. But it should not. The games entered into by our party during our long tour of the world, were played rather for the interest and enjoyment they held for us, than for gain. During such a journey there are hours that cannot be passed half so pleasantly in any other way, and if reference is made in succeeding pages to the games of "draw" indulged in upon our sleepers, or to our chances at "Calcutta pool" during our sea voyages, the reader will understand that the indulgence was the outgrowth of a desire for diversion, and not of a desire for gain. The ladies of our company, with the consideration characteristic of American women under such circumstances, generously commanded the boys to smoke whenever and wherever they pleased, with the result that the sleeper "Galesburg" became not only our sleeping apartment, but our smoking-room, our club-room and our quarters for songs, jokes, music—we having a mandolin and guitar in the party—and a good time generally. The ladies participated in our music and shared our fun, while we, in turn, enjoyed their society from breakfast until bedtime. Such was our party, and such our methods of passing time, with ample means and incidents for diversion even from this pleasant mode of travel.

Our arrival at St. Paul was the occasion of quite an assemblage at the Chicago, Burlington and Quincy depot, on Sunday morning, the boys holding a levee in the sleeper "Galesburg" from breakfast time until nearly noon. A game had been scheduled for that afternoon, President Spalding having decided to adopt a policy on the Sunday game question, according to the established customs of the cities in which we played. Sunday games had been an established institution in St. Paul for many seasons, and we consequently felt no hesitancy in playing there on the day of our arrival. It was a bit chilly for ball playing, but we put up our second game of the trip in good style, and in the presence of two thousand people. Frank Flint (Old Silver), caught for the All-Americans, in the absence of Kelly, who had returned to New York under contract with Mr. Spalding, to arrange his business affairs, and rejoin us in Denver. Kelly's name was upon the score card, however, and it was some time before the crowd discovered the fact that "Silver," and not the only Kelly, was behind the bat. Flint might have passed for Kelly very well, but he struck out five times during the afternoon, and this was more than the crowd could stand. The weather was too cold for brilliant fielding, and the game was cut short at the end of the sixth inning, that Chicago might play the St. Pauls.*

This last was the game over which the crowd became most enthusiastic, it being charged with a degree of local interest entirely lacking in the game between Chicago and All-America. St. Paul, of course, played ball for all they were worth, a natural and earnest desire to defeat so strong a combination in the presence of a local crowd, inciting them to their best efforts. Game was finally called at the end of the seventh inning, on account of darkness, with the score in favor of the St. Paul team, and Manager Barnes, of the local team, at once challenged Anson to another game at Minneapolis, on the following day. The challenge was accepted, and the visiting teams were driven to their cars.

On the following morning our special cars were run down to Minneapolis, and here the importance and character of the tour was, for the first time since our departure, declared with much pomp and dignity. A parade in a dozen landaus drawn by horses with old gold plumes and

---

* See Appendix for all Scores.

new gold blankets, behind a band of twenty-one pieces, led by a drum major with a scarlet coat and a big silver baton, emphasized our arrival, and although the day was colder than the preceding one, game was begun in the presence of 1800 people. The All-Americans turned the tables on Anson in this game, Tener being freely hit and none too well supported, while Van Haltren pitched an effective game for the opposing team. Meanwhile the crowd had been burning with impatience for the game between the Chicago and St. Paul teams to begin, and applauded enthusiastically when the players finally took the field. And what a game the youngsters did put up, to be sure. Tuckerman pitched and Earl caught for St. Paul, while Mark Baldwin, in the box for Chicago, proved a puzzle for every "Saint" who faced him. As inning after inning was played without a run being scored, the enthusiasm of the spectators knew no bounds. Pfeffer, however, finally made the winning run for Chicago in the fifth inning, reaching first on the play that put Anson out at second, stealing second, going to third on Tuckerman's wild throw to catch him off second, and crossing the plate on the play that retired Burns at first. It was a hard fight, though it lasted but five innings, and a credit to the St. Paul team though they did not win.

At seven o'clock that evening we left Minneapolis for Cedar Rapids, and after a turn at the cards, a bit of music, and the enjoyment of our cigars, the party retired—but not to sleep. It was Tom Daly's night for practical joking, and few of us escaped. He fished a piece of ice out of the water cooler and slipped it into Tom Brown's berth; he concealed himself behind the curtains of Herman Long's berth and filled the compartment with thick clouds of West Virginia "Stogie" smoke, until Long rolled from between the curtains, his eyes wet with tears, and vowing vengeance between his attacks of coughing; he artistically decorated with lampblack the good natured face of the sleeping John Healy, and perpetrated some similar outrage upon each of his fellow tourists whom he found asleep. Meantime word had been passed along among the wakeful ones that Mr. Daly was executing "a raid," and as a result a grinning and expectant face shone from between each pair of curtains, save those behind which Daly's victims slumbered.

Unfortunately for Frank Flint, his gentle snore reached Daly's ear through the berth curtains, and the joker, parting the drapings, stood looking upon the slumbering form of his unsuspecting fellow player. The opportunity was too choice a one to be treated in an ordinary way, and Tom stood for an instant with an expression on his face which told that his active brain was at work devising some crowning piece of mischief. What it would be was the absorbing question with a dozen interested observers.

In an instant he dropped the curtains and started for the rear end of the car, while a dozen pairs of eyes followed his movements. Our sleeper was the last car in the train, and Daly, stepping out upon the rear platform, detached one of the bull's-eye red lights from the railing

PRACTICAL JOKING—"SILVER'S" FEARFUL AWAKING.

and re-entered the car. The dozen watchers now divined his intentions, and with difficulty restrained their laughter. Stepping carefully to "Silver's" berth, with the lantern in his hand, the joker quietly parted the drapings, and thrusting the lantern within twelve inches of Flint's face, made the berth walls echo with a yell that would have done credit to the lungs of a Sioux warrior. "Silver," who had been pressed into taking one or two "night-caps" beyond his usual allowance, was startled from his dreams by the awful screech, only to gaze into the great red eye which Daly held steadily before his face. The lurid glare of the light blinded the old player and scattered his terrified thoughts beyond all hope of re-collection. Slowly he raised himself into a sitting posture, never once taking his wide open eyes off the horrible thing before him, and then as the climax of his fear was reached, gave a gasping, terrified howl, and plunged through the curtains into the aisle, striking his head with a resounding thump against the top of his bunk as he went. There he sat for a moment until the choking sounds issuing from a dozen compartments caught his ear, and then sprang to his feet with a dangerous gleam in his eye, as an uncontrollable and simultaneous burst of laughter filled the car from end to end. Daly had suddenly disappeared, no one knew where, not to present himself until the steward announced breakfast.

The teams were tendered a great ovation at the city of Cedar Rapids, which we reached on the morning of Tuesday, the 23d. Our cars were switched upon a track just in front of the Union depot, and from the time the boys took their seats at breakfast in the dining-car, until they entered their carriages for the grounds, they were never lost sight of by the crowds that filed past our cars in such numbers as to impart a much better idea of the city's population than any of us had entertained before. Full half a dozen special trains were run into the city from adjacent towns, each train loaded, and by noon the city presented a holiday appearance. A more beautiful day for a ball game could scarcely be imagined, and fully four thousand people flocked to the grounds to witness the game, which was well worth going to see. At the request of many, Mr. Spalding acted as umpire. The score was tied in the fifth inning and again in the eighth, the victory finally going to Chicago when Ryan crossed the plate with one man out in the ninth inning. After the game, Mr. W. C. Beake and other gentlemen, who had arranged our reception at Cedar Rapids, together with their wives and daughters, supped with us in the "Cosmopolitan," President Spalding breaking a case of "Mumm" with the boys, in appreciation of the dash and spirit they had thrown into their game during the afternoon. We left Cedar Rapids at 6.30 P. M., with the parting cheers of the crowds at the depot ringing in our ears, and reached Des Moines, the State capital, the following morning. The game at Des Moines was witnessed by some 1500 people and was the prettiest contest yet put up by the touring teams. Hutchinson and Sage, of the local team, in response to a request made by several Des Moines gentlemen, filled the points for the All-America against Chicago, and did some great battery work, while they received excellent support in the field. We were joined at Des Moines by Frank Lincoln, the well-known American monologue artist, who accompanied our party upon a professional trip as far as Australia.

From Des Moines we pushed on rapidly toward Denver, stopping en route for games at Hastings and Omaha. At the latter point we picked up Clarence Duval. Tom Burns espied the little African as the teams were on their way to the grounds in carriages, with a full military band at the head of the line. A sorry looking little "nig" Clarence was, with his dusty and tattered garments, and his badly battered cap to one side of which a thread of gold lace was clinging, the only relic of better days the poor little darkey possessed; unless, perhaps, it was the tarnished baton he carried. "Bless me!" said Tom Burns, as he caught sight of the boy, "if there isn't the little coon. Where in the world could he have come from?" and the third-base man beckoned to Clarence, who scattered the crowd in his desperate efforts to respond.

It seems that while the Chicago team were east upon a championship trip, Anson met the boy in Philadelphia, and being taken with the urchin's precocity, as well as his dancing and baton-twirling skill, had made him a proposition to travel with the team as "mascot," an offer the boy quickly accepted. He was accordingly togged out in a page's suit of navy blue with brass buttons, at Anson's expense, and promised to henceforth use his influence in favor of his benefactors. In New York, however, he came under the notice of M'lle Jarbeau, a French actress playing the country at that time, and the attractions of stage life held out to the newly appointed "mascot" were too great for him to withstand. He deserted the diamond for the stage, and the team had seen or heard nothing of him until Tom Burns caught sight of him at Omaha.

There was a merry sparkle in the waif's eye as he jumped out of the carriage at the grounds, and with prompt re-assumption of his former authority, ordered the uniformed teams to "Dress ranks, dah!" Then, as the band struck up a march, he tossed his rusty baton into the air, and, while walking in front of the line of players, went through a series of movements and tactics that caused the real drum-major of the band to rest his baton upon his arm and gaze at his youthful superior in astonishment. The exhibition caught the crowd, and it cheered the darkey for his inimitable performance, as heartily as it did the players when they drew up before the grand stand.

THE MASCOT'S MARCH TO VICTORY.

"Where'd you come from, boy?" asked Anson, in a gruff voice, as he shook hands with the lad.

"Miss Jarbeau don gimme my release dis mawnin'," was the reply.

"Well," said Anson, "you're black-listed from this party; d'ye understand? We've got no use for deserters."

"I reckon you'se right, Cap'n," was the boy's philosophic reply, "but," he added with a quick look for a bit of sympathy in Anson's face, "I'se had a mighty hahd time ob it since I left you all."

"Ahey," said Anson, "I don't doubt it in the least. You look as though you had, and you deserve it. But we're done with you," and Anson walked off to the field while Clarence strolled over to the players' bench and sat down with a very downcast expression of countenance.

It all ended, however, by Clarence re-entering the carriage with Burns and returning to the train with our party, where I found him half an hour afterwards, sobbing at having been ordered out of the car by "the old man," as the boys soon began to designate Anson. We got together, however, and took up a purse for the little darkey, and then talked to Anson until he relented and decided that Clarence should accompany us as far as San Francisco, and further, if he behaved himself. It will be seen in the ensuing pages that he proved a great source of amusement to us during hours that without him might have been dull.

The game at Omaha resulted in a sweeping victory for the All-America team. Ryan took the box for Chicago, and his slow, easy-left-handed delivery deceived the opposing batsmen under Hanlon's captaincy, until the fifth inning, when Hanlon, Hengle, Van Haltren and Long suddenly dropped to his curves and pounded him unmercifully. The exhibition of batting pleased the Nebraska people immensely, and they howled themselves hoarse, as All-America made the circuit of the bases time and again.

At Hastings, however, Chicago turned the tables upon their opponents, and with Baldwin in the box batted out a pretty victory off Van Haltren's delivery. The falling of a section of the grand stand just before the game commenced, and the unexpected precipitation of a hundred or more spectators a distance of twenty feet to the ground, proved a serious though not fatal accident, but the crowd of three thousand people who had come, not only from Hastings, but from all surrounding points, were out for a holiday and a day's fun upon the occasion of the visit of the teams to their city, and soon forgot the incident in the excitement of the game. While at Hastings, some of the boys took Clarence Duval, gave him a bath, and arrayed him in completely new apparel, and when he returned to the car, the rest of the party scarcely recognized him. He sported a light check traveling suit with a natty hat to match, patent leather shoes, new underwear, spotless linen, and carried a cane. When he led the teams upon the ground that afternoon he was certainly as much of a curiosity as the teams were an attraction, and President Spalding, who had been absent from the party on a trip to Kansas City and who returned just in time to see Clarence's *début*, decided at once to take him with us to Australia. He was made to sign an iron-clad contract, in which he agreed to undergo all sorts of horrible penalties upon the first attempt at desertion. Anson, however, would not be convinced of the little darkey's sincerity, and said, that night upon the train, as he looked the mascot over in his new clothes, "this reminds me of the new suit I gave you in Philadelphia, last spring, in which you ran away from us two days afterward. It would not surprise me a bit if you should desert us at San Francisco." Clarence looked indignant.

"Ain't I done signed dis contrack?" he asked. "Ain't me word good?"

"I should say not," replied Anson, "didn't you run away before?"

"Didn't I done tell you I was kidnapped?" replied Clarence.

"Pshaw," said Anson, contemptuously; "I believe you would desert us now for Miss Jarbeau, if she happened to run across you."

"Well," said Clarence, philosophically, "dat's because you don't know me. I habn't de slightest doubt in de world dat if Miss Jarbeau seen me now," and Clarence looked at his new outfit with an unmistakable expression of pride, "she'd say to me, 'My gracious, Clarence, whar you been? come along wid me, boy, and don't let me lose sight ob you agin.' I know she'd say jus' dat."

"And what would you say?" asked Anson, with an amused smile.

"What I say?" said Clarence, and he looked the impersonation of pride and self-confidence, "why I just say, 'Go on, white woman, I don't know you now, an' I neber did know you.' No sah, Mr. Anson, I is done wid actresses de rest ob my nat'ral life, an' you hear what I say."

He kept his word and stayed with the party until we reached Chicago on our return, but he proved so utterly worthless and so trifling that, despite his dancing powers, we should not have been sorry had he been left in America.

While en route from Hastings to Denver, we met the St. Louis train at Oxford, Nebraska, and, while we were waiting the connection, Captain John Ward, accompanied by Ed Crane and Will Brown of the New Yorks, dusty and travel-stained, but none the less welcome, rushed in upon us. Brown was on his way home to spend the winter in California, and was still suffering from the broken thumb he received in St. Louis, in the World Championship series between the Browns and the New York team. Crane and Ward, however, had come to join the Australian party as members of the All-America team. President Spalding having brought Captain Manning with him from Kansas City and telegraphed for Earle at St. Paul, our party was complete at Denver, where Hengle, Long and "Old Silver," left us, to return to Chicago.

When we awoke for breakfast on the morning of the 27th, we were rolling over the beautiful prairie lands some fifty miles east of Denver. The air was clear and exhilarating, as it always seems to be at those high altitudes, and every man of the party declared himself in splendid condition, as a result of the cool, bracing atmosphere, and the anticipation of reaching the first really important stopping-place upon our journey across the continent. While at breakfast, the ladies of the party were the first to catch sight of the great snow-capped mountains, rising like a mirage in the distance, and as we drew near Denver, the outlines of the great piles of rock, with their beards of stately pine and fir, and their glistening summits, became more and more distinct, until one of the party ventured the opinion that they were not more than six or seven miles away. "They are forty-eight, sir," said the conductor, who happened to be passing at that moment and heard the remark, "they deceive nearly every one who looks at them for the first time and who is unaccustomed to estimating distances upon the prairies in high altitudes. It is no trick at all in this country to see from forty to fifty miles, and at some seasons of the year even further than that."

Denver is, in appearance as well as in fact, the metropolis of Colorado, and also of the entire country between that State and the Rocky Mountains. It is a beautiful city, inhabited by thrifty, enterprising people, who seem to make money easily and let it go unhesitatingly. They are great patrons of amusements of all kinds, great lovers of the good things of life, and consequently enthusiastic supporters of baseball. That they had been expecting us was clearly evident on every hand. Our coming had been well announced, and the private cars which had been side-tracked for our use at the depot were surrounded by visitors during the entire morning of our arrival. The parade in Denver was a showy one, and when the teams passed through the gate into the grounds, Manager Hart was having all he could do to handle the crowd. Here, as at Hastings, Clarence Duval's drum-major performance, as the teams came upon the field, was the signal for hearty laughter and applause. The crowd soon showed that although it had not had the privilege of witnessing league games through the season, it was perfectly familiar with every player that made up both the Chicago and the All-America teams; familiar not only with his personal appearance, but with his record, his position on the field, and his especially good qualities as a player. It was the more to be regretted, therefore, that the boys should not have put up a better game than the first of the two games played at Denver.

The field upon which they played, however, was not the best in the world, being hard in one spot and soft and sandy in another, while the fact that the players were unaccustomed to playing in such a rarefied atmosphere had much to do with the exhaustion of the base-runners. Denver had been accustomed to seeing much better ball-playing than the Australian teams gave them an exhibition of; and as they expected much better playing than they had ever before seen upon the home grounds between the local teams, they were naturally much disappointed. On the other hand, the further the game progressed the more annoyed and the more discouraged the players got, and the more stubborn and erratic the spirit which moved the ball. For instance, the ball would be batted straight at Williamson, and Pfeffer, seeing a chance for a double play, would run up to take the ball from the bat, short-stop at second. Just before it got to Williamson, however, ten to one it would bound clear over his head, or shoot between his knees, with the result, not only that a double play was spoiled, but that what looked like a very stupid error had been committed, and both in-fielders would return to their positions very much out of temper, and consequently more than ever liable to make new mistakes. It was a big crowd and a very enthusiastic one at the start, but the score of 16 to 12, by which the Chicago won the game, was a decidedly unsatisfactory one to the spectators, who had been accustomed to a much better rendering of the national game.

If we played a poor game on the day of our arrival, however, we more than made amends the following day, when, I think, the boys put up one of the prettiest contests that it has ever been my pleasure to witness. The crowd was perhaps not so large, but fully 4000 people gave their enthusiasm full vent, and at least half that number left the grounds with sore throats and with voices hoarse from cheering. Billy Earle, who had just joined the party at Denver, and Ed Crane and Van Haltren did the battery work for the All-Americas, while John Ward, playing with the team for the first time, covered "short" in a style that no one but Ward has mastered. That John was not unknown in Denver was clearly evident, for when he came to the plate in the opening inning the big crowd gave him a hearty welcome of applause. His clever and strategic batting pleased the spectators as well as did his fielding and base running, and he was cheered again and again as a reward for his efforts. Crane and Baldwin were both at their best in the box, and the former only gave way to Van Haltren in the eighth inning because he could no longer continue such hard pitching against the rarefied atmosphere. Van proved as formidable as Crane, and when the ninth inning was completed, with the pitchers working their hardest and the support of each man playing ball with their teeth set and bent upon winning the game, the crowd was in a state of suppressed interest and excitement that found vent at every opportunity, in the wildest cheers.

Some of the fielding work was superb, while the efforts of the base runners, despite their shortness of breath, kept the crowd howling through both of the extra innings played. It was Hanlon's catch, however, that caused the crowd to lose all control of itself. Almost out of sight into the blue air sailed the ball, and away across the field sped Hanlon at a rate that a professional sprinter would have been proud of; Sullivan, in the meantime, made the dust fly around the runways; just once Hanlon turned to look above, and then ran on again faster, if possible, than before. Suddenly, however, he stopped, turned his face to the crowd, ran backward for fifteen or twenty feet, then threw his hands above his head; at the same instant his heel struck a hillock of sand, and pitched him headlong through the air upon his back. As he fell, however, his right hand was held above him, and as he sprung to his feet the crowd saw that he held the ball. For probably five seconds that big assemblage held its breath, and then, as the famous outfielder started in for the diamond and the balance of the All-America players turned toward their bench, such a cheer went up as one rarely hears on the ball field. For baseball enthusiasts and lovers of the

ED HANLON'S GREAT CATCH AT DENVER.

game it was, indeed, a scene for an artist, and Hanlon was cheered and cheered until he paused to raise his cap in front of the grand stand. It was a magnificent game, and completely offset the disappointment which our game of the day before occasioned.

We left Denver the same evening for Colorado Springs, where we were announced to play upon the day following. Much to our regret, our broad gauge, splendidly equipped dining and sleeping cars were left at Denver, and our combination was transferred to two narrow-gauge sleepers especially reserved for us, in which we were to make our journey through the mountains over the Denver and Rio Grande Road. Compared with the spacious carriages we left behind, the narrow-gauge cars seemed like toy cars, but they were completely equipped for all that, and we had a world of fun in them before we left them at Ogden, in far-away Utah. Indeed, the only serious ground for revolt against our new accommodations that any of our party could discover was the narrow space of the sections, which crowded to no inconsiderable extent some of our four-handed poker parties who were desirous of wooing Dame Fortune in the same section. This reminds me that the poker element in our party had received an important addition in the person of Captain Anson's father, "Pa Anson," as we soon learned familiarly to call him, in order to distinguish him from his stalwart son. According to the old gentleman's theory there were but two sources of enjoyment in life; one was a ball game and the other was a good poker game. "Why," said the old gentleman, as his portly figure and ruddy face, despite his silver hair, told that he had enjoyed every day of life accorded him, "I would rather play poker and lose right along, than not to play at all."

We received a great send-off as the train pulled out of the Union Depot at Denver; every man seemed to have a score of friends to see him off, and every traveler about the Depot staid around our cars to get a glimpse of so celebrated an aggregation of ball players.

We arrived at Colorado Springs the following morning before day had fairly broken, and of all the delightful breaks in our journey across the country our visit to this Saratoga of Colorado was perhaps the most amusing and most prolific of pleasant incidents. Mr. Spalding had very thoughtfully telegraphed from Denver to have carriages and saddle-horses waiting our party at the depot by six o'clock upon the morning of our arrival, in order that we might enjoy a ride to Manitou and the Garden of the Gods, and when the colored porters awakened us, there was a scramble among the party to see which should first get into his clothes and out upon the platform for a first choice of horses and equipages. By seven o'clock, just as the sun was gilding the very top of "Old Pike," our party had entered three comfortable park wagons and mounted a dozen bronchos with enormous saddles, which really covered fully one-third of their sinewy little bodies. It was a beautiful drive, one that none of us will ever forget. Eighteen miles ahead of us and a little to the left, arose Pike's Peak, so massive and grand in its proportions that it looked, in the clear atmosphere of the morning, scarce five miles away. The bright sunlight brought out every crag and crevice upon its rugged old sides, and as we approached it it towered before us more imposing in its grandeur than all

IN A HURRY TO CATCH THE CONVEYANCES.

the descriptions we had read of it had prepared us for. To our extreme right we could just catch sight of the peaks of towering sandstone that form the Gateway to the Garden of the Gods, while before us twined the picturesque and well-beaten roadway through the valley.

Manitou was six miles distant. It is the summer resort of wealthy Western people, who have built attractive and Swiss-like residences upon the mountain sides and in the off-shooting valleys, that they might here enjoy the cool breezes and the mineral waters during the summer months. We dismounted at Manitou and drank of the delicious waters in the Silver Springs, after which we enjoyed a splendid breakfast at the Cliff House. Then resuming our horses and carriages we passed down the picturesque mountain road and a mile below turned off into a little valley which led to the rear entrance of the Garden of the Gods. The peculiar formations of sandstone to be seen in every shape and upon every side in this remarkable spot, have been described time and again by all travelers, who have doubtless felt, just as I feel, that their duty to their friends would not be fully discharged did they fail to write something descriptive of that spot which nature has so charmingly and fancifully designed. "Punch and Judy," "The Balanced Rock," "The Mushroom Rock," "The Duck," "The Frog," "The Lady of the Garden," and "The Kissing Camels," are all wonderfully true to the objects they are fancied to represent. The piles of sandstone reaching 330 feet into the air, forming the Gateway of the Garden, impress one as no description of these wonders could, with the matchless sublimity of the creative power. After admiring the many weird and remarkable things to be seen in this play-room of Nature, we passed through the Gateway, our equipages winding away through the valleys and then up the side of a hill for perhaps two miles, to the summit. Here we came out upon a broad plateau and, as we rounded the last turn in the roadway and stood upon the topmost ridge, a chorus of admiring exclamations went up from a score of voices as we caught sight of "Old Pike" rising before us in full view, and in all its impressive majesty, upon the other side of the little valley where nestled Manitou. Cheyenne Mountain lay, dark and sullen, to the left of the great snow-capped peak. Twenty-five miles away, distinct and clear as though but ten, there stretched the far-reaching ranges of the Rockies. Six miles away lay Colorado Springs, which we had left nearly six hours before, and for which we now drove at a brisk gait.

The ride home, over the hard mountain roads and in the clear morning air, was enjoyable, refreshing, invigorating. The Park wagons bowled along at a brisk speed, while Pettit, Carrol and Tom Brown, three of the best horsemen in our party, had a great race across the plateau, Pettit finally distancing both of his competitors. This reminds me of other equestrian experiences during the morning. Several of our party, a dozen, perhaps, rode bronchos, all of which were provided with the exaggerated saddles I have mentioned. President Spalding rode a bay gelding and, as he is quite a horseman, managed the hot-tempered beast admirably. Captain Anson bestrode a cross-eyed sorrel, which I afterwards learned had been the property of a Colorado cowboy. During the ride two or three head of mountain cattle became excited by the approach of our cavalcade and dashed on in front of us over the smooth roadway. Anson's sorrel, true to his early training, stuck his stubby tail out behind him, laid his ears back upon his head, and, with a vicious squeal, started after the now thoroughly-frightened longhorns. How "the old man" managed to stop his beast I do not know, but when we came up with him a quarter of a mile ahead, Anson was sitting down at the roadside and his horse was tied to a post near by. At Manitou the sorrel was turned over to Bob Pettit, and under Bob's master-touch the old ranger, who had plenty of spirit and bottom left, proved a better nag than all the others in the party.

Mark Baldwin rode a mustang which persisted in waltzing all over the road with his rider. The animal's antics and Mark's heavy weight finally broke the saddle-girth, and the big pitcher was pitched into the dust. He promptly turned his waltzer over to Sullivan, and the latter proved himself a horseman. Ed Crane rode a bay bolter, and rode so well that no one would believe his story that he had never been in a saddle before. Carroll and Tom Brown were both at home upon the sturdy little ponies, and the style in which they cut loose over the mountain roads caused the natives we met with to wonder at their recklessness. On the way back to the Springs Ward and Crane got separated from us in some way, and half an hour later, when the boys in uniform were seated in their carriages at the depot, ready to start for the grounds, two horsemen appeared away up on the side of the mountain, coming along the roadway, evidently with more regard for time than for their personal safety. Their sure-footed ponies brought them down all right, however, and a few moments later Ward steered his mustang into a post at the depot, grasped him about the neck with both arms, and took a slide over his head that would have won him a big burst of applause had he been able to get it off in the same style on the diamond. Crane could not stop his horse at all. The animal had evidently been out on such jaunts before, and was positively bent upon repeating an old and familiar trick. With the bit in his teeth, he kept on through the town for the stable, and Crane had to roll off of him as he finally shot through the low door of the barn. We could not wait for Ward to dress, and so drove to the grounds; but John was equal to the occasion. He called a boy to hold his pony, and, donning his uniform in the car, remounted and rode

HOME RUNS OF A STARTLING SORT.

to the grounds *a la* Paul Revere, save that he wore the uniform of the All-Americas instead of the Continentals.

The Denver and Rio Grande Railway people had promised to hold the train for us an hour, if necessary, and had they done so we would have had ample time to finish the game in good style. We had scarcely begun, however, before we received word that the train could not be held over fifteen minutes, and this fact being communicated to the players they were at once seized with a desire to get through, even at the cost of good ball-playing. The result was that they became nervous. The glaring sun shone down from a confusingly "high" sky, and, to make matters worse, not a man could run bases without nearly dropping, from short wind, as the result of the rarefied air. As at Denver, the crowd knew what good ball-playing was, and naturally felt dissatisfied with such an exhibition, but there was no help for it. The boys could not have put up a better game, under the circumstances, to have saved their lives, and at the conclusion of the sixth inning, with the score 13 to 9 in favor of Chicago, we piled into our carriages amid the jeers of the crowd, which, by the way, was an extremely fashionable one, and cut loose, amidst a cloud of dust, for the depot. So great was the hurry that we might easily have left two or three of our party and not have known it. However, all the players managed to keep our carriages in sight, and our party was intact when we reached the depot.

"All right?" shouted the conductor, questioningly, as he looked at President Spalding and prepared to wave his hand to the engineer.

"All right, I guess," said Mr. Spalding, doubtfully. But just then he happened to catch sight of a cloud of dust away up the roadway, and, looking anxiously towards it, he called out to the conductor to hold on for a moment, at least. The cloud of dust rapidly became larger, and as it neared us we could see that it surrounded a horseman who was sparing neither himself nor his beast to lessen the distance between himself and our train. As he came nearer we recognized Jim Hart. Jim, it seemed, had remained behind at the grounds to settle the question of finances with the local ground authorities. When he had finished counting his cash he discovered that the party had left him. With two bags of silver, weighing probably fifteen pounds apiece, with three miles between himself and the railroad station, and with the time of departure but a few minutes off, the situation was certainly a serious one. It was by no means too small a hole for Manager Jim to pull out of, however, and, seizing the first mustang that he could lay his hands on, without regard to the arrangements of the owner, he slung his twin saddle-bags across the neck of the mustang, and commenced his race for the train. When Jim reached us he was covered with dust, the perspiration was streaming down his face, his collar was in a state of complete dissolution, his trousers had worked half-way up to his knees, and his silk hat, badly in need of an ironing, was jammed down over his face, while he clung desperately to the sacks with one hand and endeavored to guide his by no means mild-spirited mustang with the other. His appearance was too much for the risibilities of our party, and we howled with laughter as we drew his exhausted form upon the rear platform of the now moving train. I am very sure no member of our party will ever forget Colorado Springs, and it is not at all likely that Colorado Springs will ever forget the Australian Baseball party.

Soon after leaving Colorado Springs we entered the mountains, and about the hour of sunset we steamed into the Grand Cañon of the Arkansas. At the mouth of the cañon, an observation car, with a seating capacity of about 100 people, was attached to the rear of the train, and into this we crowded. Then right into the heart of the mountains plunged the puffing pair of engines that drew us. Immense walls of rock rose hundreds of feet upon each side of the track, and the head waters of the Arkansas river boiled and frothed in the mountain gorge below us, while the narrow-gauge line of railway twisted and turned upon its way through the grim chasms, so narrow, so deep, and so dark that at times we wondered if we should ever emerge from them. Soon we swung into the Royal Gorge, over the suspended bridge that spans the torrent at this point, and then on through the bowels of the mountains where the sunlight has not reached, mayhap for centuries, and as I looked upon the massive piles of rock that lie in awful disorder, or rise in towering spires,—the thought came unbidden—how fearful must have been the convulsions, and how terrible the throes through which old " Mother Earth" passed ere these imposing masses were piled in such wild confusion. We stopped at little mountain station of Solida for supper and then steamed upon our way for Marshall Pass, which may, without doubt, be classed among the grandest stretches of mountain scenery in the world. Our train was divided into two sections, of which the sleepers constituted one. Each section was drawn by two powerful engines and up the sides of these towering mountains we climbed, our trains being, perhaps, a mile apart. The moon had not risen, and the great cliffs and gorges were shrouded in impenetrable darkness.

Across the chasm on our right moved the lighted train of coaches forming the first section, four hundred feet above us, the furnace doors of the engines wide open, the smoke-stacks sending forth showers of red-hot sparks and smoke, which looked like liquid fire as they plunged into the precipice, along the edge of which the train was running.

"Is there any bottom to this chasm?" asked one of our party of the conductor who had joined us at the window.

"Well, there is no telling that," replied the officer; "a freight train rolled off there a few months ago and we never heard of any of them since, but we could see bits of the cars sticking to the sides of the cañon, not bigger than so many pieces of kindling wood. If there is any bottom to it, I never have seen the man that has found it."

Silence, like a mantle, fell upon the little group at our window as the conductor spoke, for we all knew that within a few minutes our train would be passing that identical spot, with a mass of towering granite on one side and an impenetrable chasm on the other. The wheels of our little sleeper hugged the steel rails closely, however, and ultimately we stopped on the back-bone of the great dividing range of America, 10,858 feet above the level of the sea. As the train stopped we all jumped from the coaches, and stood knee deep in the snow along the side of the tracks. Imagine it. Six hours before we had been playing ball under a hot sun at Colorado Springs, and now we were indulging in a game of snowball on the top of the Rocky Mountains. From Marshall Pass our journey was down hill, of course. We had left the country of the Missouri and the Mississippi and were descending the Pacific slope. The views of mountain scenery we had enjoyed thus far had surpassed anything that any of our party had anticipated, but the greatest of all was still to come. We were due at the Black Cañon of the Gunnison at midnight, and a goodly number of us determined not to retire until we had seen it. Ned Hanlon, Manning, Earle and myself clung to the hand-rails of the rear platform of our sleeper, and gazed in silence at the wonders of this world-famed chasm as they were revealed to us by the ruddy glare of the furnace and the light of the stars which peered through the crevices of the giant rocks. Rounding a curve suddenly, we came upon the great Currecanti Needle, a slender spire of rock that rises from the centre of the cañon until its point seems to touch the very stars above. Winding past its base our train shot into a narrow crevice, and the great needle disappeared as suddenly as it had burst upon our view. Impressive in the depth of its solitude, overpowering in its grandeur, and terrible in its suggestions as to the causes which produced it, the Black Cañon of the Gunnison is most appropriately named.

It was nearly three o'clock when we left the cañon, but no one of those who remained awake to witness its grand scenery will ever regret the sleep they lost. We awoke for breakfast at Green river, and after leaving that point entered the mountains of Utah. All day long our train wound round the base of big mud-colored hills, stopping occasionally at little settlements, the inhabitants of which were Indians, China-

CURRECANTI NEEDLE.

men and rough-looking frontiersmen. How they live or what they live upon, the passing traveler cannot imagine. On the evening of the 30th we reached Salt Lake City, and that night occupied beds for the first time since we left Chicago. Captain Fogarty, Tom Daly, Tom Brown, Mart Sullivan, Billy Earle, John Healy, Leslie Robison and myself were up bright and early the following morning, for a horseback ride through the environs of the Mormon stronghold, and, as our horses were fiery and eager to go, we did some tall riding through the picturesque country, finally drawing rein before the Parade Ground at Fort Douglas, in time to witness the dress parade of four companies of troops. After watching their evolutions for a while, we rode through the officers' quarters, and admired the pretty wives and daughters of Uncle Sam's soldiers as they sat upon the balconies of their residences, becomingly attired and enjoying the fresh breeze from the mountains. The view of the valley in which lies the city is a grand one from this point.

We found a good ball park at Salt Lake City, but a heavy storm interrupted our first game, and rendered the grounds unfit for our second. This prevented any model exhibitions of ball-playing, although the conditions under which we played were productive of any amount of fun for the spectators. Some twelve hundred people attended the first game. But a drenching rain stopped play in the first half of the fifth inning, just as All-America was beginning to bat the cover off the ball. It rained all night, and the mud in the streets and on the runways of the ball park was very soft and affectionate. Indeed, the conditions could not have been more antagonistic to good ball-playing. The outfield was in places covered with water, and the black muck on the runways was only hidden by two or three inches of sawdust which covered it; yet in spite of all, the game was full of interesting situations, and afforded two hours of good sport. Wood, Van Haltren, Manning and Ward did some beautiful infield work, and the All-America team entire had their batting clothes on from the time the game began. The black mud on the runways gradually worked itself up through the sawdust, and soon had our boys looking like a lot of street laborers in rainy weather. The white traveling suits of the All-Americas suffered sadly from the desperate base-sliding of their owners, while Tom Daly's swimming feat in centre field caused the crowd to double up with fits of laughter. It was a good game from the start to the finish, with as much kicking and warm rivalry as anybody could ask for, notwithstanding that the score was a jug-handled one in favor of the All-Americas.

We left Salt Lake the same evening, and as we assembled in the rotunda of the hotel for supper, fully two hundred people were present to shake hands with our party and bid them farewell, the boys having made scores of friends and admirers, notwithstanding their brief stay in the Mormon stronghold. While waiting for departure time, Clarence Duvall entertained the assemblage by his "baton performance and the plantation walk-around," John Healy and Fred Pfeffer acting as his orchestra. Salt Lake City had never witnessed a similar performance, and a storm of applause, together with a handful of silver, rewarded the Mascot's efforts. We got away from the Walker House in a big omnibus that was long enough to accommodate our entire combination of thirty-five people, and as we rolled through the streets to the depot, shortly after nightfall, we sang the favorite chorus of "Old Silver:"—

THE MASCOT IN REPOSE.

"Hide away; hide away;
Dere is no use to try to hide away.
Get your baggage on de deck,
Don't forget to get your check;
For dere's no use to try to hide away."

And as we drew up to the station platform, Jim Fogarty, with a preliminary call of three cheers for Salt Lake City and the people in it, led the party in an ear-splitting yell that startled a sleeping baggage-man off his truck, and caused an old lady to drop her band-boxes and make for the station, screaming "Help!" "Police!" at every jump, while the station-master for the moment seriously contemplated turning in the fire alarm.

"It is only them consarned, frisky baseball people," yelled a hackman, and then everybody but the old lady laughed. Our train was twenty minutes late, and during this interim Clarence danced for us, and somebody getting out the banjos and mandolins with which our party was supplied, we soon had the populace of the vicinity running to the station to see "the minstrel company that had just come to town," as a small boy put it. Of course, the mischief makers of the party were not idle long. John Healy stood apart from his companions with his grip at his feet, gazing at the top of a distant mountain and seemingly absorbed in reflection, possibly of home, or of the thousands of miles of our journey yet incompleted, when Tom Daly crept up behind him and dropped upon all fours. Just then Fogarty slapped the big pitcher vigorously on the shoulder, and John's heels went up in the air as he did a back somersault over Daly's back. John's training had not been neglected, however, and one of his long legs flew out in time to catch Tom under the coat tails, sending him sprawling into the crowd.

HEALY'S DAY-DREAMS RUDELY BROKEN.

At Ogden we found two special sleepers awaiting us, and departed at midnight for San Francisco. The following day seemed an unusually long one to every member of our party, for the three thousand miles which we had arranged to cover between Chicago and the Pacific slope was becoming just a bit tiresome. All day long we rolled over the prairie lands of Utah and Nevada, the great mountains looming up in the horizon, twenty and even thirty miles away. Looking from the windows of our cars we saw droves of big jack-rabbits jump from their hiding-places and cut off across the prairies. Now and then a gaunt wolf or coyote would skulk from beneath a sage bush and draw sullenly away from the train. We caught sight of one pack of half a dozen of these brutes during the afternoon. Away they ran for a little distance, and then sat with their lips turned back from their fangs, snarling at our train for having disturbed them. Great cattle ranches stretched away up the broad valleys through which we were passing, and thousands of sleek-looking animals browsed upon the grasses which grew so luxuriantly along the streams which crossed the meadows. It was, indeed, a grand section, and until one has traveled it he can form no conception of how broad, and rich, and unequaled by those of any other in the world, are the great pasture-lands of the United States.

Upon the following morning, that of November 3d, we found upon awakening that we had entered a section of country vastly different from that over which we had ridden during the preceding day. The views were not of barren rocks and mud-colored hills, like those in Utah, nor like the broad valley lands of Nevada, but of lofty mountains rich in verdure; and, as we proceeded, the elevations widened into beautiful valleys and the mountains gave way to lovely hills adorned with thousands of green trees. As we neared Sacramento we seemed to be in a veritable Garden of Eden. We partook of a delightful breakfast at Sacramento, at which the tables were loaded with rosy apples, delicious pears, yellow and red streaked peaches, and great bunches of grapes, all the product of that rich fruit-producing district. We had been expected by the baseball enthusiasts of the city, and there was quite a crowd at the depot. The cheers they sent up as we pulled out of the big station twenty minutes later reminded us of our departure from Denver and Chicago.

Beyond the city, we rolled through the rich valley of the Sacramento, through prosperous fruit ranges, and past grape vineyards that stretched away as far as the eye could reach, until our train pulled up at the little station of Suisun, thirty miles from San Francisco. Here a pleasant surprise had been prepared for us. Manager Hart, together with Frank Lincoln and Fred Carroll, had gone on to "Frisco" in advance of the party from Salt Lake City, and together with a score of Pacific coast baseball managers, and representatives of the entire San Francisco Press, had come out to bid us welcome. The first intimation of their presence was a chorus of cheers that went up as our train stopped, followed by a scurrying of feet across the station platform and the jarring of our sleepers as the delegation sprang upon them. Among those who had come to welcome us in addition to Hart, Carroll and Lincoln, were Tom Mackay, the ubiquitous and widely known passenger-man of the Burlington; Messrs. D. D. Robinson and J. F. Moran, of the Greenwood and Moran Club; Eugene Vancourt, Al Foreman, and Messrs. Dressler, Batchelder, Cory, Crawford and Bannett, representing the San Francisco Press; together with Managers Harris and Finn, all good fellows, and prominent representatives of the newspaper and baseball fraternity of California. At Port Costa the following telegram was handed President Spalding:—

"SAN FRANCISCO, November 3d, 1888.
"A. G. SPALDING, of Spalding's Australian Baseball Tour:
"We welcome you to our city and to the Baldwin Hotel. You will find carriages waiting at the foot of Market street. E. J. BALDWIN."

At Oakland we took the Steamer which bore us across San Francisco Bay to the great metropolis of the Pacific coast. We found carriages in waiting, and fifteen minutes after we landed we were quartered in our rooms at the Baldwin Hotel, but not to rest. Manager Hart had notified half a dozen of us while on the Steamer to don our dress suits immediately upon our arrival at the hotel. At six o'clock, that number of the party, in evening dress, had assembled in the rotunda, where we found awaiting us representatives of the San Francisco Press and the California Baseball League. They escorted us to "Marchand's," where we partook of a dainty supper, topped off with most delicious California wines. Those present were Mr. Spalding, Captain

Anson, Captain Ward, Frank Lincoln, Newton MacMillin, Manager Jim Hart, Managers Harrison, Robinson and Finn, Messrs. Cory, Dressler, Crawford, Bannett and myself. Lincoln's wit and the baseball reminiscences of Jim Hart and Mr. Spalding shortened the time between the courses most delightfully, and at 8.30 we arose from the table, having had our first experience of San Francisco hospitality.

Repairing to the Baldwin Theatre we joined the balance of the Chicago and All-America teams, in full evening costume, and occupied the two proscenium boxes at the performance of "The Corsair." It is needless to say that the party were objects of interest to the audience. We reached San Francisco on the evening of the great parade of the Republicans of California, and the city was fairly alive with people. Market street was a long line of colored fire and pyrotechnics, while cheers ascended in such volume as to almost deafen one. The entire populace of the city and of all California seemed to have joined in the demonstration, and it was well on toward morning before even honest people went to bed. Were the members of our party among the revellers? Well, in all probability most of them could have been found very near the centre of the city, as long as the glare of the parade, the crowds and the handshaking of friends kept them there. With our arrival at San Francisco, most of us felt that the first stage of our trip was completed. Here we were to stop for two weeks before starting on our voyage, so we felt that we were at home for a time, at least. "Two weeks," did I say? Never before did time pass so rapidly to any of us, and when the day came for final adieus, and the big steamer cast off her cables and started upon her journey of 7200 miles, there was not a man among us who would not gladly have extended his stay indefinitely.

In no section of the United States possessing the same population to the square mile are Baseball enthusiasts more numerous than at San Francisco. They can play ball there all the year round, and their championship season begins when the seasons of the League and Association end. They have turned out some of the greatest ball-playing talent in America to-day, such men as Fogarty, Brown, Van Haltren, Brown, of New York, and others of equal ability and reputation, having come from the Pacific slope to don the uniforms of the great Eastern Clubs. In San Francisco they like close scores. They want no errors, and they would rather see a sixteen innings game than shake hands with the President. The clubs of their own League, through several seasons past, have put up a wonderful number of closely-contested games, in which it has been the exception that the combined runs of both teams in a game has exceeded eight or nine in number. They seem to gauge a player in California rather by his ability to stop runs than to get them. Yet, at the time of our visit to California, many of the most brilliant, skillful, and difficult-fielding players of the ball field were comparatively unknown in California. Indeed, it was not until Jim Hart took the Louisville Team there, in 1885, that Californians were enabled to understand just what degree of perfection in team-work and fielding a ball team could attain. When the Australian party visited the coast, the infield work of Williamson, Pfeffer, Ward, Burns, and Anson was a revelation to most Californians.

Something over 13,000 people turned out at the Haight street grounds to witness our initial game in San Francisco, and it has never ceased to be one of the regrets of the tour that the game did not prove a contest, or even a creditable exhibition. The day was perfect, and thousands lined the streets through which our carriages passed in parade on their way to the grounds. Cheer after cheer welcomed the players as the gates of the grounds were thrown open and the carriages filed upon the field. The great crowd arose to its feet and shouted itself hoarse as the band escorted first the All-Americas and then the Chicagos on to the grounds. The practice work of both teams was brilliant, and had the game been anywhere near as good, the expectant and good-natured crowd would have been entirely satisfied. The boys, however, were tired out with travel and the late hours they could hardly have avoided keeping after their arrival in San Francisco. In addition, every one of them was over-anxious to put up a strong game of ball, and their over-anxiety made them the more nervous as the game progressed. I never saw men work harder or try more determinedly to play good ball; but it was of no use. Anson himself "fell down" at first before two innings had passed. Baldwin, who had pitched such a grand game at Denver, seemed to have little or no command of the ball, and Chicago's stone-wall infield seemed unable to field a little bit. The crowd was disappointed but good-natured, and generously applauded the occasional bits of good fielding that shone through the long series of errors. As for the players themselves, I do not think I ever saw a more completely disappointed lot of men. Had each of them been out a hundred-dollar note as the result of the day's play, they could not have felt more dissatisfied; but they sensibly put a bright face upon the situation and determined to show Californians what kind of a game they could put up before they left.

The second day after, the All-Americas faced the Greenwood and Moran team at the Haight street grounds and suffered a crushing defeat. Crane was unsteady in his delivery, and although his support worked hard, it made errors at critical points, while the local batsmen rarely failed to get in a hit at the proper time. Unfortunately for the All-Americas, Anson acted as umpire and gave Captain Ward's men a long way the worst of it in most of his decisions. But for this fact the score would undoubtedly have been less one-sided.

Two days later the All-Americas met the Pioneers and John Healy pitched. It would undoubtedly have been a winning game but for the poor fielding support accorded him. A total of eleven errors, most of them costly, were divided up among Hanlon, Crane, Manning, Van Haltren, Wood and Fogarty. The absence of Ward, who had yielded to an inclination to run up the bay for a day's quail shooting, made a big hole in All-America's infield, and was, no doubt, responsible to a great degree for the poor work that resulted. Purcell pitched a fine game for the Pioneers, and to his work more than to anything else was due the victory which 3000 spectators applauded heartily at the end of the ninth inning. Meantime Anson's men had gone down to Stockton, and while the All-Americas were losing a game in San Francisco, were engaged in one of the prettiest games of the tour with the Stocktons. Tener did some pretty work in the points for Chicago, Stockton's batsmen failing to get more than two clean hits off Tener's delivery. It was too dark at the end of the ninth inning to play off the tie, which stood two and two, and the game was consequently never won.

Stockton came up to San Francisco the following day, November 9th, to see what it could do against the All-Americas, and the latter, stung by two successive defeats at the hands of local California teams, turned upon the champions and gave them such a beating as doubtless left a lasting impression of the fielding and batting abilities of Ward's team. Ward himself covered short and his presence made a wonderful difference. The Stocktons pitched Baker, who at that time was one of the promising pitchers of the coast, and he was simply pounded all over the field. The game was certainly a beautiful exhibition of the strong points in baseball. Crane pitched a great game, and little Earle caught him in a style that won him many hearty bursts of applause. Hanlon covered third, while Van Haltren fielded centre, and smoother team-work than that done by the entire combination is not often seen. The base running was particularly good. Just how hard the boys worked, and how determined they were to make the Stocktons feel their power, can be seen by reference to the score, which shows a total of 17 stolen bases, of which 7 were taken by Fogarty alone. In a word, All-America taught the Californian champions a good deal that they did not before know about the game, and after that, neither the Stocktons nor the Pioneers would meet either the All-America or the Chicago teams during our stay. On November 10th the crack Haverlys had a try at Anson's men and were well beaten in a pretty contest. Incell, the star pitcher of the coast, and one whom many of the Eastern clubs were after at that time, filled the box for the Californians and pitched a good game, although his support was weak. The Californians, on the other hand, could not hit Baldwin, and the big lead Chicago had secured in the third inning, was not thereafter broken.

The work of the visiting teams against the local talent had served to offset the rather unfavorable impression created by the character of our first game in San Francisco, and there were nearly 7000 people present a week later, when, on a beautiful day, the Chicago and All-America teams met upon the Haight street grounds for their second game, which, while not without a dash of poor work here and there, was marked by fielding of a character that I have never seen surpassed for brilliancy. Tener and Van Haltren were the opposing pitchers, and each pitched effectively, although Van Haltren's in-field support was at times faulty. Chicago's in-field, however, at no time during its entire existence ever put up such a wonderful fielding game, and the enthusiasm of the crowd knew no bounds at half a dozen stages of the contest.

The following week the teams went to Los Angeles, where, upon

November 14th and 15th, they played two games in the presence of several thousand Southern Californians. All-America played all around Anson's men in both games, whitewashing them in the first game, with Healy and Earle in the box and Baldwin and Daly as the opposing battery, and beating them by a score of 7 to 4 in the second game, with Crane and Earle in the points against Tener and Daly for Chicago. The teams returned to San Francisco on Friday morning, the 16th. It was intended that a farewell game should be played the following day, on the eve of our departure for Australia. The elements decided otherwise, however, and a steady rain killed all plans for a farewell contest. Our steamer, which was to have sailed Saturday afternoon, was delayed twenty-four hours by the non-arrival of the Eastern mails, however, and we did not get away, in consequence, until the afternoon of Sunday, November 18th.

It must not be inferred from this account of our stay in California that we did nothing but play ball. On the contrary, the boys were simply overwhelmed with attentions from so many different quarters, that it became impossible to accept all the invitations extended, or to find time for sleep between the many pleasant entertainments arranged for us. The little supper which some of us had enjoyed at Marchand's on the night of our arrival, was simply a forerunner of the long line of banquets, dinner parties, receptions and theatre parties which extended over the entire period of our stay. Nearly every member of our party managed to take a tour through the Chinese quarters, and Bob Pettit, Captain Anson, Tom Daly and myself enjoyed not a few delightful rides on horseback around the picturesque environs of the city.

The remarkable sights to be seen in Chinatown proved so attractive that many of our party made two, and some of them three, visits among these Children of the Orient. I made the journey the second night after our arrival at San Francisco, in company with President Spalding, Manager Robinson and President Mann of the California League, Manager Hart and Newton MacMillan, the *Sun* correspondent, our escort being Sergeant Burdsoll of the San Francisco Police Force, and I feel that I am quite safe in saying that no pen, however clever, could adequately depict the revolting, and yet fascinating, sights we saw. The illustrations of vice and crime prevalent in the Chinese quarters of the city, which have appeared in our illustrated publications from time to time, have not been exaggerated—indeed, they have fallen far short of depicting the horror of it. Chinatown is perhaps six blocks long by three wide, and it is steadily growing. The Celestials have crowded all the white people out of their district, and have their own government, their own mercantile houses, their own water works and their own courts; and although they are under the City Authorities, to a great extent they live independently of the municipal laws. It is almost impossible to apprehend a criminal among them, and equally difficult to convict him when apprehended. They have established their gambling-houses within walls of impenetrable steel plate. The sentinel stands at the doorway, and in dangerous times gives signal, that they may shut out intruders. As we passed one of these houses Sergeant Burdsoll pointed out to me the picket on duty in front of the brilliantly-lighted passage which entered the building.

"That fellow," said the Sergeant, "looks half asleep, doesn't he?"

The Chinaman was leaning against the doorway, his hat pulled over his features and his hands tucked way under his blouse.

"Yes," replied our party, "he certainly doesn't look as though he is attending to his post."

"Well now, you just watch him," said the Sergeant, and pulling his hat over his eyes, he sauntered slowly across the street until he reached the curbstone, where he made a sudden dash for the doorway. The seemingly sleeping Celestial, however, started as though suddenly touched by an electric wire. He threw both hands across the doorway, barring the officer's progress, and at the same time uttered a peculiar cry. Ten feet beyond the doorway we could see the heavy steel-plated inner doors close with a bang, and almost at the same instant the outer doors came to with a crash, and the Chinese sentry was left standing upon the pavement in the presence of the officer. The Sergeant returned to us, and remarked, with a smile, that a Chinaman is never so watchful as when he appears to be asleep. "That fellow as he stood there," said the Sergeant, "was sweeping the street with his glance in both directions for half a block."

"Can you not batter down their doors and make prisoners of them?" I asked.

The officer smiled. "My dear sir," said he, "it would take three hours to enter these places, and when we got in, not a Chinaman would be inside. What would be the use of it, any way? No power on earth can check the crime and vice that exist in these quarters to-day. I might have arrested that sentinel whom the closing of the doors left upon the sidewalk, but what good would it have done? I could have brought him before a Police Court, and might have arraigned him upon the charge of resisting an officer, or of vagrancy, or upon some other convenient charge, but he would probably have been fined and let go; and even though imprisoned, his fine would have been paid and he would have been let go, and even while he was imprisoned there would have been hundreds of Chinamen to take his place at the Gambling House door."

The methods of living and the crowded conditions of the dwellings in the Chinese quarter are simply beyond the power of human conception until seen. Many a Chinaman, for instance, will lease a building four stories high and by deepening the foundations will make a six-story building of it. Then he will construct partitions in the rooms and hallways until he has secured accommodations for about four or six hundred Chinamen in a building which could not accommodate more than thirty or forty Americans comfortably. These apartments he rents to Chinamen for twenty-five or fifty cents a week. One room which we entered was eight by ten feet in dimensions, with a ceiling perhaps eight feet high, and in this room, reclining upon bunks arranged like the sections of a sleeping-car, were thirteen Chinamen. Their bunks are practically their rooms—their dwellings, in which they keep their personal effects, their clothing, their little tin box in which they cook their rice, their chop sticks, their slippers and their opium outfit, without which no Chinaman could exist. The streets of the entire district swarm with Mongolians, the only Caucasians to be seen being the officers of the law, or tourists like ourselves. Into foul-smelling lodging-houses, into opium joints thick with sickening vapors, down through underground passage ways, where it would be death for a white man to go alone, into Joss Houses, with their hideous idols, their burning tapers and their weird-sounding drums and tom-toms, into the din and through the fantastic surroundings of the Chinese Theatre, with hordes of almond-eyed, villanous-looking, and at times murderous faces peering at us from every nook and corner, our little party threaded its way. We grew dizzy from the overpowering odors, and were anxious to again breathe the air of a Christianized and civilized community. No religion save idolatry is known in Chinatown; virtue is unknown there. The people have brought the heathenish customs and horrible practices of their barbarous country with them to San Francisco, and cling to them with a tenacity that shows the hopelessnes of converting them to our views of life and religion and of their ever becoming desirable citizens.

The attentions of which our party were the recipients did not, by any means, come from the baseball element alone, although to the officers of the California League we are indebted for much of the warm hospitality that made our stay in their city so pleasant. The journalists of San Francisco and the merchants were equally attentive and courteous. Mr. Waller Wallace, of the California *Spirit of the Times*, entertained President Spalding, Captain and Mrs. Anson, Mr. and Mrs. Ed Williamson, Captain John M. Ward, Captain Hanlon, Newton MacMillan and myself, in charming style, at his Oakland residence; while the Press Club, on the evening of November 12th, entertained the Press representatives of our party, with President Spalding and Captains Ward and Anson, in a delightful entertainment and banquet at the Press Club rooms. Upon the following day a number of us were entertained at the Merchants' Club, by Mr. Frederick Stratton, the law partner of Ex-Congressman Miller, the Hon. Charles Alexander Bird, of the California State legislature, Mr. Al Evans, Secretary of the Bonanza and Consolidated California Mining Companies, and a number of merchants of high standing upon the coast. All seemed to be as familiar with baseball as they were with mining stocks, mercantile methods, briefs and depositions, or legislative affairs; and a more congenial company, capable of more thoroughly enjoying the many reminiscences and stories of old-time players, certainly never sat down to a two hours' dinner.

On the evening of November 17th, the day prior to our departure for Australia, Mr. Spalding tendered a farewell banquet to the members of the San Francisco Press and California League at the Baldwin Hotel.

Covers were laid for seventy-five guests, among whom were many prominent, well-known citizens. The banquet hall and tables were magnificently decorated with designs in which baseball paraphernalia and implements were a prominent feature. Perhaps, the menu card, which was the result of Frank Lincoln's ingenuity, was among the most remarkable ever laid opposite a plate. On the inner side of the " Score Card," as Frank had designated his production, was printed the list of viands, headed with the timely injunction, " Play Ball." Among the courses were "Eastern Oysters on the Home Run," " Green Turtle, a la Kangaroo," " Petit Pate, a la Spalding," " Asperges, a la Willow," " Petit Pois Française, a la 'Over the Fencé,' " " Stewed Terrapin, a la Ward," " Frisco Turkey, a la 'Foul,' " " Mashed Peaches, a la 'Soft Ball,'" "Baked Sweet Potatoes, a la 'Hot Grounder,'" " English Plum Pudding, a la 'Hard Hit,' " " Brandy, a la ' Hot Ball,' " and other equally remarkable dishes. The menu card was circular in form, its exterior representing the cover of a baseball. There were many delightful evenings spent before the tour of the American team was completed, but I am sure that none was more delightful than that of our farewell banquet at San Francisco.

The speech-making was of an impromptu order, the remarks of the speakers being filled with baseball nuggets, happy sayings and humorous incidents. " Early California ball-players," by Judge Hunt, of the Superior Court, fairly bubbled with quiet humor and bristled with quaint allusion; "The National League Champions—the New York Baseball Club," was responded to by ex-Senator James F. Grady, of New York, who paid a magnificent tribute to the great team that won the championship of 1888. "The San Francisco Press," was treated by Mr. W. N. Hart, of the San Francisco Press Club. "The Good Ship 'Alameda,'" brought Captain Henry G. Morse to his feet and gave our party our first view of the good-hearted, clever commander of the steamer which carried us 7000 miles across the Pacific. "A. J. Spalding and the Australian Trip," was responded to by Mr. Samuel F. Shortridge; "Old California," by Mr. Durkee; "The Chicago Nine," by Captain Anson; "The All-Americas," by Captain Ward; and "The Baseball Cricketers," by George Wright. In a happily worded address, President Spalding thanked the Press and the Baseball people of the Pacific coast for the magnificent reception tendered us, and for the warm hospitality that we had not failed to find in every quarter since our arrival at San Francisco.

On the afternoon of the day of our departure a number of the boys went down to the dock to inspect the "Alameda." She was by no means a large ship, but was neat and trim-looking, perfectly equipped, and with room enough to accommodate 125 passengers. The decks were spacious, and in the warmer latitudes were to be protected from the sun's rays by an awning. A well-stocked library and saloon was located just above the dining-room, and forward and aft of this were the deck state-rooms, the most desirable upon the ship in tropical climates, also a big smoking- and card-room, where the boys congregated many an evening during the voyage or spent the lazy hours of the afternoon. Altogether, we were favorably impressed with our steamer and our captain, and despite our regret at leaving the hospitable shores of California, we were anxious for the novelty of starting upon our voyage to Australia.

The day of our departure finally arrived, Sunday, November 18th, and it dawned gray and sullen, with the rain still descending in a generous shower. Toward noon, however, the clouds broke and we began to hope for fair weather. None of the boys breakfasted at an early hour, it being fully 11 A. M. before they began to show up in any numbers in the rotunda of the hotel. About noon, myself and my fellow correspondent, Newton MacMillan, or "Mac," as I shall hereafter refer to him, accompanied by several San Francisco journalists, entered a carriage and drove to the steamer. The wharf-house and the steamer itself were crowded with friends of the tourists, and a chorus of shouts went up as our party of newspaper men emerged from our equipage. Not over eighty passengers had been booked for the voyage, but several hundred were upon the steamer's deck, friends of the departing tourists, and fully a thousand more crowded the wharf. At the rail, near the staging, stood Manager Jim Hart, Captain and Mrs. Anson and Ned Williamson and his wife, chatting with scores of friends, while President and Mrs. Spalding were the centre of another group near by. The boys leaned over the rail and chatted, and joked, and laughed their farewells with friends on the dock. All was noise and confusion up to two o'clock, the hour at which the steamer was to sail, when the last call for visitors to leave the deck was given. Shortly after that hour Captain Morse took his post at the starboard end of "the bridge," his big figure set off to advantage by his gold-laced uniform of navy blue, and raised his hand to the sailors on the gang-plank, and to those who stood by the steamer's moorings on the dock. There was breathless silence on board, the quick rattling of the chains, the splashes of the cables as they fell into the water, the thud of the gang-plank as it dropped on the deck, and then the "Alameda" began to move slowly from the dock. Every passenger pressed toward the rail, and cheer after cheer went up from the deck, to be answered by those on the wharf.

FROM SAN FRANCISCO TO HONOLULU.

The big ship swung slowly out into the bay, and within a few minutes all we could distinguish of our friends on the dock was a dimly outlined aggregation, and now and then a flutter of a white handkerchief. Presently the ship headed for the Golden Gate and we were off upon our tour of the World. Ah, it was delightfully invigorating—the motion of the ship, the refreshing air that came from the headlands and rushed through the rigging as she glided rapidly over the smooth surface of the Bay, past the shipping, and around the peninsula upon which San Francisco is located, our party still lingering at the larboard-rail, loath to relinquish their gaze upon their country's shores. As we neared the bar the ocean swell became perceptible; and when we passed the bluffs that form the Golden Gate, and steamed out upon the bosom of old Ocean itself, the "Alameda" began to rise and fall with the long swell that characterizes the Pacific from coast to coast. The sun was shining when we left the dock, but the weather was erratic, and before we were fairly out of sight of the coast the land was hidden by a fog which settled around our ship and rendered necessary the frequent sounding of the whistle. Some ten miles out we stopped to let off our pilot, and then proceeded on our journey, bound for Honolulu, a distance of 2100 miles.

In addition to our own party, which numbered thirty-five, there were perhaps twenty-five others. Among the most conspicuous of these was a big, broad-shouldered, dark-complexioned man, who looked as though he would be a perfect terror in a "free for all." This was Prof. William Miller, the wrestler, whose name is known in professional circles and among lovers of athletics all over the world. He and his wife were bound for Melbourne. A somewhat effeminate, sandy-haired young man, with a weak-looking red moustache and still weaker-looking eyes, was known to our party during the first week of our voyage as Sir James Willoughby. He affected an English accent, and let it be quietly understood about the ship that he was simply out for "a bit of a tour," and expected to return some time during the course of a year or two, by way of India and Europe, to England. He was very much addicted to champagne and cigarettes, and before the trip was over afforded us considerable amusement. A tall, loose-jointed, awkward-looking man, with a gray beard and bronzed complexion, and with an eye that seemed to look through you when it looked at you, was Major-General Strange, of the English army. He had for years been quartered in India, and had taken part in that most memorable of the world's revolts, the Sepoy Insurrection. Frank Marian, and his trim-looking wife, with their over-precocious baby, were a pair of American light comedians upon their way to fill their first engagement in Sydney. Both Marian and his wife were accomplished banjoists and guitarists, and their ability as musicians contributed much to our entertainment and enjoyment.

Colonel J. M. House and a Mr. Turner, stock-yard men of Chicago, were both hale, hearty, jolly fellows, a little beyond the prime of life, and were taking a trip to Australia for business and pleasure. House was really a good fellow, and did much to afford that diversion and excitement so much needed and so much appreciated by the voyager. Before we had been out many days he instituted the old game of "Calcutta Pool," in which we all took a warm interest until the winning coterie narrowed down to so small a number that the "lambs" of the party got tired of the game and drew out. "Calcutta Pool" is simply the selling of auction pools upon the distance traveled by the steamer for twenty-four hours, ending with noon on the day in question. For instance, fifty tickets consecutively numbered from 291 to 340, this being the probable minimum and maximum of the ship's record, are issued and distributed to as many holders, in return for what is practically an entrance fee, at $1.00 each. The tickets are then put up at auction and change hands according to the degree of confidence felt by the respective bidders in their numbers. If a man held 302, for instance, and was convinced that the ship would sail 310, he would sell to some one who wanted 302, and himself bid for the latter number. The auction is, therefore, likely to increase the pool of $50.00 to $200.00, or even $300.00. Our first pool, with an entrance fee of 50 cts., was in the nature of an experiment, and was consequently a small one, aggregating $105.00; $45.00 of which went to the holder of ticket 307; $30.00 going as a second prize to the holder of ticket 302, and an equal amount going as a third prize to the holder of ticket 312. The numbers of the tickets 302 and 312, the second and third prizes, being five above and five below the number of the first prize. The pools were sold every morning after breakfast, and it was great sport until the boys began to be too much in earnest over it, when for fear of unpleasant consequences we mutually decided to drop the practice.

It took our party some time to become accustomed to the sailors' method of dividing the twelve hours of the day, and of being able to distinguish the hour by the number of bells which were sounded regularly amidship every half-hour. To the sailor the twelve hours are divided into three watches, namely: from noon to four o'clock, from four o'clock to eight o'clock, and from eight o'clock until midnight. At 12.30 P. M., half an hour after the noon hour, the ship's bell rings once; at 1 P. M. it rings twice, at 1.30 P. M. it rings three times and at 2 P. M. it sounds four times; at 4 P. M. it rings eight bells, this being the greatest number. Then it begins over again, ringing one bell for 4.30 P. M., and continuing every half-hour until it rings eight bells at eight o'clock, after which it begins at one bell again and increases up to eight bells at midnight. Our party were quite startled the second afternoon out from San Francisco, when at three o'clock the ship's bell began a horrible clanging, and we saw a lot of miscellaneously clad seamen running up from the ship's steerage and galleys, springing upon the top of the cabins and boiler rooms, where they quickly unrolled the reels of hose and attached them to the ship's hydrants, while a score or more of men stood by the life buoys and the long rows of water buckets which stood near the deck. The performance caused more than one pale cheek among the passengers not accustomed to sea-voyaging; but we afterward took a great interest in the performance, which we found, upon inquiry, to be the daily fire-practice of the ship's crew.

It requires just about a week to make the journey from San Francisco to the Sandwich Islands, and to quote a much traveled English gentleman whom I met upon the voyage, it is perhaps the most delightful sea-journey, in every way, that one can take. The great ocean, as indicated by its name, was as quiet and peaceful during those days in November, when our party crossed it, as an inland lake. The sun shone down upon us from a cloudless sky. The salt air was pure and healthful. The breezes that came to us from the spice groves and sugar plantations upon the Sandwich Islands, were warm and gentle enough to remind us of a June day at home. The surroundings and conditions of our new life upon shipboard were just novel enough to be delightful; and in looking back over our journey around the globe, I can recall no part of it that was pleasanter than those days upon the Pacific.

An ocean steamship is a world in itself, wholly apart from the rest of the world, and to the space within the limits of its hull must the voyager look for all in the way of comfort, enjoyment, entertainment and diversion. After the first four days the novelty of ocean travel is gone, and one grows a little tired, perhaps, of looking out over the rolling waters. His mind then seizes upon everything and anything that will relieve the monotony. It was so with our party. The fondness for games of chance, of all kinds that ingenious brains have hit upon, took possession of the "Alameda's" passengers before we were three days out of San Francisco. After that, it was ten to one that any man who made an offer of a bet within hearing of one or more of his fellow passengers, would not escape without having his bet booked. We bet upon everything and anything—water, wind, the kind of soup we would have for dinner, the last man to leave the table, and no one knows what not. As an illustration of the betting craze, the following instance is a good one: In the card-room, one morning, Fogarty cried out, "Twenty-five to one that the ship does not go down before we reach Honolulu."

"I will take you," said Captain Anson, plunging his hand into his pocket, and then looking foolish as he realized what he was about to bet upon.

No more interesting event can occur at sea than the meeting of another vessel. The first instance of the kind that our party experienced occurred upon our fifth day out. Ed Crane, Tom Brown, Fogarty, Daly, John Ward and myself were seated on deck near the saloon, about eleven o'clock that evening, when the entire ship and the surrounding waters were suddenly illuminated by a powerful calcium light on the top of the wheel house. We leaped from our chairs and went forward to find that we were signaling the steamer bound from Honolulu to San Francisco. She had left America before the Presidential election had taken place and so knew nothing whatever of its result, as the Hawaiian Islands have no cable connection of any kind. The signal agreed upon was one rocket in case of Harrison's success and two in case of his defeat. Two miles of ocean rolled between the two ships, but we could clearly discern the lights and hull of the "Australia" in the bright moonlight that flooded the ocean. The mate brought a big rocket from the wheel house, leaned it against the rail and touched it off. There was a flash of light, a downward shooting of yellow fire, and the great rocket ascended into the air, leaving a fiery trail across the sky, until it burst into a hundred colored stars. There is something wonderfully impressive in signaling a vessel at sea—a sort of red letter event in the voyage, made all the more remarkable by surrounding conditions. The "Australia's" lights gleamed over the waters for perhaps twenty minutes, during which time beautiful rockets crossed the heavens with as many lines of light in answer to our signal, and then the ship and her lights vanished from our sight.

Before leaving San Francisco, President Spalding was fortunate enough to meet with the English Agent at Liverpool, of the Chicago, Burlington and Quincy railroad, over whose line we had traveled from Chicago to Denver. The result of this meeting was a lengthy discussion between the Englishman, Mr. S. S. Parry, and Mr. Spalding as to the advisability of our party's returning by way of Europe. The outcome of this discussion was an arrangement between Mr. Parry and Mr. Spalding, by which, upon his return to Liverpool, Parry would visit such European points as Mr. Spalding was desirous of playing games at, and cable the result of his investigations to us at Australia. If he found that indications were favorable to our reception in London, and throughout Great Britain, in which country Mr. Spalding was most desirous of giving exhibitions of the American National Game, Mr.

Parry was to wire us to that effect, and Mr. Spalding would then determine upon a future course of action.

To return by way of Europe would necessitate the expenditure of thousands of dollars for transportation through a section in which little or no interest would be felt in Athletics. Yet Mr. Spalding did not know but that the expenditure would be a wise one from a business standpoint. The press correspondents had been taken into his confidence and given his views before leaving San Francisco, and Parry departed for New York and England about the same time that our party left for Australia. By mutual arrangement the papers represented by the special correspondents of our party were placed in possession of all the details of Mr. Spalding's plans, with the understanding that they were to be published on the Sunday following our departure from America; and no member of our party save the correspondents, Mr. Spalding himself, and Captain Anson, were apprised of our possible return by another route. After we were upon the high seas, however, the matter was allowed to leak out, with a view of learning how the members themselves felt upon the subject. The mere mention of such a possibility aroused much enthusiasm and during the balance of the voyage, and up to the time when it was finally decided, in Melbourne, probable routes were discussed with the pleasantest anticipations, and everything descriptive of the countries and people of continental Europe, Asia and Africa, that the ship's library afforded, was eagerly read by the boys.

Had we left San Francisco Saturday afternoon, the time set for our departure, we would have arrived in Honolulu the following Saturday morning. As it was, however, we were a day late, and Saturday, November 24th, passed with our ship ploughing through the ocean, 150 miles from the Hawaiian Islands at nightfall. We had been scheduled to play a game of ball in Hawaii, where there is a very large baseball element, and as Harry Simpson, our advance agent, had sailed from San Francisco a week ahead of us to prepare for our coming in the Sandwich Islands, we could, in fancy, picture the disappointment of the Hawaiians, to say nothing of the despair of Simpson and of the Reception Committee which we doubted not had been appointed to receive us, when the day dawned, and grew, and finally passed away without our steamer's being sighted; and it can be truly said that the disappointment was not wholly confined to Hawaii. All the way across the Pacific our party had hoped, against hope, that the ship might make up the day we had lost and land us in the Sandwich Islands on time, after all. This, however, could not be done, and we were compelled to content ourselves with the inevitable.

On the morning of the 25th of November, however, the lookout on the bridge of the steamer sighted land just as day began to break. Such an event on shipboard cannot long be kept from the passengers, and, while the morning was still gray, our party tumbled out of their berths and, having hastily arranged their toilets, came upon deck, anxious for the first glimpse of Honolulu. All that was to be seen at first was a faint shadow upon the distant horizon. As the "Alameda" continued on her way this began to assume more definiteness, and the rugged peaks of the mountains finally loomed up against the brightening sky. An hour later the bright green of the island's verdure became plainly discernible, and then the city of Honolulu itself, with its little fleet of shipping in the bay. Nowhere in the world, save perhaps in Ireland, have I seen foliage and vegetation of such a truly emerald hue as in the Sandwich Islands. The land is of volcanic origin, and the rugged sides of the huge mountains, which rise directly out of the sea, and between which lie beautiful valleys rich in the luxuriant foliage and verdure of the tropics, are covered by a seemingly unbroken mantle of beautiful green that is as pleasant to the eye as the sight of land, of any kind, is always delightful to the voyager. As we neared Diamond Head the ship's engine slowed down, and by the time we had left the ocean's swell for the placid waters of the harbor, all the passengers were clustered at the bow, anxious to witness every incident of the landing.

As we drew nearer, a ship's boat put off from the dock and soon reached our side. It brought to us Mr. Geoffrey, the steamship company's agent, Harry Simpson, Mr. F. W. Whitney and Mr. George W. Smith, who is a cousin to President Spalding, a prominent citizen of Honolulu and chairman of the committee appointed to receive us. Three or four dark-skinned natives followed, each bearing a basket filled with wreaths of flowers called by the natives "Leis," and indicative of welcome and good will. One of these wreaths was placed about the neck of each member of our party. Meanwhile, the steamer's cables had been made fast, and our good ship was slowly drawn to her dock, while fully 2000 people looked upon us as though we were visitors from another world. In the centre of the assemblage stood the king's band, "The Royal Hawaiian," in uniforms of white duck, which contrasted admirably with their dark complexions, and, as a cheer went up from our party in response to that of the crowd upon the dock, they began to play "The Star-Spangled Banner," "Yankee Doodle," "The Girl I Left Behind Me," "Auld Lang Syne," and other airs familiar to American ears.

It was a beautiful morning, the rising sun gilding the mountain sides and brightening the plantations along the shore, while it distinctly outlined each individual of the rapidly increasing crowd upon the dock. The officers and crew of the U. S. Cruiser "Alert," which lay a few hundred yards away, were on deck and welcomed the "Alameda" with a hearty cheer as we drew alongside. Upon our steamer all was excitement and eager anticipation. The strains of the magnificent band on the shore, the crowds of Americans and government officers attired in white duck and white straw hats, the sight of land, and a strange land at that, after seven days of continuous ocean sailing, and the realization that we were expected and that great preparations had been made for our coming, had the effect of strangely impressing every one of our party. Cheer after cheer went up from the dock, and the boys responded, but in a spasmodic, discordant chorus, that told how little their voices were at command. They were big lusty fellows, with plenty of muscle and plenty of nerve, and eyes that probably had not seen tears since the days of their boyhood, but just at this time, when they wanted to cheer their loudest and to seem their happiest, did their voices choke and their eyes fill with tears that came unbidden. Only the voyager can appreciate the joy that our party felt at landing upon that beautiful morning in Hawaii.

The crowd on the dock was characteristic of Honolulu. The Hawaiians are dark-complexioned, straight-haired fellows, with regular features and bright, intelligent faces. Their attire of white linen is wonderfully becoming and added greatly to the attractiveness of the scene as it appeared from the deck of the steamer. Score upon score of pretty girls, for the most part dressed in white, chatted with their escorts and critically sized up the stalwart fellows of our party. Our arrival at Honolulu was evidently an event of no small importance. Upon his arrival a week before Simpson had been cordially received, and the interval up to the time of our arrival had been one of pleasurable anticipation for nearly every resident of the city. Without telegraph communication of any kind, the arrival of a steamer in Hawaii is an event of interest, even upon ordi-

THE "ALAMEDA" AT HER DOCK IN HONOLULU.

nary occasions; but a steamer was doubly welcome, upon which came a score of the greatest ball-players of America, who came, too, that they might give Hawaiians an exhibition such as they had never before seen, of a game already a great favorite with them.

We had been expected, as I have said, the day before, and on Saturday morning all Honolulu was awake early to welcome us, and a big crowd assembled on the steamship docks to watch for the signal announcing our arrival. The royal band was in waiting, and the government tug "Eleu" steamed up, ready to convey a party of prominent citizens as far as Diamond Head to welcome the coming guests. Arrangements had even been made to take the port physician with the party, so that he might board the steamer at the earliest possible moment. As time passed and no steamer came, the disappointment may be imagined. The day was a fine sample of Hawaiian weather at that season, warm and beautifully clear. Business had been suspended and everybody was upon the street in holiday attire. The band upon the dock allayed impatience by playing for the crowd which watched and waited for the steamer all through the morning, and indeed we were not given up until after three o'clock that afternoon. Not having arrived Saturday, it was, for some reason, imagined that we would not reach Honolulu before Monday, the 26th, and the programme intended for Saturday was, therefore, put aside in the mind of everybody until Monday morning. No such thing, as our arrival on Sunday morning, seemed to have occurred to anybody, and, consequently, when the ship was sighted at six o'clock, the town was startled by telephone messages which went over every wire in the city, to the effect that the "Alameda" was off Diamond Head. In half an hour the streets were astir with people, and again the band had assembled with the crowd.

While our party had been shaking hands with the members of the Reception Committee the steamer had reached her berth. The companion-ways were let down and our party, descending to the dock, entered carriages in waiting. We were driven rapidly through the picturesque streets, along which grew great palm trees, banana, and stately cocoanuts, bearing their clusters of heavy-shelled fruit, and then passed on, by the palace of King Kalakuau, to the Royal Hawaiian Hotel, which, standing in the centre of beautifully-laid-out grounds, rich in every variety of tree, plant, and shrub known to tropical climates, looked more like the palatial residence of some Sandwich Island or Cuban sugar king than anything else to which I can liken it. Scarcely had we taken seats at the breakfast-table in the great, airy dining-hall, its windows extending from floor to ceiling and opening on spacious balconies that surrounded the house, than the superb band which had welcomed us at the dock began a concert at the music stand beneath the windows. This band is the musical pride of Honolulu, and is maintained at the expense of the Government. Under the leadership of Band Master Berger it has attained a reputation that reaches far beyond the Hawaiian shores; and what harmony it does make! The Hawaiian Band has few equals, and no superiors, in America. Ah, it was delightful, that breakfast in Hawaii! The tables filled with great bowls of luscious yellow oranges and juicy bananas, the moisture even yet upon

THE ROYAL HAWAIIAN BAND AT THE MUSIC STAND.

the broken stems, which had been taken from the parent branch not half an hour before; the air laden with the scent of tropical plants; the grounds crowded with dark-skinned, dark-eyed Kanakas, in their cool-looking costumes of white duck and flannel; the bright sunlight that warmed and beautified every growing thing around us, and the glorious music, all combined to make our experience more like a dream than a reality. Instead of the customary dish of oatmeal at breakfast, we were

KING KALAKAUA, THE QUEEN AND SUITE ON THE PALACE GROUNDS.

served with the native dish of "Poi," a pink-colored mush, which, when eaten with rich Hawaiian cream and a covering of sugar, is very palatable. The native method of eating "poi" is novel. The forefinger is plunged into the dish, given a peculiar twist, and withdrawn with a mouthful of the food clinging to it; the lips close over the morsel and finger, leaving the latter, when it is withdrawn, ready for another attack on the dish.

After breakfast we adjourned to the balconies and again heard the

A NATIVE FAMILY ENJOYING ITS NATIONAL DISH—POI.

sweet strains of the "Aloha Oe," or welcome song, that had greeted us at the dock. The prelude is played by the band, and then the musicians rest their instruments upon their arms, and sing with exquisite harmony their "Aloha Oe" in the melodious language of the Kanakas. Air after air was played for our amusement as we stood in the midst of our tropical surroundings enjoying every breath we breathed and every strain we heard. We were finally informed by the Chairman of the Reception Committee that His Majesty, the King, had extended our party an invitation to call upon him at his palace, 11 o'clock being the designated time. At that hour the Royal Band stepped from the music stand and formed in front of the hotel; Clarence Duval, in full drum-major regalia, taking position at the head. President Spalding and United States Minister Merrill walked down the steps behind the band, and the Chicago and All-America teams, together with the other members of our party, followed in double file, the ladies accompanying in carriages. When all were in line, Clarence tossed his baton in the air, Band Master Berger raised his hand, and the band poured fourth a burst of harmony as the procession moved down the walk toward the gate of the grounds, and then along the avenue to the King's Palace.

The grounds of the Royal Palace are a picture of tropical beauty. We entered the great gateway and proceeded up the narrow avenue to the massive porticoed entrance of the palace, where the band stepped to one side and continued playing, as with hats off we ascended the steps, Minister Merrill and President Spalding leading. We were met on the balcony by members of the King's Cabinet and were shown by attendants to the blue room of the palace, where we deposited our hats and canes and awaited developments. Presently Minister Merrill took President Spalding's arm and requested the balance of the party to fall in line. Mrs. Spalding, escorted by Mr. George Smith, followed Messrs. Merrill and Spalding, and after them came Mr. and Mrs. Frank Lincoln, Captain and Mrs. Anson, Ned and Mrs. Williamson, Captains Ward and Hanlon and the members of the Chicago and All-America teams and Press representatives. We filed across the great hall, past lines of ancestral paintings that decorated the walls and throne room, the latter an imposing apartment, perhaps 100 by 150 feet in extent. The King, attired in citizen's clothes, stood before his throne at the further end of the room, while a Gentleman of Honor, in court costume, was on either side. His Majesty extended his hand to Minister Merrill and President Spalding as the two approached, and then President Spalding introduced each passing guest as the line filed by, the King bowing in acknowledgment of each introduction. The fifty or more visitors had all been introduced and had assembled on the side of the room opposite the doorway as the King turned pleasantly to Messrs.

Spalding and Merrill and shook hands cordially with both. The three chatted and laughed for five minutes longer and then the American Minister and Mr. Spalding bowed and turned to the doorway, the entire party following them into the great hallway and saluting the King as they made their exit. Here we registered our names upon the court register, admired the royal paintings, viewed the spacious and splendidly decorated dining hall and reception rooms, and finally, assembling upon the balcony, were escorted back to the hotel by the Royal Band, which again reëntered the music stand and played airs from the popular operas and composers, while the members of our party sat upon the balconies of the hotel and enjoyed their cigars.

Upon the return from the palace, the question of a game for that afternoon began to be eagerly discussed. It was well understood that the Hawaiian law, a statute of the old missionary times, prohibited all forms of Sunday amusements, and President Spalding, in answer to questions put him on our arrival, stated that it was his purpose to respect that law to the letter. About noon, however, the members of the Reception Committee drew up a petition to President Spalding requesting him to have the team play a game of ball that afternoon, and setting forth that the signers would bear any and all expense incurred, of any kind whatever. Duplicates of this petition had been made and placed in the hotel and other public places, and within an hour half a dozen of them, bearing nearly a thousand names, were handed to President Spalding. He received them upon the balcony, glanced over them, and assured the eager assemblage that if a game could possibly be played in accordance with the municipal laws governing such matters, their request would be complied with, as both of the teams were quite anxious to play. President Spalding and the members of the Reception Committee then entered a carriage and were driven to the residence of the Marshal, where the situation was talked over and it was learned, beyond all question, that any attempt to play a game on Sunday would be in violation of the local statutes. President Spalding, consequently, adhered to his first decision, though when the fact was made known at the hotel, the crowd gave vent to its disappointment in groans and howls, and declaring that they would make an issue on the Sunday question at the next election.

That there was to be no game was a disappointment, indeed, to the Hawaiians. They had anticipated it for weeks before our arrival, and now that we were there, with twenty athletic-looking fellows fairly aching to play, the laws would not permit it. The situation certainly was exceedingly trying to the hot-headed Kanakas. They accepted it good-naturedly, however, and went to work in earnest to make our stay pleasant. Half a dozen park wagons and twice that number of saddle horses were placed at our disposal, and every member of the party took advantage of the opportunity afforded to do the city and its environs. Some of the boys accepted an invitation from the U. S. war ship "Alert" to visit the officers upon their vessel, and, from Fred Carroll's account, I imagine they must have spent a charming afternoon, all of the officers being baseball enthusiasts and admirers of the game's great exponents. Another party was taken charge of by one or two Honolulu gentlemen, and witnessed a "Hula Hula," a native dance, by a dozen graceful Kanaka women. Others of the party rode out to the Pali, perhaps the most wonderful piece of coast mountain scenery in the world.

SPLENDID COAST SCENERY ON THE PALI ROAD.

THRONE ROOM IN PALACE OF KING KALAKAUA, AT HONOLULU, S. I.

President and Mrs. Spalding and other members of the party entered a wagonette and drove south along Nuuanu Avenue, through the beautiful Nuuanu Valley; past the Royal Mausoleum where sleep the former

STATUE OF KAMEHAMEHA, THE CONQUEROR.

Kings and Queens of Hawaii, from Kamehameha, the conqueror, down to the Princess Like-Like, the last deceased of the royal family;

past the residences of wealthy Honoluluans, the broad-porticoed houses being almost hidden by masses of foliage of palm, banana and other tropical trees; on past taro and banana fields until a point was reached from which the rolling Pacific could be seen stretching away to the horizon like a great burnished mirror, while the city, thick with foliage, lay in the valley below. Returning, the party made a detour that they might pass the Queen's Hospital, built by King Lunalili in memory of Queen Emma. From the Hospital the party drove to Wai Kiki, the Asbury Park of the Hawaiian Islands, finally stopping at the residence of the Hon. A. S. Claghorn, where they met the Princess Kaiulani, a beautiful Hawaiian girl of rare accomplishments and winning manners, the next but one to succeed to the Hawaiian sovereignty. Further along we found the residence of the Hon. John H. Cummins, one of the wealthy men of Hawaii and proprietor of one of the great sugar plantations of the Island. The house was festooned with American flags, and on the broad verandahs we were entertained with music and songs by a band of

HAWAIIAN LADY IN RIDING COSTUME.

native boys with their guitars. A novelty to Americans was met with during this charming drive, in several horseback parties, the ladies of which, according to the custom of the country, bestrode their horses, being attired in a suitable and very elegant riding habit. Their grace and skill as riders were very admirable. From Mr. Cummins' house we were driven back to the hotel that we might prepare for the grand "Luau" or native feast given in honor of the Spalding party by His Majesty, and Messrs. Samuel Parker, John Ena and George Beckley.

The "Luau," or native feast of the Hawaiians, as it was given in our honor at Honolulu, was certainly the most novel, if not the most gorgeous event in which we participated during the tour. The feast took place upon the Queen's grounds, in the centre of which stood the Queen's private residence, and just as it began to grow dark our party started from the hotel and drove to the scene of the banquet. We passed the King's palace, and after a drive through an avenue of towering cocoanut palms, came unexpectedly upon the illuminated grounds of the Queen's residence, with their magnificent grove of banana, date, cocoanut, royal palm and many other varieties of tropical plants and trees. The grounds literally blazed with light. Flaming torches of oil had been set ten feet apart in one huge square around the outskirts of the park, while the softened glow of a thousand Japanese lanterns shone through the luxuriant shubbery, reminding us not a little of the *tableaux finale* in our great spectacular dramas at home. Moving about over the graveled walks and through the beautiful shrubbery we could see the figures of two hundred or more of Honolulu's residents who had been invited to meet the visiting Americans, while from all quarters of the grounds we heard the singing of bands of native boys and the sweet melody of their guitars. The scene could scarce have been more attractive, and certainly not more surprising.

The uniformed officers at the gates fell back in the most deferential manner as our party entered, and, with U. S. Minister Merrill, President Spalding, Captain H. G. Morse, and the ladies in the lead, walked toward a great tree near the centre of the grounds, beneath which stood His Majesty, the Hon. John Cummins, and members of the King's cabinet. In accordance with a very old custom in the royal families of Hawaii, a tree is planted upon royal ground at the birth of each member of the royal household, and as the tree grows in vigor, strength and beauty of proportion, or as it is destroyed by the elements or weakened by disease, the future of the child is prognosticated. The tree under which King Kalakuau stood had been planted at his birth, some fifty years before, and upon the night of our reception the King was present, in the prime of life and full vigor of manhood, while the tree towered above us, its branches far-reaching and covered with luxuriant foliage, while its sturdy trunk seemed capable of bearing the brunt of wind and weather for ages to come. His Majesty informally and cordially received his guests, after which the boys, in accordance with the royal mandate to make themselves perfectly at home, wandered away in groups about the grounds.

In one of the lattice-walled rooms of the Queen's residence stood a table bearing a hugh ten-gallon punch bowl, from which two dusky attendants were serving delicious beverage to all who requested it. Fogarty, Burns, and myself, together with several officers of the U. S. cruiser "Alert," entered to test the contents of the bowl, when, before we had reached the table, half a dozen pretty Kanaka girls, attired in gowns of some loose woven material of pure white, that contrasted beautifully with their dark hair and Italian-like complexions, approached us with a charming air of confidence, and, slipping their dusky arms around our necks, smiled into our astonished faces as they proceeded to fasten over our shoulders, "leis" of flowers—the wreath of welcome of the Hawaiians. We were all too much astonished for the moment to do much else than stare at the dusky beauties as they stood before us, their shapely arms exposed through the flowing sleeves, and the brown skin of their rounded shoulders only partly concealed by the delicate texture that covered them, and before we succeeded in recovering our self-possession the wreaths were fastened and the girls were extending the same pretty and hospitable, not to say affectionate, courtesy toward others who had entered. Outside, the scene was indescribably gorgeous, and after paying our compliments to the punch bowl a second time we joined one of the groups of Honolulu's fair daughters who had assembled in force to meet our party.

A short distance away, in the centre of a grove of magnificent royal palms, preparations for the "luau" were going on. The ground had been covered with dried rushes and native grasses to the depth of three inches. Upon these had been laid the table, in the shape of a U, the boards resting upon blocks which elevated them, perhaps six inches above the rushes. Upon each side of the table had been laid long strips of matting, upon which the guests were to sit—tailor fashion—while stationed ten feet apart stood a line of Kanaka girls attired in flowing robes of white, and waving to and fro over the table long-handled, brilliantly colored fans. The innumerable colored lanterns and the lurid glow of the oil torches which shone through the palm trees, the voices of the native boys and the sound of their guitars, the presence of a hundred white-clad Kanaka women, and the intoxicating perfume of the tropical foliage, all combined to make our experience a novel and delightful one.

An hour after our arrival the King arose from his seat beneath the branches of his Birth-tree, and offering his arm to Mrs. Spalding, proceeded toward the grove in which the tables had been laid. Following the King were H. R. H. Lilino Kalani, the King's sister; and Prince Kawanonakoa. After them came President Spalding, Captain Morse, and the remainder of the party. Thanks to the skill and experience of the royal ushers, the big party was gracefully handled, and within a very few minutes after the procession had formed we were seated, the King sharing with Mrs. Spalding a richly embroidered silk mat at the head of the table, while others occupied seats upon the native matting. Opposite each plate sat calabashes filled with "poi," while upon the platters and encased in long, coarse-fibred leaves in which they had been baked, were portions of beef, pork, veal, fish, chicken and all other viands to be found upon a moderate banquet table, but all prepared in native style. Fruit of almost every variety known to tropical countries was piled in lavish profusion from one end of the table to the other, and the usual wines were served without stint. Bands of native boys stationed upon the outskirts of the party played continuously during the feast, and not a few of us who were lovers of stringed instruments left neglected the dishes before us while we listened to the peculiar rhythm and exquisite harmony of their music.

Some of the experiences of the Americans with the native dish of "poi" were amusing. A pretty girl opposite me laughed merrily when

I transferred a spoonful of the pink porridge to my plate, and then, as if to impress me with my ignorance of Kanaka customs, plunged two rosy fingers into the dish before her, gave them an expert twist and transferred the clinging substance to her mouth. For a moment I wondered where the young woman had learned her table manners, and then as it dawned upon me that every one but myself was indulging in the same breach of table etiquette, I too fell into line and ate "poi" with my fingers, a la Hawaii, and what is more, I found it exceedingly palatable.

The "Luau" proceeded as nearly all banquets do. There was a continued hum of conversation mingling with laughter, merry badinage and the music of the native boys, until silence was finally requested by His Majesty's Attorney-General, who, speaking for the King, expressed the pleasure His Majesty felt at having been afforded the opportunity of entertaining so representative a body of Americans within his own kingdom. President Spalding responded briefly, his well-worded tribute to Hawaii and its people's generous hospitality being warmly received by the resident Honoluluans present. Some moments later the King expressed a wish to hear Frank Lincoln in some of his specialties, and in response the humorist had the King and his guests laughing heartily before he had fairly got to his feet. His satire on after-dinner speeches, his "A, B, C" oration and his artistic mixture of a "soda cocktail," which many Americans will remember, were never more cleverly given, and certainly never called forth more enthusiastic applause.

After fifteen minutes of uninterrupted laughter over Lincoln's remarks we arose from the table, the King and the members of his family and cabinet returning to the trunk of the great tree, beneath which a levee was held, the ball-players mingling with the crowd in the gardens, where scores of dark-eyed Hawaiian beauties flirted and chatted with a zest fully equal to that exhibited by the typical American girl.

It was perhaps nine o'clock—our steamer was to weigh anchor at ten—when the members of our party filed under the branches of the great tree to bid His Majesty farewell. Kalakuau had seen Clarence Duval do a plantation "breakdown" to the "music" made by the hands of Tommy Burns, Fred Pfeffer, Ryan and Ned Williamson, and

after laughing heartily at the little darkie's "pigeon-wings" and "walk-arounds," had rewarded him with a ten-dollar gold piece. He had conversed pleasantly with many members of our party, and as we passed before him he shook each one of us warmly by the hand and wished us *bon voyage*. He has a fine face, with dark, expressive eyes and a kindly expression that grows more interesting as one looks into it, and more than one member of our party afterward declared himself as having been most agreeably surprised in His Majesty—to whose generous hospi-

CLARENCE CUTTING "PIGEON-WINGS" BEFORE THE KING.

tality we were so greatly indebted. Our farewells spoken, we paused at the outskirts of the natural pavilion which sheltered the King and gave His Majesty three American cheers, which brought a smile to his face and further good wishes to his lips. Three more were given for Our Friends in Honolulu, and then Fogarty made himself the target of half a hundred pairs of admiring eyes by proposing three cheers for The Ladies of Honolulu. It is needless to say that they were given, after which we were driven rapidly to our steamer. At the dock a great crowd awaited us, the assemblage at the Queen's grounds having adjourned to the steamer's side almost in a body. The King's band was there, and even now I can in fancy hear its beautiful strains in the "Aloha" song, while the scene of the waving, cheering crowd upon the dock, illuminated by the powerful rays of the ship's calcium, and the farewells that came to us more and more faintly as the "Alameda's" head swung out to sea, are doubtless still as fresh in the memories of all our party as they are in my own.

Fair Honolulu. We strained our eyes that night to catch a last glimpse of the disappearing lights upon its shores, with regret at leaving, and hope of again seeing what many of us still remember as among the most beautiful spots upon the globe.

> Fair Honolulu, City of the Sea,
> On Oahu's shores, where stately mountains rise,
> To dwell forever there, with thee,
> Would be to live in earthly paradise.

Upon leaving Honolulu, we entered upon the longest period of our voyage across the Pacific; the distance between Hawaii and New Zealand, our next stop, with the exception of a brief wait for the mails at the Samoan Islands, being nearly 3900 miles. The trip from San Francisco to Honolulu, however, had made good sailors of most of us, and the novelty of tossing about upon the swell of the ocean having in a measure worn off, the more active minds of the party soon became restless under the inactive life we were leading upon the quarter-deck. Anson was first in an endeavor to bring about a change.

"See here, George," said he to Wright, the afternoon following our departure from Honolulu, "this kind of a life will never do for American ball-players upon a missionary tour. We shall all be as stiff as old women and as fat as aldermen by the time we reach Australia, if we don't take exercise of some kind. Can't we arrange to have a bit of cricket practice?"

George, a little later, held an interview with Captain Morse, and the result was that on the following morning, half a dozen sailors set to work to roof over and wall in with canvas the rear end of the quarter-deck promenade upon the larboard side of the ship. This was done to prevent the balls from bounding into the sea, and when completed, gave us an enclosed cricket alley about eight feet wide, ten high and forty feet long. The wickets were set in the extreme end of the alley, and the bowler, facing the opening of the tent, twenty feet beyond it, found plenty of room in which to swing his arm, and ample distance in which to "break" the ball quite effectively, despite the smooth decks and the occasional roll of the ship. Through George Wright's thoughtfulness in providing the party with a fifty-foot stretch of cocoa matting, upon which to bowl, the obstacles which the smooth oak planking of the deck offered to good bowling were overcome, and a surface almost as good as genuine turf secured. The boys began practice almost as soon as arrangements were completed, and did not afterward fail to put in several hours a day. Indeed, it was just what they all wanted, for they had begun to get a bit stiff and heavy, just as Anson predicted, as the result of three hearty meals a day and no exercise, save,

CRICKET ON SHIPBOARD.

perhaps, an early morning turn on deck, and the bowling and batting either in the warm sun outside their tent or the high temperature inside of it, brought out the perspiration freely and landed the players in Australia almost in the pink of condition.

It was the expectation when the party started out that we would play almost as much cricket as baseball, particularly in Australia, but we afterward found that we had little, if any, time left for other than the ball games arranged for by Manager Lynch. We did play one game of cricket in Sydney, and while our boys gave an exhibition of fielding with which the fielding work of the Australians could not for one moment compare, our lack of bowling and batting ability gave the Sydney Eleven an easy victory in the partly completed game played. A few of our players possessed a fair idea of batting with a straight bat, but the majority would hold on to the idea of hitting the ball hard, with a cross-bat, just as they were accustomed to do in baseball. Had they schooled themselves to do more blocking and less hitting, eight or ten of them, with continued practice and the experience of half a dozen games against the Australians, would probably have developed into very fair batsmen by the time we reached England.

Time passed so rapidly upon the voyage that we had drawn near the New Zealand coast before we realized it. The weather became warm enough, soon after we had left the Hawaiian Islands, to permit of the boys sleeping upon deck, and between the hours of midnight and five in the morning, the comfortable cane-seated steamer chairs surrounding the deck saloon, were sure to be found occupied by slumbering ball-players, attired in their flannel pjamas, and wrapped in the blankets they had brought from their state-rooms. The sailors awakened all deck-slumberers about half-past five by washing down the decks for the day with half a dozen streams of salt water, and then the boys would retire to their state-rooms, and divesting themselves of their pjamas, would reappear, *au natural*, for their salt-water baths, the water pouring from two big perforated nozzles near the smoke-stack, with force and volume enough to wash an entire regiment in half an hour. Then after a "sponge off" in fresh water, followed by a cup of black coffee and a soda cracker brought us by the cabin stewards, we would prepare our toilets for the day. The salt-water baths were a source of any amount of fun, and were besides great invigorators, the boys, when they had donned their flannel suits and straw hats, coming upon deck with hearty appetites for breakfast, and in good condition for their morning's cricket practice.

Contrary to our calculations on leaving Honolulu we crossed the equator somewhere between one and two o'clock on the morning of December 1st. Had we crossed in daylight we should have received Neptune and his suite as they came over our bow from the depths of the ocean, but as it was, we were compelled to rely upon our own resources for celebration during the hour of crossing, and our resources were by no means few. A really good literary and musical programme was given in the cabin after supper, under Frank Lincoln's supervision, in which the piano, a mandolin, two banjos, and a guitar provided very acceptable orchestra music. General Strange, the old English army officer, gave us a thrilling account of his experience in the Sepoy mutiny in India, he having been present at the siege of Lucknow, while Frank Lincoln wound up the programme with a series of his amusing specialties, after which our entire party moved our steamer chairs well up toward the bow of the ship, and under the light of a million stars, played and sang everything, from light opera to plantation darky ballads, until Captain Morse informed us, about one o'clock, that we had crossed the earth's girdle and were in southern seas.

CAPTAIN MORSE, COMMANDER OF THE "ALAMEDA."

Captain Morse, by the way, is an ideal captain. He stands six feet high and weighs 283 pounds. In his day he has been an athlete of no ordinary ability, and one of the rarest treats I enjoyed upon that voyage was getting into the big fellow's state-room, together with Ned Williamson, Tom Burns, and Ned Hanlon, to listen to the "old sea-dog's" stories of travel and adventure. He has been all over the world, and has sailed the Pacific for the past twenty-three years, until the record of his travels would make an exceedingly interesting volume. The captain sat at the head of the first table in the dining saloon, with

President and Mrs. Spalding at his right, and Mr. and Mrs. Frank Lincoln at his left; his hearty laugh and his good-natured, jovial countenance leaving no room for any such thing as a dull meal at our table during the voyage. Others at table No. 1 were Mr. and Mrs Anson, Ned and Mrs. Williamson, Captains Ward and Hanlon, the Press correspondents, Tom Burns, Fred Pfeffer, Fred Carroll, and George Wright and his chum Snyder.

On the morning of December 2d, a few hours after we had crossed the equator, the wind began to blow great guns, and by noon the "Alameda" was rolling about like a log in a mountain stream, while, to the amusement of the boys, great sheets of water dashed over our decks. Tom Daly, Pettit, Sullivan, Brown, Carroll, Earle and Healy skirmished around from one end of the ship to the other, soaked to the skin and yelling with laughter as often as a big wave would raise itself over the rail and send one of their number sprawling across the deck. At the table we were as apt to get our soup in our laps as in our mouths, and it was not an unusual sight to see a cabin steward flying down the saloon with our dinner in his outstretched hands, as though he were bent upon going through the bow of the ship. It did no good to call him, for it was utterly beyond his power to stop, so we only laughed at the poor fellow's plight and wondered if the ship's bow would be checked in its downward plunge by striking another billow before our flying steward struck the forward wall of the saloon and frescoed its polished surface with our fricasseed chicken and teal duck with jelly.

It was too wet for comfort on deck that evening, so the ship's passengers amused themselves by holding a mock trial in the saloon, with General Strange in the chair, as the presiding judge, and Sir James Willoughby as the prisoner at the bar. Charges had been preferred, to the effect that "Sir Jimmy" was not a peer of the realm, as he had declared himself to be, and that he was violating a ship's law by carrying concealed weapons. John Ward acted as counsel for the defendant, and Colonel House as prosecuting attorney, while Jimmy Fogarty as Court Crier kept the crowd in such continuous laughter that the trial proceeded with great difficulty. Each witness was sworn not to tell the truth and anything but the truth, so that the evidence was naturally of a startling character. "Sir Jimmy" had been heard to declare he would scuttle the ship, and was known to carry an eight-ton gun in his pistol pocket—several of the witnesses had seen it, and described it accurately; while as to his pretensions to nobility, half a dozen witnesses knew him to be a clerk in the ribbon department at Macy's. Other witnesses, however, testified to the defendant's wonderful tenderness of heart, and still others had been entertained in royal style at his town and country houses in England. "Sir Jimmy" was acquitted with all honor. There was afterwards some talk of bringing Tom Daly into court under "a bill of *lunatico inquirendo*," with Fogarty as "accessory to the crime," but the return and continuation of beautiful weather kept every one outside the saloon upon the decks.

Our only sight of land during our two weeks' voyage from Honolulu to New Zealand was obtained upon the night of December 3d, when we sighted the northward island of the Samoan or Navigator group, made famous during the spring of 1888 by the native war which raged at Apia, and by the destruction in a tornado of the fleet of United States cruisers anchored in the harbor. The trouble was reaching an ugly stage at the time of our visit, though its seat was some ninety miles from Tutuila, the mailing station at which our steamer touched. It had been quite stormy for several hours previous to our arrival. Captain Anson, Ed Crane, Tom Brown, Daly, Fogarty and myself were seated on the lee side of the deck, under shelter of the awning, watching for the first glimpse of a light on shore, or the first appearance of land through the darkness. Shortly after 11 o'clock we suddenly ran under the lee of a mountainous ridge of land, that rose like a black shadow out of the water, and our vessel stopped pitching almost immediately as we glided over waters that rippled gently about our bow, where five minutes before great foam-crested waves had been towering. The transition was so sudden that we all jumped from our chairs and ran to the bow just as the ship was illuminated by a signal light of green from the leeward end of the bridge. Then we saw land, and finally a twinkling light upon the shore nearly five miles away. Slowly we steamed toward it, while signal lights continued flashing their messages between our ship and the shore. We did not attempt to land, but lay in the harbor half a mile out until two boats, one a sloop and the other a little dory that bobbed about us like a cork on the waves, had come out from the dock with the foreign bound mail and two passengers for Auckland. Had we reached these islands in daytime, our ship would have been surrounded with canoes filled with natives, and we should doubtless have been able to bring away many interesting souvenirs. As it was, however, we saw nothing of the country, and caught but a glimpse of the natives as we watched them over the ship's rail. One stalwart fellow with a copper-colored skin and thick, red hair* did clamber up the side to take the purser's receipt for the mail-sacks, and we got a good view of him. He tossed off nearly a goblet full of gin, which the purser handed him, as though it were so much water, and, wiping his lips with his big, red hand, descended into the mail-boat. This was really all we saw of Samoa, for after receiving our passengers and leaving our mail, the "Alameda" moved slowly out of the harbor, and twenty minutes later was again plunging and rolling through the great waves that drenched her decks.

The weather grew cooler after leaving Samoa, and our flannel suits were discarded for clothes of a warmer texture, with light overcoats for use upon deck during the evening. Cricket practice was indulged in every day, and many delightful hours were enjoyed under the light of the southern cross, which was now plainly discernible. But despite the pleasant, lazy life on shipboard, we all began to wish for a bit of dry land to tread upon. Finally, about 3 o'clock on the morning of December 9th, we sighted the revolving light on the first island of the New Zealand group. This light, the man on watch informed me as I came out of my state-room for a solitary smoke, was just eight hours' run from Auckland. All of the passengers were on deck before breakfast, eager to catch sight of the land, that arose in beautiful green hills upon our larboard side, and at the breakfast table Major-General Strange, on behalf of the passengers, presented Captain Morse with a purse of $200 as a testimonial and in recognition of his care and guidance of our good ship upon the voyage. The big captain acknowledged the gift in a brief, though manly and well-worded speech that won him an enthusiastic burst of applause from his assembled admirers. Kind and attentive from the time we had cut loose from our moorings at San Francisco;

---

* The natives of the Navigator group have a custom of bleaching their hair with lime.

jolly, big-hearted, and an able commander, he completely won the confidence and admiration of his passengers.

Auckland harbor is second only to that of Sydney in point of picturesque beauty, and we had an excellent view of it as our ship steamed her way along a winding channel upon each side of which arose bold, irregular hills, characteristic of all countries of volcanic origin. Pretty sailboats and busy steamers dotted the bay, and upon the sides of the majestic hills were pretty, balconied residences of white stone surrounded

BIRD'S-EYE VIEW OF AUCKLAND AND ITS HARBOR.

by carefully kept grounds. As we neared the dock at the foot of the main street we were struck with the remarkable quiet of the town, and then recalled the fact that we had dropped a day from our calendar upon crossing the 180th degree of longitude, and that it was Sunday morning at Auckland, instead of Saturday, as it would have been but for the change in our calendar. We had expected to meet Leigh Lynch at Auckland, but he was unable to leave Sydney, and sent his cousin, Will

Lynch, who came on board with a big basket filled with bouquets for the members of our party. He was followed by several newspaper men, and one and all poured into our ears a wail of regret that we could not have arrived the day before, when it was reasonably certain we should have had eight or ten thousand people present to witness the game. Usually the steamers stop but a few hours at Auckland, but we were delighted to learn that the "Alameda" could not finish coaling before five o'clock the following afternoon, so we should be able, after all, to play a game in New Zealand. By way of change from steamer life, we accepted an invitation from President Spalding to take dinner at the Imperial Hotel, and the change was delightful, notwithstanding that the cuisine of our good ship was first-class. Indeed, had a Delmonico been our ship's caterer, we should have welcomed any departure from our usual bill of fare. Those who have crossed the ocean will understand this feeling.

They know how to live in New Zealand, even though they be colonists. The beef was delicious, while new potatoes, green peas, fresh from the garden, cauliflower, young radishes, English duck done to a turn, and strawberries, such as Americans have read of, possibly, but have never seen, constituted a dinner all the more enjoyable because its dishes were luxuries with Americans at that season of the year. After dinner, at the invitation of several of the representative newspaper men at Auckland, we mounted two big four-horse coaches and did the city and its environs, finally scaling the sides of Mount Eden, an extinct volcano on the outskirts of the city, and looking into its musty old crater. The country about Auckland is wonderfully rich and beautifully picturesque, and despite the drizzling rain which fell, the drive over the hard roads behind a four-in hand of sturdy English coachers was an interesting one. The clouds cleared away soon after sundown, and the "Alameda's" passengers thronged the big stone dock at which the steamer lay until long after midnight, being eager, all of us, to spend every available moment of our time upon shore.

On the following day I got a better idea of the beautiful country surrounding Auckland. It was scarcely seven o'clock when I was awakened by Bob Pettit, who informed me that a couple of saddle horses awaited us on the dock, and that we had no time to lose.

"How about breakfast?" I asked.

"Bother breakfast," was the right-fielder's reply. "If you'll move yourself in a hurry, I'll give you a breakfast at the end of the prettiest seven-mile ride you ever saw; but there is no time to be lost."

So I tumbled out of my berth, and twenty minutes later Bob and I stood on the dock attired in the pick-up riding costumes we had worn upon our first ride at Salt Lake. Two long-barreled nags awaited us, and on these we were soon riding through the streets of the scarcely awakened city, then on past the parks until we struck the hard white road that led to Manukau Cove. It was a delightful ride, for the country was green and beautiful, the air fresh and invigorating, and our horses anxious to go. We passed quaint English-looking inns and alehouses, around which groups of New Zealand farmers had gathered for business or idle chat. The "bob-carts" we have read about, driven by square-tiled yeomen, who looked at us curiously as we passed, were frequently met with, and once or twice we stopped en route for a glass of light sparkling ale from the hands of the bright-eyed bar-maids, who, instead of the white-aproned masculine bar-keepers of America, serve customers in New Zealand. Finally turning a bend in the road, we came into view of Manukau, the little village on the shore of Manukau Cove. Nearly all of the inhabitants are seafaring people, and the Manukau Hotel, which faces the Cove, is their headquarters. Without ceremony Bob and I rode into the court-yard of the inn and tied our horses to a couple of staples in the wall.

"You seem to be at home here, old man," I remarked.

"Well, I guess," replied Pettit, with all the confidence of a bred and born Yankee, "this is right where I live, and I only got acquainted last night at that. Come in, and let me introduce you to my family," with which Bob opened a side door and I followed him into the little hotel parlor, and through the doorway across the hall caught a glimpse of the inevitable hotel ale room, which we entered.

There were three people in the room and they were typical samples of colonial life. The first was an elderly, well-preserved old colonist, fat and ruddy complexioned with the ale of his own brewing; the next was a gray-bearded coast skipper, in a fore-and-aft hat and an oilskin jacket; while the third was a colonial innkeeper's wife, fat, forty and good-natured, and as thrifty and energetic as she was good-natured. And how well her name fitted her appearance, and her position as mistress of the principal tavern at Manukau, Mrs. Waterman.

Advancing toward Bob and myself with a broad smile of welcome, she gave the former a hearty slap on the shoulder as she said: "Welcome to ye, me lad; ye are out a bit early this morning, are ye not?"

"Yes, we came out for breakfast," said Pettit, "can we have some?"

"That ye can," was the hearty reply, and after an introduction to the two old skippers, we turned into the hallway just as two fresh-faced pretty girls came down the stairs, only to greet, and be greeted by Bob as though they were old-time acquaintances. They were the daughters of our hostess, and each was a typical representative of colonial beauty, with enough of wit and spirit added to their physical charms, to make them even a more interesting study for us than were our breakfasts, hungry, though we were. Mrs. Waterman sat down with us and served us from the rich juicy steak that steamed upon the platter, while we flirted with her two daughters through one of the most heartily relished breakfasts I partook of on the tour. After an hour spent over our sherry and cigarettes in the little parlor, Pettit and I bade a regretful farewell to our colonial cousins, and turned our horses' heads toward Auckland for another delightful ride. We reached the city just in time to join the party in a visit to the City Hall, where for an hour or more we were the guests of Mayor Devore.

About 12 o'clock the local band marched down the principal street to the "Alameda," where it headed a procession of carriages containing the teams in uniform and two big tally-ho coaches which carried the remainder of the "Alameda's" passengers, as invited guests at the game. The drive to the grounds was a pretty one, and the stretch of greensward within the enclosure as attractive a sight as any we saw in New Zealand. Our game in New Zealand was of the heavy batting order, and the way in which a ball rolled whenever it was batted into the smooth, velvety outfield, would have broken the hearts of a league out-field in a championship game. A dozen Englishmen sat near me, and as they had never before seen a baseball game they were completely bewildered. I explained several of the plays however, telling them how and when the side had been retired, calling their attention to the fielding, the throwing to first across the diamond and from the out-field, to double plays, base-running, and sliding, until I had them as deeply interested as ever they had been in a game of cricket. The Englishmen among our passengers who had picked up the cardinal points from the boys *en voyage*, were particularly pleased, and admitted they had never seen such fielding or remarkable base-running.

Two thousand people had assembled to bid us farewell when the "Alameda" left the dock at five o'clock that afternoon, and we watched

THE BOLD HEADLANDS OF THE SHORE OF SYDNEY HARBOR.

the picturesque coast until nightfall. An hour later the "Alameda" turned her nose west by no'r-west, heading for Sydney, 1243 miles away.

On the afternoon of December 14th, after a rough voyage, we sighted the Australian coast. By three o'clock we could discern the shore line, and at five we went down to dinner. We were not long at the table, however. Everybody dined hastily and rushed upon deck, and watched the bold headlands of the shore grow more and more distinct.

Presently we saw a thin trail of smoke across the sky, and soon we discovered the outlines of the pilots' tug as it steamed toward us. Manager Leigh Lynch's face was one of the first we saw as the pilot boat approached, and our big business manager was received with rousing cheers and hearty handshaking as he, with the old gray-bearded pilot, climbed up the ship's side. He admonished us, however, to save our voices, "for" said he, "all Sydney will be in the bay to meet you, and I want you to show them how healthy Americans can cheer."

We soon found that Lynch had but slightly exaggerated the preparations made for our reception, for as we steamed through "Sydney Heads," with schools of graceful dolphins diving about our bow, and hundreds of sea-birds that had flown out from land, as if to welcome us, circling about our masts, we discovered several steamers coming toward us at a speed that cut the water into white sheets upon each side of their bows. Nearer and nearer they drew until we could hear the bands of music with which each steamer was provided, their strains mingling with the cheers that came to us faintly across the water. Then we discerned scores of fluttering handkerchiefs, and eager happy faces, as men clung to the ropes and every other available holding place upon the little crafts and madly waved us welcome, while the ladies—and there were great numbers of them—circled their shawls and bright-colored sun-shades about their heads, determined not to be outdone by their husky-voiced escorts. Steamer after steamer dropped alongside of us, until the "Alameda" had become the centre of a puffing, cheering, banner-bedecked escort, the demonstration causing not a few eyes on board to moisten with joy and gratitude at once more reaching land, the recipients of so glorious a welcome. The lighthouse on the point was draped from top to bottom with red, white and blue bunting, and with American flags, and as we steamed up the beautiful harbor, toward the dock, two flotillas of watermen's boats, fairly covered with the "stars and stripes" and "union jacks," swung into line alongside of us, until our ship was surrounded by an hundred and fifty craft of various characters. Of course we cheered for everything any one among us could suggest, and each cheer was answered by the enthusiastic hundreds who were steaming along beside us. Indeed, no one who has not seen Sydney harbor, and who does not know the generous hospitality of the Australians, can form an adequate idea of our delightful reception. It was glorious! it was soul-stirring! It was in every way a complete surprise, in that it so far exceeded all that we had imagined it might be. Certainly no more picturesque and beautiful scenery, of its kind, exists anywhere in the world than that about Sydney harbor. The waters of the sea extend inland between jutting hills and headlands, until, when viewed from some point high above the sea level, the bay looks like a big glistening starfish, upon the back of which are moving hundreds of sailing craft of every description. Beautifully-kept private and public parks extend

PANORAMIC VIEW OF SYDNEY AND ITS SUPERB HARBOR.

downward to the water's edge, and quaintly-designed English-looking residences of white stone, with their turrets and tower-capped walls, stand upon the hillsides, partly hidden by a wealth of beautiful foliage. The sight of the picturesque harbor and its beautiful shores was alone a glorious one in the eyes of every passenger on the "Alameda," while the generous demonstration in honor of our arrival made our reception at Sydney the most delightful and noteworthy event thus far upon our tour.

Upon the quay at which our steamer was to land stood hundreds of cheering people, and the welcome they gave us was equaled only by that which we had received at Honolulu. Our party with difficulty made its way through the crowd to five four-horse tally-ho coaches, beautifully decorated with the Stars and Stripes, and through the colonial thoroughfares we rode to the Oxford and Grosvenor hotels.

GEORGE STREET—ONE OF THE COLONIAL THOROUGHFARES.

The entire party stopped first at the Oxford, the entrance to which, as well as to the dining-room, had been quite elaborately decorated in red, white and blue bunting, boughs of spruce and evergreen, and swinging colored lanterns. Brief but hearty greetings by U. S. Consul Griffin, Leigh Lynch, and President Spalding followed, and after drinking as many toasts as we thought it advisable to wet thus early in the evening, the boys repaired to their rooms to make a hasty toilet for the formal welcome to Australia arranged for us at the Royal Theatre. The Royal is presided over by "Jimmy" Williamson, a whole-souled and patriotic American, who has made a success of his dramatic enterprises in Australia. Himself and wife were in the caste in "Struck Oil" that evening, and in a farcical hit upon the evils of Chinese Immigration, as an afterpiece. The theatre had been beautifully decorated with American flags, and was filled with a fashionable audience, nearly all of whom were in evening costume. The boys were recognized and heartily applauded as they filed into the private boxes and that section of the dress circle reserved for them. After the closing act of "Struck Oil" our entire party passed through the box aisle upon the stage, where, arranging ourselves in a semicircle, we faced "the house" as the curtain arose, and stood silently for nearly a minute while the applause continued. Then Mr. Daniel O'Connor, a member of parliament and one of the most popular legislators in New South Wales, introduced us, his brief speech being full of kind words for America and everything American, and particularly eulogistic of the party of American ballplayers which had come so far upon such a mission without any guarantee whatever against financial loss, or against artistic failure, unless, perhaps, their confidence in the beauties of their national game, and in the sport-loving spirit of the Australians, was all the guarantee they wanted.

MR. DANIEL O'CONNOR, M. P., SYDNEY, N. S. W.

President Spalding responded in a manner that won him continued and hearty applause, and it is safe to say that when the curtain finally fell, the Royal contained none who were unfriendly to our party. A laughable incident, and one which shows how far a professional ball-player's fame may extend, and how small the world is, after all, occurred as the curtain fell. A voice from the gallery rang out with an unmistakable juvenile ring, "'Rah for Baby Anson." The boy may have been an American lad who had seen many a championship game at home before having drifted to far-away New South Wales, or he may have been an Australian reader of our American baseball papers, but whatever his nationality, he was a resident of Australia, and had recognized "Baby" Anson when he saw him.

HIS WORSHIP, MAYOR HARRIS, OF SYDNEY, N. S. W.

The ensuing days of our stay in Sydney were filled with pleasant incidents and unlimited entertainment and attentions. At 11 o'clock on the morning after our arrival, we assembled in the office of the Oxford for a formal call at the city hall upon His Worship, Mayor Harris. The big four-in-hand coaches, decorated with the Stars and Stripes, as upon the preceding evening, took us through the principal streets and past enthusiastic throngs of people, not a few of whom stopped to send a cheer after us as we drove by. U. S. Consul Griffin, members of the reception committee and representatives of the Sydney press accompanied us. At the City hall we were received in the council chamber by His Worship, attired in his official robes of purple and ermine, after which we crossed the hall to the mayor's chamber, in the centre of which stood a big table draped with snowy linen and loaded with refreshments, while half a dozen side-whiskered butlers broke the wires upon half a hundred quarts of Clicquot, Mumm and Pomery. The mayor received us with a cheery speech, telling us that Sydney was glad to welcome us, and would doubtless demonstrate, to our entire satisfaction, the interest it felt in the visit of so representative a body of American athletes. He believed that Australians would like baseball, and though he did not understand the game thoroughly himself, he thought well enough of it to predict that in time Australia would herself have a league embracing teams capable of coping with our American professionals. He was personally glad to see us, and tendered us the freedom of the city during our stay. United States Consul Griffin responded happily to the mayor's address, and then His Worship again arose to say that so long as Americans treated Australia with the degree of consideration they had always in the past extended, Australians would make it pleasant for their American cousins while the latter were upon Australian soil. "My reasons for believing that our athletes will emulate your baseball players" said His Worship, in conclusion, "are manifold. In the first place, we have adopted your American ideas of trotting, and we have managed to scrape up material enough to beat your best oarsmen." Here His Worship turned toward oarsman Ned Hanlan, who had quietly entered the room and taken a seat near President Spalding, and the reference was enough to secure for Hanlan a hearty burst of applause from his fellow-Americans. "And," continued the mayor, "if all Americans will yield the palm with as good grace as Mr. Hanlan has done, we will entertain as high an opinion of them as we now do of Mr. Hanlan." The Canadian was loudly cheered when, in answer to a unanimous call, he arose and told us of the warm hospitality of the Australians and his many delightful experiences during his stay among them. Responses to the mayor's address by Mr. Spalding and Leigh Lynch followed, and after drinking to the dozen or more toasts proposed, we withdrew to our equipages, with three American cheers and the inevitable tiger for the Mayor of Sydney.

That same afternoon we played our first game in Australia upon the grounds of the Sydney Cricket Association, and the boys were compelled to admit that, in whatever other respects the Colonies might be inferior to the United States, they certainly possessed athletic grounds so far superior in point of equipment and condition to anything we had in the United States at that time, that there was no room whatever for comparison. The drive to the Sydney grounds is in itself an attractive one, and the playing-field, as level as a floor, velvety with its thick covering of green turf, and surrounded by its sloping lawns and prettily-designed club houses, is a sight to delight the eye of any man who ever played cricket or baseball. Threatening weather doubtless kept many from the grounds, and the great annual foot races at Botany, together with the horse races, affected the attendance at our game to no small extent; still, there were in the neighborhood of 4000 people upon the grounds, and the strict and evidently interested attention paid by the big crowd to a foreign game, with which they were unfamiliar, was a gratifying surprise to the players and a pretty mark of

BASE SLIDING AS AUSTRALIANS SAW IT.
(From the Illustrated Paper published in Sydney, N. S. W.)

respect to our party and to America's national game. Everybody was quick to recognize and appreciate many of the stronger points of play, and all vigorously applauded the base-sliding and running, as well as the good stiff batting indulged in by both teams, all of which were well illustrated in their pictorial papers. The game was a pretty one. It was nip and tuck up to the fifth inning, when Chicago, by the capture of one run, tied the score, and it so remained until All-America sent a man across the plate in the ninth inning, with the winning run. Indeed, had the boys played it to order, they could scarcely have put up a more interesting game or a prettier exhibition of the most attractive features of baseball. During an interval of fifteen minutes at the end of the sixth inning, Lord Carrington, Governor of New South Wales, received the party in the Association club house, where His Excellency, who is a great lover of athletic sports, welcomed us warmly to the colony and wished us every success in our efforts to introduce the game into Australia. President Spalding responded, and, after three cheers for Lord Carrington, Lady Carrington, the Queen, the President, Australia and Sydney, the boys withdrew to finish the game, their reappearance upon the field being the signal for a continued shout of applause from the spectators.

The ride from the grounds was followed by an excellent dinner at the hotels, and then the boys broke away in congenial groups to see something of Sydney after dark. The theatres had all extended general invitations to our party, and each had several representatives present during the evening. John Ward, Ed Hanlan, Jim Manning and myself, under the leadership of Messrs. Allen and Murray, of the *Sydney Star* and *Melbourne Sportsman*, dropped into Larry Foley's gymnasium—the sporting headquarters of Sydney—and witnessed a by no means bad set-to of eight rounds, between two very clever middle-weights. Others of the boys were present at an athletic entertainment at the Sydney Opera House. At the close of the different performances the boys dropped into the various resorts about town, and not a few of us became interested students of that not uninteresting colonial institution, the Australian barmaid, with which no Australian café or drinking resort is unprovided. In most cases they are pretty, in every instance smart, and combining with these qualities an excellent knowledge of mankind and his weaknesses, they are more valuable to the Australian liquor dealer than our most expert beverage mixers would be, for the Australian, like the Englishman, rarely asks for other than a glass of ale or beer, or a bit of brandy and soda. It is fortunate he is so simple in his tastes, else he would suffer as does the average American who steps into an Australian bar room, expecting to be served as he would be in Chicago, San Francisco, or New York.

Our first Sunday in Australia—the day after our game—was most delightfully spent, the boys dividing into parties of six or eight, to accept invitations extended us for a drive upon tally-ho coaches through the suburbs of Sydney, some driving out to the beautiful Botany Bay district and others, including myself, going to the bluffs and shores of Coogee Bay. We drove over sloping hills and beautiful valleys with their excellent roadways, lined upon each side by pretty vine-clad, flower-embowered homes of white stone, the names "Edgewood," "Myrtle Terrace," etc., being cut into a square block of stone to answer the purpose of the ugly, unromantic "1922," ".1924," etc., which we paint upon the transoms of our doorways in America. Our road lay for the greater part along or near the shore, and we could

FARM COVE—ONE OF THE BEAUTIES OF SYDNEY BAY.

catch an occasional glimpse of Sydney Bay or some one of its many beautiful coves, to the waters of which the terraced hills descended. After an hour of such driving we came suddenly in view of the beach, and finally dismounted at the aquarium on the seashore. Our party was invited inside, and saw a collection of many hundreds of native fish—some of them remarkable specimens—in the big plate-glass tanks, into which the sea water is being constantly injected. Adjoining the aquarium is the bathing-tank, and into this the boys plunged for a sea bath that, as Fogarty declared, put them in good trim for a week's ball-playing. After our bath we enjoyed the concert in the pavilion, not forgetting to drink Manager Stafford's health before leaving, and then made our way to "The Point," a great ledge of rocks, around the base of which the sea breaks with impressive grandeur. The view of the ocean from here is magnificent, and down on the sandy beach to the right of the rocks the bathing is particularly fine. The boys were hungry when we got back to the hotel, but not too tired after supper to attend

SYDNEY'S FASHIONABLE BATHING BEACH AT COOGEE BAY.

a delightful concert at the Criterion Theatre, at which we remained until the last number had been given.

None of the boys, I am sure, will forget the first attempt at cricket by the Chicago and All-America teams in Australia. It took place upon the Sydney grounds, between 11 and 1 o'clock, the day after our drive to Coogee. Mr. Spalding, George Wright, Billy Earle and George Wade doing the bulk of the bowling, and the innings ending with a score of

67 to 33, in favor of All-America. Anson, as Captain of the Chicago team, and as one of the greatest baseball batters in America, was accordingly disgusted. All the way across he had been telling what he individually, and a team of his selection, would do at cricket, and had made not a few bets to back his assertion. Consequently, the boys listened to him respectfully as he coached them during the game, and looked upon him with great expectations when he went to bat. When he struck at the first ball bowled at him, however, and was retired on a little pop-up fly ball to Fogarty, some of the boys fell to the turf with laughter and "Anse" looked six inches shorter as he stepped to one side. He tried to "bluff" out of it, but Tom Burns told him to go and sit down, and "Anse" retired to a corner of the field to bat Mascot Duval's bowling. He was crusty enough to snap Tom Burns' head off an hour after when Tom tauntingly asked him if Clarence was "very speedy." Our second ball game in Sydney took place two hours after the cricket game referred to, in the presence of 3000 people, and like the first game, was a pretty exhibition and a close contest, resulting in a victory for All-America by a score of 7 to 5, with Baldwin and Healy as opposing pitchers.

Our first cricket game against Australian cricketers was played the following day, play commencing at 11 o'clock, and ending at 4 o'clock, with the Americans 87 runs in, and the Australians 115 runs in for six wickets, and playing as though they intended making as many more out of the remaining five. The game was brought to a close at this stage, however, to permit of the ball game being played. The latter, although close and hard fought, resulted in another victory for All-America. It was marked by little life, however, the boys being tired out as the result of their hard day's work at cricket.

I asked George Wright that evening what he thought of the showing our men had made at cricket, and he expressed the belief that had they been half as strong in bowling as in fielding, they would have been a match for the Australians. There was many a burst of applause over our fielding, but our batting was very weak, and we had no bowlers aside from Messrs. Wright and Spalding. The Australians gave us the advantage of seventeen men to their eleven.

Although tired out upon arriving at the hotel, the boys changed their uniforms for evening dress, and attended the banquet tendered by the citizens of Sydney at the Town Hall. Two hundred plates were laid, and nearly every seat was occupied. The Reception Hall of the great building, with its palatial dome, great stone columns and stained glass windows, was one gorgeous array of English and American flags. Upon one side of the room was a life-size portrait of Her Majesty, and just opposite was one of the Duke of Edinburgh. The long tables were loaded with every delicacy the *chef's* deft fingers could prepare or his skill suggest, the beauty of the entire scene being enhanced by the soft-colored lights which burned upon the table. The corridors were embowered in tropical shrubbery and trailing vines which only half hid the luxuriant divans and lounges which had been conveniently set about for the use of the guests. Soft carpets covered the marble floors, while on every side, and almost at every step, were banks of cut flowers and plants that filled the air with their delightful perfume. At one end of the hall a raised platform had been erected, and upon this a musical and literary entertainment was given at the close of the feast.

Our trip thus far had been one round of banquets and receptions, but that feast in Sydney was certainly the most elaborate and memorable we had yet enjoyed. The great room in itself, 80 feet from floor to dome and with 125 by 60 feet floor space, its magnificent ceiling of white and gold, its costly paintings, its gorgeous chandelier with two hundred and fifty crystal globes, its wealth of stained glass and its decorations of flags and flowers, was imposing beyond description, and especially so when to these adornments was added the presence of one hundred and fifty gentlemen and ladies in evening dress at banquet. Toasts were proposed, and were responded to by United States Consul Griffin, the Hon. Daniel O'Connor, President Spalding, John M. Ward, Leigh Lynch, Newton McMillan, Mr. E. G. Allen, of the Sydney *Star*, and others. They included: "The Queen," "The President," "The Governor," "Our Guests," "The Ladies," "The Press" and "The Chairman."

Following the responses to the last toast came a musical treat by some of the best amateur and professional talent in Sydney. Among the numbers given was a cornet solo, with piano accompaniment by Mrs. Leigh Lynch. Her execution was a revelation to every one present, and when she played "Yankee Doodle," "Star Spangled Banner," and other popular American airs, the guests arose from their seats and filled the room with a long and enthusiastic burst of applause, while they plucked handfuls of roses from the floral banks upon the table and showered them at the fair musician, who was encored again and again.

This brief reference to the incidents of that memorable evening falls far short of an adequate description of the generous spirit and memorable events of our last hours in Sydney. Sydney people are without doubt among the most hospitable on earth. They did not permit our party to rest an hour after our steamer reached their dock, and certainly no party of Americans ever left a city with more honest regret and kind remembrance than did ours when we took the train for Melbourne the following evening.

There had been no game arranged for the day of our departure, and we put in our time bidding farewell to many friends that each had made. During the morning the boys visited a down-town store, and each secured a neat straw hat with a band of red, white and blue ribbon. An American traveling man whom we met in Sydney also presented the boys with a button-hole badge of the stripes and stars, so that it was not at all difficult for Sydneyites to distinguish the members of our party.

An hour before train time we entered a four-in-hand drag at "The Oxford," and were driven to the "Grosvenor Hotel," where the Hon. Daniel O'Connor had invited us for a farewell to himself and other representative residents of New South Wales. The beautiful dining-room of the hotel had been prettily decorated, and was comfortably filled with the members of our party and some thirty invited guests, and the manner in which we made the walls ring with our cheers as we drank to the toasts proposed, is probably still remembered by the regular patrons of the hotel.

After three rousing cheers for everything and everybody in Sydney, we entered our drag, and were driven to the railroad station, where, thanks to the Railway Department of the New South Wales Government, we took a special train for Melbourne. The English-styled compartment-coaches were novelties to us, and for that reason, probably, we smiled good-naturedly at the discomforts we experienced. The Americans who had made it so pleasant for us at Sydney were down in force to see us off, and nearly all of them brought a package or two for the boys. The ride out of Sydney is beautiful, and with the comforts of the elegantly-appointed Pullman Sleepers to which Americans are accustomed would have been voted equal to anything at home. The land is rich and fertile, and the hills are thickly wooded, while they are well cultivated and quite generously populated. The roadbed of the railway, which is operated by the Government, is equal in solidity of construction, I think, to any I ever traveled over. We took supper at the little station of Mitagon soon after nightfall, and then the boys stretched out upon the comfortable leather-covered cushions of their compartments, and told stories and exchanged experiences over their cigars while they looked out upon the moonlight-flooded woodlands.

The only unpleasant incident of our journey from Sydney to Melbourne was a change of cars on the borders of the Colony at 5.30 o'clock in the morning, and the examination of our baggage by the Customs Authorities. These gentlemen, fortunately for us, did not think it necessary to examine our luggage very closely, however, so we escaped with but little inconvenience in this respect, and at about 6 o'clock started for Melbourne, which we reached at 11 o'clock. Our train came to a halt in a substantial-looking station at Spencer street, and as we entered, a cheer went up from fully five hundred people on the station platform, apprising us that Melbourne was ready and waiting to receive us. A number of the American residents of Melbourne being members of the reception committee appointed to meet us, and the Victorian Cricket Association also being well represented, we received a most hearty welcome on our arrival at the Victorian capital. Four-in-hand drags profusely decorated with American colors were in waiting, and as our party, wearing their straw hats with the red, white and blue bands, mounted these and drove up Collins Street they attracted general attention and not a few cheers.

We finally drew rein at the Town Hall, where Mayor Benjamin and members of the City Council were to receive us. In front of the imposing building a crowd of between two and three thousand people had assembled, and after elbowing our way across the sidewalk we passed up stairs into the great audience hall, in which has been constructed one of the grandest pipe organs I ever looked upon or listened to. The town organist, Mr. David Lee, treated us to some beautiful music, there being more than one grave face and wet eye among our party as the lovely strains of "Home, Sweet Home," filled the hall. We all arose and removed our hats as the organ sounded ."God Save the Queen." We then passed into the Mayor's private room, where a generous collation had been prepared. Among those present to receive

TOWN HALL OF MELBOURNE, AUSTRALIA.

us were the Hon. Mr. Choppin, Consul-General of the United States at the Melbourne Exposition ; Mr. Smyth, Acting Consul ; the Hon. J. B. Patterson, D. Gaunson and Messrs. Chas. Smith and Pierce, with a large number of sport patrons, cricketers and footballers. The Mayor welcomed us in a plain-spoken, hearty speech, referring to the pleasure it gave him to address such a party of Americans, who had come so far for the purpose of making Australians familiar with the game for which so much was claimed in so great a country as the United States. He could assure them of a hearty welcome to Melbourne, and trusted that they would have only pleasant remembrances of the Colonies to take away with them when they returned to their own country. Pleasant words by the Hon. Mr. Smith on behalf of the Victorian Cricket Association, by Mr. Smyth, Acting United States Consul, by Mr. S. P. Lord, who was designated as "an old colonist from America since '53," and a "baseballer," followed; and then Mr. Spalding, after being enthusiastically cheered, properly expressed his appreciation of so cordial a welcome, and expressed a hope that Victorians would take as kindly to our game as they had to its exponents. Captain Ward and Captain Anson were each called upon, and then Frank Lincoln brought down the house, as he always did, by mixing one of his inimitable cocktails. Toasts were drunk to the Victorian Cricket Association, and were followed by brief addresses by Major Wardell, Town Clerk Fitz-

MAJOR WARDELL, SECRETARY VICTORIAN CRICKET ASSOCIATION.

gibbon, Mr. David Scott, and others, and after three parting cheers and a "tigah" for the Mayor and the reception committee, we were driven to our hotel, where we secured much-needed rest and a good dinner. We were quartered at the Grand Hotel, from the doors of which could be seen the Exposition Buildings, and opposite which were the Treasury Building, Parliament Building and the Fitzroy Gardens. In

Melbourne, the Grand, the Federal and other of the most magnificent hotels of the city are termed " Coffee Palaces." They are splendidly equipped, and, in the way of appointments, surpass anything we had met with since leaving Chicago. The boys certainly had little to grumble at in their accommodations at Melbourne.

No plans having been laid for our journey beyond Melbourne—the Victorian Capital having originally been our objective point—we all looked upon it as a temporary home at least, and it was with a feeling of great relief from the almost constant travel of over ten thousand miles that the boys unpacked their trunks in their pleasant rooms at " The Grand." That same evening we accepted an invitation from Mr. Musgrove, a partner of Mr. Williamson, of the Royal Theatre in Sydney, and one of the famous theatrical firm of Williamson, Garnier & Musgrove, to attend the Princess Theatre, where an excellent English company was producing " The Princess Ida." We occupied a full section in the Dress Circle, the fashionable section of all Colonial theatres, and the boys, as they appeared in their evening suits, were certainly a magnificent-looking body of men. At the end of the third act we were called out to one of the reception-rooms, where we met Mr. Musgrove personally, and drank his health in a couple of cases of Monopole. The speechmaking was brief though hearty, and Mr. Musgrove informed us that the doors of his theatre were open to us at any and all times. It was past midnight when we finally reached our rooms at the hotel.

One feature of the Grand Hotel of which I had almost forgotten to speak was the number of pretty Colonial girls employed in almost every department of the big hotel. They answered the ring of one's electric bell, they hovered over one at the table in the dining-hall, they took one's order in the *café*, they did everything and anything, save handling the baggage and filling the duties of a porter. One of the boys—of course, it was Fogarty—made a ten-strike with these maidens within five minutes after his arrival among them, and during the balance of our stay at the Grand he came pretty near getting anything he wanted, from a *café noir*, served in his room, to a lunch at midnight. When he arrived he found, upon reaching his room, that his trunk had not been sent up ahead of him. With characteristic impulsiveness he stepped into the hall and rang every electric bell in sight, with the result that half a dozen

THE GRAND HOTEL, STOPPING PLACE OF THE TOURISTS IN MELBOURNE, AUSTRALIA.

maidens were at his door within a minute after. "Me trunk," exclaimed Fogarty, in a dramatic tone; "me kingdom for me trunk."

"Why! hasn't it come up yet?" inquired a curly-headed bell-boyess.

"In truth, no," replied Fogarty; "and now look here. I am the Star of this combination—the Star, do you understand? and me trunk I must have, or there'll be no ball game here on Saturday. Now, do I get my trunk, or don't I?"

There was forthwith a flutter of skirts and a patter of feet, and five minutes later the porter stumbled into Foge's room with two heavy trunks, while the rest of the boys were awaiting theirs in the regular course of events.

Among the first to meet the Press representatives of our party were the newspaper men of Melbourne, among whom I saw most of Messrs. Linck, of the *Sportsman*, McDonald and Kendall of the *Herald*, and Harry Hedley of the *Age*, all good fellows, and all interested in seeing baseball established in Melbourne, and throughout the Colonies.

Our first game at Melbourne took place upon the second day after our arrival, and our professional *début* in Victoria could scarcely have been a more brilliant and auspicious one. Speaking of the event afterward, with Major Wardell, of the Melbourne Cricket Club, and others, they informed me that no such large and enthusiastic gathering of Melbournites had taken place at the Melbourne Oval since the palmiest days of Cricket in Victoria, and, certainly, I have never seen a prettier picture on race course or ball field, even in America, than that which offered itself upon the Melbourne Cricket Grounds on the occasion of our initial appearance. The sky was of the bluest, and the turf carpet upon the carefully-tended field was of the greenest. Away over across the waters of the Yarrow the towers and battlements of Government House arose in picturesque silhouette against the sky, while the pretty villas of St. Kilda could be seen further down the stream. The lawn in front of the Club House was occupied by numbers of pretty women, dressed in light-colored gowns and carrying bright-hued sunshades. The Club House balconies were crowded, and two hundred members, together with their ladies, had found seats upon the roof. The Grand Stand was packed, both chairs and aisles being full, while the crowd of people which encircled the field from the far end of the Grand

Stand to the Club House grounds averaged from thirty to forty deep. In short, we played to pretty nearly twelve thousand people, and the degree of interest they manifested in the game was a gratifying surprise to each and every member of our party. The game, though not an errorless one, was of the brilliant order. The base-running would have made even an American crowd of old-time ball lovers grow enthusiastic, and when Fogarty, Manning, Hanlon, Pettit, Carroll and Geo. Wood gave some exhibitions of base-sliding, of which they are so thoroughly capable, the big crowd stood up and yelled itself hoarse, while it waved wildly everything wavable that it could get its hands upon. Baldwin and Crane each pitched a pretty game, the hits standing

GRAND STAND OF THE MELBOURNE CRICKET GROUND.

seven to eight, and the score being tied three and three up to the seventh inning. Chicago finally got a man across the plate in the seventh, as a result of Burns' three-bagger, followed by Baldwin's single, then earned another run in the eighth, as a result of Sullivan's single and Anson's great three-bagger to right centre, "Anse" being put out at the plate by Brown's magnificent throw from the outfield upon trying to make a home-run off his hit. Tom Brown's running, which to me has always been one of the prettiest features of the games in which the Californian takes part, caught the Australians to a man, and many of them expressed a wish that Brown might enter for the foot-racing events there. Altogether, it was a great illustration of the beauties of the American national game, and the newspaper comments, while not altogether eulogistic, were still of a character very gratifying to those of us who had somewhat anxiously awaited the criticisms of the Melbourne press.

If the big, fine-looking fellows of our party had excited interest upon their arrival at Melbourne, they were made far more of after their game than before, for on the diamond the Melbournites had had an opportu-

THE BIG, FINE-LOOKING FELLOWS OF OUR PARTY.
(Photographed at Melbourne.)

nity of seeing the splendid physical development of the boys and their skill as athletes—qualities of manhood which are not valued higher anywhere than in Victoria, and, in fact, throughout Australia. That evening, after their game, the boys were entertained by Mr. Charles Warner, an English actor of note, at that time touring Australia. It was with the desire to meet the boys and do what he could to make it pleasant for them, that he extended to them an invitation to dine at the *Maison Doré*, the Delmonico's of Melbourne, and the dinner was certainly a charming success in every way. There were some gems in the way of after-dinner speeches, among which was one by Fogarty, the centre fielder's native Irish wit leaving every man doubled up with laughter when he finally took his seat. Of course there were also pretty references to Americans, to the profession of ball-playing, and to the character of our visit to Australia, and when, at eleven o'clock, the boys shook hands with their generous host they had recorded the event as one of the pleasantest of the trip. Although the dinner had been a treat indeed, and although Mr. Warner was the prince of hosts, a pleasant little supplement to the affair, coming unexpectedly, as it did, added still further to the evening's program. Joe Thompson, by far the best-known man of his calling in Australia, and well known throughout England and America as a successful and wealthy bookmaker, invited a number of Mr. Warner's guests to his rooms at the Grand Hotel, and, with the assistance of his charming wife and beautiful daughters, made the "wee sma'" hours memorable ones for each of his guests.

Shortly after breakfast on the following morning, President Spalding called the boys together in the big reading-room of the hotel, and announced to them definitely his intention of returning home by way of Egypt, the Mediterranean and Continental Europe. Had it not been Sunday morning, the cheers which filled the boys' throats at this announcement would have been let out for all they were worth, and even as it was, the room was filled with bursts of applause, while every man looked enthusiastically happy. President Spalding spoke frankly and in a manner that evidently interested all. He told the boys that they were going to strange countries, and among strange people, and that they would have to be discreet as to their habits, if only to maintain their good physical health. He wanted to land the boys in New York sound and well, and with only pleasant recollections of the tour, and he hoped that each and every member of the party would coöperate with him to this end. When the boys finally quit the reading-room they adjourned to the hotel rotunda and spent the balance of the morning in discussing the experiences they would probably enjoy during the remainder of the tour—now to become a tour around the world. The trip to Australia in itself had been a stupendous affair in the eyes of us all, and now we stood upon the threshold of an experience that falls to the lot of but a favored few, and it naturally aroused delightful anticipations.

Will Lynch, our advance agent, had left a day or two before for Adelaide, to overtake the P. & O. Line steamer there for Calcutta. He went to look the ground over and determine whether or not it would be advisable for us to go across to India and Bombay, or to cut that country and put in our time in Southern Europe. I met Lynch in the office of the hotel on the afternoon of his departure, and, with Yankee *sangfroid*, he shook hands with me, as he said, "Good-bye, old boy; won't see you again for a while; I'm going over to India to-night." Only a little journey of three weeks, covering sixty-four hundred miles across the Indian Ocean. It is indeed wonderful how time and distance lose their awe-inspiring proportions to the American who has traveled oceans as he has before traveled States in his own country!

Overwhelmed with attentions of all kinds, enjoying courtesies at the hands of the press, and being the recipients of public and private banquets and dinner parties without end, the boys did not suffer for lack of means for enjoyment, aside from their ball-playing, during the stay in Melbourne. Indeed, they gradually fell into the custom of getting into their dress suits every evening about six o'clock, so that they appeared in the hotel corridors for dinner in full evening dress, and were thereafter ready for the theatre or any other form of entertainment that might come up. It was a good departure, and did much, together with the demeanor of the men, to impress Australians favorably. The great Exposition Buildings were not neglected, and though scarcely so extensive or accessible as the Exposition since held in Paris, they were still a grand exhibit which attracted almost every Australian and tourist in the country.

None of us, probably, will ever forget Christmas of 1888, spent as it was in Melbourne, with the temperature standing at 90 degrees, and ourselves, as were all others in the city, attired in suits of flannel or some other equally cool-looking texture. The store windows were filled with displays of toys and Christmas gifts, and all day and evening the streets were thronged with purchasers, just as was, doubtless, the case at home, but amid surroundings so entirely different from anything we had ever experienced that we were struck with the novelty of it all.

Our second game, played the day before Christmas in the presence of about 6000 people, pleased the crowd immensely. It was one of those hard-hitting games that we sometimes see at home during the Championship season when an opposing team have dropped to the delivery of an unfortunate pitcher and are pounding him all over the field. In this game, however, both pitchers—Ryan and Healy—were the sufferers, and the batting was exceedingly lively from start to finish. The crowd showed its appreciation by standing up and cheering when

THE EXPOSITION BUILDING AT MELBOURNE.

the ball was batted into far out-field, or sending up a great roar of laughter when some of our crack base-runners tore the top off the green turf for a distance of ten feet or more in a desperate slide to the base. The boys seemed to partake of the spirit of the crowd and slugged the ball and ran bases until they were completely tired out. Following the game, the "Professor" gave his first ascent and drop with a parachute on Australian soil. It was certainly a thrilling exhibition, and caused the big crowd, which had never witnessed anything of the kind before, to stand in open-mouthed wonder, for Bartholomew was an artist and did his work well. At St. George's Theatre that evening a baseball farce, written for the occasion, was put upon the stage, and all of our party attended. A feature of the performance was the baton twirling and plantation dancing of Clarence Duval, the little darkey being encored again and again, and made the recipient each time of a shower of silver, besides a substantial recompense from the manager of the theatre.

Christmas day we departed from Melbourne for Adelaide. It was one of the hottest days we had experienced in Australia, and the boys turned out about ten o'clock attired in negligé shirts, belts, flannel suits and tennis shoes. We left for the Spencer Street Station at three o'clock, and were delighted to find, instead of the stuffy little English apartment cars we had expected, well appointed "Mann Boudoir cars," provided with all the comforts we could have expected in a railway carriage at home; riding, therefore, was not only comfortable but delightful. Four hours after leaving Melbourne we stopped at Ballarat, where we were to play after our visit to Adelaide, and found a committee of citizens, together with any number of pretty girls, at the station to meet us.

PROFESSOR BARTHOLOMEW.

Of course the depot rang with American cheers and "tigahs," before our train finally pulled out for the balance of our interesting ride across Victoria and South Australia. We saw no kangaroos along the road, as we had fondly anticipated, but we did see rabbits by the thousands. Rabbits in such numbers and of such sizes as we had never before imagined existed anywhere. As our train proceeded, they jumped out of stone piles, fence corners, clumps of grass and from every conceivable hiding-place, not singly, but in droves, until we could easily understand how these little pests in such numbers had proved a curse to Australian farmers. The country is picturesque and attractive, though by no means thickly settled. Fruit grows luxuriantly, and at every station the boys purchased sacks of luscious cherries and apricots, with which we gorged ourselves until we were sleepy. Ed Crane, who had not thrived under the hot sun of Australia, and the ladies of the party had been left behind us at Melbourne.

We arrived at Adelaide the day after Christmas, about half-past ten o'clock. And was it hot? At first the heat seemed unbearable, but we gradually became accustomed to it and had forgotten it soon after reaching our cool-looking hotels. Upon our arrival at the depot, we were met by United States Consul Murphy and other citizens, and driven directly to the town hall, where we were welcomed to the city by Mayor Shaw. His Worship's address was a warm one, and the response of President Spalding equally hearty. After the hand-shaking was over we were ushered into His Worship's private room, back of the Council Chamber, where a long white-draped table groaned under a load of champagne bottles, sandwiches, Milwaukee beer and baskets of fruit. It was a welcome sight indeed after our long and dusty ride, and we fell to in earnest, winding up with a "shake-down" from Clarence and a bit of cheering that must have convinced Adelaideans that we "had our voices with us." Then we bade good-morning to His Worship and were driven to our hotels, the York, the Prince Alfred and the South Australian, at all of which quarters had been secured.

Our first game took place that afternoon, and it being the opening day of the races in Melbourne, not over 2000 people were present. The Adelaide Oval is equal to those of Sydney and Melbourne so far as the condition of the grounds is concerned, but the buildings do not compare with those on the grounds of the former cities. It is about ten minutes' drive from the hotels, over an even road, past a pretty artificial lake and beyond a well-kept park, a number of handsome residences overlooking the grounds from surrounding hills. The afternoon, though hot, was a good one for ball-playing, and the crowd applauded the batting and base-running—about the only points they seemed to understand. The game was of a decidedly heavy-batting order, resulting in a victory for the All-Americas.

That evening, despite the fact that the boys were all tired out, we accepted the invitation of Messrs. Williamson, Garnier and Musgrove to witness " The Magistrate," by an excellent English Company at the Royal Theatre. The boys, in evening dress, occupied the Governor's Box, a favor rarely extended to visitors, and it is needless to say were the observed of all observers during the evening, the house being crowded, and ladies as well as gentlemen being attired in evening costume.

Perhaps the most delightful experience we enjoyed in South Australia was that of the following morning, when at half-past ten o'clock we assembled at the Town Hall to accept Mayor Shaw's invitation for a drive. A big four-horse drag with a black body and red wheels awaited us, and at eleven o'clock the driver cracked his long whip, the horses started, and the drag with our party bowled down the principal street of the city toward the Sea Beach road. The weather was much cooler, and the delicious breeze, coupled with some of the most picturesque scenery in South Australia, made every rod of our drive an enjoyable one. We sang, cheered, laughed at Fogarty's witticisms and cracked a good-natured joke at the expense of every pedestrian and equestrian whom we happened to pass on the road until, at the end of a ten miles' spin, we drew up at the vineyard of Thomas Hardy & Sons, the largest grape and fruit raisers in Australia. Here we dismounted, partook of Mr. Hardy's generous hospitality, were shown through the citron and almond groves, and then passed through the borders of the extensive vineyard, where bunches of delicious grapes hung upon all sides, and which the boys swallowed by the pound. We saw olives, lemons, oranges and almost every other form of tropical fruit growing in profusion, and finally explored the wine cellars near the house. Down into the great cool vaults we descended, winding about through the stone walls and big bulging casks, until we finally stopped in the " reception room " of the cellar, and drank glass after glass of delicious wine drawn from bottles thick with dust and cobwebs. With our wine were served ripe figs, big juicy globules of fruit, and the finest olives I ever tasted, and down in this wine cellar we gave, in honor of our hosts, three cheers that made the old walls ring, not forgetting to add three more when we mounted our drag and bid the beautiful vineyards farewell. From the vineyard we drove to Henley Beach, on the shore of the ocean, and spent half an hour in picking up the delicate shells from the wave-washed sands, in quaffing mugs of ale as we sat upon the balcony of the Beach Inn, and in looking out over the grand old ocean. Then we remounted for a delightful drive back to the city, and for our game of the afternoon. At our second game the attendance was better, and the playing was especially marked by some great base-running. Fogarty, Ward, Pfeffer, Hanlon, Pettit and Ryan distinguished themselves by some exhibitions of base-sliding which made the crowd applaud enthusiastically. Chicago won handily.

The following day being the fifty-second anniversary of South Australia's existence as a Colony, it was generally observed throughout the country. The Australians, by the way, are great people for holidays, and, like the English, improve every opportunity to indulge in one. As we were to leave that afternoon, we played our farewell game in the morning, beginning at ten o'clock, in the presence of a very good crowd, the result being an easy victory for Anson's forces. After the game Sir William Robinson, Governor of the Colony, who had witnessed four or five innings of the play, stepped upon the oval and shook hands with each member of both teams, afterward welcoming them in a neat little speech, in which he complimented the boys upon their physical prowess and skill upon the field, and expressed his interest in the game as he had seen it demonstrated. After A. G.'s response and our inevitable trio of cheers, we mounted our drags and drove back to the hotel.

Few days of our journey had been more prolific of events than that following the day of our departure from Adelaide. We entered the depot at Ballarat in the morning at six o'clock, and found a committee of citizens and a four-horse drag waiting to receive us. When we were all in our seats upon the top of the conveyance, A. G., as the boys had begun to familiarly address Mr. Spalding, missed Tom Daly, and on going back to the train, found him sleeping soundly in one of the apartment coaches and securely locked in by the guard. Where he would have found himself at the end of his nap, had we not found him, it is difficult to say, but President Spalding, after a deal of hard work, found a guard to unlock the door and succeeded in getting Tom out upon the platform. Probably none of us have since forgotten what a funny looking object the Chicago catcher was as he stumbled out of the depot with his hair awry and with one eye open, making his way to the drag, which, after several vain attempts, he mounted. Tom was not the only one of us who wished that Pullman sleeping-coaches had been introduced into the Colonies before the date of our arrival.

The sun was just coming up over the housetops as we rattled through the streets of the awakening town, and finally drove up to the doors of Craig's Hotel. We made our toilets hastily and repaired to the breakfast room, where the Reception Committee had arranged for us a layout of hot coffee, sandwiches, chowchow pickles, and the inevitable brandy and soda, and in characteristically liberal quantities. We finally endeavored, after making an attempt to cheer our Reception Committee —an attempt, by the way, which ended in a disconnected and very sleepy "Rah-Rah"—to retire to our rooms for a very badly-needed nap, but that privilege was not to be allowed us. The Reception Committee piled us upon the drag again, and we started for the Botanical Gardens. The drive was a beautiful one, and the fresh air of the morning served to awaken us more thoroughly than anything else could have done. Our route lay along the shores of the extensive lake that penetrates the residence district, and then along the borders of the most beautiful public gardens I had ever seen. We dismounted at the main gate and spent half an hour looking and admiring the beautiful groups of statuary and the flowers. Our ride beyond the gardens was in a circle, so that at the end of two hours we were not far from our starting-point. Before pulling up at the hotel, however, we had a bath in the great Ballarat Swimming Aquarium, which refreshed us thoroughly and put us all in the best of spirits. On our return to the Craig a good breakfast awaited us, which we had scarcely swallowed when we were asked to mount the drag for another drive. This time we drove to the Barton Gold Mines, on the edge of the town. After attiring ourselves in overalls, canvas jackets, slouch hats and rough boots, we took a trip to the bottom of the mine, 1100 feet below the surface. Some of the make-ups of our party were indeed laughable: Captain Anson looked like a railway section boss, Bob Pettit like a day laborer, and A. G. like the king of a "white cap" organization. Our rough apparel filled the bill, however; for if there is a wet and slimy place on this earth—or rather, beneath it—it is the lower end of an Australian gold-mine shaft. A gold mine is not unlike a coal mine in appearance, and there was really little to see save the shadowy forms of the miners, with their ghostly-looking head-lamps, and the dripping walls of stone and timber. Still, it was something to have gone to the bottom of such a cavern, and all of us were interested in the journey.

From the mine we were driven to the Town Hall. Ballarat, by the way, is divided into two municipalities: East and West Ballarat. Each

THE BOTANICAL GARDENS, THE PRIDE OF SYDNEY, N. S. W.

has its separate town officers and town hall. We first called upon the Mayor of West Ballarat, Mayor Macdonald, and enjoyed the same course of feasting and wine-drinking that we had enjoyed in other Australian cities. We then bowled through the town to East Ballarat, where we were the recipients of another "lay-out" and hearty welcome at the hands of Mayor Ellsworth. Mayor Ellsworth, however, went still further: he mounted our tally-ho with us, and drove us to the Ballarat

Orphan Asylum, where we amused ourselves by throwing shilling pieces into the waters of the bath-houses for a hundred little boys to dive for. Then we drank more wine—this time with the officers of the Institution, and finally drove back to our hotel, tired out, but possessed of a fair idea of Ballarat, its people, its hospitality and its environs. President Spalding, by the way, invited all the youngsters of the Asylum to the game, and they attended that afternoon, two hundred strong.

A great crowd for Ballarat—nearly 4500—assembled to see our game that afternoon, and showed their appreciation of it by staying until the last man had been put out. The game was a good one, All-America taking the lead in the sixth inning as a result of a pretty streak of batting that was not thereafter broken. The crowd was quick to discover and appreciate the good points in the fielding and batting, and before three innings were completed, were applauding heartily. The sensation of the afternoon, however, was the ascent and fall of Professor Bartholomew. The light air of the high altitude would not sustain his weight, and the parachute fell with great rapidity for over two thousand feet. It descended in the centre of the business district, the professor striking the cornice of a roof, and gouging himself in a manner that laid him up for a month thereafter. Altogether, he met with a very narrow escape. Our departure was taken at seven o'clock that evening for Melbourne, and the five hours' ride to the Victorian Capital in the English compartment cars was certainly the most fatiguing one we had yet experienced. The boys looked a bit knocked out when they came down to breakfast next morning, but the invigorating cold showers, with which our hotel was wonderfully well provided, had an exhilarating effect, and we entered upon the day's programme, it being Sunday, with avidity.

At eleven o'clock we mounted two big four-horse drags, with the weather as fine as I have ever seen it in Australia, and started upon a twenty-five mile drive to the mountains. A Mr. J. H. Downer, a prominent and wealthy citizen of Melbourne, had asked us to be his guests for the day, and from the moment we left the hotel we were in his hands. Mrs. Leigh Lynch had her cornet with her, and as we rolled along over the country road, the "Tally-ho, tally-ho-ho" from her clear-sounding instrument caused many pedestrians to stop and gaze curiously at our big party in our gay-colored, light flannel suits, and red, white and blue rimmed hats. We saw more of the country surrounding Melbourne on that drive than at any time during our stay. It is rolling, well settled and picturesque until one gets into the bush land, when it is, like all other Australian bush districts, covered with scrub and possessed of no beauty of scenery whatever. The scrub, however, was finally passed, and we then entered the woodland at the foot of the mountains. High upon a hill sat a pretty villa surrounded by rolling lawns and prettily appointed out-buildings, a sort of oasis in the wild wilderness. From the top of one of the buildings floated an American flag, and we gave it a rousing yell as we passed it. Several handkerchiefs fluttered from the balcony of the house, and then a turn in the road hid the scene from view.

After an hour's ride we entered a picturesque rift in the mountains, and soon were sitting on the broad balcony of Mr. Bruce's house at "Fern Glen." A prettier bit of mountain scenery could scarcely be imagined. Giant trees arose on every side of the towering mountain, and Mr. Bruce's house and artistically laid out grounds appeared on the sides of the hill as if photographed there, with the mountain's growth as a frame work. Mr. Bruce, a friend of Mr. Downer, had gladly consented to entertain our party, and a big wagon-load of wines and delicacies had been sent out ahead of us that morning. The long table, with its load of good things, which had been set upon the balcony, was a welcome sight to our hungry crew, and we were not long in getting at it. It was a rich spread, embracing everything from champagne to soda and from roast turkey to sardines, and that we left little of it upon the table it is unnecessary to say. After dinner we took a walk through the beautiful glen above the house, our pathway being arched with great ferns that rose from twelve to fifteen feet high on each side of us, while a mountain stream, of crystal-like water, wound its way between their roots. At the head of the glen we seated ourselves upon a mammoth old moss-covered log, and listened to the "Star Spangled Banner" from Mrs. Lynch's cornet.

An hour later, at the house, Clarence Duval gave us another of his Alabama shakedowns to a guitar and mandolin accompaniment, and then with three cheers for Fern Glen, we turned our faces toward Melbourne. En route, we passed the stock farm of J.

J. Miller, who has undertaken the breeding of American trotting horses from imported mares and sires, on Victorian soil. It was he who had displayed the American flag to our gaze on the way out, and he now sent a messenger to ask us up to the house. It was late, but we could not refuse an invitation so offered. Upon dismounting we were cordially greeted, and were then shown the stock—Architect, by Contractor; Red Wind by Red Wilkes; Lucretia, by Mambrino Boy, Jr., and representatives of other equally celebrated strains. Then we

A JOLLY PARTY AT FERN GLEN.

were wined and toasted upon the broad balconies of mine host's pretty residence. Another exhibition of plantation dancing from Clarence, and more heartfelt cheering, and we bowled down the road, leaving mine host Miller standing at the gate. The "Travelers' Rest," the "Golden Swan," "Bull's Head Inn," and like hostelries were stopped at on our way back, for rest and refreshments, and we finally dismounted at eleven o'clock that evening in front of the Grand Hotel, where we shook hands with Mr. Downer, our host of the day.

An enticing programme had been scheduled for the last day of the year, but unfavorable weather partly spoiled it. The Carleton and St. Kilda Football teams were to play a game of football, Victorian rules, upon the pretty grounds of the St. Kilda's. Then our team was to play a game of ball with a team picked from the Melbourne cricketers, and the programme was to wind up with a game of football between the St. Kilda's and twenty of the Americans. The football game between the Australians proved a most interesting contest. There was a big crowd present, and much enthusiasm was manifested. The rules are a modification even of our most modified American college rules, and contain many points that make the Australian game in every way the most interesting of any football game I ever witnessed. As the fun proceeded our boys realized that we could make little show against the Australians, but they had no opportunity of testing their ability, as a heavy rain put a stop to the afternoon's sport.

ABORIGINAL AUSTRALIAN WOMAN AND BABE.

Two games were scheduled for New Year's day, but only one full game was played—that of the morning. The attendance was light, not more than 2000 people being present, and considering that there were 40,000 people present at the race-track, and as many more at the various cricket and athletic games going on about Melbourne, this attendance for a ball game in Australia was not unsatisfactory. President Moore, of the Victorian

Jockey Club, had invited our entire party to the races, but, as we were unable to procure a conveyance of any kind, we could not accept, and remained at the cricket grounds, where the pure air and beautiful surroundings, together with an elaborate lunch set out for us by Secretary Wardell, of the Melbourne Club, was greatly enjoyed.

After the lunch an exhibition of boomerang-throwing and rope-skipping was given for the entertainment of the crowd and our party by a number of aboriginals, and it was certainly a treat, at least to the Americans present. The degree of skill attained by the black-faced, bushy-haired Queenslanders in the use of the boomerang is certainly remarkable. That afternoon, half a dozen big fellows performed feats with the peculiar Australian weapon which our party had frequently read of, but had never before credited. The light "V"-shaped piece of wood, with its sharp edges, shot from the hands of the natives into the air for a distance of two or three hundred feet, and then, turning suddenly, described perhaps half a dozen circles about the head of the thrower, gradually narrowing the circle until it fell almost at his feet. Again it would go out in a direct line and return in a line as direct, passing over the head of the thrower and returning back again to the spot upon which he stood. The skipping-rope performance, with which the natives are wont to amuse themselves, was quite a grotesque and yet clever performance, the per-

ABORIGINAL AUSTRALIAN MAN AND BOY WITH BOOMERANG.

formers assuming all kinds of queer postures, and yet never failing to raise their bodies from the ground, and at the proper moment, to permit of the rope passing under them at regular intervals. Several of the boys tried their hands at boomerang throwing, and discovered how very little they knew of the use of the Australian weapon. After this exhibition, the Chicago team played an exhibition game with a team composed of Melbourne cricketers, and the crowd enjoyed this about as well, judging from their laughter and applause, as any game we played upon the Melbourne grounds. Rain stopped the play, however, and the players soon after returned to their hotel.

January 5th was the day set for our last game in Australia, it having been decided to sail from Port Melbourne for Ceylon the following Monday afternoon. The intervening time was consequently put in as the boys liked best, and in view of the long trip ahead of us there was much to do in the way of shopping. All articles of clothing are cheap in Australia, compared with our American prices, and nearly all of us laid in a generous provision of flannel suits, underwear and linen. Curios and mementoes characteristic of the country and people also took a fair share of our pocket money and attention. Most of us secured a kangaroo skin, an emu egg, a lump of kauri gum, and photographs of the principal Australian cities. Many of the boys visited the American exhibit at the Exposition, which was quite extensive and altogether very creditable.

The night before our departure, by the way, was an eventful one at the Grand Hotel. The two hundred and fifty guests had scarcely gotten into bed when the interior of the big court was illuminated by a red glow, and cries of "Fire," rang out upon the air. Consternation prevailed; women screamed and men shouted. Manning, of the All-Americas, stuck his head out of the window to learn the trouble and received a champagne bottle on the back of his neck, which cut him badly. Others who followed Manning's example were drenched with water from the upper windows, and it soon became evident that somebody in the building was bent upon making the night interesting for every guest in the establishment. Among the first to hear the cries and be awakened by the lurid glare from the court were Fred Pfeffer and Clarence Duval, Clarence having curled up in a blanket on the floor of

Pfeffer's room. Fred jumped from the bed with one bound and made for the door, but stumbled over Clarence on the way.

"Don't stop to talk, boy," cried Pfeffer, "but get out of here as quick as you can; don't you see the hotel is on fire?"

At this, Clarence, seeing the glow, became panic-stricken and lost no

A PRECIPITATE FLIGHT ON A FALSE ALARM.

time—though, like Pfeffer, attired only in his abbreviated night robe—in following the second baseman out into the hall and down the staircase, Pfeffer, doubtless actuated by humanitarian motives, calling "Fire," and pounding at the doors as he ran. Down the stairs went one section of Chicago's stone-wall in-field, seven steps at a time, closely followed by the little African, who was adding his cries to Pfeffer's. The cause, as it turned out, was simply the drunken spree of a couple of young tourists on the upper floor of the hotel, but it threatened for a time to be of a serious character, several ladies fainting and a number of others being greatly terrified by the uproar. When the excitement had finally subsided, and it was learned that the whole trouble had been caused by the burning of a red light on one of the window-sills, accompanied by the howls of the practical jokers, a crowd of angry men in night attire searched the halls, and many of the bed-rooms, for the perpetrators, but finally gave up the effort. Then they eagerly demanded to know who the man was who had gone through the halls yelling fire, and Pfeffer, in night attire like the balance of them, was as anxious as the rest to discover the identity of the villain, although it is said he was inwardly trembling at the time for fear that some one who had seen him as he was charitably arousing the guests from their slumbers by his warning cries, might point him out as the culprit. Clarence Duval was found crouching behind the big water-cooler in the office, trying hard to cover his black legs with a floor-rug. His only comment upon the entire performance was: "Befoh Gawd, I nevah knowed how fass Massah Peffah could run till to-night; he nevah touched de floah fum de top of dem stairs clean to de bottom, an' I knows what I's talkin' about, kase I was mighty cloas behin' 'im."

Our farewell game in Australia was played Saturday afternoon, and the assemblage of spectators present, both as to character and numbers, showed the interest which our visit had awakened in the American game. The day was a perfect one for field-sport exhibitions, and when the great crowd of between eleven and twelve thousand had filed through the gates, surrounding the beautiful oval with a living framework of humanity, the scene was indeed brilliant. The programme was a varied one, opening with a two-inning game at three o'clock between the All-America team and a team of cricketers. As in previous engagements, between the Australians and Americans, the superiority of the latter in fielding was plainly apparent. In fact, the Australians were not in the game at all, but they worked hard and evinced the deepest interest in every point of play. At half-past three o'clock, after the completion of two innings between the Australians and Americans, a football game between the Port Melbourne and the Carleton team began, and a prettier exhibition of the kind I have never seen. The Victorians have pruned down and modified the old Rugby rules in a style that has removed much of the danger to life and limb, while it has at the same time increased the opportunities for the display of skill, and has given the game a greater dash and vim than appear in our American college game. I have only one criticism to make of the Australian football teams, and that is this. If they were, as a body, to pay more attention to the selection and designs of their uniforms, they would be a much finer-looking set. The contrast between the becomingly uniformed ball-players and the pick-up costumes of the footballers was much to the discredit of the latter. But they know how to play football, for all that; and I imagine that there is a great deal of truth in the assertion that any football team from England, or America, that can go over there and beat the Australians at their own game, can carry away a cartload of money.

Following the football game, the Chicagos and All-Americas began a five-inning ball game, which was as pretty an exhibition as any we had given since leaving Chicago. Baldwin and Daly, and Crane and Earle were the batteries, and they played ball for all they were worth. When game was called at the end of the fifth inning to clear the field for the long-distance throwing contest the score stood 5 to 0 in favor of Chicago, with not a fielding error on either side, every run of the five having been earned by Anson's men, and but one safe hit scored off Baldwin. The fleetest of the All-America base-runners were unable to steal a base on Daly or Baldwin, and it was equally true that the quickest throwers to bases in the league could not have stopped the Chicago men that day in their thieving practices. Crane and Earle never watched bases more carefully or more accurately, but it was to no purpose—Chicago was out for plunder and got all it wanted, through some of the prettiest base-sliding I ever witnessed. The crowd appreciated many points of the game, which they had not seen or understood at our opening exhibition ten days before, a fact made evident from the applause created over pretty pieces of work, and when Pettit finally ended the game with a great running catch of Earle's long hit to right field, the big crowd applauded until the players had lifted their caps in front of the grand stand.

The exhibition of long-distance throwing was not less interesting than the other portions of the programme, the object being to beat the five and one-half ounce Cricket Ball, Australian record, of 126 yards 3 inches. The effort was made by Crane, Williamson and Pfeffer, and was accomplished by Crane, who sent the ball 128 yards 10½ inches. It was a magnificent throw, and elicited a yell of applause the moment the ball struck the ground, the crowd seemingly realizing that the record had been broken, before the measurements were taken. Neither Williamson nor Pfeffer was in shape for throwing, the former failing to reach 126 yards, and the latter falling several feet short of that. The Professor was to have concluded the day's sport with a parachute leap, but had not sufficiently recovered from his injuries sustained at Ballarat to make the attempt. It was nearly six o'clock when the crowd filed through the gates and on through the beautiful Fitzroy Gardens toward town, the members of our party stopping at the Club House to bid farewell to Major Wardell and the cricketers, among whom the boys had made many friends during their stay. Our last evening in Melbourne was spent by some of the boys at the theatres, by others at Martin Castello's resort, where there was a bit of fun with the gloves between middle weights. Still others dropped in at the parlors of genial Joe Thompson, where music, Pomeroy Sec, and Joe's generous hospitality made the evening a memorable one.

On the following morning the boys came down to breakfast attired in purple and fine linen, realizing no doubt that it would be the last opportunity for a display of their "store clothes" for some time to come. The rotunda of the Grand was crowded with people all day, many of them personal friends of the boys who had dropped in for a farewell chat. The day was beautiful, and some of us improved our time by a drive through the environs, or a stroll through Fitzroy Gardens, which were but a short walk from the hotel. The evening for the greater part was occupied in packing, and the following morning at 10.30 saw our luggage piled upon the two huge vans required to cart it to the depot. At three o'clock we drove to Port Melbourne Station, near Princess Bridge, where we took the train for Port Melbourne dock, seven miles distant.

This port gives superb accommodations for a fleet of fine sailing vessels and steamships, which cluster here from all quarters of the globe. Here lay the "Salier," one of the German Lloyd Steamers, which was to carry us across the Indian Ocean, and we were all soon comfortably settled in our respective state-rooms. Captain Thalenhorst and the Chief Steward and Purser, with whom we were brought most in contact on board, were affable and pleasant Germans, and had made every preparation for our comfort. On the "Alameda" the steerage passengers occupied the steerage, and the first cabin and saloon passengers were stationed amidships; On the "Salier," however, the steerage passengers

THE "SALIER" AT HER DOCK AT PORT MELBOURNE.

occupied the forward deck, and the cabin and first-class passengers were given the entire afterpart of the boat. The quarter-deck was covered with a big awning, and this furnished a magnificent lounging place, which we enjoyed during our entire voyage through the tropics. It was learned that the "Salier" would probably not sail before daybreak, and some of the boys returned to the city, but the majority remained on the steamer. The scene from the dock that afternoon, with its score or more of big sailing vessels alongside, its red-turbaned, dark-skinned Turks and Hindoos in their queerly-fashioned costumes of bright-colored cloth, together with the warm sun, the blue waters of the bay over which sea birds circled and little crafts moved hither and thither, with the picturesque shores of St. Kilda on one side and the smoke of Melbourne on the other, offered interesting studies for all. We had dinner aboard the steamer. Afterwards we sought the deck, where with our cigars, musical talent, and the company of friends who had come down to the steamer to see us off, we easily managed to put in a pleasant evening.

ON THE INDIAN OCEAN.

The "Salier" sailed from her dock at Port Melbourne at daylight on the morning of January 8th, and steamed slowly down the harbor toward the great Australian Bight. We were now fairly under way upon what most of us remember as the most delightful ocean voyage of our tour. The first week was not so pleasant, for after leaving Port Adelaide, at which we stopped twelve hours, we encountered a cold, raw wind from the South Seas, and the ocean swell was disagreeably heavy. After we had passed this portion of the voyage, however, and began to near the tropics, the air became warm, the sky clear, and the sea smooth, until more delightful sailing could scarcely be imagined. The quarter-deck of the ship, with its open-windowed smoking- and card-room, formed the assembly place of our party from the breakfast hour until midnight, and then, as upon the Pacific Ocean, most of the boys preferred donning their pjamas, and sleeping in the big, easy steamer-chairs, to going to their state-rooms. We were protected during the day by the immense awning, and at night, with a tropical moon lighting the surrounding ocean and making clear everything about the ship, our mandolins and guitars were brought out for a musical soiree on deck, which lost none of its charm for our party because of its originality, or through lack of artistic practice. The officers of the ship could not have been kinder, and it was with real regret that we parted from them when we left the ship at Suez.

There were probably 150 emigrants aboard, embracing Hindoos, Chinamen, Irishmen, Cingalese, Italians and Germans, and it was indeed interesting to take a walk through their quarters, and listen to the babble of tongues that one heard upon all sides. On the forward deck and amidships were located the scullery, the store-rooms and the stock-pens of the ship in which were kept two fat milch-cows, a number of sheep and calves and beeves, which were killed as we needed them for the table during the voyage, to say nothing of porkers, chickens, pigeons, pheasants, quail and all other animals and fowls which the purser intended for consumption by the four hundred people aboard the ship.

The cooking done on the "Salier" was really excellent, and meals were served in courses, which was at no time attempted on the "Alameda." The waiters were all German, and few of them spoke a single word of English, so that the attempts of some of our boys to make themselves understood at table were laughable. Several of us, however, were German scholars, and managed to help the others in learning sufficient German to make themselves fairly understood. We missed Frank Lincoln on this trip, he having decided to remain in Australia and take advantage of opportunities there offered. As there were not over half a dozen first-class passengers aboard in addition to our own party, we, figuratively speaking, owned the ship. The officers were not over-zealous in enforcing rules that might have been obnoxious or annoying to the boys and, in fact, allowed us to do

CAPTAIN THALENHORST, OF THE "SALIER."

very much as we chose, so that one was likely to hear a college chorus on deck at midnight, or to be startled during the quiet of the afternoon by a simultaneous cheer from a score of the boys in memory, perhaps, of our homes in far-off America.

During the afternoon of the day of our departure, I took a stroll over the "Salier" from stem to stern, and made myself familiar with every corner of our good ship, and at the same time studied her by no means uninteresting congregation of passengers. In the first-class cabin there was, in addition to our party, an Australian lady, a resident of Melbourne, who was taking her two little daughters to Germany to be left at school. There were, also, a couple of young civil engineers, who were returning home to England after a year's sojourn in Australia. But by far the greatest character on board ship was a Mr. Theophilus Green, a portly, middle-aged, red-faced, bald-headed individual, who, according to his own story, had an ample bank account, no kinsmen, and no object on earth but to hold himself up as a representative American among the various countries of the globe, which he visited as the whim or inclination might suit him to jump from Persia to Egypt, from Russia to South Africa, or from Iceland to Ceylon. He was a man possessed of quite a fund of interesting information, and yet his manner of impressing that fact upon all whom he met was so disagreeable that it detracted greatly, if it did not entirely destroy what would otherwise have made his companionship delightful. He had traveled all over the world, had seen everything, had mingled with almost every race of people under the sun, and possessed what must certainly have been a valuable collection of photographs of the different peoples and countries he had seen; but in the midst of an interesting description of Cairo, or Jerusalem and its people, he would suddenly break off to tell how smart he had been in evading the thieving and bulldozing propensities of an Egyptian cabman, or a Syrian innkeeper; and, laying his finger upon the side of his nose, would devote five minutes perhaps to telling how vastly superior was his own cunning to that of the Cingalese, Neapolitan, or Muscovite beggars who had so often appealed to him for alms. He never failed, in his conversation, to impress one with the fact that in every country, and with whomsoever he had been brought in contact, he declared himself to be a thoroughly "representative American." My chief regret was that our party of magnificent-looking fellows, with their liberal ideas, their love of fun, their fine physiques, and their genial, happy natures, were not going to some of the countries that Mr. Green had visited, so that, in the matter of representative Americans we might have shown those peoples the difference. We left the old fellow at Suez, when we departed from the "Salier" to go to Cairo, but there is a lingering suspicion in my mind that Mr. Green would have been with us all through Egypt and Continental Europe, but for the perhaps too brusquely offered snubbings which the majority of the boys extended. We never saw him afterwards, and he is probably knocking around the Orient at this writing, still posing as a "representative American."

Among the second-cabin passengers were two young Australians; big, broad-shouldered, muscular-looking fellows, of whom we saw a good deal as they paced the deck amidships for their daily exercise. They were bound for Zanzibar in Africa, and were to penetrate as far as possible into the interior upon a hunting expedition, which they intended to extend indefinitely as their health and success permitted. They were well equipped with weapons of modern construction and an unlimited supply of ammunition. They anticipated a great time, but I do not think any of our party, even had the opportunity offered, would have joined these gentlemen in facing the wild beasts and still wilder savages of Central Africa. Think of it! They expected to penetrate for 700 miles at least; to be cut off from all connection of any and every kind with civilization; to take their lives in their hands among savage tribes, who would be as likely to murder them for their weapons as not; to face the dangers of climate and poisonous reptiles, and all for their love of adventure and their desire to slay the King of Beasts in his native lair. We accepted an invitation to break a farewell bottle with them in the cabin before they finally left us at Aden, the nearest point to which the "Salier" could take them in their journey to Zanzibar. I am still anticipating a letter which will tell me of their first month's experience upon the dark continent.

Our mascot, by the way, was a great object of interest to the German waiters aboard the "Salier." On the "Alameda" he had been made to do light chores of different kinds, that he might to some extent pay for

286   ATHLETIC SPORTS.

his passage, but on the "Salier" the German waiters attended to his wants as though he had been an Indian prince. Indeed, two of them got into a difficulty one evening over a dispute as to which should serve Mr. Duval at the table, and the captain made one of the poor beggars "walk the bridge" all night, by way of penalty. The young African finally began to entertain so exalted an opinion of his own importance, however, that Mr. Spalding quietly suggested to Captain Thalenhorst that it might be a good idea to keep the boy employed. Consequently,

CLARENCE'S HUMILIATION AT THE PUNKA ROPE.

he was set to work pulling the punka rope, which swings the big tapestry fans suspended over the saloon tables; and thereafter, at meal time, the mascot sat on a chair at the end of the dining saloon pulling the rope, the picture of offended dignity, while the boys further added to his mortification by pegging an occasional ship's biscuit at him on the quiet.

Our only stop between Port Melbourne and Ceylon was that made at Port Adelaide, the second night after our departure. The Port is seven miles from Adelaide proper, a hot-looking little settlement, its buildings and streets apparently unsheltered by foliage of any kind, and we merely stopped to take on a cargo of South Australian wool. We did not finish loading, however, until two o'clock the following afternoon, and during the day employed our time by fishing over the rail of the ship, playing shuffleboard, horse billiards, quoits, and other deck games that we had picked up on the Pacific. The fishing was not bad sport, and as a dozen of us were leaning over the stern

AMUSEMENTS ON SHIPBOARD.

rail, watching the school of mackerel about our hooks, we were suddenly startled by the appearance of a shark, a big fellow, certainly not less than fifteen feet long. He lazily rolled about the stern of the ship as though in search of food, and then passed slowly out of sight. Had there been a shark hook at hand we might have enjoyed some rare sport. Shortly afterward, the black dorsal fin of the shark was seen a hundred feet from our boat as he swam slowly along, and Fogarty, Ryan, Ward and myself got our revolvers and made things so uncomfortable for his sharkship that he quickened his pace for the shore and was soon out of sight. After luncheon, we finished our loading and started on our trip across the Indian Ocean, not again to be interrupted until we had arrived in Ceylon.

The ensuing three days were thoroughly disagreeable. The sky was hidden by low, scudding, lead-colored clouds, the water was lashed into huge waves by a stiff wind, and a ground swell gave our ship a most uncomfortable motion. The ladies of the party, with the exception of Mrs. Williamson, who proved an excellent sailor during the entire tour of the world, did not appear on deck at all. Even Anson was pale and sick for the first time since leaving "Frisco." John Tener, Fred Pfeffer, the "Professor," myself, and the Mascot were the only ones who did not yield to sea-sickness. Fogarty's merry voice was hushed. He lay listlessly on a steamer chair and sighed softly to himself. About three o'clock in the afternoon he began to feel better and called for a cheese sandwich. A waiter appeared in a few moments with a big plate of sauerkraut and some steamed bologna sausages, thinking, no doubt, in the goodness of his German heart, that that which would please his own German stomach would best suit Fogarty's. "Foge" gave one horrified look at it and rolled upon the deck while he begged the Dutchman to take it away. Mrs. Anson fainted, and poor "Woody," Tom Brown, Ryan and Tom Burns all turned an idealic sea green at the same moment. John Tener fortunately happened along, however, and brought relief to the afflicted ones by grasping the tow-headed waiter by the coat collar and the slack of his trousers and hustling him, together with his plate, out of sight. It was rough and the temperature uncomfortably cool for fully four days during our journey through the Australian Bight, but after the ship had changed her course from an easterly to a northeasterly one, it began to grow warmer and the clouds gradually disappeared until the glorious sun of a southern clime warmed our party into life and genial temper. From thence on the weather grew more and more beautiful until, when we finally reached Ceylon, the Arabian Sea, and the Gulf of Aden, it could not possibly have been more delightful.

During our two weeks' voyage across the Indian, we were naturally driven to every recourse for means of passing the time. In view of our journey through Egypt, and possibly through India, the boys devoted themselves studiously to such books of travel as "An Australian Abroad," "India, Historical and Descriptive," "Jerusalem and the Holy Land," and others of like titles, but one could not read all day, and consequently each man of us utilized what ingenuity he possessed to hit upon some means of diversion. So soon as the weather became pleasant, we divided into groups of four or five and took a trip through the emigrant quarters of the ship, which enabled us to realize, from what we saw, how complete a little world in itself is a big Ocean steamer. There were the cow stables, the pig pen, chicken coops, sheep pens, pigeon coops, and the quarters where our veal and beef supply was kept. The steerage passengers sat about the deck engaged in various characteristic occupations. The German women were knitting, the Italians engaged in mending some gaudy-colored article of clothing, and the red-turbaned Turks were patiently tracing out artistic patterns in colored silk and bead work, which they afterwards sold to the cabin passengers. Anson, with his usual luck, succeeded in winning a handsome silk pillow, beautifully embroidered, which had been raffled off by an old Hindoo at a shilling a chance. The Hindoos, by the way, are an interesting lot for study. There were several castes represented among the dozen aboard, and the rigidity with which the lines of distinction were drawn was remarkable. They would eat nothing cooked by the ship's crew. In their eyes all Europeans are infidels, whose hands must not defile the food of a Mohammedan. They therefore carried their own saucepans and did their own cooking, even killing a sheep every few days with their own hands, which with their own hands they prepared for food. Fogarty early during the voyage christened the forward deck the "Zoo," and he used to show small parties of us through, as though he were the keeper of a menagerie, explaining the habits and origin of the different animals and the different races of people, to the infinite amusement of us all.

Speaking of the Hindoos reminds me that one of them, a merchant of Calcutta, died during the voyage. He had been ill from the time of leaving Adelaide, and gave up the ghost when our voyage across the Indian had been about half completed. With no ceremony whatever he was sewed up in a piece of canvas, with a bar of lead at his feet, and was laid away in his bunk. All the passengers, including those in the steerage, inquired anxiously when the burial was to take place, for all were naturally eager to witness a burial at sea. Their inquiries elicited only unsatisfactory answers, however, and the death had been almost forgotten by the first-class passengers. The following night, however, myself and my fellow newspaper correspondent were smoking a last cigar in our state-room, a few minutes before two o'clock. Through the port holes we could see the waves of the ocean as they rolled themselves into great sheets of silver under the light of a tropical moon, while the ship glided along as it had done without interruption since leaving Port Adelaide. Suddenly the screw ceased to revolve and my friend and myself were startled into silence by the occurrence of so strange an event. Before we had recovered from our surprise we heard a splash in the waters at the bow,—a splash much like that made by a log striking the water,—then all was still. As suddenly as it had stopped, the screw began to revolve again and the "Salier" proceeded on her way. "The Hindoo!" exclaimed my friend; and such it was. By the light of the stars the Hindoo's body had been quietly dropped into the blue ocean, to go down, down, into the dark depths of the sea, to its last earthly resting-place.

The smallest trifles at sea will interest an entire ship-load of passengers. For instance, a pigeon escaped from a coop during the voyage and perched upon the yardarm of the mast. Ever after, that bird was an object of the deepest solicitude to all on board. Water and food were placed within its reach, and after it had flown to the horizon in every direction searching for land, it finally gave up the effort and returned to the ship. After two days of fasting it eagerly partook of the fresh water and cracked wheat that were set out for it. In a few days it became so tame that the first officer succeeded in throwing a net over it, and the fortunate pigeon, no longer fated, as his fellows were, to lie upon a platter surrounded by mushrooms that he might delight the eye and palate of some one of our epicures, was placed in a gilded parrot cage and hung in the officer's room, to be ever afterward the pet and harbinger of good luck to this intelligent though superstitious man.

One afternoon, when it was insufferably stupid, the boys called a mock court in the smoking-room, with Fogarty presiding, and there passed a decree to the effect that, "in view of the excessively warm weather, and through consideration for the comfort and peace of mind of our entire party, Clarence Duval, our chocolate-colored mascot, must take a bath." The object of the decree fled to the uttermost depths of the steerage when he heard his sentence pronounced, but Tom Daly, Pettit, and Mark Baldwin effected his capture, and, despite his cries, thrust him beneath the salt-water shower and held him there until the tank was emptied. Clarence, on being released, went on the war-path armed with a baseball bat, but was finally dissuaded from his really murderous resolves.

One of the pleasantest reminders of home which we had during our voyage across the Indian occurred during the afternoon of January 22d, when, with our ship steaming along over waters that were perfectly placid and the boys lying about in their steamer chairs, John Ward happened to discover a sail ahead. His exclamation aroused us all. Books were dropped in haste, steamer chairs

CARRYING OUT THE SENTENCE.

were abandoned, and our entire party rushed to the ship's rail to gaze upon the stately vessel a mile ahead of us. She lay drifting about upon the waters, but with every sail set. Nearer and nearer we drew to the cloud of canvas until one of the boys read her name with a field glass— "Sam Schofield, Brunswick, Me." Almost at the same moment the stars and stripes were run up from the stranger's deck. The cheer that went up from the deck of the "Salier" as we passed the Yankee made us hoarse for at least two days, and when the cheering had died away, I discovered tears in the eyes of at least half the members of our party.

Clarence astonished us all one morning by an act that might have delayed our ship long enough to pick him out of the water, if, indeed, one of the big sharks, which we occasionally caught sight of, had not made a meal of him. It seems that he had made a bet with one of the boys that with an umbrella he could successfully imitate the "Professor's" parachute leap, and that, before the voyage was over, he would jump from the rigging at least thirty feet above the deck and land safe upon the awning. One afternoon, when half a dozen of us were lying about under the awning on the quarter-deck, we were startled by a shadow above us and then a fall, as the canvas gave a foot or two with some object that had evidently struck it on the upper side, followed by a scream of terror. We jumped to our feet and ran to the rope ladders near the smoking-room, and climbed to a point overlooking the awning. There was the mascot, making his way carefully on hands and knees to the rigging, while a reversed umbrella in a badly-damaged condition lay upon the awning.

"What in the world are you doing?" asked Fogarty of the boy. Clarence would not reply at first, but finally informed us that he had "Gist bin practicin'," and that if he had landed all right, it had been his intention to win his bet the next morning. Nothing could induce him, however, to make a second attempt.

The negro game of "craps," introduced by the mascot, soon became a popular pastime in the card-room, and in some portions of the vessel, at almost every hour of the day, one could hear the voice of Clarence as, engaged in a game with some of the players, he kept up his calls of, "Come, seben," "Come along dar eight," "What's de matter wid yo nine?" and other like expressions, without which no American negro ever engaged in his favorite method of gambling.

Captain Thallenhorst prepared a pleasant little surprise for us one afternoon after we had been out ten days, by sending the Steward on deck to announce to our half-slumbering party that a ten gallon keg of German beer, "right off the ice," had been placed on tap below. Ten seconds later there was not a man on deck. The beer keg, however, twenty minutes after the announcement, was carried forward in an empty condition.

Such were some of the incidents on the old "Salier," until the morning of January 25th, when we caught our first glimpse of the outlying islands south of Ceylon. Just as the sun came up out of the ocean we saw dimly the coast of Elephant Island, which was in all probability originally a portion of the island of Ceylon itself. At about ten o'clock we sighted the main island, and from that time on until we landed, our interest in the strange country we were approaching was kept keenly alive by all that we saw. Strange-looking, narrow-bodied native boats, called "proas," danced about in the waves and along the beach, paddled here and there by their dark-skinned, naked boatmen, while dolphins plunged and scampered through the water about our bow in great schools, and a hundred sea birds circled about our masts, keeping up their incessant cries as of welcome. We passed Point de Galle, formerly the mailing port of the Island before this distinction was transferred to Columbo, and looked with curiosity upon its ancient walls with their white cement and their background of bending, top-heavy-looking cocoanut trees. Finally, we sighted Columbo, and from three to half-past four o'clock, when we stopped at the entrance of the breakwater to receive the Harbor Master on board, we watched with deep interest the walls and harbor of the city as they became more and more distinct on our closer approach.

There is no natural harbor at Columbo, the city lying upon the open seacoast, and the Government has been compelled to construct an artificial breakwater, a massive stone wall, stretching obliquely away from the shore for a distance of nearly a mile, thus forming a quiet and deep anchorage for vessels of the greatest draught. The Harbor Master's boat, which drew alongside the ship, was manned by black fellows, the upper part of their bodies perfectly bare and the lower limbs but half concealed by a sheet-like robe that hangs from the waist. They were the native Cingalese. We were able to tell this from their long hair, brushed straight back from the forehead and rolled into a knot at the back of the neck, where it was held in place by big tortoise-shell combs. They chattered and gesticulated like a lot of monkeys, and were almost as noisy as the hordes of jackdaws and Cingalese crows which circled around the masts of our ship. No sooner had we dropped anchor than boats of every conceivable character and color put out from the shore and came toward us. There were Cingalese, Malays, and Hindoos of every caste and religion, all talking and yelling and waving their arms and long-handled paddles as they clustered about the "Salier." The queer-fashioned boats, the black bodies of the oarsmen and the red, yellow, green, orange, purple and other brilliant hues of their costumes, with the strangely constructed city and the tall groves of cocoanut palms on the shore, made the scene exceedingly picturesque.

The central object of interest to our party was a little canoe of bam-

THE ODD FISHING-BOATS OF THE CINGALESE.

boo logs upon which knelt four Cingalese boys, the youngest probably eight and the eldest twelve years of age. They paddled their craft about with barrel staves of bamboo and called to us to throw them money. Accordingly, many a sixpence and shilling piece went into the water, and in every instance the seemingly amphibious little animals would dive for them and secure them as soon as they reached the bottom. More than that, they clambered upon the rigging and dived from a distance of thirty feet or more into the water, and then dived under our ship, which was drawing twenty feet of water, and came up upon the opposite side. The "Trow it" of these little fellows, as they looked toward us with their expressive eyes, their long, dark hair dripping and their bodies glistening with the water of the harbor as they called to us to throw our silver at them, was mimicked by the different members of our party for days after we had left Ceylon. Native guards, hotel solicitors, money changers, and natives of other trades clambered over the ship and were soon objects of interest and study for us all. All was babble, confusion, and hurry, and in the midst of it all Mr. Spalding, accompanied by Leigh Lynch, started for the shore just as a drenching rain almost hid the town from view.

IN CEYLON.

At this particular time we were an undecided party. Was the "Salier" to sail at six o'clock in the morning without us, or were we to give up our trip to Calcutta and Bombay? All depended upon the word left for us by our advance agent, Will Lynch. Mr. Spalding had not obtained this when he returned an hour later, but he had made arrangements for the party at the Grand Oriental Hotel. Consequently steam launches conveyed us from the steamer to the dock, a fancifully-constructed, pagoda-like building on the shore, and, after passing through the Custom office, we entered upon the broad avenue that led directly up to the imposing entrance of the hotel, said to be the finest south of the Mediterranean. It is certainly a great structure and admirably adapted in design to the climate of Ceylon. We were shown to our respective rooms, immediately upon going into the hotel, by the dark-skinned servants in their picturesque garments and tortoise-shell combs. The high ceilings, the towering columns, the great dining-hall with its surrounding galleries, in which were Turkish divans for the use of guests, the stone balconies with their adjoining galleries, the latticed, carpetless, polished-floored bedroom—everything one looks upon reminds him of the fact that he is in a country different from any on the face of the globe save India. We enjoyed an excellent dinner. We were fanned by the great swinging punkas which were swayed backward and forward by the natives outside the walls, while we partook of tender capons, delicious curries, and juicy bananas, but turned up our noses at the foul-smelling Bombay duck, which seems to be a standard dish on this section of the globe. Our *café noir* was served us as we sat in easy chairs upon one of the big stone balconies outside the dining-hall, and we indulged in mouthfuls of tobacco smoke between sips. Then we got under our bonnets and went out to see the town.

Columbo is quite ancient, but no doubt the buildings with their white walls and pot-tiled roofs are the most comfortable for the inhabitants, if they are not as prepossessing in appearance as they might be. The streets, however, are well laid out, the parks spacious and numerous, and the people themselves as interesting a study as I had met with on the trip. The Indian shops under the hotel attracted most of our party during the best part of the evening. Every imaginable article of Indian manufacture was displayed for sale. Inlaid boxes, tortoise-shell toilet. articles, sandal-wood boxes, carvings in ebony and ivory, embroidered shawls, curtains, portières, and what-nots of a thousand names were purchased, and invariably for one-third or one-fourth the price asked by the storekeepers. An offer of one pound would be pretty sure to secure an article marked four pounds, and this rule holds good, I understood, throughout India.

One of the peculiar institutions of Columbo is the "jinrickshaw," which answers the purpose of the Hansom cabs of Chicago or New York. The "jin" is very similar to the Hansom, save that it is smaller and is drawn by a sinewy Cingalese, who trots ten, fifteen or twenty miles with you as easily and rapidly as a horse could draw you. The boys rented a lot of these and drove about town until midnight, finally ending up with an exciting race down the principal thoroughfare to the hotel. During the evening advices had been obtained by a visit to the residence of the American consul, which informed President Spalding that it would be absolutely impossible, on account of the inconvenient steamship and railway connections, while it would also be dangerous because of the unhealthy condition of Calcutta, for our party to make a tour of India, and it was that evening decided that the "Salier" would remain in the harbor until five o'clock the following afternoon, in order to give us time to play a game in Columbo, and that we should then continue on across the Arabian Sea to the Red Sea and give up our tour across India. Of course all were disappointed at this change of programme, and none more so than Mr. Spalding himself. There was the consoling thought, however, that the abandonment of our Indian tour would give us more time to spend upon the Continent and in England.

We were all up by daybreak the following morning and out upon the street eager to see everything to be seen. I remember that I was

THE JOLLY JINRICKSHAW.

awakened by the cawing of one of the big lead-colored crows, which deliberately flew down upon my railing, hopped in through the window, and, perching upon the back of a chair, startled me from my slumbers by a series of squawks, made all the more effective and discordant by the bare, frescoed walls, which echoed and reëchoed the bird's voice. I threw a boot at the intruder, but he only hopped off the chair and started on a dignified walk for the window, pausing now and then to turn around and screech at me, and, when he had finally reached the window casing, jumped to the balcony railing, and by more frantic screeching brought to his side a dozen of his fellows. I had to get up and go at them before they would disperse. These birds seem to be protected by municipal law, and they are the most impudent, and at the same time the most amusing, bipeds in Ceylon. I saw one sight that would have brought out the pencil of an artist, when, turning a corner of the hotel, I came upon a little bullock, not much bigger than a healthy

BUSINESS BOOTHS ON A COLUMBO STREET.

American calf, harnessed to an immense grass-thatched, two-wheeled cart, standing under the shade of a tree and meekly chewing its cud, while upon his back, standing sleepily upon one leg, was one of these impudent Cingalese crows. It flew to the top of a neighboring palm tree and gave me a severe scolding for shying a stone at it and disturbing its siesta.

Soon after breakfast upon the morning after our arrival most of us

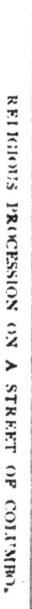

RELIGIOUS PROCESSION ON A STREET OF COLOMBO.

adjourned to a Columbo clothing establishment and purchased from one to three suits of white duck at seven rupees, or about $2.17 per suit. These secured, we added a "cumberband," or bright-colored silk sash, which was draped around the waist and, with the fringed ends hanging over the hip, gave us quite an Oriental appearance. Our straw hats were discarded for cork hats with green linings and a silk "puggery," a sort of silk scarf that passes around the crown, the ends dropping over the end of the hat brim and protecting the neck from the sun. Altogether we looked not unlike a party of returning African explorers. The costumes I have described are worn universally by the higher classes and by all Europeans living in Ceylon and India, and were found very comfortable by our party on shipboard after we had left Ceylon. Before starting out to do Columbo and its environs we were informed at the office of the U. S. Consul that the corvette "Essex," which lay in the harbor, had invited us to pay a visit on shipboard before returning to the "Salier." After appointing one o'clock for our visit to the corvette, we entered jinrickshaws and bullock carts and started upon a tour of the city. Ryan and myself took one district after another, and did it systematically. First we drove to some of the most prominent Indian shops and looked at the big cases of tempting articles on display, embracing everything from a cashmere shawl and a moonstone necklace to a carved ivory watch-charm. On the way we were beset with peddlers and beggars without number; and if there is any country on the globe where the poor have got these professions down to a fine art, it is Ceylon. A peddler will importune you for two blocks, and a beggar will follow you for two miles. "Mastah, mastah," they cry—the Cingalese always address Americans or Europeans as "master"—"Backsheesh,* backsheesh; very hungry, very hungry;" and they will put their hands upon their waistbands, while the youngsters lift up the ends of their little cotton shirts, when they have such on, that you may see how very empty are their little stomachs. The only way to get rid of them is to toss them several Cingalese coppers; and in anticipation of being thus importuned, Ryan and myself had had a sixpence changed into a pocketful of the queer-looking coins, a hatful of which would not equal the value of an English shilling.

---

* Alms.

After inspecting the shops we drove down past the British-India Hotel, and then along the beautiful beach drive to the "Galle Face," a great open lawn that extends along the ocean shore from the military barracks far beyond the Columbo Cricket grounds, until it merges into the tall groves of cocoanut trees in the distance. As we bowled along over the smooth roads and admired the beautiful view that met our gaze everywhere, the thought occurred to me that this splendid stretch of turf would be covered with juvenile ball teams on Saturday and Sunday afternoons were it located in Chicago instead of Ceylon. On the road we came across a couple of Indian jugglers and snake charmers at work, surrounded by a little crowd of people. We stopped and joined the crowd. The manipulation of the cones and balls by these dusky magicians is certainly wonderful; but what interested Ryan and myself more than anything else was the handling of the thick-bodied Cobra snakes, which spread their terrible-looking hoods and swayed their bodies to the notes of the gourd-like flutes played by the jugglers. Although deeply interested, Ryan and I took good care to stand at a safe distance from both the charmer and his pet.

THE CHARMER AND HIS PET.

Our drive through the Cingalese markets and business quarters will never be forgotten. The dusky inhabitants were thicker even than the Chinese in Chinatown, San Francisco, and their incessant chattering, mingling with the yells of the bullock-cart drivers, made the neighborhood a Bedlam. We stopped to look in at the Mohammedan barber shops, laughed at the antics of a lot of monkeys, held our noses as we passed a great pile of "Bombay duck" in one of the stalls, and paused at one of the Buddhist temples, where all good Buddhists of Columbo worship. After looking at its god-bedecked exterior (we were not allowed to enter) we gave our natives the word and were whisked back to the European quarter and to our hotel. At noon we enjoyed a well-served luncheon at the Oriental, and at one o'clock entered the gigs of the corvette "Essex" and rode out to call upon Captain Jewell and the crew. We were cordially entertained on board, the Captain's staff embracing Lieutenants Bignal, Galloway, Gearing and Walling; Ensigns Rodman and Haggatt; and Midshipmen Scales, Hudson, McMillan and Russell. Silence reigned throughout the ship and was followed by an enthusiastic applause when Mrs. Lynch played "America" on her cornet; then the hundred and fifty seamen gathered around Clarence Duval and laughed immoderately while the little African did a plantation shakedown, such as the crew of the "Essex" had probably not seen since they left home three years before. The same gigs that brought us out, rowed us from the corvette to the "Salier," and our boys having donned their uniforms returned to shore.

The native Cingalese gazed in open-mouthed wonder at the teams when they jumped upon the pier in their showy uniforms half an hour later and followed us in crowds to the doors of the Oriental Hotel, where we took, not carriages drawn by gayly-plumed horses, as we had done in America and Australia, but bullock carts and jinrickshaws, and such a scene as the road from the hotel to the Cricket grounds presented I had never imagined, and have never seen before or since. There were hundreds of howling, chattering, grotesquely-arrayed natives, with their red, white, green, blue and orange turbans, sashes and jackets; odd-looking, heavy-wheel carts drawn by ambling humpbacked little bulls, not bigger than an American calf; bare-legged Cingalese darting among the carts with their jinrickshaws; peddlers and beggars without number, and, in short, a state of wild confusion that was as laughable as it was novel to our party. I wondered if we were ever to arrive at the grounds. It certainly looked questionable, but we finally pulled up at the gates of the Cricket grounds and entered. The grounds were situated at one end of the "Galle Face," the beautiful lawn stretching away to the sands of the ocean on one side and a tall grove of cocoanut palms almost encircling it upon the other.

A diamond had been laid out in the centre of the cricket field, and around a big lawn stood 5000 people, the most picturesquely attired crowd, without doubt, that ever assembled to witness a game of ball. The officers and crew of the "Essex" took up a position in front of the Club house and yelled themselves hoarse over the five-inning game which followed our arrival at the grounds. The Englishmen, and seamen too, enjoyed the game as well, but the Cingalese broke into the wildest enthusiasm over the batting. It was laughable to see their desperate efforts to get out of the way when a ball was thrown or batted among them. They flew in all directions, tumbling over each other and chattering like a lot of magpies. During the game the military band, stationed upon the club house balcony, played between innings, and later on some Scotch Highlanders who were present entertained the crowd with their bagpipes.

Horse racing and Scotch games followed the ball game, but our steamer sailed at 5 o'clock, and we saw but little of these latter sports. The journey back to the hotel was almost as amusing as the trip out. The beggars and peddlars were just as attentive and the crowds of blacks, bullock carts and jinrickshaws just as confusing. The crew of the "Essex" cheered us in true American style as we left the pier for the "Salier," which we found again surrounded by hordes of natives. As our steam-launch neared the ship Ed Williamson, Jim Manning and Ed Crane, who had quietly slipped off their shoes, created a sensation by plunging into the water and swimming about in their uniforms among the boat-loads of natives. Our party climbed into the rigging as the screw of the "Salier" began to revolve and sent cheer after cheer to the crew of the "Essex," whose white forms we could see clinging to the rigging as we passed out of sight. The sun sank below the horizon just as we left the harbor and steamed toward the Arabian Sea and the Gulf of Aden.

AT SEA AGAIN.

As I have stated, the most beautiful weather of our voyage from Australia was enjoyed between Ceylon and Egypt. The ocean

THE "ESSEX" CREW GIVING EXHIBITION DRILL.

nowhere had seemed so indolent and so quiet in its great power and grandeur as it did here. The sky was never so blue and the atmosphere never so balmy as it came to us laden with the scent of the spice groves of Ceylon and the coffee plantations of Arabia. There was never a night when the sound of our mandolins and of Ed Crane's excellent tenor voice, as he led our choruses on the deck, ceased before midnight. Our journey, too, was not without incidents of a most memorable character. The evening after leaving Ceylon, Pfeffer, Anson, Williamson, Lynch, Mack and myself were invited down stairs by George and Bob Wilson, our Africa-bound sportsmen, where, in commemoration of the colonization of New South Wales, with the big patriotic Australians, we drank half a case of Monopole and talked with them as to their anticipated experiences in the Dark Continent.

It was late when we got to bed, but very early when we arose next morning, and doubtless our awakening will long be remembered by everybody aboard the "Salier." Indeed, there are those among our party who have not yet, and perhaps never will, forgive Lynch and Fogarty for the cruel practical joke of which they were the authors and perpetrators. Many of the boys were still sleeping when the thundering report of a cannon shook the ship, followed with cries of, "Pirates! Pirates! My God, boys, the Chinese pirates are upon us!" Then came the report of another gun. The effect may easily be imagined. The boys simply fell out of their berths, half-clad and white-faced, and rushed into the cabin in a state of panic. Treasurer John Tener grabbed his bags of gold and backed himself into the coffin-like closet of his stateroom, where he closed the door and tremblingly stood in hope that the bold sea raiders would pass him by unnoticed. Ed Crane left everything of value in his stateroom unnoticed and sprang into the cabin with a pet monkey, which had been given him by the officers of the "Essex." Captain Anson filled his mouth with Mrs. Anson's diamonds, and seizing a baseball bat swung it over his shoulder and stood at his stateroom door, as if waiting for a base hit or a pirate, while he commanded Mrs. Anson to conceal herself beneath her bunk. Ed Hanlon burst into the cabin wearing his hat and holding a pair of trousers in one hand and a valise in the other. Confusion and panic reigned supreme. We could see the smoke descending the stairway in thick volumes, and most of us got into the cabin just in time to see the flash and hear the report of the second cannon. Whether the ship was sinking, was on fire, or had really been attacked, we did not know, but in our dazed condition we were quite willing to believe that something terrible had happened, or was about to happen, until we caught sight of Fogarty galloping around upon the green table cloths that covered the saloon tables and yelling until red in the face. Then we suspected that all was not as it really seemed, and Fogarty confirmed the suspicion by finally falling in a heap upon the dining-room table, convulsed with laughter.

Upon inquiry, the frightened members of the party learned that the "Salier's" guns had been simply firing a salute in honor of the Emperor's birthday, and that Fogarty and Leigh Lynch had improved the opportunity to raise the cry of "Pirates!" There were men enough on board who were warm enough at the time to string Mr. Fogarty up to the yardarm *sans cérémonie*, and it was fully a week before some of the boys would consent to smile when the affair was mentioned. We were all pretty badly frightened, but by far the most terrified of the party was Clarence Duval. When I came out of my cabin door and into the saloon, I saw him clinging to the skirts of Leigh Lynch's pjamas, under which he was vainly endeavoring to hide himself. The whites of his eyes seemed to have extended over his entire face, and his black skin looked much as though it had been sprinkled with fine ashes. When Lynch shook him off and told him he must protect himself, the boy fell to the floor with a groan, where he sat with chattering teeth until he saw Fogarty laughing. He then disappeared, and did not show up again until evening. When asked if he had really been frightened, he said, "Yes, I reckon I was; I did'n no what *poridges* was, but I made up mah min' dat whatever dey was, dey was liable to do dis hyah niggah some h'am, an' I was lookin' foh a place ter crawl inter when I ketched sight ov dat old Mister Fogaty lafin hisself red in de face, and den I knowed it was jes one o' his tricks. Some day I's goin' to scar 'at man so, he'l be gray-headed time he gits to New Yawk."

Mark Baldwin formed a new acquaintance during the voyage across the Arabian Sea, an acquaintance which, though it at one time promised to assume most intimate relations, eventually changed to a deadly hatred. At Ceylon the engineer of the ship had purchased a big Indian monkey—one of those tall, long-legged, ring-tailed, evil-countenanced creatures, which seemed to bear an implacable dislike for all mankind. He was a powerful fellow and received Mark's advances coldly as he sat upon the grating of the engine room and glared at the big pitcher from under his shaggy eyebrows. There was a strap around his waist, to which had been attached a rope five or six feet long, and, unknown to the engineer, Mark untied the rope and coaxed the monkey out of the engine room to the deck. The monk was badly frightened at the sight of the heaving ocean and the strange appearance of the deck, and refused to advance further, but Baldwin, holding him by the end of the rope, raced up and down the deck with him, as the monk, bracing himself with stiff legs and paws, slid reluctantly over the surface of the polished floor.

Mark then took him down to the bar room and fed him beer and pretzels, after which he brought him up to the deck again and gave him another race. The monkey in the meantime never lost his expression of terror, and Mark, finally tiring of the sport, took him back to the engine room. Now, the first grating around the big steam cylinders was reached by a narrow iron staircase of five or six steps, and Mark, entering the doorway, descended the steps first. No sooner had his head got on a level with Mr. Monk than the hairy ape, with a villanous shriek, jumped straight at Mark's throat, and but for the pitcher's presence of mind would have probably injured him seriously then and there. As it was, Mark fell backward with the monkey on top of him, and the vicious brute took a mouthful of Mark's leg in his mouth and inflicted a bite that if not dangerous was at least painful. Then, chattering to himself, and his long gray whiskers standing out on each side stiff with rage, he hopped like a great kangaroo over to his corner in the grating and stood glaring fiercely at Mark. Baldwin regained his feet, and after satisfying himself as to the extent of his injuries, made one bound for that monkey. The monkey was quicker than he, however, and jumped from the grating on to the piston rod of the engine, and with every revolution of the screw he would go down into the depth of the hold and then come up again, shaking his fist at Mark and chattering like a fiend at each ascent. Although angry and burning for revenge, the situation was too comical for the Pittsburgher to withstand, and he sat down and laughed at the ape until it finally scrambled up among the crossbars and ironwork of the engine room and watched Mark until he had left the grating. Baldwin laid for the monkey during the entire remainder of the voyage, but the monkey was altogether too watchful and nimble to be caught.

On the morning of February 1st we left the waters of the Arabian Sea for those of the Gulf of Aden, the bluest, I think, of all blue waters upon the globe. We passed the Socotra Islands during the night, and sighted the volcanic groups off the African coast soon after daybreak. Passing these about breakfast hour, we slowly approached Guardafui, the great headland on the northeast corner of the coast of Africa. It rises gloomy and impressive, the waters breaking around its base as it stands looking out over the sea like some great sentinel. Until long after the noon hour we steamed along the forbidding bluff, and then as the sun began to sink we left it in the gray mist that hovered about its peak, miles and miles away. On the afternoon of the following day we sighted the Arabian coast, some forty miles away. Later on we passed an Arabian "dhow," or native sail boat, and gradually the seamed sides of the great bluffs which protect Aden from the gulf winds became more and more distinct. It was nearly dark when we dropped anchor before the little Arabian town and leaned over the ship's rail to watch the boat-loads of chattering, black-bodied fellows who surrounded the "Salier," much as she was surrounded at Columbo. It was nearly supper time, but the boys never thought of that. We wanted to stand on Arabian soil, and consequently three boat-loads of Americans were soon on their way to the shore. Of course we were appealed to for "backsheesh" the moment we landed, but we whacked the beggars with our canes and went on up the lighted street that stretched along the shore for a mile. We raided the shops for curiosities, and found any quantity of them in the way of ostrich eggs and plumes, Indian curtains, portières and handiwork of all kinds, which we brought away as mementoes of our visit to Arabia. John Tener has a cane which is part of a long Arab staff that he bought from one of a group of white-sheeted Arabs on the dock, and which John says is a divining rod for the richest of all his memories of our great tour.

We left Aden at 9 o'clock that evening, in the face of a stiff blow, and were soon on our way to the southern entrance of the Red Sea. The following morning we were startled from sleep by the sound of the gong, and sprang out of bed, not really sure but that we were to have another visitation of pirates. We were informed, however, that we were approaching the Straits of Bab-el-Mandeb, the entrance to the Red Sea, and that all who wished to see them should come up on deck. We all took advantage of the opportunity, and after hastily dressing, congregated upon the deck just as the sun broke upon the gray of the morning.

THE RED SEA.

The straits are about 2½ miles in width. Our ship passed between the coast of Arabia on the right, which arose in great elephantine-looking piles, and at the base of which the billows broke themselves into clouds of spray, and upon our left the Island of Perin, on the shores of which burned the yellow beacons of the lighthouses. Both coasts were barren and uninviting, looking as though no one but the lighthouse keepers ever set foot upon their soils. At ten o'clock that morning we passed the famous city of Mocha, which lay like a city of white walls and glistening towers upon the now far-distant Arabian coast; for the sea had widened as we left the straits behind. We watched it with our glasses until it had faded from view, with other vanished but not forgotten scenes of the many we had passed.

The voyage through the Red Sea was thoroughly delightful, although we had been led to anticipate insufferably hot weather. It was warmer than any we had yet experienced on our way from Australia, but it was by no means unpleasant, and we were sorry rather than glad when, upon the morning of February 7th, we entered the harbor of Suez and slowly steamed in the direction of the little city of the same name, which lay at the southern end of the great canal. The day of our arrival was perfect, and the bright sunlight brought into bold relief the immense bluffs of the Egyptian coasts as they looked down upon the calm waters of the bay and the seemingly limitless desert that stretched away upon the opposite shore. Several large vessels lay in the harbor, among them an English troop ship and an Italian man-of-war. And as we dropped anchor, we were soon surrounded, as in Ceylon, with native boats and a couple of little steam tugs, which towed out to the ship two or three big barges for the reception of our baggage and such freight as we might have for Suez. Again we listened to the unintelligible chatter of a new race of people, and gazed with interest on the remarkable costume of the Egyptian boatmen. After bidding farewell to Captain Thalenhorst and his clever fellow-officers, we descended the companion-way into the little steamer that lay alongside for our trip of two miles to the docks at the city of Suez. On board were several Indian jugglers and fakirs, who entertained our party with their really wonderful feats of legerdemain during the ride.

When we drew up at the pier in Suez, a crowd of Arabs and Egyptians, in long, loose-fitting gowns of blue, white and black, their

THE LITTLE CITY OF SUEZ.

feet shoeless and their heads wound about with white turban cloths, rushed toward our boat, driving before them a troop of long-eared donkeys with queer-looking, gayly-caparisoned saddles and bridles, the latter decorated with brass bangles and bright-colored ribbons. These were the donkey boys of Egypt, whose services we afterward had occasion to employ so frequently in Cairo. We had but a few moments to catch the train for the Egyptian capital, so we mounted these little beasts, none of which weighed over 275 pounds, and with the donkey boys yelling at our heels, trotted off for the railway station four or five blocks distant. What we saw of Suez did not impress us favorably, for of all the tumble-down, ramshackle, dilapidated-looking structures we saw during the trip, those at Suez take the palm. If dirt and general shiftlessness are evidences of antiquity, then surely Suez and its people are the most thoroughly antique of all the antiquities of this nineteenth century.

It was a relief to each and every one of us when the train pulled out from the station, and dodging about through the villages of mud huts, which the Egyptians are either too poor, or too much attached to, to

A PEEP AT THE GREAT SUEZ CANAL.

abandon for more comfortable and modern dwellings, we cut across country into the arid desert region, which extends northward from Suez as far as Ismalia. Our train ran parallel with the canal for a distance of forty-five miles and then branched off westward to Cairo. Gradually the country became more and more pleasant to look upon, until we entered the rich valley of the Nile, where the growth of vegetation seems fully as luxuriant as in Ceylon. Great fields of grain and clover, with here and there a grove of imposing palms or acacias, stretched away from each side of the track; flocks of sheep and goats became a common sight, and along the roadways of the irrigating canals, which overspread the valley like an immense net, the patient camels plodded along under their loads of grain or the weight of their Egyptian owners, while groups of water buffalo stood knee-deep amid the clover. Occasionally we saw evidences of the fidelity of the Egyptians

OX-POWER SHADOOF, OR IRRIGATING MACHINE OF THE NILE.

to the customs and methods of their biblical forefathers. Such, for instance, as an ox turning an old-fashioned water wheel, which lifted the water in buckets from the main canal into irrigating ditches. An American pump would have done the work in half the time, but that would not be the way in which their fathers raised the water, and therefore would not suit the Egyptian, even of this generation. At every station our carriages were surrounded by Bedouins, Arabs and Egyptians; the men being muscular-looking fellows, but servile of manner, and the women veiled to the eyes, their faces disfigured by the characteristic brass ornaments of the Egyptians, which hang from the hood of their outer garment, the "bournous," their figures being thick-set, without the faintest suspicion of contour. Most of them bore upon their heads big baskets of fruit, oranges and dates, while others carried earthenware jugs of water, from which the occupants of the dusty railway coaches quenched their thirst for the sum of a half-piastre.

Ed Crane's little Japanese monkey sat upon the carriage window-sill in his picturesque scarlet jacket, and greatly amused the ladies by his funny faces and antics. Just at dusk, as we pulled up at a station twenty miles from Cairo, Ryan invented an enlarged edition of Crane's monkey, which had the effect of causing a panic

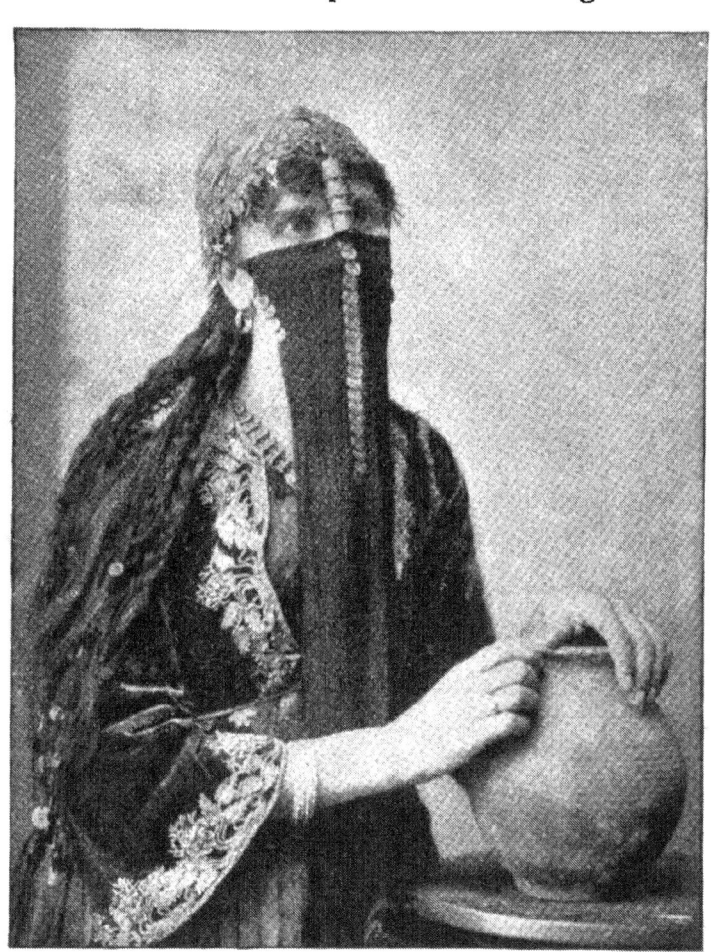

EGYPTIAN WOMAN WITH BRASS FACE ORNAMENTS.

among the unsuspecting Egyptians. Jim dressed Clarence Duval up in the latter's drum-major coat of scarlet and gold lace; he then put a catcher's mask on the boy's face and tied a rope around his waist, in regulation hand-organ style, and awaited the train's arrival at the station. As at preceding stations, the crowd rushed toward the train, and Clarence sprang through the doorway into the centre of a score of Egyptians, waddling and chattering like an angry monkey. Women screamed and men fell over each other in a wild effort to get out of reach of the terrible-looking ape, which Ryan, apparently with the exertion of great strength, held with difficulty, and finally forced back into the carriage. Then Clarence sat at the window, chattering and making faces as long as we remained at the station, and not a native would come within twenty feet of our coach. One could scarcely

CLARENCE CREATING A PANIC AT THE EGYPTIAN STATION.

blame them, for could a disciple of Darwin have seen the mascot in his impromptu make-up, his heart would have bounded with delightful visions of the missing link.

IN CAIRO.

It was dark when we reached Cairo, and no sooner had we stepped upon the station platform from our coaches than we were beset by an army of black fellows, clad in turbans and elongated night shirts, who laid hold of us and our baggage as though to carry us away bodily. Ed Crane propped one of the heathens under the chin and old Anson sent half a dozen more sprawling by a vigorous shove. Still they came at us as determinedly as ever. We were in a fair way to be smothered or pulled to pieces, when Jimmy Fogarty called out "Step on their trotters, boys, they can't stand that." Happy thought; it was cruel, but it was our only means of relief, and we forthwith proceeded to step on the bare feet of every Egyptian within reach. That settled them, and they kept at safe distance till we had reached our carriages. We were driven quickly to the Hotel d'Orient, where accommodations had been secured for the party. The Orient is not so highly fashionable as "Shephard's" or the "Grand New," but is still a well appointed hostelry, with a table that was not excelled by any that we sat down to during our tour. It faces a big, circular open space from which half a score of thoroughfares diverge like the spokes of a wheel, penetrating every quarter of Cairo.

Opposite is a big public garden in which one of the bands of the Khedive was playing as we drew up to the door of the hotel, and on every hand were booths, cafés and places of amusement without number, from roulette wheels, publicly operated, to French opera and inviting-looking *brasseries* where one can drop in for a puff at a *narghili*, or a cup of chocolate and a cigarette served by waitresses of almost any nationality in Asia or Europe, and possessed of beauty or homeliness to a greater or less degree. All these things we noticed after we had removed the dust of the Desert from our faces and refreshed the inner man with a substantial dinner. One can sit in the Eldorado at Cairo and listen to a French opera, while around him at the tables he will hear the Arabic, Hindostanee, Greek, German, Egyptian, French, Italian and English languages spoken simultaneously. Such a jargon of tongues cannot, I believe, be heard in any other city outside of Continental Europe, unless it be, perhaps, at Constantinople. Before sitting down to post up my diary that evening, I stepped to the balcony of my room, which overlooks the space in front of the hotel, and saw Cairo in the gloom of the night, its towers and minarets rising like shadows among the heavy, white-walled buildings, and the lights of a thousand booths tinting the diverging thoroughfares with a red glow, for the booths and *brasseries* of Cairo seem never to close, and their proprietors never to sleep. In the square below sat the donkey boys watching for some belated pedestrian, and there are scores of these, who might need the services of these hardy and much enduring little beasts. It is a strange land and a still stranger people, and a student of Egyptology finds, ere he has prosecuted his studies to a very great extent, that he has even more than a lifetime of work before him, every day of it filled with research, discoveries and experiences, that grow with interest as he advances.

At the breakfast table the morning after our arrival in the Egyptian capital President Spalding announced that as no arrangements could be made for a game before the day following, the members of the party were at liberty to put in their time as best suited them. Accordingly, a few of us took carriages, but the majority of the boys bestrode the little donkeys and with a donkey boy at their heels covered many a square mile of Cairo during the day. We penetrated the Arabian, Moorish, Turkish, Algerian and Greek quarters of the town, riding through the narrow streets from which the light of the sun was almost excluded by towering walls and overhanging balconies. We handled and admired the rich tapestries and works of art in the bazaars, and listened to the babble of tongues that was kept up incessantly on all sides of us. We crossed the bridge of the Nile to the Khedive's gardens, where the wealth and *élite* of Cairo in magnificent equipages go for an airing each afternoon, and it may be said that on no drive in London, or even in Paris, can so much splendor be seen as here. The foreign ambassadors, Ministers and Government officials possess the finest of Arabian stock, and their carriages are equal to any that I saw in Rotten Row or on the Champs Elysée. The effect is exceedingly Oriental, and ideally regal, as the imposing turnouts sweep down the principal avenue along the river bank, preceded by their gorgeously-liveried *avant-couriers*, attired in costumes of white broadcloth and bright-colored jackets elaborately embroidered in gold or silver, while they hold in their hands the long staffs with which they are supposed to clear the way for their masters' equipages. At the far end of the Gardens is one of the Khedive's palaces, a great imposing building of purely Egyptian style of architecture, surrounded by beautiful gardens,

DANCING GIRL OF THE ELDORADO, CAIRO.

as attractive as art and nature can make them. The Khedive, by the way, has more palaces by half a score than he visits or resides in.

The day passed only too quickly for us all, for with all we had seen, not one tithe of the great district covered by the city, or of the many interesting quarters within it, had been visited. During the evening, French opera at the Eldorado, the Algerian dances at the Byzantine, and the brilliantly lighted shops or the throngs upon the streets afforded us diversion enough. Captain Anson, by the

MACMILLAR AND PALMER MOUNTED FOR A RIDE.

way, managed during the evening to "put his foot in it." He and Mrs. Anson, wishing to see something of Cairo by gaslight, took a carriage and drove in search of the theatre. They drove down past the Grand New Hotel and the French Opera House until a palatial looking structure, its grounds brightly lighted and colored awnings extending from the streets to the doorways, attracted their attention. "Hey driver," called Anson, to the Egyptian on the box, "what is this?",

And the driver, not understanding a word of English, but properly interpreting Anson's question, replied with the single word "*Sirdar*." Whether it was the rumble of the wheels or the indistinct pronunciation of the Egyptian, I do not know, but at any rate Anson put his own interpretation upon the Egyptian's reply. "The circus, eh?" said he, "well, I guess that is just about our size. Hold on, there!" and stopping the carriage, Anson assisted his wife to alight. They passed under the canopy and by two gorgeously-attired servants who stood at the door. Music came from every direction, and the air itself was filled with the perfume of a score of fountains which spurted forth the most expensive extracts.

"Pretty swell kind of a circus this, isn't it?" questioned the old man of his better half. "I suppose, though," he continued, "that this is the way they do things over here. I have made up my mind not to be surprised at anything I see."

Within, they caught sight of a number of ladies and gentlemen in full evening dress. Still it failed to occur to the old man that he might not have properly understood his Egyptian cab-driver, and Mrs. Anson followed her lord with a confidence born of the belief that whatever he did was perfectly right and proper. Finally, Anson ran squarely against a dark-complexioned, distinguished-looking man, attired in all the magnificence of an Egyptian military costume. He glanced curiously at the Americans, and then stopped as Anson addressed him. "Can you tell me," asked Anson, "where we buy our tickets?"

"Tickets! what tickets?" asked the dark-complexioned man, in a surprised tone, but in very good English.

"Why," said Anson, a bit nervously, "the tickets to the circus here," and he made a sweeping gesture with his right hand.

Then the gentleman in military costume, partly turning away his face to hide a smile, said, "There is no circus here, my friend; this is my private residence. I am Commander-in-Chief of the Egyptian Army and am simply entertaining a few of my friends to-night. I would be very much pleased, however, if you would remain and—"

"Don't say a word, sir," replied the captain of the Chicago Club, looking very much cheaper than lovers of the game have seen him look, when, with men on bases, the Umpire has called three strikes on him.

"It's my mistake, and I hope you will be kind enough to excuse me," with which he bowed himself out, and then had to stand being laughed at by Mrs. Anson all the way back to the hotel.

That evening, in the hotel office, the following bulletin was posted: "Baseball at the Pyramids.—The Chicago and All-America teams, comprising the Spalding American Baseball party, will please report in the hotel office, in uniform, promptly at ten o'clock to-morrow morning. We shall leave the hotel at that hour, camels having been provided for the All-America players and donkeys for the Chicago players, with carriages for the balance of the party. The Pyramids will be inspected, the Sphynx visited, and a game played upon the Desert near by, beginning at 2 o'clock."

The following day, accordingly, witnessed the first professional ball game ever played upon Egyptian soil, and the scenes and incidents of that morning and afternoon rendered the 9th of February one of the most memorable of our eventful tour. Half-past nine o'clock saw twenty of the best known ball players in America in the court of the Hotel d'Orient, in uniform. Every arrangement for the day's programme had been carefully worked out. The dragoman in charge of the camels and donkeys had done his duty, as a glance at the array in front of the hotel indicated. A dozen long-necked camels, saddled and bridled, lay upon the ground, contentedly chewing their cuds, and as many gayly decorated little donks stood patiently beside the reclining travelers of the Desert. At ten o'clock the camels were drawn up in line in front of the hotel, with a line of donkeys before them, and then the fun of the morning began. The crowd of donkey boys, dragomen, guards, and venders of curios and tapestries, and photographs, and earthenware images, and fruits, and goodness knows what not, had increased to fully half a thousand, and every one of them was eagerly looking for a chance to secure, by hook or by crook, a bit of American silver. The dragoman in charge had engaged all the donkeys we needed, but other donkey boys contrived to mix up with those appointed, and succeeded in getting some of the boys upon the backs of renegade donkeys. It was when the players were apprised of their mistake that the real fun commenced, and such a hubbub as was raised in that square I never expect to witness outside of Cairo; donkeys brayed, camels trumpeted, donkey boys howled and fought and chattered, and scratched each other's faces and tore each other's gowns, and cried big tears of vexation in their efforts to hold on to their fares, while above all the noise could be heard the thwack, thwack, of the bamboo rods, in the hands of the native policemen, as they dusted the jackets of every thinly-clad Arab and Egyptian that got in their way. Those of us who had been provided with camels sat upon our reclining hump-backed beasts, doubled up with laughter, until the police had finally restored order by the free use of their bamboo sticks.

A CAMEL TRAIN READY FOR A TRIP.

In good time we were all safely mounted, All-America upon the camels, and Chicago upon the donkeys. Immediately in front of me, upon the back of a surly old camel, which lay sullenly grunting under her burden, sat Irving W. Snyder, the fat, good-natured sporting goods dealer of Nassau street. Just who had persuaded him to mount a camel I have never been able to learn, and judging from the expression of his face, when I first glanced at him, I imagined he was at that moment wondering how he could have been weak enough to allow himself to get into such a box. He had not much time, however, to

THE BASEBALL TOURISTS MOUNTED FOR THE PYRAMIDS.

devote to reflection, for the order was given for the camels to arise, that the photographer might make a picture of the party. I saw a startled expression cross Snyder's face as the big beast began to stir, and then he pitched forward and flattened his nose against old Sahara's head, as the old girl lifted her rump into the air,—the first in the remarkable series of movements a camel goes through in getting upon its feet. He only retained this position for an instant, however, for the front end of the camel immediately followed the example of the rear end, and Snyder took a tumble in the opposite direction.

When the beast finally settled itself the merchant of Nassau street looked very much as though he had just fallen off the roof of the Hotel d'Orient. Both trousers legs had worked up to his knees, and one end of his collar was poking him in the eye; but he did not worry over such trifles, even though he must have known that he was sitting for his picture. The sole question agitating his mind at that moment was that of his ability to stay where he was until help came. Alas, however, there was no help, and the incidents of the four miles ride which followed, and during which he clung to those saddle sticks as though they were the only barriers between himself and instant destruction, must be very distinctly engraved upon Mr. Snyder's memory.

Finally we got started, and with the camels and donkeys leading the line, and the carriages bringing up the rear, we moved slowly through the streets of Cairo toward the Bridge of the Nile, attracting no little attention, of course, as we proceeded. We stopped at the residence of the American Minister, and with three cheers for the flag that floated over his quarters, continued on our way toward the Nile, which we crossed, and then entered the Khedive's Gardens. At the further end of the bridge poor Snyder was overtaken by more trouble, and as his animal was just in front of mine, the halter of each camel being attached to the saddle of the camel ahead of him, I obtained an uninterrupted and most interesting view of the performance. A couple of big camels with a load of sawed lumber strapped across their humps, the ends of the twenty-four-foot boards extending out over their heads and beyond their tails, were quietly wending their way, in charge of their Egyptian drivers, along the road which our party took toward the Pyramids. Neither beast of burden noticed our cavalcade until the rear end of the procession overtook them and they caught sight of Snyder. What there was about the merchant of Nassau street to terrify the plank-laden camels I could not discover, and Snyder afterwards told me that it was the only instance in his life in which he had encountered an animal of any kind that had not shown the most marked affection for him. Be that as it may, when the bigger of the two camels saw Snyder he ran his tongue out of his mouth a distance of two feet or more and gave a trumpet that startled every camel within sight into a state of very active interest. The

THE SUPERB BRIDGE OF THE NILE.

Egyptian leading the plank-bearer turned around and endeavored to quiet his beast with a volley of Egyptian oaths and a sudden yank on the halter. The effect, however, was the opposite of what he had anticipated. The camel gave another trumpet, and then began a waltz with the swearing Egyptian at the end of the halter. A cloud of dust had almost enveloped man and beast within a few seconds after the dance began, and I could see that this miniature cyclone was slowly but surely approaching Snyder. Snyder saw it too, and judging from the expression upon his face he must have thought that this time the hour of his physical disintegration had surely come. He could only clutch the saddle sticks and look out of the corner of his eye at the approaching cloud of dust, while his face grew ghastly with dreadful anticipation. His suspense, however, was not of long duration. The waltzing camel gradually drew nearer until a final whirl brought the ends of the planks

SNYDER IN THE CONTEST OF THE CAMELS.

against the rump of Snyder's camel with a sound like the falling of a lumber pile. To say that Snyder's camel was startled would be putting it mildly. He was also indignant, for he had been soberly pursuing his way, wholly indifferent to, if not unconscious of, the antics of the other camel. When the planks struck him he let out a spiteful shriek and shot straight up into the air a distance of about four feet, and for probably fifteen seconds the air was filled with pieces of flying plank, camel legs, swearing Egyptian and Nassau street merchant, until one was almost at a loss to determine just what character of beast the whole conglomeration was. The drivers finally succeeded, however, in separating the now belligerent camels, and Snyder rode on, covered with dust and camel saliva, with his hair in his eyes and what was left of his hat on the back of his head, inwardly cursing every four-legged thing in Egypt. He was just beginning to think that after all, camel riding was perhaps not so bad as being seasick or falling off Washington Monument, when the drivers whipped the camels into a trot and Snyder's position was more uncomfortable than ever. He could not get breath enough to command the drivers to stop, and they would not have understood him had he been able to talk, so that he could only clutch the saddle sticks and suffer. Then somebody behind him fired a big, soft, juicy orange that caught him in the back of the neck. Altogether, Mr. Irving W. Snyder's ride to the Pyramids was not a howling success; but it was funny.

The road to the historic piles is a beautiful one. It runs for some distance along the left bank of the Nile, past the Khedive's palace and the Governor's residence, and then branches off across the rich lowlands of the great river, which, during the annual overflow, are covered with water, until it ends at the desolate-looking sand hills at the edge of the desert upon which the Pyramids have been constructed. Along each side of the roadway stand stately acacia trees, the branches of which meet overhead and form a leafy avenue from the Bridge of the Nile to the sand hills, a distance of eight miles. Half-way out upon the road, at Snyder's piteous solicitation, the procession stopped, and Chicago being desirous of experiencing the novelty of camel riding took the camels, while All-America mounted the donkeys for the balance of the journey. At two o'clock we reached our destination, and after ascending the winding roadway to the base of the Pyramids, partook of the luncheon that had been prepared for us in the brick cottage at the foot of old Cheops. While we were waiting, however, for lunch, we were assailed by not less than 150 Bedouins, Arabs and Egyptians, who are a nuisance to every tourist visiting the Pyramids. They besought us to buy musty-looking coins and mouldy copper

THE SPHINX IN LIVELY COMPANY.

images, which they explained had been taken from the interior of the big structures. They proved the most persistent beggars we had thus far encountered, not excepting those at Columbo, and we did not escape from them during our stay at the Pyramids.

After lunch we walked past the base of the big Pyramid to the Sphynx, and grouping ourselves about the head, shoulders and feet of the great image, were photographed by the photographer who accompanied the party. Then we passed down the hill until we reached the hard sands of the Desert, where the diamond was laid off and where, in the presence of something like a thousand people, embracing a number of tourists, but more long-sheeted Bedouins, we played the first and only game of baseball ever played in Egypt. The surface of the Desert was hard and firm, not unlike the snow crust of the North, and formed a by-no-means-poor ground for ball playing. Ward's forces were again "out for blood," and though Anson made a good start by the capture of two runs in the opening inning, All-America by good stiff batting piled up seven runs in the second and secured a lead which Chicago could not afterwards approach. The actions of the natives during the game were not unlike those of the Cingalese at our game in Columbo. When a ball was thrown wild or batted into the crowd, the entire aggregation of white-robed sons of the Desert would chase after it, capture it, and crowd around to examine it, utterly indifferent, or thoughtless of the fact that we might want the ball for playing, and as though it was one of the greatest curiosities they had ever seen. In such cases game was suspended until the teams had attacked the mob in a body and rescued the ball. At the close of the game we returned to the Sphynx and the Pyramids and looked over the great masses of stone at our leisure. A couple of Bedouins performed the dangerous task of climbing to the apex of the big Pyramid and down again within ten minutes' time, for a ten-piastre piece, and then Ward, Fogarty and Manning, accompanied by attendants, undertook and accomplished the ascent. The balance of us, however, were content to forego that experience, and soon after we were on our way back to Cairo, which we reached about seven o'clock that evening. I need scarcely say that the camels came back with empty saddles, the boys preferring the carriages and donkeys to another ride on the Egyptian beasts of burden.

Macmillan, myself and the Professor started together on three little donkeys, but the Professor objected to fast riding, and Mac and I soon left him far behind. Had it been practicable, I am quite sure Mac would have purchased his donkey and brought him back with him to New York; for he was an extraordinary donkey in several respects. His master had taught him to smoke cigarettes, and that the donkey enjoyed the habit was plainly evident by the enthusiasm with which he

AT LEISURE AT THE FOOT OF THE PYRAMIDS.

went at it. His master, a bright-faced little donkey-boy, would give a peculiar cry and then take a mouthful of cigarette smoke and start on a run. The donkey would immediately lay his ears back, whisk his tail and start after the little Egyptian until he had overtaken him. Then he would thrust his nose close to the boy's face, while the latter would blow the tobacco smoke between the donkey's lips. It was amusing to see the expression of supreme repose and delight that came over that little brute's face as he drew the white smoke into his lungs and stood there with half-closed eyes wagging his tail and rocking his body to and fro as though he wanted nothing more on earth. It was no trick at all for him to find a pocket-handkerchief in the sand after he had first scented it, and he could reach around with his teeth and unbuckle his saddle strap as neatly and quickly as his master could do it. Then with his foreleg he would paw off his bridle, and thus prepare himself for rest.

Speaking of the Professor starting with us reminds me of an amusing incident that occurred to him during the ball game. When game began, I set my camera upon the sands of the Desert and took a seat preparatory to scoring the game. The Professor happened along at that moment and, feeling somewhat fatigued after his ride, stretched himself out upon his back, and, with his head upon my camera and his hat over his eyes, was soon sound asleep. Pretty soon his hat fell off, but the Professor slumbered sweetly just the same, his sound eye closed and his glass eye staring up at the sky. Presently along came a Bedouin peddler with a trayful of coins, curios, etc., and seeing the Professor reclining upon the sand he knelt down beside him and in broken English began upon an encomium of his wares, offering the Professor his choicest bits,

THE KHEDIVE OF EGYPT.

with his most enticing grimaces and at his most tempting prices. For fully five minutes he must have talked to that unfeeling glass eye, and he would probably have continued longer had not a gentle snore from the Professor caused him to look sharply at the sleeper's face, and then

THE DAHABIE, OR PASSENGER BOAT OF THE NILE.

hurry away with his wares. "Prof." awoke fifteen minutes later, without having heard a word of the Bedouin's eloquence.

The following day and night, our last in Cairo, were spent in taking a farewell stroll through the ancient city, most of us visiting the Mosques of Sultan Hassan and of Mohammed Ali. The mosques stand upon the highest point of the city near the citadel, which is now occupied, of course, by English soldiers. Before entering we were compelled to slip our feet into ungainly-looking yellow slippers, lest our infidel heels should defile the marble floors. We tried hard to purchase the slippers we wore, but when we offered ten times the value of the ill-shaped foot-casings, we were met with a determined refusal, on the ground that such a sale would be sacrilegious. The Hassan Mosque, now several centuries old, is fast falling into decay, but the Mosque of Mohammed,

COMMON RIVER BOATS ON THE NILE OPPOSITE CAIRO.

where the Khedive worships, is in an excellent state of preservation. Its great walls of polished marble and alabaster, and the softened light of its beautiful stained-glass windows form as elegant an interior as any in Cairo. The view obtained from the citadel is without doubt one of the grandest in the world. From its walls can be seen Cairo, spread out like a great panorama, with the majestic Nile reaching away up the valley, and the Pyramids of Cairo as well as those at Sakarah, the latter twenty miles distant. One could easily spend six months in Cairo and the surrounding valley of the Nile, and then come away without having finished what must always remain one of the most interesting countries upon the globe. We managed, however, to cover considerable ground during our brief stay, and most of us doubtless brought away a fairly good idea of the city, its people, and their peculiar customs.

A NATIVE EGYPTIAN SCHOOL IN FULL OPERATION.

Some of these customs would not charm our American youngsters, notably that of the private school system, where a few boys (the girls' education not being of any account in Egypt) are grouped in an out-of-the-way corner of the Mosque buildings, squatting on the ground as they pursue their tasks, the stern old teacher sitting over them rod in hand, the petty sovereign of a by-no-means submissive and loyal constituency. The native barber-shops too, were curious in their way, and few of us cared to trust our faces to the tender mercies of their owners.

SCENE IN A CAIRO BARBER-SHOP.

On the day of our arrival in Cairo, President Spalding had, through the American Consul General, expressed to the Khedive his willingness to play a game of ball in the presence of His Highness before we left Cairo. But the Khedive had left the city for his Nile

Palace on state affairs, and sent Mr. Spalding word that, though he would be unable to return to the city, he should be pleased to receive our party at his Nile Palace and witness our exhibition there. To remain, however, would have caused us a delay of fully a week, and as we could ill spare this time we were unable to accept the Royal invitation.

We left Cairo at half-past eleven on the morning of February 11th, our destination being Ismalia, the little city on the banks of the Suez Canal, midway between Suez and Port Said. When our train stopped at the station of Ismalia we were beset, as we had been at Cairo, by natives who insisted upon taking charge of our baggage, in selling us food, or by some other means enriching themselves at our expense. A refusal upon our part had no effect whatever upon their persistency. The entire horde seemed to be under the management of a well-grown Egyptian boy of about seventeen years, and he flew from one group to another urging them on in their persecution of our party and taking the coins which they had succeeded in securing from their sales. It was not until John Healy got at the seat of the trouble, by quieting this fellow, that we were left in peace. John caught sight of him about forty feet away waving his arms and dancing about a group of little Arab boys. Unceremoniously picking up a big yellow orange from the basket of a boy who stood near, the All-America pitcher sent an "inshoot" at the Egyptian with all the speed he could put into it. The orange came in contact with the back of the peddler's neck, just at the base of the skull, and vanished into a million pieces, but it sent the Egyptian sprawling into the middle of his fellows, and he lay upon the ground with his hands to his head, probably in the belief that he had been kicked by an Egyptian donkey. Pretty soon he got up slowly, walked over to the curbing and sat down, where in a half-dazed way he watched our party until we were out of sight, but he hadn't a word to utter.

THE SUEZ CANAL.

At five o'clock that evening we boarded a small steamer and began a five hours' journey of forty-three miles up the Canal to Port Said. The night was beautiful, a full moon lighting up the blue waters of the big ditch, and the barren, weird-looking desert which stretched away on

BIRD'S-EYE VIEW OF THE KHEDIVE'S PALACE AND THE CITY OF CAIRO.

each side of us. A better opportunity for seeing this great artificial waterway could scarcely have been afforded us, and the majority of the party remained upon deck during the entire passage. The canal has a mean depth of 27 feet and varies in width from 250 to 350 feet. At the time of our passage thousands of men and camels were at work widening the canal. It is 87 miles in length, and midway between its terminal points are two natural lakes through which steamers are allowed to run at full speed. In the ordinary channel of the big ditch, however,

HOW JOHN HEALY SETTLED THE EGYPTIAN PEDDLER.

steamers are not permitted to proceed at a speed of more than five miles an hour. I was surprised to learn the rates of toll charged a vessel for passage. The "Salier," for instance, a ship of about 3200 tons burthen, paid a toll of 20,000 francs and half a franc per head on each passenger, thus making her tollage for the round trip from Bremen to Australia something over $8000. The Canal Company have fixed the toll at considerably under the cost of time and money that a vessel would be put to in going around the Cape. Thus, although the toll seems excessive, the expense is not so great as it would be for the vessel to go around Africa by the old route. We passed not less than a score of big steamers en route for the Red Sea, and the sound of our mandolins and guitars and Mrs. Lynch's cornet brought the passengers of most of them to the ship's rail as the big crafts, with their flashing electric lights, steamed slowly by us. At 10.30 we reached Port Said, the northern terminus of the canal, and climbed up the side of the handsome North German Lloyd Steamer "Stettin," where we found a hospitable lot of officers and an excellent dinner awaiting us. An hour later we steamed out of Port Said Harbor upon our journey across the Mediterranean. This voyage was the roughest we had encountered thus far, and we arrived in Brindisi twelve hours late, the result of the storms encountered. The screw of the steamer was out of water every few moments, and we rolled about at a rate that made nearly all of us seasick. The snow-capped island mountains of Crete and Candia were the only glimpses of land we secured upon this voyage. At 12.30, on the afternoon of February 15th, the "Stettin" passed through the river which leads from the bay to the Harbor of Brindisi. Finally her screw stopped before the quaint-looking and ancient little city, and a score of boats, with their Italian oarsmen, rowed out to the dock, with the Customs officers, our mail, and representatives of the various Brindisi hotels. No sight could have been more welcome to us than the big packages of letters and American newspapers which our party received. They were the first we had seen since leaving home, although I believe some of the boys did secure a few ancient copies of *The New York Herald* at the American Minister's house in Cairo. Among the letters received by President Spalding was one from Secretary of State Bayard, requesting American Consuls and Ministers throughout Europe to extend every courtesy to our party. A long letter from Walter Spalding also gave us much baseball news of a gratifying character.

ON EUROPEAN SOIL.

Brindisi is a queer little Italian town, and as we had missed the train for Naples that day, thus being compelled to remain over night at the Grand East India Hotel, we took a stroll through the narrow-winding streets, our ears being met with the sound of the guitar and mandolin at nearly every turn. At supper we were entertained by a trio of typical Italian musicians, one a dark-eyed, swarthy-complexioned, handsome Italian girl and the other two her brothers. They played as only Italians can play. All through Italy music seems to be a gift among the people, common as the gift of language. The big wood fires that burned in our rooms at Brindisi that night were very comfortable, for the raw wind of the storm still swept the coast, and most of us repaired to our apartments at an early hour to talk over the probable events of our tour through Europe. Our arrival upon European soil had put every man of our party in excellent spirits, for it seemed to us all that the greater part of our long journey had been covered, and that we were now really homeward bound.

We took our departure from Brindisi the following morning, at nine o'clock, and after an interesting ride through picturesque Southern Italy, with its vineyards, its fertile valleys and its mountains, we arrived that evening upon the shores of one of the most beautiful harbors in the world—the Bay of Naples. With the exception of four trunks and our hand baggage, all the luggage of the party had gone on to Southampton from Port Said, on one of the North German Lloyd Steamers, so that we were not hampered by the great pyramid of baggage we had carried up to that point.

Anson had the bat bag with him, however, and proposed that it should come under the head of hand baggage. With this purpose he endeavored to take it into the waiting-room of the station from which we were to be admitted to the train, and right here Anson was made to feel the power of the Italian Government. A little five-foot-two-inch, gold-laced railway official insisted that the bag was above the regulation weight, and told Anson that he must have it registered and pay extra fare thereupon. This was exactly what Anson proposed to avoid. The combat between Anson's well-known bluffing abilities and Italian authority was amusing. Here was a funny little old man, twice as aged and not one-third as big as the Captain of the Chicagoes, snapping his fingers in the latter's face. It was a species of kicking in which Anson had never before had any experience, and in which his old tactics did not stand him worth a penny. Anson had good judgment enough, however, to understand that when a traveler in Italy hits, opposes, or insults a railway official he insults, figuratively speaking, the King of Italy; so the "old man" contented himself with viciously chewing one end of his blonde moustache for a moment, after which he picked up the bag as though the bats had been so many matches, and, with a very red face, slammed it down upon the floor of the Register's office and demanded to know the amount of extra charge. It was told him, and he paid it. Indeed, he could do nothing else; but how some of Anson's old tormentors in America, who delight to sit upon the "bleachers" and howl with laughter at every misplay or "kick" the big Captain may make, would have enjoyed the situation could they have been there.

As we proceeded northward towards Naples the surrounding country became more and more picturesquely beautiful. We ran through valleys with their groves of olive and orange trees and their hills topped by white-walled villages and ancient-looking castles, the turrets and towers of which reminded one of such history as he had read of Italy in its feudal periods. During the afternoon we got well up into the mountains and ran through the first snow storm of the trip. Then we descended into the valley again, and later on, just as the mantle of night had enveloped the snow-capped peaks and the pretty low-laying glades with their flocks and farm-houses, we came suddenly into view of the Mediterranean coast. Rounding a spur of the mountain, the Bay of Naples and the beautiful "Palisade City" of the Mediterranean, Sorrento, burst upon our view with its pyramids of yellow lights and its background of shadowy mountain peaks. It was an indescribably pretty picture, and we gazed upon it with many an exclamation of admiration until a turn in the road hid it from our view. Naples was not more than thirty miles distant upon the other side of the Bay, and as we were all awaiting impatiently the first glimpse of its lights, Fogarty, who sat next to one of the windows of our compartment, in which were Hanlon, Pettit, George Wright, Mr. Snyder, George Wood and myself, startled us all with an exclamation of astonishment: "There she is, boys! There is old Vesuvius, as sure as I am a living man." In an instant we were all at Fogarty's side in the compartment, and looking through the windows we saw the great volcano standing like a beacon; its summit surrounded by a dull red halo and its crater every few seconds belching forth a sheet of lurid flame and lava. It was grand. It was awful to a degree that no description can portray. We looked and looked upon it until the guards had called out "Pompeii, Annunziata," and other historical stations about the base of Vesuvius, and until the walls of Naples itself hid the great mountain from our view.

At the Neapolitan depot we were met by Mr. Spalding and Leigh

THE PALISADE CITY OF THE MEDITERRANEAN.

Lynch, who had come on from Brindisi one train ahead of us. We were all ready for the drive to our hotel, when, much to our astonishment, we found ourselves surrounded by half a score of Italian police in their military cloaks and three-cornered hats. Finally, through the aid of an interpreter, we learned that while en route from Brindisi that afternoon, Martin Sullivan had playfully filched the horn of the guard, by which that official starts the train, a custom like that of the pulling of the bell rope, or a wave of the hand to the engineer by our American conductors. Without any idea of serious consequences, the boys had hidden the horn and had kept the guard in a state bordering upon insanity for perhaps an hour, when the horn was returned. The official's dignity had been offended, however, and he had promptly telegraphed the authorities at Naples, the terminal station of the train, with the result that we found ourselves under arrest when we arrived there. The queer feature of the arrest, however, was that we knew nothing about it until we had attempted to start for our hotel. It took the efforts of two or three interpreters and liberal promises upon the part of Mr. Spalding to straighten the affair out; and after fifteen minutes' delay we finally started for the "Hotel Vesuve," which, by the way, is everything in the way of service, equipment or location that any visitor to Naples could desire. On the way from the depot, which for a long distance led along the Bay's shore, we passed the entrance to the famous Via Roma, or "Toledo," the San Carlos Theatre, the Church of St. Francis, and the Royal Palace; finally turning upon the Bay front again, upon which, just where the "Piazza Nazionale" begins, and in full sight of Castle Ova, the Bay of Naples, and Mount Vesuvius, stands the Hotel Vesuve. We were all thoroughly tired with our long trip from Brindisi, and after a charmingly served luncheon we retired to really magnificent apartments, from the windows of which we secured our first moonlit view of the finest harbor in the world.

The bright light of a Neapolitan sun gilded the waters of the Bay the following morning as the boys stepped out upon the balconies of their bed-rooms, eager for a more extensive view of the city and its famous harbor. Castle Ova arose from the water in front of us, and further away lay the beautiful islands of Capri and Ischia, as the two points of the mainland stretched about them in the shape of a horseshoe. To our right towered Vesuvius, its summit surrounded by a great cloud of dull gray smoke that rolled away, to finally mingle with the real clouds above. We could not dispose of our coffee and eggs quickly enough, and half an hour after arising left the hotel in small parties for different quarters of the town. Some of us started through the Piazza Nazionale to the Aquarium. Others entered the Via Roma and spent the morning in promenading the famous thoroughfare, brilliant with its picturesquely attired crowds and rich shop window displays. Others attended service in the magnificent Duomo, or Cathedral of Saint Maria, while still others secured carriages and drove through the beautiful environs of old Naples, with its ancient church edifices and historical palaces. At six o'clock that evening I met Manning, Pfeffer and Leslie Robinson at the hotel entrance. They had taken a train that morning for Annunziata, and spent the day in climbing to the top of old Vesuvius, approaching as near to its smoking, belching crater as

VIA ROMA, THE LEADING THOROUGHFARE OF NAPLES.

they dared. They were tired out and covered with lava dust, but declared they would not have missed their experience for any consideration.

Of course, every one was at the theatre that evening; some preferring the ballet at Bellini's, while others went to hear Lucretia Borgia at the magnificent San Carlos. Not more than half a dozen of us had assembled in the hotel smoking-rooms at midnight to exchange our experiences of the day. Where the balance of the boys had gone and what they were doing I could only conjecture. A bulletin posted in the hotel office announced that no game could be played until Tuesday, the fourth day after our arrival. The following day was spent by most of us at Pompeii, and the scenes we beheld in the ruins of what was once a great and opulent metropolis, but which is now simply a blackened mass of ruins, will linger in our memories for years to come. I made the trip with a party composed of John Ward, John Tener, Geo.

REMAINS OF THE GRAND AMPHITHEATRE.

Wood, Ed Hanlon and "Mac." We reached Annunziata at 12.30, having left Naples at half-past eleven o'clock, and took carriages for the gates of Pompeii, distant about two miles. Here we paid our admission fee, purchased a printed description of the different objects of interest within the walls, obtained a guide and began our tour of the famous ruins. Although at the time of our visit one-third of the original city still lay buried beneath the ashes belched forth by Vesuvius, the work of excavation in the other two-thirds has been completed, and gives the visitor a fairly correct idea of the state of civilization, as well as of the customs and methods employed by the people of that unfortunate city, at the time of its destruction.

Pompeii was destroyed in 79 A.D., and at that time, the damage done by a severe earthquake was just being repaired. The shower of ashes probably came down upon the city during the night, for many of the remains recovered were found in their beds. Since the excavations

THE HOUSE RUFFA—ONE OF POMPEII'S PALACES.

began, the Government has erected a museum building near the entrance, and in this have been placed many of the interesting relics collected among the ruins. Others of these relics have been removed to the National Museum at Naples. Perhaps the most interesting of the objects in the Museum are the bodies. Of course, at the time of their discovery amidst the ashes, the flesh had long since turned to dust, but the sifting ashes had closed in around them, preserving the shapes as

352 ATHLETIC SPORTS.

though the bodies had been of bronze or iron, and when the excavators came upon any of these moulds they ceased work until the impressions had been filled with plaster. After the plaster had hardened, the surrounding ashes and lava were broken away and the plaster casts, in many of which the bones were well preserved, were removed to the Museum. The cast of a dog bent almost double, the muscles convulsed, and the bronze collar still about the neck, indicates the terror and torture the poor beast must have suffered in the agonies of suffocation.

STRADA DE ABUNDANCE—STREET OF PLENTY.

After leaving the Museum we spent several hours among the ruins, strolling leisurely along the principal thoroughfares, such as the Strada de Abundance and the Strada Stabia, and in visiting the Civil Forum, the Triangular Forum, the Temples of Jove, of Isis and of Venus, the theatres, the former homes of wealthy Pompeiians with their marble statuary, fountains and hand-painted walls, and many other points to be seen in this relic of ancient greatness. Pompeii and its history must necessarily be briefly alluded to in this volume, but there is material enough within those historical ruins to fill several volumes. While at Pompeii our party met Fogarty and Carroll. They had finished the tour of the city and were on their way to Vesuvius, bent upon climbing to its crater. I met Fogarty afterward in the Hotel Vesuve, and he told me of his experience in ascending the mountain. A railroad had been constructed up the side of Vesuvius and extended to a point not many hundred feet from its apex, but it recently took fire and had not

THE MOUNT VESUVIUS RAILROAD AS IT WAS.

been reconstructed at the time of our visit. Indeed, it is stated that the Italian guides, who for ages past have carried tourists up the mountain in sedan chairs and "palkas," destroyed the railroad upon finding that it was interfering with their old-established source of income. So Fogarty and Carroll were compelled, as were all other visitors, to make the ascent on foot. I will give Fogarty's account as he told it:—

"Carroll and I started," said he, "upon what did not seem to be such a big undertaking, but we soon discovered that the farther we progressed the farther away seemed the top of the mountain, while the steeper and more difficult of ascent it became. Time passed, and we saw that what we had laid out for half a day was really the work of an entire day. We kept at it, however, with the perspiration streaming down our faces, while one of us would every now and then stumble and fall among the brown rocks and lava; but we shortened the time by cracking jokes at the expense of our guides, and lightened the task by every now and then pausing to look back down the side of the mountain. Of course, the view of the surrounding country and the Bay and City of Naples from Vesuvius is very grand. I cannot begin to describe it, and will not undertake it, but I would not have missed it, now that I have enjoyed it, for a great deal. As we approached the summit, the ashes that had fallen from the crater grew thicker and thicker until our feet sank almost to our ankles in the drifting cinders, while the air about us was filled with a fine dust that interfered not a little with our breathing. We got around on the windward side of the mountain, however, and escaped this annoyance to a very great degree. As we continued to ascend we could smell the smoke of the volcano, and could distinctly feel the throbs of the mountain as it periodically belched forth its flames and clouds of smoke. It was awfully hard work, but Carroll and myself kept on until the guides called to us that we had ascended to as high a point as visitors usually went. Fred and I laughed at them, however, and went ahead, the guides remaining in the rear. As we proceeded, we began to notice little wreaths of smoke coming out from between the rocks, and further on we could see, not wreaths, but steady volumes of gray smoke coming out of the ground, much after the manner in which some of the scenes from Dante's Inferno have been illustrated. The mountain now not only throbbed but positively trembled. The air grew warm, and instead of the dust that had choked us before, we felt the cinders, of no delicate proportions, as they struck our hands and faces and fell round about us. Still, we kept on until we reached what I am sure must have been the outer edge of the crater, for beyond the edge over which we looked was a great basin of cinders, upon the opposite side of which I imagined was the crater proper, because we could see great masses of smoke rolling upward, while every now and then we could distinctly see the force of the explosion as flame and smoke and pieces of rock were periodically thrown into the air. Was I frightened? Yes, I was; and now that I have gone through the experience, I have no desire to repeat it. I must tell you, though, about our departure and why it was we left very suddenly, as we did. Carroll was standing near me, and we were both wondering as to the causes of the mountain's eruption, when suddenly the ground beneath us began to tremble violently. Carroll excused himself hastily and started for the foot of the mountain. I think I must have been fascinated, how-

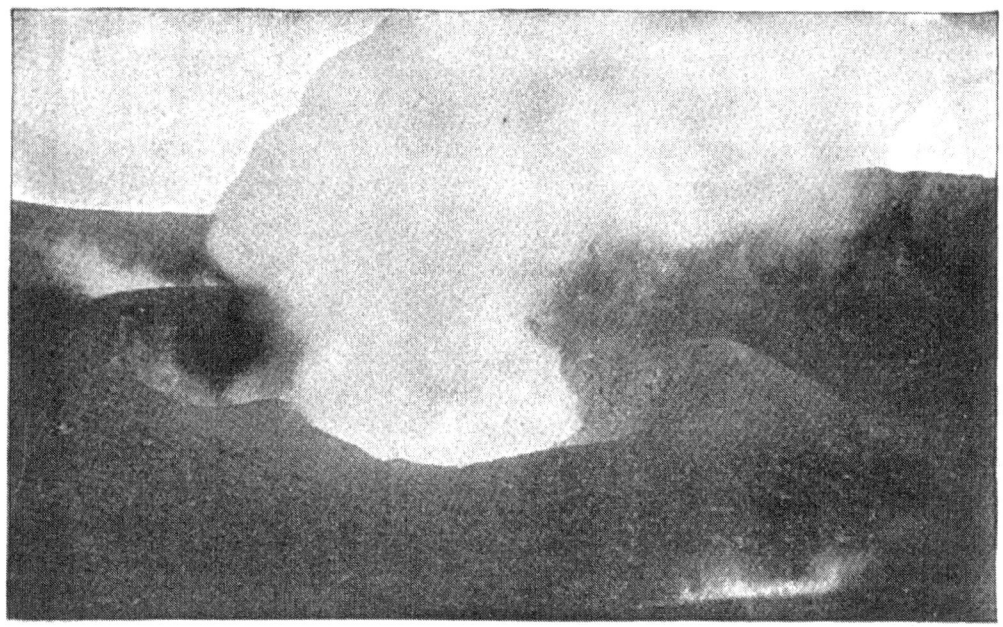

A PHOTOGRAPHIC PEEP INTO THE CRATER OF VESUVIUS.

ever, for I could not have stirred from the spot to save me. I stood there with the cinders flying and the ground trembling, not knowing just whether I wanted to remain or to follow Carroll's example, when I was suddenly startled into immediate activity. The ground seemed to actually rise under my feet. A wave of hot air almost overpowered me and then an explosion, which sounded as though the whole top of the mountain must be leaving its moorings, made me imagine my last hour had come. I did not know which way to run. But when the lava began to fall in pieces as big as my fist, and larger, all about me, I made up my mind that any place was safer than the one I was in. I accordingly started on the run, and, fortunately, having taken the proper direction, had, within a very few moments, put a safe distance between myself and the crater of Vesuvius. I never expect to make the ascent again, but if I ever do, I will not go as near the crater by a thousand feet as I went to-day."

Upon the afternoon of the 19th February we played our first game upon European soil. At one o'clock the boys in uniform entered carriages, and without any special demonstration, drove along the Via Roma and on toward the Campo de Mart, or the "Field of Mars," where the game was to be played. Upon the preceding day, United States Consul Camphausen, who was exceedingly kind and courteous to our party during its stay in Naples, had issued invitations to the members of the different diplomatic corps and to many prominent society people of Naples, and a large proportion of those invited were present. The grounds are beautifully located and are as well kept as any ball park in America. They were not enclosed, however, and there was no such thing as keeping the crowd from pressing upon the very heels of the players in their eager interest to watch every move the boys made. Half a hundred elegant equipages, and nearly as many public cabs containing many richly-dressed ladies and the official representatives of half a score of nations, were gathered upon each side of the diamond, while the crowd, beginning at the home plate, stretched away in two big lines to a point on each side far beyond the out-fielders' positions.

Tener umpired the game, which began with Baldwin and Daly and Healy and Earle in the points. Meantime, the space in which the boys were expected to play had been narrowed down by the encroachments of the crowd until batting was dangerous and fielding well-nigh impracticable. The police force present was entirely inadequate, and, besides, the officers were too deeply interested in the game themselves to admit of their discharging their duties efficiently. Minister Camphausen armed President Spalding with an Italian phrase, which he assured A. G. would have a magical effect upon the crowd, and A. G. accordingly walked up and down the line, calling, "*In di a tros; In di a tros,*" while he waved the crowd back with his hands, but the Italians only laughed at A. G.'s very bad Italian, and pressed more closely than ever about the diamond.

Then the fielders took a hand. When a ball was batted into the crowd the fielders charged after it, scattering people right and left. This had the desired effect for an inning or two, but the crowd closed in again, and just what President Spalding feared, happened in the third inning when a batted ball from Carroll took a big Italian over the eye and laid him out upon the ground. He didn't see any of the remainder of the game, for it had ended before he recovered his senses. Neither side scored a run during the first three innings, but in the fourth, Wood cracked out a single to left, got to second on Baldwin's somewhat unsteady delivery, stole third in good style, and crossed the plate on a passed ball. All-America did not long hold its lead, however, for in the last half of the fourth, Pettit got around the bases on a succession of battery errors and Pfeffer also crossed the plate. The crowd was well-nigh unmanageable when All-America came to the bat in the fifth, but after Hanlon had fouled out to Baldwin, Ward cracked out a three-bagger to centre, Brown followed with a single, and Fred Carroll next took a home run as his part of "the pie." Manning and Earle contributed two more runs, and before the inning closed the boys in blue and white had bettered their score by seven runs. At this period the crowd evidently thought the game was ended, for it rushed upon the field before the nines could change, and as none of our party were good at speaking the Italian language, we could not make them understand to the contrary. Besides, it would have been impossible for us to have handled so large a crowd had we spoken the language like natives. Ward, however, commanded his men to take their positions and claimed the game of Tener, which the latter gave him; so that, technically, the game stood nine to nothing in favor of All-America.

Our farewell night in Naples was spent by fully two-thirds of our party at the San Carlos Theatre, said to be one of the largest and certainly one of the grandest theatres in Europe. Through the courtesy of the American Minister, a dozen or more of us occupied two of the gilded boxes in the first of six tiers which lined the vast auditorium, and I am quite sure that none of us ever witnessed a more brilliant scene of the kind than we looked upon that evening. The opera was "Lucretia

Borgia." Gayorra, the great tenor, sang, and the magnificent auditorium was filled with the wealth, the beauty and the royalty of Naples, in full evening dress. There is no sham about the production of an opera in Naples. Everything, in costume, in situation, in scenic effect, is genuine, through and through. For instance, in the gladiatorial scene that evening there were not less than 600 people upon the stage, 200 of which were in the ballet and 400 or more of which constituted the spectators seated in the tiers of the gladiatorial arena. A noticeable thing about audiences in Italy, and particularly about that which filled the San Carlos that evening, was their familiarity with music and their readiness to distinguish and recognize creditable and discreditable work by the singers. Those who sat near us and about us seemed as familiar with the music as did the singers themselves, and I discovered more than one pretty Italian woman and her escort keeping time with their fingers to the singing and the orchestra, while they frequently hummed the air as the orchestra played it or as it was sung. Several times, in recognition of successful attempts at difficult executions in solo by Gayorra and his leading lady, the great crowd arose to its feet in a seemingly uncontrollable burst of enthusiasm that found vent in a wave of applause, and then was hushed immediately as the audience gained control of itself and smothered its enthusiasm for fear of drowning the succeeding notes of the singers. I had often heard it said that a singer who could sing in Naples, Venice, Florence, or anywhere in Italy, was not afraid of criticism anywhere else in the world, and after that evening spent in the San Carlos, I understood why this was true. Italians are natural musicians, from little Pepino and Jaquito who play their violins and mandolins upon the street corners, to the great Gayorra, who is wedded to his Naples, and says that he is perfectly content to sing for Neapolitans so long as his voice is left to him. He sings, I believe, three nights in a week, receiving $1600 per night, and invariably crowding the house to its utmost capacity.

We were to have left Naples the following morning at half-past eight, but on arrival at the depot, we found that the commissionaire, to whom Mr. Lynch had entrusted the all-important duty of securing our tickets, had not yet arrived at the station, so we were compelled to see our train depart for Rome with President and Mrs. Spalding, while

INTERIOR OF THE SUPERB SAN CARLOS THEATRE.

the balance of us piled our baggage in one corner of the waiting-room, and commissioning Clarence Duval as its guardian, broke away in congenial groups to put in our time as best we might until the departure of the next train, at three o'clock that afternoon. We scattered through out the city for a farewell stroll upon the Via Roma, or a visit to the Aquarium, and a stroll through the Piazza Nazzionale, while some of us took carriages and drove to San Martino, the monastery upon one of the highest eminences about Naples, and from which one of the

THE SUPERB COURT OF SAN MARTINO.

most beautiful views imaginable of the city, its magnificent harbor, and the Islands of Capri and Ischia in the distance, can be obtained. From the monastery most of the boys went for a brief visit to the Naples Museum, which is without question one of the most interesting studies in Europe. It contains within its great halls magnificent collections of marbles, bronzes, antique paintings and articles of gold and silver, embracing in all more than one hundred and fifteen thousand specimens, from which one derives an excellent idea of the manners and customs of the ancients, as well as of the high state of civilization and luxury which they enjoyed.

The great building, which one involuntarily stops to admire before entering, was begun in 1586, and was originally intended for a stable. It was abandoned, however, and left unfinished until 1610, when it was assigned to the University of Naples and used for educational purposes. Following the earthquake of 1688, it was occupied by the law

A NOVEL CONVEYANCE IN A NEAPOLITAN STREET.

courts, and during the revolutionary periods of 1701 it was utilized as barracks for the troops. Later it was again devoted to educational purposes, and in 1790, by order of Ferdinand IV, the building was largely added to and dedicated as an archæological museum for all the specimens found in the excavations at Pompeii, Herculaneum, and Stabiæ, together with antiquities from the Museum at Capo di Monte, the collections mainly of Pope Paul III. These invaluable stores of antiquities were afterward added to by the Bourbons of Naples, who finally declared the Museum to be their private property, but Garibaldi, in 1860, proclaimed the Museum the property of the country, and did much toward enlarging the collections, as did afterward Victor Emanuel the Second. The cursory and hasty glance taken by our party as we hurried through these magnificent halls and paused momentarily before such incomparable pieces of sculptor work as the Farnese Bull and the Farnese Hercules, or silently admired the great paintings of almost every school of art for centuries past, only enabled us to imagine how very many profitable and delightful hours we might have spent in this Museum had more time been at our disposal.

ROME.

At three o'clock our party entered the train at the Neapolitan station, and after another delightful ride through the picturesque rural districts of Italy, we arrived at historic Rome, the city of the Seven Hills, at nine o'clock the same evening. With little delay we entered carriages and

THE FAMOUS CORSO OF ROME.

drove directly to our hotels, the Chicago team going to the Hotel de Alamagne and the All-Americas, together with the newspaper representatives, to the Hotel de Capitol, at one end of the Corso. Rome was very much crowded with tourists at the time of our arrival, and we were exceedingly fortunate in obtaining such comfortable accommodations. The following day Mr. Spalding and Manager Lynch called upon the American Minister at Rome, Judge Stallo, of Cincinnati, and at this gentleman's office the representatives of our party received the first discourteous treatment that we had thus far met with upon our voyage around the world. I learned, from inquiries at Rome, that no more unpopular man ever represented the American Government there than Mr. Stallo, and from what little our party saw of the gentleman, we are quite ready and willing to credit the statement. He declared that he had never been interested in athletics, and did not propose to have his name made use of for mercenary purposes. As there were no enclosed grounds in Rome, and it was absolutely impossible for our teams to give an exhibition for money, there was no occasion whatever for Mr. Stallo to take such a position. Moreover, we had simply called upon him as the representative in Rome of the American Government. He did not, however, extend to us even the common courtesies which, as American citizens, we had the right to expect. Fortunately, Mr. Charles Dougherty, Secretary of the American Legation at Rome, and son of the eloquent Daniel Dougherty, of New York, proved a genial, courteous gentleman, whose efforts in our behalf the entire party appreciated. He gave us much of his valuable time, and largely to his efforts the success of our exhibition in Rome was due. Our game had been arranged for the third day after our arrival, so that we had ample opportunity for sight-seeing.

On the morning after our arrival the party divided into groups of two and three, and, chartering carriages and guides, began the pleasant experiences which most of us had hoped for all our lives, and which all of us had anticipated from the time President Spalding made known his plan to return to America by way of Europe. I think St. Peter's was the most important object of interest with us all. It requires a full day to get even a fair glimpse of the great edifice, its chapels, its galleries, and the Vatican. In the Sistine chapel; in the long galleries of the Vatican with their grand paintings and mosaics; and beneath the dome and towering arches of the great church itself, I met groups of the boys, silent and open-eyed, or inquiring and enthusiastic, as they realized with every succeeding object upon which their eyes rested how inadequate had been the descriptions they had read of this great structure. Volumes, descriptive and historical of St. Peter's, have been written by men famous in literature and journalism, and I shall not attempt even a description of that of which Bayard Taylor, Nathaniel Hawthorne, Mark Twain, and others equally capable, have given such finished word paintings. Some of the more ambitious members of our party, John Tener, Jim Manning, Mark Baldwin, and others, climbed to the ball upon the dome of St. Peter's. From the piazza this big golden globule looks the size of a pumpkin, yet it will comfortably hold sixteen people, and a grand view of Rome is obtained therefrom.

FRONT VIEW OF THE STUPENDOUS ST. PETER'S.

The following day was spent by most of our party in ancient Rome. Mack and myself took a carriage early in the morning, and amidst the ruins of the Forum ; the palace of the Cæsars ; out upon the Appian Way as far as the tomb of St. Cecilia ; at the Catacombs ; in the churches and monasteries ; and everywhere else that we happened to wander, we met members of our party. Every moment of time in Rome was improved by the Spalding tourists. To one who has read anything of the history of the world's great empire, a drive through the districts of ancient Rome is indescribably interesting. All around one are evidences of the incomparable pomp and glory of the fallen city. As one stands upon the steps of the Capitol and looks over the waste of columns and arches and magnificently carved pillars of stone of the Forum; or stands within the Coliseum and looks upon its great tottering walls; or passes under the Arch of Titus and out over the stones of the Appian Way, the same over which rolled the chariots of the imperial

THE RUINS OF THE FORUM.

rulers of Rome in the days of its splendor, he is confronted on every hand with evidences of the fact that centuries ago there dwelt on this spot a people which, in point of wealth, power, and science, was not inferior to any of the nineteenth century.

We were thoroughly tired out at the end of our second day in Rome, and after dinner, followed by a promenade on the brilliantly lighted Corso, the boys retired at an early hour so as to be ready for the game

THE BASEBALL TOURISTS AMID THE MAJESTIC SHADOWS OF THE COLISEUM AT ROME.

in the Villa Borghese the following day. In speaking of the Corso, by the way, I am reminded that among Americans generally there exists a quite inadequate conception of Rome as one finds it to-day. It is not merely a city of ancient ruins and relics of departed splendor, of sand, and beggars, and unattractive architecture. On the contrary, modern Rome is an important centre of wealth, royalty, beauty and fashionable society. Few more brilliant scenes can be imagined than that encountered on the Corso any afternoon from three to five o'clock. It is the

THE GREAT TOTTERING WALLS OF THE COLISEUM.

fashionable drive and promenade of Rome, and here the wealth and beauty of the Eternal city may be seen any pleasant day at the hours mentioned. The shop windows and their contents are marvels of the window-dresser's skill. The street is barely wide enough for two equipages to pass and the sidewalks are not over thirty-six inches across, yet I have seen as much life, as many people, as many magnificent equipages, and as much wealth, royalty and fashion on promenade in this remarkable thoroughfare as I have ever seen upon the broad surface of the Champs Elysée. Indeed, one sees a very great deal of the world on this little street. For instance, as I stood in front of my hotel one afternoon the carriage of the Prince of Naples, containing the Prince and his uncle—the son and the brother of the King of Italy, passed. The royal livery of scarlet and gold and the magnificent horses and equipage attracted general attention as it swept along. Following was the landau of the widow of a deceased California millionaire, who each winter maintains an elegant establishment in Rome and spends her summers at Nice and Paris. Next came a party of young Englishmen, who seemed desirous of seeing and being seen, and following them in a carriage almost as magnificent as that of the Prince which had just passed was a Parisian adventuress, a beautiful woman, who had won something like a million and a half francs within a week at Monte Carlo. She had taken her winnings and retired to Rome, where she was living in a state of queenly splendor.

THE ARCH OF TITUS.

One of the pleasantest incidents of our stay in Rome occurred upon the morning of February 22d, when President Spalding accepted for the party an invitation extended by Dr. O'Connell, Director of the American College in Rome, to call at the college and meet the students. Accordingly at one o'clock on the day mentioned Chicago and All-America called at the college in a body, and in five minutes after entering the gates we had all the students, some seventy or more, around us in the college garden. They were big, healthy-looking fellows representing a score of the cities of the United States ; and how glad they were to see us. Ryan and one or two others met old schoolmates among them, and the meeting under such circumstances was exceedingly pleasant to both parties. All of these boys were thorough baseball enthusiasts, and of course were present in a body at our game upon the following day. "We are fond of baseball, if we are studying for the Priesthood," said one fine athletic-looking fellow to me; "and, as I tell Dr. O'Connell, we will make good priests if we never do anything worse than harbor a love and admiration for the good old game of ball. Do we play? Oh, yes ; we get out every Saturday during the summer and have some slashing good games. Have we a good team? Yes, half a dozen of them. But we do not get half the opportunity we would like in which to exercise." After an informal chat, Clarence Duval became the centre of attraction for probably ten

THE ARCH OF SEPTIMUS.

minutes, and his exhibition of baton swinging, together with an illustration of plantation dancing, was plainly a treat to every man in the place. Afterwards we repaired to one of the class-rooms, and with a glass of Bordeaux drank an acknowledgment of the brief but hearty addresses by Bishop McQuade, of Rochester, then on a vist to Rome, Bishop Payne, of Virginia, and Dr. O'Connell, President Spalding also adding a reply. The class bell finally sounded, and when we said good-bye to the students, every one promised to be present at our game on the morrow, and it is needless to say the promises were kept.

Our game in Rome was played upon the afternoon of February 23d. During the morning, after several desperate struggles with the Italian language, I had obtained permission of the authorities to have the party photographed within the Coliseum, and when the boys drew up in front of the famous structure at half-past one o'clock, we found the photographer awaiting us. He grouped us upon the crumbling arches of the great arena and made a view that must prove a valuable memento

PANORAMIC VIEW OF ROME FROM THE SHORE OF THE TIBER.

Then we re-entered our carriages and drove to the Villa Borghese. No more beautiful spot could have been selected than that which we played upon, through the courtesy of the Prince Borghese. The Villa itself is a magnificent private park, which is thrown open to the public between the hours of two and five on Tuesday, Saturday and Sunday of each week, and the Piazza de Sienna, where our game took place, is a picturesque glade, its surface as smooth as any ball park at home, with ascending terraces on two sides and at one end. Upon these terraces, shaded by the great forest trees that have stood there for decades,

THE CHICAGO AND ALL-AMERICA TEAMS READY FOR PLAY AT VILLA BORGHESE, ROME.

assembled the representatives of the wealth, royalty and blue blood of Italy. King Humbert drove up quietly when the game was about half over and saw nearly all of the remaining innings, while of the others who remained until the last ball was batted, were the Prince of Naples, Prince Borghese and family, Princess Torlonia, Count Ferran, the Princess Castel del Fino, Count Gionatti, Senora Crispi, wife of the Prime Minister, with her daughters, Secretary Charles Dougherty and ladies, the Class of the American College at Rome, resident and visiting American and English tourists and representatives of the social and artistic circles of the city. As the teams came upon the grounds the boys of the American College gave them three rousing cheers and a "tigah,"

THE APPIAN WAY AND RUINS OF THE GREAT AQUEDUCT.

and then, after fifteen minutes of practice work, they began what was, perhaps, the most remarkable game of the trip. Each team was anxious to win the first professional game of baseball played in Rome. In order to give the spectators a couple of innings of exhibition play, the game was cut down to seven innings. Healey umpired, with Crane and Earl and Tener and Daly in the points. Chicago went first to the bat, but failed to get a man to first base, after which All-America shoved up two runs on a brilliant home-run hit by Carroll that raised the crowd off its feet. Chicago opened the second with Anson at the bat, who sent a hot one to Ward and was retired at first. Then Pfeffer cracked out a pretty double and scored on Williamson's single, Williamson next reaching second on Tener's poor throw to first, third on Burns' out, and the plate on a wild pitch. Double plays, clean hitting and brilliant fielding marked the next four innings, neither side getting a man past the plate until Tom Burns sent the ball into far right field for three bases and scored on a passed ball. All-America failed to better its score in the last half and the victory went to Anson's men by a score of 3 to 2.

The assemblage of 3500 spectators was not only appreciative but critical, and the few errors scored were received very quietly, though the brilliant fielding was enthusiastically applauded, this doubtless being due to the presence of so large a number of Americans. The two innings of exhibition work which followed were as brilliant as the invincible in-field of Chicago and the wonderful base-running of All-America could make it, and a chorus of hearty cheers went up as the boys finally lifted their caps and made their way to the carriages. Our game at Rome was a success socially and artistically.

COLUMN OF THE CONCEPTION.

On Sunday, February 24th, we left Rome for Florence, at 12.30 P. M., not a few of the boys having attended services at St. Peter's and St. Paul's during the morning. The journey was scarcely an interesting one, for, although the surrounding country was picturesque and beautiful, the day was cold and bleak and we were anxious to reach our destination. At half-past eight we entered the depot at Florence and were soon quartered at the Hotel de Europe, a comfortable inn and only a stone's throw from the right bank of the historic Arno. No one cared to inspect Florence by gaslight, under the circumstances, and all retired soon after arrival. Florence is one of the most interesting and beautiful cities we were to see in Europe, so all the boys partook of an early breakfast the following morning, and were soon after scattered through the city. The beautiful Duomo, or Cathedral of St. Maria, was unanimously voted by those of us who saw it to possess the grandest exterior of any structure we had yet seen. The Pitti and Uffiza galleries, the latter containing the Venus de Medici; the home and studio of Michael Angelo; the church of Santa Croce in front of which Savonarola was burned at the stake, and which from the time of its construction has been connected with many terrible passages of history; the palace of the Medicis;. the quiet flowing waters of the beautiful Arno, and many other celebrated points of interest were gone through rapidly, and I say this with regret, for one would fain spend

GRAND EXTERIOR OF THE DUOMO OF FLORENCE.

weeks where we spent hours, among the works of old Masters, which we had so little time to look upon.

Mr. Leroy de Koven, the scion of an American family of that name now residing in Florence, did much toward making our game in Florence a social success. The teams themselves took care of the artistic part of it, as the score will show. We played upon the Cascine, or race-course grounds of Florence, and, like the grounds of Rome, they are beautifully surrounded, being approached by a charming drive along the Arno and through one of the prettiest public parks in Europe. The game was witnessed by an assemblage which, though small, contained some of the bluest blood in Italy, royalty being well represented in the Marquisa Genora, Marquis and Marquisa Torri Giana, Baron and Baronessa Levi, Conte and Contessa Fabricotti, Conte and Contessa Geradesca, Baronessa Von de Heim, Principe Strozzi, Marquisa Balbi and many others, while visiting and resident Americans to the number of three hundred, as well as the members of the Florence Jockey Club and their ladies, embracing 'many Florentines of wealth and position, completed what was, with little question, the most fashionable assemblage of spectators that we played before during our tour of the world. The game itself was an exceedingly interesting one. Seldom have I seen better fielding, and I am safe in saying that nothing but the consideration which the boys entertained for Mr. Spalding, together with regard for their own good reputations and the presence of so many distinguished people, prevented an outbreak upon more than one occasion. As it was, there was more than one thing said "between the teeth," and many a trick was resorted to upon the field that afternoon which showed how very much in earnest the boys were and how intense was the rivalry between the teams. Chicago tried hard and desperately to win, but Baldwin did not seem to be able to

STATUE OF MICHAEL ANGELO.

BIRD'S-EYE VIEW OF FLORENCE ON THE ARNO.

get the ball where he wanted it, and the All-Americas, who ran bases like so many fiends, won the game by a score of 7 to 4.

We departed from Florence at 5 o'clock the following morning, for Nice. The weather was wet and disagreeable as our train pulled out of the station. With our departure from Florence we practically completed our stay in Italy, and that evening we slept on French soil in one of the most famous and fashionable resorts of all Europe, Nice. Sara Bernhardt and the Prince of Wales were both in the city, besides any number of people prominent in Parisian, London, New York and Chicago society, for the day following was the day of the Flower Carnival, one of the greatest of the gala days of Nice. The scenery en route from Florence to Nice is by far the most picturesque we have seen in Europe. The road runs along the shore of the Mediterranean for nearly its entire distance, one moment winding around the edge of a bold cliff, at the base of which the waters dash themselves into clouds of spray, and the next plunging into a tunnel, from which we emerged only to find ourselves upon the side of another cliff with the blue waters of the Mediterranean stretching away to the horizon.

A few hours out from Florence we entered Pisa, and obtained an excellent view of its famous leaning tower. At Genoa we stopped for luncheon, and when we stopped at the next station found that Fred Pfeffer was not with us. He had been left at Genoa, but followed on the next train, reaching Nice a few hours after we did. During the afternoon we passed through the little city of Diana Maria, which was ruined by an earthquake during the winter of '85, over four hundred people being killed or seriously injured. There did not seem to be a building in the city, and there certainly was none in sight of our train, which was not more or less damaged by the agitation of the earth's surface. Building after building stood with cleft walls and bare rafters, just as the earthquake had left it, the scene being one of indescribable desolation. Leaving this unfortunate city, we rode through some grand mountain scenery, with little villages clustered in the valleys below on one side of our train and the sea upon the other. We finally stopped at San Remo, where lay the late Emperor of Germany during his fatal illness; and then, as darkness settled down upon us, and the yellow lights began to gleam in the little harbors along the shore, we entered the station of Vingt Mille, twenty miles from Nice, on the French border.

Under ordinary circumstances we would have stopped here but twenty minutes. As it was, however, an incident, no less amusing afterward than it was annoying at the time, and similar to Martin Sullivan's experience with the Italian railway guard's horn, delayed us over an hour. It seems that Crane, Fogarty and Carroll occupied a compartment with two over-fastidious Italians, and they took offence when they imagined that the Americans were making them objects of ridicule. Accordingly, when the guard passed through the compartment they called him, and got even with the Americans by informing him that Crane had a monkey in his pocket, which, doubtless, was riding free of charge. The boys, unfortunately, had been having a little fun at the expense of the guard, and he was only too ready to seize this opportunity for revenge. He therefore insisted that Crane should pay fare for the monkey. Crane, of course, refused—indeed, laughed at the idea—for the monkey was no larger than a good-sized rat and was snugly tucked away in the New Yorker's overcoat pocket. The guard said nothing more, and we arrived at Vingt Mille, where our baggage was examined by the customs authorities. When we attempted to re-board our train, however, we were stopped, and while we were indignantly demanding an explanation, which the Italian-speaking officials could not give us, our train started out of the station before our eyes. Finally, we obtained an interpreter in the person of the cashier of the Italian dining-room in the station. We were then informed that the party could not leave the place because one of our passengers had not settled his railway fare. Upon further inquiry, we found that this passenger was Mr. Crane's monkey, and Ed was obliged to fork out seventeen francs for his Japanese pet's passage. Fifteen minutes later the official came back to us, stating that the fare for monkeys was nine francs more than he had charged us, and that he would be compelled to collect this. Crane was angry enough to have thrown the fellow through the window, and indignantly refused to pay another franc, with the result that within five minutes we were again completely surrounded by a cordon of soldiers, and Crane, alternately laughing and swearing at this imposition of Italian rule, went down into his pocket and paid the balance. Then as we were getting upon the train the interpreter mildly informed Mr. Spalding that he owed him twenty francs, or four dollars, for services as arbitrator, and if the fellow had not gotten out of the reach of Al's foot just as he did, he would certainly have felt its force.

At last we pulled out of the station and sped on toward Nice, past Monte Carlo, past Monaco, until we finally came to a halt in the station of Europe's great pleasure resort. The little city was greatly crowded, in view of the approaching " Battle of Flowers" and it was only after

PANORAMIC VIEW OF THE PRINCIPALITY OF MONACO.

some difficulty that we succeeded in securing quarters at the Interlachen Hotel. The day following our arrival was an exceedingly unpleasant one. It had rained all night and the steady downpour had not ceased for an hour during the entire day. Of course the flower carnival was suspended and the beautiful floral decorations that signaled the approach of the battle in all quarters of the city looked sorry enough. During the afternoon we learned that there were no grounds in Nice suitable for field sport of any kind and that, consequently, we would be unable to give an exhibition there. One would suppose that Nice, above all other places would be provided with well-equipped athletic grounds, tennis courts, cricket fields, and the like, but there is not even the suspicion of a cricket oval, to say nothing of a ball field within the limits of the city. The announcement of no game proved a keen disappoint-

THE SUPERB THEATRE OF MONTE CARLO.

ment to two or three hundred Americans who were in the city, but there was no help for it.

While the festivities of the Flower Carnival had been prevented, or rather postponed by unfavorable weather, rain did not in any way affect the attendance in the world-famed gaming halls of Monte Carlo, and our entire party improved the opportunity to visit them. I have been told since my visit to Monte Carlo that there is nothing else like it in the world, and this I am perfectly willing to believe. The grandeur of the great gambling hall we entered is unequaled by the interior of any theatre or public hall I saw in Europe. Beautiful grounds, made as charming to the eye as the skill of the landscape gardener can make them, and brilliant with a thousand gas jets, surround the building. On the opposite side of the plaza is a sumptuously equipped hotel, and next

ANTE-ROOM OF THE CASINO.

to that is a gorgeously fitted café to which one can escape from the heat of the gambling hall for a cooling ice or a bit of luncheon. Ward, by the way, dropped into this café during the evening and was charged the modest sum of $4.80 for a dish of asparagus, $5.20 for half a cold chicken, and $1.00 for a cup of coffee. Of course he paid it, which was the only thing he could do, but he remarked upon leaving the cashier's desk that the proprietors of the place must certainly have taken him for a gambler, and a very flush one at that. Such is the basis upon which all things are conducted at Monte Carlo. Those who have gold seem to regard it as so much dross. Those who have not gold and who cannot obtain it, too frequently end their lives as not worth the living.

Upon entering the building, one leaves his coat, hat and cane in the ante-room, in charge of a liveried attendant, passes through a magnificent lounging saloon, where gentlemen are smoking and chatting among themselves or with prettily-attired, bright-eyed, attractive-looking French women, and then on into the great gambling hall itself, with its lofty ceilings, crystal chandeliers, moquette carpets, and magnificently decorated walls. Nine big double tables are in full blast, and about each of these are gathered from 75 to 150 people, representing almost every nation of the globe, making their bets and losing or winning money. Duchess and courtesan, prince and adventurer, gentleman and confidence man, may be found jostling each other as they place their bets. Richly-dressed women, some wrinkled and gray-headed and others fair-faced and lovely to look upon, pass from table to table in search of the luck that comes to but few of them, all seemingly slaves to the one consuming passion of gambling.

I saw a gray-haired, diamond-bedecked, bony-fingered old woman sitting at a table with a pile of gold in front of her, stacked almost bosom high. Fortune seemed to smile upon her with every bet she made, and her long, slender, colorless fingers plunged in and out among the piles of gold in front of her, while her quick, restless eyes watched every jump of the ivory ball in the roulette wheel. Whether she lost or won her face never changed its expression. Opposite her was one of the prettiest, fairest faces I had ever looked upon; that of a young girl, who nervously fingered the few last pieces of money that lay upon the table before her. The old lady, I was told by my guide, was an English Duchess, who came to Monte Carlo regularly every spring for two or three months' indulgence at the gaming table. Her winnings had been enormous, and her losings equally great during the past score of years; still she came as regularly as each spring made its appearance. The pretty-faced girl opposite was one of the many pretty creatures who wander in there, lose their little wealth, and then turn to some admiring fellow who is willing to stake them to the extent of his admi-

INTERIOR OF THE GREAT GAMBLING HALL OF MONTE CARLO.

ration and his pocket book. Many a poor fellow has lost a fortune at these tables, and sent a bullet or a knife through his breast on the marble steps outside. The attendance at the Casino, by which name the great gambling hall is known, for February of 1889, is said to have exceeded, by something like 21,000 people, the attendance for the corresponding period of the year before. The number of suicides is also stated to be correspondingly heavy, nine having been known in that period, to say nothing of those which the police, for reasons best known to themselves, had failed to report. Such examples, however, do not seem to have any effect upon the frequenters of Monte Carlo. They go and come, lose and win night after night, in the face of the realization that the chances of winning are one in ninety, with almost the certainty of a suicide's grave staring them in the face at the end of it all.

Everybody, however, who visits Nice goes to Monte Carlo. An American would no more think of going to the south of France without seeing Monte Carlo than an Englishman would think of visiting America without seeing Niagara Falls, and every one who goes there becomes wicked enough for the time being to gamble, if only just a little. Monte Carlo has a history with which most of my readers are doubtless familiar. It is embraced within the Principality of Monaco and is practically under the protection of the French Government. Still it is an independent principality, as the rule of the Prince of Monaco is almost absolute, and as the greatest source of the principality's wealth is its gambling hall, there is small wonder that the evil is tolerated. It is about thirty minutes' ride from Nice, on the Rivieri, and without question is one of the most exquisitely beautiful places in the world. All of our party during our visit to the Casino wooed the Goddess of Fortune, and some of us quite successfully. Fogarty quit four hundred francs ahead; Geo. Wood did nearly as well; and Captain and Mrs. Anson each returned to Nice with a handful of gold. There were others, however, who left within the gilded walls of the Casino a considerable portion of their own cash. President Spalding "quit winner," but the merchant of Nassau street "dropped his little pile," and came away a sadder but wiser man.

The second day after our arrival at Nice, to which the flower festival had been necessarily postponed, was characterized by perfect weather. The sun shone down upon the blue waters of the Mediterranean and warmed the wet verdure and soil into bright fresh life, while thousands of people flocked to the beautiful Avenue des Anglaise, where during the entire day elaborate preparations had been going on for the event of the afternoon. This famous avenue on the shore of the Mediterranean is one of the most beautiful in Europe, and on the day of the carnival presented an attractive picture, with its magnificent private and public hotels and its gaily-decorated booths, extending for a distance of perhaps some twenty blocks. Gendarmes were stationed every twenty feet to maintain order; bright-colored ribbons and bunting were flying from every booth; French women, attired as only a French woman can attire herself, laughed with, flirted and jostled the sterner sex along the walks; while boys bearing huge baskets of flowers circulated among the crowds selling to all who would buy. About three o'clock elegant equipages literally covered with flowers began to arrive, and for two hours these promenaded up and down the avenue, while beautiful women, kid-gloved gallants and brightly-dressed children pelted each other with flowers to their hearts' content. About four o'clock, the drag containing the Prince of Wales and a dozen of his friends, among whom were several pretty American and English girls, whose names I was unable to learn, joined the procession.

PANEL DECORATION IN THE CASINO.

Of course, the Prince was the cynosure of all eyes, and if his taste is to be judged by the size of the bouquets he threw and the method with which he bestowed them, his Highness, though no longer a young man, has still an excellent eye for womanly loveliness; and he had a great array of it to select from that afternoon, for never in my life had I seen a larger concourse of beautiful women or a more brilliant picture of its kind than that of this Flower Carnival.

We all left Nice in the morning of March 1st, at six o'clock, but the majority of our party laid over at Lyons for the night. Ward and myself, however, were too eager to reach Paris to submit to any such delay, and so kept on our way, reaching Paris about eleven o'clock the following morning. There was snow on the ground at Lyons, and it was chilly and disagreeable. When we two entered the environs of Paris the next morning, however, the sun was shining brightly, and

PANEL DECORATION IN THE CASINO.

the air was as balmy and ethereal as we had left it at Nice. From the depot we drove straight to the banks of the Seine, on past the magnificent Hôtel de Ville and Cathedral of Notre Dame, into the Rue Rivoli, and thence past the Louvre into what is the most imposing thoroughfare in the world—the Avenue de l'Opera, finally crossing upon the Rue de la Paix and turning into the Rue Caumartin, where we stopped in front of the Hôtel St. Petersbourg. A. G. and Leigh Lynch met us at the door, and soon John Montgomery and I had removed all evidences of the railway ride. We found, upon arrival, that the heads of the party had experienced much difficulty in obtaining enclosed grounds for an exhibition in Paris, and it was not until we had been there for several days that the Parc Aristotique, on the banks of the Seine and but a short distance from the then unfinished Eiffel Tower, was secured. Meantime, our party saw as much of Paris as American energy and limited time permitted of.

Ward and myself managed to get into trouble before we had been in Paris two hours. On arriving at the hotel, and after having made our toilets, I asked Leigh Lynch where we could purchase some good cigars. "The best place that I know of," replied Leigh, "is at the Grand Hotel; come with me." We did so, and upon arriving at the store (which is, as are all the cigar stores in France, under the control of the Government), I stated the priced goods I wished, and the polite Frenchman, selecting an unbroken box, opened it and held it toward me. I requested Ward to help himself, and then took one myself, and handed the attendant a two-franc piece, the cigars being worth one franc each. He shrugged his shoulders, returned the money to me, laughed, and began to wrap up the box. I laid the money on the counter and followed Ward toward the door. This action brought the Frenchman after us, and he explained, in very indifferent English, that I must take the whole box. The demand was so ridiculous that I laughed; but he was very much in earnest, so I promptly put the cigar back into the box and picked up my money. Upon this, the Frenchman followed me to the sidewalk, and noticing Ward waiting for me, with the newly-purchased cigar between his lips, he walked up to the New Yorker, with true French impulsiveness, and took the weed from between Ward's teeth. Ward was too astonished to speak, but not too much so to act. He grasped the fellow's wrist with a clutch that must have given him an

NOTRE DAME, THE MAGNIFICENT CATHEDRAL OF PARIS.

excellent idea of the muscular development of American ball players, and, while holding his hand in a vise-like grip, deliberately replaced the cigar between his lips, and then told Monsieur in French that if he attempted a trick of that kind again, he would find himself in the gutter. The man threatened to call the gendarme, and looked up and down the street in search of one. Ward told him that nothing would please him better, and the fellow, seeing that his bluff game would not go, finally consented to take payment for the cigars.

THE EIFFEL TOWER AS THE TOURISTS SAW IT.

That afternoon and evening we began our tour through the streets of the city, certainly the most beautiful of all the great cities of the world. Its magnificent thoroughfares, its great institutions and beautiful boulevards, its broad public parks, its picturesque environs, with their historical palaces, its public squares, its monuments, its life, its gayety, combine to make Paris wonderfully attractive both to the Parisian and to the visitor within her gates, particularly if he be an American.

Our party arrived in Paris on Saturday. The following Tuesday was Shrove Tuesday, the closing day of the carnival festivities in Paris, and during that evening and the early hours of the following morning none of us had time or inclination for anything more serious than the Bal Masque or the glitter of the big cafés on the boulevards. Our only fear was that we should miss some part of it. We arose at a late hour on Tuesday morning, having lingered long in the cafés and the variety salons on the boulevards the night before, so that soon after we had breakfasted the fun in the streets, in commemoration of the closing hours of the carnival season, began. Masquers seemed to come from within every doorway, carriages dashed hither and thither with gloriously costumed occupants, horns were tooted, bells rung, and people jostled each other and screamed with laughter upon the slightest provocation. Paris seemed to have gone crazy. The crowd upon the streets resulted in a crush, and I remember that Mark Baldwin, Monsieur St. Claire, of the *Revue des Sportes*—who, by the way, was extremely attentive and kind to our party during its stay in Paris—passed down the Rue de la Paix to the Rue Rivoli, where we had a peep at the Louvre, and spent an hour in the book and photograph booths with which this thoroughfare is lined. Well-executed copies of the famous paintings in the French galleries can be purchased in these stalls for from ten to twenty francs apiece, and we purchased to the limit of our pocketbooks. Then back up town we strolled *via* the Avenue de l'Opera, which was so uncomfortably filled with crowds of shouting, prank-playing maskers, that it was with difficulty we got through them

THE COLUMN OF JULY.
Commemorative of the Revolution of July 14th, 1789.

and turned into the Rue Caumartin, back to our hotel. After dinner Ed Crane, John Ward, Ed Hanlon, Mac and myself deliberately laid out a programme of wickedness, and started out to see Paris on carnival night systematically. First, we drove to the Comédie Français—the home of the drama in France—whose walls have witnessed the débuts and subsequent triumphs of such lights as Coquelin and Bernhardt. We there spent an hour with French Comedy as it can be put on at this famous theatre only, and Ward was so pleased with it that we were compelled to leave him. The remaining quartet drove to the Jardin Bullier, where the students' ball was in progress.

What a crush, what wild hilarity, what exaggerated costumes, and what shockingly short skirts! There must have been five thousand dancers on the floor of that big pavilion at one time, all whirling and kicking amid the glare and heat of two thousand gas jets; yet, despite the crush, all was good nature. Lines of black-tighted students, clasping hands, would go through the crowds of dancers on the run, knocking them in every direction, yet no one lost his temper—that is, no one "kicked," in the sense that the average American baseball enthusiast would use the word. There *was* a "kick," however—a literal kick—and Ned Hanlon will bear me out in the statement. A leg encased in red silk, and belonging to a tall, well-shaped girl, shot upward just behind Hanlon, and Ed's silk hat climbed up among the chandeliers. The girl laughed, the crowd clapped its hands and rushed after Ed's hat, which they finally secured, and returned to him uninjured, but the American had had enough. "Come on," he said in a disgusted tone, "let's get out of here;" and we "got," for the students' ball of Paris is very much upon the rough-and-tumble order, aside from all else that can be said of it.

It was midnight when we reached the Eden Theatre, just off the Rue Caumartin. Here the great masked ball of the evening was shortly to commence, and as we entered, some of the prettiest women we had seen in Paris stood about the foyer, while French gallants in evening dress awaited the reappearance of their ladies from the dressing-rooms. The ball at the Eden was as select and *recherche* as the Bullier ball had been wild and reckless. The interior of the Eden is impressive. The style of the decorations and architecture is Egyptian. The parquet had been boarded over on a level with the stage floor, and a music stand, filled with a hundred musicians, stood under the proscenium arch, room being left for a passage way on each side, while a grand staircase, at a point just opposite the stage, led up to the promenades, cafés and restaurants back of the dress circle. The interior in itself was beautiful, but with the crowds of gorgeously-dressed women and their escorts it became dazzling. Our party took seats in the dress circle—front row, of course—to witness the opening, which occurred a few minutes after twelve o'clock. We had not been seated long before there was a crash of music from the orchestra, two big doors upon the stage flew open, and a hundred girls, in every conceivable costume calculated to show their figures to best advantage, filed out in a long procession, each girl bearing aloft a colored glow ball at the end of her gallant's cane. These constituted the regular ballet corps of the establishment. Most of them were pretty, and all were graceful, and the scene, as they followed their leader on a run across the parquet, up the broad staircase, through the crowds in the cafés and on the promenades, and then down to the dancing-floor again, was a brilliant one.

The programme had thus been opened, and the dancing now commenced in earnest. A dozen quadrille sets were in motion, and all around the borders of the dancing-floor sets of four, two couples, were dancing the Cancan. They evinced as great a spirit of rivalry in their dancing and were as jealous of each other's attainments as were ever two premières of the ballet, and the impulsive, excitable crowds in the room would be drawn from one quartet to another as the applause arose in different sections of the hall over some specially difficult and graceful pirouette of one or more of the dancers. Within half an hour after the dancing commenced, I saw fully half of the American party on the floor, not dancing, but eager spectators of all that was going on. Thanks to the courtesy of our Parisian newspaper friends, we were not long strangers among the assemblage, and as I glanced around I caught sight of Ed Crane, Ed Hanlon, Fogarty, Wood, Tom Brown and the "Professor" bending over the fair heads and the dark eyes of the Parisian beauties who filled the room, and who spoke, according to their own acknowledgment, "Joost a leetle Inglese"—in fact, just enough English to make them all the more interesting. It was three o'clock when the ball at the Eden had ended, and the remainder of the dancers followed those who had preceded them to the cafés on the Boulevard des Italians and the Rue Montmartre, which, when we reached them about the hour mentioned, were a blaze of electric light, brilliant costumes and vivacious women. Revelry, *bon mots*, and a good time generally seemed to be the existing order of things everywhere, until

ARC DE TRIOMPHE.
Commemorative of the Victories of Napoleon I.

approaching daylight frightened the revelers into their carriages and sent them to their apartments. One part of Paris was awaking while another was just retiring, and our party, which belonged most unmistakably to the latter class, wended its way to our rooms in the Rue Caumartin.

Ned Williamson and myself saw much of Paris in each other's company, and I found the big short-stop an excellent companion. He is well read, and nothing worthy of notice escaped his eye. Indeed, it is my impression that had Williamson chosen the journalistic profession instead of devoting the best years of his life to ball-playing, he would to-day be as prominent in one as he is in the other. His descriptive letters of the scenes and incidents of our tour to one or two American newspapers for which he corresponded were among the most interesting sent from our party. Mounted upon the big Parisian busses, which, by the way, is really the best method of seeing Paris, Ned and myself rode from the Grand Opera House to the Bastile, and from the Grand Opera House again, past the Madeleine and the Place de la Concorde to the Champs Elysées, at which we left our conveyance and walked down to the bridge which spans the Seine, at a point near the Exposition Buildings. Then we took another buss and rode to the Arc de Triomphe, which we ascended, and from which we secured a view of the French capital that is not equaled by any other save from the Eiffel Tower. From the Arc we drove to the Trocadero Palace, and from its balconies looked out over the terraced gardens and the Seine upon the incompleted buildings of the Exposition.

The others of our party were soon following our example, and, although we remained in Paris but a week, it is safe to say that we saw much more of the city than many Americans who have tarried there for a much longer period. To tell of all the incidents, or half of them, that made up our experiences in Paris, would require a substantial volume in itself, and I am not sure but it would make exceedingly interesting reading. Those who have visited Paris can doubtless imagine how much there would be for twenty-five able-bodied, fun-loving, much-traveled young Americans to see and to do, and we were seeing and doing through every available hour of our time.

The morning before our game, President Spalding and Manager Lynch, in a personal call, extended to President Carnot an invitation to attend our exhibition, and the next morning received in reply the following letter from Gen. Brugere, which, translated, reads thus:—

"PRESIDENCE DE LA REPUBLIC, Paris, March 7th.

Sir:—I have the honor to inform you that the President of the Republic is warmly appreciative of the invitation extended to him to attend the baseball match at the Parc Aristotique.

He, however, regrets that because of his numerous occupations he will be unable to be present, as he attaches much interest to the development of physical exercise in the education of our youths.

He will, however, be represented by the officers of his military staff.

Accept, sir, every assurance of my distinguished consideration.

GENERAL BRUGERE,
General of the Brigade, Secretary-General to the President.

To Mr. *Leigh S. Lynch,*
Hôtel St. Petersbourg, Rue Caumartin."

Our game in Paris, which took place on the afternoon of March 8th, was one of the memorable events of the trip. The bright sunshine, the picturesque surroundings, the pretty faces, that grew prettier with excitement and interest as the game progressed, the presence of the large number of Americans familiar with baseball, the assemblage of distinguished spectators and the spirited playing of the teams, all combined to make it so. The park is located on the banks of the River Seine just opposite the Exposition Buildings and within the shadow of the great Eiffel Tower. Walled gardens and big city residences stood high above the field, which, though small, was still large enough for some great sport and a good exhibition. The little grand stand, especially erected, had been profusely decorated with American and French flags and furnished with plush chairs for the members of the President's staff, the American Legation, and other distinguished spectators, while chairs on each side of the stand accommodated all who did not wish to remain standing.

Among those present were General Brugere and Captain Chamin, representing the President; Mr. and Mrs. William Joy, of the American Legation; Miss McLane, daughter of the American Minister to Paris; Miss Urquhart, a sister of Mrs. James Brown Potter; Consul-General Rathbone; M. G. de St. Claire, of the *Revue des Sportes;* Nate Saulsbury, and others of prominence in official, social and theatrical circles. In this game Ed Williamson was injured. He had taken his base on balls, in the second innings, and in attempting to steal second base he fell over a sharp stone, the playing surface being of sand and fine gravel, and tore his knee cap painfully. His little wife, who was among the spectators, hurried to his assistance, and together they left the grounds for the hotel, Baldwin going to first and Ryan covering Williamson's place at short. No one anticipated that the big fellow's injury would necessitate more than a few days of rest; but it kept him confined to his room in London for many long weeks, and prevented his entering upon his duties with the Chicago Club during the greater part of the championship season of 1889. Seven innings only were played in Paris, as it was necessary for the teams to depart that night for London. With the exception of Daly's single in the seventh, Chicago failed to do any hitting, save in the sixth inning, when a home run by Ryan and a two-bagger by Pettitt, together with a passed ball, netted them two runs, the only ones scored by Chicago during the game. Crane pitched a magnificent game for All-America, and his support was faultless. While the play aroused enthusiasm among the Americans present, it was "Greek" to the Parisians. All, however, admired the long hits by Ryan, Carrol, Pettitt, Wood and Crane, and applauded the base running and the brilliant fielding.

ON THE ENGLISH CHANNEL.

We left Paris at half-past eight o'clock of the same evening for our never-to-be-forgotten and eventful trip across the English Channel. We took the long route from Dieppe to New Haven, and it is safe to say that a thousand dollars would not induce any of us to go through our experience of that night again. Indeed, we were fortunate in reaching the shore at all. The Captain remarked, the following morning, that during the thirty-five years in which he had sailed those waters he had never encountered such weather and such a sea as we had passed through. Twice during the voyage he was tempted to turn around and go back to Dieppe, under the belief that it would be impossible for us to reach New Haven in the teeth of such a gale. We might very well have stopped over in Paris till Saturday, or Sunday noon, when we would have escaped the nearly all-night ride on the cars and our unpleasant experience on the Channel. We had expected, however, to play our initial game in England, at Bristol, the following day, and nothing but a heavy storm and the overflow of the grounds there prevented the carrying out of the programme. Even had the grounds been in condition, however, none of our party would have been in shape to play ball, for all of them sought their beds at once upon our arrival at the First Avenue Hotel, in London.

We arrived at Dieppe shortly before one o'clock in the morning, and bravely walked down the dock, in the face of the stiff gale, to the little side-wheeled steamer "Normande," where we made ourselves as comfortable as circumstances would permit in the somewhat cramped cabin. Very soon after, we started upon our voyage, and as the ship began to roll, probably five minutes after having left the dock, the steward, a big, ruddy-faced Englishman, came in with an armful of little tin wash basins, one of which he deposited in the vicinity of each bunk. We asked his stewardship if stationary washstands were unknown institutions in England, and were smilingly informed that washstands and the little bowls which were being deposited about the cabin were intended for entirely different purposes. He advised us, however, not to lose sight of the bowls, as we might need them. And we did. Verily, it was a night to remember! Twenty minutes after leaving the dock, the "Normande" was in the gale, and she tossed about much as an air-tight barrel upon the waves might have done. Ton after ton of water poured over her decks as the big waves engulfed us, and we in the cabin below could hear the water rushing over us as we have heard a cataract breaking over its bed in the mountains. Tom Daly, myself and several others were thrown from our bunks by the severe shocks, but all were so sick that we failed to realize the danger we were in, or, if we realized it, were wholly indifferent thereto. Goodfriend and Leigh Lynch went on deck for a breath of fresh air, soon after leaving the dock, and neither of them could get back to the cabin. With the assistance, however, of a couple of strong sailors they reached a rope bin, near the wheel house, and sat there until daylight, with the big seas breaking about them and sweeping the deck between them and the cabin hatch. About three o'clock in the morning we were all startled by a shock, as though the vessel were really going to pieces at last; the shock being accompanied by a crash of timbers and the shouting of men, dimly heard above the roaring gale. We learned the next morning that one end of the bridge had been carried away, but that the lookouts had managed to hold on. Despite the danger of our position, however, the experience was not without its laughable experiences. Mrs. Lynch insisted that she was dying, and begged for her husband; but Leigh, poor fellow, was being tossed about inside the rope bin, on deck, and could not have reached the cabin for his life's sake.

"I guess you won't die, Madam," said the stewardess, and madam did not die, but both she and Mrs. Anson looked not far from dead six hours later, when we arrived at New Haven. Poor John Healy lay upon his face, calling upon all the saints to save him from a watery grave, while John Ward and John Tener went staggering about the cabin in a dazed state, bearing with them the most wretched countenances I have ever beheld. Even Clarence Duval was sick, but not more so than the poor little Japanese monkey, which sat upon Ed Crane's breast, with its funny little head hanging over its shoulder as though indifferent whether it lived or died. Ed himself lay flat upon his back, figuratively " dead to the world."

IN OLD ENGLAND.

But the sun was shining brightly in the little seaport town of New Haven, on the English coast, when we dropped anchor there next morning at 7 o'clock. The air was clear and spring-like, and not a trace remained to recall the perilous voyage of the night, save the wretched appearance of our party—colorless, worn out, and feeling no interest in anything but the prospect of a bed and a much-needed rest. Clarence Duval turned around after having ascended the dock, and with a glance out across the waters of the channel, shook his fist at it and then at the steamer, as he said: " Hi, you Missy English Channel, you tink youself mity smaht, don't ye? and yo' *is* smaht, but you dun did well to have a *extry* good time wid us while you had de chance, 'cause yo' doan neveh get dis boy out dar agen. If eber I git back to Ameriky, I'se gwine to stay dar—yo' heah me?"

It seemed good to hear English spoken again by others than our own party, and we submitted with good grace to the Customs examination, which was hastily made. We then took the train for London town, reaching Victoria station about half-past nine o'clock, where we were met by Mr. Spalding and Mr. C. W. Alcock, of the London *Cricket* and Secretary of the Surrey County Cricket Club. Mr. Spalding smiled as he saw the pale faces that came out of the railway carriages, and was compelled to turn away with momentary laughter as we came up the platform, poor Ed Williamson bringing up the rear on crutches—as sorry a looking procession of representative athletes probably as any that ever landed in England. As soon as he had learned of our experience and Ed's injury, however, he did everything that could be done for our comfort. Drags in waiting rolled us rapidly through the streets of the city to Holborn, where we were soon quartered in comfortable rooms in the handsomely appointed First Avenue Hotel. Mr. Spalding had gone to the expense of having all our baggage shipped to London from Liverpool, whither it had gone on the North German Lloyd steamer from Port Said, so that after a forenoon nap, a raid on the wardrobe and a luncheon, most of the boys began to look themselves again by nightfall.

The spirit of sight-seeing which had clung to us ever since we had left California reasserted itself before we had been many hours in London, and the two days following our arrival were put in by most of us in obtaining, so far as possible, a general idea of the great city. All visitors, so far as

MR. C. W. ALCOCK.

I have been able to learn, are, no matter from what quarter of the globe they come, immediately impressed with the vastness and the greatness of London. The famous Strand, one of the busiest of the many busy streets in the metropolis, is but a few minutes' walk from our hotel, and as one strolls along it in the direction of Trafalgar Square, the Victoria Hotel, the Hotel Metropole and the Parliament buildings, an excellent idea of London street life can be obtained. The absence of street railway cars and the presence of the big double-decked busses, as well as of myriads of Hansom cabs, at once strike the American. Everywhere is London crowded, and no matter in what quarter one may find himself, London, to the stranger, is greater, grander, more interesting and more impressive than all other cities of the world combined. I shall not attempt to write descriptively of the world's metropolis. One might spend a lifetime there, and then not have seen all that would be well worth writing of. Unfortunately, we reached the city at a most unfavorable season of the year. It was foggy, cold, damp, penetrating, and all of us suffered more or less severely with colds, which we seemed unable to shake off. We were very pleasantly situated, however, in the First Avenue Hotel, with its luxuriously furnished smoking-rooms, reading- and lounging-rooms, its excellent table and comfortable apartments.

True to their Yankee training, the boys began bargain-hunting before we had been many days in London. Clothes, hats, canes, umbrellas, underwear, linen, and, in fact, every article necessary for a gentleman's wardrobe can be purchased in London cheaper than in any other city on the globe, and the boys consequently spent money liberally. Many of them, however, have since acknowledged that while textures may be cheap enough in London, the London tailor is a miserable failure, so far as his ability to fit an American with a suit of clothes is concerned. Not only is he unable to fit an American, but also an Englishman, and it is a noticeable fact, or was to me, that in London, Englishmen seem to be utterly indifferent to the matter of fit. They seem perfectly willing to wear their clothes as though they had been thrown at them, and while brand new and made from the finest cloths, most of the suits that I saw there would have been promptly sent back to his tailor by the average American.

Arrangements had been made for a reception and a luncheon to our party in the Club House of the Surrey County Cricket Club, at Kennington Oval, to take place on the day of our opening game in England. The Committee appointed to receive the teams on this occasion embraced the Duke of Buccleugh, Duke of Beaufort, Earl of Landsborough, Earl of Coventry, Earl of Sheffield, Earl of Chesborough,

Lord Oxenbridge, Lord Littleton, Lord Hawke, Sir Reginald Hanson, Bart., Sir W. C. Webster, Attorney-General, the Lord Mayor, American Consul-General, American Charge d'Affaires, and Dr. W. G. Grace. Tuesday, the day of our opening game, was most disagreeable and thoroughly unsuited for an exhibition of baseball. It was raining when the boys arose from breakfast, and although the down-pour ceased about noon, a typical London fog took its place, a fog which gave the towers and spires of the city a spectral and shadowy look, while but for the noise of rumbling wheels one could almost imagine himself in a community of ghosts, so dim, misty, and shadowy did everything animate and inanimate appear. Indeed, it was questionable whether the day's programme could be carried out, but the fog lifted a little by noon, and it was decided to play the game if possible. The teams accordingly entered the drags in front of the hotel at 12.30, and were driven to Kennington Oval, where, in the Club House of the Surrey County Cricket Club, a generous collation had been prepared and the boys were presented by Secretary Alcock to many, if not all, of the gentlemen named as members of the reception committee, and many prominent members of the Club. Lord Oxenbridge acted as Chairman of the assemblage, and after some of the good things on the board had been disposed of, he proposed the toasts of "The Queen" and "The President of the United States," both of which were enthusiastically acknowledged. Lord Lewisham then proposed the toast of "The American Ball Teams," President Spalding replying to the toast in his characteristically happy vein. Hon. Henry White, United States Charge d'Affaires, then brought the more formal part of the proceedings to a close, by proposing the health of the Chairman which was drunk with cheers. The boys then descended through the crowds that filled the Club House corridors and reception-rooms to the dressing quarters. Meanwhile, spectators kept pouring in at the gates until the immense oval, which is one of the most popular cricket ovals of London, and which is the personal property of the Prince of Wales, was completely surrounded by a living hedge from twenty to twenty-five feet deep, while the Club House windows and balconies were crowded to their utmost limit.

But what a day for baseball! The ground was soft, black and sticky wherever a spike cut through the green turf, and the big reservoirs of the gas company's works, which stood just outside of the walks, looked like spectral balloons in the gray fog, which was so dense that a ball knocked outside the infield could scarcely be seen. The crowd was there, however, with any number of prominent cricketers and representatives of the noble houses of England, and the Prince of Wales himself was expected; so that it was determined to proceed with the game. There was a moment of silence when the boys filed upon the field after having been photographed at the Club House steps, and then applause was tendered from all parts of the ground as the fine proportions of the men were noted. To play good ball under such conditions is difficult, almost impracticable, as almost every lover of the game in America will understand, and yet the exhibition at Kennington Oval throughout the nine innings was an excellent one under the circumstances. Healy and Baldwin pitched for their respective teams, and although the batting by neither side was heavy, many of the hits were clean and well placed, while the base-running was spirited and the fielding really remarkable, when it is considered that the ball could scarcely be seen fifty feet above the ground. At the end of the first half of the third inning a commotion was noticeable about the Club House, and a moment later the well-known face of the Prince of Wales appeared at one of the windows just behind the catcher's box. The boys simultaneously turned, walked to the home plate, and gave three cheers and a tiger for His Highness, while the crowd afterward cheered their approbation of the Americans' action.

At the close of the fifth inning, the teams, accompanied by Manager Lynch and the Press representatives, left the field at the Prince's request and ascended to the room where His Highness was seated. He arose and stood near the table in the centre of the reception room, and as President Spalding introduced the party, shook each one cordially by the hand. There was nothing affected, either in the manner or the attitude of the prospective King of England. He took the mud-stained hands of the players in his own faultlessly-gloved fingers and gave each a good strong, hearty grip and shake. Then he turned and chatted pleasantly with the boys for several minutes, calling Brown, Anson, Ward and others by name, as though he had been familiar with the

THE BASEBALL TOURISTS AT THE CLUB HOUSE, KENNINGTON OVAL, LONDON

game and its players a lifetime. He bowed pleasantly to each of us as we left, and then took his seat at the window to witness the remainder of the game. The crowd, understanding the nature of our visit to the reception room, applauded as the boys reappeared and commenced the sixth inning, while the Prince at the window asked question after question as the plays on the diamond were made, and listened attentively as President Spalding explained them.

Soon after the intermission, a representative of the *London New York Herald* asked His Highness what he thought of the game. "Here," said the Prince, "give me a card, and I will write my opinion," and he penciled the following:—

> The Prince of Wales has witnessed the game of Base Ball with great interest & though he considers it an excellent game he considers Cricket as superior.

Of course, this was very graceful and very clever, and just what His Highness should have done. He could scarcely have expressed an opinion favorable to baseball, as against cricket, even though he had desired to do so, and the best compliment he could pay the American game was to compare it with the game which England considers so vastly superior to every other field sport. I understood afterward that the Prince, during the morning, had been quite indisposed, and had been advised by members of his household to send his regrets instead of attending our game. He generously determined, since he had accepted the invitation, to make his appearance, however, and became so interested in the play that he remained a full hour at the club-house window. He was accompanied by Colonel Elliott and Prince Christian. As to the game, it was closely watched throughout, though, I imagine, more in the spirit of criticism than of admiration. The fielding, particularly catches of long outfield flies, the base-running and sliding and the batting seemed to be about the only points understood or appreciated, and these were greatly applauded. The *London New York Herald*, that afternoon, circulated among spectators hundreds of blanks, with the request that they pencil their honest impression of the game; and these, being published the following day, covered almost a page and a half of that enterprising paper. Many of the criticisms were severe. Some thought the game "child's play," others "could not see any sense in it," others thought it "too complicated in its rules to ever become widely known or popular," and all thought cricket so vastly superior in every way that there would be no room for American "diamonds" on English soil. Many, however, applauded the fine exhibition of fielding and frankly acknowledged that English cricketers might be benefited by emulating their American cousins in this respect. On the whole, the criticisms were by no means encouraging to our baseball missionaries, but I am pleased to say that before we left England there were many among the fifty odd thousand people who attended our games whose opinions changed materially, and the result of the visit to England of the American College boys, three months after the return of the Spalding party to America, has been exceedingly gratifying. The collegians played ball upon the London cricket grounds, interesting in the game many of London's best-known cricketers.

One of the pleasantest events of the trip, thus far, was the delightful little supper tendered the party the evening preceding this game by Miss Grace Hawthorne, Mr. Wilson Barrett, and Mr. W. W. Kelly, Miss Hawthorne's manager, at the Princess Theatre, in Oxford street. The teams, by invitation, attended the performance of Mr. Barrett and Miss Eastlake in "Good Old Times," occupying four of the proscenium boxes. After the performance, a collation was spread in one of the ante-rooms of the theatre, and with Mr. Barrett as Chairman of the proceedings, we spent one of the most memorable evenings of our stay in England. There were musical selections and recitations from a number of clever people, a recitation from Mr. Barrett, as well as a hearty address of welcome and wishes for our success in England, and a charming little speech from Miss Hawthorne herself, which brought down upon her golden head as big a burst of applause as she had ever received from the same number of people during all her professional life. The genial Kelly, too, came in for his share, and, as he afterward put it, was "too thoroughly broken up over it all to say much of anything."

The following morning the party, accompanied by Mr. Henry White, United States Charge d'Affaires, drove to the Parliament Buildings, and were admitted to and shown through the historical structures by the Secretary to the Chairman of the House of Commons, at that time in session, an honor rarely conferred upon visitors. We entered the great hall wherein Warren Hastings and Charles the First were tried, and which had been so badly shattered by the explosion of a dynamite bomb two years before. We visited the Crypt and the Committee Rooms, and were shown the magnificent corridors, their walls decorated with great paintings, executed at a cost of from four to five thousand pounds sterling each. We were next taken through the House of Lords, with its imposing and beautiful interior, and stood before the Woolsack and Queen's Seat, while the seats of the various members were pointed out to us by the Secretary. From the House of Lords we entered the House of Commons, where Sir William Harcourt was speaking upon "The Treatment of Political Prisoners in Ireland." Mr. Balfour occupied a seat which gave us an excellent view of his ambitious and intellectual, yet to me somewhat cold and cruel, face. It was expected that Mr. Gladstone would enter shortly, but we could not wait for even a glance at "the grand old man," and, after listening to Sir William Harcourt for a few minutes, we descended to the corridors, and, still accompanied by Mr. White, crossed over to Westminster Abbey, where we had only time to glance at its beautiful interior before mounting our drags for a drive to the grounds.

There is no question in the world that in England they can give America points on Athletic grounds. They certainly do have beautiful lawns for Cricket, and I thought, as I looked over the velvety turf at "Lords" that afternoon, of the time when, as I fondly hope, we may see at least one end of the unbroken stretch of green sward marked by the runways of a baseball diamond. "Lords" is a grand stretch of turf, and the manner in which the people poured through the gates that afternoon was a gratifying surprise to our party. There were fully seven thousand people present when play began; and what a game the boys played! It was "away up in G" from the start. All-America took the lead by capturing three runs in the second inning, and held it until Chicago, by scoring four in the eighth, as the result of timely hitting, good base-running and costly errors, forged to the front. Then

THE CLUB HOUSE.

Ward's men, by desperate base-running, which evoked burst after burst of enthusiastic applause and laughter, jumped in, and, together with the battery errors of Anson and Baldwin, won the game by one run. It was just such a game as pleased the Englishmen better than anything we could have given them, the batting being brilliant, and the base-running of a character that would have called for hearty applause even from our best-posted American assemblages. A better understanding of the game was plainly shown by the spectators, the Duke of Buccleuch, in particular, being among the first to applaud every clever bit of fielding and base-running as he viewed the play, together with a party of friends, from the Club House. That evening our party accepted the invitation of Henry Irving and Miss Terry to occupy boxes at the Lyceum, and we were present in full force. We were invited behind the scenes between acts to enjoy a glass of wine and receive the well-wishes of our host and hostess; after which we returned, some to our seats and others to the hotel.

The following day, March 14th, was the date of our game upon the Crystal Palace Grounds. These grounds, with the great palace of crystal standing in their midst, form one of the sights of London. They are located at Sydenham, some ten miles or more from Snow Hill Station—Sydenham being one of the popular residence districts about the metropolis. Our third game in London took place here, upon the grounds of the Crystal Palace Cricket Club, a beautiful stretch of lawn surrounded by stately old trees and quaint-looking English residences, which stand beyond the boundaries of the park. All-America under the captaincy of Ned Hanlon—Ward having sailed for New York upon personal matters that morning—administered another defeat to Anson's forces, in one of the prettiest games played since leaving Australia. Another big and enthusiastic crowd of over five thousand people were present. The day was fairly favorable for baseball, cool and cloudy, but still dry and fogless, and we had begun to regard even such weather as this in England as wonderfully favorable. The boys dressed in the cosy club house on the grounds, and at three o'clock began the game. More enthusiasm was manifested at this contest than at any other we had yet played in England. Englishmen actually pushed and jostled each other in their excitement, many of them calling out to the base runners, "Run, run, man, or you won't make it." In the eighth inning, when All-America scored by hard batting, the enthusiasm was such as to remind us of home. Crane cracked out a pretty double, which was finely fielded by Tener in far centre, and started to run.

"He won't get second," exclaimed one Englishman near my shoulder.

"Yes he will, yes he will," shouted another man; "see, he's got it—by Jove, he's got it."

"Yes, and he's going for third," yelled the other, waving his umbrella with excitement. "Oh! ah! look out, look out there, my hearty—you're caught."

Then he joined in the burst of applause that rewarded Tener's quick work and fine throw from the outfield. Hanlon followed with a base hit, and stole second with a slide that awakened the crowd into another burst of applause; but it was nothing to that which went up when Tom Brown picked out one of Baldwin's slow balls and sent it out of sight among the tree tops. Brown is a magnificent base runner, and he never showed up before or since that hit, to my knowledge, in prettier style. He was at the plate almost as soon as Hanlon, and Ned was not slow himself in base-running. Such interest and such applause was, indeed, encouraging to our boys, and no doubt spurred Hanlon's forces on to the capture of another run in the ninth inning, which gave them the game by a score of five to three.

DR. W. G. GRACE, ENGLAND'S GREATEST CRICKETER.

AT BRISTOL.

The following morning, at seven o'clock, we left London for Bristol, the home of Dr. W. G. and Mr. E. M. Grace, the most famous cricketers in England. As before stated, it had originally been our plan to play our first game in England upon these grounds, but a storm had rendered them unfit for use. We enjoyed a delightful ride from the metropolis in a big saloon car, especially provided for us, and upon our arrival in Bristol, at noon, were met at the depot by a committee composed of His

HIS ROYAL HIGHNESS, THE PRINCE OF WALES.

Grace the Duke of Beaufort, Dr. W. G. Grace and officials of the Gloucester County Cricket Club. We were driven at once to the Grand Hotel, where, in the parlors, we were presented individually to Dr. Grace and to the Duke. The Duke is certainly one of the finest examples of an old English gentleman I ever met; hale and hearty, yet close on to sixty, he still remains a great lover of field sports of every character. His estate at Badminten, seventeen miles from Bristol, is one of the finest in England, and here he breeds some of the greatest strains of racers extant. He shook each of us cordially by the hand, and then the entire party adjourned to the Windsor Room, where a generously covered table had been set for us. The Duke acted as Chairman, and, after the repast, the usual toasts, "The Queen," "The President," and "The American Baseball Teams," were proposed and drunk. President Spalding excited no end of laughter among our hosts and the invited cricketers present by his humorous recital of some of our adventures abroad. That little dinner and our reception at Bristol will certainly be long and pleasantly remembered by all who shared therein. With three cheers and a tiger for His Grace and our friends in Bristol, the boys left the banquet room and mounted the drags, which were surrounded by crowds of people as they stood in front of the hotel. President Spalding and the Duke of Beaufort drove out in the latter's magnificent private coach. The Gloucester Cricket Grounds are new, having been purchased and equipped but a short time before our arrival, at a cost of twelve thousand pounds sterling. Solid-looking gray walls of stone surround as pretty a stretch of turf as there is in England, and notwithstanding Bristol has but three hundred thousand people against London's four and a half millions, the latter city has no prettier cricket park than that in Bristol.

The day was the brightest we had yet experienced in England, and the grounds in excellent condition for play, yet, strange to say, the game did not show, in a single inning, a tithe of the snap shown in our London game. The boys tried their best to throw some life into it, but for some reason it progressed just as I have seen championship games at home —dead, up to the very last inning. Of course, there was batting and fielding. There was even a pretty double play by Ryan and Baldwin, and there was base-running and base-sliding, plenty of it, yet all of it seemed listless and draggy. However, the applause was liberal, and if the Bristolites enjoyed the game, we were all thoroughly glad of it. His Grace the Duke of Beaufort, with his two daughters, sat upon the press bench, to one side of the home plate, until the game was nearly finished, and watched each point of play, asking Mr. Spalding to explain what they did not understand. On the completion of the game, which ended in a victory for Chicago, Ryan and Crane, with the regular Chicago team in the field, sent the ball over the plate, while Messrs. W. G. and E. M. Grace, together with other prominent cricketers, tried to hit it. When the pitchers put any speed in the ball, not even the famous Grace brothers could gauge it. When Ryan and Crane let up, however, the cricketers found the ball perhaps a dozen times within fifteen minutes, the only safe hit being Dr. Grace's. This exhibition pleased the crowd even more than the game had done, and the boys were given a farewell round of applause as they left the field.

BACK TO LONDON.

Our farewell game in London took place Saturday afternoon, March 16th, on the grounds of the Essex County Club, at Leighton. There was another big, critical and enthusiastic crowd present, numbering something over eight thousand people. The score, twelve to six, in favor of Chicago, would have disappointed an American crowd, but was declared by the English newspaper men present to be the best game we had yet played in London. They liked it, as did the entire crowd, because there had been plenty of hard hitting and base-running. Crane did not put much speed in his delivery that day, as he was saving his arm for the long-throwing contest which had been announced to take place between himself and Bonner, the Australian cricketer, at the end of this game; and so he was freely hit by Anson's batsmen. At the conclusion of the game thousands poured upon the field and formed in a great line, that extended from one end of the oval to the other, in expectation of seeing the throwing contest. Bonner, however, did not appear, he having deliberately backed out at the last moment, and Crane accordingly gave an exhibition of throwing, sending the ball, a cricket ball, without exerting himself to any great extent, 110 yards, and following it with a baseball throw of 120 yards 25 inches. Had

Bonner been on hand, the probabilities are that the record would have been broken, as Crane declared himself in splendid condition and in the humor for throwing. On arrival at the hotel that evening the boys changed their uniforms for dress suits and repaired to the splendid buildings of the Niagara Panorama Company, where the stockholders of the institution had prepared a banquet for our party. The good old Duke of Beaufort dropped in upon us, half an hour after we had taken our seats, having come down from Bristol, as he put it, to spend the last evening with this " fine lot of fellows from America." When the toasts had been disposed of, every man of us joined in three cheers and a tiger for the old gentleman, who had been so honestly glad to see us and who had taken such sincere pleasure in entertaining us. On the following morning we fairly commenced our provincial tour in a style that excited comment and curiosity throughout Great Britain.

TOURING IN ENGLAND.

Through the efforts of Mr. S. Stanford Parry, General European Agent of the C. B. & Q. R. R., and Mr. C. W. Alcock, the London and Northwestern Railway Company had fitted our party out with a special train, the like of which had not before been seen in England. We had nine cars, two of which were dining saloons, with a connecting vestibule, two smoking and reception cars, and the remainder sleeping cars, each sleeper accommodating six to eight persons comfortably. The exterior decoration of the train was handsome, the body color being white enamel, with gold and seal brown trimmings, and the Royal Arms in gold and scarlet on the carriage doors. The interiors were even more elaborately equipped than our American vestibule trains, and contained every comfort one could ask. Each carriage was lettered in brown upon both sides, with the inscription, "The American Baseball Clubs," and the train presented a truly royal appearance as it stood beside the platform in the Euston station. It was to take us to Birmingham, Sheffield, Bradford, Glasgow, Manchester, Liverpool and Fleetwood, at which latter point we finally took the Irish Channel steamer for Belfast. There were fully five hundred people present in the station to witness our departure that morning, and with three cheers for Mr. C. W. Alcock and three more for the officers of the London and Northwestern Railway, we started on our journey through England. We were accompanied by Mr. P. G. Lane, the special correspondent of the *London Sportsman*, who was particularly courteous and attentive to our party during its stay in London and our tour through England, and by Mr. Fred W. Thompson, the Special Agent of the London and Northwestern Company, who did everything in his power to make the trip in the special a pleasant one.

BIRMINGHAM.

It was but a short run of three hours to Birmingham, where we were met at the depot by a delegation from the Warwickshire County Cricket

SPECIAL TRAIN FOR THE BASEBALL TOURISTS.

Club, who hurried us to the Colonnade Hotel and expressed their good wishes for us in bottle after bottle of "Yellow Label." Then we partook of luncheon at the Queen's Hotel, and soon after mounted two big drags and were whirled away through the streets of the city to the club grounds, prettily located and well equipped. Three thousand people were present despite the threatening weather, and we gave them a game worth talking about. Chicago opened with the capture of four runs in the first inning and All-America tied the score in the fourth. Neither side afterward sent a man across the plate, game being called at the end of the tenth inning on account of darkness. Englishmen had not seemed to like light-score games up to this point, but they entered into the spirit of this contest, and were heartily disappointed because the boys were unable to play out the game. That evening the boys attended the Prince of Wales Theatre in a body, after which we returned to our sleeping apartments in our comfortable special train.

SHEFFIELD.

We departed from Birmingham the following morning at nine o'clock, and within a few hours were steaming along through the beautiful hills of Yorkshire, at the base of which arise the towers and smoke-stacks of Sheffield, the greatest cutlery manufacturing district of England. At the station we were met by several members of the Yorkshire County Cricket Club, and were conducted to the Royal Victoria for luncheon, then, as in Birmingham, we mounted two big coaches, and with tally-hos sounding, drove to the Bramall Lane grounds, one of the oldest and most famous athletic parks in England. Full four thousand people were present when the game began in the rain. Despite the rain, however, the boys played on, and the crowd, some with umbrellas and some without, stood in the rain and watched every play until the fourth inning, when the grounds were so muddy and the rain was falling so fast that the boys were compelled to leave the field. The players waited an hour for the rain to cease, but finally gave it up and filed through the gates. That evening we attended the Royal Theatre in a body, in response to an invitation extended by Miss Kate Vaughn.

BRADFORD.

The snow was falling heavily when we pulled out of Sheffield, next morning, and started for Bradford. At Bradford we found the weather pleasanter, although the storm of the day before had left the cricket field in a deplorable condition. The grounds of the Bradford Cricket, Football and Athletic Club we found divided into two sections, one being used for cricket and the other for football. The cricket field had a fine turf surface, but the football field was covered with chopped straw and soft loam soil, a combination which no doubt made an excellent playing surface in fair weather, but which, upon the day of our arrival, was little better then so much black paste. To add to the discomfort of players and spectators, it began to rain while the boys were in their dressing room, and a chill wind swept the mist in white sheets across the field. Still, the people fought and scrambled for tickets at the gate. In America not ten people would have started for the grounds on such a day. In Bradford there were four thousand people upon the grounds at half-past three o'clock; even the members' stand being crowded with ladies in water-proofs and macintoshes. It seemed folly to attempt to play ball under such circumstances, but the Cricket Club secretary stated that three innings, if it was possible to play them, would satisfy the spectators, and as the players were willing, it was decided to make the attempt. So the boys went out and played as pretty a trio of innings on that black, sticky surface as one would wish to see anywhere. It was short, to be sure, but it was a fine exhibition, and every spectator got his sixpence worth beyond doubt. While sliding a base in the first innings, Fogarty tore the sole off one of his shoes. He had no duplicate shoe, and there was no one to take his place in left field for All-America, so, repairing to the dressing room, "Foge" wrapped the disabled member in a bath towel and played the game out. At the end of the third innings we could not get into our drags and back to our cars too quickly, and in our comfortable saloon smokers we spent a pleasant evening, while the wind blew and the rain fell outside.

GLASGOW.

When we awoke for breakfast we found ourselves in the London and Northwestern depot at Glasgow, our train having crossed the border into Scotland during the night, and had our train borne the Shah of Persia himself, it could scarcely have been an object of greater curiosity. Visitors flocked about our carriages by the hundreds. Even young women drove up to the station in their carts, took a leisurely promenade along the platform from end to end of our train, and then drove away. Until 1.30 P.M.—the hour at which we drove to the grounds—the train was surrounded, certainly not less than five thousand people having stopped to look into the windows of our cars during the morning. At noon we had luncheon in the London and Northwestern Company's hotel at the station. After luncheon, the boys in uniform, but wearing their heavy coats, for the air was cold and sharp, mounted a big double-decked, four-horse carry-all, and with nearly a thousand people assembled to see them off, started for the grounds. The West of Scotland Cricket Club's grounds are as well appointed as any outside of London, and happening to be in good condition, with fair weather for baseball, the boys put up an excellent game. All-America, by timely hitting, and by taking advantage of wild throws by Baldwin and Pettitt, won their victory in pretty style, the forty-five hundred spectators liberally according the heartiest applause at the pretty fielding work of Fogarty, Hanlon, Ryan and Pfeffer. Returning to the train, the boys exchanged their uniforms for their dress suits, and adjourned to the Grand Theatre, where, between the acts of "King Lear," they left their boxes to break a bottle of Monopole with Mr. and Mrs. Osmond Tearle behind the curtain.

MANCHESTER.

We reached Manchester for breakfast the morning of the twenty-second, having left Glasgow at midnight. All of our party were more favorably impressed with Manchester than with any Provincial town we had yet visited. In accordance with our usual custom we spent the forenoon in driving and walking about the city and inspecting the principal thoroughfares, then we returned to our train, which, as at other stations, we found surrounded by a curious crowd. After luncheon we climbed to the top of a couple of four-horse coaches and set out for the Old Trafford grounds. When I got the first glimpse of its beautiful stretch of green sward surrounded by pretty pavilions, club houses, and terraced rows of seats, the Old Trafford grounds of Manchester seemed the most beautiful in the world. The air was a bit bracing, but the boys put up one of the prettiest contests of our tour, before as distinguished and fine looking an assemblage of spectators as we had played before since our opening game in London, when the Prince of Wales was present. Had the details been prearranged, the boys could not have fought a prettier battle. In the fifth inning All-America tied the score, which stood five to five up to the time Hanlon's men came to bat in the eighth inning. Manning scored in this inning in dashing style, but Chicago again tied the score in the first half of the last, when Pettitt crossed the plate, the score standing six to six, when Hanlon came to bat for All-America's last half of the ninth. Ned cracked out a pretty single and reached second, risking his neck in a daring and successful attempt at a steal. The play sent the crowd off into one enthusiastic howl of applause, base-sliding being an entirely new feature of field sport to the majority of the spectators present. They clapped their hands, waved their handkerchiefs, and called out to Fogarty, when he came to bat, to "Hit it hard now." "Foge" picked out the ball he wanted, and sent it upon an ideal two-base journey to far left centre. Away flew Hanlon to third, and touching the bag lightly with his foot sped on toward the home plate, and then to the Club House without ever stopping, the balance of the players picking up their coats and breaking after Hanlon on a tight run, while the crowd stood upon its feet and applauded vociferously. They had seen a brilliant game, and, what is more, they had appreciated it. That evening our party was banqueted in the rooms of the Anglo-French Club, as special guests of Mr. Raymond Eddy, the European representative of the house of John V. Farwell & Co., of Chicago. A score of Mr. Eddy's friends assisted him, Major Hale, United States Consul at Manchester, acting as Chairman. Mr. Eddy proved a typical American in personal appearance, in patriotism for everything and anything American, and in the whole-souled, generous manner in which he entertained our party.

LIVERPOOL.

We departed from Manchester the following morning at seven o'clock, reaching Liverpool an hour later. Another crowd stood in the depot to see the Yankees at breakfast in their dining-cars, and to stare at the players as they emerged and made their way up town to see the city. Probably because it has so long been visited by so many Americans, Liverpool has an unmistakably American air about it. Just where or what the existing difference is between it and other English cities, I cannot say, but there is a difference, and it was noticeable to all of our party. As this was our last opportunity to do any shopping on English soil, the boys put in the morning profitably alike to themselves and to the Liverpool shopkeepers. We partook of a light lunch at the London and Northwestern Company's hotel at about half-past one o'clock, and then mounted a huge coach with seats for twenty-eight people, and bowled through the streets of the city to the Police Athletic

Club grounds for our game. With the long brass horn of the tally-ho sounding upon every block, and its notes interspersed with the sharp crack of the coach-driver's whip, we created almost as much of a sensation on our way to the grounds as our special train had done at the depot. We found the park already fairly well filled and a big crush of people at the gates. Indeed, the crowd at the gates reminded me much of an American crowd at the gates of a ball park before an important championship game. The pressure of the hundreds upon the outside of the big carriage gate finally broke it from its hinges, and nearly five hundred people swarmed upon the ground before the police could stop them. Between six and seven thousand people had finally packed themselves about the diamond when the programme began.

Five innings of baseball were first played by the Chicago and All-America teams, and the only regret of our party, and doubtless of the spectators, was that it did not last longer. Baldwin and Crane were both on their mettle, and how that ball did cut the air about the plate. Neither pitcher wanted to stop at the end of the fifth inning, when the score stood 2 and 2, but other games had been announced and the tie could not be played off. But one hit was made off Baldwin and four off Crane.

After the ball game came the game of "Rounders," which had been arranged between the local club and a team picked from the Chicago and the All-America. None of us had ever seen the game, from which it was claimed baseball sprang, and all were therefore anxious to have it begin. A picked team from the Rounders' Association of Liverpool finally went into the field against an American eleven composed of Baldwin and Earl as battery, with Tener, Anson, Wood, Fogarty, Brown, Hanlon, Pfeffer, Manning and Sullivan. The fielders were stationed much as in baseball, save that there was a fielder back of the catcher, called "long stop," and a fielder back of the third baseman. The batting is done with one hand, and the bat is like a toy cricket bat, or perhaps more like a butter paddle. The ball is the size of a tennis ball, and the bases, instead of being bags, are iron stakes protruding about three feet from the ground. A base-runner could not be retired upon being touched with the ball, but must be struck with it. Moreover, he must run the first time he strikes at the ball, whether he hits it or not. The pitching is straight armed. In the game they played against our boys, the rounder players took an unfair advantage in sending our team to bat first, and, not knowing the rules, the Americans were shut out with but six runs. The boys soon "caught on," however, and the two innings played resulted in a score of sixteen to fourteen in favor of the Liverpool players. This was all we saw of the Rounders during our tour of the world, and I am quite certain that none of our party cared to see any more of it.

Following the game of Rounders, the Americans played the rounder team two innings of baseball, simply to show them the difference. At the end of the second inning the score stood eighteen to nothing, in favor of the Americans, and would have been more, had the latter not tired of running the bases. Baldwin pitched, and after striking out three of the batsmen, let the other three hit the ball and get thrown out at first. How the crowd did enjoy this sport. They stood twenty to thirty deep in the steadily pouring rain, which had begun to fall just as the rounder game commenced, their hats on the back of their heads, and they shouting and applauding as though they were witnessing a horse race on an ideal day in June. A dozen of the biggest cranks in America could not have been induced anywhere near a ball park in such weather; and when it was all over, and the boys climbed upon their drags, the big crowd cheered the teams until we were out of sight.

Our train left for Fleetwood that evening at nine o'clock, yet the boys managed to accept two invitations after they had swallowed a hasty dinner, some of them going to the Royal Theatre as the guests of Mr. W. W. Kelley, and others to the Shakespeare Theatre, as the guests of Miss Litta. Then we hurried to the train, and bidding farewell to Liverpool, started for Fleetwood on the shore of the Irish Channel. It was but a three hours' run, and at eleven o'clock we boarded the beautiful little steamer "Princess of Wales," in which we were to cross to Ireland.

With our experience on the English Channel still fresh in our minds, none of us looked forward with very much pleasure to crossing the Irish Channel. Contrary to our anticipations, though, or rather to our fears, the trip to Belfast was one of the pleasantest voyages of our entire tour. Even before the breakfast gong sounded, the majority of the boys were on deck, eager to catch the first view of the Emerald Isle, and the announcement of breakfast failed to draw many of us down stairs. We were steaming through the Belfast Loch with the beautiful shore of County Down on one side and that of County Antrim on the other. By the time we had finished breakfast, we had entered the river Lagan, and soon after dropped alongside the stone dock in front of the Custom House. Carriages conveyed us to the Imperial Hotel, on Royal Avenue, and, for the first time since leaving Australia, the boys felt a sense of rest and relief from the rapid pace at which we had been trav-

THE JOLLY JAUNTING-CAR OF BELFAST.

eling. It was Sunday, and the players, in parties of three or four, mounted jaunting-cars, and spent the afternoon in driving about the beautiful environs of Belfast. Sunday afternoon was quiet enough to suit the severest Sabbatarian, but Sunday evening Royal Avenue was crowded with pretty girls and their escorts. The bright costumes of the Scotch Highland troops, off duty, added to the attractiveness of the scene. Rain coming up shortly after nine o'clock, however, the boys sought the big comfortable smoking-rooms of Mr. Jury's hotel, where they chatted until bedtime.

The weather on the following day was erratic. During the morning it rained for an hour, and then the sun shone for half an hour, only to be hidden by another downpour of rain, until it began to look really doubtful as to whether or not we should be able to play our game scheduled for Belfast. It cleared up about noon, however, and after luncheon the boys made their way through the crowds about the hotel doors and mounted the drags for the cricket park. The North of Ireland Cricket Club is certainly well provided with grounds. Out on the Ormeau road is a fine stretch of lawn, well fenced in on three sides and its fourth washed by the waters of the river Lagan. Beyond the river is Ormeau Park, and, altogether, the club could not have selected a prettier and more desirable site in Belfast. Despite the condition of the turf, which was too soft for base-running, the boys played one of the cleanest-cut and prettiest games I scored during the trip, and that, too, before an exceedingly attractive and thoroughly appreciative assemblage of spectators. Pretty girls in jaunting-cars, and fine-looking, highly-bred Irish gentlemen, young and old, together with large numbers of Club members and their invited guests, went to make up a crowd of three thousand people, who sat the game out through rain and shine, applauding liberally when good plays were made, and at all times showing the keenest interest. As in Manchester, the game ended beautifully. In the eighth inning it stood eight to seven, in favor of Chicago, when, in the ninth, Wood and Healy each cracked out a pretty single, both crossing the plate on Earl's fine three-base drive to far left field, and thus scoring another victory for All-America under Hanlon's captaincy. That evening the boys were banqueted by the North of Ireland Cricket Club, at the Club House, the Mayor of Belfast presiding.

We left Belfast at an early hour the following morning for Dublin, and it was while the boys were enjoying the soundest sleep of the night, shortly after five o'clock, that they were awakened from their slumbers by a voice in the hallway, which sang out as it passed our doors: " Arf pawst foive; wudge ye be gettin' oop, surrs? its arf pawst foive." Oh, the richness of that brogue! Every man of us will remember it for many and many a year to come. Hanlon rolled out of bed laughing before his eyes were fairly opened, and within two minutes a dozen grinning faces were thrust through bed-room doors into the hall, as the boys asked one another, "Did you hear that? did you hear it, I say?" Like a warden in a graveyard, Pat continued on down the hall, pausing every ten steps to raise his head in the air, and in a voice that seemed to come from his boots, call out, "Arf pawst foive." The mere repetition of that phrase by any member of our party was ever afterward certain to excite a ripple of laughter.

AN OLD IVY-COVERED CASTLE.

Beautifully picturesque indeed is the ride from Belfast to Dublin, where we arrived at eleven o'clock, four hours and a half after our departure. The carefully-cultivated farms, with their borders of stone walls or green hedges and the charming woodlands, with an occasional old ivy-grown castle lifting its towers above the tree tops, more than realized our anticipations of Irish landscape. At Dublin station we were met by U. S. Consul McCaskill and others, and driven to Morrison's

Hotel, famous as the scene of Parnell's arrest. Mr. Spalding had kindly given this day over to such of the boys as wished to visit friends and relatives in Ireland, and there was no game scheduled. Consequently, John Tener, Tom Daly, Jim Manning, and others posted off to Kildare, Kilkenny, Londonderry, and elsewhere, to visit uncles, aunts, and nieces they had not seen for years, and some of whom they had never seen. Indeed, the three mentioned left us at Belfast after the game there.

"I went to Callan, in Kilkenny," said Manning, in talking to me afterward about his trip, "Callan being a little town of about fifteen hundred people, where I have an uncle and several nieces whom I had never seen. I telegraphed my uncle that I was coming, and the 'whole town' met me at the station in jaunting-cars and on foot. Brogue? Well, you should have heard it. I wouldn't have missed it for a farm. Everybody had to shake hands with me. They looked me over as though I might have come out of the clouds somewhere. Then they took me in one of the jaunting-cars, and, completely surrounded by these little two-wheeled conveyances, I was driven to my uncle's home. Almost the first things that caught my eye were a number of pictures on the walls representing myself in costume and as my likeness had appeared in our American sporting and daily newspapers. They asked me all about baseball; wanted to know if it was played like 'Hurley'—an Irish game, something like polo—and could not understand how a man could earn a living salary by playing baseball. Of course I had a delightful time, and everything in Callan, even the scores of pretty Irish girls, was mine."

Tom Daly went down to Kildare, and his two old uncles had the little town in which they resided dressed up in gala attire to receive him. They took him over to their little home, and sat with him upon the balconies, while the town folk dropped in in instalments for a look at their neighbor's American "neffy." The conversation that took place between Tom and his uncles must have been exceedingly funny, as I got it from the Chicago catcher upon his return to the party.

"Phwat is it ye say ye'r afther doing, me boy?" asked one of the old gentlemen.

"I am traveling with the baseball party," replied Tom.

"Phwat's baseball?"

"Why, it's a game we play in America," replied Tom.

"An is it boi plain' a game that ye make ye'r livin'?"

"Certainly," said Tom. "We have thousands of people to see us in America, at from two to three shillings a head admission."

"An' it pays ye well, does it?" still further inquired the old gentleman.

"Yes," said Tom, carelessly fingering the diamond solitaire in his scarf and the diamond-studded charm on his watch chain, and then

PHŒNIX PARK, IN THE CITY OF DUBLIN.

pulling out a $350 chronometer and glancing at the hour. "It is'nt a bad business."

"Faith, an' I guess not," said the old gentleman. "Oive half a dozen of me own Oi would like to send over to yez, if ye consint t' get them inter ther same bisniss."

Tom, like Manning, owned everything within sight during this visit; and handsome John Tener, who ran down into Londonderry on a similar visit, was the lion of the day among the relatives whom he had not seen since childhood. Meantime the balance of our party who remained in Dublin put in their time to good advantage. Some went off on a stroll through Phœnix Park, and others upon jaunting-cars drove through the city and its environs, but the majority of the boys were satisfied to promenade Sackville and Grafton streets, where the crowd was thickest, and where we saw type after type of Irish beauty, such as I am firmly convinced can be seen nowhere outside of Ireland.

SACKVILLE STREET, DUBLIN.

That evening we occupied four large proscenium boxes at the Gaiety Theatre, where an excellent English Company was playing a laughable comedy known as the "Arabian Nights."

The following day was a beautiful one for the ball game, just such a day as we desired for the great game we played before taking our farewell of Old Ireland. The morning was consumed by most of the boys in purchasing black-thorn sticks, "shillalies," and other mementoes of the "old sod" for Irish-American friends at home. Shortly before noon we called at the Mansion House, and were received by the Lord Mayor of Dublin, who expressed his happiness at welcoming such a party of Americans, and tendered us the freedom of the city. After luncheon at Morrison's, the boys, in uniform, came down the stairs into the rotunda, one by one, while half a score of fair guests in the hotel, who had been waiting for this particular opportunity, leaned over the balustrade of the staircase and quietly criticised the boys as they stood

GRAFTON STREET, DUBLIN.

about in knee-breeches. Then into the drags piled the players, and off we started at a brisk pace for the Landsdown Road Grounds. Dublin is certainly a beautiful old city, our party passing along avenues on its way to the grounds that would be accounted attractive in any city in the world, while from what I saw of Dublin people during our brief sojourn, I imagined Dublin society must indeed be charming. Our party were unanimous in awarding the palm for clear complexions, beautiful faces, and attractive figures to Ireland.

The Landsdown Road Grounds, where our game was played, are more properly tennis and football grounds than cricket or baseball grounds; still they answered our purpose very well indeed, and the boys put up a game that must have fired the blood of every American present. Crane and Baldwin were again "out for keeps," and how they did pitch; while Hanlon, Carroll, Fogarty and Manning ran bases as I had rarely seen them run even in championship games. Cipher after cipher went up on the score board, until each team had six opposite its name. The Dublinites could not understand why eighteen great big fellows like these could not score a run, and when finally Pettitt, by luck and hard hitting, got around the circuit, and by great sliding threw himself upon the plate, just as Pfeffer's sacrifice ball to Brown was returned, there was a noticeable bit of sarcasm in the applause—a sort of "Ah-ha, he has scored a run at last" tinge—whereas in America they would have yelled for a good five minutes. Then All-America scored, tying the game, and Burns and Baldwin also crossed the plate, leading Hanlon's men by two runs. But in the ninth, Earl's three-bagger, Hanlon's base on balls, Tom Burns's fumble of Brown's hit, and Carroll's pretty double settled the game and killed Chicago's chances.

One of the prettiest scenes imaginable was that upon the avenue outside the grounds after the game. Nobby jaunting-cars, with the prettiest of Dublin's girls perched upon them, crowded the thoroughfare, and cabs, coaches, carriages, carts, and people in hundreds made the assemblage a large one. Some of the richest brogue I ever heard and some of the sweetest faces I ever saw it was my pleasure to hear and see in that crowd. It was also distinctly representative of the wealth and intellect of Dublin. Among the notables present were Lord Londonderry, Lord Lieutenant-Governor of Ireland and daughter; Prince Albert, of Saxe-Weimar, commander of the forces in Ireland, and party, in an English drag; the Lord Mayor of Dublin and party; American Consul McCaskill and representatives of other foreign powers.

When we went to the railway station that evening, we found, thanks to the courtesy of the great Southern Railway Company, three elegantly appointed coaches at the disposal of our party. Each plate-glass window of every coach was decorated with an American flag, on which was the inscription, "Reserved for the American Baseball Party." Our train pulled out of the station at eight o'clock, and we arrived in Cork at two o'clock the following morning. We drove immediately to the Victoria Hotel, and after a refreshing sleep of five hours, the majority of the boys tumbled out of bed for a cup of coffee and a picturesque ride in Irish jaunting-cars to the village of Blarney, five miles distant. On the outskirts of the village stands the famous Blarney Castle, majestic, ancient and ivy-grown, and as no good Irish-American visits Ireland without touching the Blarney stone with his lips, Healey, Daly,

THE FAMOUS OLD BLARNEY CASTLE.

Fogarty, Manning, Carroll, Tener, and others of the boys who can trace their lineage back to the green sod, ascended the long winding stairs, and leaning over the parapet, with the assistance of others, went through the performance that is supposed to make an Ingersoll or a Depew of the veriest dunce.

At this castle the party encountered a typical old Irish bogman. The old fellow's costume alone would have been worth a trip to Dublin for any of our American dime museum managers. He wore a veritable coat of many colors, and the seat of his ancient trousers sagged downward a distance of a foot. A battered and time-stained hat, with a pointed peak, sat upon the back of his head, and his "lilac" whiskers peeked out from beneath the folds of an old gray woolen scarf about his neck, while a tattered silk vest, that had once been of a delicate canary hue, the gift, no doubt, of some benefactor, completed his make-up. He spotted our party immediately as visiting Americans, and we, in turn,

"A FINE OULD IRISH GINTLEMAN."

gathered around him, as deeply interested as we had been in anything we had met with in Ireland. Fogarty asked him how long he had been a dynamiter, and this seemed to tickle the old man to death, for he laughed and slapped his knee and batted his peaked hat from the top of his head, as he gave a twirl to the white-thorn shillaly he swung between his fingers.

"How did ye know that?" he said.

"Ah, I saw it in your eye," said Fogarty; "I never mistook a dynamiter in my life, and I am always glad to meet 'em," and with that Foge and the Irishman shook hands.

"It's a fine morning," said John Healy.

"Shoore, an' it's a beautiful mornin' for singin'," said the old man.

"Can you sing?" inquired Healy.

"Naw, but I kin dawnce," quickly replied the bogman, and, as if to put weight in his assertion, he commenced a breakdown in the middle of that dusty road, timing himself with a low, crooning rhythm that would make famous any actor who could reproduce it upon the American stage. The finish of the dance was the signal for a handful of silver and applause from the boys, and then Healy told him that if he would sing them a song he could have as much more. The Irishman looked sad for an instant, and then a sparkle came in his eye as he said, "I can never sing unless I be half-slugged."* Then he paused, while his eyes wandered away across the hill to a little red brick house on the roadway. Pointing to this, he said, "Doo yez see thot tavern yonder? Well, Oi'm goin' there now, an' Oi'll be ready to sing in tin minutes," and taking off his battered hat to the boys, he ambled away to the tavern as fast as his legs could carry him.

After a long look at the beautiful view from the tower of the castle, the boys returned to the hotel, and drove to the station where the train left for Queenstown, leaving behind us the quaint old city of Cork, and

> The bells of Shandon,
> That sound so grand on
> The river Lee.

We skirted the lower end of the city and then struck the bank of the river, alongside of which we ran to Queenstown, eleven miles distant— and a beautiful ride it was! No artist, it seems to me, could ever reproduce the picturesque beauty of this river and its shores, with their lovely lawns, their fine old mansions and crumbling, ivy-grown castles. It is the prettiest scenery, by far, that we saw in Ireland. Half an hour's ride took us to Queenstown. The railway station is right at the dock, and it was but a few steps from the train to the little tender which was

---

* Under the "exhilarating influence."

to take us to the White Star steamer in the offing. While the steamer was loading with the mail, the boys improved the opportunity to purchase more black-thorn canes and shillalies and sprays of shamrock, which were offered by old Irish men and women on the dock. Just as I had completed the purchase of a fine white-thorn shillaly, I felt a tug at my sleeve, and turning partly around, beheld a little old Irish woman, with the most sorrowful expression imaginable. She had a little basket filled with sprays of shamrock, the roots attached, and still protected with clumps of Irish soil.

"Are yez goin' back to Ameriky?" said she.

"Yes," I replied; "can I do anything for you there?"

"Do yez know me boy?" said she.

"What is your boy's name?" I asked.

"Larry Donovan," said she, "as foine a bit of a boy as ever left old Ireland, and Oi hav'n't 'erd from him foor a year pawst."

"Where is Larry?" I asked.

"Shure Oi don't know," said she, "but if ye wud coome acrosst him, will ye' take him this bit of shamrock from his old mither, and tell him that ye got it from her at the dock at Queenstown?"

"Certainly," I replied, fancying, for the instant, how glad I should be able to make Larry feel, in case I should run across him, at receiving the bright little memento of his country's soil which his old mother handed me. "Certainly, and if I hear from Larry, I will see that he writes to you."

"May the Saints bless ye," said the old lady, "may the Saints bless ye," and then, as I turned away, she tugged gently at my sleeve. "An' shure Oi knows yez air goin' to leave somethin' for the old leddy, before ye go." How could I refuse? Of course I presented her with the last English coins I had, and soon we were aboard the steamer. A moment later our bow was cutting the waters of Queenstown harbor, and as we drew near the White Star steamer "Adriatic," the sight of the American flag at the ship's masthead drew forth three cheers and a "tigah" from the boys, and these were followed by three more, as the passengers, including Mr. Spalding's wife and mother, who had embarked at Liverpool, rushed to the rail to welcome us. Two faces we missed. Ed Williamson was still confined to his room in London from the injuries he received in Paris. He was attended by his faithful little wife, who bravely nursed him back to strength, although alone and three thousand miles from home. Telegrams were received at the steamer from many friends, bidding us "Farewell" and "God speed." On entering the saloon an hour later, we were pleasantly reminded of our London friends by a magnificent floral piece representing a home plate, and bearing upon its face, in immortelles, the inscription: " May you reach home in safety." Attached to this was a broad crimson scarf of silk, which bore the letters, " With compliments of Grace Hawthorne, London, March 27th, 1889, To the All-America and Chicago Baseball teams."

Soon after boarding the "Adriatic" we got under way and started upon the last of our voyages. We encountered exceedingly unfavorable weather, and for two days our ship made scarcely seven knots an hour. The "Adriatic" weathered the storm beautifully. She would bury her pretty nose in many an angry wave that hid the entire forward section of the ship, as it broke into big clouds of spray before her, only to come up again, ready, and seemingly anxious, for the next one.

After leaving Queenstown the boys were feverishly impatient to reach home, and fairly counted the hours. It was rough voyaging, but we bravely made the best of it. Every evening we assembled in the big smoking-room on the hurricane deck for the enjoyment of our after-dinner smoke, and for a turn at poker, yarn-spinning, or Fred Carroll's roulette wheel, which he had purchased in Nice. When Clarence Duval happened in, half a dozen of the boys would start "a-patting," and forthwith Mr. Duval's feet would begin to move, until finally he was dancing a "hoedown" with all his energy and ability. Captain Cameron and Purser Russell did everything in their power for the comfort of our party, and with fair weather our voyage would have been in every way delightful.

Our friends in New York had been expecting us for three days, and the "Adriatic" was sighted off Fire Island at a very early hour Saturday morning, April 6th. By sunrise we were at Quarantine. Meantime the enthusiasts on shore, who had prepared to welcome us to Manhattan Island, had been apprised of our arrival, and just as the sun peeped over the Brooklyn housetops and the sunrise gun on Governor's Island boomed out its accustomed good-morning, the steamer "Starin," with about one hundred and fifty people aboard, cut loose from her moorings at the barge office and steamed down the Bay. The tugboat "George Wood" bore half a hundred more. The party on the smaller boat had picked up a German band on the way down Broadway, and this, together with the steam whistles and the voices of two hundred cheering people, made noise enough to startle every one of our party out of bed and bring them on deck in a hurry. Among those who clung to the ropes aboard the visiting steamers we recognized the faces of Walter Spalding, George Floyd, F. L. Lane, Al Johnson, W. W. Kelly, Marcus Mayer, John W. Russel, Digby Bell, DeWolf Hopper, Joseph Donohue, John Kelly, Nicholas Engle, Henry Anson, J. W. Curtis, James Hart, John Ward, Colonel W. T. Coleman, and many others, including a number of ladies, the wives and daughters of their escorts. Cheering began when the vessels were half a mile apart, and was kept up for fully half an hour. As the "Starin" made fast to the ocean steamer, the cheering was loudest, even the emigrants on the "Adriatic," a thousand in number, joining in the welcoming howl. Whistles blew, the Dutch musicians on the small tugs almost straightened out their horns in efforts to drown the whistles, and hats, canes, handkerchiefs and umbrellas were waved and thrown wildly in the air. Many of the boys were too overcome by the demonstration and their joy in landing to speak, and I discovered tears coursing down the cheeks of not a few of them. Henry Anson, the father of Captain Anson, clasped the big ball player in his arms as the latter climbed upon the deck of the "Starin," and fairly cried for joy. Our entire party boarded the "Starin" and proceeded to the Twenty-first Street dock, from which we were quickly driven to the Fifth Avenue Hotel, where accommodations had been reserved, and it was when we stood in our rooms at the famous old hostelry and looked out over Madison Square that we felt once more at home, and were able to look back upon our great tour of the world as an accomplished fact.

The demonstration which began in honor of our arrival in New York harbor was but the beginning of the series of ovations tendered us until we disbanded at Chicago, two weeks later. Our first evening in America was spent at Palmer's Theatre, where, as the guests of Colonel McCaull, we saw "The May Queen," with De Wolf Hopper, Digby Bell, and other prominent lights of the operatic stage in the cast. The boxes had been elaborately decorated with flags, and from the proscenium arch hung an emblem of all nations, a gilt eagle and shield, with crossed bats, a pair of catcher's gloves and a catcher's mask. Bell and Hopper were irresistibly funny during the evening, and kept the big audience in almost continual laughter by their happy references to the return of the party and their jokes at our expense. There were frequent calls during the evening for Ward and Anson, but both remained modestly in the background, content to let the comedians upon the stage do all the talking.

THE ALL-AMERICA TEAM AFTER THE GAME AT BROOKLYN.

The first game after the return of the tourists took place Monday afternoon, April 8th, upon the Brooklyn grounds. Not more than 3000 people were present, as the weather was cold and unfavorable for ball-playing, but these received the players warmly. All-America won the game by one run. Immediately after the game the boys returned to the Fifth Avenue, and exchanged their uniforms for evening dress, Monday night having been set for the banquet tendered our party by admirers of the game in Gotham.

The supper took place at Delmonico's, and was indeed a notable gathering of representative American manhood and intelligence, in honor of the returning tourists and of the game of which they were the exponents. The decorations, menu cards and souvenirs were beautifully designed and typical of the game. The table of honor had been set crosswise of the room, and from it extended six others, plates having been laid for over 300 people. The walls of the hall had been festooned with American flags, and between them hung large and handsomely framed photographs of the party, taken in Egypt, Rome, Naples, and other foreign cities. The tables were profusely decorated with flowers and large confections, each of the latter being surmounted by the figure of a ball player in action. In the balcony had been stationed a full orchestra, which played almost constantly during the evening. Presiding at the table of honor, sat A. G. Mills, ex-President of the National League and one of the authors of the National Agreement, under the protection of which baseball has attained its present high standard of organization. Upon the right and left of Mr. Mills were seated Mr. Spalding, Hon. Chauncey M. Depew, Hon. Daniel Dougherty, Henry E. Howland, W. H. McElroy, U. S. Consul G. W. Griffin, who represented our country at Sydney at the time of our arrival there, Mayor Chapin, of Brooklyn, Mayor Cleveland, of Jersey City, Erastus Wiman, Mark Twain, Leigh S. Lynch, and the Rev. Joseph Twitchell, of Hartford. At the remaining tables sat representatives of a dozen Yale College classes; popular members of the New York Stock Exchange; the presidents and prominent members of the New York Athletic Club, the Manhattan Athletic Club, and other of the crack gentlemen's athletic organizations of New York City and vicinity. Shortly before Mr. Mills arose to call the assemblage to order, the ladies who had accompanied us around the world entered the balcony overlooking the room, and were greeted with a prolonged ovation. Then Mr. Mills, arising, reminded his hearers of the occasion that had brought them together, and during his eulogy of the game, of Mr. Spalding, and of the teams, which followed, was frequently compelled to pause until the applause had ceased.

Mayor Cleveland, of Jersey City, who followed, had his hearers laughing before he had been upon his feet many seconds. He concluded his very happy speech by saying: "Six months ago, these young men went abroad to fight, not like gladiators covered with armor, but covered with their American manhood, and they have come back covered with laurels, to place them on the fair brow of the American girl. Gentlemen, I now welcome home, in the name of the 20,000 residents of the little city across the river, this double team, as I call them, of American athletes."

Mayor Alfred Chapin, of Brooklyn, among many bright and witty things, said: "When we over in Brooklyn receive invitations to banquets, and especially to Delmonico's, we respond with alacrity, and we also make some sort of a speech, in return for a kindly dinner. In looking over the toast list I find that we are seven who will give the welcome, to be followed by a picked nine of intellectual athletes, who might safely make an after-dinner tour around the world and would not find a single foreign team who could catch them in an error."

Mr. Depew was enthusiastically cheered when he arose to his feet and smiled quietly upon the assemblage before him. He said:—

"Representing, as I do, probably more than any other human being, the whole of the American people who were deprived, by a convention that did not understand its duty, of putting me where I belong; and representing, as I do, by birth and opportunity, all the nationalities on the globe, I feel that I have been properly selected to give you the welcome of the world. I am just now arranging and preparing a Centennial oration which I hope may, and fear may not, meet all the possibilities of the 30th of April in presenting the majesty of that which created the Government which we boast of and the land and country of which we are proud, but I feel that that oration is of no importance and sinks into insignificance compared with the event of this evening. Washington never saw a baseball game; Madison wrote the Constitution of the United States, and died without seeing one; Jefferson was the author of the Declaration of Independence, and yet his monument has no tribute of this kind upon it. Hamilton, the most marvelous and creative genius, made constitutions, built up systems and created institutions, and yet never witnessed a baseball game. I feel, as I stand here, that all the men who have ever lived and achieved success in this world have died in vain. I am competent to pay that tribute, because I never played the game in my life, and never saw it but once, and then did not understand it. A philosopher, whom I always read with interest, because his abstractions sometimes approach the truth, wrote an article of some acumen many years ago, in which he said that you could mark the march of civilization and rise of liberty and its decadence by the interest which nations took in pugilism. The nations of the earth which submit to the most grinding of despotisms have no pugilists. The nations of Europe which have never risen in their boasted establishments to a full comprehension of Republicanism, have no pugilists. While Ireland and the Irish people, who can never be crushed, who have poetry, song and eloquence that belong to genius, have the most remarkable pugilists. England, which has a literature which is the only classic of to-day, which has an aristocracy and a form of government which is nearly democratic, has remarkable pugilists, and when you reach the seat of culture in America—Boston—you find the prince of pugilists. Now, that philospher was right on the general principle, but wrong in the game. Civilization is marked, and has been in all ages, by an interest in the manly arts."

In conclusion, Mr. Depew eulogized the returning teams and ended with a brilliant panegyric in favor of the national game.

In response to the toast, "The Influence of Manly Sports," the Honorable Daniel Dougherty delivered an address that won him a burst of applause at the finish. He said, in conclusion :—

"There are no happier moments in the life of man, and especially an American, than when, after a foreign sojourn, he is conscious that he is once more a part of his country and an inmate of his home. Such men a country that holds liberty dear must have, and such men the athletic spirit of the generation is breeding for the future defence of the country against foreign foes. In sports on sea and land we more than hold our own, for an American yacht still keeps the cup, and our boys, who are back with us to-night, have taught new pastimes to the athletes of far-distant lands. I glory in the triumphs of the scholar, yet gladly admit the body has its honors as well as the brain. Open-air sports are conducive to health and hardihood. They give vigor to the arm, fleetness to the limbs, alertness to the eye and nerve to the heart. They ignite the fires of emulation, create thirst for distinction, the longing desire to win a name that will mark them among their fellows. These qualities combined rear a race fit for peace and war. In peace to grapple with the tough adversaries of every-day life, and in war to endure the privations of the camp, the fatigue of the long march in advance or retreat—to do daring deeds, leap into the imminent deadly breach, and, if needs be, fall like the immortal band of Lacedæmonians, who played their gymnastic games on the very spot where the next day they died for their country."

President Spalding was heartily cheered when he arose to give an outline of the tour. He attributed the success of the enterprise to the excellent conduct and ball-playing ability of the players who composed the Chicago and All-America teams. Captains Ward and Anson responded briefly when called upon, but the oratorical gem of the evening was Mark Twain's response to the toast of "The Grand Tour." Beginning in a vein of humor that excited the continued and hearty laughter of his hearers, he concluded his response with a word-painting of the beautiful Hawaiian Islands, so full of poetry and sentiment, and so true to nature as our party had seen it, that the assemblage sat spellbound under the charm of his words. Chairman Mills, in introducing Mr. Clemens, spoke of him as a native of the Hawaiian Islands, and the speaker said :—

"Though not a native, as intimated by the chairman, I have visited the Sandwich Islands— that peaceful land, that beautiful land, that far-off home of profound repose, and soft indolence, and dreamy solitude, where life is one long, slumberless Sabbath, the climate one long, delicious summer day, and the good that die experience no change, for they but fall asleep in one heaven and wake up in another. And these boys have played baseball there!—baseball, which is the very symbol, the outward and visible expression of the drive and push and rush and struggle of the raging, tearing, booming nineteenth century! One cannot realize it; the place and the fact are so incongruous; it's like interrupting a funeral with a circus. Why, there's no legitimate point of contact, no possible kinship between baseball and the Sandwich Islands; baseball is all fact, the Islands all sentiment. In baseball you've got to do everything just right, or you don't get there; in the Islands you've got to do everything just wrong, or you can't stay there. You do it wrong to get it right, for if you do it right you get it wrong; there isn't any way to get it right but to do it wrong, and the wronger you do it the righter it is.

"The natives illustrate this every day. They never mount a horse from the larboard side, they always mount him from the starboard; on the other hand, they never milk a cow on the starboard side, they always milk her on the larboard; it's why you see so many short people there—they've got their heads kicked off. When they meet on the road they don't turn to the right, they turn out to the left. And so, from always doing everything wrong end first it makes them left-handed—left-handed and cross-eyed; they are all so. In those Islands, the cats haven't any tails, and the snakes haven't any teeth; and, what is still more irregular, the man that loses a game gets the pot. As to dress, the women all wear a single garment, but the men don't. No, the men don't wear anything at all, they hate display; when they wear a smile they think they are overdressed. Speaking of birds, the only bird there that has ornamental feathers has only two, just barely enough to squeeze through with, and they are under its wings instead of on top of its head, where, of course, they ought to be to do any good.

"The native language is soft and liquid and flexible, and in every way efficient and satisfactory—till you get mad; then, there you are; there isn't anything in it to swear with. Good judges all say it is the best Sunday language there is; but then all the other six days in the week it just hangs idle on your hands; it isn't any good for business, and you can't work a telephone with it. Many a time the attention of the missionaries has been called to this defect, and they are always promising they are going to fix it; but no, they go fooling along and fooling along, and nothing is done. Speaking of education, everybody there is educated, from the highest to the lowest; in fact, it is the only country in the world where education is actually universal. And yet every now and then you run across instances of ignorance that are simply revolting—simply degrading to the human race. Think of it—there, the ten takes the ace! But let us not dwell on such things, they make a person ashamed. Well, the missionaries are always going to fix that, but they put it off, and put it off, and put it off, and so that nation is going to keep on going down, and down, and down, till some day you will see a pair of jacks beat a straight flush.

"Well, it is refreshment to the jaded, water to the thirsty, to look upon men who have so lately breathed the soft air of those Isles of the Blest, and had before their eyes the inextinguishable vision of their beauty. No alien land in all the world has any deep, strong charm for me but that one; no other land could so longingly and so beseechingly haunt me, sleeping and waking, through half a lifetime, as that one has done. Other things leave me, but it abides; other things change, but it remains the same. For me its balmy airs are always blowing, its summer seas flashing in the sun, the pulsing of its surf-beat is in my ear; I can see its garlanded crags, its leaping cascades, its plumy palms drowsing by the shore, its remote summits floating like islands above the cloud rack; I can feel the spirit of its woodland solitudes, I can hear the splash of its brooks; in my nostrils still lives the breath of flowers that perished twenty years ago. And these world wanderers who sit before us here have lately looked upon these things! and with eyes of flesh, not the unsatisfying vision of the spirit. I envy them that!"

Following the responses to the toasts there was a call for De Wolf Hopper and Digby Bell, both of whom had come directly from the stage to the banquet hall. Both of the popular comedians responded as they only could do, Hopper portraying in verse the troubles of the New York Club in their efforts to hold on to the "Polo" grounds at 111th street, and then, in response to an encore, giving "Casey at the Bat," in his own inimitable style. Digby Bell followed with a description in verse of the arrival of our party in New York harbor, and was compelled to pause between verses for the applause to cease. The lines, written in the rhythm of "Paul Revere's Ride," and entitled "Spalding's Ride," ran as follows:—

Up from down town the other day,
Bringing my chambermaid fresh dismay,
Elongated Hopper a message bore,
In a voice that was crossed between grumble and roar,
Telling the season was on once more,
With Spalding twenty miles away.

Oh, the excitement that message brought!
Oh, the wild fervor that came unsought!
I cast on my slumbering wife a glance,
And with silence burglarious slipped on my pants;
While Hopper impatiently 'gan to prance,
Lest he should be left by the waiting boat.
His broad breast heaved with a wheezing note,
But soon we stood out in the dawning day,
And Spalding was twenty miles away.

Now, there is a road from way uptown,
A good broad highway leading down
To the dock where the waiting tugboat lay,
To bear all the ball cranks down the bay.
And there I beheld a noisy Dutch band,
With boisterous Floyd in proud command,
A temporary baton in hand.
And he gave his stentorian voice such play
That the Dutch wind-jammers were led astray—
But Spalding was twenty miles away.

On the boat we marched with steady tread,
The enthusiastic Floyd ahead.

"Cast off!" the impatient captain cried,
And the boat swung out in the river's tide
With a jerk that unsteady Hopper floored,
And Manager Mayer with excitement roared,
And the Dutch well nigh fell overboard.
But what care we for mishaps to-day,
With Spalding twenty miles away?

We passed down the stream with a mighty rush,
That would put Jay Gould's steam yacht to blush;
And with every wave's majestic swell,
Our gallant gang, with a lusty yell,
Awoke the rest of the sleeping town.
Steam whistles salute as we pass them down,
And Nature's visage wears never a frown.
And what is the cause of this joy to-day?
Why, Spalding is fifteen miles away.

The Laura M. Starin we overtake,
And soon she is left in our foaming wake.
Our glasses we point through the dawn so dull;
On the deck of the tug there's an ominous lull,
As we search for the ocean steamer's hull.
She is there, large as life, down at Quarantine!
And each of us makes up in smile serene.
We cheered as we looked where she calmly lay,
For Spalding was only ten miles away.

The miles decreased as the moments flew,
And soon the ship's deck sprang into view.
Familiar faces are waiting there,
And cheer upon cheer stirs the morning air,
And the Dutch band brays with its tuneless blare.
We can make out big Anson, and Tener, and Crane,
And we yell ourselves hoarse till our vocals we strain,
For our two teams of heroes are back again.
There's a blizzard of joy on this breaking day,
For Spalding is only ten feet away.

Hurrah, hurrah for our Spalding bold;
Hurrah, hurrah for his well-won gold;
And when New York has its baseball ground,
May his statue of bronze on the field be found,
And upon it inscribed: "From the baseball cranks,
Who in manner befitting express their thanks,
To Spalding, who, freighted with ardor sublime,
Played our national game in every clime
From 'Frisco, globe-circling, to New York Bay,
In lands ten thousand miles away."

It was nearly two o'clock when, with a farewell cheer for the friends who had accorded them so generous and hearty a welcome, the boys sought their hotel to rest for the game on the morrow.

Our second game also was played in Brooklyn, in the presence of 3500 people. The game was a rather uninteresting exhibition, Chicago taking the lead at the start and holding it throughout the nine innings. Crane was given poor support by All-America, their errors, without exception, proving costly. We departed the same evening for Baltimore, and played a game upon the Association grounds there the following day. Something over 5000 people were present, the assemblage including many of the most prominent society people of Baltimore, and the teams were given a great ovation when they came upon the field. The game was a most interesting contest. All-America was prevented from tying the score in the final innings only by Bob Pettitt's brilliant running catch of a fly to right field. The crowd was enthusiastic, and, by its liberal applause, incited the boys to some great base-running feats.

At 11 o'clock the following morning we arrived in Philadelphia, where we found a committee composed of the officers of the Philadelphia Club, and representatives of the Philadelphia papers. We were at once escorted to carriages, and were driven down Chestnut street to the South street ferry, where we took the boat for Gloucester. The ride down the river was delightful, and at Thompson's we enjoyed a planked-shad dinner, after which we listened for half an hour to the bright repartee of Messrs. Lynch, Spalding, Chadwick and John I. Rogers, and then re-boarded our steamer for the return ride.

We reached Philadelphia shortly after 3 o'clock, and were driven directly to the grounds of the Athletic Club, where the Athletics and Bostons were playing an exhibition game. The grounds were filled with people, there being 10,000 present. When our party arrived, during the third innings, play was temporarily suspended, and as the returned tourists filed upon the grounds, led by Messrs. Spalding, Reach and Pennypacker, to the strains of "Home Again" by the band, the enthusiasm of the crowd seemed to know no bounds. Ten thousand people stood upon their feet, waving hats and handkerchiefs and yelling at the top of their voices. The Boston and Athletic players had arranged themselves in line, from the home plate to third base, and, with heads uncovered, gave our players three times three cheers as we passed them. The procession moved across the diamond, and, circling about third base, left the field for the grand stand, where seats had been reserved. At the conclusion of the game the party were driven to the Continental, and, after donning evening dress, were escorted to the Hotel Bellevue, where, at 8 o'clock, they took seats at the banquet tendered by the Philadelphia *Sporting Life*.

In addition to the wealth of flowers, flags, and trailing vines in the hall, the dazzling display of cut-glass and silverware upon the table, and the vari-colored glow of a hundred fairy lights, the iron pillar in the centre of the room was surrounded from floor to ceiling with polished bats, catcher's masks, blazers, caps, base bags, and other paraphernalia of the American game all artistically arranged amidst festoons of vines and banks of flowers. The orchestra was hidden behind a pyramid of tropical plants in one corner of the room, and, as the party entered, began the appropriate and familiar air of "The Day I Played Baseball."

Editor Frank C. Richter occupied the chairman's seat, and at his right and left sat Mr. Spalding, Colonel A. K. McClure, of the Philadelphia *Times;* Colonel M. R. Muckle, of the *Ledger;* John I. Rogers, A. J. Reach, and Harry Wright, of the Philadelphia Club; Captain A. C. Anson and John Montgomery Ward; C. H. Byrne, of the Brooklyn Club; President W. M. Smith, of the City Council; and Thomas Dando, President of the *Sporting Life* Company. There were over three hundred guests in all, and it was fully ten o'clock before we had discussed the last dishes upon the elaborate menu card. At that hour the boys lighted their cigars, and until after midnight were entertained by the wit, eloquence, and baseball logic of the speakers present.

After brief welcoming addresses by Chairman Richter, Mr. Dando and President Smith, Mr. Spalding was called upon, and, after the cheers which his name aroused had subsided, first took occasion to thank our hosts of the evening, and then entered into an outline of our experiences abroad. In concluding his address Mr. Spalding said :—

"We found at Honolulu that they had four established clubs; that baseball was well under way and fully appreciated. If it had not been for an accident, in reaching them on Sunday, we would have had the largest crowd in Honolulu of any at our games since we left home. At New Zealand, I have every reason to believe they will take up baseball, and that it will become one of their established games. It will become one of the games in Australia. While being the most hospitable people in the world, they are also the greatest sport-loving people, and their climate is peculiarly adapted to baseball. They can play the year round. Cricket does not seem to reach the masses. It is a game more for the aristocracy, who have the time, means and inclination to enjoy it. Baseball is for the masses. The requirements for the game are simple, and the grounds necessary are not so elaborate and do not require the same expense of keeping up.

"As to Ceylon, it is of very great doubt whether it will ever become popular, for the climate is very much against them. In Arabia there is no more chance for a game than for a blacklisted player to get to Heaven. In Egypt it is doubtful and in Italy extremely doubtful. We found in Italy and in every country outside of the English-speaking people the uttermost indifference to athletic sports. I think the time is not far distant when baseball will be played in France. I have been asked, 'What do you think of baseball being established in England?' I reply that that is a difficult question to answer. An Englishman is a very conservative individual and does not readily take to a new idea, but judging from the immense crowds we had there, and the great attention we received from the press—the comments, in the main, being favorable—I believe in the near future England will have its ball clubs and leagues."

When Captains Ward and Hanlon arose to respond to the toast of "The Chicago and the All-America Teams" they were applauded vociferously. In introducing Anson, Chairman Richter referred to him as "Mr. Spalding's faithful lieutenant, whose fame has grown with our national game, and who is universally recognized as one of the greatest batsmen and ablest captains baseball has ever known."

The "Old Man's" reply was characteristically blunt and outspoken. He said:—

"I am proud at being thus honored by my friends in Philadelphia, for I played ball here once, although that was a good many years ago. I began to play here in 1872, and played four seasons, after which, as you all know, I went out to Chicago with Mr. Spalding. As to the tour we have just completed, I don't know that I can say anything Mr. Spalding has not already said. But I wish to pay a compliment to the ball players on the trip. Each and every member has certainly behaved himself as a gentleman. I saw some statements made to the effect that in all probability they would not come back in good condition. Well, I think if you look down along the line you will see that there is no ground for fear."

In introducing Captain Ward, Chairman Richter said :—

"Of course our next toast is to the other half of Spalding's combination, the All-America team, which picked team, without the advantages of long association and preliminary training, won a record that made it the wonder of the baseball world. It seems to me the most fitting to respond is he who so ably welded this team together and so skillfully handled it, Mr. John Montgomery Ward, famous in baseball, famous in literature, and to be famous in law."

In response Captain Ward said :—

" There is no period in my professional life that I will look back to with more genuine pleasure than upon the six months past. I am glad to have been a member of this pioneer combination and proud to have been a member of the All-America team. In my entire experience as a player I have never been associated with a more companionable lot of boys, and I am sure when the memory of our struggles on the field have faded from us we will recall with affection the many happy hours we have spent together."

"On behalf of the All-America team I wish to thank Mr. Richter, the chairman, the man to whose enterprise and intellect as editor of *Sporting Life* the success of that journal is due. I also wish to thank Mr. Harry Palmer, whose genial and able pen has added so much to the tone of the trip. I should not allow the occasion to go by without saying something of the liberality which Messrs. Lynch and Spalding have shown the players on this trip. It has been a delightful tour."

Colonel John I. Rogers, as a member of the Board of Arbitration and an official of the Philadelphia Club, then held the attention of his hearers in one of the most interesting speeches of the evening. Referring to the unquestioned honesty and integrity of the game, he said :—

"There is no professional sport, there is no game of hazard, there is no athletic exercise which men follow for a livelihood in which there is such an absolute assurance of a game on its merits as in our national pastime. I had a distinguished jurist, Judge Thayer, ask me some time ago, ' How do you know the game is played on its merits ?' I said, ' Because it is the one unpardonable crime I know of in this wide world—dishonest ball-playing. Arson, murder, highway robbery—aye, treason, may be pardoned, and are pardoned, but for dishonest or crooked ball-playing it has been proven there is no pardon under Heaven.' I said, ' Your Honor, I am a member of the supreme court of baseball, and we have had before us petitions signed by mayors of cities, governors of commonwealths, United States Senators and distinguished citizens, saying that Mr. So-and-so, ten or twelve years ago, in the old order of things, was found guilty of crooked ball-playing; that he has expiated his crime; that he has a family dependent upon him for support, and he has no other means of earning a living ; we ask you for mercy, ask you to restore this man. With all due respect, after due consideration, we respectfully returned the application as denied. And why ? Because the integrity of this game, the honesty of its play, is the foundation stone—nay, the keystone of our arch.'

"We have improved our legislation and reformed abuses. We have not yet reached perfection, but perfection is our goal. We have brought in all the minor leagues, until in all the

States of the Union are clubs formed and banded into leagues and organizations, all of them taking the law and bending their heads to the mandates of the greater organizations for the benefit of this national pastime.

"No man can afford to despise a game that is popular with the people. I have heard that governments, both national and municipal, had aided clubs by the provision of ground and the freedom from taxation, in order to encourage among the people a love for athletic sports, because a sturdy and more manly race will follow. So will it be in America when the great national game shall have established itself so firmly that no American will follow the example of that official in Rome who refused to recognize the representatives of this great institution— who had not time to have baseball talked in his office.

"While the National League only claims to be the pioneer in this work, I believe you will see we shall, with the coöperation of not only every baseball man, but every newspaper man and every citizen, show you that baseball is not the least of American institutions."

Following Colonel Rogers, Mr. C. H. Byrne's stirring address was frequently interrupted by outbursts of applause. He said:—

"I should like to pay to Mr. Spalding the tribute he deserves. The man who conceived and organized and carried out this marvelous enterprise is worthy of all consideration. Aside from him, this venture would have been unsuccessful if he had not been supported, maintained and encouraged in every step by these magnificent specimens of American manhood. They have carried themselves like gentlemen, like American citizens, animated by a purpose and a spirit which has been a surprise to everybody. They have been accompanied by the representatives of the most prominent papers in America, who have watched their career; and I have yet to see one line or word approaching a censure of any of these gentlemen. It is a surprise and a pride to me. I never knew what a legitimate, upright, manly business I was in till Mr. Spalding landed these gentlemen in the city of New York last Saturday night.

"You don't know what you have been doing. You have laid the foundation of something you cannot appreciate as yet. When the sere and yellow leaf comes along, it will be your pride and pleasure; when the national game is carried out to the extent Mr. Spalding has predicted, when we have the international game, you will say : 'I was one of the band who went around the world and showed the world what the national game was capable of.'"

No more glowing were any of the tributes paid the national game that evening, than was the address of Colonel McClure, of the Philadelphia *Times*, in response to the toast "The Press." The Colonel said:—

"I do not know of any other institution in the country that the American press is so much indebted to, without being compelled to give any return, as baseball. A baseball player is the only man who aspires to any distinction that the newspapers cannot serve. He has to serve himself. In all the other efforts of life where men are constantly struggling for distinction, we are often compelled to make very bad bricks without straw. Any one who knows anything about a newspaper office knows how politicians assail us in every possible way, and appeal and beg, and cajole and threaten, to induce us to make them famous, and we are often very sorry for the things we do. We very often make men, and after they are made we find them disgracing themselves and us. The baseball player cannot be served by the press at all. It is the only line of American distinction in which public notoriety, such as the newspaper gives to many, many men, cannot possibly aid him in his advancement. The baseball man must advance by merit alone. If all the newspapers in the world should undertake to put a man above the standard, or what seems to be the nearest approach to a legal standard, it could not affect the judgment of any one except upon merit.

"That is a very high compliment, indeed, to be paid, which perhaps most of you know, but which I must confess not to have known until it was presented to-night by Mr. Rogers. It is a marvel, indeed, that a great institution in which young men enter with all the energy and ambition that characterize men in every direction of life, that every man enters it to-day with the most perfect knowledge that only by integrity and honest merit can he be promoted. What a frightful clearing-out that would make among the politicians, wouldn't it? I would like very much to get a little of this baseball theory into our politics; I would like to get it introduced into social life—into the churches. I do not know a place or thing, system or class or method that would not be improved by your code of ethics. I am sure that no organization in this country, religious, social or political, could make the assertion that has been made here to-night with reference to the integrity of baseball.

"And then I am delighted with another thing. If it were not for baseball I don't know what the newspapers would do during the summer season. We have presidential elections only once in four years and between times the elections do not catch on. The people do not care about elections and politics. The most of them denounce politics. Here we have a perpetual source of public interest. If we can have a first-class display of a first-class baseball game we are sure to have a very interested community willing to read the newspapers. I regard the movement you have made as one of great significance, and one for which you are entitled to the thanks of every American citizen and newspaper. I bid you Godspeed, for an institution that teaches a boy that nothing but honesty and manliness can succeed, must be doing missionary work every day of its existence. It will not only make a high standard of baseball men, but make the whole world better for its presence. I came here to give you hearty welcome. Having known and heard of you, I say not only welcome, but thrice welcome to the hospitality of Philadelphia."

In response to the toast, "The Rise and Progress of Baseball," Henry Chadwick, the veteran writer upon baseball topics, gave an interesting sketch of the game and its growth in popular favor since 1850. He was followed by President Reach, of the Philadelphia club, Harry Wright, Tim Murnane and Leigh Lynch, after which Fogarty gave a recital of his experiences abroad that kept his hearers in continuous laughter for ten minutes or more. Before adjourning, the following resolution, drafted by Mr. Chadwick, was unanimously adopted:—

"RESOLVED: That the sincere and hearty thanks of all lovers of baseball in America be, and they are hereby, extended to Mr. Charles Dougherty, the present Secretary of the American Legation at Rome, for his kindness and attention to the American representatives of the national game on their recent tour around the globe; that his thoughtful and unselfish friendship, rendered the more conspicuous by the ill-mannered conduct of his superior officer, United States Minister Stallo, shall be treasured as one of the most enjoyable and delightful memories of our tour around the globe."

It was long past midnight when, with three cheers for Editor Richter and *Sporting Life*, the boys shook hands with their generous hosts and departed for their hotels.

The following afternoon, Mayor Fitler received the teams in his office, and after warmly shaking hands with each of the players, said: "I am very glad to welcome you to Philadelphia. I have carefully watched your career as you have traveled around the world, and you have not only done justice to yourselves and your profession, but you have been a credit to your country. I assure you, gentlemen, that so long as I am Mayor of Philadelphia, I will do all in my power to encourage the great game of baseball." President Spalding responded with appropriate words, and after his Honor had accepted an invitation to be present at the game that afternoon, the boys entered carriages and were driven to the grounds of the Philadelphia Club. The spectators present, owing, doubtless, to the threatening weather, numbered only about 3500 people, but a more select crowd had never before been seen at a ball game in Philadelphia. Each player was warmly cheered upon stepping to the plate for the first time, George Wood, Fogarty, Tom Daly and Earle, as Philadelphia players, receiving the lion's share. The game abounded in pretty plays, was closely contested from start to finish, and was, in fact, just such a game as both teams were anxious to put up in return for the generous treatment they had received at the hands of Philadelphians.

The tourists left Philadelphia that evening for Boston, and on arrival at the "Hub" it transpired that catcher Earle had been left upon the platform in Philadelphia while talking with a group of admirers, and as Pettitt and Healy had been granted leave of absence, the party was left short-handed. Sam Wise, however, consented to play first base for All-America, while Carroll did the catching; and Hugh Duffy, happening to drop around to the hotel, wore Pettitt's uniform and played a good short for Chicago. The game, while one-sided, was not uninteresting. A brilliant triple play by Duffy, Tener and Anson, and a quick double play by Manning and Wise, aroused much enthusiasm. Tom Brown was received with a big volley of cheers when he came to bat, and Ed Crane was the recipient of a handsome basket of flowers, which he received at the plate.

The following evening the party started on its trip westward to Chicago, stopping *en route* at Washington, and then proceeding to Pittsburgh, Cleveland and Indianapolis. The boys were warmly received at every point, and, save at Washington, put up an excellent sample of the ball we played abroad. At Washington, Chicago beat All-America "out of sight;" played a tie game with them at Pittsburgh; beat them again in a pretty game at Cleveland; and were finally beaten by All-America in a hard-fought game at Indianapolis. After breakfast at the Arlington, in Washington, Mr. Spalding was notified of the President's desire to receive the party at the White House. The boys accordingly entered carriages and were escorted to the Executive Mansion by General Williams and Walter Hewitt, the former a personal friend of the President. After shaking hands with Private Secretary Halford and Russell Harrison, the party were invited into an adjoining room and were introduced to the country's Chief Executive, Secretary Halford introducing President Spalding, and he, in turn, introducing each of the tourists. President Harrison expressed his pleasure at meeting the party. Mr. Spalding then extended an invitation to the President to attend that afternoon's game, but the Chief Executive expressed a fear that it would not be possible for him to do so. "I used to go to the games once in a while at Indianapolis," said he, "and also at Chicago. I enjoy seeing a good game, but I do not see how I can spare the time to go to-day. Mr. Halford, however, is a baseball enthusiast, and I am sure will ably represent the Administration." The President then bid his guests good-morning, and the boys, reëntering their carriages, were taken for a drive through Monument Park.

We left Indianapolis, Friday noon, in a special car provided by the officers of the "Monon Route," and reached Chicago the same evening. At Hammond, Indiana, twenty-six miles from the city, we were met by a party of Chicago enthusiasts and newspaper men who had come down from Chicago in a special. Hundreds of questions were asked, and as many answered, as the members of each party came together with hearty hand-clasps and words of welcome, and, before we were really prepared for it, we were rolling into the Union depot at Chicago. Fortunately for us, Mr. Spalding had been notified by wire at Indianapolis, to have the boys attired in evening dress upon their arrival.

We had accordingly made our toilets before reaching Hammond, and so were ready for the programme arranged for us. Not a few of our party had predicted that Chicago would out-do all other places in the welcoming reception it would extend, but not a man among us anticipated anything like the final demonstration made in our honor. The great crowd that filled the railway station could not be controlled by the police or the station guards. As our party stepped from the platforms of the coach, hundreds of cheering baseball enthusiasts swarmed over the iron railings and through the gates, until they picked us up, whether we would or not, and carried us to the carriages in waiting. There were sixty-five of these, and, as quickly as we could enter those reserved for our party, we were driven east to Peck Court and Wabash Avenue, where the lined formed. Finally, the last carriage had been filled and the procession began to move up Wabash Avenue and across Harmon Court to Michigan Avenue, amidst a blaze of pyrotechnics. The great crowd that filled the depot, that crushed about our carriages, that lined the streets along which lay our line of march, and howled and cheered at the sight of each familiar face in line, as well as the music, the calcium lights, the colored torches, and the rockets and Roman candles that burst above our heads, all combined to make the reception tendered us the most enthusiastic ever given any body of athletes upon American soil. When the last carriage had turned into Michigan Avenue, the line stopped until the illuminated procession, embracing sixty-odd amateur ball teams and representative amateur athletic organizations of Chicago, all in uniform, and provided with half a dozen bands of music, filed past us and took the lead. Then, amidst redoubled cheers and fresh bursts of pyrotechnics, our party moved on past the big auditorium building and, via Wabash Avenue, to the Palmer House, where we found the crowd as dense as at the railway station. Inside the famous hostelry we found nearly three hundred admirers of baseball and its players awaiting us, the reception committee embracing Judge H. M. Shepard, Judge H. N. Hibbard, Potter Palmer, John R. Walsh, Frederick Ullman, L. G. Fischer, D. K. Hill, C. L. Willoughby, C. E. Rollins, F. M. Lester, J. B. Kitchen, J. B. Knight, M. A. Fields, Dr. Hathaway, L. M. Hamburger, Louis Manasse, and C. F. Ginther.

The corridors and parlors of the great hotel were filled with guests all eager to shake hands with the arriving "globe-trotters," and bid them welcome home. Half an hour after our arrival we entered the banquet hall—the main dining-room of the Palmer House. This had been magnificently decorated with flowers of every variety, in huge baskets, garlands, wreaths and banks, while designs in flowers and confections, symbolical of the game and its accoutrements, confronted one at every turn. The menu and the wines provided were in keeping with all other details of the committee's work—elaborate and ample; and the menu cards, their different pages emblematic of the various stages of our tour, were the handsomest, both in design and execution, ever seen at a banquet in Chicago. In the body of the hall had been laid twenty-four tables of twelve plates each, and at these sat the players, scattered among their friends. Along the north side of the room, at an elevation of three feet above the tiled floor, stood the speaker's table, at which were seated the Hon. DeWitt C. Cregier, Mayor of Chicago; Hon. Carter H. Harrison, ex-Mayor of Chicago; Rev. Dr. Thomas; James W. Scott, President Chicago Press Club; A. G. Spalding, George W. Driggs, and others. The assemblage was thoroughly representative of the business and commercial interests of Chicago, and of the financial interests, too; for not less than twenty millions of money was represented.

It was, perhaps, ten o'clock when, the last course upon the card having been finished, coffee served and cigars lighted, Mayor Cregier called the assemblage to order, and in an able address welcomed the guests of the evening, not alone as ball-players, but as representatives of free America and the great city of Chicago. President Spalding responded, referring to the many courtesies and attentions tendered us abroad, and complimenting Chicago upon having capped them all with three great receptions—one at the railway station, another upon the streets of the city, and the third in the banquet hall. The party had enjoyed a grand experience, one that its members could refer to with pleasure for many years to come, but all were overjoyed at once more returning to their own country.

The Rev. Dr. Thomas responded to the toast of "Baseball as a National Amusement," and then "His Royal Highness, the Prince of Wales," brought Captain Anson to his feet, amidst a hearty burst of applause. While "Old Anse" was pulling down his décollete-cut vest and sipping a preparatory mouthful of water, an enthusiastic stockbroker proposed "Three cheers for the 'Old Man!'" and they were given with a roar and a wild waving of napkins. Then Anson drew himself up to his full height, and began. He said he was glad of an opportunity to say something pleasant about the Prince of Wales, for the heir to England's throne had treated them most royally, and by his recognition and presence at the opening game in London had, beyond doubt, added greatly to the public interest in our tour through Great Britain. Such recognition, Anson believed, had had the effect of raising the social standard of the national game to the highest point it had yet attained. "Anse" concluded his remarks with an honestly-meant tribute of praise to the habits, conduct and ball-playing ability of both the Chicago and All-America teams.

Major Henry L. Turner followed in a stirring response to "The National Value of Athletics," and then John Ward was enthusiastically cheered as he rose to his feet to talk upon "The World as I Found It." John expressed himself as thoroughly confident that the world was composed of land and water—principally water—as he had never before seen so much of that liquid. That it was round was evidenced by the fact that our party had started from Chicago, and, after traveling west continuously, had finally reached Chicago again. No grander tour had ever been conceived in the history of athletics, and baseball owed much, indeed, to Mr. Spalding's pluck and enterprise in carrying it to so successful an issue.

Ex-Mayor Carter Harrison was warmly received when he rose to respond to the toast, "My Own Experience." He kept his hearers in a broad smile by his humorous comparisons of his own tour of the world with that made by our party. He had gone around the world himself, he said, for the same purpose Mr. Spalding had in view—to advertise Chicago. He had filled all the foreigners he had met full of Chicago, and did not doubt but that the ball teams before him had done the same. He had told Englishmen, Scotchmen and Irishmen about our big fire, about our parks and boulevards, about our unrivaled climate, and about our crack ball team, and Messrs. Spalding, Anson and Ward had gone around the world to verify all he had said in praise of the national game and its great exponents. Mr. Harrison then gave an interesting account of his own voyages, and finally concluded with a glowing tribute to America and everything American.

"Public Opinion of the Game," "Australia," "The Humor of the Trip" and "The Press," were responded to in an interesting manner by Leigh Lynch, James W. Scott, George Driggs and others; and then, after an informal commingling and exchange of greetings, the banqueters separated for their respective apartments.

The last game of the tour took place upon the Chicago grounds on the following day, in the presence of eight thousand people. Tired out with the events of the demonstration on the night before, and impatient to get home to wives, mothers and sisters they had not seen for months, the teams did not put up a very spirited exhibition. All-America began to size up Baldwin's delivery at the start, and Mark, seeing that Ward's men were bent upon hitting, put the ball over the plate and let them peg away at it. The result was just twenty-two clean hits for All-America, with a yield of as many runs, the score standing 22 to 9 at the finish. After the game, the boys shook hands in the club house, and by midnight many members of the Spalding party were on their way to join their respective clubs.

Thus ended a tour the like of which had never before been undertaken, and which probably will never be duplicated. In conception, it was bold; in execution, it is worthy of admiration; and too much can scarcely be said in eulogy of the nerve, the enterprise, the managerial ability and the sound business judgment displayed by Albert Spalding as its projector, and to whom, more than any other, the national game of America owes its present high standard of organization and unquestioned reputation for honesty and integrity. Much praise is also due the players for their invariable good nature in the face of a thousand and one annoyances attendant upon a journey of thirty-two thousand miles through foreign lands and waters, and for their willingness to play ball under such conditions as, it is quite safe to say, no other ball teams ever played under. Indeed, the great tour, from beginning to end, must ever remain a credit to its projector and to each and every man who participated in it.

III.

LAWN TENNIS IN ENGLAND.*

PART I.

THE man responsible for the movement which culminated in the perfection of lawn tennis—taking it for granted that, as now played, the game is perfect—was an Englishman, Major Wingfield. I have heard a legend to the effect that Major Wingfield derived his idea from seeing some such game played in Russia, though we can see ball games of the tennis family played by the Basques, in Southern France, and all over Italy. Wherever he got his idea from, certain it is that Major Wingfield brought the game into public notice.

The game, as he introduced it, was wofully imperfect; he gave it an impossible name—*sphairistike*. Unfortunately, he was a man who would not listen to reason. He insisted that the shape of a court must be that of an hour glass, and by that he resolved to stand or fall. He fell. Why he fell is easy to explain. The game was taken up warmly by a body of gentlemen whose leisure had been mainly devoted to the cultivation and practice of the magnificent but extremely difficult game of tennis. They immediately pointed out the defects in the new game, and suggested alterations. These not being accepted by the inventor, they carried them out themselves, and, as the public preferred them to Major Wingfield's crude scheme, the Major soon dropped out of notice. This body of tennis players was the origin of the All England Lawn

---

* By "Banshee," London, England.

Tennis Club, grafted on the parent stem of the All England Croquet Club, croquet disappearing rapidly as lawn tennis came in. And so to the committee of the A. E. L. T. C. is due the perfecting of the game.

The first change was to curb the license of the server. Wingfield gave him such powers that he could score a game right off, for he fired into any part of his opponent's court he chose. The service line at one time stood many feet nearer the base line than it now does, and it was only after lengthy discussions that it was moved to within twenty-one feet of the net—an absolute necessity when the net was finally lowered to the present height. Other evolutions that have taken place have occurred entirely in consequence of the advance made in the play. The "man-at-the-net" question promised at one time to become a national one. The old plan of playing doubles was for one player to stand close at the net, not occasionally, as the Messrs. Clark do, but as a regular thing. This question was settled, not by writing and squabbling, but by players becoming so proficient in their ground strokes as to be able to pass the man at the net. Then he retired, and he was seen no more. The volley was evolved naturally. The Renshaws are supposed to have invented the volleying game; that is, running in for the express purpose of returning the ball on the fly; but this is wrong. The first man to use it so as to attract attention was Spencer Gore, whose volleying at the net contributed largely to his victory in the first championship. But that the Renshaws perfected the use of the volley, there is no doubt. Their names have always been intimately connected with that stroke, for, inasmuch as they could do more with it than any one else, they naturally used it oftener.

But they did not begin as volleyers. When lawn tennis first came in, the Renshaws, then mere striplings (they were born on January 3d, 1861, Ernest twenty minutes before William), tried it, but, like most other boys, left it when the novelty wore off. Living at Cheltenham, however, a place where the game took early root, they were induced to try it again, and soon attained a great skill in it. At Cheltenham a large covered building was speedily utilized as indoor court, and it still remains the best in England. There the Renshaws would practice, and there, in the autumn of 1879, when the twins were not yet nineteen years of age, they made their first notable appearance, W. Renshaw defeating the Irish champion, V. "St. Leger," by three sets to one. "St. Leger's" real name was Goold, and his anonymity has been wonderfully well kept. He was an Irishman, and in mere execution had no superior in his time; but he lacked stamina, and was not heard of after 1880, when W. Renshaw took the Irish championship from him.

"St. Leger" out of the way, the Renshaws had no rivals in dexterity, while from then till now they have always excelled in grace. Like most twins, they bear a very strong resemblance to one another. This feature is less prominent than it was a few years ago, when they were continually mistaken for one another, and when playing together one always wore a blue belt and the other a red one—a variation which, for the majority of spectators, was the only means by which one could be distinguished from the other. Ernest is five feet, ten and a quarter inches in height, and William is five feet, ten inches; but Ernest looks the bigger man, as he actually is, his weight being 154 pounds, while William's is 150. Both are natural athletes and when sixteen years old they ran a dead heat for the Cheltenham college quarter-mile race, Ernest, on the same day, clearing the splendid long jump, for a boy, of twenty feet, eleven inches—quite good enough, indeed, for some championships at that time. Being very well off, however, they took life easily, and their athletic powers were never cultivated, for they did not go to either of the universities. They made their first appearance in London as lawn tennis players at the Maida Vale covered court, where the best play was seen, and, though comparatively unknown, it did not take long for the listless demeanor of the few spectators to change into one of intense interest, for these gentlemen made surprising returns. They were then playing a back court game, and, because the opportunity had not come, the "Renshaw smash" was not even in embryo. Other pairs of brothers —and twins, too—have since made their appearance in the lawn tennis world, and have had every advantage in the way of practice, but none of them have got beyond respectability.

William Renshaw from the first went ahead of his brother. This has been a mere question of mind, or, as it is called in games, head. William has, for many years, been taken as the elder of the two, and many who know them well, found themselves betrayed into referring to Ernest as "Young Renshaw," whereas, as I have stated, he is the senior by twenty minutes. William has always seemed to me to be really more earnest than his brother. He made his reputation the first time he appeared in public, and he always feels that it must be maintained. When he goes into court, his expression denotes that business only is meant, and business it generally is. If you have not played against him before, his first service will probably make you feel glad that the service line is where it is, and not a foot or two farther from the net. No man has studied harder than Renshaw to make the service an attacking stroke. He told me that it took him a full year to get it as good as it is, and he has certainly made it a very dangerous medium of offense. In my opinion, there is no one anywhere near him in service. Many good players affect to despise the swift service. They pretend to think that it does not pay to serve hard, the server tiring himself for nothing. Pace is, of course, essential to scoring by service, and many have this and nothing else. William Renshaw adds accurate placing to pace, and therein lies his quality. I know of no other player who—at will, and not by accident—can so regularly serve the ball at top speed, close to the side line, quite a couple of feet inside the service line. Such a service is a certain score, for no one standing in the usual position for receiving the service can get anywhere near the ball, much less return it. But let the striker-out edge ever so little to the right or left, with the object of getting these wide services, and the ball will be placed, to a certainty, within six inches of the half court line, and beat him on that side. I am afraid that the Champion does not always receive the credit due to him for his fine serving. He seems, from his pure and graceful style, to play so much by the light of nature that few give him credit for having thought things out the way he has. As a matter of fact, every ball served by him is placed, though, of course, many go wrong, or he would serve the game every time.

As every one must who would make a hard service effective, he throws the ball sufficiently high to be struck by the racket when he is on the full stretch. He does not waste any time swinging the racket behind his back, but throws the ball up first, and, when it is nearly in the proper position, makes a lunge at it, the effect invariably taking him off his toes; but he is always on them again as the ball is struck. Many people think he makes a foot fault, but that is rarely true. There is a downward drag of the racket which no other player has. The effect is that of the server's whole body being stretched to its utmost an instant before the ball is struck, the effort being necessary, because every inch is of value. If William Renshaw stood six feet, his service would be something terrible to face. His second service is rarely anything but an underhand one, the ball dropping close to the service line and being carried by the curl put upon it well to the base line. If this good length were not kept, then it would be open to severe punishment.

As striker-out, or when receiving the service instead of giving it, the Champion, when the service is a very hard one, has to do the same as any one else, and make the best return he can of it; that is, put it back near the base line. As a rule, off the second service he rarely attempts to score. Whether it comes to the forehand or the backhand, nine times out of ten he places it at a moderate pace along the side line, of course at a good length, and runs up. If, however, the second service is near the half-court line and the least bit short, Renshaw pounces on it like a cat on a sparrow, and, taking it at its highest, overhand, puts it past you, according to how you are moving. If I am certain of anything in connection with W. Renshaw's play, it is that no player can approach him in the rapidity with which he detects the leap of his opponent's body. Time after time the uninitiated spectator sees the ball returned at a moderate speed quite close to the opponent, who, however, makes no attempt to return it. His body has just started to go the other way, and he cannot recover himself in time. Renshaw also knows pretty accurately where the ball is coming, which accounts for the fact that he is seen running about the court less than any one else. Unless the stroke is an important one, he is not fond of going for a distant ball, contents himself with making a mental note of the circumstance which led up to the stroke. This player possesses the gift of cutting a ball so that it falls over the net so dead that it rises only an inch or two from the ground. This applies to hard strokes as well as soft ones, for I have seen him so treat a stroke of Lawford's from close to the base line, Lawford standing at the other base line looking at the ball. This stroke is nearly always done backhanded, and nearly in front of the body. Its success depends upon the delicacy with which the racket is held. William Renshaw has sometimes shown form on great occasions of a very inferior nature for him, but at his best he is still well ahead of any one else. Generally he plays about one set per year at his absolute best, and he always wins that. But it is poor sustenance for his admirers to live on for twelve months. He declines to train, saying that he is never going to make himself a slave to any game, and, consequently, cannot play his very hardest for three sets. If he could, I am of the opinion that a fourth set would rarely be necessary.

Ernest Renshaw is best described as an erratic W. Renshaw.

"You haven't been playing much lately," I said to him once.

"No," he replied; "I got tired of knocking a ball backward and forward over a net."

And, verily, in every match in which he has since played in my presence, I believe this abstract view of the case has come upon him. A man who gives me the impression of suddenly weighing in his mind, in the middle of a match, the engrossing question: "Is lawn tennis worth playing?" is bound to be somewhat erratic, and I should never be surprised to see Ernest Renshaw suddenly cease playing and put on his coat, with the remark that he was sick of it. Physically, I do not see how a man could be more fitted to excel at the game. His activity about the court is only equaled by Hamilton's, Renshaw possessing the advantage of never appearing to be in a hurry, and always returning the ball to good advantage when he does reach it. When he goes for a distant ball, he does so by means of huge strides, two of which carry him across the court to all intents and purposes, and those who have tried both methods know that the big striding man is more collected than the short striding one. As an illustration of this, your own Dr. James Dwight, one of the "cutest" but shortest of good players, invariably progressed in bounds when after a ball.

Ernest Renshaw's service is a very hard one, perhaps the hardest known, and I believe his brother's would be quite as fast but for the controlling influence I have alluded to. Unlike William's, however, it rarely drops in the right court, and so is wasted. When it is "right," it is pretty certain to be wrong for the opponent. He throws the ball to a good height, and the racket is well flourished behind the back, the ball being met with a bang that often sends it on the fly among the spectators. Ladies sitting on a line with the Renshaws' service generally have an uneasy time of it, and when their parasols are riddled, shift to more peaceful neighborhoods. I have seen a lady appear round the corner of a stand only to receive, before she had seen anything at all, a lawn tennis ball, traveling at the rate of forty miles an hour, full in the mouth. At Dublin, where there is a large attendance and people are seated very close to the courts, the Renshaws are sometimes answerable for any number of parasol wrecks, the ball bursting the silk. Ernest's second service is overhand and decidedly weak, the ball bounding so as to give an easy return, and he has his great activity to thank for the easy way in which he so often gets out of trouble. His smashing is as erratic as is his first service. He seems to fail to measure his ball, and bangs at it apparently at haphazard. If the ball goes over the net all return is hopeless; but it is almost as probable that he will just tip the ball, or miss it altogether, and as likely as not recover himself and return it off the ground.

In all except one thing he is an inferior edition of his brother, the exception being in lobbing. As a lobber, Ernest Renshaw is *facile princeps*, and to this stroke, in the opinion of many, he owes his championship of 1888. The exactitude with which he returns ball after ball in the air, backhand and forehand, to within a yard of the base line, is wonderful. It would be difficult to execute this stroke more correctly. This player also has an original return of his own. When the ball is moderately near the net and is being taken off the ground, he takes it at its highest point with a turn-over action, the object being to put a top curl on the ball which keeps it down. No one else does the stroke this way. He very rarely plays a hard stroke off the ground, but when he does, and it comes off, it is like his service—no one can see which way the ball goes. At one time both Ernest and William Renshaw played a more "slashing" game than they do now; but their recklessness is nearly gone, and, like all other good players, they aim at accuracy in placing. William Renshaw knows his brother's play to an inch, and is always too much for him, Ernest never having beaten William.

H. F. Lawford does not now come next in point of ability. Being thirty-seven years of age, his day is past, and he can never again be the player he was, though on hard ground he is still the master of many good ones, and was good enough this year to win a set from William

Renshaw. But no attempt at the history of the game is complete without reference to him, and in the development of play he deserves a place along with the Renshaws, with whom he has physically nothing in common. He stands five feet eleven inches, and weighs one hundred and eighty-two pounds, but he used to train down much below this. In place of the activity of the Renshaws, he has great strength, and, in addition, was perhaps the only man who came properly trained into court. The secret of his play lies in the terrible certainty and pace of his underhand drive. The attachment of this stroke did not come about by mere accident or regulation; it was the result of practice, deliberately undertaken, for the attainment of a given object. He told me himself that it took him three years to bring the stroke to perfection, one of his objects being to get a top spin on the ball, which would keep it low and cause it to shoot on touching the ground. His tactics are simplicity itself. He hammers away with his powerful ground stroke, which is invariably of good length, until, supposing that he himself does not make a mistake, his opponent does. Playing from the base line, he cannot do very much in the way of placing, but a fast, low ball well in the corner of a court generally causes the opponent to play in the net or make a short return. No one among the men plays lower over the net than Lawford, and he practices it well. As I have said, his tactics are simple enough, but they can only succeed when carried out to perfection. Practically Lawford has no backhand. Of course, he plays balls which come to the backhand with his racket held on that side; but, instead of turning his wrist as others do, so that the back of the hand is outward, he turns the racket over, so that the head hangs down. To a less powerful man this would be a serious disadvantage; but Lawford gets considerable pace on the ball, and is, moreover, able to get on some of his beloved top curl. But delicate finesse strokes at acute angles over the net are to him impossible, while he is always to be beaten by balls placed well on his left, even though he can reach them, for he cannot pick them up. With such a very clumsy backhand it is wonderful, indeed, that Lawford has succeeded as well as he has, and his success must be taken as a very strong proof of the high value of a severe and accurate forward drive, unquestionably the groundwork of the game.

What is known as the volleying game, in which the player always volleys when he possibly can, is Lawford's pet aversion; but no one knows better how to finish a rest with a smash. For some years I took minute records of every big match that was played, noting down every stroke, and, on the occasion of the 1886 championship, I was able to astonish a number of people by showing that Lawford won more strokes by the final volley than did his opponent, William Renshaw, the first exponent of the volley and the "Renshaw smash." It is not his superiority in volleying that gave William Renshaw his supremacy over Lawford, who beat him one only, but his skill in all points of the game. For some time it was understood that Renshaw was willing, nay anxious, to play Lawford, all vollying being barred, and I remember his making the offer to do so in a private game, on the A. E. L. T. C. ground. My statistics also prove what had been patent to me for some time before, that no man scored oftener off weak second service than Lawford. I think I may go so far as to say that he won his solitary championship in 1887 by his punishment of Ernest Renshaw's second service, which, as I have hinted, invites it. Getting his elbow well up, Lawford would take the ball nearly at its highest, and back it would go close by one of the side lines, at a terrific pace, either to win the stroke then and there, or necessitate an easy return that could be smashed. Herein is a great difference between the playing of Lawford and the Renshaws. Lawford always punished a weak service, the Renshaws only occasionally. The Lawford system was to pound his adversaries into a difficulty at once; that of the Renshaws, to invite a bout to see who was best all round.

Ireland has produced many fine players, but none have brought to it such fame as W. J. Hamilton. This player is twenty-four years of age, stands five feet eight and three-quarter inches in height, and weighs 142 pounds, so he is of the light order. In addition he is very pale, and always looks overtrained. His crowning achievement was his dual defeat of the Renshaws this year, for the Irish championship. As he had beaten William Renshaw last year, at Wimbledon, he is the only player who has defeated him twice, single handed. It is difficult to pick out any particular stroke of Hamilton's and say that he excels in that. It is also not easy to speak of his style, for he has none. His play is imbued with his Irish character. Except on rare occasions of emergency, he does not hold his racket by the extreme end, as does nearly every other player, good and bad, but from about an inch and a half from the butt to half way to the head. Then his forehand stroke is not at all according to form, the racket being held out nearly horizontally at times, but never perpendicularly, as it is held by driving players. The exception is when he is making a distant ball on his forehand, when it is neck or nothing about his being in time. Then the racket has to be held by the extreme butt end, perpendicularly.

"How beautifully he makes that drive!" exclaims everybody. And he does, because, for once in a way, he has his racket in something like the proper position for driving. When the ball is returning by the stroke, it invariably flies at a great pace, low over the net, and is sure to score if the opponent has not anticipated it. In that case, if he is a good volleyer, he will prove to the driver that if he had left the ball alone he would have been the gainer by considerable amount of "win." Hamilton's speed about the court is one of his greatest troubles. He is always going for distant balls, and, of course, comes to grief over the majority, for the "Irish drive," as it is very aptly called, for more reasons than one, can come off only now and then. He is distinctly a volleyer, and puts as much "head" into his volleys as any one. Then he is very accurate in his placing, and can work up for an opening, with some prospects of success in consequence. One stroke he has always made his own from the first, and that is a delicate drop just over the net. This stroke is rendered the more deceptive because Hamilton can make it almost from the base line—a very difficult thing—and, if it does not score, the opponent has to run up so close to net that he is often to be beat by a pass over his head to the back of the court. This drop stroke is, however, made very clumsily, the head of the racket being up, and if more wrist were put to it, the ball would be struck so as to rise very little. Hamilton is noted for making good strokes by unaccepted methods. He is weak on the backhand, not having cultivated wrist, and always runs round a ball when he can, so as to take it forehanded. In the matter of temper, Hamilton is the most imperturbable player ever seen. Nothing puts him out, and during the most important match he will be bandying quaint Irish witticisms with the line umpires. The Renshaws visibly get very disgusted with themselves when they make bad strokes. Hamilton makes a good joke about it. Thus he is always in a good temper with himself, and the more he is behind the more he is determined to pull himself together and go on and win. I believe the chief secret of his success is his ability, from these causes, to play one consistent game all through, and not in fits and starts, *au* Renshaw. That he will never play a very much better game than he does now unless he materially alters his style, I doubt. Playing at Dublin in May and at Wimbledon in July are rarely anything like the same things. I would be the last to diminish the glory of any of Hamilton's victories, but I will never believe that he would have beaten William Renshaw as he did last year, if at all, had the ground been hard instead of soft and untrue. Dr. James Dwight, on your side of the water, knows as much as any one about Irish turf in May. "They are always looking for the ball in the mud in Ireland," he said, and there is much in this remark. It was Dr. Dwight who, when playing Hamilton in Dublin courts that were in a state of slop, insisted on having new balls when those in use got brown, and some seven or eight dozen were used in the course of the match.

Some few years ago the attention of tennis players in London was directed toward two boy players, one of whom was E. L. Williams, and the other E. W. Lewis. Williams is now in the United States, his last appearance (when unfit and out of practice) being in the covered court championship, which he won in 1886 and in 1887. Virtually he did not play after April 1, 1886. He was a mere slip of a lad, but he had a very long head, and was afraid of no one, beating Lawford in the covered court. Up to 1886 he had always beaten Lewis, of whom he had a start, but the latter was overhauling him fast. Lewis, being of larger build, took longer to fill out, and it will be some few years from now, when he is twenty-two years of age, before he is thoroughly set. He stands five feet nine and a half inches, and weighs about one hundred and fifty-four pounds. Lewis is a player who occasionally performs very startling feats. To return a ball behind his back around his leg on the half volley gives him no concern; he can apparently do absolutely what he likes in this direction, and I am not sure that appearances are very far in advance of the actual truth. In his manipulation of the racket he has no superior, but he has not the natural grace of a Renshaw, though he is by no means clumsy. He still looks like the boy he is. If his profession, that of medicine, does not interfere, as it probably will, he may become champion some day, but never, I think, so long as the Renshaws or Hamilton continue playing up to their present form. He has one fatal fault, and that is a poor forehand stroke. He places it very well, but there is never any "devil" in the ball. His forehand stroke cannot really be properly termed a drive at all, for the ball is not driven in the proper sense of the term. He has a very varied service, which fact is, however, never shown except against inferior players. I have seen him, in a handicap, win three consecutive strokes by a forehanded twist service, a backhanded twist service and a backhanded overhand service, the last named being rarely used by any one, though distinctly very useful, for it has a curl on it, though coming fast, and always alights close to the side line.

H. Grove is the last of the first-class English players whom I shall mention. He has been seen in the United States. He is a very light man, standing over five feet ten inches, and yet weighing only one hundred and forty pounds. He is twenty-seven years of age. The many winters he has spent with the Renshaws, at Cannes, have done much toward perfecting his game, which is, at times, the most brilliant imaginable. His stroke, par excellence, is a low drive, just skimming the net, and when he is in the vein, he will bring this off with unfailing certainty whenever the least chance offers. His drive is the most correct of any one's; that is, it is made according to the book, the ball being taken when very near the ground, and "lifted" over. Players have to get at the ball so soon now that the theoretically correct method is disregarded in the majority of cases, but not in Grove's case. He is, I suppose, absolutely the best stayer we have. He can, and does, play all day and never seems tired, but is always ready for one more match. This is a useful quality at country tournaments, where men begin in the morning with several matches at singles, and then pass the afternoon at doubles of various kinds. His place is below Lewis's, who would now always beat him.

An admirable opportunity was this year offered at the English championship for instituting comparisons between the play of six years ago and now. In 1883, as in 1882, the final round was between the Renshaws, and the volleying game, pure and simple, was then at its height and weakest. Time after time the two players would warm, and, separated by a few yards only, volley the ball backward and forward. The range was so short that there was only time to return the ball, and none to place it. In these volleys, William almost invariably came off best, a slight turn of the racket diverting the ball sufficiently from the straight line to beat his fraternal opponent. Now one never sees such a thing as two men close up to the net. Side-line play and lobbing have become too accurate for that, and the service line is now the recognized "position" for the volleyer, and, unless he has given his opponent a difficult return to negotiate, he has rather the worst of it. Where they used to be always "fiddling" about near the net, the Renshaws are now found hovering on the base line.

The superiority of fine back play to fine volleying was never better shown than in the match in the 1888 championship, when Ernest Renshaw beat E. W. Lewis, whose forte is volleying, though he is by no means the superior of the Renshaws in this direction. Ernest Renshaw seemed to have changed his style, and time after time he refused to volley where a couple of years before he would have volleyed in order to get more time for accuracy by taking the ball off the ground. With the exception of Lawford, all the mentioned experts are great adepts at four-handed play. They are all good volleyers, and volleying is bound to play a prominent part in four-handed matches, for whereas in a single a player has to cover twenty-seven feet, in a double it is under eighteen feet—that is, the half of thirty-six.

Except when very determined back-court players are engaged, the recognized opposition of all four players is at or about the service line, directly after the delivery of the service, and from here rests of volleys and half volleys follow, until a lob sends everybody scuttling back to the base lines. The Renshaws have always won the four-handed championship, whenever they have played for it, and this has been due more to their individual cat-like activity than to any combination. They play too rarely together to have any concerted plan, but their thorough knowledge of the game seems to compensate for this. The broadest court enables them better to bring off volleys and other strokes of a fancy nature, while their own speed prevents others from retaliating to an equal extent. William Renshaw has played a great deal with E. de S. H.

Browne, another Irish player, and these made an almost invincible pair. Browne's safe volleying and superior smash are of the greatest service in this style of game, and he never yielded to the temptation to slacken off. Lewis is another fine double player, and he has won many matches, partnered with a back-court player, pure and simple, who has never won a dozen strokes by the volley in his life. Partnered with any first-class man, Hamilton would always be bad to beat, for it is difficult to get past him, with only eighteen feet to do it in.

PART II.

The earliest records of the English country tournaments tell us that the ladies took to playing in public from the first, and it is not surprising to learn that Cheltenham, whence the Renshaws blossomed out as finished players, was answerable for the earliest women players of any note. It was even related how Miss Renshaw, sister of the celebrated brothers, showed very fair promise. The boast of Cheltenham was that it could produce four best lady players in the United Kingdom, and I think that boast would have been sustained had actual play been resorted to to prove it. One of these ladies is now Mrs. E. de S. H. Browne, mentioned in the previous article, and plays with her husband in mixed doubles. Another, Miss Marshall, still plays with success. Marriage has ended the playing career of the other two.

The first lady to show any exceptional form was a Miss Coleridge, of London. This player is below the medium height, even for a woman, but has well-built shoulders, which give her power. Then the game was not a severe one, and strokes won by good playing were far outnumbered by those lost on the ball being placed in the net or out of court. Thus Miss Coleridge's want of reach on the ground was not such a severe handicap, while her activity helped her in the case of a high ball. She had a remarkably good overhand service, severity being obtained purely by the swing of the racket, which, at the first part of the stroke, swung right back behind the player. This, in itself, was in these times a great advantage, but it was backed up by one of the best backhand strokes ever seen; indeed, I doubt if this lady's service and backhand have ever been surpassed by those of another lady.

But this lady's reign was somewhat short, for Miss Maud Watson, the daughter of a clergyman in the Midland counties, and an exceedingly clever mathematician of Cambridge University fame, began to carry all before her, and for a time was absolutely invincible. The possibility of W. Renshaw being some day caught napping by one of his contemporaries was always a matter for speculation, but that Miss Maud Watson would ever suffer defeat did not enter the head of any one. There was, in the lawn tennis world, a Maud Watson fever, just as there was in rowing circles a Hanlan fever. "The like of either would never be seen again," etc. Miss Watson and Miss Coleridge met in the final of the Ladies' London championship, and the former won all the way. Miss Coleridge married Mr. Cole, and after a couple of years retirement she came out in the All England championship, and afforded the last opportunity ever given of a perfect contrast between the old game and the new. She played as well as ever, bringing off her beautiful backhand stroke as unerringly as before, but her first game showed her that her opponent was a head and shoulders above her. Since then she has not played in public.

As I have said, Miss Watson, for some time, had matters completely her own way. She owed her superiority to her all-round excellence. Her service, like that of Mrs. Cole, was a very severe overhand, the racket being swung back also as far as it could possibly go. The racket is held by the extreme butt, rather loosely in the fingers, the blow being given by the swing of the racket merely. This method is recommended in preference to any of those which may be subsequently described, because, while being very severe, it is not exhausting. The ball is not thrown very high. There is also the fact, in connection with this service, that the downward sweep puts a certain amount of "stuff" on the ball, which a blow full in the centre does not, the result being confusion to the striker-out if the ground be at all treacherous from wet or other causes, and besides at all times a lower bound. This lady invariably won many strokes in a match by service direct. Her backhand was more safe than brilliant, while she was capital on the volley. Her weak point, in the eyes of the *cognoscenti*, was her forehand stroke. There was nothing to complain of in its accuracy, for that was its chief merit; but Miss Watson had acquired the habit of giving the ball an undercut stroke. The effect of this was to put the ball with great precision well into the backhand corner, where it deviated, on the bound, from the straight line. This settled all the inferior players; but the fact existed that the action of the racket took away from the pace of the ball, and also caused it to rise to a greater height than was advisable. It was this stroke which undoubtedly led to Miss Watson's ultimate defeat; but that did not happen until the player arrived who could take full advantage of it. Before the advent of that young woman it was found a very difficult thing to pass Miss Watson, who covered a great deal of court, and generally managed to get in front of the ball when returned at the pace then prevailing. This power of getting the ball back, and a general all-round ability, coupled with plenty of determination when things were going wrong, gave her her place at the front of lady players, more than any super-excellence in any one particular point.

Ireland, in the meantime has nearly perfected some formidable rivals in three sisters, the Misses Langrishe. The best of these was Miss May Langrishe, and when the Ladies' championship of Ireland was first introduced, in 1883, she won it. Slim and graceful, she plays with great ease, has a lovely backhand stroke, with a very free play of the racket, which adds force to the blow, and serves overhand and what is termed "cleanly." All the Langrishes have an excellent forehand drive—when it comes off. Then it generally scores; but Miss Watson's less effective but much more secure return, and her greater determination, gave her an advantage which on the mere play about the court she scarcely possessed. In brief, the English and Irish natures were opposed to one another, and the steadier won.

Simultaneously a London lady was worthily filling the place of Mrs. Cole, and predestinating herself for the highest honors. This was Miss Bingley. Without disparaging this lady's play in the court, it is not too much to say that her chief merit is her indomitable pluck and total ignorance of when she is beaten. Then comes her tremendous forehand drive. There is a good deal in the comparison of Miss Bingley (now Mrs. Hillyard) with Lawford, as each owes success to precisely the same things. Mrs. Hillyard's service is never intended to win a stroke. It is overhand, but only so, I truly believe, because it came more natural and easy than any other method. To neither backhand nor volley does she make much, if any, pretence. They are both defensive tactics, used as rarely as possible, and all the scoring is done with the hammering drive, and, whenever there is time, she runs around the ball to get it on the forehand. Being very light, she covers the court well, and can stand a large amount of play without fatigue. As Miss Bingley, Mrs. Hillyard played in the first Ladies' championship in 1884, and actually won the first set off Miss Watson, when they met in a preliminary round. In the following year Miss Bingley was winner in the championship up to Miss Watson, whose sun then shone to all the effulgence of setting. The following year she won the championship, beating Miss Watson in the final, sheerly from the way she got hold of the ball from those faulty forehand strokes I have alluded to, and drove it low over the net at express speed about the court. It will be seen that there can be no power in the stroke, it being delivered half-armed.

Ireland was also providing a lady player of exceptional calibre to support Miss May Langrishe. This is Miss L. Martin, in whom we have a player totally differing in style from those already mentioned. This lady is very powerful, and deals out a tremendous service. But beyond its pace it is a simple affair enough, the ball being struck plump in the middle without any art. Miss Martin's backhand is equally powerful and equally simple, while her volleying is far superior to that of most male players. Perhaps those are right who say that she practices the volley too much. Possibly she has found out what has been patent to others all along, that her forehand drive has nothing in it. The ball goes back at a fair pace, and that is all. It is scarcely ever low, and rarely too well placed. But what with her excellent volleying, strong backhand and power of covering the court, Miss Martin gets a very large percentage of balls back, at which the majority of ladies would break down; and this, as most lawn tennis players find out, more often than not leads to victory. Miss Martin first came into prominence at the Irish championship in 1885, when she beat Miss Langrishe, to everybody's surprise, and won a set from Miss Watson. The next year Miss Langrishe won, beating Miss Martin in the final.

I have now reached the point where I can no longer help mentioning a lady player who was to transcend anything yet dreamed of. I allude to Miss Lottie Dod. While the Misses Watson, Langrishe, Martin and Bingley were interchanging victories and defeats, leaving it very doubtful with whom supremacy would eventually rest, this young lady was enjoying steady practice at home. Born in September, 1871, she was not yet fourteen years old in June, 1885. And yet, in that very month she played Miss Watson so closely in the northern championship that the lady champion could win two advantage sets only. This was by no means Miss Dod's first appearance, for two years previously, when under twelve years of age, she had shown wonderful play for one so young. This young woman certainly owes something to nature, for she is magnificently built, and in any part of the world, by any race, of any color, would her figure be looked upon with admiration. She fully bears out the description of the Indian maiden of Fenimore Cooper, "tall and straight as a pine," though I doubt whether Cooper's maiden, or any one else, could carry herself as does Miss Dod. She is, too, the personification of health and strength, late hours not having at any time formed part of the programme of her daily life. Her appearance in the court is in itself a pleasurable incident before a stroke is played. Her play is built upon very correct lines, and the chief secret of success is the regularly perfect and very severe forehand drive which she possesses. This drive has been gradually developed upon that made court at home. As the stroke grew harder, so the ball went out of court, and then was introduced the invaluable element of "lift." I described how Lawford practiced to get top curl on his ball, and Miss Dod studied to attain the same object, and succeeded, perhaps, as no one succeeded before. To see this drive made for the first time is a revelation. As the ball approaches, the left foot is slightly advanced, and the racket held back as far as it will go, consistent with the arm, wrist and hand all remaining in a straight line. Then, as the body is brought evenly forward, swish! comes the racket to the front, meets the ball as it is well on the drop, and finishes in an absolutely perpendicular position. Nothing could be more perfect than the way in which the weight of the body is put into the stroke, and the apparent ease with which the whole thing is done. Once acquired, it is far the easiest and least exhausting method of making the drive. Swing and weight of body provide motive power; practice supplies the accuracy. I go to great lengths over Miss Dod's drive, and say that nothing like it has been shown by any other player, male or female, when ease, grace and effectiveness are taken into combined consideration, while greater accuracy could not be obtained much short of absolute infallibility. Almost from the first this young woman volleyed well. It mattered little to her whether she took the ball off the ground or on the fly. She volleys in any position with equal accuracy. The backhand stroke has always been a *bête noir* with her, more or less, and it has always struck me as curious that a player of such intelligence should have neglected to discover that the racket in her case does not have swing enough. This stroke she has greatly improved of late, but it will never be a backhand like that of Miss May Langrishe's or Miss Martin's.

Miss Dod's service surprises all who see it for the first time. One might be excused for supposing that so terrible a player would commence with a nerve-destroying service, but nothing could be more encouraging to her generally nervous opponent than the gentle and apparently very easy service that is delivered. It is a plain underhand service, but given very close to the net, where the fault is usually made, and at as great a pace as can be given without putting the ball through the service line. Miss Dod's theory is that in the case of ladies a hard service does not pay, with which I quite agree, if we take as an example the service ordinarily in use. But with my own eyes I have seen that it paid remarkably well in the cases of Miss Coleridge and Miss Maud Watson, for the simple reason that the stroke was made in such a way as to entail the minimum of fatigue upon the server. There is very little difference between Miss Dod's first service and the second, and in each the ball has a slight twist upon it.

It was at the tournament at Bath, in 1886, that this young lady made her mark distinctly and indelibly. The Bath meeting is second on the list, succeeding the Irish championship, and for years it has been patronized by the best players. Its presentation prizes for the Western

England championship, ladies and gentlemen, are extremely valuable, and so appreciated is the ladies' challenge badge which goes with the championship, that Miss L. Dod always wore it when playing in public, so long as she held it. In 1886 the entry for this event included the names of Misses Watson, Martin, Bingley and Dod. Miss Watson met Miss Dod in the final. How well I remember that match! Everybody was prepared for a good game, and I remember that, in consequence, I sat at the umpire's table and took down particulars of every stroke played. We were all so accustomed to see Miss Watson win, that anything else seemed out of keeping with the unities—and then Miss Dod was so young. Miss Watson played her usual forehand drive, without any "devil" in it, and whenever it came at all short, Miss Dod would step up, and across it went on the volley. It was this stroke that won the match. There was no getting near it, especially upon the part of a lady, and I have seen many gentlemen beaten by it. Both Miss Dod and Mrs. Hillyard owe their success to the fact that they play men's strokes, that require all men's unfettered activity to return, but have lady opponents on the other side of the net. The next year Miss Dod had grown so powerful as to be irresistible, and I shall not soon forget the power of those drives by whose agency Miss Watson was beaten at Bath again, although playing a fine game, and causing the sets to read 7–5, 6-4, just as they did on the previous occasion, and later on for the northern championship, at Manchester. Not Lawford himself could have sent the ball harder across the net than did Miss Dod on the latter occasion. Since that time the worst that has happened to Miss Dod has been to lose a set to Mrs. Hillyard on two occasions, and it says a great deal for Mrs. Hillyard's play that she is the only lady who can really make her great rival play up. Miss Dod has won the ladies' championship twice, but did not appear this year, although she would have won the trophy outright by a third victory, she being on a yachting excursion at the time. It was a great disappointment to London, but it is nevertheless a commendable thing that few of the big players go after "pots."

I have insisted a good deal on Miss Dod's play, because I want our lady players to understand that no lady can have a really strong game who has not a good forehand drive as a foundation. Particularly should this be inculcated in the minds of beginners. It is no more difficult to learn how to make a good drive than a bad one.

This year an Irish lady player has made her appearance who is destined, I think, to make a name. She is Miss L. Rice, who, at Dublin and Wimbledon, gave Mrs. Hillyard considerable trouble in the Irish and All England championships. Indeed, at Wimbledon she was within a solitary stroke of being lady champion for 1889, and this at her second public appearance. One who can make such a *début* is bound to be very formidable with riper experience. She plays a fine all-round game, steady and sure.

Several ladies play an excellent four-handed game, and it is not surprising to find that in several instances sisters play well together. Thus the matches between the Misses Langrishe and the Misses Watson, in Dublin, excited the keenest interest. Miss Maud Watson's partner was her senior, and was particularly good at the net. Then Miss Lottie Dod plays with her sister, also her senior, and also good at the net, at times excellent, cutting the ball dead on the volley. The best double game of all is played by the Misses Steedman, who go up and volley in the orthodox Renshaw style, playing a four-handed game that is about thirty better than either plays single-handed. The champion pair consists of Miss Lottie Dod and Miss Langrishe, and well it may, for they are splendidly matched, playing all strokes well. Some ladies' doubles are considered quite a feature at meetings, especially as the gentle sex predominates among the spectators, always excepting the All England championship.

There have also been some splendid matches at ladies' and gentlemen's doubles. I have seen W. Renshaw playing with Miss Maud Watson, which was by far the finest mixed pair of that, if not of any time. Miss Watson was always grand in a double, where coolness and a belief in one's partner goes for so much. I might mention, since I have seen it discussed in American papers, that it would be highly *infra dig.* for a gentleman player to make any difference in his service in an important match because he was serving to a lady. Ladies not only don't expect, but would resent, any modification of strength in their favor. I have seen it mooted that it would not be etiquette to serve one's hardest to a lady. Try it in England, and see what your partner will think about it!

As to where these young women stand in comparison to the male experts, that may be calculated by a review of the matches between the champions of either sex. These will show that the women's play is really of a high order.

At the Exmouth tournament in 1888, Miss Dod faced Ernest Renshaw, then the champion, she receiving the odds of 30. She took the first set by 6 to 2, but the gentleman won the next two by 7–5, 7–5. In the same year, however, the lady champion met William Renshaw at Scarboro, at the same odds, and beat him by 6–2, 6–4. This year William Renshaw is again champion and playing in great form, yet it may be said to be very close between him and Miss Dod at 30. And there is never any nonsense at those games on the man's part, it must be remembered. He plays to win, as though his antagonist were the male champion himself, with all the severity and effort of which he is capable.

Wouldn't that bring Miss Dod up to within 15, or better, of your own Dr. Dwight? And what a lot of men there are who fancy they are game, and not without reason, to whom Dr. Dwight could give 15 and win in a canter!

The contest for the doubles championship is played in England after the singles, and not before, as in America. This year's match between the Renshaws and Lewis and Hillyard proved to be full of excitement and very close. The two pairs had already met once this season—at the Irish championships, where Mr. Lewis and his partner defeated the brothers and afterward won the Doubles Championship of Ireland. In the English battle, however, the Renshaws succeeded in turning the tables on their former conquerors, after a rather in-and-out match, by three sets to two. The day was fine, and the conditions, with the exception that the court was somewhat slow, were eminently favorable. Ends were changed every game, and the service came from the end nearest the entrance. The match opened with a double fault by Mr. Hillyard, and the first game went to the Renshaws after deuce had been called once. The next three games also went to the brothers in quick succession, their opponents winning only four strokes. The tide then turned in favor of Messrs. Lewis and Hillyard, who took three games without allowing the Renshaws to reach deuce. Each pair then took a game in turn, bringing the score 5-4, in favor of the Renshaws, who next secured the tenth game, and with it the set.

The last stroke of this set was won by a hard overhead volley of Lewis's hitting his partner. The play in the first set was rather tame, Mr. Hillyard being the weakest of the four. The second set went to the Renshaws by the same score as at first, 6-4, though the games were more evenly contested. The Renshaws got to 3-1 in the third set, and the match then seemed to be virtually at an end. But just here a well-timed effort on the part of their adversaries altered the aspect of affairs. Five games in succession were won by Messrs. Hillyard and Lewis, who then secured the third set by 6-3. Mr. Lewis played splendidly in this set, and Mr. Hillyard improved vastly.

A sensational incident marked the first game of the fourth set. During one rest Mr. Lewis made a marvelous return of a ball which dropped short, and in doing so he ran a considerable distance past the umpire's chair, so that Mr. Hillyard was left to defend the court alone. This he succeeded in doing until Mr. Lewis returned from his little expedition in time to take part in the rest, which was eventually won by a back-handed smash by Mr. Hillyard. In the same game Mr. Lewis cleverly returned a ball behind his back. This set, the fourth, finally went to Messrs. Lewis and Hillyard, their play having been irresistible. The Renshaws, after the first few games, seemed to give up attempting to cope with it, and played rather slackly.

Curiously enough, in the last game Ernest Renshaw hit his partner in precisely the same way as Lewis had done in the first set. Mr. Lewis and his partner had now taken eleven games in succession, and the chances seemed to be very much in their favor; but the Renshaws evidently had something in reserve, and, aided by the glorious uncertainty of the double game, were enabled to win the last set, and with it the match. The score was 6-4, 6-4, 3-6, 1-6, and 6-1. The brothers Renshaw have now won the Doubles Championship of England for the seventh time since 1879.

IV.

LAWN TENNIS IN AMERICA.*

PART I.

ABOUT fourteen years ago Boston's athletic circles introduced into their variety of pastimes a charming debutant of English parentage—the game of lawn tennis. Brought into prominence by men of culture and skill, its qualities became gradually appreciated throughout the land as a wholesome amusement and a vigorous athletic sport. In the former capacity it certainly has no superior among our popular pastimes, and, while now well established as an athletic sport, its environments are of a nature most refined and devoid of the objectionable features that detract from the enjoyment of many other sports. Young and old of either sex can find in tennis an interesting means of exercise, while the most vigorous athlete needs all his physical strength and skill to acquire an excellence in the game that can secure him tennis honors.

It has been said that no game played requires so continuous and violent a use of the muscles of the body in a given length of time as tennis; and, furthermore, not alone one set of muscles are requisite, but every fibre of the muscular system is brought into play. Those who excel in tennis are invariably men of intellect, as well as good physique, and this happy combination of mental and physical adaptation is the great secret of the game's success. To be satisfied as to the popularity of the game, one has but to enter the parks of our great cities. Acres of lawn, with

---

* By F. A. Kellogg.

rectangular marked courts adorned with graceful players of both sexes, present a most enchanting picture. Nearly four hundred people have regular membership in the clubs at Central Park, New York, while at Prospect Park, Brooklyn, on a Saturday afternoon will be seen hundreds waiting for courts to be vacated. Households and summer cottages are well regarded as incomplete without lawn tennis equipments.

The true history, however, of tennis in this country lies not in the popular playing, but in its great records as a sport. The contests have in the main been amateur, and from its incipiency tennis has been surrounded by a social halo that no other game (except polo, perhaps) can boast. The first tournament of any importance in America took place at Nahant, Mass., in 1875. Dr. James Dwight, the father of lawn tennis in America, met in finals Mr. Fred Sears, elder brother of the now celebrated champion. The former won, and for two or three successive years was successful there. To Dr. Dwight is due the chief credit for the American introduction and development of the game. He is our oldest expert player, having won many prizes in England, where he spent several months every season, and he has been ranked second only to Mr. R. D. Sears, the ex-champion. As a patron of tennis here Dr. Dwight is to be held always in high honor.

DR. JAMES DWIGHT.

From Nahant and many private tournaments emanated the first Newport contests. These events, previous to 1881, were not open tournaments. Subscribers to the Casino only were allowed to enter. In 1880 Mr. Gray won. Neither Dr. Dwight nor Mr. Sears was in the tournament. The same year a double tennis tournament was held at the Staten Island Cricket and Baseball Club. Messrs. Dwight and Clark were defeated by much inferior players, owing to the use of tennis balls considerably under size and otherwise defective. In this lies the suggestion and formation of the United States Lawn Tennis Association. The objections and appeals of the Boston men as to the balls gave rise to months of discussion, finally culminating in a call, signed by Dr. James Dwight, representing the Longwood Club, of Boston; C. M. Clark, of the Young American Tennis Club, of Philadelphia, and E. H. Outerbridge, of the Staten Island Club. This call brought delegates from eighteen or twenty clubs, and a meeting at the Fifth Avenue Hotel was held in January, 1881. The attendance and enthusiasm at that meeting was a surprise, and augured well for the future. The Association was then formed with less than twenty, and now includes eighty, clubs. General Robert Oliver was the first president; and the honor now is held by Mr. Joseph S. Clark, of the Young American Tennis Club, of Philadelphia.

With the formation of the Association, American tennis traditions developed into nine years of well-defined history. The benefits of the organization were immediately felt. Means of communication were opened, and lively competition among its members gave rise to the many tournaments which have now become annual fixtures. It would be impossible to give any estimate of the number of tennis clubs now in existence. The great majority of them are not members of the Association, but to the latter class our information is limited. It is but fair to state, however, that many large and flourishing clubs do exist apart from the Association, and some, too, which figure now as important members are but recent acquisitions to the ranks of the larger body.

The Longwood Club, of Boston, deserves first mention, chiefly from the reminiscences of the early days of tennis and the associations connected with it. Its grounds are most picturesque, its courts of well-kept turf, and its members are of a class preëminently refined and cultured. Associated with this club are the names of Dr. James Dwight, the father of tennis in America; Mr. R. D. Sears, the great champion; Mr. Fred Mansfield, the Southern champion, and others who for many years have graced its courts. While no open tournaments are held at Longwood, some of the most brilliant private matches have there been witnessed while Mr. Sears and Dr. Dwight were in their prime and playing their best.

Nothing proves more conclusively the strong hold that tennis has among our sports than the fact that many great athletic clubs have made it their prominent pastime. The Staten Island Cricket and Baseball Club is a conspicuous example, and, without doubt, is the most enthusiastic and important member of the United States Lawn Tennis Association. Its membership is large, and includes gentlemen, ladies, and junior members. The commodious club house is fronted by acres of excellent turf, most of

JOSEPH S. CLARK.

which is laid out in courts. Beyond is a grand stand, newly erected, and intended principally for the ball games. But at the great match for the double tennis championship, in July, 1889, its usefulness for tennis came in play. The court was laid out in front of the stand, which made it a most desirable place for the many hundred people witnessing the contest. There they enjoyed the game and delightful society at the same time. About fifty feet to the left of the grand stand is the ladies' club house. Though small, it is exceedingly pretty, and is accessible to men only when the fair members see fit to give an afternoon tea. Beside the double-tennis championship, on these grounds are annually held contests in ladies' singles. The former event had been held yearly at Orange, N. J., until 1888, and Mr. E. H. Outerbridge is to be thanked for this beneficial change, in addition to his many other services to the club and association. Mr. H. W. Slocum, Jr., is an active member of this club, as well as Miss Adeline K. Robinson, the most expert lady player of this country.

The St. George's Cricket Club is noted for its distinguished membership, and for the superior courts at Hoboken, adapted as well for cricket and tennis. Probably more expert players practice on these grounds than on any other grounds in the country. An afternoon in June or July will find Messrs. Slocum, Taylor, Beeckman, Knapp, Deane, Miller, J. W. Raymond, and others busy with racket and ball. The Orange Club has also been prominent as the scene of many tennis contests. All the clubs mentioned use grass courts, which are acknowleged to be superior to any other kind, when properly kept. The practical difficulty of making good turf courts has, however, given rise to the adoption of clay courts by many of the leading tennis clubs in America. The Nahant Sporting Club, of which Dr. Dwight and the Sears brothers are members, is a conspicuous example.

The best clay court in this country belongs to the New Haven Lawn Club. It fronts on a beautiful little club house, and on it have been played many important matches. This club is said to have the largest membership of any in the country. While surrounded by a halo of college society, no students, unless residents, have the privilege of membership; yet it is here that the annual intercollegiate tournament is held. The New England championship tournament is also held at New Haven, and few tournaments are so well attended and so popular as this. I have attended almost every prominent tournament for several years, but none have been so well conducted as those at the New Haven Lawn Club. The committee work has been perfect, which can be predicated of no other club committee.

Much might be said of the Springfield, Rochester, and Chicago Clubs, the Brooklyn and New York Tennis Clubs; but the examples cited are enough. In general, we find in a large club from five to a dozen courts, a commodious club house, lockers, shower baths, reading rooms, etc. Once or twice a year local or club contests are held, and prizes are awarded. Progressive tennis has been introduced by ladies, which, ending with an afternoon tea, adds sociability to the game. In large clubs it has been the custom often to arrange a system of handicapping, thus classifying the men. This gives the opportunity of frequent contests, the results of which day by day change the relative ranking of the players. The difficulty of adjusting these odds among men playing in friendly contests often brings about surprising and interesting results.

Several years ago, at the New Haven Lawn Club, an ingenious system of handicapping was devised by Professor Hadley, of Yale College, and Mr. A. S. Osborne, both members of the club. The players divided, somewhat arbitrarily, into five classes. A member of any of the first four classes, by giving the odds of half fifteen to a fellow member, could, if successful, put him into the class next below. Contrariwise, a member of a lower class could challenge one in the class above, receiving odds of half fifteen, and, if he won, he became promoted into the class of his opponent. Interesting events of this kind do not convince the unsuccessful of inferiority in skill, and, at the same time, the winners are spurred on to wider fields wherein to display their prowess.

PART II.

This ambition for higher honors in tennis, as in other athletic sports, cannot be satiated by private or club contests, and so it happens that open tournaments are the natural results. For nine seasons competitions of this sort have taken place throughout the country, under the auspices and rules of the United States Lawn Tennis Association. Members of clubs belonging to the Association are alone eligible to participate in these events, which debars the possibility of the least taint of professionalism. In 1889 there were twenty-nine official fixtures between June 3d and October 6th. Only a few dates conflicted, so that a complete sporting circuit was the result.

The season is ushered in by the tournament of the Flushing Athletic Club, and, for one so early, has been very successful. It is like a return from a long vacation, where the players meet in mutual admiration and exchange greetings. A casual observer might be amazed at a party of tennis players, if he should come across them on the trip from Long Island City to Flushing. Of the dozen men you meet with dress-suit cases and rackets, each is asking of the other or answering questions like this, almost in unison :—

"In how many tournaments are you going to play?"

"Do you want to double up with me at Staten Island?"

"Who's going to be at New Haven?" etc.

R. LIVINGSTON BEECKMAN.

This little tournament inaugurates the year's play. It was this year won by Mr. Clarence Hobart, of the New York Tennis Club. On the following week comes the contest for the Middle States championship. In 1887 this honor belonged to R. L. Beeckman, but it was wrested from him the following year by E. P. MacMullen, who, in turn, lost it again this year to Howard A. Taylor. With such perfect grounds, this should be one of the leading events; but access to it from New York is not easy, and a strong wind many times interferes with the play. The New England championship comes next. A beautiful cup, offered first in

1887 by the New Haven Lawn Club, was won and successfully defended for three years by Mr. H. W. Slocum, Jr., the United States champion, and this year it became his property. The runners-up were successively, Messrs. F. G. Beach, E. P. MacMullen, and R. P. Huntington, Jr. And so on throughout the summer months tournaments of greater or less importance occupy each week. At the meeting of the association held at the Hoffman House, New York, early this spring, the date of the annual double championship contest was changed from September to the first week in July. Much has been said of the apparent decline of the double game during the last few years, and this action taken by the association proved to be both wise and beneficial.

The skill displayed by Dr. Dwight and Mr. Sears, who so long held the championship, did not seem to pass to their successors, although in singles tennis improvement was generally apparent. In 1888 Mr. Slocum and Mr. Foxhall Keene, as well as Messrs. Clark and Taylor, were defeated, while the younger players, Messrs. Hall and Campbell, secured the championship, through superior team-work. By this change of date more zeal was put into the contests, and greater interest was taken both by players and the admirers of the game. The result was that the finest match in doubles ever played in America took place at Staten Island in July last. Five remarkably close sets were required to decide it, but Messrs. Hall and Campbell, after a display of tennis even more creditable than that made by them the previous year, were obliged to relinquish the championship to Messrs. Slocum and Taylor. In closeness of score it was only rivaled by the celebrated match at Orange between Messrs. Dwight and Sears and Messrs. Taylor and Brinley, in 1886. The volleying was wonderful. During many of the "rests" the ball passed the net eighteen or twenty times before the concluding stroke was made.

Let us now visit Southampton, Long Island, where another local championship is yearly decided. The chief conquests there are made by the many pretty girls who flock to the courts daily in soft-colored muslins. Within a stone's throw of the ocean stands a club house, picturesque from without and elegant in all its appointments. In front are the tennis courts; well in the rear is attached the pretty ball room, the scene of the concluding festivities of the week's tournament. From the spacious porches of the Meadow Club it is pleasing to watch Southampton's aristocracy emerge from their delightful villas every morning of the tournament, arriving with seaside promptness, some on foot, some in their "traps." Tennis from ten-thirty to one o'clock, then to the beach and lunch, and at three-thirty more tennis. This, indeed, is a model tournament. Everybody is interested, nobody excited, and, under the management of Messrs. Cryder and Humphreys, no hitches can occur. This event increases yearly in popularity. It was won by Mr. Taylor, and, in point of social enjoyment combined with superior tennis playing, no tournament has its equal.

RICHARD D. SEARS.

The three weeks preceding the great Newport championship are taken up by three important tournaments: The Wright and Ditson tournament at Newcastle, N. H., the Nahant, and the fashionable event at Narragansett Pier. Their results are watched with especial interest, both as affecting the chances at Newport and as important factors in the individual ranking of expert players. Yet they are but preliminary skirmishes in comparison to the final battle at the Casino, where for nine seasons from thirty to forty men have met in the championship struggle. Two men only have ever secured the proud title of champion, Mr. Richard D. Sears, of Boston, and Mr. Henry W. Slocum, Jr., of Brooklyn. The former held it for seven successive years, beginning with 1881, relinquishing it by default (caused by physical inability) to Mr. Slocum in 1888, who, after another victory at Newport, retains the championship in 1889.

One cannot imagine a more suitable spot for a great tennis contest than the beautiful Casino at Newport. For those who have not visited it a glimpse as it appears on the morning of a great match may not be out of place. It fronts on Bellevue Avenue, and long before time of play the elegant equipages of Newport are gaily rolling up to the arched entrance, and swarms of beauty and fashion are passing in through the pretty vestibule, with a merry hum of conversation and eagerness to secure a good place for viewing the match. On the left, as we enter the vestibule, are exhibited the costly and beautiful prizes, including the Championship Cup. Passing through the club house, we come upon a large circular lawn, enclosed completely by picturesque buildings. The Casino café occupies the left, and straight ahead is a covered pavilion, and within an orchestra, rendering choice music, while beyond we arrive at a large expanse of lawn, interspersed with pretty clusters of trees and shrubbery. Here are laid out the tennis courts, which are considered the finest in the land. In the extreme rear is a building, wherein are the little Casino theatre, a ball room and the tennis court, and its broad piazzas and balconies afford a view for many spectators. The most popular and desirable position, however, is near the court itself. For the final contests a well-rolled court is reserved, and ropes at a liberal distance from the lines define a beautiful rectangle of green, surrounded by a deep border of fashionable frocks and fair faces under parasols of delicate tints. The scene is one not to be forgotten, for thousands of Newport's society people lend their delightful presence and enthusiastic admiration to a Casino contest.

An incident that impressed me strongly at the final match of the recent tournament is this: During the exciting play a man prominent in social and financial circles, who had been a daily witness of the games, asked of me the names of the two contestants. Without doubt, to the uninitiated, players in their conventional suits of flannel look alike, and it is a significant fact that the play itself merits the principal attention of spectators. On the other hand, the inclination to hero worship is a part of human nature, and, either from sentimental or speculative reasons, each man, woman, and even child chooses a favorite on the tennis court. It is invariably the younger player whose strokes are rewarded by the greater applause. Messrs. Shaw and Campbell were the two most popular contestants at Newport, and deservedly so from their achievements.

HENRY W. SLOCUM, JR.

No prouder knights ever stepped into the lists in days of chivalry than they, when they appeared on the court at the Casino. Mr. Shaw's clear complexion and graceful carriage impress one in his favor. Mr. Campbell is slight in build, and nineteen years old. He generally appears in striped flannels, a checked shirt adorned with a necktie tastily tied in a bow knot. The straw hat is old, but has long been worn by him as a "Mascot." His cheerful demeanor on the court, even in adversity, adds to his popularity. Both Mr. Taylor and Mr. Chase are short men, and, in strong contrast to the latter, Mr. Taylor has light hair and blue eyes. His pleasant face and his graceful appearance have long been admired on tennis courts.

The most distinguished of all in looks is Mr. Slocum, the champion. While he is the recipient of less popular applause, his manly air is impressive of power and skill. He is athletic in build, and dark. Seldom with a cap, his hair—black as an Indian's —never loses its part during the severest matches. Another conspicuous tennis player this summer at Newport was Mr. E. G. Meers, the Englishman, a man of forty years, and of medium height and build. He has a small black moustache and dark skin, and his expression is rather serious and mature compared with the younger men. Eye-glasses and a helmet hat

CHAMPION TENNIS GAME AT NEWPORT, R. I., 1889.

distinguish him from the others on the courts, and in gentlemanly demeanor he is inferior to none. So much for their looks. What they did is equally creditable, and much more important to the tennis world.

The wonderful success of the younger players not only demonstrates the recent rapid development of the game, but also points out to every young man the possibility of gaining tennis glory by proper and persistent practice. There were thirty-two entries in the all-comers' tournament, the winner of which was pitted against Mr. Slocum, the defender of the championship. But of these only eleven men stood any chance of winning, and they are divisible into three classes—Messrs. Taylor, Chase, Clark, Mansfield, and Knapp representing the older class of crack players: Messrs. Shaw, Campbell, Miller, Wright, and Huntington were the leading men in the younger class, while Mr. Meers, who ranks sixth among the English experts, constituted the third class. In the history of tennis during the last decade, most of the championships and prizes have been taken by what are named "the old cracks." These monotonous results had come to be a decided detriment to the progress of the game and a discouragement to younger and less experienced players, so that a young expert, on entering at Newport, feels morally handicapped. Added to this was the prestige and skill of Mr. Meers, who, by English experts, was expected to win the all-comers' and possibly the championship. What was the result? Surprise hardly expresses it. Mr. Shaw defeats Mr. Chase and Mr. Knapp, while Mr. Campbell puts out Mr. Taylor, the strongest favorite, then Mr. Clark, and finally, after a close and brilliant struggle, Mr. Meers is obliged to yield to one twenty years his junior. After these wonderful achievements the young experts met in finals, and Mr. Shaw gained the victory. Still, Mr. Campbell is credited with having done the best work in the tournament by defeating three of the hardest players entered. The difference in total strokes won and lost in the final match was only nine, and Mr. Shaw's thirteen successful aces by swift service were alone enough to decide the match for him.

By the rule adopted by the United States Lawn Tennis Association in 1884, Mr. Slocum did not play in the tournament, but met Mr. Shaw, the winner in the championship match. It was not surprising nor discreditable that Mr. Shaw should meet with defeat from an opponent so preëminently the peer of any tennis player in America. Mr. Shaw's play was extremely brilliant, but cool judgment, backed by experience and skill, gave Mr. Slocum an easy victory and the championship for another year. It is thought, not only by the writer but by many better versed in the game, that had either Mr. Taylor, Mr. Meers, or Mr. Campbell met Mr. Slocum on August 28th, a closer score would have resulted, and, perhaps, the final issue might have been different.

THOMAS PETTITT.

Before leaving Newport's gay whirl another tennis event of importance is to be noticed. On the day following the National tournament occurred the first professional match in the annals of American tennis. Above all other games the game of tennis has been distinguished by its total freedom from professionalism. The social halo surrounding tennis abhors any element of this nature, even to a prudish degree. But it is not within my province to discuss the advisability of encouraging such contests. Such a match did take place on the courts of the Casino, August 29th, 1889. The contestants were Thomas Pettitt, the American professional and court tennis champion, and George Kerr, the British professional. "Tommy" Pettitt is a shining light at Newport. For years Messrs. Dwight, Sears, Slocum, and others have played with him for practice, as well as for instruction. He is agile, wields his racket with great skill, and, while his general form of play is on a par with that of our best amateurs, some of his strokes are executed with marvelous skill and ingenuity. He was quite the favorite, and everybody was surprised and disappointed at his terrible defeat by Mr. Kerr. This was the first in a series of best three in five matches to be played in this country. Mr. Kerr displayed less grace, but more force and determination in his strokes. Every fibre of his body seemed to be exercised as he struck the ball, and his skill and judgment were in no way lacking. From a technical point of view Mr. Pettitt certainly made a mistake in running close up to the net and attempting to block the terrific drives of his opponent, although these tactics would have been successful with a player of less swiftness. As a matter of fact, Mr. Kerr had not displayed any such qualities in his practice previous to the match, and Mr. Pettitt had depreciated his opponent's abilities. From the first it was evident that Mr. Pettitt was beaten. His court-tennis strokes availed him little, while his swiftest cuts were handled by Mr. Kerr with ease. By more practice and the use of different methods Mr. Pettitt may yet be a match for Mr. Kerr. The attendance at this contest was not so great as at the former amateur contests, though the interest was good.

When these players met for the second time, at Springfield, Mass., September 21st, the plucky Englishman met a Waterloo at the hands of the Bostonian. They played in a cold northwest wind, under lowering skies, on a damp court, with the turf spongy and water-soaked. The first set was won by Mr. Pettitt, 6–4. Mr. Kerr took the second set, but that was all he could accomplish, for his adversary won the others, 6–3 and 6–4. In this contest it was seen that Mr. Pettitt could meet the Englishman's clever plays with improved skill. Mr. Kerr's deliveries were swift and vigorous, and it was a pretty contest from start to finish.

The third match of the professional series occurred September 25th, at the Longwood Club, Boston. The attendance was larger and the interest greater than at the previous events. Kerr won with considerable ease, taking three straight sets, by the score, 6–3, 6–3, 6–4. The concluding match occurred October 2d at the same grounds. This decided the professional championship of the world for Mr. Kerr. It was a brilliant contest. Pettitt showed improvement in his ability to meet Kerr's violent drives, and, instead of blocking them, as had been his tactics in previous matches, he took the aggressive, driving the ball with nearly as much force as his opponent. Yet it was too late in the series for Pettitt to bring his "form" to the high standard of Kerr's. In point of skill, in the use of the bat, and knowledge of the methods of tennis, little disparity exists between these men. Steadiness and greater strength in strokes seemed to have turned the balance decidedly in Kerr's favor. The latter won by the score: 6–0, 3–6, 6–2, 6–3.

Within the last few years local associations have been formed in the West and South, which might have proved threatening to the successful existence of the National Lawn Tennis Association if allowed to remain separate from that organization. For self-protection and unity, it became advisable for the United States Tennis Association to amend its constitution at the annual meeting in March, 1889, so as to admit as members not only clubs, as heretofore, but also associations of clubs. This action insured a centralization of power important for the making of uniform rules and laws regarding tournaments, as well as general play. While applying to the Western and Intercollegiate Associations as well, the immediate purpose of this move was to affect the Southern Association, where championships had for several seasons been won and lost without the auspices of the National Association. In 1886 Mr. Bonsal was the Southern victor, but was defeated in 1887, at the tournament of the Baltimore Cricket Club, by Mr. A. H. S. Post. The latter defaulted in the fall championship, but in the spring of 1888 was an easy winner of the tournament given by the Southern Lawn Tennis Association, and, meeting Mr. Bonsal, took from him the championship cup.

In these events Northern players had not been participants. Southern interest in tennis, in the meantime, had increased. The climate and facilities for playing favored the development of the game. Still, from records and the advancement of the Northern experts, both in skill and experience, those who had the interests of the game at heart advised the holding of a tournament, open alike to Northern and Southern men. Such an event took place for the first time under the auspices of the Southern Association, in the fall of 1888, and with a recognition of the National Association. It was held at the Highlands Country Club, a short distance from Washington, and proved to be eminently successful, both as to play and sociability. The men from the North were entertained at the Highlands Club. Mr. Fred Mansfield, of Boston, won the first prize and the championship of the Southern States in singles, while he and his partner, Mr. Hoppin, won in doubles. The effect of this tournament has been a decided improvement in the Southern players, who now stand on a more even footing with the experienced Northern cracks.

The position of Mr. Post was peculiar. The acknowledged champion of the South, by his defeat of Bonsal, he enters the Highland tournament and submits to defeat and the loss of the championship. Waiving all prior rights to that honor, he showed the extreme courtesy of a Southern gentleman, by which his reputation for skill is not lessened, while his popularity is enhanced. This event has now become a fixture, and will yearly attract leading players to Washington.

Another tournament is held earlier in the season at the Capitol, limited to District players.

FRED S. MANSFIELD.

This event deserves comment from the fact that it this year had for its entries sixty-three men, which exceeds in number any tournament entries ever known in the North.

This year an increased number of Northern men visited Washington, and the Southern championship was successfully defended by Mr. Mansfield. The final matches were played at the grounds of the

Bachelors' Club in Washington, instead of at the Highlands, where the rest of the tournaments took place. While the grounds at the Bachelors' are superior to those at the Highlands, a change of this kind is not in accordance with the rules regarding the holding of tournaments. Certain exigencies may furnish excuse for such an innovation, but the object of the committee in this instance, to increase the gate receipts by the change, was not favored by the players. Mr. C. J. Post won the singles, and, with his partner, Mr. M. F. Prosser, secured the doubles prize. A pleasant visit to the Columbia Athletic Club, the leading tennis club in Washington, was enjoyed by many of the contestants, and it is hoped that next year this organization may undertake the holding of the Southern tournament and promote further the interests of lawn tennis in the South.

The subject of Southern tournaments would not be complete without the mention of the so-called Tropical Championship, held annually at St. Augustine, Florida. It occurs in the month of March, and attracts many expert players. This year the entries included Messrs. O. S. Campbell, Deane Miller, A. E. Wright, R. V. Beach, E. A. Thomson, and Stuart Smith. It was my pleasure to witness their merry departure from New York by boat. Less merriment may have characterized the stormy voyage, but their visit was both memorable and enjoyable. Mr. Campbell won first prize, and, meeting the then champion, Mr. Trevor, easily gained the title of Tropical Champion.

The last event in the lawn tennis season is the Intercollegiate tournament, held soon after the college terms begin in the fall. It was for this that the Intercollegiate Association was formed. Two or more representative men are sent each fall from the leading universities and colleges, to fight for tennis laurels for themselves and their *alma mater*. The neutral grounds chosen are those of the New Haven Lawn Club, and the event there has now become an important fixture. As most all our crack players either are or have been college men, the subject of collegiate tennis blends with the general history of the game.

The greatest experts have not, as a rule, reached the acme of their skill while in college, and to those who there have excelled in the game, interest does not cease on receiving their diplomas, which is likely to happen in the case of the college ball player or oarsman. Mr. Philip

S. Sears, of Harvard, stands preëminently ahead in these contests, having defeated in finals, in 1887 and 1888, Mr. O. S. Campbell. The latter, however, with Mr. Hall as his partner, last fall secured for Columbia the double prize. A remarkable feature that has characterized these events is the absence of the boyish spirit of rivalry that amounts even to animosity in many other college sports. "Rah! Rah! Rah!" is not heard, and brilliancy in play never lacks applause, given alike by the wearers of blue or crimson. It was a pretty sight in years past to see Messrs. Brinley and Paddock when matched against the Sears twins. The former played with superior skill, but in point of grace nothing has won more admiration on the tennis courts than the play of these two brothers. They used to look alike, and always appeared on the court in similar dress; and to tell which was Philip and which Herbert has often been an interesting problem for the spectators.

The following is a list of the American championships and the winners:—

HOWARD A. TAYLOR.

Singles.—United States championship, 1889, Henry W. Slocum, Jr.
Middle States championship, 1889, Howard A. Taylor.
New England States championship, 1889, Henry W. Slocum, Jr.
Western States championship, 1889, Charles A. Chase.
Southern States championship, 1889, Fred Mansfield.

Long Island championship, 1889, Howard A. Taylor.

Intercollegiate championship, 1889, R. P. Huntington, Jr.

Doubles.—United States championship, 1889, Messrs. Slocum and Taylor.

New England States championship, 1889, O. S. Campbell and Valentine G. Hall.

Southern States championship, 1889, C. J. Post and M. F. Prosser.

Long Island championship, 1889, Howard A. Taylor and J. S. Clark.

Intercollegiate championship, 1889, O. S. Campbell, and A. E. Wright.

From 1881 the winners at Newport and runners-up are as follows:

WINNER.	RUNNER-UP.
1881—R. D. Sears.*	W. E. Glyn.
1882—R. D. Sears.*	C. M. Clark.
1883—R. D. Sears.*	Dr. James Dwight.
1884—R. D. Sears.	H. A. Taylor.
1885—R. D. Sears.	G. M. Brinley.
1886—R. D. Sears.	R. L. Beeckman.
1887—R. D. Sears.	H. W. Slocum, Jr.
1888—H. W. Slocum, Jr.*	H. A. Taylor.
1889—H. W. Slocum, Jr.	Q. A. Shaw.

PART III.

The degree of prominence that the game of lawn tennis has gained among our sports in so short a period calls for an explanation other than the records of tournaments, and players can furnish. It lies in the merits of the game itself. A mere diversion wins popular favor temporarily, and games of skill are admired by all, especially when combined with it are the elements of strength and agility. I affirm that in the game of tennis all four of these qualities—namely, diversion, skill, strength and agility—are most happily united. This proposition

---

* These years the champion played in the all-comers.

applies not to the batting of a ball without design, or even desire for exercise, on a so-called tennis court of ruts and side hills, but to the game of a club player of average ability and earnestness, and with suitable equipments.

When Major Wingfield invented the game of tennis in England, he little thought of the scientific developments in store for it, nor did he live to see the game as it is now played. He used a net six feet high instead of three feet (the present regulation), and the method of play was otherwise crude compared with that of to-day. A study and analysis of the methods and rules of tennis shows it to be most perfectly designed at once for athletic exercise, interesting amusement and unlimited use of skill and judgment.

All the good points of the ancient hand-ball, of court tennis and racquets are involved, to a greater or less extent, in lawn tennis. The first principle of the game is to pass a ball by use of a bat or racket over a net into the opponent's court. The ball weighs about two ounces; the bat, about fourteen; the net is three feet at the center and three and a half at the ends, while the opponent's court (in singles) is a rectangle thirty-nine feet by twenty-seven feet.

These measurements appear arbitrary, but they are really not so, for any slight changes in them would, in my mind, tend to defeat the purposes of the game—namely, exercise, exertion of skill, and strength.

Running is an important feature in tennis. The theoretical possibility of a man's reaching difficult balls is now far from a reality, and a foot more in width or length would increase the running at the expense of skill or strength in the strokes, while to contract the size of the court would transform the game into a volleying game, exclusive of other strokes. Next, it is asked why the net should be three feet high. Various answers may be given. One is, that experience proved that the six-foot net of Major Wingfield was too high. Then, again, swift balls must be gauged in accordance with the limits of the court, and, if they pass a net much over three feet, are liable to go out of court. Volleying, too, requires a net about waist high. In fact, this is the minimum height for a net, and it is the perfect correlation in the dimensions of both net and court that adapts these elements to the player and the game.

In playing, the racket should be held by the extreme end of the handle, and in such a way that both fore-hand and back-hand strokes may be executed with slight, if any, movement of the grip. Nor is it necessary that a tight grip be taken until just before hitting the ball. The racket is an additional third joint to the arm, and, like the elbow, should vary in rigidity as occasion requires. The variety of strokes to be made is infinite, and, at the approach of the ball in play, judgment and quick decisions are required.

E. G. MEERS.

A novice at the game invariably puts a ball far outside the court lines, but by practice his strokes become tempered, not in force but in direction. The first impulse of a beginner is to hit the ball, regardless of his position or the manner in which he plays the ball. This is not, technically speaking, a stroke. Plenty of time should be taken before the actual contact of ball and racket, wherever possible, for a few seconds then are exceedingly useful for determining the direction of the stroke and planning out the next method of most effective play.

Mr. E. G. Meers, while watching the game of Mr. Shaw, at Newport, was heard to make the expressive and terse remark: "He plays strokes," These three words are instructive as defining what is called good form of play, and, coming from so great an authority as Mr. Meers, should be of weight. Antithetical to the word "strokes" is the slang expression, "stabs;" and here we have in a nutshell the secret of superiority of practiced tennis players over men of capability, but with want of form. "Stabs" may be successful in single cases, and well executed "strokes" may fail to score.

An incident is told of W. Renshaw, quite to the point. In driving a ball it often hits the top of the net, and then goes over. At a famous match at Wimbledon, Mr. Renshaw won a decisive point in this manner. His opponent made a remark after the match, implying that it was a lucky stroke, at which Mr. Renshaw was exceedingly indignant, and rightly so. He made the "stroke" properly. His duty was done. The difference of an inch or two in the elevation of the ball was alone to decide the issue. Had it fallen into the net instead, no criticism could be made of its skillful execution, nor could the plea of luck be allowed by Mr. Renshaw.

Years of practice may be needed in acquiring a high degree of skill in this respect. Agility and quickness in the movements of the body are necessary. Design, also, is an important factor. Strokes are of three kinds—volleys (that is, playing the ball before it reaches the ground), half-volleys (or when the ball is taken on a half-bound), and ground strokes proper (where the ball is allowed to bound its full height). To decide which of these methods to adopt in a particular case requires keen judgment.

Outside of the laws of lawn tennis mentioned further on, no rules exist governing an individual's play. The variety of methods and styles noticeable among our best players is acquired by ingenuity and by habit. It is a proof, too, of the scientific nature of the game. How to play in good form cannot be learned from books, nor from the "cheap wisdom of advice." Practice and observation are the two great teachers of tennis. The writer is out of practice, but his opportunity and pleasure of several years' observation on tennis courts may convey some hints as to the style of the leading players.

Mr. R. D. Sears, in his seven years of supremacy, was an ideal tennis player. To criticise him is to attack the theory of tennis. His strokes are clean, seldom cutting the ball except in service. With a preference for volleying whenever possible, his position is close to the service line. In running he takes short steps, thus maintaining always that erect position of body so characteristic of him. A significant saying is ascribed to him: "Keep your eyes on your opponent, and both feet on the ground." In the use of his bat the elbow, when possible, is held pretty close to his body. His grace and skill in making difficult strokes, with his body nearly erect, and his eyes directed toward his opponent, are inimitable but instructive.

Dr. Dwight's long experience in this country and in England upon courts makes him an authority on, as well as a practical exponent of, "form." He puts force in his strokes as much from the use of his body as by wielding his bat. In volleying he reaches well forward, not waiting for the ball to reach him, by which the weight of his body comes in play. This avoids too much exertion of the forearm and wrist, which might lessen the accuracy of the stroke.

Mr. Slocum is a splendid runner, and makes few errors. His volleying is not so strong as are his ground strokes. Using the best possible method of taking the ball, he almost always returns it. Some of his drives are very swift, but are made always with care and intent. Unlike Dr. Dwight, Mr. Slocum relies chiefly on strength of arm, and executes the stroke like Mr. Sears, with his elbow near the body. His service is both graceful and easy.

Mr. Shaw's brilliancy is in his swift and effective driving. He waits

Q. A. SHAW.
(Winner of "All-Comers," Newport, 1889.)

generally till the bounce of the ball is about three-quarters over, and then, with a free swing of his racket, takes the ball as it descends. His service is second in violence only to Mr. Taylor's.

Mr. Campbell serves a slow ball, and at the first opportunity runs up to the net and volleys. By a quick movement of the bat he drives a ball across the court in a direction least expected by his opponent. He is not so strong in ground strokes, but, being light on his feet, he covers the court successfully.

When Mr. Taylor serves a ball, spectators tremble for safety. He takes two strides from behind the base-line, delivering a terrific first service. If it strikes in the court, an ace is likely to be scored for him. He drives balls far back into the court, and high ones are smashed by him with violence.

Many other characteristics, better noticed than described, mark the game of these and other of the leading cracks. If the elements of luck or mere brute strength entered into tennis to any extent, it is evidently impossible that so few of the large field of experts could year after year excel. Young men have indeed come to the front, but at the same time an increased steadiness in form and the methods of Mr. Sears and Dr. Dwight are noticeable in their achievements. What other explanation can there be of the victories of Mr. Sears? For seven years he was holder of the championship. Others during this period possessed certain qualities in tennis equally as brilliant as his. But the secret is here: Every movement of Mr. Sears is designed. No useless exertion of strength is made by him, while his method of making strokes is the result of consummate skill.

The constitution, by-laws and rules adopted by the United States National Lawn Tennis Association, the "Decisions" of Dr. Dwight, and "Points" by Mr. Slocum and Mr. Hall, together with certain customs and traditions, constitute the common law of tennis. Yet it would not require more than an afternoon's playing for a novice to grasp all the salient points of the game and understand the knotty questions sometimes arising. To the spectator it is quite different. Those who can watch with indifference a good tennis match are invariably those who have never played themselves nor acquired knowledge of the game. An urchin perched upon a neighboring tree or shed appreciates a "base hit" or a "double play" as keenly, perhaps, as any occupant of the grand stand. But tennis, like billiards, requires of its spectators some slight knowledge of the points of the game in order to discern the leading player, while the better they are versed in its technicalities, the more absorbing is the interest.

It must be admitted, however, that this feature has been a drawback to popular excitement over tennis matches; but, in spite of this, these contests have increased greatly in popularity, purely upon the merits of the game. Any discussion of the rules would neither interest nor enlighten those ignorant of the game, and the average player has already acquired all that is practically necessary. I may cite, however, one peculiar case that happened in July last during the match for the Waterbury cup, which had never been anticipated in the official rules nor covered in any "decisions" or "points for umpires." Mr. Slocum and Mr. Taylor were the contestants. The popular definition of a "return" is to play the ball over the net (striking the net, perhaps) into the boundaries of the opponent's court. The rules contain the expression, "falling in the court." At the time of this match, a gale of wind was blowing. The net consequently bagged, and appeared like a vertical section of a horizontal cylinder. The convex side being toward Mr. Taylor, he played a ball, hitting the top of the net. The ball went over, but lodged in the bottom of the net. The umpire gave the point to Mr. Taylor. I differ with this decision. The ball did not "fall in" Mr. Slocum's court, nor could it be considered a "let." Had the net blown down, a "let" might have been claimed; but here the unusual condition of the net existed throughout the match, so that such a claim was waived by both contestants. In point of fact, the ball resting in the net would, if allowed to drop, have fallen in Mr. Taylor's portion of the court.

One other subject pertaining to the rules deserves mention; that is, foot-faults. "The server shall serve with one foot on the base-line or perpendicularly above said line." This rule, if not followed, requires a fault to be called. It is very easy to step an inch or so over the line, and this strictly constitutes a foot-fault; yet to a player nothing is more annoying than to have a fault of this nature called when he has made no intentional error. Custom, therefore, has modified this rule, so that it is usual and proper for umpires to give at least one warning to the server in such cases.

The office of an umpire in a tennis match is by no means a sinecure, nor is it an enviable position during a five-set match on a hot day. . The difficulty of detecting positively where a swift ball strikes is vastly greater than it seems to those who have not served in that capacity. The importance, too, of these decisions is often vital to the results in close contests. It is often the case that gentlemen who are good players make poor umpires. Promptness in decisions is needed, and under no circumstances should an umpire call out while the ball is in play, unless in answer to the player's request, for, if in a close decision he calls "good," the utterance may be mistaken for "out" by a player, who accordingly discontinues his play. Any delay in the giving of a decision is very aggravating to players who possibly, by continuing the game, have exerted useless strength and skill. A loud voice is another requisite in a model umpire.

During the past season I have devoted some little attention to scoring, and the studying of English methods, together with the opportunity of practically applying them, has been an interesting task. The ordinary plan of taking games and sets in the order won is generally sufficient to show the results and the closeness of the match. But by the English method a complete analysis and summary is given of strokes won and lost. There are two methods now used in England. The first is to take note of every stroke made in each game of each set, crediting it to the winner by a symbol indicating how the point was won. On this method the results arrived at may be shown as follows:—

Points won: A, 161; B, 144:—

	A.	B.
Played out of court,	42	54
Played, but not over net,	48	69
Not played, *i.e.*, passed by opponent,	51	36
Double faults,	3	2
Total points lost,	144	161

Added to this may be a record of aces won in service.

The second method of analysis is much more complex, and in the same degree more interesting to players. In this analysis, by strokes won we do not include those won by errors of the opponent, but limit it to those strokes which, by accuracy of placing, swiftness or otherwise, are almost impossible to be returned; and by strokes lost are meant balls knocked out of court or into the net by error—that is, where a use of reasonable skill might have avoided the errors. Double faults are also included, and, in addition, a classification of strokes into volleys and ground strokes can be made. By this method, using, of course, more symbols in scoring, we can get the following summary:—

STROKES WON.	A.	B.
Ground strokes,	16	10
Volleys,	9	4
Services,	11	3
Totals,	36	17

STROKES LOST.	A.	B.
Ground strokes out of court,	15	27
Ground strokes into net,	14	16
Volleys out of court,	20	19
Volleys into net,	17	22
Double faults,	4	1
Totals,	70	85

Points won, A, $85 + 36 = 121$.
" " B, $70 + 17 = 87$.

This last method can be of use to players, if not of popular interest, giving to the former a means of knowing just where their weakness and their strength may lie.

PART IV.

An attractive feature of the game of lawn tennis is its adaptability to both sexes as a sport, as well as a pastime. It is perhaps the only outdoor sport of an athletic character that invites the skill of lady contestants, and at the same time assures perfect conformity with the rules of propriety and of etiquette. The graceful exercise, aside from any high developement of skill, makes the game exceedingly popular with ladies, so that in point of numbers little disparity exists between the players of each sex. In fact, in visiting the great parks of New York, Brooklyn, and other cities where tennis is daily played during the season, we find a decided predominance of female players. Yet in the history of our tournament playing they figure less prominently, in consequence of the violence of exercise required in match games. Skill is not lacking, but the physical exertion is the retarding element in these contests.

In the case of English lady players it is quite different. English girls begin tennis practice while very young, and from that very fact excel. Miss Lottie Dod, the champion lady player of England, is a remarkable instance. Athletic training and constant practice early in life have made her, though still in her teens, the leading female tennis expert of the world. The custom in America has been in marked contrast. Young ladies, not girls, play in our tournaments, displaying abilities that, if put in use earlier, might have rivaled those of the female experts of England; and yet so few have devoted many years of practice to tennis that we can boast of comparatively few lady "cracks" in this country.

An annual tournament for the championship in ladies' singles takes place at Philadelphia. This event is held under the auspices of the Association, and the records made in the last three years are briefly as follows: At the Wissahickon tournament in September, 1887, given by the Philadelphia Cricket Club, Miss U. F. Hansell won the title of champion. The following year Miss Bertha L. Townsend, as challenger, defeated Miss Hansell with ease. This contest took place at the Chestnut Hill Lawn Tennis Club Tournament, Philadelphia, June 12th. In 1889 the championship was successfully defended by Miss Townsend, who by these victories ranks as the best lady tennis player in America.

Next to her should be mentioned Miss Adeline K. Robinson. She was defeated at the Chestnut Hill tournament by Miss Townsend, in June, 1888, after a very close match, and, though she did not appear at the championship contest this season, her numerous victories at Staten Island and elsewhere entitle her to a high position among lady experts.

Of the other skillful and successful lady contestants may be mentioned Miss Gertrude Williams, Miss Voorhees, Miss Smallwood, the Misses Roosevelt, Miss Lente, and Miss Wright. Besides the singles annual events occur in ladies' doubles and in mixed doubles. Less violent exercise is required in these latter contests, and this conformity to a woman's physique adds both popularity and interest. Between September 19th and October 17th, 1887, no less than seven ladies' tournaments were held at the Belmont Cricket Club, Philadelphia. The handicap doubles was won by Miss Townsend and Miss Ballard. During the same week the Misses Roosevelt carried off the double prize at the New Hamburg Invitation Tournament, while a similar prize was taken by Miss Robinson and Miss Clark at the New York Tennis Club grounds. The next week Miss Hansell and Miss Knight were successful at Wissahickon, and at the open tournament of the Ladies' Out-Door Sports Clubs, held at Livingston, Staten Island, a brilliant double match was won by Miss Robinson and Miss K. Smith, the former also taking the single prize. The same team followed up this victory by again winning at the contests of the Far and Near Lawn Tennis Club Tournament, Hastings-on-Hudson, N. Y.

The seasons of 1888 and 1889 were not so brilliant in respect to double tennis among ladies, though many good matches have been witnessed. The Misses Roosevelt came to the front as the most successful team by defeating Miss Robinson and Miss Ward, after a closely contested match at the Chestnut Hill Tennis Club in June, 1888. Their success is due greatly to their custom of playing together. The changing of partners, so frequent in double tennis, both in these and in male contests, is a drawback to any high development in team playing. Men have, as a rule, better opportunity to practice together in the double game, while with the other sex it is seldom the case that any long practice is had in team playing. In consequence of this diversity of partners, no championship events are held in ladies' doubles in America, as they are in England; yet it is not unlikely that such contests will soon be authorized by the National Association, in view of the fact that the double game is eminently suited to female players.

Mixed doubles have in the last few years taken a prominent place in the history of tennis. These contests annually take place among the other events of our largest tournaments, forming an interesting feature. Assisted by a gentleman partner, the lady has less running to do, and what muscular exertion is required of her may be modified according to her physical strength and the ability of her partner. Narragansett Pier,

Staten Island, Southampton, New Hamburg, and the grounds of the Philadelphia and New York Clubs have been the frequent battle fields for these interesting contests. From the natural fact of a man's superior strength, a team of mixed doubles is not evenly balanced in respect to the skill of the two partners, and the delicacy or etiquette (whichever it may be called) which moderates a man's play against a female opponent is another important factor that detracts from the scientific value of this form of tennis. Yet what is lacking in skillful display is more than counterbalanced by the pleasant and exciting diversion. A social interest is always attached to these, as well as other events in which ladies participate, and the existence of such contests in connection with our large tournaments is in a great measure a means of preserving the refinement and unprofessional character that distinguish lawn tennis.

With the playing of the Intercollegiate Tournament at the New Haven Lawn Club in October, the American tennis season is brought to a close. In-door tennis, however, is indulged in by enthusiastic experts throughout the winter. Playing on boards differs widely from the game on turf or earth courts. The light is not so good, and the bounds of the ball are at a smaller angle from the surface of the court, though accurate in direction. From in-door tennis much pleasure and exercise have been derived, not only by experts, but also by men to whom confinement to office work affords no other recreation during the winter months. For this purpose armories are best adapted. That of the Seventh Regiment, in New York, and the Twenty-third, in Brooklyn, have been annually used for tournaments, as well as daily practice. In addition to these facilities is the Tennis Building on Forty-first street, New York, where regular in-door tennis clubs meet on certain days of the week, having the exclusive use of its courts. Besides the many leading out-door players, Messrs. Le Roy, Raymond, and Trevor have shown especial skill upon boards.

The records of in-door tennis from 1885 are: At Seventh Regiment, January 1st, 1885—Singles, won by H. G. Trevor; Doubles, won by R. L. Major and W. P. Wurts. At the Tennis Building, February 22d, 1885—Doubles, won by H. S. Le Roy and T. Maitland. At Tennis Building Tournament, February 22d, 1886—Doubles, won by H. W. Slocum, Jr., and J. W. Richards. At Seventh Regiment Armory,

December 25th, 1886—Singles, won by V. G. Hall; Doubles, won by Messrs. Hall and Trevor. At the Seventh Regiment Armory, February 22d, 1887—Doubles, won by H. W. Slocum, Jr., and G. W. Richards. At the Tennis Building, February 22d, 1888—Doubles, won by C. E. Sands and Le Roy. At the Twenty-third Regiment Armory, December 25th, 1888—Singles, J. W. Raymond.

PART V.

In accounting for the rapid growth in popularity of lawn tennis and its present status of success, we have not only to consider the merits of the game, already discussed, but also to recognize the great variety of pleasant relations and events incident to the season's playing. From a pastime of this nature pleasant acquaintances are often made, either in participating in private games, or in the associations incidental to membership in tennis clubs. Community of interest in occupations of any kind promotes instinctively a fellow feeling. This is preëminently true in the case of those devoting themselves mutually to the acquirement of skill upon lawn-tennis courts. Even in the most important contests animosity between opposing players is entirely absent, and the heat of rivalry mars but temporarily, if at all, the friendly relations so conspicuously existing. Moreover, among our tournament players a sort of affinity exists. They comprise only a small portion of the tennis players in the country, yet, coming as they do from different sections and meeting under so many varying circumstances, they become allied into a strong band, piratical, perhaps, in respect to prizes, but most congenial in their personal relations. The defeated console one another, while the winners are mutual admirers of one another's prowess.

Another most delightful feature is the intercourse between members of different clubs, promoted by visiting players at tournaments or otherwise; and, aside from the social aspect, this has an important bearing upon the development of the game. In the case of a local club, it is wonderful how great a stimulus is given to the general play of the members, either by an open tournament or by the playing of one or more visiting experts. New strokes are invariably seen and learned. To none is it more beneficial than to the younger or junior members of the local club whose imitative faculties are more active. As language is said to change with the seclusion of a class of people in one locality, so the dozen or more men playing with one another exclusively fall into habits of carelessness that may distort the character of the game. The stronger players do not always exert themselves by practice with the less skillful, and find themselves unconsciously copying their erroneous methods. But after a tournament, or the chance of even watching superior playing, a marked improvement and increased zeal are shown. In this connection may be mentioned the influence that English experts have had over the game in this country. The years spent abroad by Dr. Dwight, while his absence was much regretted, proved of inestimable benefit to tennis in this country. Derived from him and his experience were the most important precepts that have guided American tennis from its infancy to its present vigorous development. The opportunity of Mr. R. D. Sears to meet the Renshaws and others in the South of France had a like beneficial effect, besides enhancing his individual skill. Yet from the many less valuable descriptions of the play, as is likely where information is derived from hearsay, a number of erroneous ideas became formed regarding the English game. A conspicuous example was in the case of the "Lawford stroke," and many matches have been lost by players attempting this form of play. Mr. Lawford, by long practice, acquired skill in executing a body stroke which caused the ball to revolve in such a way that it would drop into court like the downdrop in baseball. Those using the so-called "Lawford" here, not having had the practical opportunity of witnessing Mr. Lawford's play, erred principally in a too free swing of the arm, in most cases fatal to the success of the stroke. The recent visit of Mr. E. G. Meers, and his participation in the Newport championship tournament, was an important step in the promotion of international contests. His playing was of great merit, and instructive in many ways. By observation of his methods, a practical illustration was given of the English game. From his high ranking in England, his defeat here by Mr. Campbell has no doubt been a great surprise to English players, who have heretofore depreciated the merits of our players.

In general, everything connected with lawn tennis points to a great future for the game in this country. The merits of the game itself, as one of science and skill, alone warrant this prediction, apart from other considerations. But we find convincing evidences when we contemplate the endless number of pleasant features of tennis that distinguish it from other sports or pastimes. Its wonderful freedom from disagreeable features is also marked. Much credit is due the officers of the National Association for their excellent management during the last nine years. The fact that, so far, no serious controversies have arisen does not lessen the importance of these officers. The greatest care should be used in the selection of both officers and committees. Dangers of professionalism or analogous evils that lower the tone of the game are to be constantly warded off, and it may readily be conceived how one or two ill-chosen men on the National Committee might mar, even by their influence, the present degree of refinement characterizing the game. The same care should be observed in choosing officers of individual clubs, and especially in the choice of representatives.

Lawn tennis is still young in America compared with its mature development in England. A glance at the London *Pastime* discloses column after column of tournament records in fine type, together with able editorials and interesting items on the subject. We are not too sanguine in expecting such an improvement in the tennis journalism here before many years, as the clubs and tournaments increase in number and importance. It is not likely that the general public will rave over match games of lawn tennis, as has been the case with baseball games, nor, indeed, is it desirable in any sense.

The strictly amateur character of tennis, in company with the careful guardian of society, has kept this beautiful and healthful sport free from contamination, and raised it to its present high position in popular esteem. In consideration of all these enviable qualities and merits, those interested in the game feel a manifest pride in its welfare, sacrificing time and expense in its advancement. We have, therefore, the assurance that the speed of its progress in future will, as in the past, be redoubled by the devoted energies both of players and of all lovers of lawn tennis.

V.

LACROSSE. *

LACROSSE, though barely forty years old as a white man's game, has nevertheless been played by the Indians for many years. In its old form whole tribes took part, and, with the curious looking sticks, two in number, carried by each man and spurred on to victory by the lashes of the attendant squaws, whose duty it was to urge on the tired or weak hearted braves in the pursuit of the ball, the game waxed fast and furious over the miles of prairie in the northwestern portion of the continent. For many years the game was unknown to the whites, and it was not until about thirty years ago that such men as Dr. G. Beers, now a prominent practicing dentist in Montreal; W. L. Maltby, President of the Montreal Amateur Athletic Association, and others of that kidney braved public opinion and reduced what was then a brutal game to the line of a successful and scientific sport.

The first men who played lacrosse had many difficulties to overcome. At that time there were no enclosed grounds in Canada, the home of the sport, and many times after protracted struggle for victory these pioneers of the game had the lustre of a victory lessened or the poignancy of defeat embittered by the loss of their outer wearing apparel. The first steps to make the game one for white men were taken by Dr. Beers, who is recognized throughout Canada as the father of the sport. Clubs for its practice sprang up; but one of the first to be recognized as a leading spirit was the Montreal Lacrosse Club, which in later years formed the basis and most supporting branch of the now famous Montreal Amateur Athletic Association.

Early in the '60s the Caughnawauga and Saint Regis Indians were the leading exponents of the game, and, following in their footsteps, soon came the Montreal, Toronto and Shamrock Clubs. In those days the Indian was considered the peer, if not the superior, of the white man at the game, and he was allowed to play on an equal footing, the amateur laws not then being so clearly defined as at present—if, in fact, they were defined at all. Increased legislation on this point placed the Indian outside the pale of the amateur, and his presence was only tolerated in the game as a preceptor or a teacher of the art. The improvements to be expected in such a game naturally placed the inquiring white mind on a higher level than the average aboriginal instinct, and in later years we find the white man rapidly assuming the ascendancy and the Indian having descended to the plane of not being the equal of his former pupil. As late as three or four years ago an agitation was raised against the employment of Indians in competition against white men, and slowly but surely they have been ousted from the game of which they were the originators. Now only a solitary match or two in the course of the year proclaims the fact that the Indians were ever experts at the game.

The rules of play are multitudinous, and, from the fact that succeeding conventions of the National Amateur Lacrosse Association and its sister bodies have so tinkered or altered them, the voluminous array is easily represented by many less hundred words of detail. The first rule relates to the crosse (*lacrosse*) which, it is enacted, shall be formed of stick and gut. The stick is in the form of almost a shepherd's crook, and is strung from the point of the crook to about half way down the straight side of the stick. Between that leading string and the stick are woven meshes, on which the ball is deftly caught, retained or thrown.

The game calls for twelve men on a side, who are arranged and technically designated as follows: Goal keeper, point, cover point, three defence fielders, centre fielder, three home fielders, outside home, and the inside home. These, with a thirteenth man as captain, who directs the attack or rallies the defence, as occasion requires, without being allowed to interfere with the ball in any way or carry a stick, form what is known as a full team. The game is started by the two centre fielders facing; that is, kneeling in the centre of the field, with faces turned toward the attacking goal; the backs of their sticks are laid flat on the ground, so that the backs of the gut will be laying against each other. Between these the umpire lays the ball, and, at the command: "Play," the sticks are drawn sharply past one another, and the ball is then in play. There is no rule of off side in lacrosse, and, apart from the fact that the game requires that each man shall be checked or covered by his opponent, there is absolutely no restriction as to the position the men will take during the game. Long experience has proven that a team, to be successful at a game of lacrosse, has to combine its efforts. In this line a number of unwritten rules have come into force, which are thoroughly recognized and acted upon by leading exponents.

DR. GEORGE BEERS;
(Father of the game.)

Lacrosse is practically a contest of man against man from start to finish. Immediately after the ball is taken out at the face it is thrown up to the home of the player who has been successful at the preliminary stage of the game. At each end of the field, about one hundred and twenty yards apart, are placed goals, two in number, six feet high and six feet apart. To score, it is necessary that the rubber ball with which the game is played be put between these posts from the front side, whether by an opposing player or after hitting one of the defence sticks is not material, the fact of its going through constituting one goal. The defence, as its name implies, is entrusted with the task of protecting the flags from the assaults of the opposing fielders. It is arranged as follows: Between the flags stands the goal keeper, who is alone. In front of him stands the point "covered," as the technical term has it, by the inside home of the opposing side. The defence has cover point covered by the outside home, and the fielders in their order are similarly attended by the corresponding home fielders. Thus on each end of the field it can be seen that the goal tender is alone, and, in cases of a close rally at the flags, there is one extra man left uncovered The point is to work down the ball from side to side, and, by successfully uncovering, or, in other words, getting away from their man, to give the fielders a chance to have a short goal with nobody to interfere with its passage through. The ground rules by the National Amateur Lacrosse Association enact that in stopping a player an opponent must not strike at the body, head or face of the incoming player, but must try and check the stick, or oppose his body from the front in such a way as to impede the course of the attacking fielder. It is the neglect of this rule wherein the objection to lacrosse comes, and which has made it unsuccessful with many classes of American athletes. The ball is made of solid sponge rubber, and is about three quarters the size of a baseball, while weighing fully as much. It is not deadened, and is a dangerous missile among inexperienced players. In matches it is provided by the home club, and, as in the case of baseball, it becomes the property of the winning club. The only other points necessary for the public to understand in connection with the game is the fact that for fouls a player may be ruled off the field and his side compelled to finish the game or match alone without him at the discretion of the referee.

The game is under the control of an official selected by the captains of the opposing teams, whose duty it is to see that the opposing players do not wear spikes in their shoes, have nothing but wood or gut on their sticks, and fully comply with the other requirements of the game. In him is vested the right to call the game on account of darkness, suspend play for any infringement of the rules, and apply the penalties in such cases made and provided. He is the sole judge of all points of field play, and has the duty of reporting to the National Amateur Lacrosse Association executive the result of all matches in which he has been empowered to act. Before the game he is handed by the opposing captains a certificate of authority, accompanied by a list of the players, with a written declaration from the president and secretary of the club, which they represent, that they have been *bona fide* members of those organizations for thirty days prior to the match, and that they are members in good standing of the club. In case that either captain is not satisfied that the requirements have been lived up to, he has the right of challenge, and, should he have sufficient proof at hand, he may protest the playing of the game, and can follow up this action with a statement of the case to the executive of the governing body and have the point adjudicated on. An umpire is stationed at either end of the field, whose duty it is to say if the ball goes through the goals.

IN FULL RUN AT LACROSSE.

Up to 1885 the system of running lacrosse matches in Canada was regulated by challenges, the system allowing a club to play once every six weeks for the flags, and not playing oftener with any club than in that time, nor could they play if any club ranked as a senior had a challenge in ahead of them. Thus, when the Shamrocks of Montreal, the Montrealers, the Torontos and the Independents, of Montreal, were the only clubs in the championship series, the few contests then played for the championship were gala occasions, and were attended by the sport loving citizens of the Dominion from far and near. Those were the days when the Shamrocks of Montreal were in their glory, and for fourteen years, with very few exceptions, they held the coveted pennant which represented the championship of the world. They were composed of mechanics, who, with the strength and agility of the descendants of the Emerald Isle, lent to the national game of Canada a power which left far in the rear the skill of the clerical classes of the Canadian athletes. They almost had a monopoly of the game of lacrosse, and Canadian athletes of the present day speak in feeling terms of the early days of John Hoobin, Con Maguire, Johnnie Farmer, McKeon and others who won for the Shamrock Lacrosse Club the premier honors of the lacrosse world.

WM. G. HODGSON, OF MONTREAL TEAM.

With the advance of the game came the desire for more lacrosse and a better system of playing it. It was then that the National Amateur Lacrosse Association had its meeting in the spring of 1885, and decided that in future the championship should be determined by the result of a series of three games, in which all the clubs entitled to the senior ranks should compete with one another. At that time the clubs eligible to the honor were the Shamrock, Montreal, Toronto, Ontario, and Cornwall. Of these, two clubs were located in Montreal, two in Toronto, and one on the borders of Ontario, near the boundary line of Quebec. The Montrealers opened that season with a match in Toronto against the Torontos, and, with one of the weakest teams that ever represented "the winged wheel," they were beaten three straight games on the Rosedale grounds of the Toronto Lacrosse Club. This defeat occasioned the strongest feelings of discontent among the members of the Montreal Club, and from the ranks of the juniors were taken W. Hodgson, James Michaud, and Thomas Carlind, who were destined to become three of the best known of the Canadian Lacrosse players. It was a wonderful season for the club, for the record shows that of twenty-eight games played but one was lost, that being on the occasion of their first appearance. They celebrated the year's victory by a trip through the United States, on which I had the honor of being one of the players. Since that time the series has been adhered to; but, in the year 1887, for a palpable injustice, the Toronto Lacrosse Club seceded from the parent association, and, with the Ontario Lacrosse Club and the Western Clubs, formed the Canadian Lacrosse Association. The split of interest thus occasioned was most disastrous to the financial standing of the Torontos, and was also a serious drawback to the welfare of the Eastern Clubs, so that it was not strange that this season found amalgamation again with representation by the Montrealers, Shamrocks, Torontos, Ottawas and Cornwalls.

In their difference from the Canadian Lacrosse Association the Toronto Lacrosse Club instituted a new style of regulating the game. Under the old system a match was won when one of the teams engaged won three goals, or if the match was determined by darkness and the score was two to nothing in either team. It often happened that in a game, through the element of chance, which enters into lacrosse more than into any other game, the spectators had reason to complain that they did not see the worth of their money. In one case which I recall to mind, the game was over before the stream of people had finished getting into the grounds. The match was that ever memorable one between the Torontos and Shamrocks, on the grounds of the latter. With this in view, the Toronto Lacrosse Club strongly favored legislation that would allow of a game being divided into two time limits, similar to that in vogue in football, and reckoning the result of a game by the number of goals won inside the allotted space. Thus a certain amount of play was insured, and the opposite extreme of a game of seven hours was an utter impossibility.

The game in the United States never amounted to very much, for many reasons. Perhaps the chief of these has been that Americans have really no idea what the game is like. The teams which have played it in the United States have always been of the "scratch" order, and on the occasions when good teams have visited us, they have been matched against those of such inferior calibre that a contest was out of the question. To illustrate this point, I might refer to the visit of one of the Montreal teams, in 1885. On that occasion the team was made up of seven of the regular men and five substitutes, who would not have found a place upon a third or fourth rate team in the home of the game. This team started from Canada after the close of a very hard season, and, though the discipline of the team was, as upon all similar occasions, greatly relaxed, and the proverbial "seeing the town" did not tend to elevate the physical standard of the men, they had no difficulty in walking away with what were then very strong representative American teams. They played games in New York, Baltimore, and Boston, winning all with the greatest of ease. In the former city, the matches were against the Staten Islanders, then called the New York Lacrosse Club, under the direction of Erastus Wiman. They were complete walkovers. The next games were against the Druids of Baltimore, who were promising aspirants for the championship of the United States,

WILLIAM A. DAVIS.

They were almost as easily defeated. Next came the Harvard team at Boston, and so complete was the mastery of the Canadians that the team never changed ends in the match, their defence acting as the home in successive goals. The last game of the tour was played against a picked team of Boston players, including such strong men as Messrs. W. A. Davis, the Ross brothers, J. K. Stimson, Clancey,

Boardman, and Andy Ritchie, the latter a Canadian who promised to become one of the best players in the country.

By far the most important event in the history of Lacrosse in the United States, was the visit of the American team to the British Isles in 1884. The head of the scheme financially was Erastus Wiman, and the management rested in the hands of H. H. Balch, of New York, who as a Canadian newspaper man gained his knowledge of the game. He was also captain of the team and with Hermann Oelrichs, deserves credit for the work done. The team was made up as follows: Goal, F. S. Wheeler, N. Y. L. C.; Point, David Brown, N. Y. L. C.; Cover Point, H. G. Penniman, Druid L. C.; Defence Field, E. P. Cottle, Yale U. L. C.; W. A. Davis, Union L. C. of Boston, and J. C. Gerndt, N. Y. U. L. C.; Centre, Dr. J. K. Simson, Union L. C.; Home Field, G. C. Nichols, Harvard; J. A. Stuart, Calumet L. C., of Chicago, and S. J. Poe, Princeton L. C.; Outside Home, A. D. Ritchie, N. Y. L. C.; Inside Home, S. M. Johnson, Union L. C.; Substitutes, H. W. Hall, and J. A. Hodge, Jr., of Princeton.

This was a very strong combination from goal to inside home, and was particularly good in the defence and home fields. W. A. Davis was probably the best all around athlete on the team and one of the finest American players I have seen. Had he been "raised" in Canada, he would have been on a champion team. As an all around athlete he was a great success, having won thirty-two prizes out of thirty-five starts. David Brown was another very fine player, and though he never had support of a very high order, he played the position finely. Poe would have made a good lacrosse man, and to this day I can remember the mauling I got when playing against him at Baltimore. He was very short, but wonderfully strong, and had he been a good stick handler, would have made his mark. "Andy" Ritchie, was one of the best Canadian players ever making the United States his field of labor. He was one of the best stick handlers I have seen, was fast and a good judge of long drops. Before the team left for England they played six matches. They beat Yale, Princeton, Harvard, Baltimore, Philadelphia, and a picked team. They sailed May 3rd, and returned to New York, July 6th. The average weight of the team was 153 pounds; age, 23 years, 4 months, and height, 5 feet 9½ inches.

This was a strapping dozen, and during their trip they only lost eight out of fifty-six goals. The record was as follows:

TEAM.	AT	SCORE.	DATE.
Cheshire County,	Liverpool,	4—1	May 19.
Lancashire,	Manchester,	4—0 and 5—0	May 21 and 24.
Yorkshire,	Sheffield,	8—0	May 26.
Notts,	Nottingham,	6—0	May 28.
South of England,	Hurlingham,	7—0	June 7.
Middlesex,	Wanstead,	0—0	June 11.†
Cambridge 'Varsity,	Cambridge,	6—0	June 9.
All England,	Private Banks,	2—0	June 10.
All Ireland,	Belfast,	3—2	June 13.
United Kingdom,	Belfast,	3—5	June 14.*

* Lost.   † Drawn.

Thus they played eleven matches, of which nine were won, one lost, and one drawn.

On their return they met the Torontos, who at that time had just been victorious over the Montreal Shamrocks and were the champions of Canada. The game was on the Polo grounds, and the Toronto team was: Ross MacKenzie, W. S. Hubbell, W. C. Bonnell, J. S. Garvin, J. Drynan, Al Blight, E. H. Gerry, F. W. Garvin, C. A. McHenry, E. Smith, F. Dixon and R. McPherson, with R. B. Hamilton, captain. George Massey was the referee, and the Torontos, as was to be expected, won easily.

American teams have always been composed of a couple of Canadian players, with a number of novices to fill out the twelve, who were depended upon for their knowledge of the game from the not over zealous teachings of their playmates. The game at the American college serves as a sample of that usually played on this side of the border. There every man has been trained to play an individual game, and against the combination of Canadian teams the effect was disastrous. As I have already stated, the difference between the first-class team and one of lesser pretensions lays wholly in the amount of combination which the men show in their work.

To illustrate how the game of Lacrosse should be played, and the composition of a team, I do not know any way to so thoroughly show what I mean as by taking a few of the sample teams which have won fame in Canada, and pointing out the physical ability of each man and his adaptability to his position. Probably the finest and best balanced team that ever played the game was that which the Montreal Lacrosse Club placed in the field in the first year of the series in 1885. That was composed of twelve men, who seemed naturally fitted for the places to which they were assigned, and it is a noted fact that no team has ever played the combination game shown by them. They were perfectly fitted to work together, and the speed of their fielders was never equalled on any other team. In goal was W. D. Aird, who has been recognized as one of the most skillful players ever seen. A magnificent long distance thrower, which is one of the greatest requisites to a goal keeper; a sure stop of thrown balls, and an expert in the art of dodging, he lent strength to the most critical position in the game. Before him stood William J. Cleghorn, known all over Canada as "the horse," from his untiring work and his herculean strength. A man with an enormous reach and wonderful stride, he was able to carry out the inside home of the opposing team in a contest for the ball, and generally left a clear field for a shot at goal, a point of which Aird never failed to take advantage. Thus the inside home had generally to perform the impossible feat of being at two places at once, and the fact that during the season of 1885 a great percentage of the games as won by the Montrealers without losing a goal shows the value of such a combination. John Louson, the cover point, was a heavy set man with a good turn of speed, great strength and a bull dog tenacity of purpose, which earned for him the name of the heaviest checker known to the lacrosse world. In struggles for the ball at close quarters he was invariably victorious, and his wonderful powers of endurance, backed up by those of Cleghorn, made the fate of any home fielder with whom they come in contact anything but enjoyable. Edward Shepherd, who played the position of first defence, had absolutely no speed, but he was one of the most wonderful stick handlers that ever played. From a crowd of three or four players he would invariably secure the ball by the most wonderful dexterity. He had a great faculty of throwing the ball in a very small space, and from his position would lob the ball with unerring certainty in a direct line to his opponent's flag. James Michaud, one of the recent additions to the team from the ranks of the Montreal Juniors, the then invincible champions of the junior series, was a slightly built but powerful young fellow, with wonderful judgment in locating the fall of the ball, and a good deal of speed. His judgment was so great that he usually had the start of five or ten feet on his opponent, and to that end was one of the hardest men to cover on the field. Before him stood Norman J. Fraser, a speedy runner and a very hard man to cover. This defence usually played a very deep game—that is, drawing their opponents a good distance from goal, so as to allow of the great average speed of the men being taken full advantage of. Little did it benefit any team of home fielders to try and close up on the flags, for the stick handling ability of such men as Louson and Shepherd made it almost an impossibility for the ball to pass them. In centre field was David Patterson, one of the coolest players who ever occupied that position. His was no regular position, for at times when the defence needed strengthening he was on hand to relieve them, while, should the home be pressed, or in need of an extra man, he was always there, covering a vast amount of territory and one of the surest stick handlers on the team. The first home field was played by Thomas Carlind, who has never had an equal in the art of dodging. I have seen him carry the ball past six successive players, and, though possessed of no great speed, his training on the Montreal Juniors had been of the kind in which Michaud had been taught, and he usually reached the ball even with, if not before, the men possessed of more speed. He was the kind of player to worry a defence not possessed of the most perfect combination. The only defect he or Patterson had was that neither could make a straight shot at goal, and they were always under the necessity of passing the ball to one of the other fielders, a fact which made them less dangerous than they otherwise would have been. John Patterson, who played the next position and who was later replaced by Archie McNaughton, was a man of great speed, but not with the judgment possessed by his brother. He did the State some service in his day; but in the year 1885, of which I speak, he was not the man he had been. Archie McNaughton, who had been a member of the Montreal Garrison Artillery and who had been one of the first of Montreal's young men to respond to the cry "To Arms" in the Rebellion headed by Louis Riel in the Canadian Northwest, was one of the fastest sprinters ever playing the game. His speed was phenomenal; but perhaps his most dangerous point was his wonderful shots for goal, which were made on the dead run and came in with the force of more than double that of a line throw from third base to the home plate. The next man on the team was W. Hodgson, one of the most perfectly built specimens of humanity I have ever seen. His only fault was that he was too good-natured. He was a perfect lacrosse player, from the fact that he never fouled and never unduly used his great strength. I have never seen his equal. He was a magnificent stick handler, a man almost as fast as McNaughton, and as sure a thrower at goal. He was a tower of strength, and in many games in which he played scored all the goals for his side. One incident in this connection serves to show his ability. I accompanied the team to Toronto on one occasion when the team played against the Ontarios of Toronto. I offered Hodgson a gold medal if he would score the three goals necessary to win the match. It was like the offer to a man to make three home runs in three times at the bat, and Charles Hagar, then one of the strongest adherents of the Montreal team, offered him a medal if he would make two goals. Hodgson got the ball only three times during the game, and scored the three goals. Thomas L. Paton, a young man, but a veteran on a first-class team, plays the difficult position of outside home, and is the trickiest of the lot of home fielders. With only a fair turn of speed, he is the most dangerous man to have the ball in front of the flags at short distance. The inside home of that famous team was John Grant, a medium-sized but powerfully built man, with the wonderful tenacity shown by Louson. He absolutely did not know the word *fail*, and, except that he was a very rough player, was an ideal man in the position.

At the time I speak of the feeling was very strong, as it in fact has always been, between the Toronto and Montreal players, and one little story, which I well remember, will serve more to show how the men regarded each other than volumes of description. W. Hubbell played point for the Torontos, and, of course, covered Grant. They got so bitter in their feeling towards one another that I have seen them at the fence with the ball laying between them, and both so intent on wrestling each other that it lay unheeded. One day, in a match on the Rosedale grounds in Toronto, the men had chaffed each other a good deal about the number of times they would take the ball from each other. At last, after a good deal of rough playing on both sides, Hubbell threatened to lay out his opponent, and when they went to the fence both were so intent on struggling for the mastery that two other men started from their positions and had the real contest for the ball before the other two could make up their minds to look for it.

At the head of the team that year was Fred M. Larmonth, who, as a player himself, thoroughly understood the game, and was determined to win the championship. He schooled his men early and late, and was responsible for much of the combination which gained for them the great record of twenty-seven matches won in twenty-eight played. With him that year was associated W. H. Whyte, who, as president of the club, was naturally very much interested in their success. In every match in which they played Mr. Whyte saw that they were handled by their clubmates with the care given to a race horse, and throughout the season the men were in a perfect state of physical training, without which it is impossible for men to play the game.

There have been many great teams in Canada, but none to my mind which could compare in general excellence with the famous one noticed. The others were chiefly conspicuous for the wonderful power of their defences, while their field and the greater part of their home was weakened thereby. One of the most wonderful instances of this was the Cornwall team, which had a defence equal, if not superior, to that of the Montrealers. In goal was Frank Lally, who had occupied that position for years for the Shamrock Lacrosse Club when they were at their best. A great long distance thrower who propelled the ball with an underhand swing from end to end of the field, a very fair runner in his earlier days, and a magnificent stick handler, he filled the flags well. Before him stood the only colored man who has ever played lacrosse on a champion team in Canada. This was Al Lewis, a clever stick handler, but at times a very vicious player. Hughey Adams occupied the position of cover point, and his magnificent work in playing up to the limit of a man like Hodson, of the Montreal team, earned for him the name of a great defence player. These three men, with George Crites, a wonderfully speedy runner and a man of good judgment, formed what was known as the "stonewall defence," which, after the training of two years in the senior series, was responsible for winning the championship for the town of Cornwall. The only man on the home of exceptional ability was George Tudhope, a player of the Carlind order, with a little more speed than that possessed by the Montrealer.

Another example of a defence team was shown in the Torontos, when Ross MacKenzie was a member. He really was a defence in himself, and I never yet saw the man who could get the ball from him if he ever reached it first. In fact, it was the work of two men to thoroughly check this giant, who stood six feet two, and weighed 190 pounds in condition. For a man of his size he was possessed of great speed, and as a stick handler he had very few superiors. He held the long distance record for throwing a lacrosse ball, and on one occasion threw a ball from behind the flags on the old Ontario Grounds in Toronto clean over the fence, a distance close to 150 yards. His point at that time mentioned was "Watty" Bonnell, who afterwards made a mark as a home player. He was also a very big man, standing six feet and weighing about 165 pounds. He was very speedy, and one of the most dangerous men in a scuffle on the team. Wm. Hubbell, who replaced Bonnell at point, was one of the cleverest

ROSS MACKENZIE.

generals who ever played the position, though he was not generally credited to be. He was not a fast runner, but was a sure catch, and could throw in a very small space—in fact, something of the style of Shepherd of the Montrealers. James Garvin, who played cover point, was a very young man when he joined the team, but, with a tenacity which is a characteristic of him, he stuck to his work until he became one of the best known of the great team which bore the blue of the Toronto Club. These three men, with John Drynan, formed a very strong defence, and, up to the time when Ross MacKenzie gave up lacrosse, it was a terribly hard team to beat.

In the face of an earlier statement that the Shamrock Lacrosse team held the championship with almost no breaks for years, it may be asked how it was that the team of that day was not the finest that ever played the game; but I think this is accounted for by the fact that the tactics of the Shamrocks were really never understood up to late years, and their wonderful combination won more games for them than the individual excellence of the players. They had not by any means a fast team; but every man did his share of the work, and where the ball lit it was almost invariably the case there were two red shirted Shamrocks to one of the opposing side. Their victories were really all won by the concentration of their power, and the game of that time had not been brought to the state of excellence which was found in it in later years. The team was composed of working men, who were held in awe on account of their sturdy make-up by the slighter built clerical classes, and indeed they won on many occasions from the fact of this feeling as much as by superior force of play,

One of the most notable lacrosse matches ever played in Canada was at the close of 1886, when the Montrealers and Torontos had to play off one game in Montreal. This was the basis for the disagreement which made the Toronto Lacrosse Club leave the parent Association and form one on its own account. I need not go into the merits of the case at this date, but will refer merely to the match itself. It was played on neutral grounds at Montreal late in October, and I well remember that the snow was piled up against the fences, while the centre of the field had icy patches which would have made the game a farce if it had not been so sternly real. The Montreal

THE MONTREAL LA CROSSE TEAM CHAMPIONS FOR 1889.

players came on the field with their old colors, but over so many additional wraps that their forms were ludicrous in the extreme. The Toronto players, with less taste for the beautiful, wore overcoats, and the Montreal public, or the few of them who were foolish enough to visit the grounds of the Shamrock Lacrosse Club on that occasion, saw the most melancholy attempt at sport ever perpetrated on an unoffending public. As might be expected where the feeling was so bitter and the conditions so wretched, there was no chance of finishing the game, and, after playing all the afternoon and the Montrealers only scoring one goal, the question was left just where it was, and the match was ordered to be a draw. A few weeks later the executive body of the National Amateur Lacrosse Association ordered the Torontos to come to Montreal again and replay the match. This the Torontos refused to do, and the Montreal Club stepped on the field and won the championship when John Lewis, the referee appointed by the executive body of the association, awarded them the match by default. Happily, the chagrin of the Torontos was not of long standing, for this year they are again found competing in friendly rivalry with their old time opponents.

In the earlier part of this article I stated that the game of lacrosse was subject more to the laws of chance, or rather the disregard of those laws, than any other game in existence. An instance will prove the point. In the year 1887, when, after covering themselves with glory for two years, the Montreal team fell into a rut of poor playing, they had to play a match against the Shamrocks. The game was fixed for the home grounds of the Montreal Club, who had lost their own stand and were playing on the exhibition grounds, a very uneven patch of land in the northern portion of the city. The Shamrocks had a very strong team, and when it came to the Montrealers turn to make up a team they found that the players had so little interest in it that two or three of the best players had not taken the trouble to report at the grounds. Thus, with the team notoriously weak that year, and with three vacancies to be filled by men not considered good enough for the regular team, weak as it was, the Montrealers took the field. The betting was one hundred to thirty on the Shamrocks, and I remember that even money was bet against the chance of the Montrealers taking one game. They went on the field with two of their junior players and another old timer who had not handled the stick for a year. When, after the lapse of five or ten minutes playing, the Montrealers took the first goal, it was thought that the Shamrocks were merely letting them down easily. But when, in an incredibly short space of time, the second and third games were added to the Montrealers' record, the greatest surprise ever seen on a lacrosse field had been passed over, and the Shamrocks could not realize that such a thing could have happened. In a less degree this experience has been repeated, and the glorious uncertainty of baseball is almost an unerring certainty compared to that of the Canadian national game.

WILLIAM L. MALTBY.

In the rise of the sport there are very many names, but four or five will live as long as the game is known. First and foremost is that of Dr. George Beers, the father of lacrosse. When the game was in its infancy hard was his struggle against popular sentiment, the old time idea of lacrosse, as well as of every other sport, being that a young man engaged in its practice was on the straight road to perdition. That the example of such a man as Dr. Beers has been fraught with the greatest good is evidenced by the fact that in every prominent town and city, from the northwest to the eastern coast, inclosed grounds have been set up, and upon Saturday afternoon, the gala day in Canada, the game of lacrosse is witnessed by thousands of people. Another pioneer was Wm. L. Maltby, an old player and a steadfast friend of the game. He held the position of president of the Montreal Amateur Athletic Association, and was largely instrumental in giving the grounds to the Montreal Lacrosse Club, which, for athletic purposes, are second to none in the world. R. B. Hamilton, captain and president of the Toronto Lacrosse Club, when in their prime; Dr. Guerin of the Shamrocks, of Montreal and M. J. Polan of the same club are also men who have a good deal to do with the history of lacrosse. Among the players who will remain in the history of the sport are the Hodgsons, Ross MacKenzie, the Garvins, Con Maguire, Johnnie Hoobin, and W. D. Aird, with others whom I will mention later on.

WM. D. AIRD.

Some of the notable points in the history of the game have been the organization by Dr. Beers of trips to Great Britain and Ireland, and the return of an Irish team to this country. On the first expedition, which was taken in 1876, the idea of Dr. Beers was to advertise Canada through its sports. That the trip was fraught with the greatest good cannot be denied, and though the game of lacrosse was established in England, where there is a vast field for it, the good to the country at large was greater than the mere establishment of the game. This trip was duplicated, but on a more extensive scale, in 1883, when Dr. Beers took a team of Canadian gentlemen and twelve Indians to show how the game was played in Canada. Among the many men who formed the teams on those occasions, the most notable were Ross McKenzie, the star of the last trip; Sam Struthers, Sam McDonald, who now fills an important position in the Central Vermont Railroad office, in Boston; W. Griffin, G. S. Hubbell, F. McIndoe, David Nicholson, F. Garvin, W. D. Aird, Walter Bonnell, J. Craven, W. Cleghorn, T. Hodgson, J. Green, R. Summerhayes, and F. Massey.

Among the red-skins who accompanied the team on both occasions were the famous Big John and his twelve Caughnawauga Indians, including White Eagle, well-known as a long distance pedestrian; Louis Hamrocks, Michel Lefebvre, Cross the River, the Dalliebout Brothers, Strong Arm, and Angus Thomas. The Indians, in 1876, were worthy opponents of the white man; but in 1883, although the team was by no means a strong one, and had been selected more . with an outlook to the physical proportions of the men, than to their lacrosse ability, the Indians were outclassed.

The return trip of the Irish team, in 1887, was looked on with a great deal of interest, as showing how far the pupils of the lacrosse pioneers had improved in the game. As was expected, their first-class team compared very unfavorably with third and fourth rate Canadian combinations, and, while some of them showed individually a good deal of cleverness, their combined effort was not what it might have been.

Among the army of players who gained fame in the lacrosse field are some who have stood pre-eminent in their positions. To take a number of the men and describe them as they were will show a vast difference in their make-up, proving that a man's physical appearance is not always a good criterion for judging. They have been of all sizes, and their work has been characterized by many differences, though in all cases, in the game of lacrosse, as in all games requiring a steady eye and field judgment, the factor of brains has told the tale. Of *goalkeepers*, who like poets are born, not made, there have been five of exceptional ability. First on the list comes Ross MacKenzie, of whose prowess I have spoken before. W. D. Aird was of another stamp, a lacrosse player pure and simple, lacking the bodily strength of MacKenzie, but giving to his work the finish of the most expert stick handler of his day. Thomas Prior, whom death claimed all too early, was a goal-keeper who deserved the title "great." He never intentionally fouled a man, and his hard and earnest work gave strength to the Shamrocks when they needed it most. Of Frank Lally I have already spoken, and to this day he is the stand-by of the Cornwall Club. A goal-keeper who ranks with any of his predecessors in ability is A. Shanks, a student of McGill College. He made his debut in that school which has turned out so many good players, the Montreal Juniors;

and when W. D. Aird gave up the game he assumed the guardianship of the flags, after having been tried and successfully on the home end of the field. He is the fastest goal-keeper playing the game, and his judgment cannot be called in question. Sam Martin, now with the Torontos, is also a clever goal keeper. He is of the type of Shanks.

At *point* more men have made their mark, and a first-class home fielder has the necessary requirements for this position, although it does not necessarily follow that a good point can play on the home end. Among the very best who have ever played the position are J. Hoobin and M. Cregan, who have figured in that position for the Shamrock Club at different stages of its existence. When Ross MacKenzie gave up playing lacrosse, Walter Bonnell assumed the position of point, and his strength and wonderful lacrosse ability gained for him a good name in the position. W. J. Cleghorn is one of the best men that ever played point. He now holds the position of captain of the Montreal Lacrosse team, to which the transition from player is but a step. Lewis, the colored point of the Cornwalls, is another sample of a first-class player, and when at his best he was a star of the first magnitude. *Cover point* is a position for which the requirements are strength and bull-dog courage. Probably the finest man who ever played the position was Toby Butler, who played for the Shamrocks up to about four years ago —a man of great strength and wonderful powers of endurance. He, Hugh Adams, and J. Louson are close contestants for the position of the star at cover point.

Among the *defence fielders* a number have shown wonderful skill, but the latter day has produced more who could play the position scientifically than any of the olden day. One of the best was Con Maguire, who played first defence fielder for the Shamrocks for many years. He was about five feet, ten inches in height, of slight build, but with immense staying powers. In his palmy days there were few men who could run for the ball with him, or who had better judgment in locating long drops. He was a good stick handler, and saved many a game for the old time champions by his coolness and untiring work. One of the men of the present day, who ranks with the very best in the position, is Allan Cameron, who plays on the Montreal team. He is about five feet, seven inches in height, slight but extremely muscular, and one of the fastest men who ever played lacrosse. He came into prominence by his work on the Montreal Juniors, and since his appearance on the senior team he has won golden opinions. He is very speedy and a powerful check. Another man of the same order and similar style of play is James Michaud. George Crites, one of the famous stonewall defence of the Cornwall Juniors, is a more heavily built man, and is, perhaps, a better stick handler than either Michaud or Cameron. He bore the heaviest part of the defence of the Cornwall team in 1887, and was at a disadvantage from the fact that he had to do the most work of any of the defence fielders.

Of the *centre fielders*, which is one of the hardest positions on the field to play, there have been four or five men who have stood out pre-eminently among the best men in the country. David Patterson and Tom Devine were, perhaps, two of the best samples of the way to play the position in the country. Neither possessed very much speed, but no men was better qualified to know what to do in a close position, and in an emergency they could always be counted upon. It was a most interesting sight to see the struggle between the two men when they opposed each other, as they often did, and to choose between them in point of excellence would be a very hard matter.

The *home fielders* have had many first-class men; but among the lot the names of the Hodgson brothers, John Heelan, Archie McNaughton, George Tudhope, Ross Eckhart, Fred Dixon, Charlie Ellard, Cregan, Wattie Bonnell, and Bob McPherson will recall more of the fine points of the position than any other names that can be suggested. W. Hodgson and Heelan were lacrosse players, pure and simple; but the former might have been found at his best position at point, instead of upon the home field. Heelan was probably the finest man who ever played on the home field. He and W. D. Aird divide the question as to which was the harder shot at goal, and Heelan had more judgment than Aird. The outside home has had few better exponents than Tom Paton, the veteran of the Montreals, who has received description already with the famous 1885 Montreal team.

At *inside home* there have been three to whom it is hard to give any special honor over the other. A. Stowe, of the Toronto team, Jack Grant, of the Montrealers, and Tom Daly, of the Shamrocks, were three men to whom it was difficult for any defence player, no matter how great his capabilities to give odds. They were very hard men to check, all being of the terrier class, and depending for their success on the amount of worry that they could give the opposing defence.

Having now disposed of the technical points in the game of lacrosse, I might say a word of the future of the game and its possibilities.

There is no question that lacrosse is one of the most exciting field sports ever seen. I firmly believe it would be an enormous success in the United States, if properly handled. It can never be played as an amateur game, but were teams located in the prominent cities it would have an undoubted success. As a professional game it would allow no lack of interest, and no contest in existence appeals so strongly to the element of excitement.

VI.

POLO.*

IT is generally conceded that the game of polo originated in Japan. Nobody knows just how long ago. A few hundred years more or less did not count for much in that country, before the Western barbarians gave the natives an idea of what progress meant. But the game is of very recent introduction in this country. It was first played here in 1873 or 1874, when it was imported directly from England. Since then it hasn't spread like wildfire, by any means, but it is evident it has come to stay. It can never be a game for the many, because only those can afford to play it who have plenty of leisure, plenty of cash, plenty of pluck, plenty of agility. The two latter qualifications will avail nothing if the two former be lacking. Therefore it must always remain an exclusive game. Yet it is a magnificent game to look at, and is as full of absorbing interest as a sensational novel.

The Westchester Polo Club was the pioneer club on this side of the Atlantic. Among the earliest players in that club who still retain their interest in the game are August Belmont, Jr., Francis R. Appleton, H. L. Herbert and Theodore and Elliot Roosevelt. The leading polo clubs at the present time are the Rockaway Club, the Meadow Brook Club, the County Club, the Orange Club and the Oyster Bay Club. There is also a club at Buffalo, and another at Philadelphia. In recent years polo has been played at Harvard and at Dedham, Mass. Still more recently a club has been organized at Morristown, New Jersey.

---

* By E. L. Snell, of the *New York Herald*.

A BRILLIANT DASH IN POLO.

The Rockaway Club, probably, has the best team. It certainly has the best individual player in the country—Foxhall Keene. In skill and boldness of play, as well as in brilliancy of horsemanship, no other player equals him. He plays to win, and he cares nothing for show. When chasing the ball his two arms work like pump handles, as though he were actually lifting his pony over the ground. It doesn't look very graceful, but it seems to be highly effective in getting there. He is ably supported by Messrs. Cowdin, Hitchcock and others. The leading lights of the Meadow Brook Club are August Belmont, Jr., W. K. Thorne, Stanley Mortimer, H. C. Richmond, Francis R. Appleton and Dudley and Edgerton Winthrop. The first team of the Orange Polo Club is composed of Charles and Emil Pfizer, Douglas Robinson, Jr., Charles L. Knoedler and Powers Farr. The Oyster Polo Club is an offshoot of the Huntington, L. I., Association. The Roosevelts, Frank Underhill and W. E. Tuckerman are among its most active and prominent members. At present the chief activity in polo is at Newport, R. I. The polo player likes a good audience. He gets it at Newport. There his courage and skill are applauded by girls who are as rich as they are pretty.

One of the most interesting features of polo is the dexterity and intelligence displayed by the ponies. They are far from being mere machines. They actually participate in playing the game, and play it, too, with vim and enthusiasm. To play polo creditably to himself and to do justice to the animal he rides, a polo player requires three ponies. These will cost him an average of about one hundred and fifty dollars each. When to this is added the cost of attendance, stabling and transportation to the place where the game is to be played, it can be readily seen that only comparatively wealthy men can indulge in it. It requires leisure. That is the reason why the game has not been transplanted out West. There, if they are not all too poor to play it, they are all too busy. Under the rule of the game a polo pony must not be over 14 hands and 1 inch high. This limit has been adopted because with bigger animals the game would become too dangerous. If a big horse were to jump in among a lot of polo ponies he would knock them and their riders over like ninepins. Besides, increased size is gained at the expense of handiness. Bigger animals would not be nearly so dexterous as the nimble little ones, and with them, therefore, the game would lose much of its charm.

The ideal pony should be full fourteen hands, one inch high, and as stockily built as possible; not young; with a mouth like velvet, that will not pull a pound on the bit; heavy quarters; entirely supporting himself when wheeling on a full run on his haunches; turning as well to the right as to the left; ready to jump ten feet upon the lifting of the rein and the inclination of the rider's heel to his side; not trotting or walking, but going upon the full run from the start; gait low and smooth—what in polo parlance is known as "daisy clipping," and both speedy and hardy. It won't do to sacrifice too much of either of these qualifications to the other. A pony that is extremely hardy and fairly speedy is, in the opinion of most players, better than a pony that is very speedy and not so hardy. The latter is apt to be rank, to plunge and pull too heavily on the bit. If it were necessary to take green ponies and train them for the game, it would take so long that it would be practically impossible to find ponies enough to play the game. But, in fact, they are first trained at something else—herding cattle. A pony that has stood the racket of cattle herding on the plains for six or seven years is already almost qualified to begin polo playing at once, and will pick up the point of the game in no time. The discipline is not dissimilar. At herding cattle the pony acquires speed, strength, endurance and hardness. He learns to wheel rapidly; his intelligence is cultivated; he finds out what he is being used for, and learns to stick close to the steer that is being chased. In polo the ball takes the place of the steer. Then the use of the long whip in herding cattle accustoms him to the subsequent use of the polo mallet about his eyes, ears and forelock.

The ponies used for polo here are the pick of the ponies used by the cowboys in herding cattle. They come from the plains of Wyoming, Indian Territory, Montana, Oregon, the Pan-Handle region of Texas, the vicinity of San Antonio—in fact, from anywhere where a business is made of cattle herding. But the best polo ponies are to be got from the mountainous districts of old Mexico, because traveling on uneven ground sets their bone and muscle better than work on a level stretch of country.

VII.

FOOTBALL.*

IN the good old days when Homer, and Xenophon, and Plato, and any number of other wise chaps were writing text-books for the distress and cultivation of young fellows in undiscovered America, various stalwart contemporaries—unknown, alas! to fame—were establishing a sport that has come to be universally associated with institutions of learning. Such light as history gives upon the subject tends to show that the great academic game of football originated with the nation that furnished also the classic literature which forms the basis of study in the higher schools of to-day. It was a very crude kind of football that the Greeks played—they called it ἐπίσκυρος (episkuros)—and none of the historians of Greece thought it worth while to leave any record of games played or the names of powerful players. All we know is that the ball was an inflated bladder, and that it was propelled entirely by the foot. There may or may not have been goals and a well-defined field, but there were no clubs, and it is not probable that there were any regulations as to the number of players on a side, time of game, and the like.

It is quite possible, of course, that the Greeks introduced the game from some other country, but there is no evidence of it, and the actual origin is of little consequence; yet it is interesting to note that the Romans, in adopting the sport, improved upon it by adding that important and striking feature known as seizing and carrying the ball. They called the game *harpastum*, and in course of time introduced it into Great Britain. There it has ever had a most extraordinary popularity, especially in Scotland, where to-day it is no uncommon thing

---

* By FREDERICK R. BURTON, *New York Sun.*

to find 20,000 people assembled to witness a match. It was not until comparatively recent years, however, that the game came to be recognized as a regular sport and its play was reduced to rules. During the first 2000 years or so of its existence it was little more than a kind of invigorating exercise. It is mentioned by a writer whose book was published in 1175, as a game much indulged in by young men after dinner. In the fourteenth century it was honored twice by royal prohibition, first by Edward III, in 1365, and later by Richard II. These worthy monarchs got into a state of mind over the decline of popular interest in archery, and they made it a crime to play football, in the hope that young men would therefore devote more attention to the bow. Another English sovereign, James I, took objection to the game on other grounds, and his attitude seems to find sympathy with some people of to-day. He thought it altogether too rough, and, in forbidding the heir apparent to play at it, he wrote that the game was " meeter for laming than making able the users thereof."

Before football was reduced to a systematic, not to say scientific, game, there was ample ground for offence at its roughness. Broken limbs were, unhappily, frequent results of play, and fatal accidents were not unknown. Even in the first quarter of the present century the playing of football in England was attended by extraordinary precautions against accidents. Shrove Tuesday had come to be recognized as "Football Day." It was an out-and-out football festival. Everybody played, old and young, men, women and children. People living near the public greens and squares barricaded their houses, put heavy shutters against windows, and made their doors fast. So far as I have been able to learn, there were no generally recognized rules of play, but there must have been lots of fun. It cannot be that the battered, bounding bladder was dangerous to windows or passers-by. The trouble came, doubtless, in the hurly-burly and excitement incidental to getting a chance to kick the wind-blown thing. Fancy several hundred, if not thousands, of people scrambling, running, pushing, jumping, falling over a common in wild pursuit of the ball, anxious only to send it again out of reach by a vigorous kick. Imagine several balls banging about in the same field. Think of a collision of two groups of players if two balls should chance to fall side by side under the eaves of a dwelling. What a turmoil must have ensued, and what a chance there was then for stray elbows to burst through ground-floor windows, for misdirected toes to caress sensitive shins, for clumsy bodies to tumble to the earth and get trodden upon! Out of all the wrangle, in which we may be sure there was a deal of shouting and screaming and grunting, the ball or balls got away again, chased as before by frenzied, perspiring players, leaving the fallen to nurse bruised joints or dispute with a house-owner about the bill for damages. It is an exhilarating picture, beside which the violent struggles on the quadrangle of to-day are gentle, orderly moves in a scientific game.

The vigorous glories of Shrove Tuesday disappeared between 1825 and 1830. Since the latter year the festival has been practically unobserved, but the game has advanced immeasurably. It took football more than twenty centuries to get out of its swaddling bands, but it is well matured now, and I believe it has come to stay.

For thirty years after the abandonment of the football festival, the game was kept alive in British academies, where it was still played in an irregular fashion. There was no authority on the subject, no recognized rules, no attention to style of play. Such rules as existed were local in their application, and the game differed materially in the various schools. In 1860, there was developed in England a widespread interest in amateur athletic sports of all kinds, and out of this grew the Football Association, founded three years later. Men who enjoyed the exercise, and believed in the game, saw the wisdom of reducing the hap-hazard play to rule. Meantime, the famous school at Rugby had developed a game of its own, which had many admirers, and a result of the newly-awakened interest in the sport was a division of taste and opinion regarding style of play. The division still exists, though there have been many modifications in each of the games during the past thirty years. Rugby's game was similar to both the Roman *harpastum* and the Shrove Tuesday play, as it allowed carrying the ball, and the charging, tackling, and holding of runners. At Harrow and Winchester, kicking alone was allowed as a means of propelling the ball. The game at Eton combined both styles after a fashion, and was probably similar to the style of play familiar to Americans. We play now what is known as the Rugby game, though there are points of difference between our game and that actually played at Rugby. The game authorized by the British Football Association, and known as the Association game, calls for a ball shaped like a perfect sphere. It is made of inflated India-rubber, covered with laced leather. Kicking is the only means of propulsion allowed, except in case of certain plays by the goal-keeper. The goal posts are 24 feet apart, and the cross-bar is eight feet from the ground. To score, the ball must be kicked between the posts and under the bar. In 1871 the Rugby Union was formed by players who did not favor the Association game. The regulation field was declared to be 330 feet by 160 feet. The goal posts are 18½ feet apart, at least 11 feet high, with the cross-bar 10 feet from the ground. The original game called for fifteen men on each side, divided as follows: Ten forwards, or rushers; two half-backs; one three-quarter-back; two full-backs. Some years after the organization of the union the present style of eleven players to a team was adopted.

I am not able to say whether one game or the other is more favored in Great Britain, but from personal observation I can assure the reader that football as a sport is wonderfully popular there. Some admirers of the game call it the "National" British game, but this claim, strictly speaking, cannot be substantiated. The national game of Scotland is golf, and of England cricket, though many thousands more turn out to see football in Scotland than to see golf; and it is my impression that the same holds true in comparison with the national game of the southern country. In the United States, football annually attracts a deal of interest, coming into prominence as it does immediately after the baseball season, when all lovers of vigorous, manly sport are hungry for an out-of-doors contest; but the game, nevertheless, cannot be called popular. The games in which the public takes a lively interest are confined wholly to contests between college teams. There are other games worth seeing, especially in the vicinity of New York city, and regular series for "championships" are played every autumn; but compared to baseball audiences the attendance is slight. Inasmuch as the game is one that healthy men admire, and is readily comprehended by an observer, the reason for the comparative lack of interest may lie in the fact that the football season begins too late. It is a grand good thing on chilly November days to bang around the quadrangle as a

A LIVELY TUSSLE IN FOOTBALL.

shin-risking rusher. The blood flows gaily, the breath comes hard, and the whole system tingles with life and warmth. The spectator on the grand stand, however, hugs himself in a vain effort to keep warm, and in his appreciation of the play imagines that he is having a good time. In his heart he prefers to read about the game, his feet on the radiator, in the next morning's newspaper. In Scotland, where there is no baseball league to stretch the season of out-of-doors sports to the utmost, they begin their great football matches early in September, and sometimes in August. Our game must continue to suffer from its late season, and in all probability the deserved popularity of baseball will prevent football from ever assuming any such place in public esteem here as it holds across the Atlantic.

Until 1875, football, even in the colleges, was loosely played, and no importance was attached to it as a sport. Such game as there was before that year was played with a rubber sphere, and was more of a Shrove Tuesday scramble than anything else. It was called the "Harvard" game, because at Harvard College there was some semblance to system in the play. In 1875 a Harvard man went over to Rugby, and brought back a book of rules, and interested his fellow-students in the improved game. A team of fifteen players was selected and trained, and, meantime, correspondence was begun with Yale with a view to introducing football as an intercollegiate contest. Yale was willing, and, accordingly, Harvard's team went down to New Haven to teach the blues how to play. The Yale men stood up and accepted a courteously administered defeat in full payment for their instruction; for since that year Harvard has never succeeded in defeating Yale. Games have been played in every year since then, except 1877, when a dispute about the number of men to a team was waged so bitterly that neither party would compromise. Yale wanted to play with thirteen men, and Harvard insisted on the established number of fifteen. In 1880 both colleges adopted the present make-up of team, eleven players, and other colleges and athletic associations throughout the country speedily followed suit. As at present constituted, the eleven are disposed thus: Seven rushers, one quarter-back, two half-backs, one full-back. This arrangement is due more to Mr. Walter C. Camp, Yale, 1880, than to any other man. Mr. Camp distinguished himself early in his college career as a football player, and he made a careful study of the game in all its aspects. The result is that he became the leading player and authority on the game in this country. He still retains a lively interest in the intercollegiate contests, and lends his assistance as an adviser to the men who hustle for Yale.

The dimensions of the Rugby field are retained in the American game, but the goal posts must be at least twenty feet high, instead of eleven. The Rugby, or oval, ball is used in all American games, and the rules adopted by the colleges prevail in the general athletic associations. Rugby retains the old style of scoring, by which the game is decided by the number of goals made, or in case of no goals, or a tie, by the number of touch-downs. Several years ago the colleges adopted the following regulation for scoring:—

> Goal obtained by touch-down, ... 6 points.
> Goal from field kick, ... 5 "
> Touch-down, failing goal, ... 4 "
> Safety by opponents, ... 2 "

Men of nerve and brawn are required for football, but the game is by no means so rough as some of its critics claim. It is a trial of strength, courage, and cleverness, and since the introduction of the Rugby game many changes in the rules have been made with a view to eliminating features of unnecessary roughness. A "down" resulting from a tackle by six or more men at once looks far more severe from the grand stand than it does on the spot itself, and soiled trousers and jackets at the end of play are not trustworthy evidence of physical injuries. It is hardly worth while to discuss the question of roughness, or, as some choose to call it, "brutality," in football. The character of the men who play it should be sufficient guarantee to the uninformed that the game is worthy of its place. For my own part, with all respect for baseball, I do not know of any sport better calculated to infuse vigor to the system, or to cultivate manliness, courage, determination, and good temper in circumstances where every energy is devoted to gaining a victory or preventing a defeat. We have to look to the colleges for the names of great players in this country. Mr. Camp has been mentioned. He stands easily ahead of all others, not necessarily that there were not stronger men and more successful players in various teams, but because of his long-continued activity and the leading part he has taken in bringing the game to its present satisfactory condition. Captain Baker, now a Western merchant, gave Mr. Camp his first training in football in 1876, when Harvard's lesson was read backward by the Cambridge fifteen. The sensational player in that game was Mr. O. D. Thompson, a half-back, deeply loved by his fellow-students for his kicking. He won the game by kicking a rolling ball over the goal. Two years later he added another laurel to his foot, so to speak, by kicking the ball from a puddle on the Boston baseball grounds. It sprinkled muddy water over half the length of the field, and scored a goal. One of the men whose name is still heard in the football traditions at New Haven is "Jack" Harding, now a lawyer at Wilkesbarre, Pa. He played centre-rush from 1877 to 1880. This very important position is generally assigned to a large man, but Harding, who is about the size of Captain Beecher, the little wonder of recent years, made himself famous in the sport by his cleverness in "snapping back." Walter I. Badger, a Boston lawyer, was the first quarter-back at Yale when Camp invented that position. The team of 1880 was, perhaps, the best that Yale ever put in the field. Camp and Badger were there, and with them Robert Watson, the captain and half-back, Bacon, full-back, and E. B. Storrs, a tremendous strength in the rush-line, now a professor of law in a Japanese university. Eugene Richards, a New York lawyer, and Wyllis Terry, associated with a warehouse company, were famous kickers from the field in 1882.

Among Harvard's strong players, first mention is deserved by Robert Windsor, 1880, now with Kidder, Peabody & Co., of Boston. Windsor was recognized then as the best goal kicker known, and it is doubtful if anybody has equaled his record since. He seldom failed to score a goal from touch-down, even under the most disadvantageous circumstances. Livingstone Cushing was captain and half-back in 1878 and 1879. He was one of the phenomenons, playing a fine game, though his weight did not much exceed 125 pounds. In contrast to him with respect to physique was Robert Bacon, a very powerful man and popular player around 1880. Another player who is kindly remembered at Harvard was Frank Holden, though his contemporaries will more readily recognize him by the nickname, "Skeeter" Holden, a title affectionately conferred, it is to be presumed, for his "get there" qualities. He was very agile, determined, and a good runner. William Manning, 1882, played a good game throughout his entire course, and captained the eleven in 1881. Princeton can claim the best full-back yet seen in the field, in the person of Moffat.

These five colleges make up the American Intercollegiate Football Association: Harvard, Yale, Princeton, Wesleyan and the University of Pennsylvania. The championship series, played every autumn, consists of one game with each college. Yale is far ahead of the others in games won, and Harvard and Princeton stand about even next below. The championship of 1889 was captured by Princeton, whose eleven played the decisive game with Yale, fairly defeating the wearers of the blue in a most exciting and scientific contest, on the Berkeley Oval, New York. This game will go down in history as creating an unexampled interest and attracting the largest crowd ever gathered at a football contest in this city.

There are few quotable records in the game, as the system of scoring does not necessitate the keeping an account of personal play. It might be a good plan to enlarge the score, so that at the end of a season each player could be rated according to touch-downs made and goals kicked. The greatest score ever made on the American point system was in a game between Harvard and Exeter, played in 1886: Harvard, 158; Exeter, 0. The greatest in England was played in Derbyshire, March 30th, 1881, the Nottingham Foresters' match, when the winners scored 17 goals to 0. These individual performances are worth noting: William P. Chadwick, at Exeter, N. H., November 29th, 1886, sent the ball 200 feet, 8 inches, by a place kick with run; the best kick of this kind in Great Britain was made at Glasgow, July 2d, 1881, by R. Young, 187 feet, 10 inches. The best distance by drop kick, 172 feet, 8 inches, was made by F. Hardgrave, in October, 1882, at Queen's Park, Brisbane, Australia.

VIII.

COLLEGE BASEBALL.*

BASEBALL is the leading sport in our colleges. Though attempts have been made in some of the leading institutions to frown upon it, and to induce the students to abandon it for some other pastime, all such endeavors have failed, and the game continues to flourish. It is in the colleges that the purely amateur part of the game thrives. The amateur clubs, so called, in the principal cities hire players to a greater or less extent. It is customary for them to hire a pitcher and a catcher for the season, paying them a certain sum per game for their work. The scientific character of the game, especially in the pitching and catching departments, has increased to such an extent that this is the only way for such clubs to secure competent men. In the colleges, however, the game remains pure. Naturally, any college is loth to part with a good player, and, when he has graduated, every attempt is made to induce him to return and take a post-graduate course. This has been done in several instances. Then it not seldom occurs that a fine ball tosser is induced to enter college for no other reason than that he is a good ball tosser, and in more than one instance a young man ambitious to shine in baseball has been unable to obtain ingress because he failed to pass the examinations. Tricks to obtain good players and to keep them in college have not been wanting, it may be seen. Then there is no little rivalry to induce men to enter one institution rather than another. The new players generally come from the large preparatory schools, and the friends of the big colleges wax eloquent in their advocacy of the respective institutions of learning. The inducements offered some of the incoming baseball talent are very often most questionable from an amateur standpoint, but of course there is no detection, and there is nothing done about the matter.

*By J. C. MORSE, *Boston Herald*.

The great charm to the spectator of a first-class college contest is that he knows it is played on its merits, and that every man is straining every nerve to win. The game that the amateur plays is far different from that of the professional. A contest between two nines such as Harvard and Yale is an event not to be missed. It is the greatest treat to the lover of the game that can be imagined. The best professional contest ever played almost pales into insignificance aside of it. Imagine a magnificent ball field as level as the finest lawn and so long that the ball cannot be knocked out of the lot by the heaviest drive possible, and an idea will be had of the extent of the Harvard and Yale ball fields. The attendance is the very finest to be seen anywhere. Nowhere are there such select and representative crowds as gather to witness the contests at Harvard and Yale. The spectacle of the ladies radiant in their array of their favorite colors is alone worth the trouble of attending. The students are seated on opposite sides of the field, and from the very first appearance of their favorites to the last out in the game they make the air ring with encouraging cries, which are kept up not only with every play, but with the calling of every ball and strike. The game fairly bubbles over with enthusiasm if the score is at all close. Every fine play of the home club is greeted with continued cheering that often interrupts the game.

The conclusion of the contest sees a scene of the wildest excitement, the victors being borne off the field on the shoulders of their friends. The jubilation does not end until a late hour in the evening, the event being celebrated in the most elaborate manner possible. Then there is no such "kicking" at the umpire in the college game. The men selected to umpire the games are always competent, and know how to do their duty. Their decisions are accepted as a matter of course. It must not be understood that the college player fails to enter a protest when he thinks that his side has been misused, but it is of a mild kind, and there never have been witnessed in the games of the best college clubs the scenes that have so often disgraced the professional diamond. There was a time when the college nines could cope with the best professional talent there was in the country. The game has grown so in science that this is no longer true. Before the League came into existence it was not at all surprising for a college nine to win from professional clubs. Now, such a victory is a great feat. Professionalism has grown to that extent that the college nines are no match for even the minor league clubs, and there are plenty of so-called amateur nines, which are nothing else than semi-professional organizations, that can give the college clubs all they want in the battle for victory. It is exceptional for a college club to have such a pitcher as Stagg, who is really superior to most of the professional pitchers in the field. With such a player at the head of a nine it is almost invincible. When Harvard had the famous battery, Ernst and Tyng, it was almost invincible, no matter what club entered against it. Now and then some other college club would develop some great player. Mainly it was a pitcher who was of such great value to his nine. Such men were Mann to Princeton, Avery to Yale, Richmond to Brown, Nichols to Harvard. The skill of these players was of the highest kind. Any of them could have places in the professional ranks, and offers were not a few. Of those mentioned, Richmond was the only one to avail himself of an opportunity. For awhile he did finely and made a great reputation for himself, but he did not last very long, and retired to devote himself to the practice of medicine. One of the best players that ever graced the diamond was Herbert C. Leeds, short-stop of the club in 1876, when the Harvards wrested the college championship from the Yales, with one of the strongest nines that Harvard ever placed in the field. He was a great player, a heavy hitter, a fine fielder, and a dashing base runner, and he compared well with the professionals against whom he played. Leeds still takes the greatest interest in the game as played by collegians, as well as by professionals. It was his idea to improve the game by doing away with the foul-fly, but his suggestion was only followed so far as the tip was concerned. One would not think to look at this big hearty fellow of to-day that he was at one time one of the leading players in the business. Before the time of Leeds, Archie Bush, the catcher, was one of the crack players of the Harvard nine. He was a fine backstop as well as a great hitter, and he was behind the bat when his club made the famous trip through the country in 1870, playing the strongest clubs that could be found anywhere and defeating most of them. It was in a game in Cincinnati in this season that the local club, then the strongest professional club in the country, narrowly escaped defeat at the hands of the Harvards. Pitcher Goodwin of the Harvard nine was injured in the last inning, and this led to the scoring of no fewer than eight runs in the last inning by the Cincinnatis, who won the game, 20 to 17. Fred Thayer of Harvard was in the college at the same time that Ernst and Tyng were there. He was one of the best captains that Harvard ever had, and he had to contend against some of the strongest nines that Yale ever put into the field. He was a worker and a dashing player. Thayer was the inventor of the mask, which has ever since played so conspicuous a part in the game. One season Thayer lost the two first games that his club played, and then went in and won three straight and the championship. It was done by great ball playing and by the best of generalship.

After Thayer left college his place was left vacant until Sam Winslow, of the class of 1885, came along. Winslow was not much of a player, but he was another worker, and knew how to handle men and get all there was in them into the play. Winslow, when captain, won no fewer than ten straight championship games. Coolidge was a crack second baseman, but he was not a success as a captain. He covered a great deal of ground, and he compared in his position with some of the best professionals. He had a splendid eye for the ball, and he was not afraid of any pitcher in the business. Yale had some very strong players, who can be placed aside of those mentioned that have obtained renown at Harvard. Camp has been one of the very best men who ever played in a college nine. There have been few men who have done so much for the sport and the advancement of the interests of Yale as Camp. He was a pitcher and an outfielder. In fact, he was an excellent all around player. He made the game a study, and he inculcated the results of his observations into his companions. They profited by them then and ever since, as Camp has been very valuable to the athletic interests of his college ever since. It is very rare, indeed, for him to absent himself from some great athletic event of the college. He is very quick to look over a man and find out his merits or demerits. He knows how to handle men, too. "Jumping Jack" Jones of Yale was a very effective pitcher. He was so called on account of the peculiar jump he made while delivering the ball. He joined the professional ranks and was for a time very effective. Yale had in Terry a fine player. He was as skilful in handling a football as in the use of a bat and base ball. Hutchinson of Yale was a strong player. He excelled as a pitcher and as a batsman. He played with the Union Pacifics of Omaha, and afterwards with the DesMoines club, that made so excellent a record in the West. He was secured by the Chicagos for the season of 1889 and made a splendid showing. Sam Bremner was one of the Yale captains who displayed great skill in his outfielding, and was one of the best base runners in the college nines. He won more than one game for Yale by the speedy and dashing way that he found his way around the bases. Dartmouth had one of the best batteries in Rundlett and Cram that ever wore college uniforms. Cram was a strong and accurate thrower and a good hitter. Dartmouth had a great first baseman in Partridge. He was very tall and an immense reach, while he had few superiors as a hitter. Stuart of Amherst made his mark on the professional diamond as well as on the college field. He covered a great deal of ground, making many brilliant catches and throwing well to bases, while as a batsman he ranked with the best. Brown had a great player in Bassett. His home position in his college club was catcher, but when he left college and became a professional he played second base. He has been for several seasons with the Indianapolis club, and he has been rated as one of the best and most reliable second basemen in the land. In the season of 1889 he ranked third among the League's second basemen and his average was .937. He is one of the most successful players who ever joined the professional ranks. He is a thrifty young man, owns his own home and has a snug sum in the bank beside, and, being still a young man, he has a glorious career before him. Not a few players have earned money during their vacations by playing ball, rejoining their college clubs in the spring. The larger colleges have severe rules against professionalism, but they can be easily winked at, as it is very hard to prove in the case of the semi-amateur clubs whether a player is paid or not, and there have been many cases in the crack college clubs where men have been paid for baseball playing. There was no little stir created when the Harvard faculty, about eight years, ago debarred its nine, not only from any contact whatsoever with professionals, but even forbade the playing on the grounds of the latter. Such a provision did no good, and it hampered the success of the Harvard nine. The pitchers were, however, coached in Boston, and the spirit of the rule was evaded in more ways than one. The nine had in 1889 an opportunity to play with professional clubs as formerly, but it did not avail itself of the privilege to any considerable extent. What made this antagonism against baseball all the more striking was that professionals were in the employ of the University to teach the students gymnastics, and athletics, but the line was drawn at baseball, in which the students were more interested than in any other pastime. The crusade against professionalism did not extend outside of Harvard. In baseball and other athletic matters Yale has been far more liberal than Harvard. This may be largely due to the fact that the instructors there take so much interest in the sports, and enter heartily into their spirit and do not consent to hamper the athletic interests of the University. At Yale there has been no attempt made to direct the students what they should and what they should not do, but all has been left to their sober judgment, and with the best results. The Yale men have shown themselves to be entirely worthy of the confidence reposed in them. Yale, too, has labored under far more disadvantages than Harvard. The grounds are farther from the college, and there is more difficulty in obtaining leave of absence. Yale has triumphed in face of all difficulties, and the feeling of unity that has prevailed there and of democracy has kept that college in the front in athletics and in baseball, not to speak of boating. There is better management at Yale, and that perhaps sums up the whole matter. Yale is now ahead of Harvard in about everything, and, the latest thing of all, it has outstripped Harvard in lawn tennis, which Harvard was the first to popularize as a college sport. In the last inter-collegiate tournament at New Haven, Harvard failed to obtain a prize. There was no objection interposed in any of the denominational colleges to the nines playing against professionals, and, had Harvard exercised as much care about the welfare of its students in other directions as in baseball, the results would have been far more satisfactory. It does not pay to try to rule the students in one department of athletics, as was the case in baseball. Now the nine has a regularly engaged professional, who visits the gymnasium of the college regularly in the late winter and early spring to train the pitchers. The popularity of the contests can well be seen by the immense receipts. When Harvard has a good nine in the field an attendance of 8,000 people is not at all extraordinary. The charge for admission is fifty cents, and there is an extra charge of as much for reserved seats. As the players are not paid, as is the case with professionals, the immense profit realized can be easily figured. Not unfrequently some of the profits are given to the university crew. The attendance at the Harvard games is far in excess of that seen at Yale, for Harvard has a far greater population to draw from, and, also, has more students than Yale.

There are now in the field two principal college associations. One is composed of the nines from Harvard, Yale, and Princeton, and the other of nines from Williams, Dartmouth, Trinity, and Amherst. The division became necessary. The smaller colleges were at times able to cope with the larger ones, but in the long run they could not show the requisite degree of skill. Then it was anything but delightful to make the trips to such places as Dartmouth and Amherst. Brown was once a member of the Intercollegiate Association, and went with the Amherst and Dartmouth only to drop out of the new college league. The club made a very poor showing in the league of the minor colleges, and this doubtless lead to its being withdrawn at the instigation of the faculty. The ill success of the club was largely the cause. Then the series of games, when the college clubs played together in one league, was but two games—one on the home grounds and one away. In the three-cornered series between Harvard, Yale, and Princeton, four games constitutes the series, two games at home and two on the opposing grounds. The other clubs in their league play, on the same plan, a series of four games. Trinity, like Brown, has found the pace too hot, and has withdrawn from the league. This club cannot put forth such an organization as the other colleges in the league, and will do much better independently than in a league. There are other minor college leagues. New York for several seasons has supported a college league of New York State colleges. There has also been a college league in the West. The Maine State League has been in successful operation for many seasons, with nines at Orono (Maine State

College), Lewiston (Bates), Waterville (Colby), and Brunswick (Bowdoin). In fact, for several years these college nines gave to Maine about all of the baseball there was in the State, and were prosperous, while the attempts to organize professional nines were abortive. The University of Pennsylvania has had a strong nine in the field for several seasons, which has played independently, making trips to the various colleges in the East, and playing the same games on their own grounds, when such could be arranged. Pennsylvania has also, but in vain, tried to obtain admission to the same league with Harvard, Yale, and Princeton. The players on the Pennsylvania nine are mostly graduates of other colleges, who come to the university to take the advanced courses. Columbia has at times had a ball nine, and at one time was a member of the league with Harvard and Yale, but it survived only a few games, and its career was most inglorious. While the club was independent it did finely and made a great reputation for itself. Its pitcher, Ayrault, covered himself with glory by shutting out the Harvards in one contest on their own ground. This was in 1886, and Columbia then had a nine fit to cope with any of the college clubs. The New York League Club has annually offered a pennant to the college club making the best showing against it. Until last year a great deal of the interest that would naturally attend such an offer was lost by the fact that the Harvard nine was not allowed to play, and last season the weather prevented Harvard from entering into the competition. When Harvard and Yale were playing independently for the supremacy of the two colleges it was the crimson banner that was carried to the fore the greater number of times, but since a league was formed the aspect of things has been changed, and ever since then it has come to be almost the regular thing for Yale to win the championship.

The Intercollegiate Association was formed December 6, 1879, Amherst, Brown, Dartmouth, Harvard, Princeton, and Yale being the members. Yale withdrew, on account of the refusal to submit to the playing of professional players in the league. Princeton won the championship, taking six games out of eight, though there was no doubt of the superiority of Yale, which won seven games out of eight played independently with Harvard, Princeton, and Amherst. The wearers of the blue defeated the champion Princetons most decisively, 9 to 0 and 8 to 1. Yale won in 1881, 1883, 1884, 1887, 1888 and 1889; Harvard won in 1882 and 1885. Princeton won in 1881, and came in third in every one of the other years excepting 1889, when it finished second. The record of the Yale nine during this period has been something remarkable. It has won 75 games and lost but 19 since 1880, while Harvard has won 53 and lost 39 and Princeton has won 48 and lost 44. Yale's record by seasons has been as follows: 1880, won 7 lost 1; 1881, won 7 lost 3; 1882, won 8 lost 3; 1883, 7-1; 1884, 9-2; 1885, 7-3; 1886, 9-2; 1887, 8-1; 1888, 6-2; 1889, 7-1. In no fewer than four seasons Harvard was just one game behind Yale. In the last three seasons Princeton has made a very poor showing. In 1887 it won but three games and lost six; in 1888 it won one game and lost seven, and 1889 it won three games and lost five. Harvard has only once before made so poor a showing as it did last season, and that was in 1883, when it won but two games out of eight. In 1881 Harvard won the first six games, and then lost the next four and the championship. It will be noticed that even when Yale lost the championship its record was nevertheless very creditable. In no season has it lost more than three games, and in no campaign has it lost more games than it won. Dartmouth won the championship of the other intercollegiate association in 1887, and Williams won it the next two seasons, its battery, Wilson and Clarke, proving to be one of the best batteries in the college arena. Besides winning the championship in its own league, the Williams nine succeeded in defeating Harvard in 1888. These intercollegiate games do no little good in bringing students of the colleges together, and through them many friendships are formed that are of value in after life. It is a boon, too, to belong to a college nine, for not only does the student who plays ball have a chance to visit the different colleges, but he is given a standing among his classmates that is of the greatest value. It is worth while to train for the nine and go through all the trouble that it entails for the advantages derived from it, for the reputation of the best scholar in the class does not amount to much compared to that of the crack ball tosser. At Harvard and Yale, the members of the university nine, as well as the freshmen players, are distinguished by the wearing of a specially prepared ribbon on a straw hat. In almost all of the colleges there is played a series of games for the class championship, and these class nines are the feeders of the university nine. By these class nines the players are enabled to keep up their practice after their freshman year, and in case of need such a practice is most beneficial, as there is always somebody to be had in case of emergency. Some excellent material has thus been developed even after the player has been passed by in his first year. This was the case with Downer, of the Harvards, who pitched so successfully for the nine last season. He was a member of his freshman class nine, but it was not until he was a junior that he was given an opportunity to pitch on a university nine. He made a magnificent showing, and with good backing he would have brought victory to his club in every contest that he pitched. The freshman nines are recruited from the preparatory schools. Such schools as Phillips Andover Academy at Andover, Mass., and the Philliks Exeter Academy at Exeter, N. H., bring out splendid ball tossers, and the rivalry between these schools, akin to that between Eaton and Harrow on the other side, stimulates the interest in the game not a little. The Boston Latin School nine also has furnished good players, and recognizing the importance of these nines as feeders, a number of Harvard graduates living in and around Boston organized an Inter-Scholastic Base-Ball Association, in order to induce the schools to bring out the best base-ball talent possible in their institutions. The scheme worked very well last season. The college players ought to help the game, but unfortunately they fall far short of it. Instead of making such rules as would best suit their purpose, the legislators of these intercollegiate leagues take their rules almost bodily from the professionals, following almost directly in their wake. This should not be. The college boys ought to do their own thinking and endeavor to better the game all they can according to their own way of thinking. This could easily be done. Such men as Camp of Yale and Leeds of Harvard ought to be invoked. They have been great ball players, they have watched the professionals, and they have also kept an eye upon the collegians, and their views would be of the greatest value in the councils of the collegians.

IX.

THE PRESS AND SPORT.*

SUCH a volume as this would hardly be complete without some reference to that powerful factor in the amazing growth and splendid development of sport—the daily and weekly press; hence these lines, which it is a pleasure to indite, considering that the writer, as a journalist, and as founder and editor of the acknowledged leading baseball and sporting paper of the country, the *Sporting Life* of Philadelphia, has the privilege of being one of that notable body of men—of whom account is given elsewhere in these pages—whose pens have been so valiantly, so well, and so incessantly employed in the cause of sport, and whose great service in their particular field of journalism forms the text for this chapter in what is undoubtedly the best, most comprehensive, and most valuable book the literature of sport has yet produced.

In England, the original home of most manly sports, from time immemorial the press has given more or less space to sporting topics and treated them in thorough fashion; but in America until within a very recent period the attention and space given to sporting matters of even greatest moment has been exceedingly small, and not so very many years ago racing news and college sports almost monopolized what little room was accorded sporting affairs in the daily press. Baseball, for instance, which to-day leads all other sports in the attention devoted to it and the space given it by newspapers of every grade, less than a decade ago received almost no notice at all; and every man familiar

---

* By Francis C. Richter, founder and editor of *Sporting Life*.

with the progress of the game can remember the time when in New York, Philadelphia, Brooklyn, Pittsburgh, Baltimore, St. Louis, and many other of our larger cities, a baseball score could not be found in any newspaper, when a baseball reporter in all those places was unknown, and when the publication of a score by innings was a priceless boon to the managers of struggling clubs who were only too willing to be their own scorers and messengers to boot. As for other sports, they received even less notice than baseball, with the solitary exception of horse-racing, and that was merely looked after in a desultory manner, according to local demands or events. In fact, the regular weekly sporting press had the field of sport almost exclusively to itself, and that field was necessarily contracted, because, without the stimulus of the daily press, no general public interest could be aroused or maintained.

This was less than ten years ago, and yet to-day the American press not only rivals the English press in the thorough manner in which all sports are covered, but actually outstrips it; and so well does it do it that the daily journals of the larger American cities may easily be considered as sporting papers. In fact, there is nothing a weekly sporting paper can offer that the daily press does not supply except in amplitude and a reliability in matters of record and statistics that the rush and roar of a daily paper and its ephemeral character does not permit of. But for all practical purposes the press of this country may be considered as essentially a sporting press, because there is not a paper of any pretensions whatever that does not give a great deal of attention to sporting matters continuously and copiously, and in most of them one sport alone—baseball—exceeds in the space allotted to it that given to any other subject. Glance over any great daily during the season and observe how the affairs of the nation, the most interesting local events, the vast field of music and drama, and very often even the editorial columns, shrink into comparative insignificance contrasted with the space and attention given to baseball. And what this means can better be estimated when I state that from a journalistic standpoint the importance of news is to be measured by the position and space accorded to it. In every newspaper there is a constant pressure for space, and year in year out, in the wee sma' hours of the morning, the most perplexing problem that vexes the soul of the editor as he directs the make-up is what to choose for insertion from the enormous amount of set-up news matter before him. That being the case, baseball and sporting news must be the most important news of the day in editorial estimate, because it is not only never or hardly ever cut down, but actually takes precedence over many other departments in the manifold field of news and discussion. In the metropolitan press, for instance, baseball and horse-racing share honors, and between them as a rule monopolize an entire page each day of the season. In the press of the other American cities baseball distances all other sports, and nowadays no paper of any standing, from the daily of the large cities to the less pretentious (but equally influential locally) dailies and weeklies of the towns and villages of the entire country, would think of omitting a baseball column from its pages. And in every well-regulated paper of the first-class a competent sporting editor and baseball reporter is an important and indispensable adjunct of the editorial staff. Truly a marvellous change—from no sporting news to columns; from inertia to the employment of such vast energy in the collection of sporting news and opinion that it is quite safe to say that, great as is the capital invested in baseball and other regularly organized sports, enormous the amount contributed in support by the public, it is almost equalled by the aggregate sum spent by the newspapers of the country in the salaries of reporters, the collection of special and general news, the cost of composition, and the other expensive incidentals in the single department of sport.

The causes of this great change are patent. Primarily it was due to the fact that our American people have been slowly but nevertheless surely and generally awakening to the need of recreation and relaxation from the incessant nerve and health-destroying pursuit of the almighty dollar. But this was supplemented by the organization of professional sports upon business lines, and notably was this so with baseball, which game, owing to its peculiar and distinctively American characteristics, easily stands at the head of all sports in popularity in this country. When this game was rescued from the hands of blacklegs and guerillas by the National League, established on business principles, and conducted on lines of rigid honesty, the first and most important step was taken which led to a gradual revival of public interest. Next came the organization in 1882 of the American Association, which widened the territory dominated by baseball, and brought about the National Agreement—a compact which bound all the various baseball organizations of the country together for mutual advantage and protection against crookedness and other disintegrating forces. Honest sport was the result, and this led to such a tremendous popular interest in and enthusiasm for this game that all other sports felt the effect and profited thereby, and the hitherto dormant press was compelled to give baseball, and gradually other sports also, more and more recognition, until that mighty engine, which at first to some extent merely followed the public demand for news, recognizing the merit of genuine manly sport, its power for good when properly directed, and its immense resources as health and pleasure-giving amusement, soon assumed the lead, and to-day is foremost in helping the development of sport, creating new interest, keeping warm the enthusiasm, checking the encroachment of evils, and is constantly doing grand work in elevating the standard of all sport, shielding it from baneful influences, and checking that tendency to degeneration to which sport, whether amateur or professional, is so peculiarly susceptible.

What was at first with the press merely a perfunctory performance of duty has become very largely a labor of love, and in addition to mere news-gathering well-edited papers now treat sport as one of the factors of modern life, worthy of special consideration and comment, and editors vie with each other in paying tribute to the various manly legitimate sports and to their leading exponents. Management is editorially commended or criticised as the case may call for by papers that a few years ago would have considered it beneath their dignity to even refer in their editorial pages to sporting subjects, to say nothing of devoting lengthy space thereto in leading articles. There has been an evident desire to elevate baseball, athletics, rowing, horse-racing, and the other minor sports; and there has been a manifest determination to keep them honest by flashing the fierce journalistic light into all the dark places and obscure corners, and dragging such few rascals as may desire to degrade healthy, honorable sport to their own base level into the light of day, to scourge them and drive them out of the rank of sportsmen. In pursuance of this policy severe criticism of sporting men and measures has sometimes been necessary; but if occasionally too severe, it has at least been well meant in all cases, and is in the direction of conserving the best interests of sport and its professional or amateur exponents; and to the credit of the latter be it said criticism is usually accepted in the proper spirit. Indeed, the importance of the press as a factor in the success of any important affair is recognized by no class so quickly as the sportsmen; hence, commendation is eagerly sought, and criticism as a rule brings forth but renewed exertions to merit the acclaim of the public and the approval of the press.

The good effect of the grand support and encouragement of the press has been to educate our people in a wonderful measure to the importance of healthful sport and recreation as a great factor in human health and happiness, and to elevate the sports to such a degree as to justify the rapidly, steadily growing interest and to continually increase the vast army of active or passive devotees of legitimate sport, which army embraces in its ranks all manner of men from every station in life—the mechanic, the artisan, the clerk, the merchant, the educator, the physician, the lawyer, the clergyman, the politician, the journalist; and whose fascination in some of its manifold forms even the ladies cannot resist.

Further, through the efforts of the press there has been developed a class of writers, who as specialists are not excelled, if equalled, by any other class of literary specialists in the world, and of whom this volume treats more fully in other pages; a distinctive line of literature has been created which claims in its service many men of eminent ability, whose talent in versatility, depth, expressiveness, copiousness, and general scope will not suffer by comparison with any special class of newspaper or magazine writers, however able, learned or brilliant.

So, while the real secret of the wonderful popularity of American out-door sports, particularly ball sports, is the admitted integrity of purpose and execution, and the undoubted honesty of the mass of the exponents of sport, these prime elements of success are almost wholly due to the encouragement, support, advice, criticism, and watchfulness of the press, and the latter, therefore, is the chief factor in the successful conduct and maintenance of any sport which contains intrinsic elements of popularity; and just so long as this needful, all-powerful engine—the public press—exerts its protecting, nourishing, and developing influence for the cause of sport in fullest degree as now, just so long will sports in the aggregate suffer no material decline. Rather, with the continued assistance of the grand press of this blessed country, ever ready to assist in the elevation of sports, ever eager to guard against dishonesty in any form, and to stamp out threatening evils, there is no reason why the legitimate sports of the future should not surpass in popularity and resources the sports of the present, as these now surpass the sports of ten years ago. This is a progressive age, and grand as has been the development of the instinctive human interest in sport, it is capable of still further development and extension—a task which may however safely be left to that power which has hitherto so successfully guided the destinies of sport—the press.

X.

SKETCHES OF PROMINENT BASEBALL WRITERS.

HENRY CHADWICK.—It is not an exaggeration to say that there is no man who has done more to promote the game of baseball, or who has worked harder for the truest interests of honest sport in connection with it, than Henry Chadwick. He has been so long identified with the game as to have earned the honored title of "Father of Baseball," a soubriquet which rests most happily upon him. Mr. Chadwick is easily the Dean of America's corps of baseball writers, and is fairly entitled to lead these sketches of them, not only by reason of his long service, but also by his pre-eminent ability in this line of work. Henry Chadwick was born at Exeter, England, in 1824. His father was James Chadwick, editor of the *Western Times*, an English journal, and his brother was Edwin Chadwick, the noted sanitary philosopher. Mr. Chadwick came to this country when a boy of thirteen. He first resided in Brooklyn in 1837. Six years later he wrote articles for the *Long Island Star*. In 1856 he became a regular reporter on the *New York Times*. His special line was sporting matters, principally cricket. In 1858 he accepted a position on the *New York Clipper*, with which journal he continued for a period of over thirty-one years, resigning in 1888. In 1859 Charles A. Dana, then on The

HENRY CHADWICK.

---

* By W. I. Harris.

Tribune, sent him to Montreal to report the English cricket matches. In addition to his work on *The Clipper*, Mr. Chadwick has at different times been connected with nearly every morning newspaper in New York city, being the first man to report baseball on *The Herald* in 1864. He first began to write of baseball in 1858. He is now on the editorial staff of *Outing, Sporting Life,* and the *Brooklyn Eagle*, having held the latter position for over twenty-five years. Mr. Chadwick's services to the cause of baseball have been great. All his life he has boomed the game, and the credit of securing its proper recognition from the press is largely his. He has ever been vigilant in his watchfulness for the honesty of the sport, and his ever-ready pen has unmasked crookedness, or actions tending to demoralize the game, wherever they have sought a foothold. Mr. Chadwick was chairman of the Committee on Rules in the old National Association up to the time of its disbandment, and since then his suggestions as to the rules and methods of the game have always received careful attention. He is specially noted as a statistician. Mr. Chadwick edited Beadle's "Dime Book of Baseball" thirty years ago. He also edited Routledge's "Book of Sports," the "Umpire's Guide," and, since 1880, has edited "Spalding's League Guide." Mr. Chadwick's style is convincing, but he is not brilliant or humorous as a writer. His writings of recent years have been largely reminiscent, but are none the less interesting on that account. Mr. Chadwick holds his age well. Although sixty-five years have silvered his hair, he can yet play cricket. He is a fair billiard player and a good manipulator of the chess men. He is still in active service, as his letters to the *Sporting Life*, his work as official scorer of the Brooklyn Club, and on the *Eagle*, bear witness. All true supporters of the game unite in trusting that it will be yet many years before the Great Umpire shall declare "out" this "grand old man."

ALFRED H. WRIGHT.—One of the veterans of the game of baseball, both as a player and an authority, is Alfred H. Wright. He was born March 30th, 1842, at Cedar Grove, N. J., but has resided nearly all his life in Philadelphia and in New York. He was educated in Philadelphia, graduating at the Central High School in the same class with the late Isaac P. Wilkins (who was for many years short-stop of the Athletic Club of that city) and George Alfred Townsend, the well-known journalist. His father was a prominent publisher and bookseller, having establishments in New York, Philadelphia, Baltimore, and Boston, besides being the editor of several weekly and monthly periodicals. Mr. Wright played at town-ball while attending school, and was one of the first to introduce the game of baseball in Philadelphia. Taking up a residence in New York in 1858, he played for ten successive seasons with leading baseball clubs of the metropolis, filling at various times every position on the field except pitcher and catcher, generally guarding second base, however. He was also corresponding secretary for several clubs, besides being their delegate at annual conventions. He also played for several seasons with the Manhattan Cricket Club.

Mr. Wright's journalistic career commenced in 1868 on the staff of the Philadelphia *Sunday Mercury* as assistant to Mr. Charles H. Graffen until his death, when Mr. Wright succeeded him as editor of the baseball, cricket, and dramatic departments of that paper. He was eleven years with the *Mercury*, until January 1st, 1879, when he went to New York as baseball editor of *The Clipper*, which position he has held ever since. Mr. Wright's best work on *The Clipper* was the preparation of a condensed but perfect history of the national game,

ALFRED H. WRIGHT.

which appeared in "The Clipper Annual" of 1884. This article has since proved a mine of information. During his residence in Philadelphia he did other journalistic work, being dramatic correspondent of the *New York Clipper* and baseball correspondent of the *Boston Herald, New York World, Chicago Tribune,* and other leading papers. In the *Mercury* Mr. Wright printed a history of the Athletic Club from its organization in 1860 to the close of the season of 1871, when it won the championship of the first professional Association, which, by the way, Mr. Wright helped to organize. He also compiled the averages of the leading professional clubs from 1867 to 1875, and was the first to use the checker-board arrangement now universally used to show the progress of the championship grade. He suggested the principal clause of the first championship code, that the pennant should belong to the club having the greatest percentage of victories to games played. Prior to that the pennant went to the club which should defeat the nominal champions two out of three games. Mr. Wright has also assisted a great many players to fame and fortune during his many years' connection with the game, but his work has always been a labor of love. For eleven years he was secretary and scorer of the Athletic Club, and in that capacity accompanied the club in its visits to almost every section of the country, and also on its tour to England with the Boston Club in 1874. Mr. Wright managed the Athletics in 1876. He was also manager of a co-operative professional team in 1878 known as the Athletics, it being the predecessor of the present American Association team of that name. In 1874 Mr. Wright organized for its projectors the original representative professional team of St. Louis. He also assisted in organizing and played with the celebrated I Zingari Cricket team of Philadelphia. Mr. Wright has been engaged in writing about baseball for twenty-two years, and is second to Henry Chadwick only in length of service. Mr. Wright is still in active work. He possesses the respect and confidence of all the veteran players, and his decisions on points of play and records of the past in *The Clipper* are accepted as authoritative and final.

TIMOTHY H. MURNANE.—The only retired professional ball player who now makes a living by his pen is Timothy H. Murnane, baseball reporter for the *Boston Globe*. "Tim" Murnane, as he is best known far and wide, was born at Waterbury, Conn., June 4th, 1850. His first playing of any account was with the Norwalk Club as a catcher in 1869. The next year he caught for a club at Stratford, Conn., for which Jim O'Rourke was the short-stop. The first big game he ever saw was between the New Britains and Pequots for the championship of the State. There were 10,000 people present, and the scene made such an impression on Tim that he determined to become a ball tosser for good. Murnane went to Savannah, Ga., and played as catcher from December, 1870, to August, 1871. During this time the Savannahs made a tour of the Eastern cities. While in the East, Murnane engaged with the Mansfields, of Middletown, Conn. Jim O'Rourke, Mike Dergan, John Clapp, Jim Tipper, Ed Boothby, and other well-known players were members of this team. In 1873 and 1874 Murnane played first base for the Athletics of Philadelphia, and was a member of that team when it visited England in 1874. In 1875 he left the Athletics for the Philadelphias. In 1876 he signed a contract with the Boston Club. He remained two years, and then signed to play first base for the Providence League team of 1878. In 1879 he played with the celebrated Hop Bitters team. Andy Leonard, Jack Manning, Dick Higham, Fred Lewis, Harry Schaefer, Ed Rowan, Harold McClure and Billy Smiley were members of these roving advertisers. In 1880 Tim played a few games with the Albanys, and then, as he says, "threw up the sponge as an active player." But Tim's playing days were not really over. After three years' experience in the billiard room and saloon business, he took hold with Mr. Lucas, and organized the Boston Unions, and played with the team in 1884 as Captain and Manager. When the Union Association collapsed Murnane played with the Jersey Citys a couple of months, and then retired for good. Mr. Murnane started the Boston Blues in 1886, and then sold the franchise to Walter Burnham. For some time previous to this Murnane had been running an occasional sporting sheet called *The Boston Referee*, devoted to baseball, Polo and "a stray advertisement" now and then. He also wrote a few specials for the *Clipper* and other papers. When Mr. Harris retired from the *Boston Globe* Murnane was engaged, together with John J. Drohan, to do the baseball work. Mr. Drohan soon left, and Tim was given full charge. Murnane writes the stories of the games, and travels with the Boston Club. When at home he gets up the baseball notes. Mr. Murnane has for years been the Eastern agent for the Chicago Club. During his time Tim, who is one of the best judges of players living, has brought out many of the great players of the day. Among them may be mentioned Crane, Slattery, McCarthy, John Irwin, Morgan Murphy, "Cyclone" Ryan, Martin Sullivan, Pat Hartwell, Johnnie Shaw and Joe Sullivan. Duffy and Farrell, of the Chicagos, were put into that team by Murnane.

Mr. Murnane has made a remarkable record during his two years' service as a writer on baseball. His style is original and bright. He calls things by their proper names, and distributes blame and censure with great fairness. It was said of him as a player: "He played the game for all it was worth." The same earnestness implied in that apt illustration Mr. Murnane puts into his newspaper work.

REN MULFORD, JR.—Ren Mulford, Jr., baseball editor of the *Times-Star* of Cincinnati, is a born Buckeye, and has lived in Queen City all his life. He came to the town November 30th, 1859, and has been a baseball enthusiast ever since he took off short dresses. He came by it naturally, for his father was ruptured while a youth in Jersey playing ball. He has early recollections of playing "hookey" to eye the great game through a mortgaged knot-hole. During Cincinnati's last year in the League he was baseball editor of the defunct *Gazette;* was the first to give much prominence to the game in that staid old family journal. Mr. Mulford has been a specialist in baseball only about three years, but has been in active newspaper work for a decade. He has a style peculiarly his own. It consists of making base hits on the evils of the game, and wise suggestions for its welfare through the medium of funny paragraphs and witty stories. Mr. Mulford possesses a hobby. He believes that the men who give the game and its players prominence—the baseball writers—deserve recognition for meritorious work, and he inaugurated a system of personal credit which has been adopted by others—a system advantageous to writer and paper alike, and in strict accordance with his belief in personal journalism. Mr. Mulford was also the organizer and president of the Miami Valley League—a successful amateur organization. He is an able scorer, and has twice represented the Scorers' League before the Joint Committee on Playing Rules.

REN MULFORD, JR.

ALBERT MOTT.—This gentleman was born in Saratoga county, N. Y., May 14th, 1844. His connection with baseball commenced in New York when he was only fourteen years of age. Suffering from too constant attention at desk work, however, he organized a baseball club at Baltimore in 1873, uniformed and equipped it, and paid all expenses. The venture proved a paying one, however, in lieu of physicians' bills. The name of the club was the Creighton, and it achieved considerable local fame. Mr. Mott occupied the positions of catcher, manager, and captain, and was unequalled in his territory as an amateur player. The club existed five years, and developed for the professional ranks Jake Evans, Lewis Dickerson, William Smiley, Hugh Daly, John Morgan, and others. The discipline in this club was equal to that of any professional team, and was due to Mr. Mott's force of character, and the "pull" given by the command, "Take off that uniform!" as the penalty for grave offence. In 1883 Mr. Mott began writing baseball for the *Sporting Life* as its regular Baltimore correspondent, under the transposed letters of his name, thus, "T. Tom Trebla." Eventually the *nom de plume* dropped to "T. T. T.," and by those alliterative initials he is now known to baseball history. Mr. Mott is not a "newspaper man," he having a civil connection of over twenty years' standing with the Corps of Engineers, United States Army. He is also an enthusiastic bicycle rider, and is chief Consul of the Maryland Division of the League of American Wheelmen. He is popular among his fellows, and his opinions command the respect of everybody connected with the national game.

ALBERT MOTT.

SIMON GOODFRIEND, late baseball editor of the New York *Evening Sun*, is a thorough New Yorker. He was born in the great city, educated in its public schools, graduated from the city college, and, for a while, taught the young idea how "to shoot" in its evening public schools.

He afterwards "made a bluff" at studying law, but finally went West in 1878, and followed commercial pursuits in Arizona. Just how many years it took all this to happen is not definitely known, but to judge from "Goodey's" baseball reminiscences he was contemporary with "Rhiny" Walters, of the old Mutuals, Dick McBride, of the famous Athletics, and the perennially youthful Bob Ferguson. He acknowledges to being less than thirty-five, but he went to baseball games when he was "so young," and has such a vivid memory, that he talks of "old timers" in a way that makes colts like Tom Burns and Ed Hanlon blush with envy. Goodfriend drifted into journalism from choice, and did his first active professional work on the Tucson *Star*, and then on the Brooklyn *Citizen* about eight years ago.

SIMON GOODFRIEND.

His salary was small, but he worked from sixteen to eighteen hours a day, wrote four columns of local news every day, edited all the telegraphic, read all the proofs; and even this did not cool his journalistic ardor or raise his salary. Later Mr. Goodfriend became connected with the San Francisco *Chronicle*, reporting and for a time being coast editor. While on the *Chronicle* he secured a great "beat" in exposing the infamous traffic, then long-existing, of selling white girl babies to Chinamen for ultimate infamous purposes. He not only discovered the vile old woman who supplied the babies from her asylum, but with the aid of his paper brought the woman to justice, and had the pleasure of seeing her convicted. Drifting homeward, Goodfriend secured a position on the Chicago *Tribune*, and did general reporting. He became connected with the *Evening Sun* shortly after it started, two and a half years ago. He began writing on baseball matters in 1887, beginning with the first venture of the *Sun's* sporting extra. He was given entire charge of that department in 1888. He was one of the fortunate newspaper men who took the big trip around the world, pluckily going at his own risk after being deprived of an assignment to make the trip for his own paper at the last moment. He corresponded for a syndicate of strong papers, and during the trip through England did the cabling for the New York *World* and *Sun*. He is now a theatrical advance agent.

FRANK H. BRUNELL, sporting editor of the Chicago *Tribune*, is twenty-nine years old, and was born at Maidstone, Kent, England, but has been an American for sixteen years, and likes it. He saw his first ball game in 1878, left a bookkeeper's desk in 1882 to go into journalism, became baseball editor of the old Cleveland *Herald* in 1883, and was appointed official scorer of the Cleveland League Club the same season. When the *Herald* was absorbed by the *Plain Dealer* in 1886, he held his old desk, and, at the beginning of 1889, became city editor of the paper, resigning in August to accept a place on the staff of the Chicago *Tribune* as sporting editor. Cleveland fell out of the League during the winter of 1884–5, and Brunell fought the League for wrongs wrought the club, which drove its officials to resign. Previously, with O. P. Caylor, he had fought the Union Association tooth and nail, and it was the concessions made to its founder, H. V. Lucas, of St. Louis, that caused him to turn against the League. He was secretary of the Cleveland Western Club in 1885, and with James A. Williams secured Cleveland its Association franchise at the Cincinnati meeting of 1887. He was official scorer of the club during its two seasons in the Association, boldly fought the cliques within it, and in the summer of 1888 announced, through the *Plain Dealer* and *Sporting Life*, that Cleveland had had enough of the Association, and wanted a League franchise. He drew Presidents Stearns and Robison, of the Detroit and Cleveland Clubs, together, and out of their meeting came the withdrawal of Detroit, the sale of its players, partly to Cleveland, and the election of Cleveland to the National League of 1889. Of the present team of "Spiders" Brunell secured Faatz, Zim-

FRANK H. BRUNELL.

mer, Bakely, and McKean. When James A. Williams resigned the management of the Cleveland team, in 1888, Mr. Brunell was instrumental in securing Tom Loftus as a manager. Mr. Brunell has always written fearlessly and conscientiously about the game, denounced its evils, and hit out whenever and wherever a blow was needed. He says: "I would rather be right than be popular." His opinion is respected; he writes of what he knows; he writes well, and always interestingly.

HENRY F. BOYNTON, sporting editor of the Chicago *Inter-Ocean*, was born in New York city in 1849. In 1858 he went to Chicago, and in 1866 graduated from Eastman's National College, at Poughkeepsie. Entering commercial life in the same year, he employed his leisure hours in writing for the press as a correspondent. Sporting events seemed to give ample opportunity for his efforts, and after a few years he adopted journalism as a profession. He perfected himself in the *technique* of the business, from the press-room to the editorial floor. Although chiefly occupied on sporting work, yet in his fifteen years' experience his assignments have ranged from a dog-fight to the inauguration of a president. Mr. Boynton was for many years connected with the Chicago *Times*. He began writing on baseball as far back as 1869, and travelled with the Excelsior and White Stocking Clubs. For six years he wrote for the *Turf, Field and Farm*, over the *nom de plume* of "Harry B. Free." He has been sporting editor of the *Inter-Ocean* for eight years, but recently, as the several departments have enlarged, has selected baseball as a specialty. He is a director of the Chicago Press Club. His other accomplishments are a wife and boy—the most effective domestic battery in the world. In point of continuous service, Mr. Boynton is the senior sporting editor in Chicago.

HENRY F. BOYNTON.

HARRY M. WELDON.—Circleville, Ohio, was the place of Mr. Weldon's birth, on December 4th, 1856. He began his newspaper career as local editor of the *Union Herald*, a weekly paper in his native city. He joined the local staff of the Cincinnati *Enquirer* in 1880, and two years later took charge of the sporting and baseball departments of that journal. In addition to his newspaper duties he served as official scorer of the Cincinnati Unions in 1884, and in 1885 was secretary of the Chester Park Trotting Association. In 1886 he was the secretary of the St. Louis Browns. He returned to the Cincinnat *Enquirer* in 1887. During the past three years he has been assistant secretary of the Cincinnati Club. Mr. Weldon is a vigorous writer, and has made his department on the *Enquirer* one of the features of baseball journalism.

HARRY M. WELDON.

BYRON B. JOHNSON, although in the younger corps of writers on sporting matters in the West, has already acquired a reputation in his particular department that is not frequently or readily achieved, even by those whose advantages and experience have been of a more comprehensive and lengthier nature. Mr. Johnson is a Cincinnatian by birth, and displayed his fondness for athletic sports during his college days, not, however, to the disadvantage of a liberal education. His writings are characterized by fairness and excellent judgment, and his style is vigorous and picturesque. His attributes of candor and honesty have gained for Mr. Johnson a wide and rapidly increasing circle of friends. He is young, affable and industrious, and his work in the sporting department of the

BYRON B. JOHNSON.

Cincinnati *Commercial Gazette* has become not only an interesting but a reliable feature of that popular journal.

THOMAS S. FULLWOOD.—A bright cherub of a boy baby was born at Greensburg, Pa., on Washington's birthday, in the year 1854. That cherub became the present sporting editor of the Pittsburgh *Leader*, Thomas S. Fullwood, affectionately known among the fraternity as "Sly Tom Fullwood." Greensburg was too small for the scope of Tom's genius, and his parents moved to Pittsburgh. Tom went to school there, and then finished his education during a seven years' sojourn "in the country," as he designates the city of Philadelphia. In 1873 he returned to Pittsburgh, and entered the newspaper business. "My first journalistic work," writes he to the historian, "was washing galleys." From this it will be seen that he began in the composing room. He passed through the various branches of mechanical work, and finally graduated as a sporting reporter on the *Leader*, which position he has held with slight interruptions since 1876. In 1878 he managed the Allegheny Club in the International League, with which club Jack Glasscock played his first professional engagement. In 1886 he was editor of *The Referee*, a weekly sporting journal on which the Pittsburgh Club directors lost considerable money. While it lasted it was a first-class paper. Mr. Fullwood is known throughout the country as a hustler after news, and he can prepare it for the printer in bright and attractive form. He is a versatile writer, although inclined to be facetious. He always strikes a hard blow when he aims at abuses in any branch of sport. As a baseball writer he stands well. He understands the game thoroughly, knows a good player when he sees one, and does his work without fear or prejudice. Personally he is very popular, not only among the men he writes about, but with everybody with whom he comes in contact.

THOMAS S. FULLWOOD.

JOHN P. CAMPBELL was born at Hackensack, N. J., August 18th, 1850. He graduated from Pennington (N. J.) Seminary in 1868, studied law with Hon. Manning M. Knopp, and was admitted to practice at the New Jersey bar in 1872. He took charge of the baseball department of the Philadelphia *Item* in 1880. He was active in the formation of the American Association, and was elected secretary and official scorer of the Athletic Club, which position he fills at the present time. Mr. Campbell took charge of the amateur clubs of Philadelphia, organized them into leagues, and boomed amateur baseball to a large degree. He was also active in the formation of the Philadelphia Scorers' Association, having been its secretary almost from its inception. Mr. Campbell took great interest in baseball while yet at school, and when studying law organized and was president of the Hackensack Stars. Readers of baseball news are familiar with his weekly screed in the *Sunday Item* under the *nom de plume* of "The Veteran." Mr. Campbell has always been a warm friend of the players.

JOHN P. CAMPBELL.

HARRY CLAY PALMER.—The baseball oracle of the Chicago *Tribune*, the best known of the Lake City corps of baseball writers, is Harry C. Palmer, who was born at Covington, Ky., September, 1861. His early years were passed in Cincinnati, where he acquired his education. Mr. Palmer began his career as a journalist in 1880, as a general reporter with a local press bureau at Chicago. His work attracted attention, and two years later he was made police reporter for the Chicago *Times*. Soon afterwards he was promoted to the position of sporting editor. In 1884 he was induced to accept a similar position on the *Tribune*, and about the same time was appointed a correspondent for the *Sporting Life*. Mr. Palmer remained with the *Tribune* until 1886, when he accepted a place upon the staff of the Chicago

Evening Journal. He introduced into this paper what it had never had in a staid and eminently proper career of over forty years—a sporting department, which he conducted in an able manner until October, 1888, when he severed his connection for the purpose of making the tour of the world with the Spalding excursionists. Before leaving Chicago Mr. Palmer's associates on the *Journal* tendered him a complimentary banquet, at which nearly every employé of the paper testified his regard for him. On the trip around the world Mr. Palmer did an immense amount of work. Besides collecting material for his elaborate history of the trip, he represented the Philadelphia *Sporting Life*, New York *Press*, Boston *Herald*, and Chicago *Times*. In addition, during the latter part of the trip, he covered the tour for the New York *Herald*, sending that journal a daily account and full scores by cable. His letters to *Sporting Life* were the most complete and detailed record of the tour published in this country. On Mr. Palmer's return he accepted his present position of baseball editor of the Chicago *Tribune*. He is a most fluent and graceful writer, is especially strong in descriptive work, possesses a very complete knowledge of his specialty, and is counted among the ablest of the baseball journalists.

HARRY C. PALMER.

JOHN D. PRINGLE was born in England, at Newcastle-on-Tyne. In 1852, when but ten years of age, he worked in the north of England coal mines. He was very studious, and began to collect a library, the first book in which was Adam Smith's "Wealth of Nations." While yet in his teens he was urged to enter the Methodist ministry, and really made some preparations for it. At the age of twenty he began to write articles on political economy. In 1878, while still working in the mines, Mr. Pringle attended night lectures and won a Cambridge University certificate for proficiency in political economy, being first in a class of sixteen, not one member of which even suspected that he was a miner. He soon became a prominent official in the mines, and also took an active interest in outdoor sports. He also continued journalistic work. In 1881 he was sent to America, and located in Pennsylvania, to write up industries for the *Newcastle Weekly Chronicle*. In 1882 he returned to England, and in London took charge of a politico-social movement, in which the late Dean Stanley, Thomas Hughes, and other eminent men were interested. In 1883 he returned to America and had a hard time of it, being compelled, while waiting for an opportunity, to labor at mining. Finally he obtained

JOHN D. PRINGLE.

a position on the Pittsburgh *Times*. He has worked for the *Post*, also, and is now sporting editor of the Pittsburgh *Dispatch*. He has made a solid reputation as a sporting writer, although he has not confined himself solely to that work. He is careful, well-informed and intelligent, and is ever ready to break a lance in defence of his opinions.

WILLIAM M. RANKIN.

WILLIAM M. RANKIN is a native of Pennsylvania, having been born in the southern part of that State prior to the war. He removed to Brooklyn when but a lad. He learned to play ball in 1866, and played with a number of noted amateur teams until 1872. In the meantime he learned the trade of job printing. His journalistic career began in 1872, but he did not make baseball writing a specialty until the latter part of 1875. Since then, however, he has been connected with the New York *Times, Daily Witness, Tribune, World, Mail and Express, Sporting World, Evening*

Sun, and *The Clipper*, besides doing the baseball work for the United Press, as well as for many daily and weekly papers. He also writes special sporting letters every week, which are syndicated. Mr. Rankin has written a history, "Our National Game," which was printed in nearly all the leading newspapers of the country. His collection of baseball literature is a rare one, and embraces everything of importance up to date from the year 1853, when the game was yet in its infancy, and when Senator Cauldwell, of the New York *Sunday Mercury*, first gave it prominence in his paper.

PHILIP F. NASH is baseball and sporting editor of the Philadelphia *Daily News*. Mr. Nash is a Pennsylvanian by birth, and a journalist by choice. He was born at Pottsville, January 9th, 1858. His early mental training was acquired in the public schools of his native town, which he left to learn the trade of a printer. He remained two years at this work. He then became a student at St. Mary's University, from which he graduated with honors in 1880. He then decided to enter the ministry, and devoted eighteen months to study in a Catholic seminary, but, becoming convinced that he was unfitted for the priesthood, he turned to journalism. He first became a reporter on the Philadelphia *Times*, then went to Atlantic City as a hotel clerk, and soon after became manager for a book concern. But he could not divorce himself from newspaper work, and in 1884 he went to work on the *News*, writing special articles. In 1885 he was given charge of baseball, which has been his specialty ever since. Mr. Nash is also assistant city editor of the *News*, and has charge of its dramatic department. He is therefore a very busy man. He is personally popular, is a writer of much originality, and his Sunday letters on baseball over his signature have attracted considerable interest throughout the country.

PHILIP F. NASH.

ALFRED R. CRATTY.—This gentleman is the Pittsburgh correspondent of the *Sporting Life*, and is known as " Circle." He was born at Butler, Pa., September 8th, 1864. Mr. Cratty's family removed to Pittsburgh when he was six years old, and he was educated in that city. As a boy he was quite a ball player, making a capital local reputation as short-stop for the H. H. Kane Jr's. He began life as an office-boy for the *Commercial Gazette*, of which paper his father is cashier. When sixteen years old Alfred was made a reporter. He did good general work. Afterwards he went to the *Times*, and about five years ago became baseball reporter for the *Chronicle-Telegraph*. Mr. Cratty is quite a hustler, and is one of the best news-gatherers in the smoky city. His letters to *Sporting Life* are very readable. Mr. Cratty made the only outside suggestion adopted by the Joint Rules Committee two years ago. It was giving a player a stolen base when he left a base after a fly ball and beat it to the next base. Mr. Cratty is the Pittsburgh correspondent of the New York *Press*.

ALFRED R. CRATTY.

FRANK HOUGH, of the *North American*, was born in Philadelphia on October 4th, 1857. It is not on record that there was any seismic convulsion on that day, but if the earth knew a good thing when it saw one all nature must at least have smiled. He received a common school education, and early in his youthful career took a fancy for the stage. From 1870 to 1875 he was off and on in the show business, which he finally abandoned to enter a printing establishment. In 1877 he went to the *North American*, with which paper he has remained ever since. In 1884 the *North American* wanted a baseball reporter, and the choice very happily fell upon Mr. Hough. It was soon evident that no mistake had been made. His originality attracted attention at once, and in a very short time no feature of the *North American* was better known than its baseball column. His description of a game is invariably bright and impartial, and has a vain of humor through it that lends an added charm to the story. Mr. Hough has the custody of the Philadelphia baseball news for the New York *World* and Boston *Globe*. His bright squibs, or, as he not inaptly terms them, "passed balls," have acquired for him a reputation for wit that is not possessed by any other writer on the game. One admirer has called him the "Bill Nye" of baseball, but that is a mistake. He is an original if there ever was one.

WALTER O. ESCHWEGE is one of the youngest of the New York baseball writers. He is a native of Brooklyn, and still makes his residence in that city. His first journalistic work was done in 1885, when, as Captain of the Nassau Athletic Club of Brooklyn, he wrote athletic and baseball items for the Brooklyn and New York dailies. When the New York *Sporting Times* was founded, in 1886, Mr. Eschwege obtained on that paper his first regular position as correspondent, covering the Brooklyn athletic and baseball territory. His Brooklyn letters were printed over the pseudonyme "Archer MacDougall." In the following fall he was put in charge of the dramatic department of that paper, and for two years conducted its theatrical interests in addition to his baseball work. In the spring of 1888 Mr. Eschwege was engaged by the New York *Press* to cover the Brooklyn baseball news, and when the dramatic season of 1888–89 opened he was made assistant to Dramatic Editor William I. Harris. He is still identified with the *Press* in both capacities. At the beginning of 1889, when Mr. Geo. H. Dickinson assumed the sporting editorship of the New York *World*, he appointed Mr. Eschwege Brooklyn baseball correspondent. Mr. Eschwege's letters in the *Sunday World*, signed "Archer," are very readable, and have added much to his reputation as a shrewd observer of and commentator on the national game.

WALTER O. ESCHWEGE.

PETER J. DONOHUE, who is widely known in the world of sport as " P. Jay," is a New Yorker by birth, and is about thirty years of age. Early in life Mr. Donohue became interested in athletic sports, and about ten years ago was noted as an amateur pedestrian. His experience in athletics led him into the paths of sporting journalism, and, after serving an apprenticeship on the New York *Sportsman*, he accepted a position on the staff of the New York *World*. That was in 1881, and he soon became celebrated as an authority on field sports. In 1884 Col. Cockerill, managing editor of the *World*, induced Mr. Donohue to assume charge of the baseball department of that paper. In a very short time " P. Jay " became known wherever baseball is played. His trenchant pen made spicy reading at times for the lovers of the national pastime, and the causticity of his writings oftentimes caused a twinge to players who were derelict in their duties, and to managers who fell from grace.

PETER J. DONOHUE.

Mr. Donohue was largely instrumental in the admission of Henry V. Lucas and the St. Louis Club to the League. To him, also, in a measure was due the credit of causing the League to ratify the famous " big four " deal, by which the Detroit Club secured from the Buffalo Club the services of Richardson, Rowe, Brouthers, and White. To him, also, in a measure does Roger Connor owe his position as first base man of the New York Club, for it was " P. Jay " who negotiated with McKinnon for the transfer of the latter's services to St. Louis. Connor was then playing second base for New York's team, and, on the sale of McKinnon's release to St. Louis, Connor was placed on the initial bag. In 1886 Mr. Donohue, in company with J. C. Kennedy, John B. Day, and James Mutrie, started the *Sporting Times*. Mr. Donohue is now what is known in journalism as a " free lance," and his articles on baseball and other sports are always entertaining. He writes for the New York *Press*, Philadelphia *Press*, Chicago *Tribune*, Cincinnati *Enquirer*, St. Louis *Post-Dispatch*, and other prominent journals.

O. P. CAYLOR.—The editor of the New York *Sporting Times* is O. P. Caylor, a bright and vigorous writer, and one of the most independent and fearless men who ever put pen to paper. For years he has been connected in some way with the game, and his letters to *Sporting Life* during their continuance in that journal were widely and eagerly read. He was born near Dayton, O., December 17th, 1849. He graduated, being first in his class, at the Dayton High School in 1870. Two years later he was admitted to the bar in Cincinnati. In connection with his practice he began a newspaper correspondence which quickly attracted attention. In 1874 he was regularly engaged on the staff of the Cincinnati *Enquirer*, and remained there until 1881, when he resumed the law business. During his connection with the *Enquirer*, he gave ample evidence of his merits as a thorough journalist, his reports and criticisms on baseball being particularly clever, and in a peculiar but happy, readable style.

O. P. CAYLOR.

Mr. Caylor was one of the men who proposed and organized the American Association. He was the Cincinnati Club's representative at the first meeting of the Association in Cincinnati, November 2d, 1881, and continued to represent it in the years '82, '83, '84, '85, and '86. During the latter year he was manager of the Cincinnatis. In 1887 he went to New York and managed the celebrated Metropolitan Club. In the spring of 1888 he published and edited in New York a rather bright baseball publication, known as the *Daily Baseball Gazette*, and later in the season he migrated to Carthage, Mo., where he assumed the entire charge of a daily and weekly paper.

JACOB C. MORSE.—The most rapid baseball writer in America is Jacob C. Morse, of the Boston *Herald*. His aptitude for figures is marvellous, and his capabilities for hustling seem unlimited. In addition to these traits he is a writer of marked ability, and a scorer of great accuracy. Mr. Morse was born at Concord, N. H., in June, 1860. His family moved to Boston in 1866, and he has been a resident of that city ever since. He was a member of the Harvard College Class of 1881; entered the Boston University School of Law in the fall of 1881; graduated in 1884, and was admitted to the Suffolk Bar the same year. Always having been very fond of the national game, he reported the baseball games at Harvard for the Boston *Herald* for several years, and at the same time was Boston sporting correspondent of the New York *Clipper*, a position he held for eight years. After practising law for a short period, he decided to devote himself to journalism, and has been a regular member of the *Herald* staff ever since. Mr. Morse is the Boston correspondent of the New York *Sporting Times*. He has been interested in the success of the Boston Press Club from the start, and is its first vice-president. Back in 1883 he was the first baseball editor of the Boston *Globe*. As a statistician few men can touch Mr. Morse. He has edited several guides on baseball, and also a short history of the game. During the past season he travelled over the circuit with the Boston team, and his stories of the game were very popular in New England because of their completeness, and the impartial treatment he accorded, not only to the Boston players, but to those of other teams.

JACOB C. MORSE.

CHARLES JUDD MERRILL, the baseball editor for the *Evening World*, of New York, was born at Warsaw, N. Y., October 17th, 1867. He removed to Boston in 1875, and spent five years in the public schools of that city; fitted for college at the Holdermen School, for boys, at Plymouth, N. H.; was for three years at Dartmouth College, and entered journalism as a general reporter on the *Evening World* in 1887. He went to California in the winter of 1887–8 as private secretary to Mr. Joseph Pulitzer. In 1888 he was given charge of the baseball department of the *Evening World*, and has since covered the games of the New York team both at home and abroad. At college Mr. Merrill was a very enthusiastic ball player. He is, therefore, well conversant with all the fine points of the game. He observes closely, judges fairly, and his stories, most of which are written for immediate transmission by wire, are discriminating and always bright and interesting. He frequently writes the morning stories for the *World*, and these show him to be a man of ability as well as originality. His reports are written under high pressure, and are all the more remarkable for that reason. Mr. Merrill is the elder son of W. H. Merrill, formerly of the editorial staff of the Boston *Herald*, and now a leading editorial writer on the New York *World*. In point of personal popularity with managers, players, and associates, there is no writer who possesses it in a higher degree than Charley, or, as he is familiarly known by his intimates, "Dally" Merrill.

CHARLES JUDD MERRILL.

ALEXANDER M. GILLAM was born June 25th, 1858, at Troy, Bradford county, Pa. He commenced newspaper work on the Boston *Post* in 1880. In 1882 he did baseball work for the *Post*, while also acting as assistant city editor. He was made city editor, and resigned that position to accept the sporting editorship of the Philadelphia *Record* in 1883. Mr. Gillam is a very conservative writer. Quiet and reserved, he is liked by everybody. He is thoroughly versed in sporting matters; is a most reliable scorer, a picturesque writer, and one of the most impartial men who ever told the story of a ball game.

ALEXANDER M. GILLAM.

JOHN H. MANDIGO.—Among the prominent figures in baseball journalism stands John H. Mandigo, the well-known baseball editor of the New York *Sun*. He was born in New York city nearly thirty years ago, and received his early training in the public schools. In 1875 he entered the office of the New York *Sun* as a clerk. He held this position until 1880, when he succeeded Henry Chadwick as baseball editor of that paper. During the nine years he has held this position Mr. Mandigo has been a firm friend to the best interests of the game. With the aid of a chief who never asks the cost, Mr. Mandigo, who is a hustler of hustlers, has made his department as complete a chronicle of daily events as it can possibly be. He is not what you would call a brilliant writer, but he is clear, ready, and precise, and gives all interests a fair show. The *Sun* is seldom left in the facts in any local news. Mr. Mandigo is very industrious, and has been known to prepare for publication ten columns of baseball matter in one day, the larger portion of which he wrote entirely himself. He assisted in the formation of the National Scorers' Association, and is the treasurer of that organization. In addition to the baseball, Mr. Mandigo edits all of the miscellaneous sports which are published in the *Sun*.

JOHN H. MANDIGO.

ROBERT M. LARNER, or Bob, as he is better known to baseball readers, was born at Washington, D. C., July 14th, 1856, and, with the exception of about a year, he has resided continuously at the National Capital. When quite a youth he was appointed a page in the United States Supreme Court, his endorsers being President Grant, Vice-President Wilson, and Senator Zachariah Chandler. After leaving the court he apprenticed himself to the *Sunday Herald*, published at Washington, and served four years at the case. During the evenings while he was learning his trade he put in the time reporting local events, and was subsequently assigned to reportorial work on the *Herald*. His duties were to look out for department news, and he then became an attache of the United Press, and "worked space" for a while on the New York *Herald* during the times succeeding the assassination of President Garfield. While thus employed Mr. Larner was offered a position in the Washington Bureau of the Baltimore *Sun*, and for the past eight years he has devoted his time and talents principally to the service of

ROBERT M. LARNER.

that famous newspaper. During the sessions of Congress he is assigned to the capital, and has a large and valuable acquaintanceship among the leading members of the National Legislature. He is also the regular Washington correspondent for the Charleston *News and Courier*. Bob is one of the most active members of the Gridiron Club, composed exclusively of Washington correspondents, and he has developed a talent as a composer of topical songs. Mr. Larner's connection with the National pastime dates back to the time when baseball contests occurred every afternoon on the grounds south of the White House, and he established quite a reputation as a twirler for the Creightons, the junior champions of Washington. In addition to his other newspaper work he finds time to furnish the latest baseball gossip from Washington, the headquarters of the League and of President N. E. Young, to several leading papers.

WILLIAM H. VOLTZ, baseball editor of the Philadelphia *Press*, was born at Cleveland, O., December 2d, 1858. He graduated from the Cleveland schools when sixteen years of age, after which he studied law and acted as sporting editor of the Cleveland *Voice* from 1875 until 1877, when he became sporting editor of the Cleveland *Leader*. The college years of 1877 and 1878 found him a law student at the University of Michigan, Ann Arbor. He forsook the law for journalism, again taking charge of the sporting department of the *Leader* in 1880, where he remained until the fall of 1882. He then organized the Toledo Club, which won the championship of the Northwestern League in 1883, and was the first man to bring Barkley, Welch, and O'Day prominently before the public. In 1884 Mr. Voltz organized and managed the Cleveland Reserves, which developed Ed Seward, Campion, and several other prominent players. He also managed the Chattanooga Club in 1885, the year Ramsey created such a furore while pitcher of that team. He became baseball editor of the Philadelphia *Press* in the spring of 1886. Mr. Voltz was very active last season in organizing the Middle States League, and conducted its affairs with tact and discretion. Mr. Voltz is a fluent talker and writer, and an expert news-gatherer. His opinions on the game have been widely quoted. His work for the *Press* is a monument to his perseverance and industry.

CHARLES F. MATHISON was born in Detroit, of rich and respectable parents, July 27th, 1856. In the intervals of playing "hookey" and baseball, for which latter sport he early conceived an inordinate fondness, he managed to acquire a fair education in the common schools of Detroit. He began his career when quite a lad as "devil" in the composing-room of the *Free Press*. In leisure moments, and some that were not, Mr. Mathison played baseball, and it was a struggle between newspaper work and baseball as a profession. Baseball got left in the shuffle, and "Mat" became, first a compositor, then proof-reader, then telegraph editor. This was in 1881. In 1884 he was made sporting editor, a position he still holds. Since 1886 he has been official scorer of the Detroit Club, and the Detroit correspondent of the *Sporting Life*. Mr. Mathison is one of the brightest and best-informed of Western writers on the game. He is very enthusiastic, and perhaps the most loyal man to a home team of all our writers. Still, he never hesitates to speak the truth about the players, and is a foe to anything that tends to lower the game. He is one of the few

CHARLES F. MATHISON.

men in the West who oppose Sunday ball-playing, and indeed one of the few of any section who print their opinions on the subject. Mr. Mathison's strong point is in broad, humorous descriptive, his work in that line keeping pace with the well-known reputation of the *Free Press.*

GEORGE H. DICKINSON.—One of the latest additions to the bright corps of special writers on baseball connected with the New York dailies is George H. Dickinson, of the *World.* In six years Mr. Dickinson has attained distinction in his profession. It was only during the past season, however, that he devoted any considerable portion of his time to baseball. He was born at Baltimore, June 24th, 1860. He was educated in the public and private schools of Baltimore and Charlestown, N. H., and was also a student at Dartmouth College. His first newspaper work was as a correspondent of the St. Albans (Vt.) *Daily Advertiser* in 1879. From 1879 to 1883 he worked as a telegraph operator, edited the Cottage City *Star*, and entered the office of the Boston *Globe.* He was a member of its editorial staff from April, 1884, to October, 1886. He then became night editor of the Boston *Post*, and later of the Boston *Herald.* In June, 1887, he went to New York as resident correspondent of the *Globe.* When the Evening *World* was started in 1887 Mr. Dickinson was made its telegraph editor. In the spring of 1889 he was made sporting editor of the Morning *World.* He still holds this position, and also retains the New York correspondence of the *Globe.* The New York news service of the *Globe* under his direction has never been surpassed, and time and again has that journal, as well as the *World*, profited by his skill, pluck, and energy. As a writer on the national game, he has shown independence and ability, proving himself a man who has the best interests of the game at heart, though tempered

GEORGE H. DICKINSON.

with an earnest desire to treat all connected with it with absolute fairness.

EDWARD S. SHERIDAN was born at Camden, Ind., in 1862. He is the son of a Methodist clergyman, and received a good early education. In 1880 he was working as a compositor on the Cincinnati *Commercial Gazette*. He then went to De Pauw University, from which institution he graduated with honors in 1885. He was always very fond of baseball, and while at college was pitcher for the University team. His first newspaper work was reporting on the St. Louis *Republican*, in 1885. In 1886 he was given charge of the baseball department of the paper, and during the two years he held this position the *Republican* was seldom, if ever, beaten on baseball matters.

EDWARD S. SHERIDAN.

In 1889 Mr. Sheridan went to Indianapolis to accept a position on the Indianapolis *Journal*. In March, 1889, he accepted his present position on the *Sentinel*. Mr. Sheridan is the official scorer of the Indianapolis Club. He does not now report baseball for the *Sentinel*, but still writes on the subject for out of town papers. Mr. Sheridan writes well, and has a reputation for great fairness. He has always taken strong ground in favor of maintaining baseball upon a high level, and his opposition to Sunday games was one of the reasons that caused him to leave St. Louis.

The celebrated author of the Millennium plan, which has created such an immense amount of comment, and whose ideas are forming the lines of all baseball legislation now, Francis C. Richter, editor and founder of the great baseball weekly, *Sporting Life*, of Philadelphia, is still a young man. He was born in Philadelphia, January 26th, 1854. He has lived his life in the city of his birth, and has been connected with newspapers in various capacities since his early youth. Mr. Richter has been an ardent lover of baseball since childhood, but first became prominently connected with the game when he assumed charge of the baseball department of the *Sunday World* of Philadelphia in 1880, and there first started the boom for the national game which led to a great revival of local baseball enthusiasm, and put the Athletic and Philadelphia clubs upon their feet. Mr. Richter established *Sporting Life* in April, 1883. Since then the paper has made the most rapid and remarkable strides. To-day it has a circulation among baseball people possessed by no other weekly, and it wields an influence that speaks well for the ability of the man who has made it what it is in the short space of five years.

FRANCIS C. RICHTER.

The paper is a recognized authority on the sport, and its editorial opinions on all topics connected with the game are eagerly read, and have weight because they are uniformly wise and conservative. Mr. Richter wields a trenchant pen, and is independent and fearless. That he is easily in the front rank of brainy writers of the sport is shown by the Millennium plan, which provides a scheme by which, its author claims, "baseball may be benefited and made a permanently successful institution." This scheme, aside from the question of its practicability, is a marvel of ingenuity. Several of its features have been already adopted by the major leagues, and others probably will be. Mr. Richter's pen has rendered great service to the national game, and is ever used on the side of honest sport. He has always been fair in his treatment of disputes between clubs and players. The latter are never abused, and are sure to get a hearing. This policy has won great popularity for *Sporting Life* and its able and progressive editor.

WILLIAM D. SULLIVAN.—The leading baseball authority of New England, and the fairest and most entertaining writer on the game in that section, is William D. Sullivan, assistant city editor of the Boston *Globe* and Boston correspondent of *Sporting Life*. Mr. Sullivan was born in Somerville, near Boston, and has always resided there. He is about twenty-eight years of age. He took high honors at the Somerville High School, and stood well at Harvard College, graduating there in the class of 1883. During his last year in college he was Harvard reporter of the *Globe*, and went to work on the regular staff of that paper in July, 1883. In 1884, made famous in baseball history by the organization of the Union Association, Mr. Sullivan reported baseball for the *Globe*. He displayed such aptitude that in the fall of that year he was made sporting editor of the paper. During his conduct of that department the *Globe* established itself as the

WILLIAM D. SULLIVAN.

sporting daily of Boston. April 1st, 1888, Mr. Sullivan was selected for his present position, in which he has shown marked ability. Mr. Sullivan still writes special articles for the *Globe* on baseball, under the *nom de plume* of "Feather Weight." His letters in *Sporting Life* are signed "Mugwump." For several years Mr. Sullivan has reported the Harvard-Yale boat races at New London for the *Globe*. He is an authority on rowing, football, and all branches of college athletics. It is said of Mr. Sullivan that he hasn't a real enemy in the world, and yet, unlike most men of that kind, he never hesitates to tackle a player or club that he thinks is wrong, never truckles to anybody, and calls things by their true names. His immense popularity is the best evidence of his fairness and personal worth, and his position as a baseball writer without an enemy is unique because it is unparalleled.

JAMES C. KENNEDY is the baseball editor of the New York *Times*. He is a native of New York, having been born in Williamsburg about thirty-two years ago. He has been a sporting writer in the metropolis for ten years. Although not now connected with it, he was one of the founders of the New York *Sporting Times*, in connection with John B. Day, James Mutrie, and P. J. Donohue, and was editor of that journal for the first two years of its existence. He made a bright and newsy paper. He is a direct and forcible writer and never beats about the bush, but goes right to the point. "Jim" Kennedy is one of the best known sporting writers in New York, and is very popular in baseball circles and among sporting men.

JOSEPH C. PRITCHARD, the St. Louis correspondent of *Sporting Life*, is a prolific writer on baseball when one considers that he is not directly connected with a daily paper. "Joe," as he is best known among baseball people, is an enthusiast and a steadfast advocate of Von der Ahe's Browns. He knows everybody in the West connected with the game, and his letters to *Sporting Life* fairly teem with news, so much so that, with the addition of his bright comments, these letters are a most important and valuable feature of the journal in which they appear. "Handsome Joe," as Mr. Pritchard has been called in the West, was born at Terre Haute, Indiana, and is forty-three years old.

JOSEPH C. PRITCHARD.

It is said of him that "he is a newspaper man from the ground up." There is some foundation for this, because when a boy he did a rattling business selling newspapers. At eleven years of age he became a printer's "devil," and he has been identified with the newspaper and printing business all his life. Fifteen years ago he went to St. Louis. Shortly after he went to New York, became associated with now Manager Gus Schmelz, of Cincinnati, and both did type-setting in the offices of the New York *World, Tribune*, and other papers. After three years Mr. Pritchard removed to St. Louis, and for twelve years he has been identified with the Merchants' Exchange *Price Current*, the oldest commercial publication west of the Alleghenies. Mr. Pritchard is also well known as an agent for signing ball players, in which he has had some very satisfactory success, and he is also the vice-president of the Scorers' League.

GEORGE ERSKINE STACKHOUSE, baseball editor of the New York *Tribune* and *Morning Journal*, is a Kentuckian, in all that the word implies. He was born at Louisville, August 27th, 1860, and began his education in the public schools, finishing at the Simpsonville Seminary, in his own State. He settled in New York in 1879, and was employed by the *Tribune*. He was a clerk in the office at first, and his earliest reporting was done in covering the races. Soon after he was given charge of the baseball department, and when the *Morning Journal* was founded Mr. Stackhouse did the same work for it. He still edits baseball for several papers, and reports it for the Associated Press. During the winter he does football, bowling, and horse racing. Mr. Stackhouse is a free writer and a good news-gatherer. He is best known outside of New York by his letters to the *Sporting Life*, of which he was New York correspondent for several years. He resigned this position in May, 1889, in order to do editorial work on the New York *Sporting Times*. Mr. Stackhouse is secretary of the National Scorers' League, and was largely instrumental in organizing that association at Cincinnati in 1887.

GEORGE ERSKINE STACKHOUSE.

EDWARD F. STEVENS is the baseball editor of the Boston *Herald*. He is one of the oldest writers on the national game now in active service. His age is not far short of fifty years, and he has been a local reporter in Boston for a long time. In the winter season he does general assignment work. He has made the baseball department of the *Herald* one of the best in the country. He has long been official scorer for the Boston Club. He is the Boston correspondent for the

Philadelphia *Press*, and in the early days of baseball, before the Associated Press covered the ball games, he was Boston correspondent for at least twenty papers. Mr. Stevens is a vigorous writer, who gives facts and makes no pretensions to brilliancy. He has been so long identified with baseball that he is known everywhere. In 1887-8 he was secretary of the New England League. He is a pronounced Prohibitionist, has many times been a candidate for office on the temperance ticket, and is a prominent officer of the National Temperance organization.

WILLIAM M. CROUNSE.—Few men who have covered the baseball news in Washington have attracted more attention by the quality of their work or made more reputation than Mr. Crounse. He is at present the Washington bureau of the New York *World*. He was born at Milwaukee, Wis., July 17th, 1861. He was brought East when very young, where he has since resided. He passed through the public schools of Washington, and was fitted for Harvard at the famous "Gunnery" preparatory school at Washington, Conn., the institution that figures so largely in Dr. Holland's Arthur Bonnicastle as "The Birdsnest."

WILLIAM M. CROUNSE.

He left college before graduating to go into business, and drifted into journalism quite naturally, as his father was one of the old war correspondents, and for ten years chief of the New York *Times* Washington bureau. He was "brought up" in a newspaper office, so to speak, and began writing, or rather scribbling, very early in his career, contributing to the provincial press of New York State. In 1883 Mr. Crounse started a series of letters on sporting topics, which were somewhat widely printed, and he has since contributed more or less matter to nearly every leading Eastern daily that pays any attention to out-door sports. A story that attracted no little attention was a page display printed in several papers, giving instantaneous illustrations of the pitchers of the National League in the act of delivering the ball. Mr. Crounse has made his reputation as a writer on baseball mainly through his interesting and able letters to the *Sporting Times*. He is always entertaining, and, as he has the confidence of President N. E. Young, rarely gets left in official news. Mr. Crounse's theory is that anything that is worth doing at all is worth doing well, and he takes as much pains with a baseball story as he would in handling senatorial debates or presidential messages. He enjoys the most intimate relations with all the baseball magnates, and he holds it simply by his rule of respecting confidences. He is popular everywhere, is a member of most of the noted clubs of the capital, and is an amateur oarsman of no mean ability.

A. B. RANKIN has been for many years a baseball and sporting reporter on the New York *Herald*, and has been official scorer of the New York Club since its formation. He is about thirty-three years old, and is one of the best known all-round newspaper men in New York city. It is doubtful, however, if one person in fifty could tell you his initials, so universal is the nickname he has carried from childhood. "June" Rankin everybody knows and likes. Why he was called "June" is a mystery, but it probably arose from his sunny disposition and balmy temper. "June" is so popular that it is doubtful if an important sporting event in the pugilistic line could take place in New York without his being furnished with the tip. Mr. Rankin is connected with several sporting weeklies in New York, and has had the correspondence of a number of out-of-town papers. He is a bright and ready writer, and for years, while he had entire control of the *Herald's* baseball, made it interesting and reliable. During the past two seasons his baseball work on that paper has consisted of furnishing the scores and local news, one of Mr. Bennett's periodical "shake-ups" having placed another man in charge of the department.

HENRY H. DIDDLEBOCK, whom everybody calls Harry, was born in Philadelphia, June 27th, 1854. He is one of the veteran baseball scribes of his native city, and holds high rank as a news-gatherer and as a commentator on the national game. He was vice-president of the National Association of amateur baseball clubs in 1876, and was also the manager of the Philadelphia Club of that year. He did a great deal to keep baseball alive in the Quaker City during 1877-9, during which time he managed the local teams under the names of Athletic and Philadelphia Clubs. When the Eastern League was organized, in 1883, Mr. Diddlebock was made president and secretary, positions which he held in 1884 and 1885, and during these years was a member of the Arbitration Committee. He has been a continuous writer on baseball since 1876, in which year he was on the Philadelphia *Item*. In 1877 he worked for the *Press*. In 1880 he joined the *Times* staff, and in 1884 was made sporting editor of that paper. His work in that position attracted much attention. He made baseball a great feature of the *Times*. In March, 1889, Mr. Diddlebock accepted the position of sporting editor of the Philadelphia *Inquirer*.

HORACE S. FOGEL was born at Macungie, Lehigh county, Pa., March 21st, 1861. The Fogel family is one of the oldest in that county, and its members have held numerous offices of trust. At the age of fifteen Horace learned telegraphy. He was appointed by Congressman Bridges to a scholarship in the Naval Academy at Annapolis, but was rejected on account of defective eyesight. On returning home the Reading Railroad offered him a position at telegraphing, which he accepted. Promotion followed, and he was stationed in the main office at Philadelphia. About that time he received a scholarship in Pierce's College through Hon. Samuel J. Randall. He attended the night sessions for two years and the day sessions one term, in the meantime keeping up his work in the telegraph office. He expected to enter Mr. Randall's law office in 1881, but, acquiring a taste for journalism, he accepted the position of news editor on the Baltimore *Day*,

HORACE S. FOGEL.

which paper lasted about six months. Mr. Fogel then went to New York, and worked on the *Times*, and for the Western Union as cable operator. Returning to Philadelphia in 1883, he was offered a position on the *Press*, taking charge of its telegraph service and receiving extra salary for doing its baseball work. At that time none of the local papers devoted more than a few sticks to the great game, but Mr. Fogel was soon printing several columns a day, and other papers quickly followed suit. In 1884 Mr. Fogel was appointed secretary and official scorer for the Athletic Club, which position he held for two years. While with the Athletic Club he was lucky in "finding" young players who developed well. In 1886 he advocated a "Battery Assist," and aided largely in the agitation which resulted in the present "sacrifice hit" rule. During the last half of the season of 1887 Mr. Fogel was the manager of the Indianapolis team, but, like everybody else who had before or has since tried to manage that club, he made only an indifferent success. During the three months he had charge he enforced strict discipline, and, after making the Hines deal and signing Shreve and Buckley, he resigned the management to accept the post of associate editor of *Sporting Life*. In addition he conducts the baseball department of the Philadelphia *Public Ledger*. He is official scorer of the Philadelphia League Club, and correspondent for a dozen out-of-town papers.

WILLIAM INGRAHAM HARRIS, the sporting and dramatic editor of the New York *Press*, was born at Washington, D. C., September 28th, 1857. Although prevented under medical advice from systematic study, Mr. Harris had the advantage of early home instruction from his mother, who was a woman of remarkable educational attainments. He began his career as a wage earner at the age of thirteen, as office boy for a real estate broker. In 1871 he was in the book business, and in 1872 was appointed to a position in the Treasury Department. For six years he remained in the office of the United States Treasurer, where he made a record for industry and integrity. In 1878 Mr. Harris migrated to Massachusetts, worked six months on a dairy farm at Walpole, regained his health, and, going to Boston, made a new start as a book-keeper in a business house. In 1884 he went on the road as a travelling salesman, and it took him a year to satisfy him that drumming was not his strong point. While in Washington Mr. Harris had done some work for New York story papers and published an amateur newspaper. During his last three years in commercial life Mr. Harris wrote for the 'cycling press, and was bicycle editor of the Boston *Star* for six months, and filled the same position on the Boston *Globe* for two months. He secured a regular position on the *Globe* reportorial force, January 1st, 1885. During his three years on the *Globe* Mr. Harris was intrusted with many important assignments in all reportorial and special lines, and established his standing as a good and reliable reporter. He was made baseball editor of the *Globe* in 1886, and filled that post for two seasons. In April, 1888, he accepted the position of sporting editor of the New York *Press*, of which paper he has since been made dramatic critic. Mr. Harris has been a prolific writer on baseball topics, and his articles have given him a national reputation. In addition to his duties on the *Press* he is the New York baseball correspondent for *Sporting Life* and other journals.

WILLIAM INGRAHAM HARRIS.

XI.

AQUATICS.*

PART I.

THE amateur sculler is the pride of aquatics. To him is due the credit for all those bright ideas which have improved and advanced the pastime. There is more genuine spirit and earnestness in the humble amateur than can be found in the whole rank and file of the professional. The public, that critical factor which the average sportsman fears so much, is a staunch believer in the doings of the amateur, and supports in every way his lightest works; whereas, in the case of the professional, crooked deeds and shady methods have severed the ties between him and the masses. That's why the amateur is fostered and the professional is cursed. And yet, while it is true that the amateur always remains within bounds, it cannot be said with any degree of truthfulness that it is of his own sweet will. There are some four hundred amateur rowing organizations throughout the United States. Sixty per cent. of these are governed and live by rules and regulations laid down by what are called father associations. The most important of these bodies are the National, the Mississippi Valley, the Northwestern, the New England, the Harlem, the Long Island, the Passaic, and the Kill-von-Kull. The National is the ruling spirit among these, and has a larger membership and greater influence than all the others as a unit. A frown from the Executives of the National Asso-

---

* By W. S. Quigley, New York *Mail and Express*.

ciation means a great deal to any amateur. The Association law is rigid, unlimited, sweeping, and generally unalterable. Its standing rules to govern contests on the water are of the highest order, and are frequently used by professionals in their races. The amateur lawbreaker seldom escapes punishment, and this is one of many reasons why the Association is looked up to by all other governing associations, including the big Canadian organization. There have been some serious mistakes made by the Executive Committee—there's no getting over that fact. But what do these mistakes amount to when compared to the great and grand work which the body has done for the pastime? If we hadn't any National organization, there wouldn't be any genuine amateur champion. Why? Well, the money-making rogues who are invariably to be found clinging to the coat-tails of the successful rower would turn the honest sculler, in spite of his objections, into a bare-faced thief. The National Association stops all this. It has swept away the riff-raff or "professional-amateur," and it holds the gold certificate of the public—confidence and respect. An amateur champion might thrive for a time as a result of wrong-doing, but he is bound to fall into the Association fly-trap sooner or later. It isn't long since the Association was hauled over the burning coals by the newspapers for its disqualification of half a dozen good rowers who competed against John J. Murphy, a marked man. The writer hasn't always upheld the findings of the Association, but in this Murphy case the yardstick was a yard long.

When the National Association came into the world in 1872 the best aquatic writers of the day hazarded the prediction of its early demise. Like good spirits, it has gathered strength. In 1878 it was decided to limit its membership to clubs located in the United States. Those in the organization now consist of an aggregate membership of 25,000, and their "floating" property is roughly estimated to be worth over $1,500,000. The Association has many peculiar laws to govern boat-racing, but on the whole they are better than those of any other ruling body. Even the professionals who are credited with "knowing it all" have the greatest faith in the National Association rules. According to the National idea, a sculler becomes a senior by rowing in a senior, or winning a junior, scull race, whether that race be for single or for double sculls. In the majority of other governing associations a man remains a junior until he has won a senior race.

At the present time there are two or three men who claim to be amateur champions of America. Dennie Donohue, of Hamilton, Ont., won the honors in August last, beating some of the best representatives of the States and Canada. Donohue is a member of the Nautilus Rowing Club. It is he who rowed Chas. G. Psotta, the Cornell University and New York Athletic Club man, to a standstill on the Susquehanna in 1888. It will always remain a vexed question concerning the result of this race. The college man received the judgment award, but to this day his victory is questioned. Hundreds have maintained since that race that Donohue is Psotta's superior in points of speed and style. In personal appearance the men are as different as a steam yacht and a canal-boat. Psotta does not look so big as he really is. He is a son of a millionaire parent, and has been brought up with all that care, education, and refinement can bestow. If he has any fault, it is his lack of civility to strangers. Donohue, on the other hand, is the essence of all that's polite. Like Pugilist John L. Sullivan, his strength is all above deck—that is, about his shoulders. He has a stocky neck, a well-shaped head of good size, immense shoulders, and large, prominent features. Hard work has given him a rough appearance. But he is a diamond of the first water. At play or at work his fine manly traits are ever visible. As game as a fighting-cock, as honest as "they make 'em," and as strong as a steam-engine, Donohue may always be depended on to win. In one respect only is he like Psotta. He has a big heart; none of the white specimen so common among some athletes these days, but a blood red, which, when belonging to an oarsman, says: "I'll never give in; I'll never give in; you have to kill me in my boat before I'll give in." Those who witnessed the race between the two men at Sunbury will recall that it was fought out in hammer-and-tongs style from the start. Donohue was nearly swamped at the go-off, but he kept plugging away at it, and never for a moment dreamed that he wasn't in the hunt until his wash-box was swept away and the sea commenced to "come aboard." The finish between the two will dwell forever in the memory of amateur aquatics. There were thirty thousand spectators on the banks, urging them on when the finishing flags loomed up a hundred yards ahead. Psotta's head fell back clear over his shoulders with every stroke, and Donohue had the strength of despair in every catch. The Canadian was all awash, the water which had been shipped floating clear over the runners of the sliding seat. Psotta had a new boat, and his washboards remained intact, so that the rough water played no important part in his discomfort. The men were in even water 100 yards from the finish. At that stage of the race all the gambling was done. The Canadians are the best gamblers in the world, and they carried the Americans right off their feet the way they threw down the cash. It was even money at first, and finally the Kanucks knocked it down to $100 to $40 on Donohue. And even after the decision was given, contrary to expectation, the Canadians continued to trust in Yankee honesty and back their opinions. After that race the writer was empowered to make a special match between the two men, but the Ithaca champion would not come to the scratch. His absence in Europe last season prevented any negotiations looking to a settlement of the question of supremacy.

Psotta was born on Washington's Birthday, twenty-four years ago. His first appearance in public was at the Passaic Association regatta at Newark on July 5th, 1886. There he won the junior sculls by half a dozen lengths in the creditable time of 9 minutes 28 seconds. At the same Association's regatta on June 11th, the year following, he tried for the senior championship, but was laid out by Wm. Goepfert, the ex-amateur. At the People's regatta on the Schuylkill on Independence Day, 1887, he was fouled and had his shell broken, but managed to finish second to F. B. Baltz, of the Pennsylvania Boat Club. His next appearance was at the National Association regatta on Chautauqua Lake, July 26th, 1887. He finished third, being beaten by J. F. Corbett, of the Farragut Boat Club, Chicago. On September 28th of the same year he captured the senior sculls at the Potomac river regatta, winning by ten lengths in 9 minutes 51 seconds. In the spring of 1888 he reappeared at the Passaic Association regatta and won a splendid race from E. J. Mulcahy, of the Mutual Boat Club, Albany. His time here was 9 minutes 14 seconds. On June 18th he went to the New England Association regatta at Lake Quinsigamond, and over a two-mile course defeated the two Boston champions, Corcoran and Cummings. His time here with the turn was 14 minutes 7¼ seconds. His next exhibition was at the People's regatta at Philadelphia on July 4th. He won by a trick here, it is thought, although it is not believed he had any hand in the deal. This is the race in which his old rival, J. F. Corbett, made such a miserable showing. His next entry was at Sunbury in his race with Donohue. Psotta's final race for the year 1889 was at Washington, where he again won the senior scull event. The story of his gallant victories in the heat races for the diamond sculls at the Henley regatta, and his defeat in the final by A. McKalls, the famous Oxford oarsman, and Guy Nichalls, the Cambridge crack, who in '88 won the Wingfield sculls and the championship of the Thames in the record-beating time of 23 minutes 36 seconds, have only recently occurred, and are too well known to bear repetition.

The public career of Donohue does not extend back many years. It is only within the past four years that he has taken a prominent position in aquatics. It was not until 1886 that he took a fancy to the single sculls. The sweeps are not calculated to better the condition of the average sculler, but Donohue appears to have been greatly benefited by his trials in company. The sweeps gave him his first genuine lesson in the knack of ripping the water properly, and also taught him how to best utilize his wonderful bursts of strength. When he finally turned out good speed with the sculls he made up his mind to "hit at the biggest tree and finish the job one way or the other," as he himself characteristically put it; so in '87 he went to Chautauqua Lake and won the junior single championship of the National Association. He is a cigarmaker by trade, and his greatest trouble has been to spare the time necessary for training. Donohue has often practised and trained after nightfall and on Sunday. But he is a faithful athlete to his admirers and himself, and he has readily mastered that which Psotta, with his many hours of daily practice, has not yet learned—the knowledge of a graceful and accomplished stroke. To an experienced eye the movement of Donohue on the water looks professional all over. There is a cleanness and finish about it that few men in the amateur ranks can attain. The "life" of the stroke is just as powerful at the finish as at the catch. At the last National regatta on Calumet Lake his most formidable opponent was his brother, Jerry. It was the same way at the Mississippi Valley Association regatta on the same sheet of water. Corbett, the Chicago sculler, who was Psotta's superior while the good game lasted, was in both of these races, but in name only. The Donohue boys made a show of him. Dennie is two years older than his brother, but the younger has been rowing for ten years. As a double, he and C. Furlong, another handy man with the blade, won the double-scull shell championship at the Canadian regatta in 1881, and at Sunbury in 1888 he captured the junior championship of America. Thus it may be seen that the Donohues are a great rowing family. There are very few honors left for the older Donohue in the amateur line, and it may be that one of these days he will launch into the professional ranks. If he does I venture the prediction that a great many good men will give way to his skilful oar. As a double he and his brother could beat anything in the amateur fold.

Considering that the Harlem river is the rendezvous for eight of the finest racing organizations of the country, it is really surprising that a more perfect strain of single sculler is not put before the public. The stuff is there, but somehow or another the talent does not understand how to bring it out. Of the Harlem men who have won laurels of recent years on the water in singles, a few only are of more than ordinary material. Their best time would be creditable to a sculler of a fresh pond only. Within the past ten years the Harlem has "done itself proud" in turning out only half a dozen first-class men. These consisted of Wm. Goepfert, James Pilkington, Robert O. Morse, and Ollie Stephens. Goepfert was in his day the superior of any of these. He was remarkably fast in a single at a mile, but he was a "dead quitter" at any greater distance. His style of locomotion was perfect and pleasing to the eye, and the members of the Metropolitan Rowing Club, the same that boasted the celebrated eight of years ago, were justly proud of his powers. It was he who gave Psotta his first defeat; that was at the Passaic Association regatta in '87. Goepfert in a single won everything worth winning except a National Association championship. As a double he captured the National and Canadian championships, however. This National race was at Chautauqua Lake in 1887, and his partner was John O. Reagan, one of the best of good fellows, and a capital oarsman. Their opponents were Weinand and

Korf, the famous Delaware Boat Club crew, of Chicago. Reagan and Goepfert as a double crew knocked down all the big pins, including those of New England, during that year. Reagan abandoned rowing after that, and the year following Goepfert took Jim Pilkington as a partner. At the sixteenth annual regatta of the National Association on the Susquehanna there was a scandal, and Goepfert, who with Pilkington had entered for the double contest, disappeared from Sunbury and returned home. He was tried by the Association, charged with an attempt to sell his race, and was disqualified.

R. O. Morse won the majority of his races as a member of the Nassau Boat Club. He is still an ardent supporter of that organization, but has not competed in any open events for several years. He won the junior championship in 1882, and the year after came out strong and captured the senior single event of the Harlem fall regatta. This championship he held until 1886, when Goepfert took it from him. During 1883 he rowed double with P. W. Page, a club-mate, who won the senior single race at the Harlem spring regatta of that year. As a double Morse and Page won the honors of the Harlem and the Passaic for 1883 and 1884.

James Pilkington, of the Metropolitan Rowing Club's forces, has led a varied life as an oarsman. When he became proprietor of Oak Point, and operated a sort of sporting resort and excursion grounds for the people of New York, he had business relations with all the professional scullers, and this naturally put him under the bane of the National Association. He was not disqualified by the body, but, after he gave up Oak Point and resumed rowing, it became necessary for him to appeal to the National Executive Committee before the Harlem Association would permit him to compete in its races. Pilkington has rowed in every style of boat and race. He was a very fast man in his early days, as may be judged from the fact that he won thirteen distinct prizes in a one day's regatta at Saratoga Springs. He is a tall, lank veteran, and in street costume looks anything but a good sculler. He has a collection of some seventy medals. Though aged, as a wildcat, Pilkington has plenty of the old grit and speed left, and to this day can show the way to a number of the young flyers. He rowed double last season with John Nagle, a brother of the old-time oarsman. Together they showed up in splendid form and rowed a dead heat with the Bayside Boat Club crew, of Toronto, at the National regatta at Pullman, Illinois, on August 9th, 1889. The Canadians refused to row the race off, so certain were they of defeat at the hands of the New Yorkers. The following day the Metropolitan crew won the double championship of the Mississippi Valley Association, defeating the champion Ravenswood Boat Club crew, Buschman and Platt, of Long Island City. On Labor Day, at the regatta of the New England Association on the Charles river, the last-named crew turned the tables on Pilkington and his partner, and beat them by a sixteenth of a mile. The Metropolitan crew labored under a disadvantage in this race. The last appearance of Pilkington and his partner was at the fall races of the Harlem Association. Pilkington stroked an eight-oared crew of the Metropolitan Club, and Nagle rowed at No. 7. The crew was defeated after a bruising contest by the second eight of the Atalanta Boat Club.

Ollie Stephens is without question the fastest single sculler regularly attached to the Harlem river at the present time. There are one or two other fast men, members of Harlem clubs, but they do not reside in New York, and are seldom seen about the Nursery, as the river is called. Stephens is a member of the New York Athletic and Union Boat Clubs. All his rowing the past year has been done under the New York Athletic Club colors. He started in to row in 1885, and at the spring regatta of the Harlem in 1886 won the junior single scull contest. In the fall regatta of the same Association the year following he secured a seniorship. On both these occasions he was entered by the Union Boat Club. He successfully defended the Diamond Scull championship of the Harlem three consecutive times, and lost it this fall to John Ryan, the Bradford Boat Club sculler, of Boston, who was entered in that race by the Union Boat Club, Stephens' old "standby." Stephens was never pushed to any degree until he met his Waterloo at the hands of Ryan. At the People's regatta on the Schuylkill last Independence Day he won the senior single race without any particular display of a fast oar. Stephens is twenty-six years old, and is noted for being the only present-day champion who revels in the possession of a bearded face.

Of the other amateurs outside of the Harlem who have won fame on the single sliding seat, much more credit is deserved because their laurels were won under greater difficulties and in more decisive style. Take, for instance, Martin F. Monahan, of Albany, J. F. Corbett, of Chicago, J. J. Ryan, of Canada, E. J. Mulcahy, of Albany, and F. D. Standish, of Detroit. They fought out their aquatic battles in the good old days of this decade, when the young blood was warm for competitive action, and when half a dozen of the pick of the county came to the starting line in each event. Monahan has rowed all his races from the Albany Boat Club. He has one hundred medals, cups, and banners to show for his work in the shell. He commenced his career in 1880, and the year after won a junior race. In 1883 his designs on the senior championship were accomplished at the Passaic Association regatta, and three years later at Albany he won the National Association seniorship. The year previous to this he and his brother took the National double scull championship by forfeit. Monahan is still a warm supporter of aquatics. Corbett has been away "off form" for a couple of seasons, and has not captured a prize of any value since the National regatta was held at Long Point, Chautauqua Lake. Corbett launched his first winning shell from the Pullman Boat Club, of Chicago. He won the junior and senior championships in the one day at the 1885 regatta of the Mississippi Valley Association. After these victories he was taken under the wing of a rival organization, the Farragut Boat Club, and in 1886 he rowed his first race in its colors. He was successful in this event. It was at the annual regatta of the Northwestern Association, and he defended his senior championship. He repeated the performance at the Mississippi Valley regatta the same year, and the season following he took another prize from that association, as well as the championship at the National regatta. Since then he has not set anything on fire by his success on the water.

Standish, the Detroit champion, is a member of the Excelsior Club, and has been rowing for eighteen years. His first race was on July 12th, 1871, at the third annual regatta of the Northwestern Association. This regatta was held at Oconomowoc, Wis., and Standish was one of a six-oared crew. Since then he has participated in all the regattas of the association until now he is just as lively as ever. As a proof of his wonderful lasting powers, it may be said that at the last Northwestern regatta held on Reed's Lake, on August 2d, he pulled in the winning pair-oared shell. He is the only man who has remained a winner for eighteen years. With E. Talfer and J. H. Clegg, as partners at different times, he has won National, Northwestern, Canadian, and Mississippi Valley championships. With the pair-oars, the National honors fell to him at Washington in 1881, the Canadian the year following, again in 1885.

Double-scull shell rowing has of late years taken the place of the pair-oared shell contest. The latter was very popular in its time, but these are not the days of Bulger and Moseley, Smith and Eldred, the Gorman brothers, and Freeman and Weldon, and the style of craft is falling into obscurity. It is a question of a few years only when both the National and Canadian Associations will obliterate the event from their entry list altogether. Last year the Seawanhaka Boat Club's crew, Pelton and Fogarty, of Brooklyn, rowed over for the prizes attached to the event at the National, and this year the contest failed to receive any support save from the New York Athletic Club. It was a similar story at the Canadian regatta of 1883 and 1884. There is too much "wobble" about the pair-oared craft to suit the all-round oarsmen. As a result of this disusage, the double-scull shell has taken a firmer hold on aquatic devotees, and in future will assume a more important position in all the great regattas than has ever been the case in the history of the sport. At the last spring regatta of the Harlem there were half a dozen crack doubles in one event, and at the last National ten crews came to the line for double-scull honors.

Single and double-scull competitions are of course attractive and interesting, but for catching the public eye let us have crew racing. The most popular style of craft to show in company is an eight-oared shell. A man can sometimes stand and watch good single and double-shell rowing for weeks without arousing a "sporty feeling," but let him be a spectator at even an ordinary contest between eight-oared shells, and his enthusiasm will flow all over. There is something sublime and grand in seeing eight swarty men move backward and forward with perfect machine-like regularity. The man with the weak heart may be prosperous in the single and double, but he has no right in an eight-oared boat. There is no lagging for the handlers of the sweeps, once the word is given, and the seven men forward of the stroke have to keep "step" to the movement, no matter how fast the eighth man "whoops it up." The champion eight of this country is enrolled in the Atalanta Boat Club, of the Harlem river. This is the oldest rowing organization of America. The Atalantas have held an annual meeting every year since 1848. The club was organized on May 5th of that year. Its first boat-house was situated at the foot of Thirteenth street, North river, New York. It was only a narrow shed, hardly wide enough to accommodate an eight-oared barge which the club originally owned. The structure was quite a contrast to the fine boat-houses of the present day. In 1851 the club moved to the foot of Christopher street, on the same river, where it remained until it located on the Harlem. The first boat owned by the club was a heavy four-oared barge, twenty-seven feet long. In the summer of 1848 the club sold this craft, and purchased from the Castle Garden Amateur Association the Gazelle, an eight-oared barge. During the first few years of the Atalanta's career, the George Washington, Manhattan, Conover, and Duane were the only boat clubs in existence. These four clubs are now dead. There were no regattas in those days—only barge parties and "launches." In 1860 the Hudson Navy gave a series of races, and this was the inaugural of racing about Manhattan Island. The first president was Robert Livingston, and he was succeeded in turn by the following gentlemen: W. D. Nichols, Frank Charlton, J. W. Avis, C. A. Peverelly, J. R. Hay, W. Roberts, Jr., B. Frank Curtis, C. Ingalls, W. H. Webster, H. H. Dyer, A. S. Swan, D. Banks, Jr., R. Parker, Jr., G. B. Deane, Jr., and M. V. B. Smith. During the forty odd years of the club's existence, no one has been elected to the presidency except by a unanimous ballot, and there never have been two candidates for the office in the field at the one time. The club has been at its best the last three years, and its gallant victories on the water reflect great credit on all its members in general, but on Theo. Van Raden in particular. Mr. Van Raden is the captain of the club, and there is none better at the head of any organization. He comes of the genuine Yankee stock, is a big, out-spoken fellow, full of hope and full of life, and one who has enterprise and ambition enough to get every pound of effort out of every pound of flesh. He has a superior knowledge of the rowing business, knows the qualifications of the men under his charge, and his experienced eye can pick out raw stuff for rowing material in any crowd. It would not be truthful to say that the high standing of the club is due to Captain Van Raden's efforts alone, but his "trick at the wheel" has resulted in the club's possession of the crack eight and four of the States. He brought them to the organization, and he gave them their positions in the craft which they have so often since paraded to victory. The eight-oared crew has yet to feel the pangs of defeat. There is only one crew in the country that can make it hustle. That is the Bradford Club eight, of Cambridge, Mass. H. B. Cashim occupied the bow seat in the champion eight, with George N. Storm, No. 2; John H. Chambury, No. 3; Benjamin Van Clief, Jr., No. 4; C. A. Lunjack, No. 5; Fred Freeman, No. 6; John Weldon, No. 7; Matthew T. Quigley, stroke, and Edward P. K. Coffin, coxswain. That is the personnel of the crew that has swept everything before it. Each member of the crew is a finished oarsman, and has a "breast-plate" of gold medals to show his victories in all manner of races and style of boat. Freeman and Weldon have been partners in the pair-oared shell since 1883, and have won two National Association championships, two Passaic Association championships, and one Harlem Association championship. In their early races they rowed for the Ariel Boat Club, of Newark, then for the Eureka Boat Club, of the same city. They left the Eureka for the Atalantas. Quigley and Chambury have also won fame in the pair-oared. They formed the famous Institute Boat Club crew of '86. Quigley is the gamest man that ever took a stroke seat. At the last New England Association regatta, on the Charles river, he beat all the cracks, and received a junior championship at single sculls. Cashim is another graduate of the Passaic river, and was bowman in the Ariel Boat Club six-oared crew that was famous in '83, '84 and '85. He has won many single prizes. Lunjack also came from the Institute Club, and Van Clief has been in many hot races for the Ariel, Eureka, and Passaic Clubs. Storm comes from the old Valencia Club of Hoboken. Lunjack is the tallest man of the crew. He is six feet four inches high. Chambury is the "short one," five feet six inches high. Cashim is the light-weight, 140 pounds, and Weldon tops off the crew with 172 pounds. As a four, Quigley, Freeman, Lunjack, and Chambury, won two grand races in '88, the National championship at Sunbury and the honors of the Potomac Association at Washington. On these occasions they wore the colors of the Passaic Boat Club, of Newark. As an eight, the crew captured last year the Long Island Association championship on Bowery Bay, and the Labor Day race of the Staten Island Athletic Club on the Kill-von-Kull, the latter in the wonderful time of 4.42. In this last race they defeated the celebrated eights of the Fairmount Rowing Association and the Schuylkill Navy, of Philadelphia. On May 18th of this year the champion New York Athletic Club crew gave way to them in a match race on the Harlem. In another match race on the same river on June 18th, the Columbia College 'Versity eight was pitted against them. It was a two mile contest, and the Atalantas won as they liked. At the Long Island Association regatta on June 22d they were again victorious. It was the same story at Albany on Independence Day. Then the crew went West to the National regatta, and laid out the supposed invincible Bradford crew, going the mile and one-half in 7.41, and beating the still water record by forty-two seconds. This was a gallant contest, and both crews were ready to "drop dead" in their craft at the conclusion. It was the last appearance of the crew on the water. Speaking of the crew, an aquatic writer says: "They are a foxy, iron-muscled, time-seasoned set of fellows. Matty Quigley, the stroke, has a style of his own. It is something like the Fairmount stroke. It has the same vim and jump to it. The recovery is slow, the reach long. The stroke is long, too, but it is torn through the water as if every man was mad, and the finish is very hard."

The champion four of the Atalantas is composed of a happy family, the Dempsey brothers, John Aird and Guy C., and the Lau brothers, Max and William. Captain Van Raden says of the crew that it is unbeatable because it is formed of the best of Irish and German blood. Before joining the Atalanta forces the Dempsey brothers rowed double in gig races on the Hudson. The Lau brothers did likewise for the Valencia Club, of Hoboken. The two crews joined the Atalantas about the same time last year, and then came the question of superiority. After several severe contests between the crews, Captain Van Raden reached the conclusion that both were about equal as regard power and speed. He then decided to boat the brothers in a four. Their first victory in that boat was at the Fourth of July regatta at Albany, when they defeated the fast Metropolitan Rowing Club crew, Maloney, Heraty, Nagle, and Pilkington. The big National regatta at Pullman, Ill., was next visited, and there they were defeated by the Winnipeg Rowing Club four, of Manitoba. The Atalantas rowed a "hogged" shell in this race, which mainly caused their defeat. At the Mississippi Valley regatta, on August 11th, the four was successful, "laying out" some first-class crews. The crew finished its season's rowing on Labor Day by defeating the King Philip Boat Club four, of Fall River, and Reid, Dunn, Johnson, and McGrath, the Varuna Boat Club four, of Brooklyn, at the New England Association regatta on the Charles river. A total of the prizes won this year by the Atalantas numbers ninety-nine. They consist of the Harlem Cup, the Ladies' Plate and Grand Challenge Cup, trophies given in trust by the Harlem Association, eighteen small silver cups, fourteen banners, and sixty-four medals. Captain Van Raden wants to know why the championship should not be put down as another trophy, and so make the prize list an even hundred. With a record like the above, is there any reason for withholding the palm from the Atalantas?

The American Rowing Almanac, in speaking of the early amateur races, says: "The first race on record in this country is described as having taken place at the mouth of the Hudson river. The winning boat, Knickerbocker, four oars, was placed in the Museum and destroyed at Barnum's fire in 1865. Another prominent four-oared boat, the American Star, was presented to General Lafayette upon his departure for France. The two crews, American Star and gig crew of the English frigate Hussar, whose race resulted in a fine victory for the Americans, were exhibited on the stage of the old Park Theatre on the evening after their race. About 1834 the Castle Garden Amateur Association was organized, composed of the wealthy and aristocratic portion of young men. They held regattas every year until 1842, the more prominent clubs being the Ware, Gull, Gazelle, Cleopatra, Pearl, Halcyon, Ariel, Minerva, Gondola, etc. In nearly the same period another association was formed, styled the Independent Boat Club Association. Their rules were less stringent; they were out oftener, and enjoyed themselves more. Their prominent boats are well remembered, among them the Disowned, Wizard, Skiff, Lafayette, Masaniello, Vivid, Spark, Metamora, Triton, D. D. Tompkins, Sylph, Erie, Duane, Eagle, Thomas Jefferson, Fairy, Washington, Brooklyn, and Edwin Forrest." Newburg has been famous for its regatta as early as 1838, and in the work referred to above some very interesting accounts of them are preserved. Stephen Roberts was the champion sculler in 1837. He rowed four match races with Sidney Dorlon, was defeated in the first, won the two next, and came in first in the fourth; but, Dorlon being interfered with, the race was declared off. The boat Gull, of the Castle Garden Athletic Association, was the first boat ever rowed to Philadelphia.

Fifteen years ago there were half a dozen amateur rowing clubs for every one now in existence. Around New York in particular there was to be found a grand galaxy of renowned organizations. Every available foot of water front was in the hands of an earnest band of aquatic lovers. The majority of these clubs have died away, and their liberal supporters are too heavy of limb now to longer appreciate the delights and sorrows of the exhilarating sport.

There have been few International crew races among the amateurs for the last ten years. One which set the tongue of the aquatic gossip talking was rowed in England on September 16th, 1882. It was between the Hillsdale crew, of this side, and a crack four of the Thames Rowing Club. The visitors were derided and insulted in every possible way while abroad, and when they were beaten it became painfully evident that International races were at an end for a time.

PART II.

ROWING was not a flourishing institution with the native colleges much before the first half of the fifties. About that time the clear-headed students of the two foremost universities of America commenced to realize the importance of physical culture. The more the students thought of it the more they became convinced of the necessity of a gymnasium where, in the whirl and excitement of dignified recreation, the hardships of a sedentary life would be forgotten. Of course there was the natural opposition on the part of the faculty and parents to any innovation that might divert the mind for a single moment from the books and tasks; but gradually the opposition faded away, and then came the general scramble for physical development. In 1851 there were three first-class boat clubs attached to Yale University. Harvard rejoiced in the possession of one organization only, but that one was the superior, both for membership and prowess, of anything that Yale could produce. The initial contest between these two colleges took place in the midsummer of 1852, and from that race the craze for aquatic glory sprang up; a craze that has held a firm root ever since. And in this thirty-seven years of glorious victories and honorable defeats, what grand strides have been made! It is no longer a battle between the rudely constructed boat and its undeveloped rowers, but a fight of the cultured giants in the finest specimen of craft that can be found. Everything is down as fine as a hair's point. Thousands of influential citizens who carried stout hearts under sturdy constitutions in after life traced the secret of their long life and grand physiques to their early intuition in the college rowing craft. Take Brayton Ives, Prof. Alex. Agassiz, Benj. K. Phelps, once District Attorney of New York; R. S. Peabody, the noted architect; Geo. W. Smalley, the journalist; the Rev. James Whiton, Richard H. Dana, Edmund Coffin, Wm. Blaikie, Dr. C. H. McBurney, Wm. A. Copp, and the three Crowninshields, Casper, Francis and B. W., as prominent illustrations of what the sport has done. This list does not represent any more than a bare fraction of the number of great men who have taken pride in being classed as veterans of the college sweep.

Although all the big colleges have had a voice in the growth of the sport, Yale and Harvard are justly credited with the distinction of having given it its permanent importance. The sport will never die while the blue mingles with the magenta colors. The first race in which the blue and the crimson participated has gone down into the history of the colleges as an inter-collegiate affair, but such it really was not. It was not until six years after, or in 1858, that formal arrangements were made for "an inter-collegiate regatta." It was Harvard which opened the negotiations, and Yale, Trinity, and Brown were not slow in responding. All the preliminaries had been attended to and perfected when an unfortunate disaster caused the postponement of the race. This was the drowning of Geo. E. Dunham, the Yale stroke, at Springfield, on July 17th of that year. The accident completely unnerved the men, and the blow was felt for some time after. It was not until the following year that a regular race for the inter-collegiate championship took place. The previous contests were of a scrub nature, so much so that they aroused but little interest outside college circles. The initial battle between Harvard and Yale was decided on August 3d, 1852. The race came about through a challenge from the blue to the Oneida Club, the Harvard organization.

Great minds had not considered the power and importance of anything superior to a big, stout barge at that time, and in this style of boat the first race was rowed. Yale owned two or three fairly good boats at that time, but Harvard had only one. This was the Oneida, and she is described as being the finest model of her kind at that time. The craft had originally been built for a race between two Boston clubs, and she was purchased from them in 1844, the year in which the Harvard lads first fell to rowing. The craft was of the lap-streak construction, thirty-seven feet long, and her chief features were a straight stem and no shear. In width she was three and a half feet. Her thole pins were of wood, plain and flat. The boat was floored with wooden strips half way up to the gunwale, and a grating made of hard, unpainted wood decorated each end. These gratings were the beauty spots of the craft in the minds of those interested, and the members of the crew used to take turns in polishing them up. For stretchers there were plain bars of wood, the stationary seats were covered with a cushion of red baize, and the tiller-rope was encased in painted canvas. To assist in the navigation of this craft the crew used eight white-ash oars, twelve feet long for the men stationed forward, and thirteen feet six inches in length for those amidships. This was the craft used for the first time by Harvard. The race was rowed in the Centre Harbor, Lake Winnepeseogee, N. H., at four o'clock in the afternoon, the start being taken from the third blast of a noisy bugle. The course was two miles to windward and straightaway. Not more than a handful of collegians were spectators at this contest, and when the Oneida, of Harvard, defeated the Shawmut or Halcyon, of Yale, a craft thirty-eight feet long, by two full lengths in ten minutes time there was scarcely any excitement. Harvard was much elated over this victory. The men had rowed together a dozen times only before the race, "for fear of blistering their hands," as one of them afterwards put it. The blue took its defeat with good grace, and before the oars were dry in the boat-house intimated another race. After some wrangling the Connecticut river, Springfield, was chosen as a course, and the distance was increased to three miles, or one and a half miles down stream and return. Harvard put two boats in this race, the Iris, an eight-oared barge, and the Y. Y., a four-oared barge. Yale showed up in two six-oared barges, the Nautilus and the Nereid. In this contest, which was rowed on July 21st, of 1855, outriggers were introduced for the first time, although as early as 1846 they had been used in the Oxford-Cambridge matches abroad. The Y. Y. was of St. John manufacture, outrigged and furnished with spruce oars instead of oak. The eight-oared barge of the college was only slightly outrigged, plain pieces of wood being spiked to the gunwales. The two Yale craft also had wooden outriggers, but bent a trifle and running from the bottom of the craft across the gunwale. They were braced like a wherry, and altogether better fitted than the craft of the crimson. There were great preparations made for the second race, and after weeks of figuring it was ascertained to the satisfaction of both colleges that eleven seconds for each one of the smaller craft would be about the proper handicap. The Yale boys showed before the race that which was then considered to be an excellent display of good judgment. They arose earlier than usual the morning of the race, and taking their craft to a quiet nook potleaded them thoroughly from the water-line down. Then they returned the boats to the house, and for hours before the contest "laughed up their sleeves" over the bright idea. Strange as it may appear, the poorest equipped boat of the fleet won that day, the Iris coming in ahead in twenty-two minutes, with the Y. Y. second, three seconds behind. The Nereid finished third in twenty-three minutes thirty-eight seconds, and the Nautilus occupied the tail end, an even minute behind the Nereid. The contest took all the moral courage out of Yale, and two and a half years stole by before her athletes would listen to a proposition for another race. But, as hinted at above, Harvard threw down the gauntlet on this occasion, and the death of young Dunham terminated the season's programme. The first race of the genuine inter-collegiate series was rowed on July 26th, 1859. Lake Quinsigamond at Worcester was adopted as a central course. The distance was the same as in the race of 1855.

In November of 1857 Harvard had constructed the first six-oared

HARVARD BOAT CREW AT THEIR TRAINING GROUND.

shell ever put together on this side of the Atlantic. The craft was only forty feet long, cut short, as her builder said, to facilitate an easy turn of a stake mark. She had twenty-six inches "beam," not much more than is in use these days, and rigged she tipped the scale at 150 pounds. White pine was for the most part used in her construction, and the frame was set off by iron outriggers, another great novelty at the time. There was no coxswain.

The second and last regatta for a period of ten years in which more than two colleges took part was rowed on the Quinsigamond course on July 24th, 1860; Harvard winning in eighteen minutes fifty-three seconds, Yale second in nineteen minutes five seconds, and Brown twenty-one minutes fifteen seconds. After that contest Brown rowed a big boat, and refused to engage in other contests. The faculty of Yale and Harvard also put a barred gate in the way, and the war breaking out there was no contest between the colleges for four years.

Want of space prohibits a detailed account of the other great races between that time and this, but, for the benefit of those who desire to preserve the records of the battles lost and won, a carefully prepared list of races from the beginning of the second period in 1864 to the present time is subjoined:

Second Period—1864 to 1870.

Date.	Crews.	Time. m. s.	Date.	Crews.	Time. m. s.
1864	Yale, winner	19 01	1868	Harvard, winner	18 28½
	Harvard	19 43½		Yale	18 38½
1865	Harvard, winner	18 09	1869	Harvard, winner	18 02
	Yale	18 42½		Yale	18 11
1866	Harvard, winner	18 43½	1870	Yale, winner	18 45
	Yale	19 10		Harvard	20 30
1867	Harvard, winner	18 12¾			
	Yale	19 25½			

This closed the series which had been so disastrous to Yale, she having won but two races to the crimson's seven. The next series took place on the Connecticut river over a three mile straightaway course. Here's how they resulted:

Third Period—1871 to 1875.

Date.	Crews.	Time. m. s.	Date.	Crews.	Time. m. s.
1871	Mass. Agr., winner	16 46½	1873	Wesleyan	17 01
	Harvard	17 23½		Harvard	17 11
	Brown	17 47½		Dartmouth	17 27½
1872	Amherst, winner	16 33		Amherst	17 32
	Harvard	16 57		Columbia	17 53½
	Mass. Agr.	17 10		Bowdoin	18 07¼
	Bowdoin	17 21		Mass. Agr.	18 19½
	Williams	17 59		Cornell	18 24
	Yale	18 13		Trinity	18 42
1873	Yale, winner	16 59		Williams	19 25½

AQUATICS.

In 1874 the course was changed to Saratoga Lake, and two races on a three mile straightaway course resulted as follows:

Date.	Crews.	Time. m. s.	Date.	Crews.	Time. m. s.
1874—	Columbia, winner	16 42½	1875—	Columbia	17 04¼
	Wesleyan	16 50		Harvard	17 05¾
	Harvard	16 54		Dartmouth	17 10¼
	Trinity	18 23		Wesleyan	17 13¾
	Princeton	18 38		Yale	17 14¼
	Dartmouth	17 08¼		Amherst	17 29¾
	Williams	17 31		Brown	17 33¾
	Cornell	18 00		Williams	17 43¾
1875—	Cornell, winner	16 58½		Bowdoin	17 50¾

At the conclusion of the last pointed regatta, Yale and Harvard joined hands and decided to have a private trial of speed over four miles each year, and to bar all other colleges. Since that agreement thirteen races have been decided. The record of these is appended:

FOURTH SERIES—1876 to 1889.

Date.	Place.	Winning Crew.	Time. m. s.	Date.	Place.	Winning Crew.	Time. m. s.
1876—	Springfield,	Yale	22 02	1883—	New London,	Harvard	25 46½
1877—	Springfield,	Harvard	24 36	1884—	New London,	Yale	20 31
1878—	New London,	Harvard	20 45	1885—	New London,	Harvard	25 15½
1879—	New London,	Harvard	23 48	1886—	New London,	Yale	20 31¼
1880—	New London,	Yale	25 09	1887—	New London,	Yale	22 56
1881—	New London,	Yale	22 19	*1888—	New London,	Yale	20 10
1882—	New London,	Harvard	20 47½	†1889—	New London,	Yale	15 37

*Best on record. † Three miles. Time over full course 21 m. 30 s.

PART III.

ENGLISHMEN rightfully claim that the defeats of their professional oarsmen in mixed national regattas are more than counteracted by the victories of their collegiate and other amateur scullers at international contests. Her Majesty's subjects point with pride to the accomplished and finished style of their college crews. Some day it may come the good fortune of an American college crew to lower the colors of the representative oarsmen of English universities, but up to date the foreign collegians have invariably whipped their American cousins in rowing contests. Harvard once essayed to meet a representative English 'Versity crew in four-oared racing, but was defeated. Columbia, however, earned success in a race at Henley several years ago, but not against a representative English university eight. There is no getting away from the fact that Oxford and Cambridge are the fountain-head of eight-oared rowing. Of the two, eight-oared rowing was first introduced at Oxford, but long before that time it was practiced at Eton College. After Oxford took it up it made its way to the River Cam, where Cambridge adopted it.

In 1826 the first eight-oared boat for Cambridge was built at Eton, and belonged to St. John's College. The earliest college races on the Cam were rowed in 1827, when five boats contested, one ten-oar, one eight-oar, and three six-oar. The proposition for the first university race between Oxford and Cambridge came from the latter in February, 1829, and was rowed over a distance of 2¼ miles, from Hambledon Lock to Henley Bridge on the Thames. The boats were much shorter than they are at present, an eight of that period being no longer than a single scull-shell of to-day. The time of the first race was variously stated as from eleven to fourteen minutes, but it was agreed that Oxford won by between four and five lengths, time not being considered so much a factor as the distance by which one crew beat the other. The 'versity oarsmen were not so heavy then as they are at present, Cambridge being represented by an eight whose average weight was 155¾ pounds. Five years elapsed before Cambridge again essayed to demonstrate superiority over her sister university, and a challenge was then sent to Oxford, with the stipulation that the course should be from Westminster Bridge to Hammersmith. This was objected to by Oxford, for the reason that the course on which the first race was rowed was preferable for many reasons. This disagreement caused an abandonment of the race for two years more. In 1836 Cambridge and Oxford challenged simultaneously, and the race took place on June 17th from Westminster Bridge to Putney Bridge. Cambridge won by one minute. Cambridge beat her own time on that occasion by five minutes, and in 1832 Oxford covered the distance in thirty minutes forty-five seconds, or almost six minutes faster than the time made by her crew in 1836.

The 1889 race between the Oxford and the Cambridge crews was the forty-sixth contest rowed by the representatives of these two great English universities. Of these Oxford has won twenty-three, Cambridge twenty-two, and one resulted in a dead heat in 1877, when Oxford pulled the last mile with only seven men, their bow having broken an oar. In 1849 there were two contests, Cambridge winning in March and Oxford in December on a foul. The race in 1859 was rowed despite the fact that the weather was so bad as to make the water very dangerous for even a stout craft. The Cambridge boat sunk a mile from the finish, and all the members of the crew were saved, though one of them could not swim a stroke.

The following is a table of the aquatic contests between these famous universities:

Year.	Date.	Winner.	Time. M. S.	Won by
1829	June 10	Oxford	14.30	Easily
1836	June 17	Cambridge	36.00	1 minute
1839	April 3	Cambridge	31.00	1 minute 45 seconds
1840	April 15	Cambridge	29.30	¾ length
1841	April 14	Cambridge	32.30	1 minute 4 seconds
1842	June 11	Oxford	30.45	13 seconds
1845	March 15	Cambridge	23.30	30 seconds
1846	April 3	Cambridge	31.05	2 lengths
1849	March 29	Cambridge	22.00	Easily
1849	December 15	Oxford	00.00	Foul
1852	April 3	Oxford	21.36	27 seconds
1854	April 8	Oxford	25.29	11 strokes
1856	March 15	Cambridge	25.50	½ length
1856	April 4	Oxford	22.35	35 seconds
1858	March 27	Cambridge	21.23	22 seconds
1859	April 15	Oxford	24.40	C. sunk
1860	March 31	Cambridge	26.05	1 length
1861	March 23	Oxford	23 30	48 seconds
1862	April 12	Oxford	24.41	30 seconds
1863	March 23	Oxford	23.06	43 seconds
1864	March 19	Oxford	21.40	26 seconds
1865	April 8	Oxford	21.24	4 lengths
1866	March 24	Oxford	25.35	15 seconds
1867	April 13	Oxford	22 40	½ length
1868	April 4	Oxford	20.56	6 lengths
1869	March 17	Oxford	20.05	3 lengths
1870	April 6	Cambridge	22.04	1¼ lengths
1871	April 1	Cambridge	23.05	1 length
1872	March 23	Cambridge	21.15	2 lengths
1873	March 29	Cambridge	19.35	3¼ lengths
1874	March 28	Cambridge	22.35	3 lengths
1875	March 20	Oxford	22.02	10 lengths
1876	April 8	Cambridge	20.20	Easily

Year.	Date.	Winner.	Time. M. S.	Won by
1877	March 24	Oxford } Cambridge }	24.08	dead heat.
1878	April 13	Oxford	22.13	10 lengths
1879	April 5	Cambridge	21.18	3¼ lengths
1880	March 22	Oxford	21.23	3¼ lengths
1881	April 8	Oxford	21.51	3 lengths
1882	April 1	Oxford	20.12	7 lengths
1883	March 15	Oxford	21.18	3½ lengths
1884	April 7	Cambridge	21.39	2¼ lengths
1885	March 28	Oxford	21.36	3 lengths
1886	April 3	Cambridge	22.29	⅔ length
1887	March 26	Cambridge	20.52	2¼ lengths
1888	March 24	Cambridge	20.48	7 lengths
1889	March 30	Cambridge	——	2 lengths

In addition to the above, the universities have contended five times in the same heat at Henley regatta for the Grand Challenge Cup, with the following record:

Year.	Date.	Winner.	Time. M. S.	Won by
1845	June 7	Cambridge	8.30	2 lengths
1847	June 17	Oxford	8 04	2 lengths
1851	June 17	Oxford	7.45	6 lengths
1853	June 11	Oxford	8.03	1½ length
1855	June 25	Cambridge	8.32	2¼ lengths

Also at the Thames National regatta, on June 22d, 1844, when Oxford beat Cambridge.

PART IV.

It is like saying that black is white to make the statement that the professional oarsman is improving in a worldly way. There will always be a question about the physical improvement of the modern sculler over his old time brethren, but there is hardly any room for doubting the depressed condition of the former's finances. "There is no money in the business," is a familiar cry these days among the little band of athletes who feather the water and send forth sweet music from the row-locks for a living. A great deal has been said and written about the fabulous financial resources of the present day sculler, and though it may not be believed by the public it is nevertheless true that few, if any, of our professional oarsmen get more than a bare sustenance from the whirl of the sculls. I know of half a dozen who are doing the bread-and-butter act in plain, ordinary, every-day walks of life at so much per day. You couldn't convince them that there is a future for the professional sliding-seat any more than you could convince them that there is luck in the possession of a moonstone. It is perfectly natural to signal out Ned Hanlan and one or two others as an evidence of the reputed prosperity of the business, but the money-owning professional reaped his harvest in the golden sunset of a full decade ago. Since that time the occupation has been declining, steadily and gradually, but surely, until now a man must be a king-pin at the top-notch to make the shekels ring. It doesn't require the services of a new fangled telescope or even an investigating committee to understand why 'tis thus. The public has played one part in the downfall, but that task was merely to finish up what the rowers themselves began. It's cruel to say that dishonest practices and an utter disregard for the rights of a patient public had all to do with the stifling of that intense interest that was once showered on the sport, but when it's true what's the use of denying it? The record of crooked races won and lost is a mighty card in the hands of that public, and it will be held aloft as a death knell to the professional oarsmen's financial success until such time as these devotees of the shell re-establish themselves in the confidence and esteem of the masses.

For the first time in a number of years the aquatic world realizes that the question of supremacy as applied to the professional ranks is settled for a time. In the defeat of William O'Connor, the Canadian crack, by Henry Ernest Searle, of New South Wales, the last spark of hope in the American breast simmered away. The Yankee blood centred more than a passing interest on the young Kanuck. His manly exhibition on the Potomac last fall, when he extinguished John Teemer's light, showed that he was made of the right stuff. In that contest he tried his best to establish his fondness for fair play, and how well he succeeded is shown by the history of the event. Twice before the start did the McKeesport sculler try to command an unfair advantage over his opponent, and O'Connor would have "let it slide" had his admirers not interposed in his behalf. Teemer lost a great many staunch friends by his conduct during that race, and it is a burning blot on the record of the American that he refused to shake hands with the Canadian after the contest had been decided. What a striking difference there was when this same O'Connor fell before the mighty sweep of Goliah Searle! Ill and weak at heart, with his tower of fame pulled asunder, O'Connor sought the victorious Antipodean, placed his brawny hands within his own, and said, so that all could hear: "You are my superior in every way, Henry; on tide water I'd be willing to lose any day to you." May be it was this sample of genuine manliness that brought forth the ringing three cheers and a tiger from the British public when the Canadian started to row back to his headquarters.

It was Bob Cook who once said that Ned Hanlan had done more for professional racing than any other man in the business. The famous coach of Yale University never spoke a truer sentence. The equal of Hanlan as an ardent and conscientious worker in the hum and drum of the professional life has not yet fully declared himself. There were any number of enthusiastic workers before Hanlan's time, but they were freighted down with old-fangled notions that did more harm than good. There was no bombast about Hanlan's efforts, however. He never believed in show, and a great many things which have come as a result of his deep, quiet thinking have been attributed to the brain of other followers of aquatics. One can admire Hanlan without even knowing him in a personal way. But to appreciate the goodness of the man it is necessary to know him thoroughly. If one knows him in public life one has a pretty accurate idea of his private character. Always pleasing, ever kind and generous, and never vulgar—such are the home and public traits of one of the best of fathers and scullers. If the man ever had a hobby outside the confines of the rowing paraphernalia, it was to own a grand home. His hand has never been that slow or his purse that spare but what he could buy some trinket to bedeck his castle. "My wife is the gem and my home the setting," he has often said. Yes, his wife is the gem. She is for Ned Hanlan first, last, and all the time, and he has won many a dollar through her wholesome advice and never failing assistance. I have seen her as a spectator at races where Ned was in a bruising contest, her large blue eyes all aglow with a mellow softness, her beautiful form towering backward and forward in terrible suspense as if she and not he were sliding the seat, and her bloodless lips moving in silent prayer for the success of her heart's idol. If it wasn't pure, honest devotion, let somebody else call it by its proper name.

Next to Hanlan, Charles E. Courtney ranks as a veteran and chief figure in American aquatics. The Union Springs' sculler is now the trainer and mentor of the oarsmen attached to Cornell University. That his hand is still dextrous and his mind active and alive to the hour is evident in the wonderful success of late years of the Ithaca College oarsmen. Courtney has never believed in the supposed superiority of big oarsmen over the little fellows, and that is his only explanation for putting a light-weight eight-oared crew on the market last year—a crew stroked by a young Sandwich Islander, and which beat Columbia and the University of Pennsylvania 'Varsity crews on the Thames last June, and smashed the best time on record on the Schuylkill on July 5th. Courtney's early races were rowed from the Union Springs' Boat Club. His first prominent race was with Joseph Seeley, whom he defeated on Cayuga Lake, August 6th, 1868. His time for the three miles was thirty-three minutes. After that his victories as an amateur were all but numberless. His reputation in the professional ranks is too well known to be given here. He was at the "head of the pack" when the boat cutting incident levelled him to the ground, and he has rowed only a few good races since.

Even to-day you can find hundreds of sporting men who forget their childhood lessons in forebearance whenever the name of Courtney is spoken. These are unchangeable in the opinion that he had a direct hand in the cutting of that shell. They did not see him do it, of course, but they put two and two together to suit their own purposes, and offer very one-sided arguments to prove their case. But when it comes down to cold, plain facts the boot is on the other foot, and there is really no just cause for affirming that the Union Springs' rower had a hand in the dastardly outrage. Since that memorable occurrence Courtney has lived under a heart-beating cloud. He has often insisted that the public had not given him a fair hearing, and that he was condemned and punished without mercy. Gazing at that sawed boat in 1887, Courtney said to the writer: "That shell brought me blasted hopes and a name that God knows I never deserved. But I'll live it down, I'll live it down, and I'll show these hounds who are now so willing to cast their cowardly aspersions at me that I remain what I have always been—an honest oarsman and a loyal friend."

Henry Ernest Searle, the champion, has written a short sketch of himself which, with his permission, is used in this work. "I was born" he says, "on July 14th, 1866, at Grafton, on the Clarence river, New South Wales. Both my parents are of English birth, and settled in Australia when Grafton was founded. I was a mere boy when my father changed his home to Esk Island, forty miles from Grafton. He purchased the island, and began farming. The nearest school-house to the island was three and one-half miles away. My father was a poor man, but he had the proper idea of education, and insisted upon my going to school. I learned very little at school, but I acquired the knowledge of how to pull a boat, because I had to row to and from school, a distance of seven miles, every day. This task made me strong, and when at thirteen years of age I found myself a big, strapping fellow, full of life and full of confidence, I told my father that the farm had no attraction for me. In 1883 my whole body was afire with the desire to figure as a great oarsman. I had rowed in a number of scrub races with schoolmates who were no match for me. So in the fall of 1884 I entered for a race in the watermen's skiffs. It was rowed at Chatsworth on November 9th, and I won. There was a young fellow named F. Fischer in the contest who gave me a tight push, and after the race we agreed to form a partnership to row double. Our first race together was in a regatta at Hardwood Island in May, 1885. Three pairs started, and we finished second; but the first boat was disqualified on a foul and we received the prize. The following January, on the same course, I entered in an all-comers' race. It was rowed in light skiffs over a three mile course, and I beat M. Wallace and M. Driscoll, then good oarsmen. Wallace, however, bested me in the final race of the day—a mile contest. I finished second, and G. Baker was third. I forgive Wallace for that defeat, for I have beaten him many times since. The following April, in a light skiff race at Chatsworth, with a level start, I out-rowed A. Baker, M. Wallace, G. Bush, and L. Pringle. Two days after the Chatsworth Island race I competed at Yamba. Here I was compelled to carry ten pounds as a handicap, Baker and Wallace starting at feather-weight. The water was very rough, and I shipped a half boat full, and once or twice I was nearly swamped. Still, I managed to get second place, Baker beating me out at the finish.

"When I reached my twentieth birthday I was as I am now, 5 feet 10 inches high, with a chest measurement of $41\tfrac{3}{4}$ inches and 175 pounds of flesh. My training weight now is 162. In 1886 I was doing regular work at the farm, seeing to things and generally assisting my father; but I would take half an hour in the morning or in the evening for practice. My race after Yamba was at Palmer's Island. I then had sixteen pounds handicap, A. Baker sixteen pounds, Wallace ten pounds, and G. Baker feather-weight. I won, with Wallace second. I rowed again at Palmer's Island with twenty-eight pounds handicap, A. Baker eight pounds, Wallace seven pounds, and Reid feather. After a good race, in which I led for a mile, my weight began to tell, and Baker passed me, though I pressed him home a good second. Then I rowed a match with M. Wallace, at Chatsworth, over a two and a half mile course, and won easily. A fortnight later I rowed a match with S. Davis over the same course. It was a clinking race for the first half mile, but I beat him with ease at the finish. It was, I think, in 1887 that I rowed Maclean a time-allowance skiff race, receiving twenty seconds from D. McDonald, one of the best scullers for his weight that ever got into a boat. He was a small man, but game as a pebble. He was in the Trickett, Laycock, and Rush set, so that this occasion afforded my first chance of seeing what I could do against men of world-wide reputation. Two others were also in the race, A. Baker, with twenty-six seconds start, and M. Wallace, with forty-five seconds. I soon caught up with Baker, and after a mile and a half passed Wallace, leading easily home, McDonald coming in a good second. A month or two later, at Chatsworth, I rowed my first skiff race.' I was handicapped thirty-five pounds, against A. Baker, twenty pounds; R. J. Brown, fifteen pounds, and M. Wallace, feather-weight. It was a good race to the first stake-boat; there Brown and I fouled. I got the worst of the foul, all getting around before me, and I had to renew a stern chase, which was not, however, as long as the proverbial one, for I came up, hand over hand, and won by about two lengths, with a bit up my sleeve. Wallace was second.

"I now took to rowing in wager boats for the first time, and on the 2d of January, 1888, rowed at my birthplace, Grafton. The following entered for the race: Hanlan, scratch; C. Neilson, three and one-half lengths' start; W. Hearn, the New Zealand champion, four and one-half lengths' start, and myself, who received seven lengths. We all paddled to the scratch and got to our moorings, when, just as the flag was about to fall, Hanlan quietly says: 'I guess I won't start; I don't feel well,' and off he went a quarter of a mile ahead of us all, determined to see the race if he did not take part in it. We got the signal, and off we went at a rattling pace. I kept my distance throughout, and won by just the number of lengths I had received. How I wished Hanlan had rowed! The race was a terrific struggle for a mile between Neilson and myself, but I pulled through at the finish. Neilson was second.

"After this race I took a trip to Sydney, 350 miles from the Clarence river. I there met for the first time my friend, Neil Matterson. He arranged a match for me with Wolf. The stakes were £100 a side, and we decided on the Parramatta river course. I showed him the way home. A fortnight later I met on the same course James Stansbury for £100 a side. This was the hardest race I ever rowed in my life. After the severest struggle I just managed to get in first, beating all records, for I did the three miles 330 yards in 19 minutes 58 seconds.

"In September of the same year I rowed over the same course against C. Neilson for £200 a side, and won rather easily. A fortnight later I rowed W. Hughes, at Newcastle, Hunter river, for £100 a side, and allowing him ten seconds start. The day was very rough, and when we had gone about half a mile my boat sprang a leak and began to fill rapidly, so that I had to make the best use of my time to get to the post. I need scarcely say that I did so, but just before getting home the plug flew out of my boat, and I was compelled to take off my cap to stuff up the hole with. I got home twelve lengths to the good, but only just in time for all that, for just as the post was passed my boat went down below the water-line, and I alone remained visible. I was now matched against Peter Kemp, the champion sculler of the world, over the championship course on the Parramatta river. We rowed October 28th, 1888, and a great day that was for me, for, after a pretty good race for a mile, I went ahead, and when the post was passed I was left in the proud position of champion, and the dreams of my early boyhood had come true."

William O'Connor is not only a beautiful sculler, but he is a lucky one. The career of Hanlan, Beach, Laycock, Trickett, Teemer, Gaudaur, and in fact all the professional champions, shows that they were obliged to climb step by step the ladder of fame. Not so with O'Connor. He rowed a few races only, and reached the point. His races with Teemer, Gaudaur, Lee, and Henry Peterson, of San Francisco, were the only ones to which he can point with any degree of professional pride. Still, without the ability he could not have beaten these men. And O'Connor has the ability. There is no oarsman in this country, Canada or the United Kingdom and Continent of Europe to whom he has to pay homage. He is the peer of any of them, and, although Searle lately defeated him, there are hundreds who saw that race who think that the Canadian, properly boated, would be found too fast for the Antipodean on dead water. O'Connor is a very unhappy man in street costume. He looks and acts clumsy in that garb. But on the sliding-seat he is graceful and unabashed. He is never at a loss what to do with his hands and feet there. His movement is exceptionally fine.

The victories of William Beach are almost as numerous as those of Hanlan. The honors of Trickett, Laycock, Boyd, Morris, and a dozen other good men had fallen to Hanlan when Beach jumped into fame. During 1883 he defeated E. A. Trickett three times on the Parramatta course, making the three miles and 330 yards within twenty-one minutes each time. The following February he suffered his first genuine defeat. Trickett was the man who did the trick. The April after that Beach again finished in first of his old rival. Hanlan went to Australia in 1884, and on August 16th was bested by the big Antipodean. After beating T. Clifford in 1885, Beach again laid out Hanlan, and N. Matterson followed. Beach went to England in 1886, and defeated Gaudaur and Ross. When he returned to Australia the next year he put his third defeat of Hanlan on record. Hanlan seemed unfit to meet Beach after that, and when the Australian showed the way to the Canadian a fourth time on November 27th, of 1888, Hanlan was undone.

Lack of space prevents an extended history of John Teemer, Jacob G. Gaudaur, George Lee, George Hosmer, Henry Peterson, James Ten-Eyck and a number of other professionals of note. Teemer had a great future before him once, but now he finds it all an up-hill fight. The McKeesport sculler was always a peculiar man. His ideas of training are indeed liberal, not because the practice is advantageous, but because it is much easier to prepare under his rule and system than under any other. Wallace Ross once told me that Teemer could never hope to remain a champion long. "He is killing his stomach, mind and body by his utter disregard of the rules of nature," Ross said. "He never masticates his food; he simply dumps it down in wholesale fashion. Pastry, meats, beer, tea, coffee, everything or anything, it makes no difference to John—all go." Gaudaur is just the reverse. He has a horror of anything that might "put him on his beam end." He knows what he likes and he likes nothing that is not beneficial. There was a time when, in common with many other oarsmen and athletes, he considered animal flesh the elixir of life. Experiments, however, showed him the folly of this belief. He found that meat made him decidedly nervous, and that when partaken of before or after a heavy practice spin he could not rest at night. Teemer was rowing at his best in 1885. On October 24th of that year he met Hanlan for the first time. The race was rowed on the Pleasure Bay course, at Albany, and to use an expression of a prominent writer of that day "turned out to be a championship fizzle." Hanlan was overmatched and out-rowed, and failed to finish the race. Teemer covered the course in twenty-one minutes thirteen seconds. Hanlan explained his defeat by saying that in turning his stake-boat he miscalculated the current and carried his shell against the mark and was thrown into the water. His judge, Dan Breen, assisted him back to his boat. After a long line of contests, crowned with many victories, Teemer lost the championship to O'Connor on the Potomac river course, November 24th, 1888. Gaudaur met Teemer again at the Point of Pines, May 30th, and at

Round Bay, Md., August 9th, 1888, and Teemer won in each case. The last time that Gaudaur and Teemer met was at McKeesport, on September 13th, 1889. Gaudaur finished first, but Teemer was fouled by Al Hamm, and the referee decided the race a draw. There is hardly any question but that Teemer has seen his best day. Jake Gaudaur is now his superior as a sculler. In fact Gaudaur is almost as good to-day as he was in 1886 and 1887, when he defeated both Teemer and Hanlan. When the Indian half-breed met Beach in England, on September 18th, 1886, and was defeated over the British championship course he was in anything but good condition. The same state of affairs existed when O'Connor defeated him at Sturgeon Point, August 22d, 1888.

George Lee has had an up and down sort of life since he began with the sculls. Originally a Newark amateur he started out well, winning the National Association championship. He was very fast in 1886, when he out-rowed Neil Matterson on the Putney-Mortlake course, and continued so up to the time he met and defeated Hanlan at Toronto, and again on San Francisco Bay.

James A. TenEyck, of Peekskill, N. Y., probably had a better record as an amateur than as a professional. As a youngster he beat John McNiel, Ferryman, Skidgel, Thomas Murphy, Gilbert Ward, James Shean, and many other good men.

For the benefit of those who desire to preserve the record of the more celebrated sculling matches which have been decided here and abroad, the following tables are compiled from that sterling and reliable publication, *The Clipper Annual:*

INTERNATIONAL SCULLING MATCHES.

Date.	Winner.	Loser.	Where.	Distance. Mls. Yds.	Time. M. S.
1866.... July 4.........	H. Kelly.........	James Hamill....	England.....	5 000	32 45
1866..... July 5..........	H. Kelly.........	James Hamill....	England.....	5 000	36 00
1868..... October 21......	Jno. McNiel.....	O'Niel..........	United States.	2 000	15 51
1869.... November 19....	Walter Brown...	John Sadler.....	England.....	3 000	21 50
1871..... September 1....	Joseph Sadler....	Brown..........	Halifax......	3 000	25 02
1871..... September 11...	Joseph Sadler....	Kelly..........	United States.	4 000	30 18½

INTERNATIONAL SCULLING MATCHES—*Continued.*

Date.	Winner.	Loser.	Where.	Distance. M. Y.	Time. M. S.	Date.	Winner.	Loser.	Where.	Distance. M. Y.	Time. M. S.
1880	E. C. Laycock	Th. Blackman	England	4 440	26 13½	1886	G. Bubear	C. Neilson	England	4 440	——
1880	E. C. Laycock	G. H. Hosmer	England	4 300	26 08½	1886	G. J. Perkins	P. Kemp	England	4 440	24 40
1880	E. C. Laycock	J. H. Riley	England	4 440	25 04	1886	G. Bubear	P. Kemp	England	4 440	24 20
1880	E. Hanlan †	E. A. Trickett	England	4 440	26 12	1886	N. Matterson	G. J. Perkins	England	4 440	25 12
1880	W. Ross	E. A. Trickett	England	4 440	23 42	1886	G. W. Lee	N. Matterson	England	4 440	24 25
1881	E. Hanlan	E. C. Laycock	England	4 440	25 40	1886	W. Beach	J. Gaudaur †	England	4 440	22 29
1882	E. Hanlan	R. W. Boyd	England	3 563	21 25	1886	W. Beach	W. Ross †	England	4 440	23 05
1882	E. Hanlan †	E. A. Trickett	England	4 440	27 58	1886	J. Largan	C. Neilson	England	4 440	27 30
1882	E. C. Laycock	R. W. Boyd	England	3 880	17 28	1887	G. Bubear	J. A. TenEyck	America	3 000	20 16⅛
1882	J. Largan	H. Pearce	England	4 440	24 40	1887	G. Bubear	W. Ross	America	3 000	20 00
1884	W. Ross	G. Bubear *	England	4 440	26 10	1887	C. E. Courtney	G. Bubear	America	††	19 35
1884	E. Hanlan	E. C. Laycock	Australia	0 000	22 45	1887	W. Beach	E. Hanlan †	Australia	3 440	19 55¾
1884	W. Beach	E. Hanlan †	Australia	3 330	20 29	1888	P. Kemp	E. Hanlan †	Australia	3 330	21 36
1885	E. Hanlan	T. Clifford	Australia	3 330	21 04	1888	E. Hanlan	Ed. Trickett	Australia		
1885	W. Beach	T. Clifford †	Australia	3 330	26 01½	1888	P. Kemp	E. Hanlan †	Australia	3 330	21 25
1885	W. Beach	E. Hanlan †	Australia	3 330	22 51¼	1888	W. Beach	E. Hanlan	Australia	3 330	21 15
1886	G. J. Perkins	N. Matterson	England	4 440	——						

* Received ten seconds start. † Championship of the world. †† Course short of announced three miles.

AMERICAN SCULLING CHAMPIONSHIP.

Date.	Winner.	Loser.	Distance.	Time. M. S.	Date.	Winner.	Loser.	Distance.	Time. M. S.
1859 Oct. 11	Joshua Ward	T. Daw, etc.	5 mls.	35 10	1875 Oct. 16	E. Morris	H. Coulter	†	35 20
1862 Aug. 13	Jas. Hamill	J. Ward	3 mls.	22 27	1876 Oct. 21	W. Scharff	E. Morris	5 mls.	*
1862 Aug. 14	Jas. Hamill	J. Ward	5 mls.	37 39	1877 June 9	E. Morris	Wm Scharff	5 mls.	36 45
1863 July 23	J. Ward	J. Hamill	5 mls.	42 29	1877 Oct. 13	E. Morris	P. Luther	5 mls.	37 05
1863 Sept. 28	J. Hamill	J. Ward	5 mls.	37 38	1878 June 20	E. Hanlan	E. Morris	5 mls.	37 00
1864 July 19	J. Hamill	J. Ward	5 mls.	40 46	1885 Oct. 24	J. Teemer	E. Hanlan	3 mls.	21 13
1867 May 21	W. Brown.	J. Hamill	5 mls.	46 30	1886 June 12	J. G. Gaudaur	J. Teemer	3 mls	21 20
1867 Sept. 9	J. Hamill	W. Brown	5 mls.	Sunk	1887 May 30	J. G. Gaudaur	E. Hanlan	†	19 32
1868 June 19	J. Hamill	H. Coulter	5 mls.	37 26	1887 July 23	E. Hanlan	J. G. Gaudaur	3 mls.	20 33
1868 Sept. 9	W. Brown	H. Coulter	†	34 28½	1887 Aug. 13	J. Teemer	E. Hanlan	†	19 26
1874 July 8	Geo. Brown	Wm Scharff	5 mls.	*	1887 Oct. 28	J. Teemer	J. G. Gaudaur	3 mls.	20 28⅛
1874 Sept. 26	Geo. Brown	E. Morris	5 mls.	37 00	1888 Nov. 24	W. O'Connor	J. Teemer	3 mls.	20 33
1875 Sept. 11	E. Morris	H. Coulter	†	*					

* No official time taken. † The course measured less than the announced distance.

ENGLISH SCULLING CHAMPIONSHIP.

All races rowed straightaway, with tide. Previous winners appear in *Annual* for 1884.

Date.	Winner.	Loser.	Distance. M. Y.	Time. M. S.	Date.	Winner.	Loser.	Distance. M. Y.	Time. M. S.
1831 Sept. 9	C. Campbell	Williams	——	——	1877 May 28	R. W. Boyd	J. Higgins	4 300	29 00
1846 Aug. 19	R. Combes	Campbell	4 300	25 15	1877 Oct. 8	J. Higgins	R. W. Boyd	4 300	24 10
1852 May 24	T. Cole	Combes	4 300	25 15	1878 Jan. 14	J. Higgins	R. W. Boyd	3 713	Foul
1854 Nov. 20	J. Messenger	Cole	4 300	24 25	1878 June 3	J. Higgins	W. Elliott	4 300	24 38
1857 May 12	H. Kelley	Messenger	4 300	24 35	1879 Feb. 17	W. Elliott	J. Higgins	3 713	22 01
1859 Sept. 29	R. Chambers	Kelley	4 300	25 25	1879 June 16	Ed. Hanlan	W. Elliott	3 563	22 01
1865 Aug. 8	H. Kelley	Chambers	4 300	23 26	1880 Nov. 15	Ed. Hanlan	E. A. Trickett	4 440	26 12
1866 Nov. 22	R. Chambers	J. Sadler	4 300	25 04	1881 Feb. 14	Ed. Hanlan	E. C. Laycock	4 440	25 40
1867 May 6	H. Kelley	Chambers	5 000	31 47	1882 April 3	Ed. Hanlan	R. W. Boyd	3 563	21 25
1868 Nov. 17	J. Renforth	H. Kelly	4 300	23 15	1886 May 24	G. J. Perkins	N. Matterson	4 440	——
1874 April 16	J. H. Sadler	R. Bagnall	4 300	24 15	1887 Feb. 7	G. Bubear	G. J. Perkins	3 563	23 34
1875 Nov. 15	J. H. Sadler	R. W. Boyd	4 300	29 02	1888 Feb. 13	W. Ross	G. Bubear	4 440	23 16

AQUATICS.

SCULLING RACES IN AUSTRALIA.

Previous winners appear in *Annual* for 1884.

Date.	Winner.	Loser.	Distance. M. Y.	Time. M. S.	Date.	Winner.	Loser.	Distance. M. Y.	Time. M. S.
1883 Jan. 13	D. McDonald	J. Largan	3 330	21 50	1885 Mch. 28	W. Beach	E. Hanlan	3 330	22 51¼
1883 Feb. 17	T. Clifford	H. Pearce	3 330	29 50	1885 May 29	N. Matterson	C. Messenger	3 330	23 51½
1883 Mch. 10	E. C. Laycock	M. Rush	3 330		1885 Dec. 12	C. Neilson	C. Matterson	3 330	22 35
1883 April 21	G. Perkins	C. Messenger	3 330	26 15	1885 Dec. 18	W. Beach	N. Matterson	3 330	24 11¼
1883 July 28	E. A. Trickett	W. Beach	3 330	21 15	1887 April 29	W. G Brett	D. Green	3 330	24 15
1883 Aug. 18	W Beach	E. A. Trickett	3 330	20 50½	1887 July 4	P. Kemp	N. Matterson	3 330	22 21½
1883 Aug. 27	W. Beach	E. A. Trickett	3 330	20 44	1887 Nov. 26	W. Beach	E. Hanlan	3 440	19 55¾
1883 Dec. 1	E. A. Trickett	M. Rush	3 330	25 17	1888 Feb. 11	P. Kemp	T. Clifford †	3 330	23 47¼
1883 Dec. 8	W. Beach	E. A. Trickett	3 330	20 58	1888 May 5	P. Kemp	E. Hanlan †	3 330	21 36
1884 Feb. 1	E. A. Trickett	W. Beach	3 330	27 00	1888 June 13	E. Hanlan	E. Trickett		
1884 Feb. 2	T. Clifford	H. Pearce	3 330	22 05	1888 July 13	H. Searle	J. Stansbury	3 330	19 53
1884 April 12	W. Beach	E. A. Trickett	3 330	23 19	1888 Sept. 14	H. Searle	C. Neilson	3 330	21 34¼
1884 May 10	W. G. Brett	Wood	3 330	25 46	1888 Sept. 26	N. Matterson	C Neilson	3 330	25 09
1884 May 22	E. Hanlan	E. C. Laycock	0 000	22 45	1888 Sept. 28	P. Kemp	E. Hanlan †	3 330	21 25
1884 Aug. 16	W. Beach	Ed. Hanlan	3 330	20 29	1888 Oct. 27	H. Searle	P. Kemp †	3 330	22 44½
1884 Sept. 12	W. G. Brett	A. Sharland	3 330		1888 Oct. 29	P. Kemp	N. Matterson	3 330	22 26½
1885 Feb. 7	E Hanlan	T. Clifford	3 330	21 04	1888 Nov. 27	W. Beach	E. Hahlan	3 330	21 15
1885 Feb. 28	W. Beach	T. Clifford	3 330	26 01½					

† Championship of the world.

PART V.

No name in the annals of aquatic sports was more famous about 1860 than that of Josh Ward. Even in these days he is referred to as the paragon of excellence as a single-scull oarsman. He was for a long time the single-scull champion of America, and was the most noted of the four Ward brothers, Ellis, Gilbert, and Henry, who gained fame and emoluments by taking the world's championship from their English competitors on Saratoga Lake in 1871. Josh is now the proprietor of a well-patronized hostelry, near the water's edge, at Cornwall-on-the-Hudson. The advance of time has made but little change in the personal appearance of the veteran, and the witnesses of his youthful accomplishments would find no difficulty in recognizing in the Josh Ward of to-day, the tall, raw-boned, smooth-faced youth, with sloping shoulders and lithe muscular figure, "who set the pace on the waters of the world" over a quarter of a century ago.

Ward is prone to talk of his early achievements, but never in a bombastic fashion. In a recent conversation, Josh said with his eyes resting on a crayon drawing of himself over the fire-place of his Hudson river hostelry—a picture made right after he had wrested the championship from his English adversaries—that a championship contest in singles was the race of his life. The official time of the race was thirty-five minutes and ten seconds, which has never been beaten. The contest was for $100 and the championship belt.

In single-scull contests, Andy Fay, of New York, Tom Dorr, of Brooklyn, and John Hancon, of Cornwall—all of whom he defeated—were not the least vigorous of Ward's competitors. After his race with Fay, Ward said that the New York man was the best he had ever met. Fay was about the same build as Ward, and rowed the same stroke—between thirty-six and thirty-eight to a minute. Tom Doyle, of Boston, was another strong adversary of the "Father of American Scullers." Though Doyle was a superior oarsman, he seemed fated never to reach first place in a race, but he made a very close second in all his contests. In 1859 he was defeated by Ward on the Charles river in a close struggle.

Another famous defeated competitor of old Josh in his younger days was William Stevens, the stroke of the then well-known "Stranger Four, of Poughkeepsie." John Hancon had gained reputation before Ward met and beat him at Troy. A complete list of Josh Ward's victories would include the names of John McGrady, John Biglan, J. Bash, John McKiel, all the oarsmen of any prominence in the fifties, sixties, and seventies. His brother Ellis, the coach and trainer of the University of Pennsylvania, is also a shining light among the Schuylkill oarsmen, and, like Josh, he is never happy save when he is employed in advising youth or turning out a good solid rowing oar.

In the Saratoga Lake International regatta, which Josh is very fond of discussing, the Tyne or Renforth crew, of Newcastle, England, the Biglin-Coulter crew, of New York city, the Taylor-Winship crew, of Newcastle-on-Tyne, England, the Burger-Stevens crew, of Poughkeepsie, and the McKee Club crew, of East Birmingham, Pa., started. The course was four miles and the prize $2,000. The Hon. John Morrissey was referee, and gave an additional prize of $750. The Ward crew were pushed to the last, but won handily, the others finishing in the order in which they are named. The other celebrated races of the crew were numerous, as were the individual victories of the brothers, but must be passed over at this time.

AQUATICS.

Possibly no one place on the globe has turned out more famous oarsmen than the city of Halifax, N. S., nor any waters witnessed more exciting or record-breaking aquatic contests than the waters of Halifax harbor and the adjoining Bedford Basin. Warren Smith and George Brown were prominent oarsmen from this vicinity. The fathers of both were Halifax fishermen, and the boys were early trained in their fathers' profession. In his early manhood Brown was a harbor pilot. No sailing craft were employed by pilots in those days, the pilots putting off from the shore to a vessel in a heavy row-boat. This experience made Brown proficient in the use of an oar and venturesome at sea. In 1863 he jumped into fame as an oarsman. For several years previous John Lovitt, a local fisherman, had successively won the championship of Halifax harbor in the annual boat-race. A massive gold belt was the trophy. This was to be the permanent property of the oarsman who won it in five annual competitions. Lovitt had captured the prize three successive years prior to 1863. In this year Brown was prevailed upon to try his skill in the contest. He entered the regatta and came in a close second to his famous rival. For an inexperienced sculler and an untrained competitor his performance was looked upon as marvellous. Preparatory training the following year, when the belt was within the grasp of Lovitt, made Brown a dangerous rival. Expectations were realized and Brown carried off the honors and the belt. For four years thereafter Brown entered the annual race with a like result, and with the belt he was awarded the championship of the country. During his subsequent connection with aquatic matters he numbered among his competitors John Biglin, Robert Fulton, Henry Coulter, William Scharff and Eph Morris.

From Sadler, in 1871, and as a victim of mean jockeying, Brown suffered his single defeat of note. The only other time he lost was when he first rowed against Lovitt for the local championship. Brown subsequently challenged Sadler to meet him, but a race was never arranged. Brown's complete record is a good one and covers many events. In his final competition with Morris on the Kennebec, in 1874, Brown was ill and really had no business on the water. The race was a tight one, but Brown won the race by a length. In less than a year he died and was interred in the Herring Cove Churchyard at the age of thirty-six years. His heirs divided between $3,000 and $4,000.

Warren Smith, as a professional sculler, received his first training in the now defunct Halifax Rowing Association. He came prominently to the front as a competitor of Wallace Ross on the Kennebaccasis in 1878. An accident caused his defeat in this contest. The following year he won his first prominent race, defeating Eph Morris after a severe struggle on Silver Lake. The next year Smith again met Wallace Ross on Bedford Basin. Barrels of money changed hands on this contest. The race was a game one, but Ross had now met his superior and was beaten out of his boots by the Halifax fisherman. A second race was, a few days after, arranged between Smith and Eph Morris over the Basin course, and Smith again came out victorious. The above events were Smith's greatest victories. After the last-mentioned race he considered himself the master oarsman of the world. He was finally lost at sea in a fishing vessel that went down in a gale off the coast of Halifax. Al. Hamm and Pete Conley, two men well known in the United States, were also protégés of the Halifax Rowing Association.

Less than fifteen years ago the coming man in the aquatic arena was Wallace Ross, now known as the New Brunswicker. Born and reared in St. John, Ross early took to rowing and easily vanquished all local aspirants. When Ross sprung into notice Hanlan, having defeated E. A. Trickett, was the champion of the world. With the self-confidence and hardihood of men of his race, Ross determined to strike for the championship. He met Hanlan and was defeated. A second effort proved disastrous, and then Ross came to the United States. Ross' best race was his defeat of Trickett in England in 1880. His time for the four miles and four hundred and forty yards was 23.42, unusually fast for that period. Ross' last race heat with Bubear was in 1888, and the New Brunswicker finished in the van.

NED HANLAN, THE WORLD'S CHAMPION OARSMAN, 1876-1882.

XII.

NED HANLAN ON ROWING.*

IN December of 1888, I, together with the players of the Chicago and All-American ball teams, met Edward Hanlan in Sydney, N. S. W., and as Ned was one of the prominent Americans in Australia at that time, our party saw a good deal of him. "If ever you get anywhere near Toronto, after I have returned to America," said the oarsman when I shook hands with him upon the departure of our party for Melbourne, "don't fail to drop in upon me, and I will show you the prettiest inland harbor in the world and give you a bit of my history that has not yet been seen in print."

Happening to be in Boston eight months later, and reading of Hanlan's return from Australia and his arrival in Toronto a day or two before, I determined to accept the invitation tendered me 10,700 miles from the centre of Massachusetts' old Commonwealth, and leaving Boston that night reached Toronto the following afternoon. Inquiring at The Queen's Hotel for Hanlan I was given the number of his residence on John street, but was told, upon driving there, that I would find him "over at the Island." I had heard of "Hanlan's Island," even before I had met the oarsman himself, and having located my man did not rush matters further, but after a supper, partaken of quite leisurely, I walked down to the shore of the beautiful bay, across which I could see the electric lights upon the Island. Even the levee at Toronto is well ordered and in cleanly condition, and as I walked down to the dock at which was moored a busy, energetic looking little steamer, the tall,

---

* By Harry Palmer, from a recent personal interview.

well-constructed buildings; the spacious, substantially-built railway station; the broad thoroughfares, and the glimmer of hundreds of electric lights which threw a great white glow upon the sky above, bespoke the location of a modern, thriving and enterprising city, destined to one day become the most populous and important north of the chain of great lakes. Never has a city been more favored by nature than is Toronto. Its climate is delightfully cool during the summer months, and invigorating and bracing during the winter season. The city lies directly upon the lake shore with a gently rolling country behind it, through which are some of the most charming suburbs imaginable. Opposite the city, just far enough away to form a harbor large enough for the needs of a city of a million souls if necessary, is the island, crescent-shaped, and about seven miles long.

Hanlan owns about seven acres upon the west end of the island, and has made his property the most popular public resort about Toronto. A handsomely constructed hotel with surrounding cafés, walks, bandstands, dancing pavilions, merry-go-rounds, and other provisions for pleasure and recreation, to which are added boat-houses, with gracefully built, modernly equipped, and softly cushioned row-boats, the whole fanned by cool breezes and surrounded by emerald-hued, wave-tipped waters, make the island one of the pleasantest spots upon the borders of Ontario. The island was simply a breakwater, a barren reef, in fact, until Hanlan, who had inherited about half of his present acreage, developed one portion of it as a breathing spot and pleasure resort. During the past three years, however, the land has been selling by the foot instead of by the acre, and for residence and resort purposes that locality promises ultimately to become the most valuable about Toronto.

I happened to arrive in the city while its inhabitants were enjoying a civic holiday, and when I took the little steamer at the dock that evening, for the island, I was but one of an hundred or more, the party including dozens of fresh-faced Canadian girls and their escorts. At the island there was a crush. Hanlan afterwards told me that fully 25,000 people had visited the island that day, and I believed him, for there seemed to be all of that number there when, after a trust-to-luck search of nearly an hour I found the oarsman seated with his wife and a party of friends upon one of the upper balconies of the hotel.

I found Hanlan looking much the same as when I had left him in Australia; perhaps a little more fleshy, but the same jovial, entertaining, hospitably inclined fellow that he has been all his life. It is unnecessary to say that I was warmly welcomed. Hanlan joined me in a stroll about the premises and pointed out the improvements he intended making during the next year, and after enjoying the Canadian's hospitality, listening to the music, and watching the great crowd as it moved about under the electric lights, I left the island for my hotel, having made an appointment with Hanlan for the morrow.

Hanlan's Island is interesting from one standpoint, and his pretty, yet modest residence in the city proper, doubly interesting from another. At his home are to be seen the trophies and memorials of more than 160 contests upon the water in England, America, and Australia, and it was in the midst of these, with every object doubtless recalling to him some interesting event of his career, that I held one of the most interesting interviews upon athletics that it has ever been my good fortune to enjoy. I will give it verbatim, and in Hanlan's own words, for no dressing with which I might clothe it could be half so interesting. Naturally my thoughts first turned to Hanlan's achievements in that part of the world where I had last met him, and I said: "I remember some time ago you did not want to row in Australia, but in England, on account of the climate; what was there in that?"

"I went to Australia the latter part of 1883," replied Hanlan, as he settled back in his chair in a manner that indicated an interesting bit of explanation by way of reply, "and arranged a match with Laycock for the championship of the world. He and I rowed this race on the Nepean river, New South Wales, and after that I gave exhibitions in Melbourne and every colony of Australasia, and was received with great honors. The Stars and Stripes I do not suppose were ever hoisted more freely than during my visit. After all the wine suppers, balls and pic-nics at every place I visited, I found I was out of condition, and I refused to make a match with Beach because I was not feeling right. I had simply overtaxed my powers by over indulgence, and I thought I would be doing wrong, under the circumstances, to make a match with Beach. He kept challenging me, however, every day, and people finally said I was afraid to meet him. Then I accepted his challenge, and only gave myself five weeks in which to prepare to row Beach on the Paramatta river. I trained as carefully as I could, but not as correctly as I should have done, for the simple reason that there were from one thousand to two thousand people a day coming to my boat-house to see me, and bringing their lunches to eat out there on the banks of the river, and every party coming up would pay me a visit and perhaps I would take a mouthful of champagne and explain my boats to them. This, of course, interfered considerably with my work, but it went on until three or four days before my race, and then my constitution seemed to leave me all at once, and I seemed to go down, until I said to myself, I am beaten, sure. But, notwithstanding this, I went out and rowed that race, although I was not fit to row with anybody. These were the causes of my first defeat. The time of that race was about 21 minutes 50 seconds, over three miles and 330 yards against the strong flood tide. Beach beat me about three boat lengths. I led him for two miles in the condition I was in. He could not overtake me in that two miles, although he tried hard. I think if I had kept it up another hundred yards I would have won the race, but my constitution would not allow it. If I had rowed as well in the last as I did in the first part of the race I would have beaten him. I could have done nothing else. My defeat was owing to the enjoyment of too much hospitality at the hands of the Australian people. After that, the climate took hold of me and I could not do anything.

"I consider Beach one of the greatest men that ever sat in a boat," continued the ex-champion. "His performances and record will show that. He came out late in years, being about thirty-one or thirty-two when he started. In five years he won seven championships of the world, defeating such men as myself, Gaudaur, Teemer, Neil Matterson and Thomas Clifford. In fact, he defeated every good man he met when in his prime. He defeated me on my second visit to Australia. We rowed on the Nepean. The race came off on the 26th of November, 1887, over the Nepean championship course, three miles 330 yards, for a stake of one thousand pounds. It was a terrific race. In fact, at the finish of the race there was hardly a boat length's daylight between us. Beach was so thoroughly exhausted that his friends had to come down the bank and lift him out. I was as fresh as when I started.

I should have shoved my race stronger half the distance from the start. If I had pressed him harder I do not think he would have been able to finish. I rowed in reserve too long. Then he retired after that and would not row. The cause, as I think, was the race I rowed, which about finished him. He thought he had better let well enough alone. He gave the championship over to Kemp. He claimed to have that right. I don't think he had. As soon as he said he had retired, his friend Kemp, whom he taught to row in Australia, challenged Beach at once, and as Beach did not accept Kemp claimed the championship and Beach retired. I challenged Kemp for a race on the Paramatta river about three months after. I do not know what got into me. I do not suppose I could have beaten a good amateur after I had been in Australia two or three months. I was very well for about two or three months in that climate, but after that my constitution seemed to leave me and I did not feel so strong as I ought to have felt. I think the climate of Australia will act on any other athlete similarly. You are just as good for the first three or four months, and after that you are not one-half the man you were when you went there. It acted the same with me the last time as it did the first. After the first two or three months of my stay there, I believe the amateurs of Australia could have beaten me. I would now be well pleased, however, to row any of them, if they would row on the Thames or here. There is no reason why I should not row as good a race now as before, but I have got to prove that. A young man starting in at twenty-three lasts until about thirty-three. I notice also that where a man goes in at thirty or thirty-two he lasts about five years. Beach and Laycock lasted about five years each. The vitality seems to leave an athlete after that many years of hard work. Young athletes last about ten years."

"What about Searle, Ned; where did you first see him and what were your first impressions of him?"

"Searle was brought up on the banks of the Clarence river, New South Wales. I think it was about a year and a half ago, in the month of January, I first saw him; it was when I went up to row in a handicap-distance two miles. I was scratch. Nelson had three boats and a half start of me; Heren, from New Zealand, four boats start. It was Searle's maiden race. He had seven lengths start. I noticed Searle rowing around a bit. I had been seasick for two days coming up to Grafton from Sydney, and consequently on account of my not being in proper condition I was forced to draw out of the race. That was the first place I saw Searle. He won the race, of course. He was given such a start because it was his maiden race. He was in his infancy then as a sculler. Before that he had won three or four local sculling races. Some one told him he would make a great sculler, and the consequence was he sent to Sydney, bought a racing boat and entered this race. He had no trouble winning at all. He is a natural born athlete, a great sculler. Not only is he gifted with the oars but he has a wonderful physique. He is a model of human nature; a better built man I never saw in my life for a sculler, and a fearfully strong fellow. He is a most remarkable man. He is about twenty-three and a half years of age and has a great future before him. He does not take liquor of any description except a little champagne now and again. However he dissipates more than I did when I was his age. Perhaps his habits grow on him, just as they do on everybody else.

"What gave Beach success was his constitution, his physical force. Beach was a blacksmith before he took to rowing. From the hip to the shoulder and arms, Beach was the finest man, I think, who ever sat in a boat—that is, for endurance and strength."

"In what waters do you think the best time can be made?"

"Well," replied Hanlan, "boat-racing is different from horse-racing, and there is only one country in the world where we can get the accurate time of oarsmen, amateur or professional, and that is America, because we have such beautiful fresh lake water and still water. In the Thames and Tyne, in England, the tide some days runs four miles an hour, and some days three and a half; some days five miles. Of course they follow the tide as carefully as they can, and get it to a certain height when they call it dead smooth water. You cannot get the accurate speed of the men where there is a rise and fall of the stream. It is also the same in Australia, on the Paramatta and the Nepean. I could never get my accurate speed. I would be either too fast or very slow. I could never get within two or five seconds of home time, on account of the rise and fall of the stream."

"You think, then, that the finest courses are in America?"

"Yes, by far. We have such lakes as Lake Quinsigamond, Seneca Lake, Greenwood Lake, Saratoga Lake, Calumet, at Pullman; Crèvecœur Lake, at St. Louis; Toronto Bay, Burlington Bay, Kempenfeldt Bay, at Barrie; and Lachine, at Montreal; Kennebeccasis, at St. Johns, N. B.; Bedford Basin, at Halifax, and other places that no wind or great storms can get at. The water is always smooth, and we have the correct distance. There are 100 lakes through New York you can row in. We never select the place here, we have so many to choose from. We can row in Toronto Bay; on the courses in New York; Silver Lake, Boston; or Seneca Lake in New York State, and Saratoga Lake. We have so many different courses here, and they are so far ahead of anything in England that we look on the rivers there as nothing more than ditches compared with what we have in America. The Australian courses do not compare with ours either, except one, and that is the Nepean river. Another good course they have is in Rockhampton, the Fitzroy river, in Queensland. They all have tides, however."

"How much has the three-mile time been reduced in the last ten years?"

"I have been looking as far back as 1865, when Hamill, Walter Brown, John Keele, Joe Sadler in England, and Renforth rowed. Sadler came to England in 1871, and his four-mile time was 28 minutes 28 seconds, and his three-mile time was about 22 minutes. Such men as Hamill, Walter Brown, John Keele, Ellis Ward, and others of that school, thought that three miles rowed in 22 minutes was remarkable time. It stopped so until 1876, when John O'Neil made three miles in 21 minutes 19½ seconds in Saratoga. Then I came out and rowed in the World's International Regatta on the Schuylkill, at Philadelphia, in 1876, and won in 21 minutes 9 seconds, which broke the record. That race was for the aquatic championship of the world, $800 first and $400 second money. It was the first race of my life away from home. I thought I was rich when I won my $800. I had so much confidence in myself, that before I started from here I told every friend I had I would only have to go down there and get it. I felt that way, for the simple reason I knew how fast other men could row, and I knew we had a correct distance here on Toronto bay, and consequently that I was so much faster. I could then row three miles in 20 minutes. I knew my speed from trials with my own watch, and that was what took me to Philadelphia. I went to my sisters for assistance to take me. My father and mother died when I was very young. I wanted to get sufficient money to take me away. They would not give me one shilling, not a farthing. I said to myself, Here I am; I have no friend or anybody to help me, and I must help myself. I had a race-boat that George Warren built in 1875, which cost me $90, new. I paid that $90 out of my own little purse. I practiced in that boat and won several little local events in 1875. I defeated everybody around Toronto, and winning those races and the little trials I rowed to myself gave me confidence that I could beat anybody. The year 1876 came along, with the regatta at Philadelphia. There were fifteen picked men of the world to row. My people didn't want me to go; in fact, tried in every possible way to keep me at home. They thought I could never return; still, I stole away. Three weeks before this race I bought myself a little ten-cent note book and went over to Mr. Collins, who is dead now—he was the editor and owner of the *Canadian Sportsman*—and said to him: Mr. Collins, I am an inexperienced boy, and I want a little assistance. I am locally known as an amateur oarsman, and I have so far beaten everybody here. I want you to write me a heading in this note book to get the requisite funds to take me to Philadelphia."

"All right, my boy," he said, "I will."

"He wrote me a heading as I told him, stating that I went to represent Toronto in the World's International Regatta at Philadelphia, on the Schuylkill river, and that I wanted the people of Toronto to subscribe their names on my book and give so much toward my expenses. He did that and off I went. It took me three weeks to get $250 together. Everybody I went to said, 'You little fool, what do you want money to go and row in that big race for?' I can remember now all the chaff and fun they poked at me. 'Audacity!' 'Against renowned aquatic champions;' 'Kid,' etc., etc. Never mind, I said, I will come back with something. I collected about $250. Never more than $5 from anybody. Colonel Shaw gave me $5, and Dave Ward and others $5. I got as low as 25 cents. I accepted everything. When I got the $250, I went and borrowed a better boat than I had. Mr. Thomas

Lowden here had an old race-boat called 'The Duke of Beaufort,' the boat in which Joe Sadler beat such men as Ellis Ward, Harry Coulter, of Pittsburgh, and George Brown, of Halifax. Thomas Lowden bought it from Joe Sadler, and he brought it to Montreal to row in a regatta there. He had it there then and I went to him. 'Tom,' I said 'I want you to assist me a little. My boat is not good enough for this race. I will give you $20 to loan her to me to take to Philadelphia.' 'All right, Ed,' he said. So I gave him the $20 for the loan of the boat, sculls, etc.

HANLAN'S EASY VICTORY IN THE CENTENNIAL INTERNATIONAL REGATTA.

Off I went and entered, and the result was I won as I liked. Whether it was English, American, or Canadian, I could row the best of them there as if they were sticks of wood."

"How much did you beat the second man by?"

"I had to win two heats before I was admitted into the final heat. The first heat they put me against Harry Coulter and Thomas, of England. I recollect it well. When the gun was fired you would swear, if you saw that race, that somebody had a rope and pulled me along. In ten strokes I was two lengths ahead. I said to myself, these people are just letting me have this start. Well, I said, I am far enough ahead and I will stop here. I kept that distance and every now and again I would stop and have a drink out of the water. I created more amusement on that river in my race than in all my other races put together. I had a drink at the end of every half mile. The people sitting in their boats in the river were all laughing at the easy way I was rowing; they could not help it. As soon as they came up I would be off like a shot. My second heat with Plaisted and Luther was similar; did as I had a mind to. Brayley, of St. Johns, won both his heats and he and I were brought into the final. I beat him just the same. I hadn't to row any harder. I had to row about ten strokes to get ahead and then I would stop there. When Brayley and I were on the home stretch, and were about three quarters of a mile from the finish, I remember there was a large weed patch into which he was deliberately running. I was leading then about six lengths. I said 'Look out Brayley, don't run in there.' He pulled his right and rowed himself clear. It was very funny I had only the reputation of a local boy. Nobody outside of Toronto had ever heard of me. I remember Colonel Shaw gave me a letter of introduction to the President of the Association. When I presented it he looked at me in astonishment and said 'The idea of an innocent kid like you rowing in this World's Regatta!' I had no moustache and didn't weigh more than 137 pounds stripped. The race was against the best men in England and the world. So easily did I win that I never shed a drop of perspiration from my brow during the race."

"How do you account for it?"

"In this way. I was a better sculler than any of them, in a scientific point of view, and I had a better rig than any of them. I had studied the art of sculling and improved my fittings. I had a longer slide than any of them, I had a shorter foot-brace than any of them, I had also shorter oars; the ones I rowed with were nine feet six inches in length and blades six and a quarter inches in width. They were rowing with oars ten feet three inches in length and five and a half blades, and their slides were about eight or nine inches in length, while mine were twenty-four. Everything they had was on the lines of the old style of rowing. I improved on the old English rigging; I altered the rigging of my boat, except the old thole pins. Swivel rowlocks were not thought much of then. I made considerable alteration in the old English rig, even with the old thole pins. I bought myself new oars, about nine feet six inches with blades about six and a half in width, and altered the angle of my foot-brace from about twenty inches to an angle of about forty inches, and these little things helped me. I did this without any previous teaching. My style of rowing was then far ahead of that of anybody else, and with the alterations I had made it would have been a wonderfully strong young fellow who would have beaten me. The reception on my return was enough to bring tears into one's eyes. It was more suitable for the President of the United States. Here is a watch the people of Toronto gave me on my return," said the ex-Champion, producing a magnificent time-piece bearing this inscription; "Presented by the citizens of Toronto to Edward Hanlan, Champion of the World, Winner of the professional sculling race, Centennial Regatta, 1876."

"I came to Niagara by rail," continued Hanlan, "and from Niagara to Toronto by the Steamer 'Chicora.' We arrived too late that night, on the boat, to give me a reception by water, but there was a torchlight procession in Toronto, one of the grandest given to anybody in this country. It was about eight in the evening. There were about five thousand people, with torches, parading the streets. On my arrival from the steamer, Angus Morrison, the Mayor of Toronto, was the first man to grasp me by the hand; and he said, Mr. Hanlan, I welcome you back to your native home and to the freedom of the city for six months. They then escorted me up the end of the wharf and hoisted me up on a fire escape and ladder wagon, and my boat was put up there and I was placed in her. This was the boat I learned to row in, not the one I actually rowed the race in. I crawled up into my delicate resting place, about twenty feet in the air. They then escorted me all round the city; up York street to King street, and along King to Church, and up Church to the Horticultural Pavilion, situated in the principal garden of Toronto. They tried to charge an admission fee of ten cents to get into the grounds, for the 'Hanlan fund.' This went on very well until I got into the Pavilion, and then the crush was so heavy they broke away fences, posts and everything else, and everybody got in for nothing. That was my first experience before an audience. Alderman Harry Piper introduced me to the people. Making a speech was the hardest thing I ever attempted. I would rather have rowed ten boat races than have talked to an audience ten minutes. I recollect the tears in my eyes. I was half frightened out of my life. I could win a boat race and think nothing of that, but after my clothes were almost torn off my back, and I was hustled around with so much

WHY THE ADMISSION FEE WASN'T COLLECTED AT HANLAN'S RECEPTION.

excitement and then brought on the platform, it was as much as I could do to say 'I thank you, ladies and gentlemen, for this great reception.' And when I sat down I commenced to cry, with the life and soul fairly scared out of me. Take any young fellow and put him in such a position as I was, all at once, and he will be frightened to death."

"Do you look for a very great decrease in the three-mile time?"

"We have got that decrease now. My race with Gaudaur on Lake Calumet, at Pullman, shows that it was a record race, 19 minutes and 30 seconds. I was beaten by Gaudaur then, by a length and a half. I attributed my defeat to having a very small boat; my speed was interfered with. I was about a quarter of a mile from home, with a terrific wind that came up there, which caused my boat to run under the waves, and Gaudaur went past me as if I were standing still. I was leading him two and a half to the buoy. On the return, however, I was shoving the water from my boat while his boat easily rode the waves, and he got in about a length ahead of me. This was the 31st of May, 1887. I made another race with him for the 25th of July, the same year, over the same course, and didn't have any trouble in beating him. Gaudaur could never live on the same street with me when I was right. I am the only champion of the world who ever lived in this country, that is, the United States and Canada. Gaudaur never was champion of the world, neither was Teemer, and although I defeated Gaudaur a great many times, the only time he defeated me was the time I have mentioned. I lost the championship to Beach."

"Do you think three miles will remain the popular length of course?"

"Yes, the popular championship distance is long enough and short enough to test a man's speed and endurance; it is too far, however, for constant rowing, that is, for five, ten, or fifteen races in a season. I think for exhibition regattas, which are nothing more than an exhibition of rowing, that two miles is far enough, and I think it would have a tendency to advance the speed of a racing boat to adopt this distance, because where men have to do a mile they regulate their boats for two miles; for three they will have to make a different alteration. I am satisfied if men only rowed mile races, in a year we would improve ten seconds in a mile, that is, they would be rowed ten seconds quicker than now. I can to-morrow rig a racing boat for any one, as well as for myself, to row a mile ten seconds quicker than if I were training that man to row three miles. I would have to fit him to stand strong pulling for that distance; the length of the oars, the length and width of the footbrace, and the support of the outriggers from rowlock to rowlock. We have to regulate our boats to take us over our various distances. I can fit a man in a boat to row for a day without feeling it. I have made a study of this. It would be easy for a professional oarsman to handicap an amateur. I can tie a man up in the rigging of his boat so that when rowing he can scarcely move. An experienced professional will sometimes take hold of an amateur and undertake to teach him, and perhaps the professional does not know any more than the amateur himself. I have had a great deal to do with teaching oarsmen, and they give me a great deal of credit in Australia for teaching them nearly all they know in that country about rowing. Although they have won races from me, they always gave me credit for teaching them. They said as much as this, that only for Hanlan they would not know as much about rowing as they do to-day."

"Do you think the condition of the amateur oarsman in America is a healthy one to-day?"

"Yes. They cannot help being so where the professional improves by making alterations in the rigging of a racing boat; the boat builder must have the rig, length of oar and any alterations, before he can properly fit it. The consequence is, the amateur will write to the same boat builder to build a boat for him and fit her as Hanlan's, or some other particular oarsman's boat is fitted; and thus the amateur gets the benefit of the professional's study and experience. I think amateurs are improving more rapidly than the professionals, because there are more of them. They must improve, because they get our experience, and they get our rigs, etc. Very few men thoroughly understand how to row. How the ideas came to me was in this way: when I was training for my race with Ross, that was rowed on the 15th of October, 1877, after my big race at Philadelphia, for a thousand a side, I was backed by Toronto people, friends of my own, and of course I then started to study how to improve myself as much as possible. Although I was blessed with a wonderful constitution, and was a good, strong, hearty oarsman, and had won the great race at Philadelphia, I knew that I could improve myself considerably by being more scientific. Ross had a tremendous reputation for beating everybody he rowed with. He was a very large, powerful man. His friends came up with tons of money, I suppose as much as $150,000 to wager on the boat race alone. I saw there was a great chance of losing money for my friends, and took every precaution to improve myself. The very first thing I noticed when I began the study was that every race-boat is built to have a certain water line, to displace a certain amount of wetted surface. A race-boat is thirty-one feet long, ten and a half inches wide; depth of centre five and three-quarters inches, two inches aft, three inches in the bow, so you can imagine how frail a craft a race-boat is. A boat is built so as to suit the weight of the man who has to row in her. If the boat is not rowed on her water line the consequence is she displaces more water than she ought to, and it is consequently more difficult to propel her through the water than if she rowed on her proper lines. The manner in which I learned to accomplish this one thing, to row a boat on her water line, was this: when I came forward with my body, which is aft in the boat, I noticed the stern of the boat would dip down and the water would come up on the canvas about a foot. She would go half an inch under, and I said, this boat cannot be running correctly, because if the stern goes down the bow must come up. The consequence is, she is not running on the lines she is built to run on. So in order to keep the stern of the boat up I brought my body into a certain position, in order to reach forward for my strike, which took all the weight from the foot-brace and away from the stern, and in about two months, although I did go forward, the stern of my boat would be up on the water line. When I accomplished that one thing the bow corresponded with the stern, and the consequence was my boat ran true. It seemed to go easier and more gracefully. It brought my stroke also into a more graceful finish. I was also trying to learn perpetual motion of the body, to imitate the pendulum of a clock, and thought if I could get my body to go as easily and gracefully as that it would be a great advantage. I noticed my sliding seat used to touch at the aft end and check a little, and once the sliding seat checks it retards the motion of the boat. When I noticed this I altered the slide at once, and put about three and a half inches to the end of my slide. It was then that the pendulum idea was wandering in my head from daylight till dark. Those are the two things that taught me to row so scientifically. I am the originator of the long slide. I improved on that so much that if a man were to go back and row on the old slide of eight or nine inches, I don't care how good he may be, and with the old rig they had twelve or fifteen years ago, I could take a third-rate man in Toronto who would run away from him. No man without a sliding seat has got any business to row against a man with one.

"Another great thing the length of the slide has done is in the benefit it has given to the constitution and health. You never hear of death from heart disease from rowing, now. For years and years the upper portion of the body, from the heart up, was doing all the work, but now the whole body comes into full play."

"What advice would you give to amateur oarsmen in their training, and in their physical culture, and in their improvements in their methods as oarsmen, and what would you tell them to avoid?"

"That is not an easy one to answer. Men are not constituted alike; every man changes in his training; what you would give one man another cannot stand; to talk to a multitude of people is a delicate thing to do; what would make one man would kill another. Training differs among athletes. All men should know how to treat themselves according to their constitutions. A great many start out for training without taking any medicine to clean out their system. The consequence is that in about two or three weeks a boil appears, the tongue becomes coated and the eyes have a sleepy look, the skin has not the ruddy complexion of health, and the athlete becomes drowsy, discontented and cannot sleep. It is because all the bad matter which has been lying in the system becomes disturbed, and works through the blood and through the flesh. The liver gets out of order. The doctor will give a tonic. I have gone through all this; perhaps the patient will feel well next day, and the next day or two he will be as bad as ever again; the old feeling will come back, whereas, if he went to work in the first place and said to the physician: 'I am going into training and want my system put in order,' he might train for six months after treatment and not want any more medicine. He will eat heartily, feel fresh and sleep well. What has hurt so many young men is that in starting out they do not go through a course of physic and get their system thoroughly in order. Another thing is, never to work too hard, or leave the race on the track, or on the river, as the saying goes, that is, before it comes off. A good many overwork themselves, and their constitutions do not last. Many give out and leave their race on the track before the day comes off; their constitutions have been overworked; they are trained too fine."

"You would advise amateurs, then, to be careful in their selection of a trainer?"

"By all means. I have not a good opinion of trainers. I have always had to be cautious in listening to my trainers. They sometimes give you too much work, and want you to do all sorts of absurd things not required at all, whether it is in training to run or to row a race. Perhaps another will be just the reverse and give you nothing to do, and try and prevent you from working, and when you are on the race-track you are not in condition to row at all. The trainer sometimes does not know as much as the pupil himself. Perhaps if the rower was left to himself he would be in better condition than with a trainer. There are few trainers who understand the man they have under control, and, in my opinion, it will take a trainer a year to understand a man's constitution; that is why I say it is a great risk to put yourself in charge of another, whom you have perhaps never seen before, and whose method of training does not suit your constitution at all. Sometimes trainers do a great deal more harm than good, by not knowing the constitution of an athlete."

"Which was the greatest race you ever witnessed, that you remember most distinctly?"

"I have great ideas of races beforehand, and I have pictured to myself and imagined wonderful things, but as most of my races were so easy, and I have won so many of them, it is hard just to think which was most exciting. Perhaps, however, it was the race Trickett and I rowed on the 15th of November, 1880, for the aquatic championship of the world, on the River Thames. I was not at all well when I started; I was very light, a difference of five or six pounds lighter than my usual weight, 147. He stood six feet $3\frac{1}{2}$ inches and weighed 190 pounds. I had to be very cautious in rowing my race; no overtaxing of my constitution. Trickett started away with a stroke of forty to the minute, and I started with a stroke of about thirty-five. At the first half mile he was leading a nice half boat's length. The water was like a mirror, beautiful and smooth; thousands of people were on each side of the river; the scene and excitement was enough to turn anybody's head. Steamboats whistling, and people shouting, etc. I recollect saying to myself, this fellow is leading half a length, I had better exert myself a little more. I recollect I put more power into my stroke and drew myself slightly up, although I did not extend my full speed, as I was reserving every particle of force I could to bring myself to the finish. I saw I was gaining. It took me about a quarter of a mile to get that half length. Once I saw I was gaining it satisfied me. As soon as I got on his bow and placed myself half a length ahead, I kept there until he would put on a tremendous spurt, running from thirty-six to forty, in sprints. This would last until he gained the half length. He would row about twenty strokes and bring himself up level. I noticed he had to put on three or four strokes more to bring himself up. I never altered my stroke at all, and as soon as he came up level he would be compelled to ease again. No sooner did he lessen his strokes than I regained my position. Perhaps he would row that way for another quarter of a mile and he would place himself level again. I never altered my stroke at all. We kept this up for a mile and a half. The last spurt he put on was between the soap works and Hammersmith Bridge. I have rowed against the picked men of the world; but I never saw the muscles of any man put to such a strain as Trickett's. I would like to have a photograph of those muscular movements of his back. I can see him yet, and what a huge man he was—190 pounds. That man rowed in sprints, and just at Hammersmith Bridge he put on the last spurt, but I still kept a half a length in front. Suddenly Trickett collapsed and fell right over on his knees, it is a wonder he did not fall out. I have seen a great deal of excitement, but I never saw such a scene. In England they have eight-oared cutters following with a coach sitting face to face with the contestants, and these men were looking at each of us. They were only twenty feet behind and five steamers were following the race, loaded with people. The cheering and hallooing of our two coaches were deafening. They were beckoning with their handkerchiefs. If they want you to go to the left they beckon that way, and if to the right they make a motion in that direction. Our two coaches were yelling and screeching. It was the first race I ever rowed where there was so much excitement, the coaches kicking up such terrible noise, screeching and hallooing, and the people on the banks of the river shouting and the steamboats whistling and trying to make us increase our speed. We could not row another inch faster if we got twenty million pounds. It was my constitution, I think, brought me in the winner of that race, although I am lighter than Trickett by about forty pounds. He only paddled home. A third-rate amateur could have beaten him the rest of the distance. He felt his defeat terribly. When I got through Hammersmith Bridge, I must have been ten lengths in front. I went in close to the Surrey side, thousands shouting 'Good boy, Hanlan.' Of course, I heard this and I began to think

HANLAN PLAYING DEAD.

I would like to fool my backers on the boat and the people on the shore. All at once I laid on my back in the race boat as if I were dead, for about ten seconds, never a move. There were all my Canadian friends and friends from the United States, thinking I was dead and had fallen over in the boat, and that they were going to lose the thousands of pounds they had placed on me. The scene was something that defies description. Trickett came right up and was almost passing me. You can imagine if you had a thousand pounds on the race and your man dead in the boat, how you would feel. Suddenly I sat up and started off again. I could see my backers on the referee's boat with faces white as chalk and as long as to-morrow, and what a shout they set up when I started. I did not think of the consequences of what I was doing when I laid down; but when I saw my backers, I thought what a terrible thing it was to do. I started off again and went home as I liked.

"All of my races have had a little incident of that kind connected with them. My first race with Boyd, on the river Tyne, on the 3d of April, was something of that description. It was my maiden race in England. Ross rowed an International race on the Thames, and our Canadian people sent me as the Champion of America; and I went and rowed John Howden from the High Level Suspension Bridge. During my training they thought I could not row fast enough to beat little sticks floating on the Tyne, my style was so different from theirs. Howden was the first man of my size, height and age I ever rowed with. He weighed about 150 pounds. Well, I said, here is the first man I ever got my own size, physique and age. I had been rowing against six-footers of 180 and 190 pounds. I said to myself, what a picnic I have got to beat that fellow. We started by mutual consent, that is, Howden's trainer held the stern of his boat while my man held mine. We broke away together. Everybody expected to see a life and death struggle; and everybody was on expectation to see a wonderful race. In four strokes I was about two lengths in front; you could have heard a pin drop in the water, the excitement was so pent up; they could not think a man could leave another so quickly. I beat him as if he were a little boy, and never saw a boat. When we got two miles from the start in the meadows, it became terribly rough; the seas began to wash over my boat as if it were a breakwater. I had three big sponges in my boat, and as soon as I would fill up I would stop and sponge out. One big wave came on and they told me I could not be seen for about a second and a half; it took it that long to pass me. I came out of the wave shaking my head and sponging my boat out. I could hardly see

Howden, he was so far behind. The descriptions of my sponging my boat out and antics were very funny. Every one thought I was drowned; that I was not waterman enough to manage my boat in such lumpy water."

"What is the hardest fought race you ever saw?"

"I have never seen a Harvard and Yale race rowed; and strange to say I have been in England three or four times, and never saw the Oxford and Cambridge rowed, and those are the races that are rowed and fought as a great struggle."

"I refer only to professional races."

"All that I have seen, so far, have been races where the winner got ahead and remained there.. Searle's race was a mere walk-over from the start. Searle did a very clever thing when he rowed Wolfe in Australia; not one in ten thousand would have had the nerve to do it, and it was his maiden race, too, on the Paramatta. The race was rowed for one hundred pounds a side, and from the start he let Wolfe go away from him. At the mile Wolfe led by a boat's length, and at two miles by a couple of boat's lengths. Wolfe was leading by forty-five feet within a quarter of a mile from home, and Searle suddenly looked at him and then commenced to row; marvellous to say, he passed Wolfe as if Wolfe was anchored, and the way he went past the finish was a sight to see. It was great fun. I was in the swim, and knew how fast he was. There were only two or three on the referee's boat knew of it, and they laid odds of two and three to one on Searle beating Wolfe. Searle is without question the coolest man I ever saw. He has a wonderful nerve. During the race, and before he pulled alongside Wolfe, he said: 'Mr. Wolfe, I will wager my boat, and the takings of the steamboat, that I beat you in this race.' 'All right.' Searle won the race, got Wolfe's boat, the stake money and the takings of the steamer. In every race he did the same thing. In the race with Stanberry he wagered the steamer's taking and his boat, and he also got them. He did the same thing with Nelson, except the steamboat takings, which Nelson would not back. He won Nelson's boat, won four boats in all. He let this man Wolfe lead him so close to the finish that there are very few men who would have the nerve to do it. I am satisfied that if O'Connor beats him, he must be a marvellous man. Searle is, without question, the greatest oarsman I ever saw. I have seen him do some really wonderful things on the Paramatta."

"Can an oarsman regulate his time accurately in a race? Do you ever sit with a watch in front of you?"

"In trials I do, but not in a race. I think a man would be benefited by it if he could keep his course; but a man has to turn round to look where he is going. I have many and many a time went on a strange lake in America, and I have been told it was a mile to such a place, and a half mile to some other, and I have struck that distance and never looked until I have given a certain number of strokes, and I have stopped within ten feet of the place where I wanted to. I know just where I am most of the time. When I have had dead water as near as possible, I could tell when I started how many strokes it would take me to finish. I have done this so often that I have not varied more than four or five strokes, when I have undertaken to time my strokes; 575 is my pace for three miles and 330 yards. One time 580 would take me over the same distance, never over 600. If I got a little breeze to assist me I would go very much quicker. With a back breeze I have done it in 570. That very thing helps regularity in the motion of the boat; you count your strokes, and it is a great benefit."

"What is the lowest you ever expect to see three miles reduced to?"

"We are comparatively in our infancy, yet; in five or six years rowing will be down to 19-15. We have not come to a standstill, yet. Fifteen seconds is a big reduction at the present standard. To reduce it fifteen seconds more will be the extreme. We have advanced so rapidly during the last few years I do not see where we are going to make greater changes. I think, however, we can reduce it fifteen seconds. When we row short races and teach ourselves to go quicker, it will advance speed so much, perhaps, that our constitutions will be able to continue."

"What do you think of Melbourne, Sydney, Adelaide, and Ballarat; of Australia, and Australians generally?"

"As for Sydney, from a boating standpoint, I do not think there is a city in the world that excels it. Their models of sailing yachts are equal to anything I have seen in this country, or in England. I have seen the finest yachts in Canada, England, and the United States, and their models in Sydney compare favorably with any of them. It is wonderful for a young country to be so far advanced. The models of their little steam launches are really beautiful, and the amount of speed they get out of them is equal to anything they get here. They are built by Australian boat builders, and they can build as good a shell there as in America or England. They build also a large iron clad steamer in New Zealand, for traffic, which is a remarkable boat. They build ocean boats also to ply from Sydney to the New Zealand coast, which are fine specimens of their class. The race boats they build in Sydney are remarkable. Their system of bracing a race boat is better by far than the system here. In their race boats they have a wonderful brace. It is not what we call a supplementary gunwale, but it is a gunwale concaved that acts as a wonderful brace up and down and does away with the supplementary gunwale. A race boat if not built strongly will twist lengthwise. That concaved gunwale is of the utmost benefit, and strengthens the boat more than anything we put in here. They also brace her by triangular braces. They also put a very light rib in the Australian boat. A heavy skin and a light frame is better than a heavy frame and a light skin. When you have a heavy frame and a light skin, the boat will not keep her proper lines in the water, as well as a boat with a light frame and heavy skin; and you can get a better polish on a light frame and heavy skin. I believe boat builders are wrong in the construction of the rib. We should not have a perpendicular rib at all around the skin; we should have a rib running from one end to the other. A triangular piece of whalebone, for instance, from gunwale to kelson, which is attached to the kelson and then to the gunwale; this would be better than a near rib running on the skin to the gunwale and kelson. It would not only strengthen the boat, but it would be lighter and safer. You must have practical ideas on boats to be able to dictate to the best boat builders, and tell them about boats.

"In a sporting sense, the Australian system is perfect in management; not only in boat races, but in the athletic field. Their grounds are really superb; they are magnificent. The management is correct. In the spring races there are thousands of pounds given in prizes. Five thousand dollars at one International Handicap, and there are four or five every year. Five or six hundred men will enter for one of these handicaps; the distance being 130 yards, and the limit mark 20 yards. Every man who runs a good trial from his mark and has a chance to win, will be backed from fifty to a hundred thousand dollars. There are five or six hundred entries, and about four hundred starts. The entrance is $2.50. If you start you pay $5. Every part of the race-track is illuminated with beautiful electric lights. They have seating capacity for twenty thousand people. Those are the Carrington grounds which are lighted up and open at nights.

"At the Putney grounds they have a foot-race track, but the racing all takes place in the daytime. I suppose Frank Smith, who is the proprietor of the Putney ground, has spent fifteen or sixteen thousand dollars for pavilions, etc. That sport is carried on in Australia in a systematic manner. A stranger without a reputation cannot enter there and get the limit, but has only three or four yards start. He has to work his way up, foot by foot, until he gets to where he thinks he can win, when he will be backed for thousands. The amount of money wagered on the races is wonderful. They are extremely fond of boating there, and they will wager more money on a boat race than on anything else. The amount of money Searle's backers won on his three races was surprising. His individual friends must have won from three to four hundred thousand dollars on the result of his different races.

"Horse races are also a surprising institution there; the Sydney cup being a grand meeting. But the greatest track in Australia is the Melbourne. The Melbourne Derby is run on a Saturday; then they start in Monday and run right up until the next Saturday or Wednesday, then Melbourne cup. On the cup day there are from a hundred and fifty to a hundred and seventy-five thousand people from the city of Melbourne, and from all parts of Australia, who come to the Melbourne cup run. A finer race-track I do not think there is in the world than this. The lawn is a quarter of a mile long, and so careful are they of the grounds, that if you were caught eating even a sandwich there you would be ordered off at once. You cannot imagine the magnificent dresses to be seen there. The women are the finest dressed I have ever gazed upon. The names of the best dressed are given in the newspapers, with descriptions of their dresses, and that has, I think, a tendency to bring the finest women in the country to the races.

"Australian horses are as good as any in the world. Their system of training is really splendid; they do everything in so systematic a manner. They have the comprehensive force of the English combined with the enterprise of the American, and they are the most hospitable people on the globe. Dinners, balls, and presentations—there was no end of them. No man ever went to the colony of Australia and had better receptions than I had. The Prince of Wales might have been

THE ROWING COURSE IN ALBERT PARK, MELBOURNE.

better received, but for an athlete my reception exceeded everything. In Melbourne, at the Albert Park, I gave an exhibition of rowing, and twenty thousand people came to see it. Then I went to Ballarat, and gave an exhibition there on Lake Windere, and had eight or ten thousand—the whole town. They said a gang of burglars might have robbed the city without being molested. It is a lovely spot. The buildings are very costly for a small place. I gave an exhibition, also, at Sandhurst. They gave me one hundred pounds to row. They had two hundred and fifty pounds clear money after paying me. Every place I went I had guaranteed amounts. I went from there to Queensland, where I received for an exhibition race five hundred pounds. In each place I was well received. You can look almost anywhere in these parlors and see evidences of that fact for yourself," said the oarsman, with a sweep of his hand toward the cabinets of silverware, the framed memorials upon the walls, and the articles of virtu and bric-a-brac, the gifts of friends upon two sides of the earth's surface.

"There is a picture of Toronto Bay as it was taken July 15th, 1879.

MAIN STREET IN BALLARAT.

on my return from England to Toronto after my race with Elliott. I am standing on the pilot house of the 'Chicora.' There were 4000 pleasure boats and every steamer about Toronto, as well as yachts, canoes, and craft of all kinds on the water that afternoon. I went to England in January of 1879; arrived there on the 9th of February. Went from Liverpool to Manchester and was met there by friends and Colonel Shaw, the American Consul in Manchester at that time. We proceeded to Newcastle-on-Tyne in company with my trainer, Mr. James

Hasley. Went to Newcastle to see the championship race rowed between Elliott and Higgins, and then my friend Colonel Shaw matched me to row John Hawdon. That race came off on the 3d of May, 1879. I won very easily. It was for £200 a side. On the 16th of June I rowed Elliott for the championship of England. Won that also on the Tyne Championship course from High Lever Bridge to Scotswood Suspension Bridge. I rowed the local match first and challenged Elliott afterwards and took the championship of England from him. This is the picture of my reception on my return, July 15th, 1879. Here is a very handsome address also in connection with that presented by the citizens of Toronto. The race was rowed in England on the 16th of June. That address," pointing to a framed memorial, "represents my race when I defeated Morris for the championship of America. It was presented by the citizens of Toronto. Here is a very handsome picture, also, of my return home, with Toronto in the background. I am supposed to be out rowing in the Bay here. Here is a souvenir presented to me by the citizens of Toronto on my return from Australia, June 24th, 1885, after my first defeat. It is an address by all the leading political men of Toronto, principal officials and citizens. Here is a handsome picture of the Henley course. That is the scene of the Henley Regatta rowed about four years ago. The only regatta course where American amateurs go and row. It is on the Thames at Henley. There are three eight-oared crews coming down the course in the picture.

"Here is a walking stick in this corner. What is it? That is a cabbage stalk. It looks like a heavy stick, but it is as light as a feather. It was presented by friends in Newcastle-on-Tyne. Here is a clock given me by the citizens of Toronto, when I came back from England after winning the championship. This will give you an idea of my reception through the north of England. This is a picture of a reception at Sunderland, November 24th. Enthusiastic reception at Mr. John Beattie's hotel. This is a picture taken in front of my boat-house on the Paramatta river, in Australia. There is a steam launch paying a visit to me. This is about five miles up the river from Sydney city. Here is a picture of some of my presents taken in Toronto, silverware, cups, watches, medals, etc Here is a photograph of myself, TenEyck, and W. Kennedy, of Quincy, Ill., as we sat in the broiling sun on Lake Quinsigamond. Here is a photograph of my hotel at Toronto Island. Here is a wine and cake-basket presented to me by C. B. Baillie, in Sydney, April 23d, 1885.

"Here is my first diploma at the Centennial. The easiest but most important I ever won. Here is a souvenir from Detroit," pointing to a large frame containing a dedication to Hanlan of a fantaisie called "The Magic Boatman," and which was signed by over five hundred people. "Here is a souvenir from Stockton, on the river Tees, England (pointing to an address), and one from the citizens of Orillia, Canada. Here is the scene of the high level bridge, where they start the races on the river Tyne, England. Over yonder is an illuminated address, presented by the citizens of Windsor, and beside it a copy of one from the citizens of Ottawa, the original having been destroyed by fire." And so we could have gone on until now, probably, looking over the many objects of interest that filled the apartment. I finally shook hands with the ex-Champion, however, and said, as I turned to go,—

"They say that you are getting old now, Ned, and that you have had your day; that you have been victorious, and that you ought to give up and let the young oarsmen have a chance."

"A man never feels he is getting old," replied the oarsman, with a smile. "I am doubtful, however, whether I will row any more; I have done enough. I have not the same ambition I used to have for it.

"What I think of doing in future is to settle here in Toronto, on the Island, and take some regular though gentle exercise, thus getting a good rest and plenty of out-door pastime in walking, ice-boating, and possibly a little shooting. I want to do this the more as I am troubled a little with dyspepsia, through eating here and there, drinking the different waters of the world, and living high generally."

The correctness of Hanlan's judgment, as stated above, in reference to the Australian sculler, Searle, was demonstrated on September 9th, 1889, a few weeks after the interview, when, in the race for the world's championship, upon the Thames, Searle beat O'Connor by ten lengths; and the opinion of all observers was that it was a good race fairly won. Searle's subsequent death, of typhoid fever, in December, 1889, was a sad blow to his many admirers.

CRICKET

LEARNED men who have gone [into the question admit] that the game of cricket is o[ne of the few of] which we have any definit[e...] avoid disputing over the [...] same learned men seem to [agree, on one point] at least, for the majority of them [...] among them, admit the identity of [... with the] sport called Club-ball. Now this [...] the vicinity of the fourteenth c[entury...] English form as Han[d]-ly-an [...] esque and illustrative than the [...]

There have been a m[ost plausible...] origin and license of the word cr[icket...] credited than that which, upon goo[d authority,] is found in the Saxon *cryce* or *c* [...] this method of reasoning is tr[...] bat, which is now made straight [... was formerly] as quite crooked, showing that lo[ng...] of games that have derived [... manner in] which they are played. Base-ba[ll...] other easily quoted verification[s...]

England lays undisputed and [...]

XIII.

CRICKET.*

LEARNED men who have gone back into very musty records agree that the game of cricket is one of the most ancient pastimes of which we have any definitive knowledge. While they may never avoid disputing over the doubtful derivation of the term itself, the same learned men seem to meet on one common ground of concession, at least, for the majority of them, perhaps I should say the best posted among them, admit the identity of the present game with the old English sport called Club-ball. Now this latter pastime flourished somewhere in the vicinity of the fourteenth century. It was better known in its early English form as Handyn and Handoute, a title that is far more picturesque and illustrative than the present mysterious term, is it not?

There have been a multiplicity of explanations advanced as to the origin and license of the word cricket, but no argument is more easily credited than that which, upon good authority, states that the derivation is found in the Saxon *cryce* or *creag*, meaning a crooked stick. Indeed, this method of reasoning is further strengthened from the fact that the bat, which is now made straight, is represented in old prints of the game as quite crooked, showing that here is another of the obvious instances of games that have derived their names from the implements with which they are played. Baseball, foot-ball, hand-ball, and lacrosse are other easily quoted verifications of this theory.

England lays undisputed and unswerving claim to cricket as its truly

---

* By J. A. Fynes.

national game. Played rudely for the first century or two of its existence, it gained steadily in followers until we find it, about 1740, accounted a fashionable sport, guarded by careful rules, dignified by printed scores, and already possessing its crack exponents. Those were picturesque days, surely, and we may not wonder that the game quickly spread until it found in Scotland and in Ireland a devoted and gradually increasing body of admirers. To-day its wide acceptance in Victoria's domains is hardly less, all the circumstances considered, than that of our own phenomenally progressive baseball. Few towns, fewer villages, and no schools in England are without their own private cricket grounds; the rank and file of its amateur exponents, indeed, are not easily reckoned in calculating figures.

Yet cricket in America does not flourish, never has flourished, and, I am not afraid to forecast, will never make conspicuous progress in popularity here.

The history of its earlier days in this country antedates by far that of baseball, or even the various rude progenitors of baseball; for we are accurately able to ascertain that cricket was played prior to 1747 in the vicinity of what is now Fulton Market, New York. More than that, we know that the attempt to win favor for the game was steady rather than spasmodic, for we possess clear records of a contest on those same grounds four years later, when elevens composed of New Yorkers and Londoners contested fiercely, and with results adverse to the foreign team.

Naturally, as an outcome of these olden time games, it is fair to presume that clubs or other bodies for the practice and promotion of cricket were organized in due season. New York could hardly have been without its quota, though we possess no absolute knowledge of the details connected with the earliest organizations; but we know that as far back as 1809 Boston had its crack club, whose printed rules and by-laws are among the *ana* jealously preserved to this day in the library of a well-known cricketer. English residents in Philadelphia organized the Union Cricket Club about 1832, and by 1854 there were three other clubs in existence in that city—the Philadelphias, Germantowns, and Young Americas, the first native American cricket clubs. The St. George Club of New York directly resulted from the jubilation and *esprit du corps* consequent upon a game won by a representative New York eleven from a representative Long Island eleven in October, 1838. The New Yorkers banded together for years, and it is interesting to know that their first grounds were in the neighborhood of Broadway and Thirtieth street. Needless to say, they could hardly play there now. I suppose a prime article in cricket grounds in that locality at this day would be quoted at from $5,000,000 to $10,000,000. But, with all other growing movements in Gotham, the cricketers later moved their grounds northward.

In all these early progressions of the game here, English residents, or their direct descendants, were the ones most actively interested. They formed the nucleus of the fraternity of cricketers in America, and only in Philadelphia was there at any time an exception to this rule. The Quaker City is still famous as the principal thriving place of American cricket, but I have yet to hear a plausible explanation of this rather odd circumstance. With us, cricket has been known in nearly all localities where sports in general find a following; but the mere acquaintance does not ripen so fast as our English cousins would wish, and it seems useless to deny that with each succeeding year the prospect for a wider adoption of the game becomes less hopeful.

For a half century or more our little congregations of cricket clubs here and there have gone through their somewhat conventional yearly series of friendly contests, developing a degree of skill of which we need not be ashamed, pleasing the circles of their immediate friends and admirers, receiving from the newspapers a generous measure of space and intelligent comment—yet still never arousing the public at large from its apathy towards cricket. We have placed to our credit in these matches some good aggregate and individual scores, we have done some extraordinary run-getting, and in bowling we have not been without distinction. So that lack of proficiency, at least, cannot be pressed as an excuse for the indifference of the multitude.

At rare intervals, however, something really like enthusiasm has illumed the rather dreary record of American cricket. These spasms of actual interest have been when the spirit of patriotism has been aroused—I dare say, love of country affecting most of us a great deal more than love of cricket—by visits from foreign teams. A series of international matches in the years 1859, 1868, 1872, 1881 and 1882, count among the most memorable events in our cricket history. In 1859 a challenge from this side of the water brought hither without much delay an English eleven (or, rather, twelve), captained by George Parr, and representing the flower of British professionalism at the wicket. They played five games, at Montreal, Hamilton (Canada), Hoboken (New Jersey), Philadelphia and New York city, winning them all and returning to England " covered with laurels," as a London writer has proudly recorded it. The second party from the other side came under Captain Willsher in 1868, and, after defeating all the teams who met them in the States, were forced to take a draw with a Canadian twenty-two at Montreal, owing to a rainstorm. W. G. Grace led the third English team (amateurs in this case, however), who, in 1872, visited eight of our cities and won in seven, the contest in the eighth (Boston) being called a draw on account of darkness.

But a change was to come in the discouraging record of American defeats. In 1878 the Australian cricketers, fresh from a tour of victory in England, stopped in transit long enough to engage in contest the Hoboken, Philadelphia, Detroit, Montreal and San Francisco Clubs, but winning from only four of them, the other two games being fairly drawn. In 1879 a visiting team of Irish amateurs met with defeat in Philadelphia, while in 1881 a team of English professionals, captained by Alfred Shaw, encountered three draws to vary the monotony of their victories.

Games between the United States and Canadian clubs have also had their weight in keeping alive interest in cricket on this side of the Atlantic. As early as 1844-5-6 New York and Philadelphia were allied against teams of Montreal and Toronto. The games in the first series were mostly won by the Canadians. From 1853 to 1860 there were annual contests, the United States eleven winning five and losing only two of this series. In 1879 the second series commenced, and this time only actual natives of the United States were upon its eleven. The balance of victories in this series has also been to the credit of Uncle Sam's citizens.

XIV.

'CYCLING.*

PART I.

'Cycling is a general term, and has come into latter-day service to cover everything connected with the sport of wheeling. In the same manner, the term 'cyclist may be applied to a bicycle, tricycle, or safety rider; to a lady or to a gentleman. This sport of 'cycling has some phenomenal aspects, not only in the development in the style and manufacture of wheels, but in the remarkable increase of its votaries, which shows an amazing gain every year.

'Cycling was a development. Between the years 1800 and 1816 there must have been a very large number of men who believed that a man-motor, or vehicle driven by man power, was a possibility. No public mention was made of such a vehicle until 1816, but there is reason to believe that numbers of men were experimenting, and that more or less crude forms of manumotors were in use in the early years of the century. The patent records of all countries will show the most curious collection of man-power vehicles that one could well look upon. 'Cycling began as a wonder, degenerated into a "fad," was revived as a sport, and to-day occupies an important place in the history of outdoor recreation.

In the perfection of the 'cycle, England, France, Germany, and America join hands. The French conceived the idea, the Germans went them one better, the English carried the idea to a greater degree of progress, and, finally, America furnished a few essential ideas which gave the finishing touch and produced the bicycle as we know it to-day.

The first form of man-motor was a three-wheeled velocipede, invented by Blancharde and Magurier. This wheel was exhibited in the Place de la Concorde, Paris, before the members of the French Academy and

---

* By F. P. Prial, Editor of *The Wheel* and *Cycling Trade Review*.

other distinguished spectators. An account of the proceedings appears in *Le Journal de Paris*, of July 27th, 1779. It seems to have been of complicated design, and had no merit of any kind, outside the mere idea. Between that date and 1816, when the general idea of the bicycle appeared, there were numbers of wheels produced, all without merit, and for the most part complicated masses of metal. They were known under the various names of mechanical carriages, perambulators, accelerators, passepartouts, mechanical horses, propellers, velocipedes, etc.

To the German race is to be credited the rudimentary bicycle. It was invented in 1816 by the Baron Von Drais, a landscape gardener of some reputation, who was master of the forests of the Grand Duke of Baden, at Manheim-on-the-Rhine. He was, quite probably, an "odd genius," and he conceived the idea that, with the aid of a velocipede, a man could support the weight of his body while on the level, and could make good pace by coasting down grades. His invention was called the "Draisine." It consisted of two wheels, one in front of the other, connected by a perch, with a rude contrivance to control the front wheel. The rider sat astride the perch, propelled the wheel by thrusting his feet on the ground as if pushing the ground behind him, and lifting his feet and coasting down grades. On this peculiar and primitive vehicle the Baron perambulated about the Duke's grounds to the admiration of the few and the consternation of the many.

The Baron's "Draisine" appeared in Paris in 1816, when an exhibition was given at the "Tivoli Gardens," a famous resort of the day. Patents were taken out in France, in which country the machine was called the "Célérifère." The wheel did not show in England until 1818, when it was immediately improved by one Dennis Johnson, who took out patents on a "Pedestrian Curricle." Johnson's wheel had an adjustable saddle, which could be moved forward or backward, to suit the convenience of the rider. It also had cushioned rests for the forearms, and the handles were of more convenient form. Johnson's improved wheel created a furore in England, and many wheels were ridden. The Baron Drais' wheel was also very popular throughout Germany and France. It was called the Draisina, Draisine, Célérifère, Pedestrian Curricle, and Velocipede. The most popular name for it in England was the "dandy-horse," or "hobby-horse."

In 1819 the "dandy-horse" was brought to New York, and immediately became the craze, not only in the metropolis but in other cities. In June, 1819, one W. K. Clarkson was granted a patent for an improvement, but the papers disappeared in the Patent Office fire of 1836, and the nature of Clarkson's improvement has never been learned. In 1821, Louis Gompertz, an Englishman, patented an important improvement. Gompertz practically retained the lines of the "Draisine" and Johnson's "dandy-horse," but, by the use of a sequent rack gearing into a pinion on the front wheel, the rider was able to drive the wheel by drawing the handles toward him. So that Gompertz was the first man to produce a velocipede which could be driven without the use of the limbs as propellers. From 1821 until 1865 but little progress was made in 'cycle invention. In March, 1865, a Frenchman, named Marischal, obtained a patent for a "double-running" velocipede. Marischal describes his velocipede as consisting of a frame connecting five wheels, each having an independent axle, the ends of which are provided with foot cranks bearing loose pedals; each wheel to be mounted and driven by its rider, who was seated directly over his wheel. The front wheel was used as a steering wheel, so that it was practically a five-seated velocipede, with one rider guiding and the other four seated two abreast and helping to propel.

In 1865 Messrs. Woirin and Leconde took out French patents on a wheel which was simpler than Marischal's, and which approached the modern bicycle more closely than any previous device. It was a three-wheeled velocipede, a large front wheel and two smaller rear wheels, the latter on the same axle. The axle of the front wheel terminated in two cranks, projecting in opposite directions. To these cranks were affixed loose pedals. The frame was of wood, and shaped like a horse, the hind legs forming the rear forks of the machine, and the fore legs forming the front forks, between which the large driving-wheel revolved. It will be noted that these men were the first to make a three-wheeler driven by cranks and pedals.

The next step in 'cycle invention was the discovery that the foot-crank method of propulsion would work as well on two as on three wheels; that two rear wheels are not necessary to maintain equilibrium. This discovery was made in 1865, by Pierre Lallement, a French mechanic.

Lallement perfected his wheel at odd moments, and it was exhibited at the Paris Exposition in 1865. In 1866 Lallement came to the United States, and removed to New Haven. Being out of employment, he built two of his wheels and gave exhibitions in that city. The wheel attracted the attention of a man named Carroll, and on November 20th, 1866, an American patent was obtained by Lallement and Carroll.

Lallement's wheel was the immediate forerunner, and contained the essential ideas, of the modern bicycle. Shortly after introducing his wheel, Lallement sold his interest in the American patents and returned to France, where he became a manufacturer for a time. Of late years he has been an employé in the Pope Manufacturing Company's factory at Hartford. In 1868 Lallement turned out a rather better style of a wheel, with some of the parts made of iron and bronze, instead of wood, and his wheel was exhibited in the Champs Elysées and Tuileries, and caused a great furore.

Lallement's title as the inventor of the primitive bicycle is disputed by Edward Gilman, an Englishman, who obtained patents in the British Patent Office on August 1st, 1866. In Gilman's device the weight of the rider was of material service in propelling the wheel, and greatly increased the power applied.

These improvements of Lallement and Gilman brought the velocipede into great popularity; indeed, riding became a craze in England, France, and the United States. During the years 1867-8-9 the English made steady progress, many improvements of a minor kind being patented. On March 31st, 1868, L. F. P. Riviere, a resident of the county of Middlesex, produced a machine in which the front wheel was "somewhat larger than the rear one." In November, 1868, C. K. Bradford, an American, added the suggestion of a rubber tire, and in December, 1868, Edward A. Paver, an Englishman, introduced the suspension wheel and anti-friction bearings; and so the modern bicycle was perfected.

PART II.

The modern 'cycle dates from about 1875 in England, and from the 1876 Centennial Exposition in this country. The first real impetus to the introduction of modern 'cycling was given by John Keen and Dave Stanton, two English racing men, who came here in 1876 and gave exhibitions throughout the country. A bicycle was also on exhibition at the Philadelphia Exposition. The first bicycle ridden by a native was brought to Boston on May 29th, 1877, by Alfred D. Chandler, a law student. In November, 1877, Cunningham & Heath, a Boston concern, began to import bicycles, the pioneer rider being Frank Weston. In the fall of 1877, Colonel Albert A. Pope rode a bicycle, and became so much interested that he imported eight bicycles and sold them at his store. At the time the Colonel was in the air-pistol business. In July, 1878, the first wheels were manufactured for Colonel Pope by the Weed Sewing-Machine Company, at Hartford. The total sales of bicycles for the year 1878 were ninety-two. Within a year there were one hundred regularly organized bicycle clubs in this country, and from that time the growth of 'cycling has been phenomenal.

The wheels used in this country are imported from England, or manufactured here. The types of wheels may be generally grouped as bicycles and tricycles. The bicycles are of several styles, as: ordinary, which is the name applied to a two-wheeled vehicle, with a large driving or front wheel, with a diameter of from forty to sixty inches and a rear wheel averaging from eighteen to twenty-two inches. The other important division of bicycles is the safety, or dwarf, in which both wheels are about equal in size and have diameters of twenty-six to thirty-two inches, and are driven by a direct crank action, by chain and cog wheel, and by other power devices, the feature of the dwarf being that the front wheel is the steering wheel and the rear wheel the driver, hence they are called rear-drivers.

A division of the rear-driving bicycles are the rear-driving or tandem safeties, an equal-wheeled two-seated vehicle, the rear rider sitting directly behind the front rider. This form of bicycle may be constructed so that three, four, or more riders may use it. Modifications of the tall or ordinary bicycle are the Star and Eagle bicycles.

Tricycles are of various forms, some simple, many complicated, the most popular form being a three-track vehicle, two wheels of about twenty-two inches, and a small front steering wheel, with a chain and ratchet arrangement for driving power. Other forms of the tricycle besides the single tricycle described are the sociable, the tandem, the triplet, and the quadricycle. The feature of the sociable is that the two riders sit side by side, but this has been found to be an awkward arrangement, and the sociable tricycle has fallen into innocuous desuetude. The tandem tricycle provides that one rider shall sit behind the other. Its two principal forms are the bicycle, or direct-steerer, and the "Humber" type, which is easiest to drive, but is not without danger on account of its peculiar construction. The triplet is a four-wheeled vehicle with seats for three. It has not come into practical use, but remarkably fast time has been made upon it. The quadricycle, which has as yet attracted no very great publicity or popularity, is a four-wheeled vehicle providing seats for two. These types are the principal ones, though there are scores of variations, a mere sketch of which would make a big book.

The American 'cycle trade still centres around Boston, although "the Hub" is not the centre of 'cycling that it once was, and it is rapidly losing its prestige as the 'cycling trade centre. Perhaps a more careful statement would be that there is now no trade centre at all. In past seasons the heart of the trade certainly was in the City of Culture, but the advent of so many new concerns in various parts of the country has detracted from the premier position which Boston once held.

The first three years of the American trade might be sketched in a few brief paragraphs, but a history of the trade as it is to-day would make a bulky volume. The 'cycle industry is divided among manufacturers and importers. Some of the manufacturers have their own plant, while others have their wheels made by contract. The importers either represent some English houses, or have their wheels manufactured to special order by English concerns. In two cases, English houses have established American branches, and import and sell their own wheels direct.

The wheels are sold through agents, who are allowed a discount according to the amount of their sales. Most of the agents deal only in 'cycles, and have the exclusive agency in their city or town for one or more styles of wheels. It is the custom for an agent to make a "leader" of one style, and he devotes his best energy to pushing that make, making but little effort to sell the other lines he carries, and only showing them upon demand. The relations between the agent and the parent houses are quite close, and he is quite frequently financially aided by them. Besides selling new wheels, he rents wheels by the hour, repairs, buys, sells, and exchanges second-hand wheels, and sometimes lets storage room to riders who are not members of clubs. Within the past year the agency business has been developed, and some of the larger dealers now have exclusive control of a wheel for one or more States. Besides dealers who confine their business to 'cycles are others who are in the hardware or sporting goods line, and who have bicycle departments. Two of the most successful dealers in the country made a reputation in the retail sewing-machine business before they commenced to sell 'cycles.

The 'cycle trade has many peculiarities found in no other business. The fact that a maker or importer depends on what are called "novelties" and "improvements" for advertisement and popularity has developed certain conditions—despicable conditions—which will disappear with the growth of the industry. At the present time many members of the trade carefully watch each other's movements, and at the present time an alert man can easily keep *au courant* with all the deals that are on or off. He knows, or feels that he ought to know, how much longer A will hold on; whether Company E's capital is all paid up; what H is going to put on the market next season; whether it is or is not true that J made $25,000 this year, and how many unsold wheels K has in stock at the end of the season. For the reasons stated above, important makers, importers, and sellers are very guarded in statement, and it is difficult to get at the status of a firm, to learn the amount of its capital, the approximate number of wheels sold, the market value of its stock, and what modifications in styles it may introduce.

There are at the present time eighteen manufacturers and nine importers in this country, making a total of twenty-seven 'cycle concerns, and these will be increased to at least thirty before the season of 1890 is opened, which will be about February. The makers turn out eighty-two different styles of wheels, while the importers bring over seventy-nine styles, a total of one hundred and sixty-one different types. The makers have about $2,250,000 invested, while the importers employ about $350,000, or altogether about four millions are used in the business of making and importing. These four millions represent the money invested in manufacturing plant, in material, in machines, and actually used in carrying on the business. There are probably 2,000 agents in the country. Of these 2,000 many derive a large portion of their profit from profits on exchanges, buying and selling second-hand wheels, repairing, etc., and sales of lamps, gongs, and other cycling accessories. The average agent makes nothing more than a good living. The average profit would be about $2,000, the large majority running at about $1,500, with a constantly decreasing number netting above the sum named up to $20,000 and $25,000. They marketed in the aggregate about seven million dollars. A fair estimate of the number of 'cyclists of the country would be from 115,000 to 130,000. They spend $7,000,000 for new wheels, $750,000 on second-hand wheels, $300,000 for club dues, $600,000 on repairs, and $1,750,000 on uniforms, cycle sundries, etc., a total of over ten millions. Besides this there is $1,500,000 invested in club property, and the total value of 'cycling stock is about $18,000,000.

PART III.

The style of wheel which a 'cyclist should purchase depends upon several circumstances, as sex, age, physical condition, kind of roads over which the wheel is to be ridden, and other special conditions. Of course the state of one's pocket-book must be taken into the account. The choice of a person between the ages of fifteen and fifty should be between an ordinary, or a safety of high grade, ranging in price from $125 to $135, or a medium grade wheel, which may be bought for from $75 to $100. For a man who does most of his riding by daylight, and has good roads, the average light roadster ordinary, having a weight of about thirty-eight pounds, will be found to possess many advantages. He will find that it takes much longer to learn to ride the ordinary than the safety; the tall wheel is more dangerous than the dwarf. Of course, a skillful rider will reduce this danger to a minimum, and will guide his ordinary over the most difficult places, but the average rider never takes the time or the thought to develop this mastery of his wheel. Besides, the feeling of unsafety which is always consciously or unconsciously in the rider's mind takes a deal of stamina out of him and largely contributes to the fatigue occasioned by the muscular effort. Notwithstanding the drawbacks to which I refer, many riders will use none but a tall wheel. It takes less muscular effort to drive it, the wheel lasts longer, and the pleasure of driving a tall wheel is in slight degree greater than that experienced on a safety. There are a half score of tall wheels sold in this country, all of which are of high grade make and the matter of selection becomes merely a whim. One man will prefer a particular feature of one style, such as a ball head, a tangent spoke, a direct spoke, etc., while another rider will consider this same feature a drawback to the wheel.

By far the larger number of young male riders prefer the safety bicycle. Indeed, the popularity of the dwarf wheel has amounted to the proportions of a "craze," not only in this country but in England, France, and Germany. The makers are turning out ordinaries, but their greatest ingenuity and capacity are devoted to making safeties. During some months of the spring of 1889 it was impossible to obtain safeties of certain popular styles.

The safety runs almost as easily as the ordinary bicycle, and can be made as light in construction. It is lighter than the tricycle, is practically free from headers, and is easily mastered. The average type of safety is two wheels of equal size or thereabouts, about thirty inches in diameter, though the sizes run from 26 to 32 inches, and sometimes the front wheel varies from the rear wheel to the extent of a couple of inches. The safety is the wheel for night riding, and for rough country. It has the advantage of being geared up to different powers, so that the rider may have a wheel geared all the way from 54 to 60. The strongest form of safety is the diamond-frame, which is constructed to take up the strain. The upper joint of the diamond is generally made detachable, so that the wheel may be ridden by a lady, when the bar is removed. The weights of wheels run from thirty to fifty-five, six, or seven pounds. The wheels turned out by American makers run at a few pounds over fifty. A fifty-pound wheel geared to 54 or 57 inches will be found most suitable for the ordinary country roads. A man of light weight or of delicate physique may ride a 38 to 45-pound wheel with advantage. A wheel weighing in the neighborhood of forty pounds is quite heavy enough for Park, asphalt or good macadam riding. Most young riders who use light wheels gear them as high as 60 and even up to 64, but such a wheel is not worth much after a season's hard riding, and the extra gear, especially if it is higher than 57 inches, is scarcely an advantage, as the muscular effort necessary to overcome the high gear, especially if there is any hill work, leaves one rather ragged after a good run. The safeties on the American market differ in many points. One is fitted with an anti-vibrator device, while almost all differ in the following points: Length of wheel base, size of wheels, style of saddle, shape of handle-bars and handles, slant of handle-bar post and front forks, form of frame, shape of seat-rod, etc.

In purchasing a wheel the rider should consider that a large part of the fatigue of a ride is caused by the vibration, not only in the arms and hands, caused by the vibration of the handles, but over the entire body. This vibration also causes great wear and tear of the 'cycle, and shortens its life. The common minimizers of vibration are: Special anti-vibration devices, arrangement of the saddle on springs, and the use of heavy rubber tires. A wheel that is too stiffly or too rigidly built has more vibration than one which has some spring both in the machine itself and in the form of construction. Generally speaking, a good saddle and heavy rubber tires are depended upon to absorb the larger part of the vibration, but, in addition to these, many makers use special devices. These American makers use springs in the front forks, which do their share to absorb the vibration. Other makers use springs coiled into the bottom of the forks, or connect the forks to the hubs by strong springs. The two latest anti-vibration devices are: A detachable handle-bar and a pneumatic tire. The latter device, which has created somewhat of a sensation, consists of a rubber tire inflated with air so that it passes over obstacles and rough roads without jar. The drawbacks of this tire are its large size and the necessity of replenishing the air to keep it properly distended.

To sum up, the ideal safety should not be geared too high, should be geared to 54 or 57 inches—except in the case of strong riders, while the tires should be heavy, the cranks fairly long, and the saddle the most comfortable that money can buy.

The fair sex who go about on wheels are called lady 'cyclists, though "cycling for women" is a permissible and proper combination. The types to which a lady may confine her selection are the tricycle and the safety bicycle. Tricycling has always been popular with ladies since man first took up wheeling, for where man goes woman will follow, or at least make the attempt. By far the largest number of lady riders use bicycles, though many ride with either lady or gentlemen friends on the tandem bicycle or tandem tricycle.

PART IV.

In the early days, the 'cyclist was regarded as a boyish man, as a person with a screw loose; and, as the general public dislikes cranks, it took special pleasure in making the life of the 'cyclist as miserable as possible. Of course, this sort of thing is rapidly disappearing. The number of cyclists has become so great that the sight of one no longer excites the deviltry inherent in all small boys. The hoodlum has learned, through the policy of silence, that the cyclist either despises his meanness or pities his ignorance, and as for the men who go abroad on wheels, and who are called road-hogs, or the men who want the earth, they have been restrained by the insinuating but potent influence of the law, which has long since placed the cyclist on the same footing with the modest buggy, the cumbersome barouche, and the pretentious tally-ho, not to forget all manner of vehicles of trade, from the skittish butcher cart to the furniture van.

It may be stated, with truth, that the cycle is in use all over the civilized world, and, since Thomas Stevens completed his remarkable journey around the globe, it may be added that, in certain byways of the world, the bicycle is familiar where the modern family coach has never been seen. The home of the sport is in England, where there are probably 400,000 wheelmen. It has the finest roads of any country. It has thousands of agents and hundreds of factories. Its cycling journals are the oldest and the largest published. Its manufacturers send wheels to America, to all the European countries, Australia, India, and even to Africa. The cycle is very popular in both France and Germany, and even this year a German rider scampered off with the one-mile bicycle championship of England. Almost all the countries where cycles are extensively used have organizations, the main planks of whose platforms are the protection of cyclists and the advancement of their interests. The Cyclists' Touring Club, of England, has a membership of over 20,000. The League of American Wheelmen numbers 12,000. The Cyclists' Society maintains a salaried secretary, publishes a monthly magazine, prints cyclists' hand-books and maps, and lists of hotels at which cyclists receive special discounts. The American association has a constitution as perfect in its outworkings as the United States Constitution. It has a President, who, with the First and Second Vice-Presidents, forms an Executive Committee. It is governed by a National Assembly, composed of about ninety members, apportioned to the various States. Its work is carried on by various standing committees. The Racing Board makes the laws of the race-path, adjudicates on all questions raised, and preserves a state of strict amateurism. The Rights and Privileges Committee look out for the legal interests of cyclists, influence legislation in favor of wheelmen, carry on suits against drivers who have injured wheelmen, against turnpike companies who make unjust charges, and prevent city, town, and park authorities from passing illegal restrictions and ordinances. The Transportation Committee secures special rates from railroads, and has induced all the principal lines to transport wheels free when accompanied by their owners. The Roads Improvement Committee have long been educating the people on the necessity and benefits of good roads, and are about to introduce roads improvement legislation in several States. Each " State Division " comprising this League has a controlling body called the Board of Officers. Its head is the Chief Consul. Each of the National Committees mentioned above are also duplicated in the State, the whole working in harmony. The League maintains a salaried Secretary-Editor at Boston, and each of its members receives weekly a cycling paper, in which all official news is published. The National Assembly meets every February to transact the business of the League. The national body holds an annual meet every summer, which is much in the nature of a reunion. The States also hold their annual meets, and many of the larger Divisions have published road-books, in which are outlined routes between the principal cities. Besides the two organizations whose work has been sketched, are cyclists' associations in Scotland, Ireland, France, Germany, Australia, and Canada.

The early oppression, suppression, or persecution of wheelmen developed a fraternal, live-together-or-we'll-die-separate feeling which was productive of numerous clubs. The Pickwick is the oldest club in England, and was organized in 1869 or thereabouts. The oldest club in America is the Boston Bicycle Club, which was organized in 1879. The English club is a club in name only, while the American organization is anything from a weekly meeting at the cross-roads of a few riders bent on taking a run to an organization of perhaps two hundred men, having a club-house palatial in size and appointments. There are perhaps a thousand clubs, at least half of which have club headquarters or rooms furnished more or less elegantly. About two hundred clubs have club property, each representing investments from five to forty thousand dollars. The greatest wheel city is Washington, which has so many miles of asphalt pavements and so many Government clerks who have time to ride. The wheel is used to go to and from business, as a delivery wagon by retailers. Ladies shop on it, and wheels are as common a sight as car horses. The number of cyclists in the Capital City has been estimated from eight to twelve thousand.

Chicago has about fifteen salesrooms, a like number of clubs, and about six thousand riders. Its splendid boulevards are the cause of this activity. Boston and its suburbs afford riding to about twenty thousand riders. In the Orange, N. J., district, in which nearly all the roads are well-kept macadam, are four thousand riders. Roughly estimating, the number of riders in other large cities is as follows: New York and Brooklyn, about five thousand; Philadelphia, three thousand; Cleveland, Indianapolis, Cincinnati, Pittsburg, Scranton, Baltimore, St.

Louis, San Francisco, Buffalo, Denver, and Omaha have from eight to fifteen hundred riders each. A city of fifty thousand will contain about two hundred riders, and this is about the proportion of 'cyclists to the total population, except that where the roads are good the number of wheelmen is much larger than the average named.

New York city supports five clubs, all renting large private houses and having an aggregate membership of nearly a thousand. Brooklyn cyclists maintain three superbly appointed club-houses, with a membership of five hundred and an investment of about seventy thousand dollars, of which the wheelmen owe forty thousand. Jersey City supports one club-house; Boston, one; Washington, three; Philadelphia has several clubs, supports four houses, three of which are worth eighty thousand dollars, and are equal to anything in the country. Baltimore has a palatial club building, facing Druid Hill Park. Chicago has three large club buildings and several smaller clubs. Cincinnati, Cleveland, Pittsburg, San Francisco, and Scranton have club-houses. A general and accurate statement would be that all towns with a cycling population have from one to a dozen clubs; that at least one club has meeting-rooms, and where the number of clubs runs over three, at least one of these has a specially built house, which it either leases or owns outright.

The more pretentious club buildings are architecturally fine as to front, and commodious and richly furnished as to interior. The basement is used as a wheel-room, the first floor as a parlor and reception-rooms, with an alcove reading-room, the next floor a locker and billiard-room. Some large houses have bowling-alleys, gymnasiums, card and committee rooms, janitors' quarters, etc. The well-conditioned club has club runs on Sundays and holidays, holds stag rackets, smoking concerts and receptions during the winter, and the rooms are the social headquarters of the members.

XV.

APPENDIX.

I. STATISTICS OF BASEBALL.

The first series of games played for the championship of the world occurred in 1884 between the Providence club and the Metropolitan, of New York. It consisted of three games, all of which were won by Providence, the scores being 6–0, 3–1, and 12–2.

In 1885 the Chicago and St. Louis teams fought for honors, with this result:

Oct. 14, St. Louis vs. Chicago, at Chicago (8 innings) . . . . 5—5
" 15, Chicago vs. St. Louis, at St. Louis (6 innings) forfeited . . . . 5—4
" 16, St. Louis vs. Chicago, at St. Louis . . . . 7—4
" 17, " vs. " at " . . . . 3—2
" 22, Chicago vs. St. Louis, at Pittsburg (7 innings) . . . . 9—2
" 23, " vs. " at Cincinnati . . . . 9—2
" 24, St. Louis vs Chicago, at " . . . . 13—4

Total victories for Chicago, 3; for St. Louis, 3, with one game drawn. Total runs scored by Chicago, 43; by St. Louis, 41.

In the contest of October 15th, at St. Louis, the umpire awarded the game to Chicago in the sixth innings by 9 to 0, and this award was concurred in by the St. Louis club. When the match was arranged Messrs. Spalding and Von der Ahe placed in the hands of the editor of *The Mirror of American Sports* a written document to the effect that the sum of $1,000 was to be paid to the club winning the series. The money was divided, although the St. Louis club claimed that Captain Anson had agreed to waive his claim to the forfeited game and let the game of October 24th decide the series.

In 1886 the same clubs again contended for the world's pennant. This time the St. Louis Browns won by taking four out of six games, winning October 18th, 12-0; October 21st, 8-5; October 22d, 10-3; and October 23d, 4 to 3 (10 innings). Chicago won the first game October 20th, 11-4. The series was generally considered something of a hippodrome, because after the second game certain players of both teams agreed to divide their share of the receipts, no matter which team won the pennant.

In 1887 the contestants were the Detroit and St. Louis teams. Fifteen games were played, the Detroits winning ten. The following table shows the results:

DATE.	WINNER.	SCORE.	WHERE PLAYED.	ATTENDANCE.
Oct. 10, ...	St. Louis	6-1	St. Louis	4208
" 11, ...	Detroit	5-3	"	6408
" 12, ...	"	2-1	Detroit	4509
" 13, ...	"	8-0	Pittsburgh	2447
" 14, ...	St. Louis	5-2	Brooklyn	6796
" 15, ...	Detroit	9-0	New York	5797
" 17, ...	"	3-1	Philadelphia	6478
" 18, ...	"	9-2	Boston	2891
" 19, ...	"	4-2	Philadelphia	2389
" 21, ...	St. Louis	16-4	Washington (A. M.)	1261
" 21, ...	Detroit	13-3	Baltimore (P. M.)	2707
" 23, ...	St. Louis	5-1	Brooklyn	1138
" 24, ...	Detroit	6-3	Detroit	3389
" 25, ...	"	4-3	Chicago	378
" 26, ...	St. Louis	9-2	St. Louis	659—51,455

The receipts were $42,000, and the expenses $18,000. The price of admission was one dollar, and the teams traveled in special Pullman cars. Each club received about $12,000, and each member of the team received a liberal share of the receipts, the Detroit players getting about $500 each.

In 1888 New York and St. Louis played for the world's pennant. New York won the series October 25th. The last two games were practically exhibition contests, as the New Yorks were short handed and made no pretense of trying to play ball. The following table shows the record:

DATE.	CONTESTING CLUBS.	CITIES.	PITCHERS.	In's.	Scr.	Rec.
Oct. 16	New York vs. St. Louis	New York	Keefe . . . . King	9	2–1	$2,876
" 17	St. Louis vs. New York	" "	Chamberlain . Welch	9	3–0	3,375
" 18	New York vs. St. Louis	" "	Keefe . . . . King	9	4–2	3,530
" 19	" " "	Brooklyn	Crane . Chamberlain	9	6–3	1,562
" 20	" " "	New York	Keefe . . . . King	8	6–4	5,624
" 22	" " "	Philadelphia	Welch . Chamberlain	8	12–5	1,781
" 24	St. Louis vs. New York	St. Louis	King . . . . Crane	8	7–5	2,624
" 25	New York vs. St. Louis	" "	King . Chamberlain	9	11–3	2,365
" 26	St. Louis vs. New York	" "	King . . . . George	10	14–11	411
" 27	" " "	" "	{ Chamberlain, Titcomb, Hatfield }	9	18–7	212
	Total					$24,362

Total Runs—New York, 64; St. Louis, 60.

Pitchers' Victories—Keefe, 4; Welch, 1; King, 2; Chamberlain, 2; Crane, 1.

Pitchers' Defeats—Keefe, 0; Welch, 1; Crane, 1; Titcomb, 1; King, 3; Chamberlain, 3.

The world's pennant was won by New York in 1889 by defeating the Brooklyns six out of nine games. The record follows:

DATE.	WINNER.	SCORE.	WHERE PLAYED.	ATTENDANCE.	PITCHERS.
Oct. 18	Brooklyn	12–10	New York	8848	Terry . . . . Keefe
" 19	New York	6–2	Brooklyn	16172	Crane . . Caruthers
" 22	Brooklyn	8–7	New York	5181	Hughes . . . Welch
" 23	"	10–7	Brooklyn	3045	Terry . . . . Crane
" 24	New York	11–3	"	2901	Crane . . Caruthers
" 25	"	2–1	New York	2556	O'Day . . . . Terry
" 26	"	11–7	"	2584	Crane . . . Lovett
" 28	"	16–7	Brooklyn	3312	Crane . . . Terry
" 29	"	3–2	New York	3067	O'Day . . . . Terry
			Total	47,666	

The profits were equally divided between the clubs and the players, each club paying its own expenses. The New York players received $380.13 each, and the Brooklyn men $389.85 each. The clubs got a little over $6,000 each.

The games in which more than the usual quota of nine innings are played, are, of course, the most closely contested and exciting of each season. One of the first extra-inning games on record required sixteen innings before it was decided, the contestants being the Gothams and Knickerbockers, of New York city; the date, June 30th, 1854. The same clubs met again late in the season of 1854 and played twelve innings, with the score a tie at 12 each, the preceding prolonged contest having been won by the Gothams. Eleven years elapsed before another remarkable contest occurred, and the match played between the Gothams and the Enterprise of Brooklyn, July 6th, 1865, required thirteen innings before it could be decided in favor of the former by a score of 19 to 18. Two noteworthy games were played July 8th and 10th, 1876, in Louisville, Kentucky, between the Mutual and Louisville clubs. On the first day, Saturday, they had played fifteen innings, with the score still remaining a tie at 5 runs each, when darkness caused a postponement to the following Monday. No fewer than sixteen innings were played when they again met before victory was secured by the Mutuals by a score of 8 to 5. On May 11, the Manchester and Harvard College teams played twenty-four innings without a run being completed when darkness caused a cessation of play. Very few hits were made outside of the infield in the entire twenty-four innings. Tyng, the catcher of the Harvards, put out thirty-six men, and assisted twice, this being the greatest number ever put out by any player in a single game. Coggswell, of the Manchesters, put out thirty-one men at first base.

The next longest game in regard to the number of innings played was that which took place on the ball field of Girard College, in Philadelphia, June 29th, 1878, between the college nine and an amateur club called the Yeager. So evenly matched were the two nines, that no fewer than twenty-one innings were necessary before the question of superiority was settled in favor of the Yeagers by a score of 10 to 7.

The most remarkable game in the history of the league, and one of the longest professional contests on record, was played August 17th, 1882, in Providence, R. I., between the Providence and Detroit clubs. Not until the eighteenth inning was a run made. Radbourn led off in the last half of the eighteenth with a home-run hit over the left-field fence, thus winning the game for Providence by a score of 1 to 0.

Two games of nineteen innings each have been played. One was played June 26th, 1881, in Louisville, Kentucky, between the Eclipse club of that city and a professional nine hailing from Akron, Ohio, darkness causing a cessation of play after nineteen innings had been completed, and each had made 2 runs. The home team tied the score in the eighth inning, but neither nine could get a man across the home-plate during the remainder of this remarkable game. The other game was played August 22d, 1882, between the Actives, of Reading, Pa., and the Merritt club, of Camden, N. J. The Merritts tied their opponents in the third inning, and after the nineteenth inning had been finished, and each club had been blanked sixteen successive times, darkness caused the game to end in a draw, the score standing even at 3. An eighteen-inning game was also played on July 9th, 1877, the contestants being the Tecumsehs, of London, Ontario, and the Buckeyes, of Columbus, Ohio. Each club had scored but one run at the close of the eighteenth inning, and then the contest was declared a draw on account of darkness. The next longest game in regard to the number of innings played was that between the Providence and Chicago clubs, in Providence, R. I., June 4th, 1880, when each had scored one run at the end of the sixteenth inning. The contest between the Metropolitan and Philadelphia clubs, June 24th, 1882, in Philadelphia, ended in a draw, with a score of 2 to 2, after an exciting and prolonged struggle of fifteen innings.

A game between the Dayton and Ironton clubs, played September 19th, 1884, in Dayton, O., is noteworthy as being the quickest played on record, only forty-seven minutes being occupied in playing the entire nine innings.

One of the slowest run-getting games between first-class clubs that we can find recorded was played July 30th, 1862, when the Unions, of Morrisania, and the Eckfords occupied four hours in scoring twelve runs—an average of three runs an hour.

About the longest game on record was played at Carrollton, Ky., during the season of 1868, which was commenced at ten o'clock in the morning, and was called on account of darkness at six o'clock that evening, with only seven innings completed.

The work in the field of the St. Louis Browns in 1886, is, in point of the number of games played and the continuous service on the diamond, an unprecedented record in the annals of baseball, as during their seven months' season, from March 27th to October 31st inclusive, the St. Louis team played in no fewer than 175 games. O'Neil and Welch each took part in 175 games.

The largest number of runs ever made in a game was that credited to the Niagara club, of Buffalo, N. Y., June 8th, 1869, when they defeated the Columbia of that city by the remarkable score of 209 to 10. The runs were rather evenly distributed among the winners, two of the Niagaras scoring 25 runs each; and the least number of runs by any one batsman amounted to 20. Three hours only were occupied in amassing this mammoth total. A game was played in 1867, in which the winning club made 123 runs, 51 in the last inning, and the losers 91 runs. A remarkable game was played May 17th, 1870, in Cleveland, O., between the Forest City and Atlantic clubs of that city. At the end of the fifth inning the game stood at the unprecedented score of 132 to 1 in favor of the Forest City.

The Athletic club, of Philadelphia, on October 20th, 1865, defeated the Alert club, of Danville, Pa., by one of the largest scores on record, viz., 162 to 11. This score is all the more remarkable on account of the Athletics having played a game the same morning with the Williamsport club, in which they made 101 to 8. In the afternoon game all the bats that could be procured were broken by the Athletics, and they were compelled to use the handle of a shovel as a substitute for a bat at the finish. Al Reach in these two games made thirty-four runs. The Athletics in 1865 and 1866 played nine games, in which they scored over 100 runs, with a grand total of 920 to 63 made by their opponents. The Athletics have made such scores as 162, 131, 119, 118, 114, 107, 106, 104, 101, and 101, while the highest score ever made against them was 51 by the Atlantics, of Brooklyn. An overwhelming defeat was sustained by the Nationals, of Jersey City, in a game with the Athletics September 30th, 1865, when the Philadelphians won by a score of 114 to 2, although the Nationals had anticipated but little difficulty in winning. A somewhat similar game took place at Pottsville, Pa., August 19th, 1869, when the Athletics defeated the local club by 107 to 2, although the home team were confident of victory before the game commenced.

The Forest City club, of Rockford, Ill., gained considerable notoriety by a victory over the Nationals of Washington in 1867, and when the Athletics visited Rockford on June 18th, 1868, they expected to be troubled to escape defeat. The game, however, proved to be a signal victory for the Athletics by a score of 94 to 13.

The most one-sided contest between professional clubs was June 18th, 1884, when the Mutuals vanquished the Chicagos by 38 to 1.

The largest score on record in a game between professional nines marked the game between the Atlantics, of Brooklyn, and Athletics, of Philadelphia, on July 5th, 1869, when the former won by a score of 51 to 48. Fifteen thousand spectators were present. The Atlantics made six home-runs and the Athletics three. The greatest number of runs to an inning yet recorded in a first-class match was scored by the Atlantics, of Brooklyn, in a game with the New York Mutuals October 16th, 1861, when they were credited with 26 runs in their third inning. Geo. Wright umpired a game between amateur clubs in Washington, D. C., in 1867, in which the winners made 68 runs in an inning—the largest total ever made. The greatest number of home-runs in any one game was credited to the Athletics, of Philadelphia, September 30th, 1865, when they made twenty-five against the National club, of Jersey City, Reach, Kleinfelder, and Potter each having five home-runs. The Athletics were credited with nineteen clean home-runs May 9th, 1866, while playing an amateur club in Newcastle, Del. Harry Wright, while playing with the Cincinnatis against the Holt club, June 22d, 1867, in Newport, Ky., made seven home-runs, the largest number ever scored by any individual player in a game. Lip Pike made six home-runs—five in succession—for the Athletics against the Alerts, July 16th, 1866, in Philadelphia, Pa.

Several clubs have accomplished the wonderful feat of retiring their opponents in nine consecutive innings without a man reaching first base in safety. Games without runs are common; games without base-hits have often been played; but a contest without a base being run was unprecedented until June 12th, 1880, when the Worcesters retired the Clevelands in one-two-three order nine successive times, a wild throw being the only error in this exceptional contest.

The Boston, Cleveland, Providence, and Metropolitan clubs in 1883, each once accomplished the feat of playing an entire game without an error of any kind—passed balls, wild pitches, or bases on balls.

John Hatfield, in July, 1868, in Cincinnati, O., made six successive throws of 123, 129, 132, 127, 127, and 126 yards. The first three throws were made with a slight breeze, and, as some said it helped him, Harry Wright got him to throw the ball in the opposite direction, which he did three times with the above-mentioned results. At the baseball tournament in October, 1872, on the Union Grounds, Brooklyn, a throwing match took place, the entries including Hatfield and Boyd, of the Mutuals; George Wright and Leonard, of the Bostons, and Fisler and Anson, of the Athletics. Each competitor was allowed three throws. Hatfield was ahead on each trial, and in the last one he eclipsed all previous records, and cleared 133yds., 1ft., 7½in. The best throws by the others were: Leonard, 119yds., 1ft., 10in.; Wright, 117yds., 1ft., 1in.; Boyd, 115yds., 1ft., 6in.; Fisler, 112yds., 6in.; and Anson, 110yds., 6in. The second longest throw ever chronicled was 132yds., 1ft., by E. N. Williamson, September 9th, 1882. Pfeffer's best throw out of three trials was 132yds., 5in. Edward Crane, of Boston, Mass., claimed the credit of throwing 139yds. in July, 1881, but failed to produce any witnesses of his alleged feat.

The remarkable pitching feat of retiring a professional club in nine successive innings without a solitary safe hit being made has been accomplished many times. Richmond, the left-handed pitcher, who made a great reputation in 1879 by twice blanking the Chicagos—on one occasion without their getting even a safe hit—eclipsed all his previous performances with the ball June 12th, 1880, when in nine consecutive innings not one of the Clevelands reached first base, on either safe hits or fielding errors. Ward, of the Providence club, repeated the same wonderful feat June 17th, 1880, when he pitched so effectively that not a single safe hit was made off him by the Buffalos, who were retired in one-two-three order in nine consecutive innings.

Twenty-three of the Dubuque club were retired on strikes off the pitching of Dorr, of the Union Pacific club, in a game played August 12th, 1882, in Omaha, Neb. Salisbury struck out twenty-one of the B. and M. club, of Omaha, Neb., June 16th, 1883, including fourteen out of the first fifteen men at the bat. Kilroy struck out twenty in an amateur game September 1st, 1883, in Philadelphia. In a ten-inning game played January 6th, 1884, in San Francisco, Cal., the pitchers—Morris and Chas. Sweeney—each retired nineteen men on strikes, an unparalleled feat.

The wonderful feat of striking out three men in succession off nine pitched balls was performed once each by Flynn, Fitzgerald, Hudson, and Van Haltren in 1886.

Prior to 1858 in every match there were two umpires—one chosen by each club—and a referee. As the umpires, in a majority of cases, decided in favor of their own clubs, the decision had ultimately to be left to the referee. In March, 1858, that plan was abolished, and in its stead was adopted the system of having only one umpire.

The first notice of baseball by the press was published in the Sunday *Mercury*, of New York, May 1st, 1853. It began as follows: "Cricket and Baseball.—The season for the enjoyment of both these healthful and most excellent games is now at hand, etc., etc." The same paper, on July 10th, 1853, published a short report of the game, written by Mr. William Cauldwell, one of its proprietors. This was the first game of baseball ever reported, and it read as follows: "Baseball.—The Gotham and Knickerbocker clubs played a match game, on the grounds of the latter, at Hoboken, on the 5th inst. The Knickerbockers won. Gotham, 18 outs, 12 runs; Knickerbocker, 18 outs, 21 runs—21 runs constituting a game."

The first code of rules for baseball was adopted by the Knickerbocker club September 23d, 1845. Here they are:

The bases shall be from "home" to second base, 42 paces; from first to third base, 42 paces, equidistant. The game to consist of 21 counts or aces, but at the conclusion an equal number of hands must be played. The ball must be pitched and not thrown for the bat. A ball knocked outside the range of the first or third base is foul. Three balls being struck at and missed, and the last one caught, is a hand out; if not caught, is considered fair, and the striker bound to run. A ball being struck or tipped, and caught either flying or on the first bound, is a hand out. A player, running the bases, shall be out, if the ball is in the hands of an adversary on the base, as the runner is touched by it before he makes his base; it being understood, however, that in no instance is a ball to be thrown at him. A player running, who shall prevent an adversary from catching or getting the ball before making his base, is a hand out. If two hands are already out, a player running home at the time a ball is struck cannot make an ace if the striker is caught out. Three hands out, all out. Players must take their strike in regular turn. No ace or base can be made on a foul strike. A runner cannot be put out in making one base when a balk is made by the pitcher. But one base allowed when the ball bounds out of the field when struck.

From these primitive rules have grown up the present elaborate manual of the game.

Previous to 1864, a man was out if the ball was caught on the bound. In 1864 the "fly catch" was adopted.

II. Scores of Games on the World's Tour.

During the tour, the Chicago and All-America teams played fifty-three games of four innings and upwards. Three of these were tie games, and of the remaining fifty, All America won 28 and Chicago 22 games. In addition to these, the Chicagos played two games against the St. Paul team at Minneapolis and St. Paul, and both Chicago and All America played exhibition games with the teams of the California League, at Stockton, Los Angeles, and San Francisco. A summary of the results of all games played, from the date of leaving Chicago until the date of the team's return, follows.

At Chicago, October 20, 1888.—Chicago, 11; All America, 6. Pitchers, Spalding and Tener for Chicago; Hutchinson for All America. Catchers, Daly and Kelly. Attendance, 3000.

At St. Paul, October 21.—Chicago 9; All-America 3. Pitchers, Baldwin and Healy. Catchers, Daly and Carroll. Attendance, 1500.

At Minneapolis, October 22.—Chicago 3; All-America 6 (four innings). Pitchers, Tener and Van Haltren. Catchers, Flint and Carroll. Attendance, 1500.

At Cedar Rapids, October 23.—Chicago 6; All-America 5. Pitchers, Tener and Ryan for Chicago; Hutchinson for All-America. Catchers, Flint and Carroll. Attendance, 4500.

At Des Moines, October 24.—Chicago 2; All-America 3. Pitchers, Baldwin and Ryan for Chicago; Hitchinson for All-America. Catchers, Flint and Sage. Attendance, 2000.

THE WORLD'S TOUR.

At Omaha, October 25.—Chicago 2; All-America 12. Pitchers, Tener and Ryan for Chicago; Healy for All-America. Catchers, Daly and Carroll. Attendance, 3500.

At Hastings, October 26.—Chicago 8; All-America, 4. Pitchers, Baldwin and Van Haltren. Catchers, Anson and Flint. Attendance, 3500.

At Denver, October 27.—Chicago 16; All-America 12. Pitchers, Tener and Healy. Catchers, Flint and Carroll. Attendance, 7500.

At Denver, October, 28.—Chicago 8; All-America 9. Pitchers, Baldwin for Chicago; Crane and Van Haltren for All America. Catchers, Daly and Earle. Attendance, 6000.

At Colorado Springs, October 29.—Chicago 13; All-America 9. Pitchers, Ryan and Healy. Catchers, Anson and Earle. Attendance, 1200.

At Salt Lake City, October 31.—Chicago 3; All-America 9 (four innings). Pitchers, Tener and Crane. Catchers, Daly and Earle. Attendance, 2500.

At Salt Lake City, November 1.—Chicago 3; All-America 10 Pitchers, Baldwin and Healy. Catchers, Anson and Earle. Attendance, 2000.

At San Francisco, November 4.—Chicago 4; All-America 14. Pitchers, Baldwin and Healy. Catchers, Daly and Earle. Attendance, 10,500.

At San Francisco, November 11.—Chicago 6; All-America 9. Pitchers, Tener and Van Haltren. Catchers, Daly and Earle. Attendance, 6000.

At Auckland, N. Z., December 10.—Chicago 22; All-America 13. Pitchers, Baldwin and Crane. Catchers, Daly and Earle. Attendance, 4500.

At Sydney, Australia, December 15.—Chicago 4; All-America 5. Pitchers, Tener and Healy. Catchers, Daly and Earle. Attendance, 5500.

At Sydney, December 17.—Chicago 5; All-America 7. Pitchers, Baldwin and Healy. Catchers, Anson and Earle. Attendance, 3000.

At Sydney, December 18.—Chicago 2; All-America 6 (five innings). Pitchers, Tener and Healy. Catchers, Daly and Earle. Attendance, 2500.

At Melbourne, December 22.—Chicago 5; All-America 3. Pitchers, Baldwin and Crane. Catchers, Daly and Earle. Attendance, 10,000.

At Melbourne, December 24.—Chicago 13; All-America 15. Pitchers, Ryan for Chicago; Healy and Crane for All-America. Catchers, Daly and Anson for Chicago; Earle for All-America. Attendance, 6000.

At Adelaide, December 26.—Chicago 14; All-America 19. Pitchers, Tener and Healy. Catchers, Daly and Earle. Attendance, 2000.

At Adelaide, December 27.—Chicago 12; All-America 9. Pitchers, Baldwin for Chicago; Healy and Ward for All-America. Catchers, Daly for Chicago; Carroll and Earle for All-America. Attendance, 2200.

At Adelaide, December 28.—Chicago 11; All-America 4. Pitchers, Ryan and Simpson. Catchers, Anson and Earle. Attendance, 2000.

At Ballarat, December 29.—Chicago 7; All-America 11. Pitchers, Baldwin and Healy. Catchers, Anson and Earle. Attendance, 4500.

At Melbourne, January 1, 1889.—Chicago 14; All-America 7. Pitchers, Tener and Healy. Catchers, Anson and Earle. Attendance, 2500.

At Melbourne, January 5.—Chicago 5; All-America 0 (five innings). Pitchers, Baldwin and Crane. Catchers, Daly and Earle. Attendance, 11,000.

At Columbo, Ceylon, January 26.—Chicago 3; All-America 3 (five innings). Pitchers, Baldwin and Crane. Catchers, Daly and Earle. Attendance, 4000,

At Cairo, Egypt, February 9.—Chicago 6; All-America 10 (five innings). Pitchers, Tener and Baldwin for Chicago; Healy and Crane for All-America, Catchers, Daly and Earle. Attendance, 1200.

At Naples, Italy, February 19.—Chicago 2; All-America 8 (five innings). Pitchers, Baldwin and Healy. Catchers, Daly and Earle. Attendance, 3000.

At Rome, February 23.—Chicago 3; All-America 2 (seven innings). Pitchers, Tener and Crane, Catchers, Daly and Earle. Attendance, 4000.

At Florence, February 25,—All-America 7; Chicago 4. Pitchers, Healy and Baldwin. Catchers, Carroll for All-America; Anson and Daly for Chicago. Attendauce, 2000.

At Paris, France, March 8.—Chicago 2; All-America 6 (seven innings). Pitchers, Tener and Crane. Catchers, Anson and Earle. Attendance, 3000.

At Kennington Oval, England, March 12.—All-America 4; Chicago 7. Pitchers, Healy and Baldwin. Catchers, Earle and Daly. Attendance, 8000.

At Lords' Cricket Grounds, March 13.—Chicago 6; All-America 7. Pitchers, Tener and Beldwin for Chicago; Crane for All-America. Attendance, 7000.

At Crystal Palace Grounds, March 14.—All-America 5; Chicago 9. Pitchers, Healy and Baldwin. Catchers, Earle and Daly. Attendance, 6000.

At Bristol, March 15.—Chicago 10; All-America 3. Pitchers, Ryan for Chicago; Brown and Crane for All-America. Catchers, Anson and Earle. Attendance, 3000.

At Layton Grounds, London, March 16.—All-America 6; Chicago 12. Pitchers, Crane ahd Baldwin. Catchers, Earle and Daly. Attendance, 8000.

At Birmingham, March 18.—Chicago 4; All-America 4 (ten innings), Pitchers, Baldwin and Healy. Catchers, Anson and Earle. Attendance, 3000.

At Glasgow, Scotland, March 21.—All-America 8; Chicago 4 (seven innings). Pitchers, Crane and Baldwin. Catchers, Earle and Anson. Attendance, 3000.

At Manchester, England, March 22.—Chicago 6; All-America 7. Pitchers. Tener and Healy. Catchers, Anson and Earle. Attendance, 3500.

At Liverpool, March 23.—Chicago 2; All-America 2 (five innings). Pitchers, Baldwin and Crane. Catchers, Daly and Earle. Attendance, 6500.

At Belfast, Ireland, March 24.—All-America 9; Chicago 8. Pitchers, Healy and Tener. Catchers, Earl and Anson. Attendance, 2500.

At Dublin, March 27.—All-America 4; Chicago 3. Pitchers, Crane and Baldwin. Catchers, Earle and Daly. Attendance, 4000.

At Brooklyn, April 8.—All-America 7; Chicago 6. Pitchers, Healy and Baldwin. Catchers, Earle and Anson. Attendance, 4000.

At Brooklyn, April 9 —Chicago 9; All-America 6. Pitchers, Tener and Crane. Catchers, Daly and Earle. Attendance, 3000.

At Baltimore, April 10.—All-America 2; Chicago 5. Pitchers, Healy and Baldwin. Catchers, Earle and Anson. Attendance, 6000.

At Philadelphia, April 12.—All-America 4; Chicago 6. Pitchers, Healy and Tener. Catchers, Earle and Daly. Attendance, 4000.

At Boston, April 13.—All-America 10; Chicago 3. Pitchers, Crane and Ryan. Catchers, Carroll and Anson. Attendance, 4000.

At Washington, April 15.—Chicago 18; All-America 6. Pitchers, Baldwin and Crane. Catchers, Anson and Earle. Attendance, 3000.

At Pittsburg, April 16.—All-America 3; Chicago 3 (nine innings). Pitchers Healy and Tener. Catchers, Earle and Daly. Attendance, 3000.

At Cleveland, April 17.—Chicago 7; All-America 4. Pitchers, Baldwin and Crane. Catchers, Anson and Earle. Attendance, 4500.

At Indianapolis, April 18,—All-America 9; Chicago 5. Pitchers, Healy and Tener. Catchers, Earle and Anson. Attendance, 2000.

At Chicago, April 20.—All-America 22; Chicago 9. Pitchers, Crane and Baldwin. Catchers, Earle and Daly. Attendance, 3700.

2. Scores of Incidental Games.

At St. Paul, October 21, 1888.—Chicago 5; St. Paul 8. Pitchers, Tener and Duryea, Catchers, Flint and Earle. Attendance, 2500.

At Minneapolis, October 22.—Chicago 1; St. Paul 0 (six innings). Pitchers, Baldwin and Tuckerman. Catchers, Daly and Earle. Attendance, 2000.

At San Francisco, November 6.—All-America 2; Greenhood and Moran 12. Pitchers, Crane and Anderson. Catchers, Carroll and Hardy. Attendance, 3000.

At San Francisco, November 8.—All-America 4; Pioneer 9. Pitchers, Healy and Purcell. Catchers, Earle and Ebright. Attendance, 4000.

At Stockton, November 8.—Chicago 2; Stockton 2 (nine innings). Pitchers, Tener and Harper. Catchers, Daly and Stockwell. Attendance, 4000.

At San Francisco, November 9.—All-America 16; Stockton 1. Pitchers, Crane and Baker. Catchers, Earle and Ebright.

At San Francisco, November 10.—Chicago 6; Haverly 1. Pitchers, Baldwin and Incell. Catchers, Daly and Swett. Attendance, 5000.

CPSIA information can be obtained
at www.ICGtesting.com
Printed in the USA
LVOW03s1110071116
511948LV00005B/119/P